Banned Books:
Challenging Our Freedom to Read

Robert P. Doyle

Banned Books:
Challenging Our Freedom to Read
Robert P. Doyle

Sponsored by: American Booksellers
Association, American Booksellers
Foundation for Free Expression, American
Library Association, American Society
of Journalists and Authors, Association
of American Publishers, Comic Book
Legal Defense Fund, Freedom to Read
Foundation, National Association of
College Stores, National Coalition Against
Censorship, National Council of Teachers
of English, and PEN American Center.

Endorsed by:
Center for the Book in the Library
of Congress
Project Censored

American Library Association
Chicago, Illinois

Cover design by
Pressley Johnson Design,
Chicago, Illinois.

2014 Design and publication
composition by Sam Silvio Design Inc.,
Chicago, Illinois.

Printing by Aspen Printing Co.,
Naperville, Illinois.

This publication was composed using
QuarkXPress, Adobe Illustrator,
and Adobe Photoshop for the Macintosh.
The primary typeface used is Constantia
and Gotham.

ISBN 978-0-8389-8688-2
ISSN 0888-0123
LCCN 88-659709

This paper meets the requirements
of ANSI/NISO Z 39.48-1992
(Permanence of Paper).

Banned Books:
Challenging Our Freedom to Read

Table of Contents

Notes on the 2014 Edition

This edition of *Banned Books* compiles a comprehensive database of 1,890 titles, published between 387 B.C. and 2014. Books published after 2010 are new to this edition, and include titles such as the bestselling *Fifty Shades of Grey,* by E. L. James and many others. Many titles previously listed have new incidents to report. Information on banning, removal, suppression, or challenges to these titles is drawn from a wide variety of published sources and includes chronology, listing of prizes and awards, and geographic information on where the incidents occurred.

Whether you're surprised by finding a classic or favorite author or looking for a specific reference, the book's new design invites you to scan, search, or browse. Along with the wealth of information, sections on insight and interpretation deepen your understanding and offer practical tips and tools. Seeded with ideas for both reflection and action, *Banned Books* is a resource for reference and a manual of instruction.

What's Inside at a Glance

Part 1 | Introduction
How It All Began
If you're new to the subject of Banned Books Week, this surprising story will fill you in on the background and bring you up to date on the current state of book banning in America.

Part 2 | Insights
The Challenge of Censorship
This introduction establishes a framework for understanding literary censorship and the danger it poses to our First Amendment freedom to read.

Part 3 | Interpretations
The First Amendment
Study the singular beauty of this unprecedented and inspiring document to grasp the power of the original words penned on paper in 1791.

Freedom of Expression
Discover the principles beneath the ongoing interpretation of the law that protects our uniquely American freedom of expression. Gain an overview of the issues that have come to symbolize First Amendment rights.

Freedom to Read
Read the key documents of the American book community applying the First Amendment principles to booksellers, librarians, and publishers.

Part 4 | Information
First Amendment Timeline
Get a sense of the First Amendment unfolding over time. From the ratification of the U.S. Constitution in 1787 to present-day Supreme Court opinion, a chronology puts it all in order. This well-researched, concise timeline will help you put the significant events in perspective.

First Amendment Notable Court Cases

This section describes some noted legal precedents concerning freedom of speech. Use these to launch further research, and you'll have ample information to support your programs, presentations, articles, and displays.

First Amendment Glossary and Acronyms

Straightforward, precise, and relevant, you'll want to keep this glossary close at hand. Familiarize yourself with these definitions and soon you'll be using these essential words and phrases like an expert.

First Amendment Quotations

Summing up the value of the First Amendment can be difficult for the layperson, especially compared to these eloquent and memorable expressions by notable individuals. Don't hesitate to use these quotes to elevate your celebration and illustrate your displays. Incorporate an unconventional utterance into your press materials or even print an erudite expression on your T-shirts or tote bags.

First Amendment Action Guide

Without our constant attention, the First Amendment freedoms that we so often take for granted—the right to read, explore ideas, and express ourselves freely—are at risk. This guide presents three ways that you can get involved.

Part 5 | Incidents
Top Ten Challenged Books of 2013

It should come as no surprise to find Toni Morrison, Sherman Alexie, and Dav Pilkey among the Top Ten. To find out who the other contenders are, along with the top categories of objection, take a look at the Top Ten page.

Banned and Challenged: Dangerous Books

This extensive list includes books banned or considered controversial from 387 B.C. to 2014. Designed with the reader in mind, the entries are easy to scan visually to find the information you need. Awards are prominently noted. Browsing through this list leads to valuable ideas for creating an exhibit or preparing for discussions, presentations, and writings.

It should be noted that this bibliography is limited to documented challenges to free speech and expression. Surveys indicate that approximately 85 percent of such challenges to library materials receive no media attention and remain unreported. Moreover, this list is limited to books and does not include challenges to magazines, newspapers, films, broadcasts, performances, electronic publications, or exhibits.

Indices

The three indices to the comprehensive *Banned and Challenged: Dangerous Books* list can help customize an exhibit or program by identifying challenged books by title, location, and category. For example, if you want to create an exhibit of books banned or challenged in your state or city, use the geographic index to find the titles. Or, if you want to have a program on children's literature or gay literature, check the topical index. Using these tools will help create an event targeted for your audience or community. Please note that the bibliography entries are numbered sequentially and the entry number (not the page number) is used in all three indices.

About the Author

Acknowledgements

Part 1
Introduction

"The history of persecuted writers is as long as the history of literature itself."

Toni Morrison, novelist, winner of the 1988 Pulitzer Prize for Fiction and 1993 Nobel Prize in Literature (1931–)

Organizing events to call attention to the banning of books is a relatively new idea, but one that has taken hold. The events themselves gave rise to documentation and building a living history of the action taken to keep books out of the readers' hands.

This introduction tells the story of the first Banned Books Week and the annotated lists that eventually became the basis for this book.

How It All Began

In the spring of 1982, thousands of onlookers in Anaheim, California, greeted the concept of three well-respected twentieth-century women behind bars with disbelief. Their individual imprisonment would have been improbable enough; even more baffling was imagining what the three "prisoners" could have in common. What crimes were committed by an African-American poetess, a German-Jewish adolescent, and an All-American Hollywood star?

The crowds surrounding the padlocked cells that day nearly thirty years ago found themselves imagining Maya Angelou, Anne Frank, and Doris Day surrounded by a display of their books. The three imprisoned authors apparently did have a crime in common—they were guilty, at least in the opinion of some individuals, of creating controversial content. In particular, Maya Angelou's *I Know Why the Caged Bird Sings* was objectionable because it preaches "bitterness and hatred against whites," *The Diary of Anne Frank* because it was "a real downer," and *Doris Day: Her Own Story* because a group found the content shocking "in light of Miss Day's All-American image."

To call attention to the practice of book banning, The American Booksellers Association (ABA) had included these three titles in a selection of recently banned books displayed in a series of cages at their annual convention. Up until that day when they witnessed the display of books behind bars, the members of the professional association—the authors, publishers, booksellers, librarians, and journalists attending the convention—were all unaware that so many books and such familiar titles were removed from bookstore and library shelves because an individual or group thought the printed matter unfit for others to read. To the spectators the implication was clear—it was readers who were being caged, not just books.

As a result of the attention to the display and the conversations and questions it provoked, the first Banned Books Week was held several months later in the fall of 1982. It was then, and is still, sponsored by the following organizations and endorsed by the Center for the Book of the Library of Congress:

- American Booksellers Association
- American Booksellers Foundation for Free Expression
- American Library Association
- American Society of Journalists and Authors
- Association of American Publishers
- National Association of College Stores

This coalition selected the first full week of September as Banned Books Week to coincide with the beginning of the school year, because so many of the challenges occur in schools throughout the country. The ABA and the cosponsoring National Association of College Stores (NACS) sent out a promotional packet to members that included a list of more than five hundred banned books, a poster titled "Caution! Some People Consider These Books Dangerous," a sample press release, and background information for booksellers. The American Library Association (ALA) endorsed the week and publicized the event to its members.

With an enthusiastic response from the local and national press, book censorship became a front-page story for dozens of newspapers, radio, and television stations. During that first Banned Books Week in 1982, the press and the library community frequently posed the questions, "Why was the book banned?" "Where was it banned?" "When was it banned?" "What can we do?" Without annotations or explanations, the list of banned books distributed that first year left many of the questions unanswered.

The following year, working for ALA's Office for Intellectual Freedom, I prepared the first annotated list of banned books for the Banned Books Week celebration. Titled "A List of Books Some People Consider Dangerous," that first list in 1983 contained 404 titles compared to this year's list of 1,890. The increase in the number of challenges and bannings is more the result of better reporting of such incidents, rather than an indication of their proliferation. Each entry in the list includes a brief explanation of the reasons, location, and dates for the challenged, restricted, or banned titles; and the information is cumulative, offering a chronological history for each title. Each year, the list is updated, revised, and published in an abbreviated version as a brochure.

In 2010, the following organizations joined the coalition: Comic Book Legal Defense Fund, Freedom to Read Foundation, National Coalition Against Censorship, National Council of Teachers of English, and PEN American Center. And it was endorsed by Project Censored.

The intent of Banned Books Week is three-fold: to draw attention to the importance of the freedom to read, to publicize threats to that freedom, and to provide information to combat ignorance and lack of awareness. The provocative title, Banned Books Week, has sometimes generated controversy, but rarely has it failed to attract attention—its primary reason for being.

Occasionally, individuals have misinterpreted the name as a celebration of the legal prohibition of books; worse, others have thought the book community was actively engaged in banning or advocating the removal of books from publication, purchase, or library circulation. Banned Books Week has even been accused of being fraudulent because, in many cases, the banning is requested but doesn't actually take place.

Suggestions to rename the week inevitably arise from time to time, but mostly they carry the same potential confusion and dilute its central message—that readers are banished when a book is banned and the threat of banning can be as dangerous as the actuality.

Since 1982, Banned Books Week continues to uphold one of the world's greatest visions of the right to free expression—the First Amendment to the U.S. Constitution. Judge Oliver Wendell Holmes, Jr., an eloquent spokesperson for the role of free speech in a democracy, characterized it as "freedom for the thought that we hate." Resisting the temptation to curb such thought, lest our own be curbed as well, is the basis for this book and the annual week of celebrations from which it draws its name.

Part 2
Insights

"A point of view can be a dangerous luxury when substituted for insight and understanding."

Herbert Marshall McLuhan, Canadian sociologist (1911-80), from *The Gutenberg Galaxy: The Making of Typographic Man.* Toronto: University of Toronto Pr., 1962, p. 216.

Even in the digital era, books are an unsurpassed medium for sharing ideas and influencing others. It's no wonder then that books continue to be an irresistible target for the undeniably human urge to censor.

Insights offers a perspective on the desire to censor literary expression and the danger of disregarding it.

The Challenge of Censorship

Censorship is nothing new; it has always been with us. The urge to censor is primordial. The instinct isn't limited just to those in positions of power who are driven to control access to information. The truth is, almost everyone wants to censor something at some point in time. Adults often censor to protect children, and children sometimes to protect their parents. If you believe something to be true, you may have the impulse to suppress or censor expression to the contrary, finding it to be inaccurate or harmful.

Recognizing the difference between an individual restricting his or her own choices and action by a governmental or public body is at the root of any discussion of censorship. The first is an exercise of freedom, while the second is its reverse. We may use the word "censor" to describe both actions, but it is the action of the government that is the concern of this book.

Censorship is everywhere. It isn't restricted by geography or ideology, nor limited to certain religious practices or political beliefs. Although it may be more commonly found where narrow viewpoints are the norm, it surprisingly still appears in open societies and circumstances.

Censorship is current. It didn't disappear with the end of the Inquisition or other repressive regimes. But unless it somehow comes up in conversation, people tend to dismiss it as a thing of the past. Censorship? It couldn't possibly still be happening today, not in a society as tolerant, diverse, and sophisticated as ours, could it? It seems remote until it happens in our hometown, or to someone we know, or we overhear a conversation at work or school.

Censorship is captivating. Even when we oppose it, we're intrigued by it. It prompts our curiosity, and in its own way, creates bestsellers. Challenging, restricting, removing, banning, or burning a book arouses as much fascination as fear, maybe more. Contrary to the censors' original intent to limit exposure, banning generates interest, increases sales, and provokes discussion.

In the United States, the freedom to choose what we read, to select from a full array of possibilities, is more pronounced than in most societies. Firmly rooted in the First Amendment to the U.S. Constitution, this right protects freedom of speech and freedom of the press in our country. Despite constitutional guarantees, however, these precious rights are vulnerable to erosion. Our freedom is only as secure as we make it. And what makes those rights secure is the body of law developed gradually over time—through the dedicated efforts of readers, publishers, booksellers, librarians, and others.

Books aren't the only form of expression subjected to censoring, but they may well be the most significant. Even in the digital age, we endow books with a certain aura of permanence and authority that gives weight to their content. Gossip and news are transitory by nature, easier to ignore than to ban. Movies and performances often have limited life spans, during which ticket sales peak and then plummet after a few short weeks or months. But books stick around. Their popularity endures. They're not so susceptible to the whims of fashion. We can find them in library stacks and on bookstore shelves, making their ideas accessible to a growing audience for years to come. So it comes as no surprise that attempts to censor books are more robust and often take the form of "challenges"—the formal, written requests to remove them from library shelves or otherwise restrict public access.

As noted earlier, censorship pressures come from all quarters and all political persuasions. No matter how well intentioned, the practice of censorship limits the freedom of others to choose what they read, see, or hear. Sex, profanity, and racism remain the primary categories of objections; and most challenges occur in schools and school libraries.

Challenges are often motivated by the desire to protect children, but deciding what we get to read has broader consequences; if the government can restrict access for one reason, it can extend it to another. Supreme Court Justice William Brennan, in *Texas v. Johnson,* said, "If there is a bedrock principle underlying the First Amendment, it is that the Government may not prohibit the expression of an idea simply because society finds the idea itself offensive or disagreeable." Individuals can choose for themselves and their children, but if governmental or public agencies are called on to make that choice, we all ultimately forfeit our own right to choose.

The challenges documented in this publication are not merely expressing a point of view or exercising the right to choose; rather, they are formal requests for removal of materials from schools or libraries, restricting access to them by others. Even when the eventual outcome allows the book to stay on the library shelves, the censorship attempt is real. Someone has tried to limit another person's ability to choose.

Challenges are as important to document as actual bannings that result in removing a book from the shelves of a library or bookstore or from the curriculum at a school. Challenges—or attempts to censor—can eventually lead to a narrowing down of the range of books available for us to read. The constant pressure from those determined to censor our reading materials can have a chilling effect on publishers and editors who might decide that certain topics are simply too incendiary, so that some books may never make their way into print. Even librarians, booksellers, and educators might find it easier to avoid controversy and aggravation by staying away from certain authors or subjects altogether.

Readers everywhere can take heart from the fact that challenges are often met with successful resistance, keeping reading materials on the shelves where they belong. The everyday vigilance of ordinary people prevents censorship from encroaching upon our hard-won freedoms. The freedom to read, as promised by the First Amendment, is ours to use or to lose. This book is one small part of the ongoing endeavor to preserve our freedom to read and to promote understanding of the precarious nature of our irreplaceable right to learn.

Part 3
Interpretations

"All human knowledge takes the form of interpretation."

Walter Benjamin, German-Jewish philosopher, sociologist, literary critic, translator, and essayist (1892-1940), *Briefe* 126 (December 9, 1923).

In spite of the permanence of written documents, the meaning of words on paper changes over time. No matter how precise or powerful the language, every expression of thought—from the Bill of Rights to a scientific theory to a lullaby— is open to interpretation.

Interpretations chronicles the milestones of the emerging First Amendment taking shape over the generations—in the courts, in the literature, and in the language.

The First
Amendment

"Congress shall make no law respecting an establishment of religion, or prohibiting the free exercise thereof; or abridging the freedom of speech, or of the press; or the right of the people peaceably to assemble, and to petition the government for a redress of grievances."

The First Amendment of the Bill of Rights to the United States Constitution, 1791

The Freedom of Expression

Freedom of expression is a uniquely American tradition, at least to the degree it is practiced here. Whether born out of the founders' desire to make sure they wouldn't have to leave their new land when and if the new government became as oppressive as their old one, or simply a political strategy to get the new Constitution adopted by states unwilling to surrender their sovereignty, it put notions into law that hadn't been there before.

Governments were thought to reign supreme and criticizing them considered a crime. And for much of the First Amendment's history, its protection primarily extended to political expression, and even then was reluctantly employed by the courts. Development of First Amendment law has been a slow process of each decision building upon the cumulative pattern of earlier ones, each lending its weight and voice to what has become a solid foundation for the right of writers and speakers to express themselves freely without fear of repercussion.

As Supreme Court Justice John Marshall Harlan continued in his opinion for the majority in a 1971 case about the right to protest, albeit profanely, during the Vietnam War:

"The constitutional right of free expression is powerful medicine in a society as diverse and populous as ours. It is designed and intended to remove governmental restraints from the arena of public discussion, putting the decision as to what views shall be voiced largely into the hands of each of us, in the hope that use of such freedom will ultimately produce a more capable citizenry and more perfect polity and in the belief that no other approach would comport with the premise of individual dignity and choice upon which our political system rests. . . . That the air may at times seem filled with verbal cacophony is, in this sense, not a sign of weakness but of strength."
U.S. Supreme Court Justice John Marshall Harlan, *Cohen v. California,* 403 U.S. 15, 91 S.Ct. 1780, 29 L.Ed.2d 284 (1971).

Both the Supreme Court and the rest of the country generally ignored these constitutional rights until well into the twentieth century. And the first time the Court cited the First Amendment in defending freedom of speech it was in a dissenting opinion. But even dissenting opinions are part of the process that builds the body of law. A series of dissents authored by Justices Oliver Wendell Holmes, Jr., and Louis D. Brandeis in the 1920s began to change what the award-winning journalist Anthony Lewis called "the old, crabbed view of what the First Amendment protects." Lewis went on to say:

"It was an extraordinary change, really a legal revolution. And it showed the power of words to change minds. Holmes and Brandeis had only two votes of nine. But their rhetoric was so powerful, so convincing, that it changed the attitude of the country and the Court."
—from *Freedom for the Thought That We Hate: A Biography of the First Amendment*

It was in one of these opinions that Holmes coined the phrase we still use today to describe the fundamental nature of free speech—"freedom for the thought that we hate." Supporting expression of ideas with which we agree is easy; much harder, and more important, is supporting expression of ideas we condemn. Jailing of socialists and unionists, burning of German-language books during World War I and detention of Japanese-Americans during World War II, treatment of communist sympathizers during the Cold War, and even the rights of Nazis to march in Skokie, Illinois, in the 1970s were all issues that came to symbolize First Amendment rights. More recently, the threat of terrorism in the wake of September 11, 2001, has led to suppression or suspension of some of these rights, not by the courts, but by other units of government.

Fighting for the freedom to read is not an isolated act. It is part of all these other battles waged, most of which were eventually won in front of the Court, though victory often followed earlier defeats. The right to publish and to read "the thought that we hate" has been the basis for resisting demands to remove books and reading materials from libraries, schools, bookstores, and other public places. It has finally and firmly been embraced by the Supreme Court.

The Court's first key decision to apply this reasoning came in *Stromberg v. California* in 1931. Even though this decision established the principles the Court still observes, case law continues to evolve. The amendment did not come with specific instructions, but was rather "a sweeping command," as Justice Holmes termed it, left to each generation and set of circumstances to define and refine.

Much of the attention to defining the parameters of free speech occurred in cases involving the press, often dealing with the protection of journalists and their sources. The role of a free press in limiting the government's power to put its own spin on information became a particular area of interest and was largely upheld by the Court, though stopping short of making journalists a special or privileged class.

In fact, sexual rather than political content is what ultimately brought books and their banning to the attention of the Court. In the early twentieth century, literary classics such as D. H. Lawrence's *Lady Chatterley's Lover,* Theodore Dreiser's *An American Tragedy,* and James Joyce's *Ulysses* were found to be obscene and frequently banned, bans upheld by local, state, and federal district courts. In one such case in 1933, the presiding judge set a new test for obscenity, judging a work by its effect on an average reader. Applying that test, Judge John M. Woolsey found *Ulysses* was not obscene, and the test was widely adopted.

An obscenity case before the Supreme Court in 1948 was the last to allow a lower court ban on a serious book to stand, and even then in a split 4-4 decision. Subsequent decisions attempted to separate free speech and obscenity, guaranteeing one while placing the other outside the amendment's protection. Two great friends of the freedom that libraries claim for their readers were Justices William O. Douglas and Hugo Black, both contending that this freedom is one that individual citizens are capable of exercising without governmental support or interference. Douglas said he had "the same confidence in the ability of our people to reject noxious literature as I have in their capacity to sort out the true from the false in theology, economics, politics or any other field."

This tradition of First Amendment law, handed down by the U.S. Supreme Court, has built a strong foundation for the freedom to read. While it may seem secure in legal precedent, at least at the national level, it remains subject to local pressure and the continuing evolution of ideas under our societal blueprint, the U.S. Constitution. Librarians, booksellers, lawyers, judges, journalists, readers, and writers have all helped define this precious freedom. This book looks at many of the examples in which they've succeeded, some in which they've failed. All are part of the beautiful and textured fabric of the First Amendment, embroidered with words, phrases, and ideas from some of the world's bravest hearts and best minds.

An opinion authored by Justice Robert H. Jackson in 1943 in reference to saluting the flag makes it clear that all First Amendment cases have much in common, whether they address literary, political, or other forms of expression:

"Compulsory unification of opinion achieves only the unanimity of the graveyard.... We can have intellectual individuals and the rich cultural diversity that we owe to exceptional minds only at the price of occasional eccentricity and abnormal attitudes. When they are so harmless to others or to the State as those we deal with here, the price is not too great. But freedom to differ is not limited to things that do not matter much. That would be a mere shadow of freedom. The test of its substance is the right to differ as to things that touch the heart of the existing order."
—*West Virginia Board of Education v. Barnette* (1943)

The Freedom to Read

Just like the courts, the American book community did not become serious advocates of First Amendment freedoms until well into the twentieth century. The first expressions of concern were in the 1920s and 1930s and were typically related to the exclusion of political ideas, whether through library policies about what could be placed on shelves or tariffs on imports or ideas in specific publications. Responses were isolated and sporadic, and neither unanimously held nor widely publicized.

Efforts to ban John Steinbeck's *The Grapes of Wrath* in the late 1930s brought about adoption by the American Library Association (ALA) of *The Library's Bill of Rights,* which focused on unbiased book selection and open meeting rooms and didn't even mention censorship or book banning. The document evolved, however, through the general climate of political repression in the 1950s and civil rights issues of the 1960s, eventually becoming *The Library Bill of Rights,* the profession's basic policy statement on censorship.

The role of ALA has evolved as well, with expanded services to librarians who find themselves on the front lines of censorship issues. While ALA's Committee on Intellectual Freedom provided a forum for philosophical discussion and policy formation, creation of the Office for Intellectual Freedom (OIF) in 1967 and the Freedom to Read Foundation in 1969 positioned the association to provide support to librarians through continuing education, publications, court cases, and even direct financial support.

The approach throughout has been one that seeks to reflect both the views of the profession and to offer leadership for the positions taken. The Freedom to Read statement, originally adopted in 1953, has been maintained as a bedrock document, subject to minor revision and interpretation, but steering clear of major shifts and swings. Like the Constitution itself, it is a living document, meant to be applied to changing realities but holding fast to basic principles.

Library
Bill of Rights

Library Bill of Rights

Adopted June 18, 1948; amended February 2, 1961, and January 23, 1980, by the ALA Council. Inclusion of "age" reaffirmed January 23, 1996, by the ALA Council.

The American Library Association affirms that all libraries are forums for information and ideas, and that the following basic policies should guide their services.

1. Books and other library resources should be provided for the interest, information, and enlightenment of all people of the community the library serves. Materials should not be excluded because of the origin, background, or views of those contributing to their creation.

2. Libraries should provide materials and information presenting all points of view on current and historical issues. Materials should not be proscribed or removed because of partisan or doctrinal disapproval.

3. Libraries should challenge censorship in the fulfillment of their responsibility to provide information and enlightenment.

4. Libraries should cooperate with all persons and groups concerned with resisting abridgment of free expression and free access to ideas.

5. A person's right to use a library should not be denied or abridged because of origin, age, background, or views.

6. Libraries which make exhibit spaces and meeting rooms available to the public they serve should make such facilities available on an equitable basis, regardless of the beliefs or affiliations of individuals or groups requesting their use.

The Freedom to Read Statement

The Freedom to Read Statement

This statement was originally issued in May of 1953 by the Westchester Conference of the American Library Association and the American Book Publishers Council, which in 1970 consolidated with the American Educational Publishers Institute to become the Association of American Publishers.

Adopted June 25, 1953; revised January 28, 1972, January 16, 1991, by the ALA Council and the AAP Freedom to Read Committee.

A Joint Statement by: American Library Association & Association of American Publishers.

The freedom to read is essential to our democracy. It is continuously under attack. Private groups and public authorities in various parts of the country are working to remove books from sale, to censor textbooks, to label "controversial" books, to distribute lists of "objectionable" books or authors, and to purge libraries. These actions apparently rise from a view that our national tradition of free expression is no longer valid; that censorship and suppression are needed to avoid the subversion of politics and the corruption of morals. We, as citizens devoted to the use of books and as librarians and publishers responsible for disseminating them, wish to assert the public interest in the preservation of the freedom to read.

We are deeply concerned about these attempts at suppression. Most such attempts rest on a denial of the fundamental premise of democracy: that the ordinary citizen, by exercising critical judgment, will accept the good and reject the bad. The censors, public and private, assume that they should determine what is good and what is bad for their fellow-citizens.

We trust Americans to recognize propaganda, and to reject it. We do not believe they need the help of censors to assist them in this task. We do not believe they are prepared to sacrifice their heritage of a free press in order to be "protected" against what others think may be bad for them. We believe they still favor free enterprise in ideas and expression.

We are aware, of course, that books are not alone in being subjected to efforts at suppression. We are aware that these efforts are related to a larger pattern of pressures being brought against education, the press, films, radio and television. The problem is not only one of actual censorship. The shadow of fear cast by these pressures leads, we suspect, to an even larger voluntary curtailment of expression by those who seek to avoid controversy.

Such pressure toward conformity is perhaps natural to a time of uneasy change and pervading fear. Especially when so many of our apprehensions are directed against an ideology, the expression of a dissident idea becomes a thing feared in itself, and we tend to move against it as against a hostile deed, with suppression.

And yet suppression is never more dangerous than in such a time of social tension. Freedom has given the United States the elasticity to endure strain. Freedom keeps open the path of novel and creative solutions, and enables change to come by choice. Every silencing of a heresy, every enforcement of an orthodoxy, diminishes the toughness and resilience of our society and leaves it the less able to deal with stress.

Now as always in our history, books are among our greatest instruments of freedom. They are almost the only means for making generally available ideas or manners of expression that can initially command only a small audience. They are the natural medium for the new idea and the untried voice from which come the original contributions to social growth. They are essential to the extended discussion which serious thought requires, and to the accumulation of knowledge and ideas into organized collections.

We believe that free communication is essential to the preservation of a free society and a creative culture. We believe that these pressures towards conformity present the danger of limiting the range and variety of inquiry and expression on which our democracy and our culture depend. We believe that every American community must jealously guard the freedom to publish and to circulate, in order to preserve its own freedom to read. We believe that publishers and librarians have a profound responsibility to give validity to that freedom to read by making it possible for the readers to choose freely from a variety of offerings.

The freedom to read is guaranteed by the Constitution. Those with faith in free people will stand firm on these constitutional guarantees of essential rights and will exercise the responsibilities that accompany these rights. We therefore affirm these propositions:

1. It is in the public interest for publishers and librarians to make available the widest diversity of views and expressions, including those which are unorthodox or unpopular with the majority.

Creative thought is by definition new, and what is new is different. The bearer of every new thought is a rebel until that idea is refined and tested. Totalitarian systems attempt to maintain themselves in power by the ruthless suppression of any concept which challenges the established orthodoxy. The power of a democratic system to adapt to change is vastly strengthened by the freedom of its citizens to choose widely from among conflicting opinions offered freely to them.

To stifle every nonconformist idea at birth would mark the end of the democratic process. Furthermore, only through the constant activity of weighing and selecting can the democratic mind attain the strength demanded by times like these. We need to know not only what we believe but why we believe it.

2. Publishers, librarians and booksellers do not need to endorse every idea or presentation contained in the books they make available. It would conflict with the public interest for them to establish their own political, moral or aesthetic views as a standard for determining what books should be published or circulated.

Publishers and librarians serve the educational process by helping to make available knowledge and ideas required for the growth of the mind and the increase of learning. They do not foster education by imposing as mentors the patterns of their own thought. The people should have the freedom to read and consider a broader range of ideas than those that may be held by any single librarian or publisher or government or church. It is wrong that what one can read should be confined to what another thinks proper.

3. It is contrary to the public interest for publishers or librarians to determine the acceptability of a book on the basis of the personal history or political affiliations of the author.

A book should be judged as a book. No art or literature can flourish if it is to be measured by the political views or private lives of its creators. No society of free people can flourish which draws up lists of writers to whom it will not listen, whatever they may have to say.

4. There is no place in our society for efforts to coerce the taste of others, to confine adults to the reading matter deemed suitable for adolescents, or to inhibit the efforts of writers to achieve artistic expression.

To some, much of modern literature is shocking. But is not much of life itself shocking? We cut off literature at the source if we prevent writers from dealing with the stuff of life. Parents and teachers have a responsibility to prepare the young to meet the diversity of experiences in life to which they will be exposed, as they have a responsibility to help them learn to think critically for themselves. These are affirmative responsibilities, not to be discharged simply by preventing them from reading works for which they are not yet prepared. In these matters taste differs, and taste cannot be legislated; nor can machinery be devised which will suit the demands of one group without limiting the freedom of others.

5. It is not in the public interest to force a reader to accept with any book the prejudgment of a label characterizing the book or author as subversive or dangerous. The ideal of labeling presupposes the existence of individuals or groups with wisdom to determine by authority what is good or bad for the citizen. It presupposes that individuals must be directed in making up their minds about the ideas they examine. But Americans do not need others to do their thinking for them.

6. It is the responsibility of publishers and librarians, as guardians of the people's freedom to read, to contest encroachments upon that freedom by individuals or groups seeking to impose their own standards or tastes upon the community at large.

It is inevitable in the give and take of the democratic process that the political, the moral, or the aesthetic concepts of an individual or group will occasionally collide with those of another individual or group. In a free society individuals are free to determine for themselves what they wish to read, and each group is free to determine what it will recommend to its freely associated members. But no group has the right to take the law into its own hands, and to impose its own concept of politics or morality upon other members of a democratic society. Freedom is no freedom if it is accorded only to the accepted and the inoffensive.

7. It is the responsibility of publishers and librarians to give full meaning to the freedom to read by providing books that enrich the quality and diversity of thought and expression. By the exercise of this affirmative responsibility, they can demonstrate that the answer to a bad book is a good one, the answer to a bad idea is a good one.

The freedom to read is of little consequence when expended on the trivial; it is frustrated when the reader cannot obtain matter fit for that reader's purpose. What is needed is not only the absence of restraint, but the positive provision of opportunity for the people to read the best that has been thought and said. Books are the major channel by which the intellectual inheritance is handed down, and the principal means of its testing and growth. The defense of their freedom and integrity, and the enlargement of their service to society, requires of all publishers and librarians the utmost of their faculties, and deserves of all citizens the fullest of their support.

We state these propositions neither lightly nor as easy generalizations. We here stake out a lofty claim for the value of books. We do so because we believe that they are good, possessed of enormous variety and usefulness, worthy of cherishing and keeping free. We realize that the application of these propositions may mean the dissemination of ideas and manners of expression that are repugnant to many persons. We do not state these propositions in the comfortable belief that what people read is unimportant. We believe rather that what people read is deeply important; that ideas can be dangerous; but that the suppression of ideas is fatal to a democratic society. Freedom itself is a dangerous way of life, but it is ours.

Part 4
Information

"Whenever the people are well informed, they can be trusted with their own government."

Thomas Jefferson (1743-1826) third U.S. President (1801-9) and principal author of the Declaration of Independence, to Richard Price, 1789.

In a democratic society, people have the right to speak out, to express their thoughts, and to read the books they choose. When these freedoms are protected by constitutional guarantees, individuals with free access to information are empowered to learn and to use their newfound knowledge to effect change.

Information chronicles the milestones shaping the First Amendment as it emerges over the generations—in the courts, in the literature, and in the language.

First Amendment Timeline

Every challenge to the First Amendment has helped shape the current interpretation of Americans' rights.

1787
The U.S. Constitution is ratified on the unwritten condition by many states that a Bill of Rights be added soon afterward.

1788
The Constitution goes into effect; nine states have ratified it, with others to follow. Several states gave their approval on the unwritten condition that a Bill of Rights be added soon afterward.

1791
The First through Tenth Amendments are adopted, comprising the Bill of Rights.

1798
Fearing war with France, Congress passes the unpopular Sedition Act of 1798, curtailing First Amendment freedoms. Numerous newspaper editors were fined and jailed under the Act.

1868
The Fourteenth Amendment is adopted as one of the Civil War Amendments. The due process clause of this amendment has served as the basis for the Supreme Court to apply selectively, against actions by state governments, the checks and guarantees contained in the Bill of Rights. Up to this time, the free speech rights of the citizen of a state were safeguarded solely by the constitution and laws of the state.

1885
Mark Twain's *The Adventures of Huckleberry Finn* is banned in Concord, Mass. The book continues to be one of the most frequently challenged or banned books in the United States.

1917
The Court defines freedom of speech quite narrowly in the years around World War I, upholding the Espionage Act of 1917 in several cases.

1919
U.S. Supreme Court Justice Oliver Wendell Holmes, Jr., announces in *Schenck v. U.S.,* 249 U.S. 47, a "clear and present danger" test to judge whether the First Amendment protects speech. Using the test, the Supreme Court affirmed the wartime convictions of the defendants charged with interfering in armed forces recruitment by mailing new recruits leaflets urging them to resist conscription.

Justice Holmes demonstrates the limits of his "clear and present danger" test by dissenting in *Abrams v. U.S.,* 250 U.S. 616, which affirmed the convictions of several Russian immigrants who distributed circulars that denounced President Wilson and urged workers to unite in support of the Bolshevik Revolution. In his dissent, he argues that the "silly leaflet" of the immigrants posed no real danger to the United States or its war effort, and thus failed to present a "clear and present danger" that the government might be justified in trying to suppress.

1920
Roger N. Baldwin creates the American Civil Liberties Union (ACLU).

1923
Writer Upton Sinclair is arrested in Los Angeles after trying to read the Bill of Rights in public at a dockworkers strike. He is later charged with "discussing, arguing, orating and debating certain thoughts and theories, which. . . were detrimental and in opposition to the orderly conduct of affairs of business, affecting the rights of private property. . . ."

1925
When science teacher John Scopes challenges a Tennessee law forbidding him from teaching the theory of evolution, one of the most noted trials in U.S. history followed. Though Scopes lost the "monkey trial," his conviction was overturned later on a technicality. It is forty-three years before the U.S. Supreme Court rules on the same issue. In 1968, in *Epperson v. Arkansas,* 393 U.S. 97, the Court said that rules requiring that only Biblical or religious theories of the origin of man be taught violate the U.S. Constitution.

1925
The U.S. Supreme Court, in *Gitlow v. New York,* 268 U.S. 652, decides that rights protected under the First Amendment are among the personal "liberties" protected by the due process clause of the Fourteenth Amendment from impairment by states. Nevertheless, the Court declined to apply Justice Holmes's "clear and present danger" test and upheld the defendant's convictions under New York statutes for publishing a manifesto advocating, advising, or teaching the overthrow of organized government by force or violence.

1931
In *Near v. Minnesota ex rel. Olson,* 283 U.S. 697, the U.S. Supreme Court interprets the First and Fourteenth Amendments to forbid as "prior restraints" a lawsuit authorized by a state statute to enjoin future publication of a newspaper. The case extended the definition of "prior restraints" to include more than simply official pre-publication review that involves either licensing or censoring of particular content.

1931
The U.S. Supreme Court invalidates California's "anti-red flag" law in *Stromberg v. California,* 283 U.S. 359. The Court found the California statute that made it a felony to display a red flag "as a sign, symbol or emblem of opposition to organized government" repugnant to the Constitution.

1939

The American Library Association adopts the *Library Bill of Rights,* the profession's basic policy statement on intellectual freedom involving library materials.

1942

In *Chaplinsky v. New Hampshire,* 315 U.S. 568, the high court upholds a New Hampshire statute as a valid regulation of "fighting words," i.e., words "which by their very utterance inflict injury or tend to incite an immediate breach of peace." Fighting words, like certain other limited classes of speech, e.g., the lewd and obscene, "are no essential part of any exposition of ideas and are of such slight social value as a step to truth that any benefit that may be derived from them is clearly outweighed by the social interest in order and morality."

1943

The Bill of Rights is included for the first time in the handbooks given to immigrants to study for their citizenship tests.

In *West Virginia State Board of Education v. Barnette,* the U.S. Supreme Court overturns a law requiring schoolchildren to salute the U.S. flag, holding that the government cannot compel or coerce an individual's speech against his conscience. Justice Jackson, writing for the majority, stated that "[i]f there is any fixed star in our constitutional constellation, it is that no official, high or petty, can prescribe what shall be orthodox in politics, nationalism, religion or other matters of opinion or force citizens to confess by word or act their faith therein."

1951

During the era of McCarthyism and Communist witch-hunting, the Court weakens free speech rights by ruling that speakers can be punished for advocating overthrow of the government, even if the likelihood of such an occurrence is remote.

1953

The Freedom to Read statement is issued by the Westchester Conference of the American Library Association and the American Publishers Council, which in 1970 consolidated with the American Educational Publishers Institute to become the Association of American Publishers. The statement was subsequently endorsed by American Booksellers Association, American Booksellers Foundation for Free Expression, American Civil Liberties Union, American Federation of Teachers AFL-CIO, Anti-Defamation League of B'nai B'rith, Association of American University Presses, Children's Book Council, Freedom to Read Foundation, International Reading Association, Thomas Jefferson Center for the Protection of Free Expression, National Association of College Stores, National Council of Teachers of English, P.E.N.-American Center, People for the American Way, Periodical and Book Association of America, Sex Information and Education Council of the U.S., Society of Professional Journalists, Women's National Book Association, and YWCA of the USA.

1957

The appeal taken in *Roth v. U.S.,* 354 U.S. 476, directly raises before the U.S. Supreme Court the question of whether obscenity is speech protected under either the First or Fourteenth Amendments. U.S. Justice Brennan answered that it is not, and set forth the standard for judging obscenity as "whether to the average person, applying contemporary standards, the dominant theme of the material taken as a whole appeals to the prurient interest." The "Hicklin test," which judged obscenity by the effect of isolated excerpts upon the most susceptible persons in a community, was thus rejected.

The Court, in *Yates v. United States,* 354 U.S. 298, draws a distinction between advocacy of an abstract doctrine such as Marxism and advocacy directed at promoting unlawful action. The decision construed certain federal statutes regulating subversive political activity to permit advocacy and teaching of the forcible overthrow of the government, even with evil intent, so long as the advocacy and teaching is divorced from any effort to instigate action.

1961

In *Scales v. U.S.,* 367 U.S. 203, the Court further construes the statutes at issue in *Yates v. United States,* upholding a clause that criminalizes knowing membership in any organization that advocates the overthrow of the government by force or violence. The clause presses the limits of constitutionality, the Court observed. However, "active" members who also have a "guilty knowledge and intent"—going beyond "merely an expression of sympathy with an alleged criminal enterprise"— "unaccompanied by any significant action" or "any commitment to undertake such action" engage in illegal advocacy.

1962

The U.S. Supreme Court, in *Engel v. Vitale,* 370 U.S. 421, rules that public school use of a prayer composed by state officials and recommended as part of a program for moral and spiritual training violated the First Amendment prohibition against governmental establishment of religion. The Court found irrelevant the fact that the prayer may have been denominationally neutral or that its observance by students was voluntary.

1964

In the first libel case to reach the Supreme Court, *New York Times v. Sullivan,* 376 U.S. 254, the justices rule 9-0 that a public official may not recover damages for a defamatory statement, unless he can prove the statement was made with "actual malice."

1967

The American Library Association establishes the Office for Intellectual Freedom. The office's goal is to educate librarians and the general public on the importance of intellectual freedom.

1968

Though the Supreme Court has made clear in a series of opinions that symbolic speech may be protected by the First Amendment, in *United States v. O'Brien,* 391 U.S. 367, it identified the limits that could be placed on symbolic speech. After he burned his draft card during a public protest, Paul O'Brien was found guilty of violating federal statutes forbidding the destruction of Selective Service documents. The Court affirmed O'Brien's conviction, stating that the draft card statutes furthered an important governmental objective unrelated to the suppression of speech, were narrowly tailored to achieve the government's legitimate objective of assuring the efficient functioning of the selective service system, and left open ample alternative means for protest. Laws that did not meet this stringent test would be struck down as unconstitutional.

1969

The Freedom to Read Foundation is created. The Foundation assists groups or individuals in litigation by securing counsel, or providing funding and by participating directly or as a "friend of the court" in important and possibly precedent-setting litigation.

1969

Reversing the conviction of a Ku Klux Klan member, the U.S. Supreme Court, in *Brandenberg v. Ohio,* 395 U.S. 444, overrules its earlier decision, which had upheld criminal syndicalism statutes that proscribe advocacy of violent means to effect political and economic change. Constitutional guarantees do not permit a state to forbid such speech, except where advocacy of the use of force "is directed to inciting or producing imminent lawless action and is likely to incite or produce such action."

1971

Efforts by the U.S. federal government to stop the publication of the "Pentagon Papers," bring to a head conflicting claims of free speech and national security. The Court ruling in *New York Times Company v. United States,* 403 U.S. 713, reaffirmed the heavy presumption that a "prior restraint" of free expression is constitutionally invalid. Because the government failed to meet the "heavy burden of showing justification" for such a restraint, newspapers were not enjoined from releasing the secret history of American involvement in Vietnam.

1973

Striving to remove confusions concerning a test for obscenity requiring that the material be "utterly without redeeming social value," the Supreme Court in *Miller v. California,* 413 U.S. 15, reformulated the test. The Court's test, which still stands, involves three parts. First, the average person, applying contemporary community standards, finds that the work, taken as a whole, appeals to the prurient interests. Second, that the work depicts sexual conduct in a patently offensive way. Third, the work, taken as a whole, lacks serious literary, artistic, political or scientific value.

1977

When neo-Nazi Frank Collin and his National Socialist Party of America are denied a permit to march in Skokie, a Chicago suburb with thousands of Holocaust survivors, the ACLU fights for their First Amendment rights. The protracted legal battle concluded after the U.S. Supreme Court refused, in *Smith v. Collin,* 439 U.S. 916, to review the proceedings, resulting in Collin eventually obtaining a permit. The Party's march, however, was held in Chicago's Marquette Park.

1978

In proceedings on a complaint about an afternoon radio broadcast of comic George Carlin's seven "dirty words" monologue, the Supreme Court in *Federal Communications Commission v. Pacifica Foundation,* 438 U.S. 726, upholds an FCC order as to "possible" sanctions against the radio station, which found the monologue as broadcast "indecent" but not obscene.

1979

When the *Progressive,* an alternative newspaper in Madison, Wis., prepares to run a cover story that explains how to build a hydrogen bomb, the government takes quick action to prevent publication. After a seven-month showdown, the government backs down and the article runs.

1981

Banned Books Week: Celebrating the Freedom to Read is created. The week is sponsored by the American Booksellers Association, the American Booksellers Foundation for Free Expression, the American Library Association, the American Society of Journalists and Authors, the Association of American Publishers, and the National Association of College Stores. These groups sponsor this week to draw attention to the danger that exists when restraints are imposed on the availability of information in a free society.

1982

In *Island Trees Union Free School District No. 26 v. Pico,* 457 U.S. 853, a divided U.S. Supreme Court recognizes that a board of education's discretion to remove books from junior and senior high school libraries is more limited than its discretion with respect to classrooms and the curriculum. The plurality opinion by Justice William Brennan declared that "local school boards may not remove books from school library shelves simply because they dislike the ideas contained in those books and seek by their removal to prescribe what shall be orthodox in politics, nationalism, religion or other matters of opinion."

1982

The U.S. Supreme Court added child pornography as another category of speech excluded from First Amendment protection. The ruling came in the case *New York v. Ferber,* 458 U.S. 747, when the Court upheld the constitutionality of a New York statute prohibiting persons from promoting a sexual performance by a child under the age of sixteen by distributing material, which need not be legally obscene, that depicts such a performance.

1989

Burning the U.S. flag is a protected form of symbolic political speech, the Supreme Court rules in *Texas v. Johnson,* 491 U.S. 397. Because a principal function of free speech is to invite dispute, any interest asserted by the state in preventing breaches of the peace from outraged onlookers was found to be insufficient to support the defendant's conviction under a Texas statute prohibiting "desecration of a venerated object."

1990

The Supreme Court, in *U.S. v. Eichmann* and *U.S. v. Haggerty,* 496 U.S. 310, strikes down convictions under the Flag Protection Act of 1989, passed by Congress in response to the Court's flag desecration decision that year.

1990

The constitutionally protected right to receive obscenity, and information generally, in the privacy of one's home does not extend to child pornography, the U.S. Supreme Court rules in *Osborne v. Ohio,* 495 U.S. 103. The Court found that Ohio reasonably concluded that the state will decrease the production of child pornography, thereby protecting child victims, if it penalizes those who possess and view the product.

1992

The U.S. Supreme Court clarifies that "fighting words" is not a category of speech that is wholly outside of First Amendment protection. In *R.A.V. v. St. Paul*, 505 U.S. 377, the Court overturned a St. Paul ordinance punishing the placement of certain symbols that were "likely to arouse anger, alarm, or resentment on the basis of race, religion, or gender" after a teenager was convicted of violating the ordinance by burning a cross in the yard of a black family. The Court reversed the teen's conviction on the grounds that the ordinance unconstitutionally criminalized some hurtful expression (specifically that aimed at racial and religious minorities) and not other hurtful expression (that aimed at other unprotected groups) based on the political preferences of legislators.

1997

The first U.S. Supreme Court decision regarding the Internet, *American Library Association v. U.S. Department of Justice* and *Reno v. American Civil Liberties Union*, 521 U.S. 844, strike down provisions of the Communications Decency Act regulating "indecent" and "patently offensive" speech. Intended to protect minors, the Act was found to unconstitutionally limit adults' reading on the Internet to only "what is fit for children." The rare 9-0 decision by the Court sets forth the rule that the First Amendment applies, without limitation or restriction, to all content published on the Internet.

1998

In response to the U.S. Supreme Court's decision in *Reno v. ACLU*, Congress enacts the Child Online Protection Act (COPA), which criminalizes the online transmission of material considered harmful to minors for commercial purposes. Artists, writers, and publishers immediately challenge the new law, and the courts prohibit its enforcement. The law is eventually declared unconstitutional and overturned after a decade of litigation.

2003

The U.S. Supreme Court upholds the Children's Internet Protection Act in *United States v. American Library Association*, 539 U.S. 194, a law requiring public schools and libraries receiving certain kinds of federal funding to install Internet filtering software on their computers. The Court upholds the law as a constitutional condition imposed on

institutions in exchange for government funding because the law's provisions entitle adult patrons to ask the institution to disable the filtering software, noting that, "[w]hen a patron encounters a blocked site, he need only ask a librarian to unblock it or (at least in the case of adults) disable the filter."

2004

The U.S. Supreme Court upholds a lower court's preliminary injunction preventing enforcement of the Child Online Protection Act (COPA). The Court reasons that the use of filtering software by parents is an alternative less restrictive of First Amendment rights than COPA, which criminalized online transmission of speech protected for adults. The Court noted that parents' use of filtering was likely a more effective means of restricting children's access to materials considered harmful to minors.

2010

In *Citizens United v. Federal Election Commission*, the U.S. Supreme Court holds that corporate funding of independent political broadcasts in candidate elections cannot be limited by the government, overturning existing laws restricting what and when profit-making and nonprofit corporations may say during federal election campaigns. Writing on behalf of the majority, Justice Kennedy wrote that "[i]f the First Amendment has any force, it prohibits Congress from fining or jailing citizens, or associations of citizens, for simply engaging in political speech." The opinion was immediately criticized for holding that corporations are, for constitutional purposes, persons entitled to First Amendment rights as well as increasing the power of corporations and special interests to influence elections.

2014

Challenges to library materials continue. Among the challenged titles in the past year are *The Absolutely True Diary of a Part-Time Indian*, by Sherman Alexie; *The Handmaid's Tale*, by Margaret Atwood; *The Perks of Being a Wallflower*, by Stephen Chbosky; *Invisible Man*, by Ralph Ellison; *Anne Frank: The Diary of a Young Girl*, by Anne Frank; *Bluest Eye*, by Toni Morrison; *Persepolis: The Story of a Childhood*, by Marjane Satrapi; and

The Color Purple, by Alice Walker. Librarians, teachers, parents, trustees, students, and administrators continue to work to defend library collections.

This timeline was compiled using a variety of sources including, but not limited to: Patrick, John J. *Oxford Companion to the Supreme Court of the United States*. New York: Oxford University Pr., 1994;

Spaeth, Harold J., and Edward Conrad Smith. *The Constitution of the United States*. New York: HarperPerennial, 1991; and

Weber, Laura, and Charles Apple. "The Evolving 1st Amendment." *Chicago Tribune*, Friday, July 4, 1997.

First Amendment Court Cases

Notable First Amendment Court Cases

This section contains summaries of frequently cited First Amendment cases. Arranged by topic, they cover case law issued by a variety of courts: the Supreme Court of the United States, the Court of Appeals of different Federal circuits, the District Court of several Federal districts, as well as the highest court of several states and particular appellate courts of action.

The standard citation is given to indicate where to find the complete text of a decision. For example, *Kreimer v. Bureau of Police for Morristown*, 958 F.2 1242 (3d Cir. 1992), gives the names of the main parties in the case ("Kreimer," who sued the "Bureau of Police for Morristown"), the abbreviated title of the case reporter where the decision is published ("F.2d" for *Federal Reporter, Second Series*)—which is preceded by the particular volume number ("958") of the reporter and followed by the page number 1242 where the decision begins—and, in parentheses, the name of court that issued the decision ("3d Cir." for Court of Appeals for the Third Circuit) and the year ("1992"). Other conventions may apply, depending on which case reporter is involved.

Abbreviations

U.S.	=	United States Reports
S.Ct.	=	Supreme Court Reporter
L.Ed.	=	United States Supreme Court Reports Lawyers' Edition
L.Ed.2d	=	United States Supreme Court Reports Lawyers' Edition, Second Series
F.2d	=	Federal Reporter, Second Series
F.3d	=	Federal Reporter, Third Series
F.Supp.	=	Federal Supplement
F.Supp.2d	=	Federal Supplement, Second Series
N.W.	=	North Western Reporter
N.W.2d	=	North Western Reporter, Second Series
N.Y.S.	=	New York Supplement
N.Y.S.2d	=	New York Supplement, Second Series
P.	=	Pacific Reporter

Foundations of Free Expression: Historic Cases

Schenck v. United States
249 U.S. 47, 39 S.Ct. 247, 63 L.Ed.2d (1919)

Justice Oliver Wendell Holmes, Jr., stated in this case his famous aphorism about "falsely shouting fire in a theatre" and set forth a "clear and present danger test" to judge whether speech is protected by the First Amendment. "The question," he wrote, "is whether the words are used in such circumstances and are of such a nature as to create a clear and present danger that they will bring about the substantive evils that Congress has the right to prevent. It is a question of proximity and degree." The Supreme Court affirmed the convictions of the defendants for conspiring to violate certain federal statutes by attempting to incite subordination in the armed forces and interfere with recruitment and enlistment. During wartime, the defendants mailed to new recruits and enlisted men leaflets that compared military conscription to involuntary servitude and urged them to assert their constitutional rights.

Near v. Minnesota
283 U.S. 697, 51 S.Ct. 625, 75 L.Ed. 1357 (1931)

In this case, the Supreme Court interpreted the First and Fourteenth Amendments to forbid "previous restraints" upon publication of a newspaper. "Previous restraints"—or in current terminology, "prior restraints"—suppress the freedom of the press to publish without obstruction, and recognize that lawsuits or prosecutions for libel are "subsequent punishments." The Court invalidated as an infringement of constitutional guarantees a Minnesota statute allowing specified government officials or private citizens to maintain a lawsuit in the name of the State to suppress a public nuisance and enjoin the publication of future issues of a "malicious, scandalous and defamatory newspaper, magazine or other periodical," unless the publisher can prove "the truth was published with good motives and for justifiable ends."

Brandenburg v. Ohio
395 U.S. 444, 89 S.Ct. 1827, 23 L.Ed.2d 430 (1969)

The Supreme Court established the modern version of the "clear and present danger" doctrine, holding that states only could restrict speech that "is directed to inciting or producing imminent lawless action, and is likely to incite or produce such action."

The Right to Read Freely

Evans v. Shelma Union High School District of Fresno County
222 P. 801 (Ca. 1924)

The California State Supreme Court held that the King James version of the *Bible* was not a "publication of a sectarian, partisan, or denominational character" that a State statute required a public high school library to exclude from its collections. The "fact that the King James version is commonly used by Protestant Churches and not by Catholics" does not "make its character sectarian," the court stated. "The mere act of purchasing a book to be added to the school library does not carry with it any implication of the adoption of the theory or dogma contained therein, or any approval of the book itself, except as a work of literature fit to be included in a reference library."

Rosenberg v. Board of Education of City of New York
92 N.Y.S.2d 344 (Sup. Ct. Kings County 1949)

After considering the charge that *Oliver Twist* and the *Merchant of Venice* are "objectionable because they tend to engender hatred of the Jew as a person and as a race," the Supreme Court, Kings County, New York, decided that these two works cannot be banned from the New York City schools, libraries, or classrooms, declaring that the Board of Education "acted in good faith without malice or prejudice and in the best interests of

the school system entrusted to their care and control, and, therefore, that no substantial reason exists which compels the suppression of the two books under consideration."

Todd v. Rochester Community Schools
200 N.W.2d 90 (Mich. Ct. App. 1972)

In deciding that *Slaughterhouse-Five* could not be banned from the libraries and classrooms of the Michigan schools, the Court of Appeals of Michigan declared: "Vonnegut's literary dwellings on war, religion, death, Christ, God, government, politics, and any other subject should be as welcome in the public schools of this state as those of Machiavelli, Chaucer, Shakespeare, Melville, Lenin, Joseph McCarthy, or Walt Disney. The students of Michigan are free to make of *Slaughterhouse-Five* what they will."

Minarcini v. Strongsville (Ohio) City School District
541 F.2d 577 (6th Cir. 1976)

The Strongsville City Board of Education rejected faculty recommendations to purchase Joseph Heller's *Catch-22* and Kurt Vonnegut's *God Bless You, Mr. Rosewater* and ordered the removal of *Catch-22* and Vonnegut's *Cat's Cradle* from the library. The U.S. Court of Appeals for the Sixth Circuit ruled against the school board, upholding the students' First Amendment right to receive information and the librarian's right to disseminate it. "The removal of books from a school library is a much more serious burden upon the freedom of classroom discussion than the action found unconstitutional in *Tinker v. Des Moines School District*."

Right to Read Defense Committee v. School Committee of the City of Chelsea
454 F.Supp. 703 (D. Mass. 1978)

The Chelsea, Massachusetts, School Committee decided to bar from the high school library a poetry anthology,

Male and Female Under 18, because of the inclusion of an "offensive" and "damaging" poem, "The City to a Young Girl," written by a fifteen-year-old girl. Challenged in U.S. District Court, Joseph L. Tauro ruled: "The library is 'a mighty resource in the marketplace of ideas.' There a student can literally explore the unknown, and discover areas of interest and thought not covered by the prescribed curriculum. The student who discovers the magic of the library is on the way to a life-long experience of self-education and enrichment. That student learns that a library is a place to test or expand upon ideas presented to him, in or out of the classroom. The most effective antidote to the poison of mindless orthodoxy is ready access to a broad sweep of ideas and philosophies. There is no danger from such exposure. The danger is mind control. The committee's ban of the anthology *Male and Female* is enjoined."

Salvail v. Nashua Board of Education
469 F.Supp. 1269 (D.N.H. 1979)

MS magazine was removed from a New Hampshire high school library by order of the Nashua School Board. The U.S. District Court decided for the student, teacher, and adult residents who had brought action against the school board, the Court concluding: "The Court finds and rules that the defendants herein have failed to demonstrate a substantial and legitimate government interest sufficient to warrant the removal of *MS* magazine from the Nashua High School library. Their action contravenes the plaintiffs' First Amendment rights, and as such it is plainly wrong."

Loewen v. Turnipseed
488 F.Supp. 1138 (N.D. Miss. 1980)

When the Mississippi Textbook Purchasing Board refused to approve *Mississippi: Conflict and Change* for use in Mississippi public schools, on the grounds that it was too concerned with racial matters and too controversial, the authors filed suit. U.S. District Judge Orma R. Smith ruled that the criteria used were not justifiable grounds for rejecting the book. He held that the controversial racial matter was a factor leading to its rejection, and thus the authors had been denied their constitutionally guaranteed rights of freedom of speech and the press.

Kreimer v. Bureau of Police for Morristown
958 F.2d 1242 (3d Cir. 1992)

In detailed analysis, the court of appeals held that a municipal public library was a limited public forum, meaning open to the public for the specified purposes of exercising their First Amendment rights to read and receive information from library materials. Such exercise could not interfere with or disrupt the library's reasonable rules of operation. The court then upheld three library rules which: (1) required patrons to read, study, or otherwise use library materials while there; (2) prohibited noisy or boisterous activities which might disturb other patrons; and (3) permitted the removal of any patron whose offensive bodily hygiene was a nuisance to other patrons.

Case v. Unified School District No. 233
908 F.Supp. 864 (D. Kan. 1995)

When the Olathe, Kansas, School Board voted to remove the book *Annie on My Mind*, a novel depicting a lesbian relationship between two teenagers, from the district's junior and senior high school libraries, the federal district court in Kansas found they violated the students' rights under the First Amendment to the United States Constitution and the corresponding provisions of the Kansas State Constitution. Despite the fact that the school board testified that they had removed the book because of "educational unsuitability," which is within their rights under the *Pico* decision, it became obvious from their testimony that the book was removed because they disapproved of the book's ideology. In addition, it was found that the school board had violated its own materials selection and reconsideration policies, which weighed heavily in the judge's decision.

Campbell v. St. Tammany Parish School Board
64 F.3d 184 (5th Cir. 1995)

A public school district removed the book *Voodoo and Hoodoo*—a discussion of the origins, history, and practices of the voodoo and hoodoo religions that included an outline of some specific practices—from all district library shelves. Parents of several students sued and the district court granted summary judgment in their favor. The court of appeals reversed, finding that there was not enough evidence at that stage to determine that board members had an unconstitutional motivation, such as denying students access to ideas with which board members disagreed; the court remanded the case for a full trial at which all board members could be questioned about their reasons for removing the book. The court observed that "in light of the special role of the school library as a place where students may freely and voluntarily explore diverse topics, the school board's non-curricular decision to remove a book well after it had been placed in the public school libraries evokes the question whether that action might not be an attempt to 'strangle the free mind at its source.'" The court focused on some evidence that school board members had removed the book without having read it or having read only excerpts provided by the Christian Coalition. The parties settled the case before trial by returning the book to the libraries on specially designated reserve shelves.

Sund v. City of Wichita Falls, Texas
121 F.Supp. 2d 530 (N.D. Texas 2000)

City residents who were members of a church sought removal of two books, *Heather Has Two Mommies* and *Daddy's Roommate*, because they disapproved of the books' depiction of homosexuality. The Wichita Falls City Council voted to restrict access to the books if 300 persons signed a petition asking for the restriction. A separate group of citizens filed suit after the books were removed from the children's section and placed on a locked shelf in the adult area of the library. Following a trial on the merits, the district court permanently enjoined the city from enforcing the resolution permitting the removal of the two books. It held that the city's resolution constituted impermissible content-based and viewpoint-based discrimination; was not narrowly tailored to serve a compelling state interest; provided no standards or review process; and improperly delegated governmental authority over the selection and removal of the library's books to any 300 private citizens who wish to remove a book from the children's area of the library.

Counts v. Cedarville School District
295 F.Supp.2d 996 (W.D. Ark. 2003)

The Cedarville, Arkansas, School Board voted to restrict students' access to the *Harry Potter* books, on the grounds that the books promoted disobedience and disrespect for authority and dealt with witchcraft and the occult. As a result of the vote, students in the Cedarville school district were required to obtain a signed permission slip from their parents or guardians before they would be allowed to borrow any of the *Harry Potter* books from school libraries. The district court overturned the board's decision and ordered the books returned to unrestricted circulation, on the grounds that the restrictions violated students' First Amendment right to read and receive information. In so doing, the court noted that while the board necessarily performed highly discretionary functions related to the operation of the schools, it was still bound by the Bill of Rights and could not abridge students' First Amendment right to read a book on the basis of an undifferentiated fear of disturbance or because the board disagreed with the ideas contained in the book.

See also:
Board of Education, Island Trees Union Free School District No. 26 v. Pico, 457 U.S. 853, 102 S.Ct. 2799, 73 L.Ed.2d 435 (1982)

Smith v. Board of School Commissioners of Mobile (Ala.) County, 827 F.2d 684 (11th Cir. 1987)

Mozert v. Hawkins County Board of Education, 827 F.2d 1058 (6th Cir. 1987)

Virgil v. School Board of Columbia County, 862 F.2d 1517 (11th Cir. 1989)

American Library Association v. U.S. Department of Justice and Reno v. American Civil Liberties Union, 521 U.S. 844, 117 S.Ct. 2329, 138 L.Ed.2d 874 (1997)

Mainstream Loudoun, et al. v. Board of Trustees of the Loudoun County Library, 24 F.Supp.2d 552 (E.D. Va. 1998)

Freedom of Expression in Schools

Tinker v. Des Moines Independent Community School District
393 U.S. 503, 89 S.Ct. 733, 21 L.Ed.2d 731 (1969)

In this seminal case considering the First Amendment rights of students who were expelled after they wore black armbands to school in symbolic protest of the Vietnam War, the Supreme Court held that students "do not shed their constitutional rights at the schoolhouse gate" and that the First Amendment protects public school students' rights to express political and social views.

Zykan v. Warsaw (Indiana) Community School Corporation and Warsaw School Board of Trustees
631 F.2d 1300 (7th Cir. 1980)

A student brought suit seeking to reverse school officials' decision to "limit or prohibit the use of certain textbooks, to remove a certain book from the school library, and to delete certain courses from the curriculum." The district court dismissed the suit. On appeal, the Court of Appeals for the Seventh Circuit ruled that the school board has the right to establish a curriculum on the basis of its own discretion, but it is forbidden to impose a "pall of orthodoxy." The right of students to file complaints was recognized, but the

court held that the students' claims "must cross a relatively high threshold before entering upon the field of a constitutional claim suitable for federal court litigation."

Board of Education, Island Trees Union Free School District No. 26 v. Pico
457 U.S. 853, 102 S.Ct. 2799, 73 L.Ed.2d 435 (1982)

In 1975, three school board members sought the removal of several books determined objectionable by a politically conservative organization. The following February, the board gave an "unofficial direction" that the books be removed from the school libraries, so that board members could read them. When the board action attracted press attention, the board described the books as "anti-American, anti-Christian, anti-Semitic, and just plain filthy." The nine books that were the subject of the lawsuit were *Slaughterhouse-Five*, by Kurt Vonnegut, Jr.; *The Naked Ape*, by Desmond Morris; *Down These Mean Streets*, by Piri Thomas; *Best Short Stories of Negro Writers*, edited by Langston Hughes; *Go Ask Alice*; *Laughing Boy*, by Oliver LaFarge; *Black Boy*, by Richard Wright; *A Hero Ain't Nothin' But a Sandwich*, by Alice Childress; and *Soul on Ice*, by Eldrige Cleaver.

The board appointed a review committee that recommended that five of the books be returned to the shelves, two be placed on restricted shelves, and two be removed from the library. The full board voted to remove all but one book.

After years of appeals, the U.S. Supreme Court upheld (5-4) the students' challenge to the board's action. The Court held that school boards do not have unrestricted authority to select library books and that the First Amendment is implicated when books are removed arbitrarily. Justice Brennan declared in the plurality opinion: "Local school boards may not remove books from school library shelves simply because they dislike the ideas contained in those books and seek by their removal to prescribe what shall be orthodox in politics, nationalism, religion, or other matters of opinion."

Smith v. Board of School Commissioners of Mobile (Ala.) County
827 F.2d 684 (11th Cir. 1987)

Parents and other citizens brought a lawsuit against the school board, alleging that the school system was teaching the tenets of an anti-religious religion called "secular humanism." The complainants asked that forty-four different elementary through high-school level textbooks be removed from the curriculum. After an initial ruling in a federal district court in favor of the plaintiffs, the U.S. Court of Appeals for the Eleventh Circuit ruled that as long as the school was motivated by a secular purpose, it didn't matter whether the curriculum and texts shared ideas held by one or more religious groups. The court found that the texts in question promoted important secular values (tolerance, self-respect, logical decision making) and thus the use of the textbooks neither unconstitutionally advanced a nontheistic religion nor inhibited theistic religions.

Mozert v. Hawkins County Board of Education
827 F.2d 1058 (6th Cir. 1987)

Parents and students brought this action challenging the mandatory use of certain textbooks on the ground that the texts promoted values offensive to their religious beliefs. The U.S. Court of Appeals for the Sixth Circuit rejected the plaintiffs' claim, finding that the Constitution does not require school curricula to be revised substantially in order to accommodate religious beliefs.

Hazelwood School District v. Kuhlmeier
484 U.S. 260, 108 S.Ct. 562, 98 L.Ed.2d 592 (1988)

After a school principal removed two pages containing articles on teenage pregnancy and the impact of divorce on students from a newspaper produced as part of a high school journalism class, the student staff filed suit claiming violation of their First Amendment rights. The principal defended his action on the grounds that he was protecting the privacy of the pregnant students described, protecting younger students from inappropriate references to sexual activity and birth control, and protecting the school from a potential libel action.

The Supreme Court held that the principal acted reasonably and did not violate the students' First Amendment rights. A school need not tolerate student speech, the Court declared, "that is inconsistent with its 'basic educational mission,' even though the government could not censor similar speech outside the school." In addition, the Court found the newspaper was part of the regular journalism curriculum and subject to extensive control by a faculty member. The school, thus, did not create a public forum for the expression of ideas, but instead maintained the newspaper "as supervised learning experience for journalism students." The Court concluded that, "educators do not offend the First Amendment by exercising editorial control over the style and content of student speech in school-sponsored expressive activities so long as their actions are reasonably related to legitimate pedagogical concerns." The Court strongly suggested that supervised student activities that "may fairly be characterized as part of the school curriculum," including school-sponsored publications and theatrical productions, were subject to the authority of educators. The Court cautioned, however, that this authority does not justify an educator's attempt "to silence a student's personal expression that happens to occur on the school premises."

Virgil v. School Board of Columbia County
862 F.2d 1517 (11th Cir. 1989)

This case presented the question of whether the First Amendment prevents a school board from removing a previously approved textbook from an elective high school class because of objections to the material's vulgarity and sexual explicitness. The U.S. Circuit Court of Appeals concluded that a school board may, without contravening constitutional limits, take such action when the removal decision was "reasonably related" to the "legitimate pedagogical concern" of denying students access to "potentially sensitive topics." The written "stipulation concerning Board Reasons" cites explicit sexuality and excessively vulgar language in two selections contained in *Volume 1, The Humanities: Cultural Roots and Continuities* as the basis for removal of this textbook. The two s elections are Chaucer's *The Miller's Tale* and Aristophanes' *Lysistrata*.

Romano v. Harrington
725 F.Supp. 687 (E.D. N.Y. 1989)

The U.S. District Court found in favor of a faculty adviser to a high school newspaper who claimed a violation of the First and Fourteenth Amendments when fired following the newspaper's publication of a student's article opposing the federal holiday for Martin Luther King, Jr. The court held that educators may exercise greater editorial control over what students write for class than what they voluntarily submit to extracurricular publications.

Cohen v. San Bernardino Valley College
92 F.3d 968 (9th Cir. 1996)

A tenured English professor was disciplined for violating the college's sexual harassment policy against creating a "hostile learning environment" for his in-class use of profanity, and discussions of sex, pornography, obscenity, cannibalism, and other controversial topics in a confrontational, devil's advocate style. The court held the policy unconstitutionally vague as applied to Cohen's in-class speech, calling it a "legalistic ambush." In-class speech did not fall within the policy's core definition of sexual harassment and Cohen, who had used this apparently sound and proper teaching style for year, did not know the policy would be applied to him or his teaching methods.

Morse v. Frederick
551 U.S. 393 (2007)

In this case, the Supreme Court ruled that a principal did not violate the First Amendment rights of a student when the principal punished the student for displaying a banner across the street from the school that read "Bong Hits 4 Jesus." The Court held that school officials can prohibit students from displaying messages that promote illegal drug use, explaining that while students do have some right to political speech even while in school, this right does not extend to pro-drug messages that may undermine the school's important mission to discourage drug use, and that the highly protective standard set by *Tinker* would not always be applied. Justice Alito stressed that the decision applied only to pro-drug messages and not to broader political speech.

See also:
Evans v. Shelma Union High School District of Fresno County, 222 P. 801 (Ca. 1924)

West Virginia State Board of Education v. Barnette, 319 U.S. 624 (1943)

Rosenberg v. Board of Education of City of New York, 92 N.Y.S.2d 344 (Sup. Ct. Kings County 1949)

Todd v. Rochester Community Schools, 200 N.W.2d 90 (Mich. Ct. App. 1972)

Minarcini v. Strongsville (Ohio) City School District, 541 F.2d 577 (6th Cir. 1976)

Right to Read Defense Committee v. School Committee of the City of Chelsea, 454 F.Supp. 703 (D. Mass. 1978)

Salvail v. Nashua Board of Education, 469 F.Supp. 1269 (D.N.H. 1979)

Loewen v. Turnipseed, 488 F.Supp. 1138 (N.D. Miss. 1980)

Case v. Unified School District No. 233, 908 F.Supp. 864 (D. Kan. 1995)

Campbell v. St. Tammany Parish School Board, 64 F.3d 184 (5th Cir. 1995)

Counts v. Cedarville School District, 295 F.Supp.2d 996 (W.D. Ark. 2003)

Minors' First Amendment Rights

American Amusement Machine Association, et al. v. Teri Kendrick, et al.
244 F.3d 572 (7th Cir. 2001); cert. denied, 534 U.S. 994; 122 S. Ct. 462; 151 L.Ed.2d 379 (2001).

Enacted in July 2001, an Indianapolis, Indiana, city ordinance required video game arcade owners to limit access to games that depicted certain activities, including amputation, decapitation, dismemberment, bloodshed, or sexual intercourse. Only with the permission of an accompanying parent or guardian could children seventeen years old and younger play these types of video games. On March 23, 2001, a three-judge panel of the Seventh Circuit Court of Appeals reversed and remanded the trial court's decision stating that, "children have First Amendment rights." On Monday, October 29, 2001, the U.S. Supreme Court denied certiorari, thus letting the appeals court's decision stand.

Interactive Digital Software Association, et al. v. St. Louis County, Missouri, et al.
329 F.3d 954 (8th Cir. 2003)

St. Louis County passed an ordinance that banned selling or renting violent video games to minors, or permitting them to play such games, without parental consent, and video game dealers sued to overturn the law. The court of appeals found the ordinance unconstitutional, holding that depictions of violence alone cannot fall within the legal definition of obscenity for either minors or adults, and that a government cannot silence protected speech for children by wrapping itself in the cloak of parental authority. The court ordered the lower court to enter an injunction barring enforcement of the law, citing the Supreme Court's recognition in *Erznoznik v. Jacksonville*, 422 U.S. 205, 213–14, 45 L.Ed.2d 125, 95 S. Ct. 2268 (1975) that "speech that is neither obscene as to youths nor subject to some other legitimate proscription cannot be suppressed solely to protect the young from ideas or images that a legislative body thinks unsuitable for them. In most circumstances, the values protected by the First Amendment are no less applicable when the government seeks to control the flow of information to minors."

See also:
West Virginia State Board of Education v. Barnette, 319 U.S. 624 (1943)

Ginsberg v. New York, 390 U.S. 629 (1968)

Tinker v. Des Moines Independent Community School District, 393 U.S. 503, 89 S.Ct. 733, 21 L.Ed.2d 731 (1969)

Board of Education, Island Trees Union Free School District No. 26 v. Pico, 457 U.S. 853, 102 S.Ct. 2799, 73 L.Ed.2d 435 (1982)

Free Press

New York Times Company v. United States
403 U.S. 713, 91 S.Ct. 2140, 29 L.Ed.2d 822 (1971)

In the "Pentagon Papers" case, the U.S. government attempted to enjoin the *New York Times* and the *Washington Post* from publishing classified documents concerning the Vietnam War. Applying the doctrine of prior restraint from *Near v. Minnesota*, the Court found that the claims that publication of the documents would interfere with foreign policy and prolong the war were too speculative, and could not overcome the strong presumption against prior restraint.

Hustler Magazine, Inc. v. Falwell
485 U.S. 46, 108 S.Ct. 876, 99 L.Ed.2d 41 (1988)

Hustler magazine published a parody of a liquor advertisement in which Rev. Jerry Falwell described his "first time" as a drunken encounter with his mother in an outhouse. A unanimous Supreme Court held that a public figure had to show actual malice in order to recover for intentional infliction of emotional distress as a result of a parody in a magazine. The Court held that political cartoons and satire such as this parody "have played a prominent role in public and political debate. And although the outrageous caricature in this case "is at best a distant cousin of political cartoons," the Court could see no standard to distinguish among types of parodies that would not harm public discourse, which would be poorer without such satire.

Simon & Schuster, Inc. v. Members of New York State Crime Victims Board
502 U.S. 105, 112 S.Ct. 501, 116 L.Ed.2d 476 (1991)

The Supreme Court struck down New York's "Son of Sam Law," which required book publishers to turn over to the state any proceeds from a book written by any person convicted of a crime, related to, or about that crime. The Court said the law impermissibly singled out income only from the prisoner's expressive activity, and then only expressive activity relating to his crime, without necessarily compensating any victims of those crimes. The Court agreed that many important books—including the *Autobiography of Malcolm X,* Thoreau's *Civil Disobedience,* and works by Martin Luther King— perhaps might not have been published with such a law in place.

See also:
The New York Times v. Sullivan, 376 U.S. 254, 84 S.Ct. 710, 11 L.Ed.2d 686 (1964)

Gertz v. Robert Welch, Inc., 418 U.S. 323, 94 S.Ct. 2997, 41 L.Ed.2d 789 (1974)

The Right to Dissent

West Virginia State Board of Education v. Barnette
319 U.S. 624, 87 L.Ed. 1628, 63 S.Ct. 1178 (1943)

In 1940, the West Virginia Board of Education issued regulations requiring every schoolchild to participate daily in a salute to the flag of the United States. The Barnette children, all members of the Jehovah's Witnesses, refused to participate in the flag salute, consistent with the tenets of their religious beliefs, and were expelled from school. The Supreme Court struck down the regulation on the grounds that the First Amendment barred any rule compelling an individual to salute the flag or participate in the Pledge of Allegiance. In strong language, the Court affirmed the right to dissent: "But freedom to differ is not limited to things that do not matter much. That would be a mere shadow of freedom. The test of its substance is the right to differ as to things that touch the heart of the existing order. If there is any fixed star in our constitutional constellation, it is that no official, high or petty, can prescribe what shall be orthodox in politics, nationalism, religion, or other matters of opinion, or force citizens to confess by word or act their faith therein. If there are any circumstances which permit an exception, they do not now occur to us."

Texas v. Johnson
491 U.S. 397, 109 S.Ct. 2533, 105 L.Ed.2d 342 (1989)

In this case the Supreme Court held that burning the U.S. flag was a protected form of symbolic political speech, concluding that there is no legitimate government interest in protecting the U.S. flag where the sole act in question is destroying the flag in its symbolic capacity. "A bedrock principle underlying the First Amendment is that Government may not prohibit the expression of an idea simply because society finds the idea itself offensive or disagreeable."

U.S. v. Eichman and U.S. v. Haggerty
496 U.S. 310, 110 S.Ct. 2404, 110 L.Ed.2d 287 (1990)

The Supreme Court struck down a federal statute designed to allow the government to punish persons who burn U.S. flags. The Court held that the plain intent of the statute was to punish persons for political expression and that burning the flag inextricably carries with it a political message.

City of Ladue v. Gilleo
512 U.S. 43, 114 S.Ct. 2038, 129 L.Ed. 2d 36 (1994)

A federal court struck down a local ordinance banning the placement of signs on private property, in a challenge brought by a woman who had posted a sign on her lawn protesting the Persian Gulf War. The Court said lawn signs were a "venerable means of communication that is both unique and important," for which "no adequate substitutes exist."

R.A.V. v. St. Paul
505 U.S. 377, 112 S.Ct. 2538, 120 L.Ed.2d 305 (1992)

St. Paul, Minnesota, passed an ordinance that banned "hate speech" — any expression, such as a burning cross or swastika, that might arouse anger, alarm, or resentment in others on the basis of race, color, religion, or gender. The Supreme Court struck the ordinance down as unconstitutionally discriminating based on the content of expression: the law banned only fighting words that insult, based on race, religion, or gender, while abusive invective aimed at someone on the basis of political affiliation or sexual orientation would be permissible. The law thus reflected only the city's special hostility towards certain biases and not others, which is what the First Amendment forbids.

See also:
Tinker v. Des Moines Independent Community School District, 393 U.S. 503, 89 S.Ct. 733, 21 L.Ed.2d 731 (1969)

The Right to Free Association and the Freedom of Religion

Concerned Women for America, Inc. v. Lafayette County
883 F.2d 32 (5th Cir. 1989)

The county library that had permitted various groups to use its auditorium had created a designated public forum and thus could not deny access to groups whose meetings had political or religious content. Such a denial would be based on the content of speech and would be permissible only as the least restrictive means to serve a compelling interest. Preventing disruption or interference with general use of the library could be such an interest; library officials' first step to controlling such disruptions would be to impose reasonable regulations on the time, place, or manner of the auditorium's use, provided the regulations apply regardless of the subject matter of the speech.

Lamb's Chapel v. Center Moriches Union Free School Dist.
508 U.S. 384, 113 S.Ct. 2141, 124 L.Ed.2d 352 (1993)

The Court held that a school district that opened its classrooms after hours to a range of groups for social, civic, and recreational purposes, including films and lectures about a range of issues such as family values and child rearing, could not deny access to a religious organization to discuss the same, permissible issues from a religious point of view. Whether or not the classrooms were public fora, the school district could not deny use based on the speaker's point of view on an otherwise permissible topic.

Right to Privacy and Anonymity

Stanley v. Georgia
394 U.S. 55, 22 L.Ed.2d 542, 89 S.Ct. 1243 (1969)

A man found to possess obscene materials in his home for his private use was convicted of possessing obscene materials in violation of the state laws of Georgia. The Supreme Court overturned the conviction, holding that the Constitution protects the right to receive information and ideas, regardless of their social worth, and to be generally free from governmental intrusions into one's privacy on the grounds that the government "cannot constitutionally premise legislation on the desirability of controlling a person's private thoughts."

McIntyre v. Ohio Election Commission
514 U.S. 334, 115 S.Ct. 1511, 131 L.Ed.2d 426 (1995)

The Supreme Court struck down a state law banning distribution of anonymous campaign literature, emphasizing the long tradition of anonymous and pseudonymous political and literary speech and recognizing the right to exercise First Amendment rights anonymously as an "honorable tradition of advocacy and dissent."

Tattered Cover, Inc. v. City of Thornton
44 P.3d 1044 (Colo. Sup. Ct. 2002)

The Colorado Supreme Court reversed a court decision that required Denver's Tattered Cover Book Store to turn over information about books purchased by one of its customers. As part of an investigation, officers of the City of Thornton (Colo.) discovered two books on the manufacture of amphetamines in a suspect's residence and found a Tattered Cover mailer in the garbage. The officers, seeking to tie the books to the suspect directly, served a Drug Enforcement Agency subpoena on the Tattered Cover. The subpoena demanded the title of the books corresponding to the order and invoice numbers of the mailer, as well as information about all other books ever ordered by the suspect. The Tattered Cover then brought suit to litigate the validity of the search warrant. The court began its opinion by stating that both the First Amendment to the U.S. Constitution and Article II, Section 10, of the Colorado Constitution protect an individual's fundamental right to purchase books anonymously, free from governmental interference.

When Is Speech Unprotected? Obscenity and Indecency

Butler v. Michigan
352 U.S. 380, 1 L.Ed.2d 412, 77 S.Ct. 524 (1957)

A man convicted of selling "a book containing obscene, immoral, lewd, lascivious language, or descriptions, tending to incite minors to violent or depraved or immoral acts, manifestly tending to the corruption of the morals of youth" to a police officer appealed his conviction to the Supreme Court. The Court overturned the conviction and struck down the law, holding that the state's attempt to quarantine the general reading public against books not too rugged for grown men and women to read in order to shield juvenile innocence "is to burn the house to roast the pig." Famously, the Court ruled that the state of Michigan could not "reduce the adult population of Michigan to reading only what is fit for children."

Ginsberg v. New York
390 U.S. 62, 20 L.Ed.2d 195, 88 S. Ct. 1274 (1968)

The Supreme Court upheld a New York State statute barring retailers from selling sexually explicit publications to minors under the age of 17. Noting that the statute did not interfere with the right of adults to purchase and read such materials, it found that it was not constitutionally impermissible for New York to restrict minors' rights to such publications in light of the state's interest in safeguarding children's welfare and supporting parents' claim to authority in the rearing of their children.

Miller v. California
413 U.S. 15, 93 S.Ct. 2607, 37 L.Ed.2d 419 (1973)

In this case, the U.S. Supreme Court mapped out its famous three-part definition of obscenity. First, the average person, applying contemporary community standards, must find that the work, taken as a whole, appeals to prurient interests; second, that it depicts or describes, in a patently offensive way, sexual conduct as defined by state law; and third, that the work, taken as a whole, lacks serious literary, artistic, political, or scientific value. The Court ruled that community standards and state statutes that describe sexual depictions to be suppressed could be used to prosecute Miller, who operated one of the largest West Coast mail order businesses dealing in sexually explicit materials.

New York v. Ferber
458 U.S. 747, 102 S.Ct. 3348, 73 L.Ed.2d 1113 (1982)

In July 1982, the U.S. Supreme Court added child pornography as another category of speech excluded from First Amendment protection. The other categories excluded are obscenity, defamation, incitement, and "fighting words." The ruling came in the case when the U.S. Supreme Court affirmed a conviction against Ferber for showing a movie depicting two young boys masturbating. The film itself was not seen as obscene for adults, but the Court made the distinction between what was obscene if children were the participants compared with if adults were the leading actors.

American Booksellers Assoc., Inc. v. Hudnut
771 F.2d 323 (7th Cir. 1985) (Easterbrook, J.), aff'd., 475 U.S. 1001, 106 S.Ct. 1172, 89 L.Ed.2d 291 (1986)

The city of Indianapolis passed a statute outlawing pornography, defined as the graphic, sexually explicit subordination of women, presenting women as sex objects, or as enjoying pain, humiliation, or servility. The court of appeals struck the law down, saying it impermissibly established an "approved" view of women and how they react in sexual encounters. The law therefore allowed sexually explicit words and images that adhered to that approved view, but banned sexually explicit words and images that did not adhere to the approved view. The court called this "thought control," saying the "Constitution forbids the state to declare one perspective right and silence opponents."

National Endowment for the Arts, et al. v. Finley, et al.
524 U.S. 569, 118 S.Ct. 2168, 141 L.Ed.2d 500 (1998)

In 1990, homoerotic photographs by Robert Mapplethorpe and blasphemous ones by Andres Serrano created a furor on Capitol Hill, because both artists had received grants from the National Endowment for the Arts (NEA). As a consequence, the NEA governing statute was amended to require the NEA to consider "decency" and "respect" for American "values" when selecting future grant recipients. Shortly thereafter, performance artists Karen Finley, John Fleck, Holly Hughes, and Tim Miller were denied fellowships, because of the "decency and respect" clause, they alleged. They made this allegation in a federal court lawsuit seeking to have the clause declared unconstitutional; and they were successful at the district court and court of appeals level. The U.S. Supreme Court ruled, however, that the statute is constitutional "on its face." Writing for the court, Justice Sandra Day O'Connor did not "perceive a realistic danger that it will be utilized to preclude or punish the expression of particular views," nor did she think that the statute would "significantly compromise First Amendment values."

John D. Ashcroft, Attorney General, et al. v. Free Speech Coalition, et al.
535 U.S. 234, 122 S.Ct. 1389, 152 L.Ed.2d 403 (2002)

The U.S. Supreme Court affirmed the Ninth Circuit's judgment invalidating the Child Pornography Prevention Act of 1996 on the grounds that the act's ban on any depiction of pornographic images of children, including computer-generated images, was overly broad and unconstitutional under the First Amendment. Supreme Court Justice Anthony M. Kennedy wrote: "First Amendment freedoms are most in danger when the government seeks to control thought or to justify its laws for that impermissible end. The right to think is the beginning of freedom, and speech must be protected from the government because speech is the beginning of thought."

See also:
Stanley v. Georgia, 394 U.S. 55, 22 L.Ed.2d 542, 89 S.Ct. 1243 (1969)

Libel

The New York Times v. Sullivan
376 U.S. 254, 84 S.Ct. 710, 11 L.Ed.2d 686 (1964)

To protect "uninhibited, robust, and wide-open" debate on public issues, the Supreme Court held that no public official may recover "damages for a defamatory falsehood relating to his official conduct unless he proves that the statement was made with 'actual malice'—that is, with knowledge that it was false or with reckless disregard of whether it was false or not." The Court stated that the First and Fourteenth Amendments require that critics of official conduct have the "fair equivalent" to the immunity protection given to a public official when he is sued for defamatory speech uttered in the course of his duties.

Gertz v. Robert Welch, Inc.
418 U.S. 323, 94 S.Ct. 2997, 41 L.Ed.2d 789 (1974)

The Court applied the rule in *The New York Times* case to public figures, finding that persons who have special prominence in society by virtue of their fame or notoriety, even if they are not public officials, must prove "actual malice" when alleging libel. Gertz was a prominent lawyer who alleged that a leaflet defamed him.

See also:
Hustler Magazine, Inc. v. Falwell, 485 U.S. 46, 108 S.Ct. 876, 99 L.Ed.2d 41 (1988)

The First Amendment and New Technologies: Broadcast and Cable Communications

FCC v. Pacifica Foundation
438 U.S. 726, 57 L.Ed.2d 1073, 98 S.Ct. 3026 (1978)

In a case that considered the First Amendment protections extended to a radio station's daytime broadcast of comedian George Carlin's "Seven Filthy Words" monologue, the Supreme Court held that Section 326 of the Telecommunications Act, which prohibits the FCC from censoring broadcasts over radio or television, does not limit the FCC's authority to sanction radio or television stations broadcasting material that is obscene, indecent, or profane. Though the censorship ban under Section 326 precludes editing proposed broadcasts in advance, the ban does not deny the FCC the power to review the content of completed broadcasts. In its decision, the Court concluded that broadcast materials have limited First Amendment protection because of the uniquely pervasive presence that radio and television occupy in the lives of people, and the unique ability of children to access radio and television broadcasts.

Denver Area Educational Telecommunications Consortium, Inc. v. FCC
518 U.S. 727, 116 S.Ct. 2374, 135 L.Ed.2d 288 (1996)

In a decision that produced six opinions, the Supreme Court upheld a federal law permitting cable system operators to ban "indecent" or "patently offensive" speech on leased access channels. The Court also struck down a similar law for nonleased, public access channels, and struck down a law requiring indecent material to be shown on separate, segregated cable channels. The case is significant in that the Court affirmed that protecting children from some speech is a compelling state interest.

United States, et al. v. Playboy Entertainment Group, Inc.
529 U.S. 803, 120 S.Ct. 1878, 146 L.Ed.2d 865 (2000)

On May 22, 2000, in a 5-4 decision, the U.S. Supreme Court upheld a U.S. District Court decision that Section 505 of the Telecommunications Act of 1996 violated the First Amendment when it sought to restrict certain cable channels with sexually explicit content to late night hours unless they fully scrambled their signal bleed. In an opinion written by Justice Anthony Kennedy, the Court ruled that the government may have a legitimate interest in protecting children from exposure to "indecent material." Section 505, however, is a content-based speech restriction and, therefore, must be the least restrictive means for meeting the governmental interest. The Court found that Section 505 is not the least restrictive means.

Telecommunications

Sable Communications of California, Inc. v. FCC
492 U.S. 115, 106 L.Ed. 2d 93, 109 S.Ct. 2829 (1989)

The Supreme Court overturned a Telecommunications Act ban on indecent telephone messages, concluding the law violates the First Amendment because the statute's denial of adult access to such messages far exceeds that which is necessary to serve the compelling interest of preventing minors from being exposed to the messages. Unlike broadcast radio and television, which can intrude on the privacy of the home without prior warning of content and which is uniquely accessible to children, telephone communications require the listener to take affirmative steps to receive the communi-

cations. The failure of the government to show any findings that would justify a conclusion that there are no constitutionally acceptable less restrictive means to achieve the government's interest in protecting minors, such as scrambling or the use of access codes, demonstrates that a total ban on such communications goes too far in restricting constitutionally protected speech. To allow the ban to stand would have the effect of "limiting the content of adult telephone communications to that which is suitable for children to hear."

The Internet

American Library Association v. U.S. Department of Justice and Reno v. American Civil Liberties Union
521 U.S. 844, 117 S.Ct. 2329, 138 L.Ed.2d 874 (1997)

In a 9-0 decision, the U.S. Supreme Court on June 26, 1997, declared unconstitutional a federal law making it a crime to send or display indecent material online in a way available to minors. The decision in the consolidated cases completed a successful challenge to the so-called Communications Decency Act by the Citizens Internet Empowerment Coalition, in which the American Library Association and the Freedom to Read Foundation played leading roles. The Court held that speech on the Internet is entitled to the highest level of First Amendment protection, similar to the protection the Court gives to books and newspapers.

Mainstream Loudoun, et al. v. Board of Trustees of the Loudoun County Library
24 F.Supp.2d 552 (E.D. Va. 1998)

Adopted in 1997, the Loudoun County, Virginia, Library Board's "Policy on Internet Sexual Harassment" was designed to prevent adult and minor Internet users from accessing illegal pornography and to avoid the creation of a sexually hostile environment. To accomplish these goals, the board contracted with Log-On Data Corporation, a filtering software manufacturer that offers a product called "X-Stop." Though Log-On Data Corp. refused to divulge the method by which X-Stop filters sites, it soon became apparent that the software blocks some sites that are not prohibited by the policy. Shortly after the adoption of the policy, People for the American Way Foundation commenced litigation on behalf of several Loudoun County residents and members of a nonprofit organization, claiming the policy violates the right to free speech under the First Amendment. The suit was predicated on the theory that the policy is unnecessarily restrictive because it treats adults and children similarly, and precludes access to legitimate as well as pornographic material. On November 23, 1998, Judge Leonie Brinkema declared that the highly restrictive Loudoun County Internet policy was invalid under the free speech provisions of the First Amendment.

United States, et al. v. American Library Association, Inc. et al.
539 U.S. 194, 123 S.Ct. 2297, 156 L.Ed.2d 221 (2003)

The Supreme Court upheld the Children's Internet Protection Act, which requires libraries receiving federal funds for Internet access to install filters so that both adult and child patrons cannot access materials considered obscene, child pornography, or "harmful to minors." Chief Justice Rehnquist announced the judgment of the Court that the law, on its face, is constitutional. Speaking for a plurality of four justices, Rehnquist held that CIPA was a valid exercise of Congress's spending power and did not impose an unconstitutional condition on public libraries that received federal assistance for Internet access because Congress could reasonably impose limitations on its Internet assistance, and because any concerns over filtering software's alleged tendency to erroneously "overblock" access to constitutionally protected speech were

dispelled by the ease with which library patrons could have the filtering software disabled. Justices Kennedy and Breyer concurred with the judgment, holding that CIPA, while raising First Amendment concerns, did not violate the First Amendment as long as adult library users could request that the Internet filter be disabled without delay.

First Amendment Glossary and Acronyms

Absolutism

The position that the right to free speech is absolutely inviolable and cannot be infringed by any governmental action that would inhibit its exercise. It requires a determination whether the action at issue is "speech" (and therefore protected) or "conduct" (and therefore subject to reasonable governmental regulation).

Actual Malice

In *New York Times Co. v. Sullivan*, 376 U.S. 254 (1964), the Supreme Court defined actual malice as a state of mind in which a person or publication makes an untrue and defamatory statement about a person "with knowledge that it was false or with reckless disregard of whether it was false or not." In order to recover damages for libel or defamation, a public official or public figure must be able to show by clear and convincing evidence that the defendant acted with actual malice.

Amendment

A formal alteration or addition to a document or record. In the United States, an amendment to the Constitution is a change or addition, proposed by a two-thirds vote of both houses of Congress or by a convention called by Congress at the request of two-thirds of the state legislatures, and ratified by approval of three-fourths of the states.

Amicus Curiae

The legal Latin phrase, literally translated as "friend of the court," that refers to someone, not a party to a case, who volunteers to offer information on a point of law or some other aspect of the case to assist the court in deciding a matter before it. The information may be a legal opinion in the form of a brief, a testimony that has not been solicited by any of the parties, or a learned treatise on a matter that bears on the case. The decision whether to admit the information lies with the discretion of the court.

Anti-Federalist

An opponent of the ratification of the U.S. Constitution.

Arbitrary Distinctions

Inappropriate categorizations of persons, classes of persons, conduct, or things based on criteria irrelevant to the purpose for which the distinctions are made. For example, a rule intended to regulate the length of time an item may be borrowed should not be based on an irrelevant consideration (arbitrary distinction), such as a personal characteristic of the borrower (height or age).

Assembly

A group of persons gathered together for a common reason, or a legislative, religious, educational, or social purpose.

Bill of Rights

The first ten amendments to the U.S. Constitution. Ratified in 1791, these amendments limit governmental power and protect basic rights and liberties of individuals.

Boycott

To abstain from or act together in abstaining from using, buying, or dealing with, as an expression of protest or disfavor or as a means of coercion.

Brief

A written legal document used in various legal adversary systems that is presented to a court arguing why the party to the case should prevail.

Captive Audience

A person or group of people forcibly subjected to view or hear expression in the use of public facilities or places where they are reasonably unable to avoid seeing or hearing the expression. The government has the ability to limit speech when it is impractical for the listener to escape that speech.

Censor

To edit, expurgate, stifle, repress.

Censorship

Official prohibition or restriction of any type of expression believed to threaten the political, social, or moral order. A change in access status of library materials, made by a governing body or its representatives. Such changes include exclusion, restriction, removal, labeling, or age/grade level changes.

Certiorari (writ of certiorari)

Certiorari, meaning in Latin to "be more fully informed," is the procedure used by the Supreme Court and appellate courts to review the cases they hear. After receiving an appeal, the court decides whether to grant certiorari and review the lower court's case. If it grants certiorari, or "cert," then the higher court reviews the case. If the court denies cert, then the lower court ruling stands. In the Supreme Court, the votes of four justices are required to grant certiorari.

Child Pornography

Special category of sexual material that the U.S. Supreme Court has said can be prohibited in the interest of preventing commerce in the abusive use of children as subjects of pornography. This category does not include "virtual" child pornography, whether generated by a computer or by using young-looking adults as actors.

Chilling Effect

Term of art to describe the self-censorship that results when someone fears the actions of another; the idea that vague and overly broad rules regulating speech are likely to result in people censoring themselves, even censoring acceptable speech, since they cannot be sure whether their speech is illegal or not.

Clear and Present Danger

In *Schenck v. United States,* 249 U.S. 47 (1919), Justice Oliver Wendell Holmes Jr., articulated this test of free speech, which said that the government may suppress speech that presents a clear and present danger, as long as the government can show that that danger is both real and imminent.

Commercial Speech

Speech (as advertising) that proposes a commercial transaction.

Compelling Government Interest

A term used by courts when assessing the burden of government regulation or action upon the exercise of a fundamental right, such as freedom of speech. For such a rule to withstand constitutional challenge, the government must show more than a merely important reason for the rule. The reason for the rule must be compelling; that is, it must be so important that it outweighs even the most valued and basic freedom it negatively affects.

Constitution

The system of fundamental laws and

principles that prescribe the nature, functions, and limits of a government or another institution; the fundamental law of the United States, framed in 1787, ratified in 1789, and variously amended since that time.

Content-based Laws and Regulations
Statutory restrictions on speech that prohibit some categories of expression while allowing others. In contrast, viewpoint-based laws and regulations restrict expression because of the regulator's favoring of one opinion or side of an issue over another. For example, a ban on the publication of confidential information is content based; however, a ban on all picketing except that by labor unions is viewpoint based.

Content Neutrality
The opposite of content-based laws, content-neutral laws and regulations apply to all categories of speech and do not expressly prohibit any particular subject matter of expression. For example, although a law might be able to regulate whether pamphlets be distributed in a public school, it could not discriminate against only Christian or Muslim pamphlets. Such content-neutral regulations that interfere with speech are examined under a balancing test, comparing the state's interest in prohibiting the activity in question and the level of interference with the speaker, which is often determined by looking at available avenues of communication.

Copyright Laws
The legal rights granted to an author, composer, playwright, publisher, or distributor to exclusive publication, production, sale, or distribution of a literary, musical, dramatic, or artistic work.

Defamation
Communication to third parties of false statements about a person that injures the reputation of or deters others from associating with that person.

Dissenting Opinion
Opinion disagreeing with the majority opinion; in the context of a legal action, an opinion that dissents from the majority decision rendered by a panel of judges.

Diversity
The state of being different; a point or respect in which things differ.

Due Process
The principle, encapsulated in the Fifth and Fourteenth Amendments, that neither the federal nor state and local governments may deprive one of life, liberty, or property without appropriate legal procedures and safeguards. In the United States, this principle gives individuals a varying ability to enforce their rights against alleged violations by the government, but normally not against private citizens.

Editorial
An article in a publication expressing the opinion of its editors or publishers or commentary on television or radio expressing the opinion of the station or network.

Editorializing
To express an opinion in or as if in an editorial.

Equal Access Act
Passed by Congress to end growing discrimination against student religious groups that began to occur in public schools.

Equal and Equitable Access to Information and Services
Approach to operating that ensures that everyone the library serves is entitled to the same level of access to information and services and that all have the opportunity to avail themselves if they so choose. Equal access refers to uniform access to information and services. Equitable access refers to just and fair access taking into consideration the facts and circumstances of an individual case. Access to information and services is equal and equitable when there is a level playing field.

Established Church
A church that a government officially recognizes as a national institution and to which it accords support.

Establishment Clause
A clause in the First Amendment to the U.S. Constitution forbidding Congress from establishing a state religion.

Expression of Concern
An inquiry that has judgmental overtones.

Extralegal Pressure
Threat of legal action or pressure by community members or organized groups that results in the banning of materials. The term also refers to requests from law enforcement without proper court order and actions taken by persons in positions of authority (e.g., mayor, elected officials, school officials) to remove or restrict access to materials or services without following established policies and procedures.

Facial Challenge
Challenge on constitutional grounds alleging that no set of circumstances exists under which a statute would be valid.

Fair Use
The U.S. Copyright Act has a fair-use exemption, allowing a defendant to a copyright infringement claim to escape liability on the theory that it is only equitable that he should be able to use the original work in some manner. Fair-use inquiries are examined case by case and depend on four factors:

1. The purpose and the character of the use.
2. The nature of the original copyrighted work.
3. The amount of the original work used in the secondary work.
4. The economic impact of the use.

Federalist
An advocate of federalism who was a member or supporter of the Federalist Party; one who supported ratification of the U.S. Constitution.

Fighting Words
Those words "which by their very utterance inflict injury or tend to incite an immediate breach of the peace." Such words must be uttered as a direct personal insult in a face-to-face confrontation and are calculated or highly likely to result in an immediate violent physical reaction.

FOIA
Freedom of Information Act.

Founding Fathers
Delegates to the Constitutional Convention.

The Fourth Estate
A name often given to the public press.

Free Exercise Clause
The clause in the First Amendment to the U.S. Constitution prohibiting Congress from making any law prohibiting the free exercise of religion.

Fundamentalism
Usually a religious movement or point of view characterized by a return to fundamental principle by rigid adherence to those principles and often by intolerance of other views and opposition to secularism.

Gag Order
A court order prohibiting or limiting communication about a case. Gag orders have been imposed on the press, attorneys, jurors, and others. These orders are presumptively unconstitutional when applied to the press. Judges have greater ability to impose such orders on trial participants.

Government Neutrality
The state or policy of the government being neutral.

Harmful to Minors
Phrase used to describe sexual materials that are protected speech for adults but are deemed obscene for minors by state law. Many states have passed such "harmful to minors" obscenity statutes. The U.S. Supreme Court has held that these statutes must be quite narrow and must not limit the ability of adults to access protected speech. Consequently, applying these statutes to material on the Internet has proven to be complicated, as current technology makes it difficult to discern between adult and minor viewers.

Hate Speech
Speech intended to degrade, intimidate, or incite violent or prejudicial action against an individual or group of persons based upon their race, ethnicity, national origin, religion, sexual orientation, or disability. This category of speech receives considerable constitutional protection because the government cannot prescribe

what thoughts we may think or which political philosophies we may advocate. The U.S. Supreme Court has said that the "fighting words" doctrine is not a tool to cleanse public debate or regulate words that give offense.

Immigration
The act of entering and settling in a country or region to which one is not native.

Implied
Insinuated, expressed indirectly, hinted at.

Indecency
"Indecent" speech usually receives First Amendment protection, except when it is broadcast over the airwaves. In *FCC v. Pacifica,* 438 U.S. 726 (1978), the Supreme Court held that the Federal Communications Commission (FCC) could regulate indecent speech because broadcast media are both uniquely pervasive and uniquely accessible to children. For regulatory purposes, the FCC defines indecency as "language or material that, in context, depicts or describes, in terms patently offensive as measured by contemporary community standards for the broadcast medium, sexual or excretory activities or organs" (16 FCCR 7999, 8000).

Intrusion
Uninvited entry, infringement upon, the act of intruding or infringing on others.

Lawsuit
A civil action brought before a court in which a party (plaintiff) claims to suffer damages from another party's (defendant's) action, and the plaintiff seeks a legal or equitable remedy. The defendant is required to respond to the complaint of the plaintiff.

Libel
A written or oral slander that defames an individual and has the effect of ruining that person's reputation, standing in the community, or ability to associate with others. Because of the adverse economic consequences that false accusations can have, the courts can award damages to compensate an individual injured by those false accusations. By contrast, truthful yet harmful accusations incur no similar damage and are not actionable.

Limited Public Forum
A public place purposefully designated by the government as a place dedicated to a particular type of expression. As in a traditional public forum, only reasonable content-neutral time, place, and manner restrictions may be imposed on speech, within the scope of the designated purpose of the forum. In a limited public forum, the government may exclude entire categories of speech that do not fall within the designated purpose of the forum, but may not discriminate against particular viewpoints or restrict speech appropriate to the forum.

Lobbyist
A person who is employed by an individual, organization, association, or business to represent its interests before the legislature. The term derives from the fact that lobbyists usually frequent the areas (lobbies) adjacent to the chambers of the senate and the house, either seeking to buttonhole legislators as they walk to and from the chambers or await legislative action, which might affect their clients' interests. Individual citizens may also "lobby" their legislators on matters of concern to them.

Magna Carta
The charter of English political and civil liberties granted by King John at Runnymede in June 1215. It serves as a piece of legislation that guarantees basic rights.

Marketplace of Ideas
One of the main theories of free speech. The theory was first given form by U.S. Supreme Court Judge Oliver Wendell Holmes Jr., when dissenting in *Abrams v. United States,* 250 U.S. 616 (1919), stating that, "the best test of truth is the power of the thought to get itself accepted in the competition of the market."

Materially Interfere
A term used by the courts to describe the necessary level of intrusion, inconvenience, or disruption of an accepted or protected activity caused by certain conduct, which justifies regulation of that conduct. A material interference is much more than mere annoyance—it must be an actual obstacle to the exercise of a right.

Miller Test

The Miller test is the list of criteria used to determine whether particular material is obscene. The Supreme Court held in *Miller v. California*, 413 U.S. 15 (1973), that material is obscene if:

1. The average person, applying contemporary community standards, would find that the work, taken as a whole, appeals to the prurient interest, which means arousing sexual desire.
2. The work depicts or describes, in a patently offensive way, sexual conduct specifically defined by the applicable state law.
3. The work, taken as a whole, lacks serious literary, artistic, political, or scientific value. Court battles often focus on this third prong of the test.

Morals

Of or concerned with the judgment of the goodness or badness of human action and character.

Neutrality

Unbiased; tolerance attributable to a lack of information.

Non-partisan

Not supporting the interests or policies of any particular political party.

Nudity

The state of wearing no clothing. Obscenity and nudity are not synonymous. Although obscene materials, which depict a very narrow category of hardcore sexual acts that have a tendency to incite lustful thoughts, can be illegal, it is unconstitutional to prohibit the circulation or exposure of materials that depict or contain nudity. In 1975, the U.S. Supreme Court issued an opinion in *Erznoznik v. City of Jacksonville*, 422 U.S. 205, that struck down a law that banned nudity in movies shown in drive-in theaters when the screen was visible from the street.

Objectivity

Judgment based on observable phenomena and uninfluenced by emotions or personal prejudices.

Obscenity

For a work to be obscene, a court or jury must determine that (1) the average person, applying contemporary community standards, would find that the work, taken as a whole, appeals to the prurient interest; (2) the work depicts or describes, in a patently offensive way, sexual conduct specifically defined by the applicable law; (3) the work, taken as a whole, lacks serious literary, artistic, political, or scientific value.

Open Meetings Act

An act that ensures that public business is conducted in public view by prohibiting secret deliberations and actions on matters that should be discussed in a public forum.

Opinion

A belief or conclusion held with confidence but not substantiated by positive knowledge or proof.

Oral Arguments

Spoken presentations to a judge or appellate court by a lawyer (or parties when representing themselves) of the legal reasons why they should prevail. Oral argument at the appellate level accompanies written briefs, which also advance the argument of each party in the legal dispute. Oral arguments can also occur during motion practice when one of the parties presents a motion to the court for consideration before trial, such as if a case should be dismissed on a point of law, or when summary judgment may lie because there are no factual issues in dispute.

Oral Complaint

An oral challenge to the presence and/or appropriateness of the material in question.

Overbreadth Doctrine

Allows a court to invalidate a law as a facial challenge on First Amendment grounds if a substantial number of its applications would be unconstitutional.

Petition

In law, a request to the government to grant a particular right, or to take a specific action.

Picket

A person or group of persons stationed outside a place of employment, usually during a strike, to express grievances, protest, and discourage entry by nonstriking employees and/or customers. Picketing can also be used to promote interests other than those of workers, such as protests against racial discrimination or particular government actions or decisions.

Plaintiff

Party that files a lawsuit against a defendant.

Police Power

In law, the right of a government to make laws necessary for the health, morals, and welfare of the populace.

Political Speech

Any form of speech directly linked to the government; speech that conveys opinions and ideas about government and political and social issues. Such speech performs a valuable function as a check and balance of the government. Speaking out against government intervention or financial contributions is considered an example of political speech, as a method of expressing a political ideology.

Pornography

In legal terms, pornography and obscenity are not synonyms, and the U.S. Supreme Court has recognized that erotic messages, nudity, and depictions of sexual behavior are forms of speech protected by the First Amendment of the U.S. Constitution. The Court's obscenity decisions comprehend that sex is a subject in well-regarded literature and art and a mysterious force that commands great human attention; as a result, the Court has held that society's concerns about obscenity should not be a vehicle to interfere with serious artistic or scientific expression. As a result, materials cannot be prohibited or restricted solely because they contain erotic messages.

Prior Restraint

Prohibition on expression (especially by a publication) before the expression actually takes place.

Protected Speech

Speech that is protected from government censorship or regulation to one extent or another, depending upon the nature of the speech and the nature of the regulation. In law, it is speech that is interpreted as protected by the U.S. Supreme Court under the First Amendment. The Court has never held that the Constitution establishes an absolute right to free speech.

Public Attack
A publicly disseminated statement challenging the value of material, presented to the media and/or others outside the institutional organization in order to gain public support for further action.

Shield Laws
Laws giving journalists the ability to protect the identities of confidential sources without fear of prosecution.

Slander
A spoken false or malicious statement or report about someone. *See Libel.*

Standing
Legal right to bring an action in court. For example, a plaintiff challenging a criminal statute must have a "credible fear of prosecution." A plaintiff challenging a book removal in a high school must have a connection to the school (i.e., student) at the time of the removal and through the conclusion of the case.

Strict Scrutiny
Test applied to determine whether a restriction on speech is unconstitutional under the First Amendment. To justify a restriction on speech the government must show that 1) it has a compelling interest in enforcing the restriction; 2) the restriction is narrowly tailored to achieve that compelling interest; and 3) there is no less restrictive alternative to achieving that interest.

Substantial Objectives
Goals related to the fundamental mission of a government institution and not merely incidental to the performance of that mission. Providing free and unrestricted access to a broad selection of materials representing various points of view is a substantial objective of a public library.

Symbolic Speech
A "message" or conduct intended to convey a particular message, which is likely to be understood by those viewing it.

Tax-exempt
Not subject to being taxed.

Time, Place, and Manner
The U.S. Supreme Court has repeatedly ruled that right to free speech is not absolute and that the state and federal governments may place reasonable restrictions on the time, place, and manner of individual expression. The government cannot, however, impose speech restrictions simply because it disagrees with the message of the speaker. In other words, any government regulation of speech must be content neutral and advance a significant government interest, and must be narrowly tailored so as not to restrict any more speech than is necessary to advance that interest. An example of a regulation affecting "manner" of free speech would be a restriction on the size of signs carried by picketers.

Tort Liability
A tort is a wrong done to someone, a civil cause of action for which a standard remedy is monetary damages or an injunction. Examples of tort claims include defamation, invasion of privacy, and intentional infliction of emotional distress. Liability means that one owes another for the harm he or she has caused.

Unprotected Speech
Speech that may be limited because the First Amendment does not protect it. The U.S. Supreme Court has identified nine areas of unprotected speech in its decisions: (1) obscenity, (2) defamation, (3) expression intended and likely to incite imminent lawless action, (4) fighting words, (5) unwarranted invasion of privacy, (6) deceptive or misleading advertisements or those for illegal products or services, (7) clear and immediate threats to national security, (8) copyright violations, and (9) expression on school grounds that causes a material and substantial disruption of school activities.

U.S. Courts of Appeals (or circuit courts)
The intermediate appellate courts of the U.S. federal court system. A court of appeals decides appeals from the district courts within its federal judicial circuit, and in some instances from other designated federal courts and administrative agencies. There currently are thirteen U.S. courts of appeals. The eleven "numbered" circuits and the D.C. Circuit are geographically defined.

The thirteenth court of appeals is the U.S. Court of Appeals for the Federal Circuit, which has nationwide jurisdiction over certain appeals based on subject matter.

USA PATRIOT Act
Uniting and Strengthening America by Providing Appropriate Tools Required to Intercept and Obstruct Terrorism (USA PATRIOT) Act of 2001.

Written Complaint
A formal written complaint filed with an institution (library, school, etc.) challenging the presence and/or appropriateness of specific material.

This First Amendment Glossary and Acronyms was compiled using a variety of sources including, but not limited to:

Doyle, Robert P., and Robert N. Knight. *Trustee Facts File.* Third edition. Chicago: Illinois Library Association, 2004.

First Amendment Center, www.firstamendmentcenter.org/.

Peck, Robert S. *Libraries, the First Amendment, and Cyberspace: What You Need to Know.* Chicago: American Library Association, 1999.

First Amendment Quotations

"The burning of an author's books, imprisonment for opinion's sake, has always been the tribute that an ignorant age pays to the genius of its time."

Joseph Allen (1749–1827), U.S. politician, nephew of U.S. President Samuel Adams, Massachusetts Constitutional Convention, 1788.

"Freedom of thought and freedom of speech in our great institutions of learning are absolutely necessary… the moment that either is restricted, liberty begins to wither and die and the career of a nation after that time is downwards."

John Peter Altgeld, Governor of Illinois, (1847–1902), to George H. Shipley, September 25, 1897.

"Intellectual freedom, the essence of equitable library services, provides for free access to all expressions of ideas through which any and all sides of a question, cause, or movement may be explored. Toleration is meaningless without tolerance for what some may consider detestable. Librarians must not justly permit their own preferences to limit their degree of tolerance in collection development, because freedom is indivisible."

American Library Association, Office for Intellectual Freedom. *Intellectual Freedom Manual.* Eighth edition. Chicago: American Library Association, 2010, p. 108.

"The use of 'religion' as an excuse to repress the freedom of expression and to deny human rights is not confined to any country or time."

Margaret Atwood, Canadian poet, novelist, literary critic, and essayist (1939–).

"To view the opposition as dangerous is to misunderstand the basic concept of democracy. To oppress the opposition is to assault the very foundation of democracy."

Aung San Suu Kyi, Myanmar opposition leader and winner of the 1991 Nobel Prize for Peace (1945–). *Letters from Burma.* New York: Penguin Books, 1995.

"The freedom to share one's insights and judgments verbally or in writing is, just like the freedom to think, a holy and inalienable right of humanity that, as a universal human right, is above all the rights of princes."

Carl Friedrich Bahrdt, German theologian and author (1741–1792). *On Freedom of the Press and Its Limits*, 1787.

"The oppression of any people for opinion's sake has rarely had any other effect than to fix those opinions deeper, and render them more important."

Hosea Ballou, U.S. Universalist clergyman and theological writer (1771–1852).

"To permit every interest group, especially those who claim to be victimized by unfair expression, their own legislative exceptions to the First Amendment so long as they succeed in obtaining a majority of legislative votes in their favor demonstrates the potentially predatory nature of what defendants seek through this Ordinance and defend in this lawsuit.

"It ought to be remembered by defendants and all others who would support such a legislative initiative that, in terms of altering sociological patterns, much as alteration may be necessary and desirable, free speech, rather than being the enemy, is a long-tested and worthy ally. To deny free speech in order to engineer social change in the name of accomplishing a greater good for one sector of our society erodes the freedoms of all and, as such, threatens tyranny and injustice for those subjected to the rule of such laws. The First Amendment protections presuppose the evil of such tyranny and prevent a finding by this Court upholding the Ordinance."

Judge Sarah Evans Barker, *American Booksellers Association, Inc., et al. v. William H. Hudnut III*, 598 F.Supp. 1316 (S.D. Ind. 1984)

"Thought that is silenced is always rebellious. Majorities, of course, are often mistaken. This is why the silencing of minorities is necessarily dangerous. Criticism and dissent are the indispensable antidote to major delusions."

Alan Barth, U.S. journalist (1906–1979). *The Loyalty of Free Men.* London: Gollancz, 1951.

"As long as I don't write about the government, religion, politics, and other institutions, I am free to print anything."

Pierre-Augustin Caron de Beaumarchais, French writer (1732–1799).

"I'm in favour of free expression provided it's kept rigidly under control."

Alan Bennett, British playwright (1934–).

"Political correctness is really a subjective list put together by the few to rule the

many—a list of things one must think, say, or do. It affronts the right of the individual to establish his or her own beliefs."

Mark Berley, British entrepreneur (1930–2007). *Argos*, Spring 1998.

"In order to get to the truth, conflicting arguments and expression must be allowed. There can be no freedom without choice, no sound choice without knowledge."

David Knipe Berninghausen. U.S. librarian (1916–2001). "Arrogance of the Censor," *USA Today* 110, no. 2442 (March 1982): 63.

"The layman's constitutional view is that what he likes is constitutional and that which he doesn't like is unconstitutional."

U.S. Supreme Court Justice Hugo L. Black. *New York Times*, February 26, 1971.

"I fear more harm from everybody thinking alike than from some people thinking otherwise."

Charles G. Bolte, U.S. publisher and vice president, Carnegie Endowment for International Peace (1920–1994).

"Censorship is the mother of metaphor."

Jorge Luis Borges, Argentine novelist and poet (1899–1986).

"You don't have to burn books to destroy a culture. Just get people to stop reading them."

Ray Bradbury, U.S. science fiction writer (1920–2012). "Bradbury Still Believes in Heat of 'Fahrenheit 451,'" *The Seattle Times*, March 12, 1993.

"Without free speech no search for truth is possible… no discovery of truth is useful. Better thousandfold abuse of free speech than denial of free speech. The abuse dies in a day, but the denial slays the life of the people, and entombs the hope of the race."

Charles Bradlaugh, British freethinker and reformer (1833–1891), speech given at the Hall of Science, 1890.

"Correctly applied (the clear and present danger test), … will preserve the right of free speech from suppression by tyrannous majorities and from abuse by irresponsible, fanatical minorities."

U.S. Supreme Court Justice Louis Dembitz Brandeis, *Schaefer v. U.S.*, 251 U.S. 466, 40 S.Ct. 259, 64 L.Ed. 360 (1920).

"Those who won our independence by revolution were not cowards. They did not fear political change. They did not exalt order at the cost of liberty.... If there be time to expose through discussion the falsehood and fallacies, to avert the evil by the processes of education, the remedy to be applied is more speech, not enforced silence."

U.S. Supreme Court Justice Louis Dembitz Brandeis, *Whitney v. California*, 274 U.S. 357, 47 S.Ct. 641, 71 L.Ed. 1095 (1927).

"Experience teaches us to be most on our guard to protect liberty when the government's purpose is beneficent. The greatest dangers to liberty lurk in insidious encroachments by men of zeal, well-meaning but without understanding."

U.S. Supreme Court Justice Louis Dembitz Brandeis, dissenting, *Olmstead v. United States*, 277 U.S. 438, 48 S.Ct. 564, 72 L.Ed. 944 (1928).

"Debate on public issues should be uninhibited, robust, and wide-open and that...may well include vehement, caustic, and sometimes unpleasantly sharp attacks on government and public officials."

U.S. Supreme Court Justice William J. Brennan Jr., *New York Times v. Sullivan*, 376 U.S. 254, 84 S.Ct. 710, 11 L.Ed.2d 686 (1964).

"If there is a bedrock principle underlying the First Amendment, it is that the Government may not prohibit the expression of an idea simply because society finds the idea itself offensive or disagreeable."

U.S. Supreme Court Justice William J. Brennan Jr., *Texas v. Johnson*, 491 U.S. 397, 109 S.Ct. 2533, 105 L.Ed.2d 342 (1989).

"Everybody favors free speech in the slack moments when no axes are being ground."

Heywood Broun, U.S. journalist (1888–1939). *New York World*, October 23, 1926.

"Censorship is the tool of those who have the need to hide actualities from themselves and others. Their fear is only their inability to face what is real. Somewhere in their upbringing they were shielded against the total facts of our experience. They were only taught to look one way when many ways exist."

Charles Bukowski, U.S. writer and poet (1920–1994).

"The only thing necessary for the triumph of evil is for good men to do nothing."

Edmund Burke, British orator, philosopher, and politician (1729–1797).

"Freedom of expression is the matrix, the indispensable condition, of nearly every other form of freedom."

U.S. Supreme Court Justice Benjamin Nathan Cardozo, *Palko v. Connecticut*, 302 U.S. 319, 58 S.Ct. 149, 82 L.Ed. 288 (1937).

"If we don't believe in freedom of expression for people we despise, we don't believe in it at all."

Noam Chomsky, U.S. professor of linguistics (1928–).

"From a comparative perspective, the United States is unusual if not unique in the lack of restraints on freedom of expression. It is also unusual in the range and effectiveness of methods employed to restrain freedom of thought.... Where the voice of the people is heard, elite groups must insure their voice says the right things."

Noam Chomsky. *Index on Censorship*, July/August 1986.

"Everyone is in favor of free speech. Hardly a day passes without it being extolled, but some people's idea of it is that they are free to say what they like, but if anyone says anything back, that is an outrage."

Sir Winston Churchill, British statesman and author (1874–1965), speech, House of Commons, 1943.

"You see these dictators on their pedestals, surrounded by the bayonets of their soldiers and the truncheons of their police. Yet in their hearts there is unspoken—unspeakable!—fear. They are afraid of words and thoughts! Words spoken abroad, thoughts stirring at home, all the more powerful because they are forbidden. These terrify them. A little mouse—a little tiny mouse!—of thought appears in the room, and even the mightiest potentates are thrown into panic."

Sir Winston Churchill, speech, "Defense of Freedom and Peace," 1938.

"The public library is the most dangerous place in town."

John Anthony Ciardi, U.S. poet and critic (1916–1986).

"The fact is that censorship always defeats its own purpose, for it creates, in the end, the kind of society that is incapable of exercising real discretion.... In the long run it will create a generation incapable of appreciating the difference between independence of thought and subservience."

Henry Steele Commager, U.S. historian (1902–1998). *Freedom, Loyalty, Dissent.* New York: Oxford University Pr., 1954.

"The irony of book-banning attempts is that the publicity often causes people to read the books for the wrong reasons. If a book is controversial, perhaps the best place for it is the classroom where, under the guidance of a teacher, the book can be discussed and evaluated, where each student will be free to proclaim how he or she feels about the book and, in fact, can even refuse to read the book. The point is that free choice must be involved."

Robert Cormier, U.S. author, columnist and reporter (1925–2000). In *Banned in the USA: A Reference Guide to Book Censorship in Schools and Public Libraries*, edited by Herbert N. Foerstel. Westport, Conn.: Greenwood Pr., 2002, p. 123.

"The library is not a shrine for the worship of books. It is not a temple where literary incense must be burned or where one's devotion to the bound book is expressed in ritual. A library, to modify the famous metaphor of Socrates, should be the delivery room for the birth of ideas—a place where history comes to life."

Norman Cousins, U.S editor and essayist (1915–1990).

"What censorship accomplishes, creating an unreal and hypocritical mythology, fomenting an attraction for forbidden fruit, inhibiting the creative minds among us and fostering an illicit trade. Above all, it curtails the right of the individual, be he creator or consumer, to satisfy his intellect and his interest without harm. In our law-rooted society, we are not the keeper of our brother's morals—only of his rights."

Judith Crist, U.S. film critic (1922–2012). In *Censorship: For and Against*, edited by Harold H. Hart. Hart Publishing Co., 1971.

"Freedom of the press is not just important to democracy, it is democracy."

Walter Leland Cronkite, U.S. journalist and radio and television news broadcaster (1916–2009).

"Students throughout the totalitarian world risk life and limb for freedom of expression; many American college students are demanding that big brother restrict their freedom of speech on campus. This demand for enhanced censorship is not emanating only from the usual corner—the know-nothing fundamentalist right—it is coming from the radical, and increasingly not-so-radical left as well."

Alan Morton Dershowitz, U.S. lawyer (1938–). *Shouting Fire: Civil Liberties in a Turbulent Age.* Boston: Little, Brown, 2002.

"The function of free speech under our system of government is to invite dispute. It may indeed best serve its high purpose when it invites a condition of unrest, creates dissatisfaction with conditions as they are, or even stirs people to anger. Speech is often provocative and challenging. It may strike at prejudices and preconceptions and have profound unsettling effects as it passes for acceptance of an idea."

U.S. Supreme Court Justice William Orville Douglas, *Terminello v. Chicago,* 337 U.S. 1, 69 S.Ct. 894, 93 L.Ed. 1131 (1949).

"It is our attitude toward free thought and free expression that will determine our fate. There must be no limit on the range of temperate discussion, no limits on thought. No subject must be taboo. No censor must preside at our assemblies."

U.S. Supreme Court Justice William Orville Douglas, address, Author's Guild, December 3, 1952, on receiving the Richard E. Lauterbach Award for Distinguished Service in the Field of Civil Liberties.

"Restriction of free thought and free speech is the most dangerous of all subversions. It is the one un-American act that could most easily defeat us."

U.S. Supreme Court Justice William Orville Douglas, address, Author's Guild, December 3, 1952, on receiving the Richard E. Lauterbach Award for Distinguished Service in the Field of Civil Liberties.

"One has the right to freedom of speech whether he talks to one person or to 1,000."

U.S. Supreme Court Justice William Orville Douglas, *United States v. Auto. Workers,* 352 U.S. 567, 77 S.Ct. 529, 1 L.Ed.2d 563 (1957).

"[T]he ultimate welfare of the single human soul [is] the ultimate test of the vitality of the First Amendment."

U.S. Supreme Court Justice William Orville Douglas, *Gillette v. United States,* 401 U.S. 437, 91 S.Ct. 828, 28 L.Ed.2d 168 (1971).

"A government that can give liberty in its constitution ought to have the power to protect liberty in its administration."

Frederick Douglass, U.S. abolitionist and journalist (1818–1895).

"When books are challenged, restricted, removed, or banned, an atmosphere of suppression exists.... The fear of the consequences of censorship is as damaging as, or perhaps more damaging than, the actual censorship attempt. After all, when a published work is banned, it can usually be found elsewhere. Unexpressed ideas, unpublished works, unpurchased books are lost forever."

Robert P. Doyle, U.S. librarian (1951–). *Banned Books: 1998 Resource Guide.* Chicago: American Library Association, 1998, p. ii.

"Free speech has been on balance an ally of those seeking change. Governments that want stasis start by restricting speech.... Change in any complex system ultimately depends on the ability of outsiders to challenge accepted views and the reigning institutions. Without a strong guarantee of freedom of speech, there is no effective right to challenge what is."

Judge Frank Hoover Easterbrook, *American Booksellers Association, Inc., et al. v. William H. Hudnut III,* 771 F.2d 323 (7th Cir. 1985).

"It is evident that any restriction of academic freedom acts in such a way to hamper the dissemination of knowledge among the people and thereby impedes national judgment and action."

Albert Einstein, U.S. (German-born) physicist (1879–1955).

"Don't join the book burners. Don't think you are going to conceal thoughts by concealing evidence that they ever existed."

Dwight David "Ike" Eisenhower, U.S. President (1890–1969), speech at Dartmouth College, June 14, 1953.

"The libraries of America are and must ever remain the home of free, inquiring minds. To them, our citizens—of all ages and races, of all creeds and political persuasions—must ever be able to turn with clear confidence that there they can freely seek the whole truth, unwarped by fashion and uncompromised by expediency. For in such whole and

healthy knowledge alone are to be found and understood those majestic truths of man's nature and destiny that prove, to each succeeding generation, the validity of freedom."

Dwight David "Ike" Eisenhower, letter to the American Library Association's Annual Conference, Los Angeles, 1953.

"Censorship is advertising paid by the government."

Federico Fellini, Italian film director (1920–1993).

"If the human body's obscene, complain to the manufacturer, not me."

Larry Flynt, U.S. publisher, *Hustler* magazine (1942–).

"Students in school as well as out of schools are 'persons' under our Constitution. They are possessed of fundamental rights which the state must respect.... It can hardly be argued that either students or teachers shed their constitutional rights to freedom of speech or expression at the schoolhouse gate."

U.S. Supreme Court Justice Abraham Fortas, *Tinker et al. v. Des Moines Independent Community School District et al.,* 393 U.S. 503, 89 S.Ct. 733, 21 L.Ed.2d 731 (1969).

"Liberty is always dangerous, but it is the safest thing we have."

Harry Emerson Fosdick, U.S. clergyman (1878–1969).

"Freedom of the press is not an end in itself but a means to the end of [achieving] a free society."

U.S. Supreme Court Justice Felix Frankfurter, *Pennekamp et al. v. Florida,* 328 U.S. 331, 66 S.Ct. 1029, 90 L.Ed. 1295 (1946).

"Whoever would overthrow the liberty of a nation must begin by subduing the freeness of speech."

Benjamin Franklin, U.S. author, diplomat, inventor, physicist, politician, and printer (1706–1790), *Silence Dogood Letters,* no. 8.

"They who would give up essential liberty to obtain a little temporary safety deserve neither liberty nor safety."

Benjamin Franklin. *Historical Review of the Constitution and Government of Pennsylvania,* 1759.

"If all printers were determined not to print anything till they were sure it would offend nobody, there would be very little printed."

Benjamin Franklin, 1730.

"We state these propositions neither lightly nor as easy generalizations. We here stake out a lofty claim for the value of the written word. We do so because we believe that it is possessed of enormous variety and usefulness, worthy of cherishing and keeping free. We realize that the application of these propositions may mean the dissemination of ideas and manners of expression that are repugnant to many persons. We do not state these propositions in the comfortable belief that what people read is unimportant. We believe rather that what people read is deeply important; that ideas can be dangerous; but that the suppression of ideas is fatal to a democratic society. Freedom itself is a dangerous way of life, but it is ours."

The Freedom to Read Statement's concluding paragraph

Concerned about threats to free communication of ideas, more than thirty librarians, publishers, and others conferred at Rye, New York, May 2–3, 1953. A committee was appointed to prepare a statement to be made public. The American Library Association Council endorsed this officially on June 25, 1953, and it was subsequently endorsed by the American Book Publishers Council (ABPC), American Booksellers Association, Book Manufacturers' Institute, and other national groups. In the light of later developments, a somewhat revised version was prepared after much consultation, and was approved in 1972 by the ALA Council, Association of American Publishers (successor to ABPC and American Educational Publishers Institute), and subsequently by many other book industry, communications, educational, cultural, and public service organizations. The statement was revised in 1991, 2000, and 2004 and is available at http://www.ala.org/oif/policies/freedomtoread.

"What progress we are making. In the Middle Ages they would have burned me. Now they are content with burning my books."

Sigmund Freud, Austrian psychologist (1856–1939).

"To suppress free speech in the name of protecting women is dangerous and wrong."

Betty Friedan (Betty Naomi Goldstein), U.S. women's rights activist and author (1921–2006).

"We must learn to welcome and not to fear the voices of dissent. We must dare to think about 'unthinkable things' because when things become unthinkable, thinking stops and action becomes mindless."

James William Fulbright, U.S. senator D-Ark. (1905–1995), speech to the U.S. Congress, March 27, 1964.

"Whenever I notice that my name isn't on the list of banned and challenged authors, I feel faintly like I'm letting the side down. Although I suspect all I'd have to do to get on the list is to write a book about naked, bisexual, hard-swearing wizards who drink a lot while disparaging the Second Amendment, and I'd be home and dry."

Neil Gaiman, English author (1960–), *Badger Herald*, September 27, 2004.

"Freedom is not worth having if it does not include the freedom to make mistakes."

Mohandas Karamchand "Mahatma" Gandhi, Indian ascetic, peace activist (1896–1948). Quoted in Jerome Agel and Walter Glanze, *Pearls of Wisdom*. William Morrow, 1987.

"The First Amendment was designed to protect offensive speech, because nobody ever tries to ban the other kind."

Mike Godwin, staff counsel, Electronic Freedom Foundation (1956–).

"The First Amendment does not require silence in the face of outrage. On the contrary, freedom demands a constant assertion of values."

Richard Goldstein, media critic, *Village Voice*.

"When there is official censorship it is a sign that speech is serious. When there is none, it is pretty certain that the official spokesmen have all the loudspeakers."

Paul Goodman, U.S. novelist, playwright, poet and psychotherapist (1911–1972). *Growing Up Absurd*. New York: Vintage Books, 1960.

"Censorship is never over for those who have experienced it. It is a brand on the imagination that affects the individual who has suffered it, forever."

Nadine Gordimer, South African novelist (1923–), "Censorship and Its Aftermath," address given at the English PEN's international Writers' Day, London, June 2, 1990.

"Books won't stay banned. They won't burn. Ideas won't go to jail. In the long run of history, the censor and the

inquisitor have always lost. The only sure weapon against bad ideas is better ideas. The source of better ideas is wisdom."

Alfred Whitney Griswold, historian and educator (1906–1963). *Essays on Education*. New Haven: Yale University Pr., 1954.

"[O]ne man's vulgarity is another's lyric."

U.S. Supreme Court Justice John Marshall Harlan, *Cohen v. California*, 403 U.S. 15, 91 S.Ct. 1780, 29 L.Ed.2d 284 (1971).

"Where they have burned books, they will end in burning human beings."

Christian Johann Heinrich Heine, German critic and poet (1797–1856). *Almansor*, 1823.

"I cannot and will not cut my conscience to fit this year's fashions."

Lillian Florence Hellman, U.S. author of plays, screenplays, and memoirs (1905–1984), subpoenaed to appear before the House Un-American Activities Committee, 1952.

"To prohibit the reading of certain books is to declare the inhabitants to be either fools or slaves."

Claude Adrien Helvetius, French philosopher (1715–1771). *De l'Homme*, vol. 1, sec. 4.

"Our Constitution was not intended to be used by…any group to foist its personal religious beliefs on the rest of us."

Katherine Houghton Hepburn, U.S. actress (1907–2003). *Ladies Home Journal*, October 1991.

"The only difference between the expression of an opinion and an incitement in the narrower sense is the speaker's enthusiasm for the result. Eloquence may set fire to reason."

U.S. Supreme Court Justice Oliver Wendell Holmes Jr., *Gitlow v. People of State of New York*, 268 U.S. 652, 45 S.Ct. 625, 69 L.Ed. 1138 (1924).

"The best test of truth is the power of the thought to get itself accepted in the competition of the market…. We should be eternally vigilant against attempts to check the expression that we loathe."

U.S. Supreme Court Justice Oliver Wendell Holmes Jr., dissenting, *Abrams v. United States*, 250 U.S. 616, 40 S.Ct. 17, 63 L.Ed. 1173 (1919).

"The right to be heard does not automatically include the right to be taken seriously."

Vice President Hubert Horatio Humphrey (1911–1978), speech to National Student Association, Madison, Wisconsin, August 23, 1965.

"The vast number of titles which are published each year—all of them are to the good, even if some of them may annoy or even repel us for a time. For none of us would trade freedom of expression and of ideas for the narrowness of the public censor. America is a free market for people who have something to say, and need not fear to say it."

Vice President Hubert Horatio Humphrey, as reported by the *New York Times,* March 9, 1967, p. 42. Humphrey addressed the National Book Awards ceremony in New York City, March 8, 1967, where during his speech more than fifty people walked out to protest the U.S. role in Vietnam.

"Fear of corrupting the mind of the younger generation is the loftiest form of cowardice."

Holbrook Jackson, English writer and critic (1874–1948).

"Did you ever hear anyone say 'That work had better be banned because I might read it and it might be very damaging to me?'"

Joseph Henry Jackson, U.S. critic and travel writer (1894–1955).

"The First Amendment grew out of an experience which taught that society cannot trust the conscience of a majority to keep its religious zeal within the limits that a free society can tolerate. I do not think it any more intended to leave the conscience of a minority to fix its limits. Civil government cannot let any group ride roughshod over others simply because their consciences tell them to do so."

U.S. Supreme Court Justice Robert H. "Bob" Jackson, *Douglas et al. v. City of Jeannette et al.,* 319 U.S. 157, 63 S.Ct. 877, 87 L.Ed. 1324 (1943).

"If there is any fixed star in our constitutional constellation, it is that no official, high or petty, can prescribe what shall be orthodox in politics, nationalism, religion, or other matters of opinion or force citizens to confess by word or act their faith therein."

U.S. Supreme Court Justice Robert H. "Bob" Jackson, *West Virginia State Board of Education v. Barnette,* 319 U.S. 624, 63 S.Ct. 1178, 87 L.Ed. 1628 (1943).

"The very purpose of the Bill of Rights was to withdraw certain subjects from the vicissitudes of political controversy, to place them beyond the reach of majorities and officials and to establish them as legal principles to be applied by the courts."

U.S. Supreme Court Justice Robert H. "Bob" Jackson, *West Virginia State Board of Education v. Barnette,* 319 U.S. 624, 63 S.Ct. 1178, 87 L.Ed. 1628 (1943).

"The First Amendment says nothing about a right not to be offended. The risk of finding someone else's speech offensive is the price each of us pays for our own free speech. Free people don't run to court—or to the principal—when they encounter a message they don't like. They answer it with one of their own."

Jeff Jacoby, U.S. journalist (1959–). "Little Less Freedom of Speech," Townhall.com, January 26, 2004.

"A democratic society depends upon an informed and educated citizenry."

Thomas Jefferson, U.S. President (1743–1826).

"If the book be false in its facts, disprove them; if false in its reasoning, refute it. But for God's sake, let us hear freely from both sides."

Thomas Jefferson, letter to his bookseller, April 19, 1814.

"Books and ideas are the most effective weapons against intolerance and ignorance."

Lyndon Baines Johnson, U.S. President (1908–1973), commenting as he signed into law a bill providing increased federal aid for library service, February 11, 1964.

"The First Amendment is often inconvenient. But that is beside the point. Inconvenience does not absolve the government of its obligation to tolerate speech."

U.S. Supreme Court Justice Anthony McLeod Kennedy, *International Society for Krishna Consciousness, Inc., and Brian Rumbaugh, Petitioners v. Walter Lee; Superintendent of Port Authority Police v. International Society for Krishna Consciousness, Inc., et al.,* 505 U.S. 672, 112 S.Ct. 2711, 120 L.Ed.2d 541 (1992).

"The Constitution exists precisely so that opinions and judgments, including aesthetic and moral judgments about art and literature, can be formed, tested, and expressed. What the Constitution says is that these judgments are for the individual to make, not for the Government to decree, even with the mandate or approval of a majority. Technology expands the capacity to choose; and it denies the potential of this revolution if we assume the Government is best positioned to make these choices for us."

U.S. Supreme Court Justice Anthony McLeod Kennedy, *United States, et al. v. Playboy Entertainment Group, Inc.,* 529 U.S. 803, 120 S.Ct. 1878, 146 L.Ed.2d 865 (2000).

"We are not afraid to entrust the American people with unpleasant facts, foreign ideas, alien philosophies, and competitive values. For a nation that is afraid to let its people judge the truth and falsehood in an open market is a nation that is afraid of its people."

John Fitzgerald Kennedy, U.S. President (1917–1963), remarks made on the twentieth anniversary of the Voice of America at H.E.W. Auditorium, February 26, 1962.

"People hardly ever make use of the freedom they have, for example, freedom of thought; instead they demand freedom of speech as a compensation."

Soren Aabye Kierkegaard, Danish philosopher (1813–1855). Quoted in *The Fitzhenry & Whiteside Book of Quotations* (1981), p. 172.

"A library's role never has been, is not currently and will not be in the future to keep people from the information they need and want. If the United States is to continue to be a nation of self-governors, the people must have available and accessible the information they need to make decisions."

Judith F. Krug, U.S. librarian (1940–2009), "Intellectual Freedom 2002: Living the Chinese Curse," Luminary Lectures at the Library of Congress, May 23, 2002.

"The first step in liquidating a people is to erase its memory. Destroy its books, its culture, its history. Then have somebody write new books, manufacture a new culture, invent a new history. Before long the nation will begin to forget what it is and what it was. The world around it will forget even faster."

Milan Kundera, Czech writer (1929–). In "Memories of a Wistful Amnesiac," by Walter Goodman. *New Leader* 63, no. 23 (December 15, 1980), p. 26ff.

"I am absolutely convinced that the most important perspective is that people are obligated to respect opposing views.... If we are a poor respecter of other people's thoughts, our thoughts are not going to be well-received at another time."

James Albert Smith "Jim" Leach (1942–), former member of the U.S. House of Representatives from Iowa. *Washington Post,* March 20, 2003.

"Why should freedom of speech and freedom of the press be allowed? Why should a government which is doing what it believes to be right allow itself to be criticized? It would not allow opposition by lethal weapons. Ideas are much more fatal things than guns."

Vladimir Ilyich Lenin, communist revolutionary, politician and political theorist (1870–1924), speech in Moscow, 1920. In *A New Dictionary of Quotations on Historical Principles from Ancient and Modern Sources*, edited by H. L. Mencken. New York: Knopf, 1991, p. 966.

"Where all men think alike, no one thinks very much."

Walter Lippmann, U.S. author and journalist (1889–1974).

"Censorship, like charity, should begin at home; but unlike charity, it should end there."

Clare Booth Luce, U.S. diplomat, dramatist, journalist, and politician (1903–1987).

"Every American librarian worthy of the name is today the champion of a cause. It is, to my mind, the noblest of all causes for it is the cause of man, or more precisely the cause of the inquiring mind by which man has come to be. But noblest or not, it is nevertheless a cause—a struggle—not yet won: a struggle which can never perhaps be won for good and all. There are always in any society, even a society founded in the love of freedom, men and women who do not wish to be free themselves and who fear the practice of freedom by others—men and women who long for the comfort of a spiritual and intellectual authority in their own lives and who would feel more comfortable if they could also impose such an authority on the lives of their neighbors. As long as such people exist—and they show no sign of disappearing from the earth, even the American earth—the fight to subvert freedom will continue. And as long as the fight to subvert freedom continues, libraries must be strong points of defense."

Archibald MacLeish, U.S. poet, writer, and Librarian of Congress (1892–1982). *Champion of a Cause*. Chicago: American Library Association, 1971, pp. 228–29.

"A popular government, without popular information, or the means of acquiring it, is but a prologue to a farce or a tragedy; or perhaps both. Knowledge will forever govern ignorance; and a people who mean to be their own governors, must arm themselves with the power which knowledge gives."

U.S. President James Madison (1751–1836), letter to W. T. Barry, August 4, 1782. In *The Complete Madison*. New York: Harper, 1953, p. 337.

"It is impossible for ideas to compete in the marketplace if no forum for their presentation is provided or available."

Thomas Mann, German writer (1875–1955).

"Thanks to television, for the first time the young are seeing history made before it is censored by their elders."

Margaret Mead, U.S. anthropologist (1901–1978).

"One cannot and must not try to erase the past merely because it does not fit the present."

Golda Meir, Israeli political leader (1898–1978).

"If all mankind minus one were of one opinion, and only one person were of the contrary opinion, mankind would be no more justified in silencing that one person, than he, if he had the power, would be justified in silencing mankind."

John Stuart Mill, English philosopher, political economist, and civil servant (1806–1873). *On Liberty*. Girard, Kan.: Haldeman-Julius Co., 1925.

"Who can compute what the world loses in the multitude of promising intellects combined with timid characters, who dare not follow out any bold, vigorous, independent train of thought, lest it should land them in something which would admit of being considered irreligious or immoral?... No one can be a great thinker who does not recognize that as a thinker it is his first duty to follow his intellect to whatever conclusions it may lead."

John Stuart Mill. *On Liberty*. Girard, Kan.: Haldeman-Julius Co., 1925.

"As good almost kill a man as kill a good book; who kills a man kills a reasonable creature, God's image; but he who destroys a good book kills reason itself."

John Milton, English poet, polemicist, man of letters, and a civil servant (1608–1674). *Aeropagitica*. Christchurch, New Zealand: Caxton Pr., 1941.

"Give me the liberty to know, to utter, and to argue freely according to conscience, above all liberties."

John Milton. *Aeropagitica*. Christchurch, New Zealand: Caxton Pr., 1941.

"To forbid us anything is to make us have a mind for it."

Michel Eyquem de Montaigne, French philosopher (1533–1592). *Essays*, 1595.

"You have not converted a man because you have silenced him."

John Morley, 1st Viscount Morley of Blackburn, English statesman, writer, and editor (1838–1923). *On Compromise*, 1874.

"Senator Smoot (Republican, Ut.)
Is planning a ban on smut
Oh rooti-ti-toot for Smoot of Ut.
And his reverent occiput.
Smite. Smoot, smite for Ut.,
Grit your molars and do your dut.,
Gird up your l--ns,
Smite h-p and th-gh,
We'll all be Kansas
By and By."

Frederic Ogden Nash, U.S. poet (1902–1971). "Invocation," 1931.

"When voices of democracy are silenced, freedom becomes a hollow concept. No man or woman should be sentenced to the shadows of silence for something he or she has said or written."

Allen H. Neuharth, U.S. journalist (1924–2013).

"When information which properly belongs to the public is systematically withheld by those in power, the people will soon become ignorant of their own affairs, distrustful of those who manage them, and—eventually—incapable of determining their own destinies."

Richard Milhous Nixon, U.S. President (1913–1994). *Washington Post*, January 23, 1996, p. D16.

"Censorship of anything, at any time, in any place, on whatever pretense, has always been and always will be the last resort of the boob and the bigot."

Eugene Gladstone O'Neill, U.S. playwright (1888–1953).

"The First Amendment forbids any law 'abridging the freedom of speech.' It doesn't say, 'except for commercials on children's television' or 'unless somebody says 'cunt' in a rap song or 'chick' on a college campus.'"

P. J. O'Rourke, U.S. journalist and author (1947–). *Parliament of Whores: A Lone Humorist Attempts to Explain the Entire U.S. Government*. New York: Vintage Books, 1992.

"Who controls the past controls the future, and who controls the present controls the past."

Eric Arthur Blair, pen name George Orwell, English essayist, novelist, and satirist (1903–1950).

"That is what pluralism is: a nation where people who are different from one another are all entitled to the same rights and opportunities; the same standing before the law; the same respect, given to and received from each other.

"The First Amendment's value is linked directly to its use. To preserve it, it must be shared. Unless it is everyone's, it can be no one's."

Jean Hammond Otto, U.S. journalist (1925–2011).

"It is shared values, not shared opinions, that keep a diverse and pluralistic nation from splintering. It is tolerance for our differences that binds us. It is the First Amendment that protects the individual mind and conscience against the authority of government and the tyranny of the majority."

Jean Hammond Otto. *Social Education*, October 1990, p. 356.

"He that would make his own liberty secure, must guard even his enemy from opposition; for if he violates this duty he establishes a precedent that will reach to himself."

Thomas Paine, English-American political activist, author, political theorist, and revolutionary (1737–1809). *Dissertation on First Principles of Government*. London: D. I. Eaton, 1795.

"A censor is an expert in cutting remarks. A censor is a man who knows more than he thinks you ought to."

Laurence Johnston Peter, Canadian educator and author (1919–1990). *Peter's Quotations: Ideas for Our Time*. New York: Morrow, 1977, p. 97.

"Now that eighteen-year-olds have the right to vote, it is obvious that they must be allowed the freedom to form their political views on the basis of uncensored speech before they turn eighteen, so that their minds are not a blank when they first exercise the franchise. And since an eighteen-year-old's right to vote is a right personal to him rather than a right to be exercised on his behalf by his parents, the right of parents to enlist the aid of the state to shield their children from ideas of which the parents disapprove cannot be plenary either. People are unlikely to become well-functioning, independent-minded adults and responsible citizens if they are raised in an intellectual bubble."

Judge Richard Allen Posner, *American Amusement Machine Association, et al., Plaintiffs-Appellants v. Teri Kendrick, et al.*, 244 F.3d 954 (7th Cir. 2001).

"A free press is a cornerstone of our democracy. In the First Amendment to the Constitution, our Founding Fathers affirmed their belief that competing ideas are fundamental to freedom. We Americans cherish our freedom of expression and our access to multiple sources of news and information."

Ronald Wilson Reagan, U.S. President (1911–2004), message of the President for National Newspaper Week, October 10–16, 1982.

"Indeed, perhaps we do the minors of this country harm if First Amendment protections, which they will with age inherit fully, are chipped away in the name of their protection."

Judge Lowell A. Reed Jr., *American Civil Liberties Union, et al. v. Janet Reno*, 931 F.Supp.2d 473 (E.D. Pa. 1999).

"Where, after all, do universal human rights begin? In small places, close to home—so close and so small that they cannot be seen on any maps of the world. Yet they are the world of the individual persons; the neighborhood he lives in;the school or college he attends; the factory, farm, or office where he works. Such are the places where every man, woman and child seeks equal justice, equal opportunity, equal dignity without discrimination. Unless these rights have meaning there, they have little meaning anywhere. Without concerned citizen action to uphold them close to home, we shall look in vain for progress in the larger world."

Anna Eleanor Roosevelt, U.S. diplomat and reformer (1884–1962). From *In Your Hands: A Guide for Community Action for the Tenth Anniversary of the Universal Declaration of Human Rights*, 1958.

"If in other lands the press and books and literature of all kinds are censored, we must redouble our efforts here to keep it free. Books may be burned and cities sacked, but truth, like the yearning for freedom, lives in the hearts of humble men and women. No people in all the world can be kept eternally ignorant or eternally enslaved."

Franklin Delano Roosevelt, U.S. President (1882–1945), speech before the National Education Association, 1938.

"Free societies...are societies in motion, and with motion comes tension, dissent, friction. Free people strike sparks, and those sparks are the best evidence of freedom's existence."

"What is freedom of expression? Without the freedom to offend, it ceases to exist."

(Ahmed) Salman Rushdie, British (Indian-born) author (1947–).

"The creative act requires not only freedom but also this assumption of freedom. If the creative artist worries if he will still be free tomorrow, then he will not be free today."

(Ahmed) Salman Rushdie, *The New Yorker*, May 15, 2012.

"Men fear thoughts as they fear nothing else on earth—more than ruin—more even than death.... Thought is subversive and revolutionary, destructive and terrible, thought is merciless to privilege, established institutions, and comfortable habit. Thought looks into the pit of hell and is not afraid. Thought is great and swift and free, the light of the world, and the chief glory of man."

Bertrand Arthur William Russell, English author, mathematician, and philosopher (1872–1970).

"Intellectual freedom is essential to human society. Freedom of thought is the only guarantee against an infection of people by mass myths, which, in the hands of treacherous hypocrites and demagogues, can be transformed into bloody dictatorships."

Andrei Dmitrievich Sakharov, Russian physicist (1921–1989).

"The First Amendment cases of the 1990s and the twenty-first century will pit powerful emotional interests—such as privacy or nationalism—against our intellectual commitment to the value of information and the right of the public to freely receive information."

Bruce W. Sanford, U.S. attorney (1945–).

"All truth passes through three stages. First, it is ridiculed. Second, it is violently opposed. Third, it is accepted as being self-evident."

Arthur Schopenhauer, German philosopher (1788–1860).

"All censorships exist to prevent anyone from challenging current conceptions and existing institutions. All progress is initiated by challenging current conceptions, and executed by supplanting existing institutions. Consequently the first condition of progress is the removal of censorship."

George Bernard Shaw, Irish playwright (1856–1950). Preface to *Mrs. Warren's Profession.* Studio City, Calif.: Players Pr., 1991.

"The war between the artist and writer and government or orthodoxy is one of the tragedies of humankind. One chief enemy is stupidity and failure to understand anything about the creative mind. For a bureaucratic politician to presume to tell any artist or writer how to get his mind functioning is the ultimate in asininity. The artist is no more able to control his mind than is any outsider. Freedom to think requires not only freedom of expression but also freedom from the threat of orthodoxy and being outcast and ostracized."

Helen Foster Snow, U.S. writer promoting American-Chinese understanding (1907–1997).

"The ultimate result of shielding men from the effects of folly is to fill the world with fools."

Herbert Spencer, British philosopher (1820–1903).

"Our nation's understanding and appreciation of the First Amendment is not passed along genetically. It must be reaffirmed and defended, over and over. Keep fighting and keep winning."

Paul Steinle, U.S. journalist and cofounder of the Who Needs Newspapers? Initiative.

"The interest in encouraging freedom of expression in a democratic society outweighs any theoretical but unproven benefit of censorship."

U.S. Supreme Court Justice John Paul Stevens, *Janet Reno, Attorney General of the United States, et al., Appellants v. American Civil Liberties Union et al.,* 521 U.S. 844, 117 S.Ct. 2329, 138 L.Ed.2d 874 (1997).

"The sound of tireless voices is the price we pay for the right to hear the music of our own opinions."

Adlai Ewing Stevenson II, U.S. politician (1900–1965), Governor of Illinois, and Ambassador to the United Nations, speech in New York City, August 28, 1952. *The Papers of Adlai E. Stevenson*, vol. 4 (1974).

"Freedom rings where opinions clash."

Adlai Ewing Stevenson II.

"You see, boys forget what their country means by just reading 'the land of the free' in history books. When they get to be men, they forget even more. Liberty is too precious a thing to be buried in books, Miss Saunders. Men should hold it up in front of them every single day of their lives and say, 'I'm free—to think and speak. My ancestors couldn't, I can. And my children will.'"

James Stewart in Frank Capra's film *Mr. Smith Goes to Washington* (1939).

"Censorship reflects a society's lack of confidence in itself. It is the hallmark of an authoritarian regime."

U.S. Supreme Court Justice Potter Stewart, dissenting, *Ginzberg v. United States*, 383 U.S. 463, 86 S.Ct. 942, 16 L.Ed.2d 31 (1966).

"The ultimate expression of free speech lies not in the ideas with which we agree, but in those ideas that offend and irritate us."

Charles "Chuck" Sumner Stone, U.S. journalist (1924–). "Ethnic Groups vs. Free Speech: When Does Dissent Cross the Line and Become Illegitimate?" *Philly.com*, January 18, 1991.

"Once a government is committed to the principle of silencing the voice of opposition, it has only one way to go, and that is down the path of increasingly repressive measures, until it becomes a source of terror to all its citizens and creates a country where everyone lives in fear."

Harry S. Truman, U.S. President (1884–1972), special message to Congress on the Internal Security of the United States, August 8, 1950.

"There is no more fundamental axiom of American freedom than the familiar statement: In a free country we punish men for crimes they commit but never for the opinions they have."

Harry S. Truman. Veto of the Internal Security Act of 1950, September 22, 1950.

"In America, as elsewhere, free speech is confined to the dead."

Mark Twain [Samuel Langhornne Clemens], U.S. author and humorist (1835–1910). *Notebook*, 1904.

"It is by the goodness of God that in our country we have those three unspeakable precious things: freedom of speech, freedom of conscience, and the prudence never to practice either."

Mark Twain, *Pudd'nhead Wilson's New Calendar*, 1897.

"Everyone has the right to freedom of opinion and expression; this right includes freedom to hold opinions without interference and to seek, receive, and impart information and ideas through any media regardless of frontiers."

United Nations *Universal Declaration of Human Rights, Article 19.*

"The basis of the First Amendment is the hypothesis that... free debate of ideas will result in the wisest governmental policies."

U.S. Supreme Court Justice Fred Moore Vinson, *Dennis et al. v. United States*, 341 U.S. 494, 71 S.Ct. 857, 95 L.Ed. 1137 (1951).

"I may disagree with what you have to say, but I shall defend to the death your right to say it."

Voltaire, [François Marie Arouet], French writer (1694–1778).

"It is the characteristic of the most stringent censorships, that they give credibility to the opinions they attack."

Voltaire [François Marie Arouet]. *Poème sur le désastre de Lisbonne*, 1756.

"If I open my mouth to speak, must I always be correct? And by whose standards?"

Alice Malsenior Walker, U.S. author and activist (1944–). *In Search of Our Mothers' Gardens.* San Diego: Harcourt, 1983.

"Teachers and students must always remain free to inquire, to study and to evaluate, to gain new maturity and understanding; otherwise our civilization will stagnate and die."

Chief Justice of the United States Earl Warren, *Sweezy v. New Hampshire*, 354 U.S. 234, 77 S.Ct. 1203, 1 L.Ed.2d 1311 (1957).

"I believe in censorship. I made a fortune out of it."

Mae West, U.S. movie actress (1893–1980).

"There were a lot of things the censors wouldn't let me do in the movies that I did on stage. They wouldn't even let me sit on a guy's lap and I'd been on more laps than a napkin."

Mae West, *Index on Censorship.*

"The books that the world calls immoral are the books that show the world its own shame."

Oscar Fingal O'Flahertie Wills Wilde, Irish dramatist, novelist, and poet (1854–1900).

"An idea that is not dangerous is unworthy of being called an idea at all."
Oscar Fingal O'Flahertie Wills Wilde.

"I believe in America because in it we are free—free to choose our government, to speak our minds, to observe our different religions. Because we are generous with our freedom, we share our rights with those who disagree with us."
Wendell Lewis Willkie, U.S. politician (1892–1944).

"To suppress minority thinking and minority expression would tend to freeze society and prevent progress.... Now more than ever we must keep in the forefront of our minds the fact that whenever we take away the liberties of those whom we hate, we are opening the way to loss of liberty for those we love."
Wendell Lewis Willkie. *One World.* New York: Limited Editions Club, 1944.

"I have always been among those who believed that the greatest freedom of speech was the greatest safety, because if a man is a fool the best thing to do is to encourage him to advertise the fact by speaking."
Woodrow Wilson, U.S. President (1856–1924). "That Quick Comradeship of Letters," address at the Institute of France, Paris, May 10, 1919. *The Public Papers of Woodrow Wilson,* edited Ray Stannard Baker and William E. Dodd, vol. 5, p. 484 (1927).

"The wisest thing to do with a fool is to encourage him to hire a hall and discourse to his fellow citizens. Nothing chills nonsense like exposure to the air; nothing dispels folly like its publication."
Woodrow Wilson. *Constitutional Government in the United States.* New York: Columbia University Press, 1908, p. 38.

"The trouble with free speech is that it insists on living up to its name."
Jonathan Yardley, *Washington Post* book critic (1939–). *Washington Post,* June 17, 1996, p. CO2.

"I think you can leave the arts, superior and inferior, to the conscience of mankind."
William Butler Yeats, Irish poet, dramatist, and winner of the 1923 Nobel Prize for Literature (1865–1939). Speech, June 7, 1923, to the Irish Senate.

"Every dogma has its day, but ideals are eternal."
Israel Zangwill, English novelist (1864–1926).

First Amendment Action Guide

Take Action!
Protect Your Right to Read

Each day, all across the country, one of our most basic freedoms—the right to read—is in danger. In communities large and small, censorship attempts threaten to undermine our freedom to read. Without our constant support, the First Amendment freedoms that we so often take for granted—the right to read, explore ideas, and express ourselves freely—are at risk.

The First Amendment guarantees that each of us has the right to express our views, including opinions about particular books. At the same time, the First Amendment also ensures that none of us has the right to control or limit another person's ability to read or access information. Yet when individuals or groups file formal written requests demanding that libraries and schools remove specific books from the shelves, they are doing just that—attempting to restrict the rights of other individuals to access those books.

The rights and protections of the First Amendment extend to children and teens as well as adults. While parents have the right—and the responsibility—to guide their own children's reading, that right does not extend to other people's children. Similarly each adult has the right to choose his or her own reading materials, along with the responsibility to acknowledge and respect the right of others to do the same.

When we speak up to protect the right to read, we not only defend our individual right to free expression, we demonstrate tolerance and respect for opposing points of view. And when we take action to preserve our precious freedoms, we become participants in the ongoing evolution of our democratic society.

Act now to protect your right to read. Here are three ways that you can get involved:

1. Stay Informed

Be aware of what's happening
The best way to fight censorship is to be aware that it's happening. When you encounter it, be prepared to speak up or let others know.

Ask the people on the front lines—librarians, teachers, and school principals—if there are any current attempts to challenge or ban books or other materials. If they have support groups or information lists, ask to join them.

Legislators and public officials often introduce legislation to restrict access to books and other materials in libraries, schools, and bookstores. Let officials know that there are citizens actively opposed to demands to restrict or remove books in schools and libraries.

Attend school board, library board, and PTA meetings
You can speak up about the importance of free speech to education in a democratic society.

As a regular participant in gatherings, you have the opportunity to learn about policies governing access to books and materials. You can witness firsthand when someone demands that a school or library remove a book or restrict access to books.

Subscribe to print and online news publications
You can stay current on First Amendment rights and censorship issues.

The ALA Office for Intellectual Freedom (ala.org/oif) publishes the *Newsletter on Intellectual Freedom* and provides regular news updates via the OIF blog, Twitter (twitter.com/oif) and the IFACTION mailing list (lists.ala.org/sympa/info/ifaction).

The First Amendment Center (firstamendmentcenter.org) maintains an online First Amendment library (firstamendmentcenter.org/research-articles) and provides breaking news about First Amendment issues via its RSS newsfeed.

Join groups committed to preserving the right to read
You can participate by joining these nonprofit organizations.

The Freedom to Read Foundation (ftrf.org) is the only organization in the United States whose primary goal is to protect and promote the First Amendment in libraries by participating in litigation dealing with free expression in libraries and other venues. Members receive a quarterly newsletter, *The FTRF News.*

The American Booksellers Foundation for Free Expression (abffe.org) promotes and protects the free exchange of ideas, particularly those contained in books, by opposing restrictions on the freedom of speech.

The National Coalition Against Censorship (ncac.org) is an alliance of fifty national nonprofit organizations, including literary, artistic, religious, educational, professional, labor, and civil liberties groups, that works to educate both members and the public about the dangers of censorship and how to oppose it.

The Comic Book Legal Defense Fund (cbldf.org) works to protect free speech in comics by supporting First Amendment rights for the comics community, fans and professionals alike.

The American Civil Liberties Union (aclu.org) works daily to defend and preserve the individual rights and liberties guaranteed by the Constitution, including the freedom of speech and freedom of the press. Local chapters and affiliates (aclu.org/affiliates) provide assistance to local communities.

2. Challenge Censorship

Report censorship to ALA's Office for Intellectual Freedom
You can help raise awareness of censorship in your local community.

ALA's Office for Intellectual Freedom tracks attempts to remove or restrict books across the country. By reporting censorship incidents, you can help to identify trends in censorship cases and document responses and solutions to censorship. All identifying information is kept strictly confidential. You can file reports online by going to ala.org/challengereporting.

Attend and participate in public hearings
You can inform public officials that censorship won't be tolerated in the community.

By attending hearings, you can speak out in support of free expression and the right to read freely. You can let officials know that there are citizens actively opposed to demands to restrict or remove books in schools and libraries. Such attempts seldom succeed when concerned citizens speak out against censorship.

Write letters to public officials
You can write to public officials encouraging them to preserve the freedom to read.

Let them know that your rights and your views are entitled to the same respect as those who seek to censor books. Write to any public official that you believe can prevent the suppression of books in your community: your mayor, city council, other city officials, library board members, school board members, superintendent of schools, etc.

Send a letter or an op-ed article to local news organizations
You can update community news outlets with information and opinion.

Make sure you let reporters and editors know that there are members of the community who oppose censorship and the official suppression of ideas. Letters to public officials, letters sent to local news outlets, and comments posted on websites and blogs are effective ways to raise awareness.

Work with community groups
You can network with local organizations for support.

Inform professional associations, civic organizations, and religious groups about attempts to remove books from the community's library or school. You can ask to speak to their membership about the importance of preserving First Amendment freedoms. Or ask if you can contribute an article to the group's newsletter or website. You can speak with the group's leaders and ask them to lend public support to efforts to protect the right to read in the community.

Form a coalition to oppose censorship in your community
You can partner with others who support the right to read freely.

Even a small number of persons can form an effective group to oppose censorship. Such groups allow members to share responsibility for attending meetings and conducting outreach efforts. By joining together you can become a resource for the community as a whole. To read the story of one exemplary community

coalition, visit its website at westbendparentsforfreespeech.webs.com.

Seek assistance from national groups
You can get guidance and support from experienced organizations.

Get started by researching existing groups so that you can benefit from their expertise. Check out the national organizations listed previously for assistance, resources, and referrals whenever you or your organization address demands to remove books from libraries or schools.

3. Support your local schools and libraries

Join Library Friends groups and PTAs
You can become an advocate for community education groups.

Libraries and schools rely on volunteers and advocates to accomplish their mission of educating young people. These groups also provide information and lifelong learning opportunities to adults in the community. You can contribute by participating in Friends groups, PTAs, or volunteering directly where your help will strengthen these vital institutions.

Participate in Banned Books Week
You can promote the right to read by joining in the celebration.

Each year, libraries, schools, and bookstores across the nation celebrate the freedom to read by observing Banned Books Week. This public event in September features author visits and readings from banned books. You can show your support for the freedom to read by attending these events. Please visit ala.org/bbooks for more resources and information or connect on Facebook (facebook.com/bannedbooksweek).

Part 5
Incidents

"I begin to feel like most Americans don't understand the First Amendment, don't understand the idea of freedom of speech, and don't understand that it's the responsibility of the citizens to speak out."

Roger Ebert, U.S. film critic, journalist, screenwriter, and winner of the 1975 Pulitzer Prize for Criticism (1943-2013).

To reach their readers, authors and publishers count on librarians and booksellers to make books openly available to everyone— patrons, students, and customers. But when censors successfully intervene, readers are denied access to the books that some people consider dangerous.

Incidents documents the accumulation of book-by-book attempts to erode our freedom to read in libraries and schools across America and around the world.

Top 10 Challenged Books of 2013

Captain Underpants (series)
Dav Pilkey

Reasons
Offensive Language, Unsuited for Age Group, Violence

Fifty Shades of Grey
E. L. James

Reasons
Nudity, Offensive Language, Religious Viewpoint, Sexually Explicit, Unsuited to Age Group

The Perks of Being a Wallflower
Stephen Chbosky

Reasons
Drugs/Alcohol/Smoking, Homosexuality, Sexually Explicit, Unsuited to Age Group

The Bluest Eye
Toni Morrison

Reasons
Offensive Language, Sexually Explicit, Unsuited to Age Group, Violence

The Hunger Games
Suzanne Collins

Reasons
Religious Viewpoint, Unsuited to Age Group

Bless Me, Ultima
Rudolfo Anaya

Reasons
Occult/Satanism, Offensive Language, Religious Viewpoint, Sexually Explicit

The Absolutely True Diary of a Part-Time Indian
Sherman Alexie

Reasons
Drugs/Alcohol/Smoking, Offensive Language, Racism, Sexually Explicit, Unsuited to Age Group

A Bad Boy Can Be Good for a Girl
Tanya Lee Stone

Reasons
Drugs/Alcohol/Smoking, Nudity, Offensive Language, Sexually Explicit

Bone (series)
Jeff Smith

Reasons
Political Viewpoint, Racism, Violence

Looking for Alaska
John Green

Reasons
Drugs/Alcohol/Smoking, Sexually Explicit, Unsuited to Age Group

As compiled by the Office for Intellectual Freedom, American Library Association. The Office for Intellectual Freedom does not claim comprehensiveness in recording challenges. Research suggests that for each challenge reported there are as many as four or five which go unreported.

The Nobel Prize in Literature is generally considered to be the highest award a writer can receive for his or her work. Since 1901 when the prize was established, 106 prizes have been awarded to… "the person who shall have produced in the field of literature the most outstanding work in an ideal direction."

Many of the names are familiar to most readers, some are not. You will find works by the following twenty-one Nobel laureates listed in the Incidents section.

Nobel Laureates Whose Books Have Been Banned

Miguel Angel Asturias	1967
William Faulkner	1949
Anatole France	1921
Gao Xingjian	2000
Gabriel Garcia Marquez	1982
Andre Gide	1947
William Golding	1983
Nadine Gordimer	1991
Ernest Hemingway	1954
Hermann Hesse	1946
Rudyard Kipling	1907
Sinclair Lewis	1930
Naguib Mahfouz	1988
Toni Morrison	1993
Boris Leonidovich Pasternak	1958
Bertrand Russell	1950
Jean-Paul Sartre	1964
George Bernard Shaw	1925
Aleksandr Isayevich Solzhenitsyn	1970
Wole Soyinka	1986
John Steinbeck	1962

Challe

Banne

nged or
Books

This "List of Challenged or Banned Books" is a compilation of actual or attempted bannings, over the centuries, worldwide. All entries are books published in the English language, and emphasis is on recent U.S. incidents involving popular titles. This list of books was compiled from the following sources:

1. Bald, Margaret. *Literature Suppressed on Religious Grounds,* Rev. ed. New York: Facts on File, 2006.

2. Geller, Evelyn. *Forbidden Books in American Public Libraries, 1876-1939: A Study in Cultural Change.* Westport, CN: Greenwood Press, 1984.

3. Green, Jonathon. *The Encyclopedia of Censorship.* New York: Facts On File, 1990.

4. Haight, Anne Lyon, and Chandler B. Grannis. *Banned Books, 387 B.C. to 1978 A.D.,* 4th ed. New York: Bowker Co., 1978.

5. *Index on Censorship.* London: Writers and Scholars International, Ltd., published bimonthly.

6. Jones, Derek, ed. *Censorship: A World Encyclopedia.* 4 vols. Chicago: Fitzroy Dearborn, 2001.

7. Karolides, Nicholas J. *Literature Suppressed on Political Grounds,* Rev. ed. New York: Facts on File, 2006.

8. Karolides, Nicholas J., Margaret Bald, and Dawn B. Sova. *120 Banned Books: Censorship Histories of World Literature,* Rev. ed. New York: Checkmark Books, 2005.

9. *Limiting What Students Shall Read: Books and Other Learning Materials in Our Public Schools: How They Are Selected and How They Are Removed.* Report on a survey sponsored by Association of American Publishers, American Library Association, Association for Supervision and Curriculum Development. Washington, D.C.: Association of American Publishers, 1981.

10. Nelson, Randy F. "Banned in Boston and Elsewhere." In *The Almanac of American Letters.* Los Altos, CA: William Kaufmann, Inc., 1981.

11. *Newsletter on Intellectual Freedom.* Henry Reichman, ed. Chicago: American Library Association, Intellectual Freedom Committee, published bimonthly.

12. O'Neil, Robert M. *Classrooms in the Crossfire: The Rights and Interests of Students, Parents, Teachers, Administrators, Librarians, and the Community.* Bloomington, IN: Indiana University Press, 1981.

13. Sova, Dawn B. *Literature Suppressed on Sexual Grounds,* Rev. ed. New York: Facts on File, 2006.

14. _____. *Literature Suppressed on Social Grounds,* Rev. ed. New York: Facts on File, 2006.

15. Tebbel, John. *A History of Book Publishing in the United States.* New York: Bowker Co., 1981.

This compilation is admittedly incomplete because it is impossible to document and record all prohibitions against free speech and expression. In fact, this list is limited to books and therefore does not include prohibitions against magazines, newspapers, films, broadcasts, plays, performances, exhibits, or access to electronic resources. The professional, economic, or emotional consequences of the curtailment of an author's free expression also are not documented.

At the 1986 American Library Association (ALA) Annual Conference, the ALA Intellectual Freedom Committee adopted the following operative definitions of some terms frequently used to describe the various levels of incidents that may or may not lead to censorship. This terminology is employed by the *Newsletter on Intellectual Freedom.*

Expression of Concern:
An inquiry that has judgmental overtones.

Oral Complaint:
An oral challenge to the presence and/or appropriateness of the material in question.

Written Complaint:
A formal, written complaint filed with the institution (library, school, etc.) challenging the presence and/or appropriateness of specific material.

Public Attack:
A publicly disseminated statement challenging the value of the material, presented to the media and/or others outside the institutional organization in order to gain public support for further action.

Censorship:
A change in the access status of material, made by a governing authority or its representatives. Such changes include: exclusion, restriction, removal, or age/grade level changes.

In this bibliography, the following postal code abbreviations for states are used:

State or Territory	Abbreviation	State or Territory	Abbreviation
Alabama	AL	Montana	MT
Alaska	AK	Nebraska	NE
Arizona	AZ	Nevada	NV
Arkansas	AR	New Hampshire	NH
California	CA	New Jersey	NJ
Colorado	CO	New Mexico	NM
Connecticut	CT	New York	NY
Delaware	DE	North Carolina	NC
District of Columbia	DC	North Dakota	ND
Florida	FL	Ohio	OH
Georgia	GA	Oklahoma	OK
Hawaii	HI	Oregon	OR
Idaho	ID	Pennsylvania	PA
Illinois	IL	Puerto Rico	PR
Indiana	IN	Rhode Island	RI
Iowa	IA	South Carolina	SC
Kansas	KS	South Dakota	SD
Kentucky	KY	Tennessee	TN
Louisiana	LA	Texas	TX
Maine	ME	Utah	UT
Maryland	MD	Vermont	VT
Massachusetts	MA	Virginia	VA
Michigan	MI	Washington	WA
Minnesota	MN	West Virginia	WV
Mississippi	MS	Wisconsin	WI
Missouri	MO	Wyoming	WY

1

Abelard, Pierre.
Introduction to Theology.

1120
Published

1121
The Catholic Church condemned and burned his work in 1121. In 1140, he was charged with heresy, confined to a monastery, and forbidden to continue writing.

1559
Listed on the *Index Librorum Prohibitorum* (Index of Prohibited Books). Also listed in 1564 along with all of his writings. The French theologian, poet, and teacher is best known for his tragic love affair with Heloise, his pupil, and for the love letters he wrote to her after he entered a monastery and she became a nun.

1930
U.S. Customs lifted ban on *The Love Letters of Heloise and Abelard.*
Source: 1, pp. 163-65; 4, p. 6; 6, pp. 2–3.

2

Abernathy, Rev. Ralph D.
And the Walls Came Tumbling Down.

1989
Published

1989 CO
Burned in protest in Denver because it alleges that Martin Luther King, Jr., was involved with three women. E. Napoleon Walton, publisher of the *Denver Cosmopolitan Advertiser*, stated, "[Abernathy] has his freedom of speech, and we have our freedom to burn it."
Source: 11, Jan. 1990, p. 19.

3

Abrahams, Roger D.
African Folktales: Traditional Stories of the Black World.

1983
Published

1991 TX
Dallas school administrators told teachers to rip an offending page from the school textbooks because the story, which refers to male genitals and bodily functions, didn't fit the curriculum. Instructors were also asked to avoid teaching the first two chapters of another book that dealt in part with circumcision and puberty.
Source: 11, Nov. 1991, p. 197.

4

Adams, Carmen.
The Band.

1994
Published

1998 IA
Challenged, but retained, at the Madison Elementary School in Cedar Rapids.
Source: 11, May 1998, pp. 87–88.

5

Adler, C. S.
Down by the River.

1981
Published

1983 WA
Removed from the Evergreen School District of Vancouver along with twenty-nine other titles. The American Civil Liberties Union of Washington filed suit contending that the removals constituted censorship, a violation of plaintiff's rights to free speech and due process, and a violation of the state Open Meetings Act because the removal decisions were made behind closed doors.
Source: 11, Nov. 1983, pp. 185–86.

6

Adler, C. S.
The Shell Lady's Daughter.

1983
Published

1983
Best Books for Young Adults

2007 WY
Challenged, but retained, at the Campbell County junior high school libraries in Gillette despite "objectionable subjects: sexual relations between teenagers, sexual thoughts, promiscuity, masturbation, deceiving parents, suicide by overdosing on sleeping pills, suicide by drowning oneself and self-inflicted pain."
Source: 11, Nov. 2007, p. 241; Mar. 2008, pp. 79-80

7

Adler, David.
I Know I'm a Witch.

1988
Published

1998 IL
Retained on the shelves at Prairieview Elementary School in Elgin despite a parent's complaint that the material gives children the impression that witchcraft is "fun and harmless."
Source: 11, May 1998, p. 87.

8

Adler, Margo.
Drawing Down the Moon.

1979
Published

1997 TX
Removed from the Kirby Junior High School in Wichita Falls because of "Satanic" themes.
Source: 11, July 1997, p. 95.

9

Adoff, Arnold, ed.
Poetry of Black America.

1973
Published

1996 FL
Challenged at the Fort Walton Beach school libraries because it "promotes violence" and contains "expletives and a reference to abortion."
Source: 11, July 1996, p. 133.

10

Adoff, Arnold.
The Cabbages Are Chasing the Rabbits.

1985
Published

1992 IN
Challenged at the Deer Ridge Elementary School because the book could breed intolerance for hunters in children's minds.
Source: 11, May 1992, p. 94.

11

Affabee, Eric.
Wizards, Warriors & You.

1984
Published

1992 OH
Removed from the Fairfield elementary school libraries because of "wizardry themes." The series of books were initially challenged because they "promote violence and acceptance and involvement in occult practices."
Source: 11, Sept. 1992, p. 138; Nov. 1992, p. 185.

12

Agee, Philip.
Inside the Company: CIA Diary.

1974
Published

1974
U.S. Customs stopped delivery of imported copies of Agee's book.
Source: 4, p. 99.

13

Agrippa, Henricus Cornelius.
Of the Vanitie and Uncertaintie of Artes and Sciences.

1530
Published

1531
Banned in Rome, Italy.

1531
Denounced and banned by the theological faculty of the Sorbonne in Paris, France.

1531
Banned in Cologne, Germany.

1531
Denounced and banned by the theological faculty of Louvain, Belgium.
Source: 1, pp. 222–23.

14

Aho, Jennifer S., and John W. Petras.
Learning about Sex: A Guide for Children and Their Parents.

1978
Published

1980 KS
Challenged, but retained, at the Hays Public Library.

1981 RI
Challenged, but retained, at the Great Bend Public Library.

1994 NV
Challenged, but retained, at the Washoe County Library System in Reno because, "Nobody in their right mind would give a book like that to children on their own, except the library."
Source: 11, Nov. 1980, p. 138; Nov. 1981, p. 169; Sept. 1994, p. 147; Nov. 1994, pp. 200–201.

15

Al-Shaykh, Hanan.
The Story of Zahra.

1980
Published

1980
Banned in Saudi Arabia and other Arab countries more than twenty-five years after its publication for offending religious authorities by its explicit portrayal of sexuality and its indictment of social hypocrisy in contemporary Arab society.
Source: 1, p. 322.

16

Alderman, Ellen.
In Our Defense: The Bill of Rights in Action.

1991
Published

1998 WI
Challenged, but retained, at the Wisconsin Rapids high school despite two social studies teachers' objections to descriptions of violence in one chapter and explicit sexual details in another.
Source: 11, Mar. 1999, p. 47.

17

Alderson, Sue Ann, and Ann Blades.
Ida and the Wool Smugglers.

1988
Published

1991 MD
Challenged in the Howard County school libraries. The mother in the picture book was considered neglectful because she sent her daughter to the neighbors when she knew the smugglers were in the vicinity.
Source: 11, Sept. 1991, p. 178.

18

Alexander-Minter, Rae Pace.
Young and Black in America.

1970
Published

1983 MN
After the Minnesota Civil Liberties Union sued the Elk River School Board, the Board reversed its decision to restrict this title to students who have written permission from their parents.
Source: 11, Sept. 1982, pp. 155–56; May 1983, p. 71; Sept. 1983, p. 153.

19

Alexander, Lloyd.
The Prydain Chronicles.

1991
Published

1993 MA
Challenged as required reading at the Northbridge Middle School. The complainants said that the series of fantasy novels contains religious themes that are pagan in nature and young minds would be drawn to the allure of witchcraft and black magic that runs through the books.
Source: 11, Mar. 1994, p. 54.

20
Alexander, Lloyd.
The Wizard in the Tree.

1975
Published

1995 IN
After hearing impassioned pleas from parents against book banning, a Duneland School Committee in Chesterton voted to keep the elementary school library book on the shelves. The book came under attack by a parent because a character in the story uses the words "slut" and "damn."
Source: 11, Sept. 1995, p. 157.

21
Alexander, Ruth Bell et al.
Changing Bodies, Changing Lives.

1980
Published

1981 WI
Placed in a restrictive circulation category at the Muskego High School library.

1982 ME
Challenged in the York school systems.

1982 WI
Challenged in Amherst school system.

1984 MO
Challenged at the William Chrisman High School in Independence because it is "filthy."

1984 OR
Removed from the Sandy Union High School library due to "foul language and disregard for a wholesome balance about human sexuality."

1984 WV
Challenged at the Boone-Madison Public Library.

1986 ME
Challenged at the Gray-New Gloucester High School library because the book contains first person accounts of teenagers' sexual experiences.

1992 AK
Removed from the Kenai Peninsula Borough School District libraries in Homer because the book was too explicit.

1992 WI
Challenged at the Eau Claire Memorial High School library because of its graphic language and because the book condones abortion, homosexuality, and incest.

1994 PA
Challenged at the Council Rock School District in Bucks County because of passages that "undermine parental authority and depict sexual relations in explicit and vulgar language."
Source: 11, July 1981, p. 92; May 1982, p. 100; July 1982, p. 124; July 1984, pp. 104, 106; Sept. 1984, p. 138; Nov. 1984, p. 186; Jan. 1985, pp. 27–28; July 1986, pp. 135–36; Sept. 1992, p. 140; Mar. 1993, p. 41; Mar. 1995, p. 44.

22
Alexie, Sherman.
The Absolutely True Diary of a Part-Time Indian.

2007
Published

2007
Best Books of 2007 *School Library Journal*

2007
National Book Award for Young

2008
Best Books for Young Adults

2008
People's Literature Boston Globe-Horn Book Award

2008 OR
Suspended from a Crook County High School classroom in Prineville after a parent complained it was offensive. *The New York Times* best seller is on many recommended book lists and will remain out of the classroom until the school district can revamp its policies. The book is about a boy growing up on the Spokane Indian Reservation who decides to attend an all-white school. The protagonist in Alexie's book discusses masturbation.

2009 IL
Retained on the summer reading list at Antioch High School despite objections from several parents who found its language vulgar and racist. In response to concerns, however, the district will form a committee each March to review future summer reading assignments. The committee, which will include parents, would decide whether parents should be warned if a book contains possibly objectionable material.

2010 MO
Banned in the Stockton School District because of violence, language, and some sexual content.

2011 GA
Pulled from the Dade County library shelves and the required high school reading list because of complaints about "vulgarity, racism, and anti-Christian content."

2011 MA
Challenged at the Old Rochester Regional Junior High School in Mattapoisett as an eighth-grade English assignment.

2011 MT
Retained in the Helena School District despite a parent's objection that the book contained "obscene, vulgar and pornographic language."

2011 WA
Banned, but later returned to the Richland school district's reading list despite objections to the "coarse themes and language in the young-adult novel."

2012 NJ
Challenged as required reading in at least three freshmen English classes at Westfield High School because of "some very sensitive material in the book including excerpts on masturbation amongst other explicit sexual references, encouraging pornography, racism, religious irreverence, and strong language (including the f- and n-words)."

2013 MT
Challenged on the tenth-grade required reading list at Skyview High School in Billings because "[t]his book is, shockingly, written by a Native American who reinforces all the negative stereotypes of his people and does it from the crude, obscene, and unfiltered viewpoint of a ninth-grader growing up on the reservation."

2013 NY
Removed as required reading in a Queens middle school because the book included excerpts on masturbation.

2013 WA
Challenged at the West Valley School District because some parents found the sexual references and profanity in the novel inappropriate for high school students.

2013 WV
Pulled from the Jefferson County schools because a parent complained about the novel's graphic nature.

2014 ID
Pulled from the Meridian high school supplemental reading list (2014) after some parents complained that the novel "discusses masturbation, contains profanity, and is anti-Christian."

2014 OR
Challenged in a Sweet Home Junior High English class because of concerns about its content, particularly what some parents see as the objectification of women and young girls, and the way alternative lessons were developed and presented. Parents of the eighth-graders in the language arts classes received information summarizing the novel's most controversial issues before the unit started and had the option of asking for an alternative assignment.
Source: 11, Mar. 2009, p. 41; Sept. 2009, p. 171; July 2010, p. 156; Sept. 2010, pp. 198-99; Nov. 2010, pp. 241, 243-44; Mar. 2011, pp. 73-74; Sept. 2011, pp. 196-97; Jan. 2012, pp. 9, 13; May 2012, pp. 105-6; Mar. 2013, pp. 51-5; Sept. 2013, p. 185; Jan. 2014, pp. 10-11, 14; Mar. 2014, p. 49; May 2014.

23
Alinsky, Saul.
Rules for Radicals.

1971
Published

1987 MI
Challenged at the Plymouth-Canton school system in Canton because the book holds "Lucifer or the Devil up as a role model."
Source: 11, May 1987, p. 109.

24
Allan, Nicholas.
Where Willy Went.

2005
Published

2007 AZ
Challenged at the Chandler Public Library along with complaints about the *Phoenix New Times,* comedian George Carlin's audio book, *When Will Jesus Bring the Pork Chops?,* and a fairy tale DVD narrated by Robin Williams. A parent requested that Allan's children's picture book be moved from the children's area to a restricted parenting collection because Willy is a sperm and the book is about sex.
Source: 11, Nov. 2007, pp. 239-40.

25
Allard, Harry, and James Marshall.
The Stupids Have a Ball.

1978
Published

1993 IA
Challenged in the Iowa City elementary school libraries because the book reinforces negative behavior and low self-esteem, since the Stupids rejoice in their children's behavior.
Source: 11, Jan. 1994, p. 35.

26
Allard, Harry, and James Marshall.
The Stupids Step Out.

1974
Published

1985 WA
Removed from the Silver Star Elementary School in Vancouver because "it described families in a derogatory manner and might encourage children to disobey their parents."

1985 WI
Challenged at the Cunningham Elementary School in Beloit because it "encourages disrespectful language."

1993 PA
Challenged, removed, and then returned to the shelves in the Horsham schools. The book was challenged because it "makes parents look like boobs and undermines authority."
Source: 11, May 1985, p. 91; Nov. 1985, p. 204; July 1993, p. 101.

27
Allard, Harry.
Bumps in the Night.

1979
Published

1989 OR
Challenged at the South Prairie Elementary School in Tillamook because a medium and seances are in the story.
Source: 11, Jan. 1990, pp. 4–5.

28
Allard, Harry.
The Stupids Die.

1981
Published

1998 MI
Pulled from the Howard Miller Library in Zeeland along with the three other Allard books in the series because of complaints that children shouldn't refer to anyone as "stupid."
Source: 11, Sept. 1998, p. 140.

29
Allen, Donald, ed.
The New American Poetry, 1945-1960.

1960
Published

1976 CO
Banned for use in Aurora High School English classes on the grounds of "immorality."
Source: 11, May 1977, p. 79; 15, pp. 128–32, 238.

30
Allende, Isabel.
The House of the Spirits.

1982
Published

1994 CA
Retained in the Paso Robles High School despite objections to accounts of sexual encounters and violence.

1997 VA
Retained on the Stonewall Jackson High School's academically advanced reading list in Brentsville after being challenged for sexual explicitness.

1998 MD
Challenged as obscene on the Montgomery County reading lists and school library shelves.

1999 CA
Challenged on the tenth-grade reading list at La Costa Canyon High School in Encinitas because the work "defames" the Catholic faith and contains "pornographic passages."

2000 CA
Retained on the summer reading lists for honors high school students at the Fairfield Unified School District despite objections that the book is "immoral and sexually depraved."

2000 CA
Retained on the summer reading lists for honors high school students at the Suisun City Unified School District despite objections that the book is "immoral and sexually depraved."

2003 CA
Challenged, but retained, in the advanced English classes in Modesto. The seven-member Modesto City School Board said administrators should instead give parents more information about the books their children read, including annotations of each text. Parents can opt their children out of any assignment they find objectionable.

2013 NC
Challenged in the Watauga County High School curriculum because of the book's graphic nature. After a five-month process, the book was fully retained at a third and final appeal hearing. The bestseller was critically acclaimed and catapulted Allende to literary stardom. The novel was named Best Novel of the Year in Chile in 1982, and Allende received the country's Panorama Literario award. It has been translated into over thirty-seven languages.
Source: 11, Sept. 1994, p. 167; Nov. 1994, p. 201; Nov. 1997, pp. 169–70; Jan. 1998, p. 29; Mar. 1998, p. 56; May 1998, p. 70; Nov. 1999, p. 164; Nov. 2000, p. 195; Mar. 2001, p. 76; Jan. 2004, pp. 27–28; Jan. 2014, pp. 27-28; Mar. 2014, pp. 66-68.

31
Allington, Richard.
Once Upon a Hippo.

1993
Published

2000 GA
Challenged, but retained, in the Gwinnett County schools. A parent challenged a story in the book The Hot Hippo, by Mwenye Hadithi because of a reference to a character called Ngai, described as the "god of everything and everywhere."
Source: 11, May 2000, pp. 76–77; July 2000, p. 124.

32
Allison, Dorothy.
Bastard Out of Carolina.

1992
Published

1996 ME
Removed from the Mt. Abram High School English classes in Salem because the language and subject matter (incest and rape) were inappropriate for fifteen-year-olds.
Source: 11, Mar. 1996, p. 49; Nov. 1996, p. 196; Mar. 1997, p. 39.

33
Alvarez, Julia.
How the Garcia Girls Lost Their Accents.

1991
Published

2002 VA
Challenged, along with seventeen other titles in the Fairfax County elementary and secondary libraries, by a group called Parents Against Bad Books in Schools. The group contends the books "contain profanity and descriptions of drug abuse, sexually explicit conduct, and torture."

2006 IL
Retained on the Northwest Suburban High School District 214 reading list in Arlington Heights along with eight other challenged titles. A board member, elected amid promises to bring her Christian beliefs into all board decision-making, raised the controversy based on excerpts from the books she'd found on the Internet.

2007 NC
Removed from Johnston County school libraries after a parent challenged its sexual content and profane language. The county school's staff then launched a district-wide book title review.
Source: 11, Jan. 2003, p. 10; July 2006, pp. 210–11; Mar. 2008, pp. 59-60.

34
Alvarez, Julia.
In the Time of the Butterflies.

1994
Published

1994
National Book Critics Circle Fiction Finalist

1995
Best Books for Young Adults

2000 NY
Withdrawn from inclusion at the Paul D. Schreiber High School in Port Washington because of a drawing of a homemade bomb. The text preceding and following the handwritten diagram does not provide details or instructions. The novel was nominated for the National Book Critics Circle Award in 1995.
Source: 11, Jan. 2001, pp. 13–14.

35
Alyson, Sasha, ed.
Young, Gay & Proud!

1980
Published

1989 MI
Challenged at the public libraries of Saginaw because the book promoted acts in violation of Michigan law and "appears to qualify as obscene material."
Source: 11, May 1989, p. 78.

36
American Heritage Dictionary.

1976 AK
Removed in school libraries in Anchorage due to "objectionable language."

1976 IN
Removed in school libraries in Cedar Lake due to "objectionable language."

1977 MO
Removed in school libraries in Eldon due to "objectionable language."

1982 CA
Removed in school libraries Folsom due to "objectionable language."

1993 NV
Challenged, but retained, in the Churchill County school libraries. The controversy began after another dictionary was removed due to "objectionable language." It was removed from, and later returned to, classrooms in Washoe County.
Source: 11, Sept. 1976, p. 115; Nov. 1976, p. 145; Jan. 1977, p. 7; July 1977, p. 101; Mar. 1983, p. 39; Mar. 1994, p. 71.

37
American Jewish Yearbook.

1983
Banned from the 1983 Moscow, Russia, International Book Fair along with more than fifty other books because it is "anti-Soviet."
Source: 11, Nov. 1983, p. 201.

38
Ames, Lee J.
Draw 50 Monsters, Creeps, Superheroes, Demons, Dragons, Nerds, Dirts, Ghouls, Giants, Vampires, Zombies and Other Curiosa.

1983
Published

1994 MI
Challenged, but retained, at the Battle Creek Elementary School library despite protests from a parent who said the book is satanic.
Source: 11, Nov. 1994, p. 200.

39
Anaya, Rudolfo A.
Bless Me, Ultima.

1972
Published

1992 CA
Challenged at the Porterville high schools because the book contains "many profane and obscene references, vulgar Spanish words and glorifies witchcraft and death."

1996 TX
Retained on the Round Rock Independent High School reading list after a challenge that the book was too violent.

1999 CA
Removed from the Laton Unified School District because it contains violence and profanity that might harm students. The novel is considered by many critics to be the finest work by the New Mexico writer, widely respected as one of the leading Hispanic writers in the U.S. It was chosen by teachers who thought it would be welcomed by the district's students, who are 80 percent Hispanic.

2000 NY
Challenged at the John Jay High School in Wappingers Falls because the book is "full of sex and cursing."

2005 CO
Pulled by the Norwood Schools superintendent after two parents complained about profanity in the book. The superintendent confiscated all of the copies of the book and gave them to the parents, who "tossed them in the trash." The superintendent later apologized. Students organized an all-day sit-in at the school gym. President George W. Bush awarded Anaya the National Medal of Arts in 2002. First Lady Laura Bush has listed the book as ninth on a list of twelve books that she highly recommends.

2008 CA
Banned from the Orestimba High School's English classes in Newman by the superintendent after complaints that the book is profane and anti-Catholic. Teachers claimed that the superintendent circumvented the district's policies on book challenges and set a dangerous precedent. The book is about a boy maturing, asking questions about evil, justice, and the nature of God.

2013 ID
Retained in the Teton High School sophomore English class in Driggs despite concerns about the novel's mature content. Anaya's best-known work, it was awarded the prestigious Premio Quinto Sol. In 2008, it was one of twelve classic American novels selected for The Big Read, a community-reading program sponsored by the National Endowment for the Arts, and in 2009, it was in the list of the United States Academic Decathlon.
Source: 11, Jan. 1993, p. 29; May 1996, p. 99; Sept. 1999, pp. 120–21; Mar. 2000, p. 51; Mar. 2005, p. 55; Jan. 2009, p. 7; Mar. 2009, pp. 39-40; Jan. 2014, pp. 26-27.

40
Ancona, George.
Cuban Kids.

2000
Published

2006 FL
Banned in the Miami-Dade County Public Schools. The picture book shows a child with a rifle and children saluting the Cuban flag with the caption, "We will be like Che!"
Source: 11, Nov. 2006, p. 288.

41
Anders, Jim.
The Complete Idiot's Guide to Sex on the Net.

1998
Published

1999 TX
Challenged, but retained, at the Will Hampton Branch of the Austin Public Library despite complaints from at least three parents that the book is "obscene."
Source: 11, Nov. 1999, p. 172.

42
Andersen, Christopher P.
Madonna—Unauthorized.

1991
Published

1993 CO
Challenged at the Loveland High School library because the book has obscenities and sexual references, and one photo with Madonna posing topless.
Source: 11, July 1993, p. 97.

43
Andersen, Hans Christian.
The Little Mermaid.

1837
Published

1994 TX
An edition with illustrations of bare-breasted mermaids was challenged in the Bedford School District because it was "pornographic" and contained "satanic pictures."
Source: 11, Nov. 1994, pp. 188–89.

44
Andersen, Hans Christian.
Wonder Stories Told for Children.

1835
Published

1835
Banned in Russia by Nicholas I during the "censorship terror." Ban removed in 1849.

1954 IL
Stamped in Illinois "For Adult Readers" to make it "impossible for children to obtain smut."
Source: 4, pp. 41–42.

45
Anderson, Janice.
The Life and Times of Renoir.

1967
Published

1997 PA
Restricted at the Pulaski Elementary School library because of nude paintings in the book.
Source: 11, May 1997, p. 61.

46
Anderson, Jean.
The Haunting of America.

1973
Published

1985 FL
Challenged at the Sikes Elementary School media center in Lakeland because the collection of historical ghost stories, "would lead children to believe in demons without realizing it."
Source: 11, July 1985, p. 133.

47
Anderson, Jill.
Pumsy.

1987
Published

1989 OK
The Putnam City Elementary School counselors are forbidden to use this story of a fictional dragon because it propagates the principles of "secular humanism" and "new age religion" and that its use would "drive a wedge between children and parents."
Source: 11, July 1989, p. 129.

48
Anderson, Laurie Halse.
Speak.

1999
Published

2000
Best Books for Young Adults

2010 MO
Challenged in the Republic schools because it is "soft-pornography" and "glorifies drinking, cursing, and premarital sex," and "teaches principles contrary to the Bible."
Source: 11, Nov. 2010, pp. 243-44; Sept. 2011, pp. 175-76.

49
Anderson, Laurie Halse.
Twisted.

2007
Published

2008
Best Books for Young Adults

2009 KY
Withdrawn from classroom use and the approved curriculum at the Montgomery County High School, but available at the high school library and student book club. Some parents have complained about five novels that contain foul language and cover topics—including sex, child abuse, suicide, and drug abuse—deemed unsuited for discussion in coed high school classes. They also contend that the books don't provide the intellectual challenge and rigor that students need in college preparatory classes. The titles appeared on suggested book lists compiled by the Young Adult Library Services Association, a division of the American Library Association, for twelve- to eighteen-year-olds who are "reluctant readers." The superintendent removed the book because it wasn't on the pre-approved curriculum list and couldn't be added by teachers in the middle of a school year without permission.
Source: 11, Jan. 2010, pp. 16-17; Mar. 2010, p. 56.

50
Anderson, Lee, et al.
Windows on Our World series.

1976
Published

1987 AL
Removed from Alabama's list of approved texts—and from the state's classrooms—because the book promotes the "religion of secular humanism." U.S. District Court Judge W. Brevard Hand ruled on March 4, 1987, that thirty-nine history and social studies texts used in Alabama's 129 school systems "discriminate against the very concept of religion and theistic religions in particular, by omissions so serious that a student learning history from them would not be apprised of relevant facts about America's history. . . . References to religion are isolated and the integration of religion in the history of American society is ignored." The series includes: *At Home, At School; In Our Community; Ourselves and Others; Our Home; The Earth; America: Past and Present;* and *Around Our World.* On August 26, 1987, the U.S. Court of Appeals for the Eleventh Circuit unanimously overturned Judge Hand's decision by ruling that the information in the book was "essentially neutral in its religious content." The fact that the texts omitted references to religion was not "an advancement of secular humanism or an active hostility toward theistic religion."
Source: 11, Jan. 1987, p. 6; May 1987, pp. 75, 104–7; Sept. 1987, pp. 166-67; Nov. 1987, pp. 217–18; Jan. 1988, p. 17; Mar. 1988, p. 40.

51
Anderson, M. T.
Feed.

2002
Published

2002
Los Angeles Times Book Prize, Young Adult fiction

2003
Best Books for Young Adults

2003
National Book Award Finalist

2003
New York Times Notable Books

2012 VA
Challenged at the William Monroe High School because the book is "trash" and "covered with the F-word." A consent form was sent to the students' homes, and a notice that the class would be reading a mature book was posted on the teacher's webpage as well.
Source: 11, July 2012, p. 159.

52
Anderson, Robert, et al.
Elements of Literature.

1989
Published

1994 VA
Retained in the Fairfax County schools despite complaints that it might "plant seeds" of violence or disobedience in students. The anthology contains stories such as Edgar Allen Poe's "The Tell-Tale Heart" and John Steinbeck's "The Pearl."
Source: 11, Nov. 1994, pp. 201–2.

53

Anderson, Sherwood.
Dark Laughter.

1925
Published

1930 MA
Blacklisted in Boston.
Source: 2, p. 137; 4, p. 62.

54

Andrews, V. C.
Dark Angel.

1986
Published

1994 GA
Removed from Oconee County school libraries "due to the filthiness of the material." The school board voted unanimously at a later date to rescind its controversial book-banning order, but then rescinded that action and ordered the removal of the book.
Source: 11, Sept. 1994, pp. 145–46; Nov. 1994, pp. 187–88, 200; Jan. 1995, p. 6.

55

Andrews, V. C.
Darkest Hour.

1993
Published

1994 GA
Removed from Oconee County school libraries "due to the filthiness of the material." The school board voted unanimously at a later date to rescind its controversial book-banning order but then rescinded that action and ordered the removal of the book.
Source: 11, Sept. 1994, pp. 145–46; Nov. 1994, pp.

56

Andrews, V. C.
Dawn.

1990
Published

1994 GA
Removed from Oconee County school libraries "due to the filthiness of the material." The school board voted unanimously at a later date to rescind its controversial book-banning order but

then rescinded that action and ordered the removal of the book.
Source: 11, Sept. 1994, pp. 145–46; Nov. 1994, pp. 187–88, 200; Jan. 1995, p. 6.

57

Andrews, V. C.
Flowers in the Attic.

1979
Published

1983 RI
Challenged at the Richmond High School because the book contains offensive passages concerning incest and sexual intercourse.

1994 GA
Removed from Oconee County school libraries "due to the filthiness of the material." The school board voted unanimously at a later date to rescind its controversial book-banning order but then rescinded that action and ordered the removal of the book.
Source: 11, Sept. 1983, p. 153; Jan. 1984, pp. 9-10; Sept. 1994, pp. 145–46; Nov. 1994, pp. 187–88, 200; Jan. 1995, p. 6.

58

Andrews, V. C.
Garden of Shadows.

1986
Published

1994 GA
Removed from Oconee County school libraries "because the book encouraged sexual activity and the result of reading or seeing it might be 'incestuous relationships' and 'aggressive sexual behavior.'" The book was removed despite a recommendation from a committee of parents and teachers to retain it. The action stemmed from a complaint filed in May 1994 when eight other V. C. Andrews books were removed.
Source: 11, Nov. 1994, p. 188; Jan. 1995, p. 6; July 1996, p. 117.

59

Andrews, V. C.
If There Be Thorns.

1981
Published

1983 RI
Challenged at the Richmond High School because the book contains offensive

passages concerning incest and sexual intercourse.
Source: 11, Sept. 1983, p. 153; Jan. 1984, pp. 9-10.

60

Andrews, V. C.
My Sweet Audrina.

1982
Published

1985 CA
Rejected for purchase by the Hayward school trustees because of "rough language" and "explicit sex scenes."

1990 WA
Challenged at the Lincoln Middle School in Pullman because it deals with themes related to sexual violence.

1994 GA
Removed from Oconee County school libraries "due to the filthiness of the material." The school board voted unanimously at a later date to rescind its controversial book-banning order but then rescinded that action and ordered the removal of the book.
Source: 11, July 1985, p. 111; July 1990, p. 145; Sept. 1994, pp. 145–46; Nov. 1994, pp. 187–88, 200; Jan. 1995, p. 6.

61

Andrews, V. C.
Petals on the Wind.

1980
Published

1983 RI
Challenged at the Richmond High School because the book contains offensive passages concerning incest and sexual intercourse.

1984 GA
Removed from Oconee County school libraries "due to the filthiness of the material." The school board voted unanimously at a later date to rescind its controversial book-banning order but then rescinded that action and ordered the removal of the book.
Source: 11, Sept. 1983, p. 153; Jan. 1984, pp. 9-10; Mar. 1984, p. 53; Sept. 1994, pp. 145–46; Nov. 1994, pp. 187–88, 200; Jan. 1995, p. 6.

62
Andrews, V. C.
Seeds of Yesterday.

1984
Published

1994 GA
Removed from Oconee County school libraries "due to the filthiness of the material." The school board voted unanimously at a later date to rescind its controversial book-banning order but then rescinded that action and ordered the removal of the book.
Source: 11, Sept. 1994, pp. 145–46; Nov. 1994, pp. 187–88, 200; Jan. 1995, p. 6.

63
Andrews, V. C.
Twilight's Child.

1992
Published

1994 GA
Removed from Oconee County school libraries "due to the filthiness of the material." The school board voted unanimously at a later date to rescind its controversial book-banning order but then rescinded that action and ordered the removal of the book.
Source: 11, Sept. 1994, pp. 145–46; Nov. 1994, pp. 187–88, 200; Jan. 1995, p. 6.

64
Andry, Andrew C., and Steven Schepp.
How Babies Are Made.

1968
Published

1981 FL
Moved from the children's section to the adult section of the Tampa-Hillsborough County Public Library by order of the Tampa City Council.

1987 WA
Placed on restricted shelves at the Evergreen School District elementary school libraries in Vancouver in accordance with the school board policy to restrict student access to sex education books in elementary school libraries.
Source: 11, Jan. 1982, p. 4; May 1987, p. 87.

65
Angelou, Maya.
And Still I Rise.

1978
Published

1982 LA
Challenged at the Northside High School library in Lafayette.

1987 WA
Challenged at the Longview school system because some "students could be harmed by its graphic language."
Source: 11, May 1982, p. 83; May 1987, p. 91; Sept. 1987, p. 195.

66
Angelou, Maya.
I Know Why the Caged Bird Sings.

1969
Published

1970
Best Books for Young Adults

1971
Coretta Scott King Author Honor Book

1983 AL
Four members of the Alabama State Textbook Committee called for its rejection because Angelou's work preaches "bitterness and hatred against whites."

1987 NC
Removed from the required reading list for Wake County High School juniors in Raleigh because of complaints about a scene in which eight-year-old Maya is raped.

1988 ME
Challenged at Mount Abram Regional High School in Strong because parents objected to a rape scene.

1990 WA
Rejected as required reading for a gifted ninth-grade English class in Bremerton because of the book's "graphic" description of molestation.

1991 CA
Removed from a Banning eighth grade class after several parents complained about explicit passages involving child molestation and rape.

1992 CA
Challenged at the Amador Valley High School in Pleasanton because of sexually explicit language.

1993 FL
Challenged in the Haines City High School library and English curriculum because of objections to a passage that describes the author's rape when she was eight years old.

1993 MS
Temporarily banned from the Caledonia Middle School in Columbus on the grounds that it is too sexually explicit to be read by children.

1993 TX
Challenged in the Hooks High School in a freshman honors history class.

1994 CO
Challenged as part of the Ponderosa High School curriculum in Castle Rock because it is "a lurid tale of sexual perversion."

1994 IA
Retained as required reading for all of Dowling High School's sophomores in Des Moines. The book became an issue after a parent objected to what he said were inappropriately explicit sexual scenes.

1994 TX
Challenged at the Westwood High School in Austin because the book is pornographic, contains profanity, and encourages premarital sex and homosexuality. The superintendent later ruled that parents must first give their children permission to be taught potentially controversial literature.

1995 AZ
Removed from the curriculum pending a review of its content at the Gilbert Unified School. Complaining parents said the book did not represent "traditional values."

1995 FL
Challenged, but retained, in the Volusia County County Schools. The complainants wanted the book removed because "it is sexually explicit and promotes cohabitation and rape."

1995 LA
Removed from the Southwood High School Library in Caddo Parish because the book's language and content were objectionable. Eventually, the book was returned after students petitioned and demonstrated against the action.

1995 TN
Challenged, but retained, on the Beech High School reading list in Hendersonville.

1995 TX
Challenged at the Danforth High School in Wimberley.

1995 TX
Challenged at the Carroll School in Southlake because it was deemed "pornographic" and full of "gross evils."

1996 AL
Challenged, but retained, on an optional reading list at the East Lawrence High School in Moulton. The book was challenged because the School Superintendent decided, "the poet's descriptions of being raped as a little girl were pornographic."

1996 TX
Retained on the Round Rock Independent High School reading list after a challenge that the book was too violent.

1997 CA
Challenged at the Folsom Cordova School District because it contains sexually explicit passages.

1997 GA
Challenged as an Advanced Placement English class reading assignment at the Wayne County High School due to the novel's sexual explicitness.

1997 MN
Removed from the ninth-grade reading list at Richfield High School because some parents say it is too explicit.

1997 NC
Removed from the curriculum at the Turrentine Middle School after complaints by parents about profanity and sexual references.

1997 OH
Removed from the high school reading list at Lakota High School in Union Township because of Angelou's brief description of being raped at age eight and other sexual content.

1997 WA
Retained in the Mukilteo school district's high school curriculum after objections to the work's "explicit sexual content."

1998 FL
Banned from the Dolores Parrott Middle School in Brooksville school library and classrooms because of a passage in which Angelou tells of being molested and raped as an eight-year-old. Removed from the Brooksville eighth-grade reading list because of the book's strong sexual content.

1998 MD
Removed from the ninth-grade English curriculum in Anne Arundel County by the school superintendent after parents complained the book "portrays white people as being horrible, nasty, stupid people—if a child didn't have negative feelings about white people, this could sow the seeds." Returned to the Anne Arundel County approved reading list for ninth-grade English classes, overriding some parents' complaints that the book is too sexually explicit.

1998 NC
Removed from the Turrentine Middle School's reading list in Alamance.

1999 NH
Removed from the seventh- and eighth-grade reading list at the Unity Elementary School because the "book is too sexually explicit."

2000 MD
Challenged on the Poolesville High School reading list due to the book's sexual content and language.

2002 MT
Challenged as required reading for freshman English classes. At issue are scenes in which the author explores her sexuality through intercourse as a teenager and the depiction of a rape and molestation of an eight-year-old girl; homosexuality is another theme explored in the book that has drawn criticism.

2002 VA
Challenged, along with seventeen other titles in the Fairfax County elementary and secondary libraries, by a group called Parents Against Bad Books in Schools. The group contends the books "contain profanity and descriptions of drug abuse, sexually explicit conduct, and torture."

2006 MD
Removed as required reading in Annapolis freshman English curriculum because the book's rape scenes and other mature content are too advanced for ninth-graders. The freshman English class syllabus is sent home to parents to read at the beginning of each year. It warns them of the book's mature themes and allows parents to ask to have their children read another book instead.

2006 WI
Retained in the Fond du Lac High School sophomore advanced English class. Parents objected to teens reading Angelou's account of being brutally raped by her mother's boyfriend and an unwanted pregnancy later in life. Parents will receive notification and be allowed to decide whether or not they approve of its use by their children, according to recommendations agreed upon by a review committee and parents who objected to the use of the book.

2007 ID
Challenged in the Coeur d'Alene School District. Some parents say that the book, along with five others, should require parental permission for students to read them.

2007 PA
Challenged in the Manheim Township schools due to sexual references. The book was retained in the ninth-grade English curriculum, but it was decided to teach the book later in the school year, after a public forum was held with parents to discuss that book and the entire literary canon of the English department.

2009 CA
Restricted to students with parental permission at the Ocean View School District middle school libraries in Huntington Beach because the "book's contents were inappropriate for children."

2009 CA
Challenged in the Newman-Crows Landing School District on a required reading list presented by the Orestimba High English Department. A trustee questioned the qualifications of Orestimba staff to teach a novel depicting African American culture.

Source: 6, p. 60; 11, Mar. 1983, p. 39; Jan. 1989, p. 8; Mar. 1989, p. 38; Nov. 1990, p. 211; Mar. 1992, p. 42; July 1992, p. 109; July 1993, p. 107; Jan. 1994, p. 34; July 1994, p. 130; Jan. 1995, pp. 11, 14; Mar. 1995, p. 56; May 1995, pp. 67, 72; Sept. 1995, pp. 158–59; Nov. 1995, pp. 183, 186–87; Jan. 1996, pp. 14, 30; Mar. 1996, pp. 47, 63; May 1996, pp. 84, 99; July 1996, p. 120; Sept. 1996, pp. 152–53; Nov. 1996, pp. 197–98; Jan. 1997, p. 26; May 1997, pp. 65–66; July 1997, p. 98; Jan. 1998, pp. 13, 14, 29; Mar. 1998, pp. 41–42; May 1998, pp. 69, 72; July 1998, p. 120; Sept. 1998, pp. 143-44; Nov. 1998, p. 182; Jan. 1999, p. 20; May 1999, p. 69; July 1999, pp. 93-94; Nov. 2000, p. 196; Nov. 2002, p. 258; Jan. 2003, p. 10; May 2006, pp. 132-33; Jan. 2007, pp. 30-31; July 2007, pp. 149-50; Sept. 2007, p. 181; Jan. 2010, pp. 7, 14-15; May 2010, p.103.

67

Annas, Pamela J., and
Robert C. Rosen.
*Literature in Society:
Introduction to Fiction, Poetry
and Drama.*

1990
Published

1994 PA
Pulled from the senior literature class
at the Hempfield Area School District
after it was determined that some
passages were "vulgar."
Source: 11, Jan. 1995, pp. 13–14; Mar. 1995, p. 44.

68

Anonymous.
*Arabian Nights or The
Thousand and One Nights.*

1881
Published

1927
U.S. Customs held up 500 sets of the
translation by the French scholar
Mardrus, which were imported from
England. Continued until 1931.

1985
Confiscated in Cairo, Egypt, on the grounds
that it contained obscene passages which
posed a threat to the country's moral
fabric. The public prosecutor demanded
the book, which contains stories such as
"Ali Baba and the 40 Thieves" and "Aladdin
and His Magic Lamp," be "burned in a
public place" and said that it was the cause
of "a wave of incidents of rape which
the country has recently experienced."

1985
Judged inappropriate for Jewish pupils by
the Israeli director of the British Consul
Library in Jerusalem, Israel.
Source: 4, p. 28; 5, June 1985, p. 50; Aug. 1985, p. 51;
Oct. 1985, p. 65; 8, pp. 317–18; 11, July 1985, p. 120.

69

Anonymous.
Caroline.

1991 OR
Removed from the Multnomah County
Library because the novel contains graphic
descriptions of sexual acts.
Source: 11, Jan. 1992, p. 6.

70

Anonymous.
*The Fifteen Plagues of a
Maidenhead.*

1707
Published

1707
James Reade and Angell Carter were
prosecuted in England for publishing the
work and charged with "obscene libel."
They were acquitted after the defense
counsel asserted that the court had no
right to try the case because the defendants
were not guilty of breaking any existing
law. While the court disliked the tone and
content of the book, calling it "bawdy,"
it acknowledged that no common law or
statute existed that "could warrant an
indictment against even the filthiest book."
Source: 13, p. 71.

71

Anonymous.
Go Ask Alice.

1971
Published

1971
Best Books for Young Adults

1974 MI
Removed from school libraries in
Kalamazoo due to "objectionable" language
and explicit sexual scenes.

1975 MI
Removed from school libraries in
Saginaw due to "objectionable" language
and explicit sexual scenes.

1975 NY
Removed from school libraries in
Levittown due to "objectionable" language
and explicit sexual scenes.

1975 NY
Challenged at the Marcellus School District.

1977 NJ
Removed from school libraries in
Trenton due to "objectionable" language
and explicit sexual scenes.

1977 TX
Removed from school libraries in Eagle
Pass due to "objectionable" language and
explicit sexual scenes.

1979 UT
Challenged at the Ogden School District.
1980 NJ Removed from school libraries
in North Bergen due to "objectionable"
language and explicit sexual scenes.

1982 FL
Challenged at the Safety Harbor,
St. Petersburg Middle School Library
where written parental permission was
required to check out the title.

1983 CO
Challenged at the Pagosa Springs
schools because a parent objected to the
"graphic language, subject matter,
immoral tone, and lack of literary quality
found in the book."

1983 MN
Challenged at the Osseo School
District in Brooklyn Park where a school
board member found the book's
language "personally offensive."

1984 MS
Challenged at the Rankin County School
District because it is "profane and sexually
objectionable."

1986 GA
Challenged at the Central Gwinnett High
School library because "it encourages
students to steal and take drugs."

1986 GA
The Gainesville Public Library prohibits
young readers from checking out this
book along with forty other books. The
books, on subjects ranging from hypnosis
to drug abuse to breast-feeding and sexual
dysfunction, are kept in a locked room.

1986 MI
Removed from the school library shelves
in Kalkaska because the book contains
"objectionable language."

1988 ME
Challenged at the King Middle School
in Portland.

1993 NJ
Removed from the Wall Township
Intermediate School library by the
Superintendent of Schools because the
book contains "inappropriate" language
and "borders on pornography." Responding
to an anonymous letter in 1987, the
superintendent ordered the book removed
from all reading lists and classroom book
collections. "I thought we'd got rid
of them all about five years ago," he said.

1993 NY

Challenged as a required reading assignment at the Johnstown High School because of numerous obscenities.

1993 WV

Removed from an English class at Buckhannon-Upshur High School because of graphic language in the book.

1994 MA

Banned from a ninth-grade reading list at Shepherd Hill High School in Dudley because of "gross and vulgar language and graphic description of drug use and sexual conduct."

1995 AK

Challenged at the Houston Junior and Senior High School in Wasilla.

1995 OH

Banned from the Jonathan Alder School District in Plain City.

1995 VA

Removed from a supplemental reading list for sophomore English students in Warm Springs because of its "profanity and indecent situations."

1998 RI

Confiscated by a Tiverton middle school principal, while the class was reading it. The book was later returned by the school board.

1999 TX

Removed from the Aledo Middle School library and restricted at the high school library to students with parental permission. A parent complained about the references to drug use, vulgar language, and descriptions of sex.

2000 PA

Retained as optional reading for eighth graders at Rice Avenue Middle School in Girard. A grandmother found the book offensive because it contains "filth and smut" that she didn't want her granddaughters reading.

2008 SC

Challenged as a reading assignment at Hanahan Middle School in Berkeley County because of blatant, explicit language using street terms for sex, talk of worms eating body parts, and blasphemy. The book is about a fifteen-year-old girl who gets caught up in a life of drugs and sex before dying from an overdose. Its explicit references to drugs and sex have

been controversial since it was first published.

Source: 8, pp. 456–57; 11, Jan. 1975, p. 6; Mar. 1975, p. 41; May 1975, p. 76; July 1977, p. 100; May 1977, p. 73; May 1979, p. 49; Mar. 1980, p. 32; July 1982, p. 142; Mar. 1983, p. 52; Mar. 1984, p. 53; May 1984, p. 69; July 1986, p. 117; Sept. 1986, pp. 151–52; Nov. 1986, p. 207; Jan. 1987, p. 32; Mar. 1989, p. 39; May 1993, p. 71; July 1993, pp. 109–10; Mar. 1994, p. 54; Sept. 1994, p. 150; July 1995, p. 94; Jan. 1996, p. 12; Mar. 1996, p. 50; Sept. 1998, p. 144; Sept. 1999, pp. 119–20; May 2000, p. 92; May 2008, pp. 98-99.

72

Anonymous.
Life: How Did It Get Here?

1985
Published

1992 MA

Challenged at the Jones Library in Amherst because it is religious propaganda. "The book lists no authors or editors; there is no accountability for its statements."
Source: 11, Sept. 1992, p. 162.

73

Anonymous.
Mariska II.

1989
Published

1991 OR

Removed from the Multnomah County Library because the novel contains graphic descriptions of sexual acts.
Source: 11, Jan. 1992, p. 6.

74

Anthony, Piers.
Question Quest.

1991
Published

2000 CA

Removed from the mandatory reading program at the Norman L. Sullivan Middle School in Bonsall due to sexually explicit language.
Source: 11, May 2000, p. 76.

75

Apollinaire, Guillaume.
Memoirs of a Young Rakehill.

1962
Published

1964

The Debauched Hospodar and *Memoirs of a Young Rakehill* were seized by New Zealand Customs officers. The New Zealand Indecent Publications Tribunal concluded that, "we classify the translation of two novels written by Guillaume Apollinaire as indecent unless circulation is restricted to persons professionally engaged in the study of abnormal psychology, who desire to use them for that purpose."
Source: 13, p. 162.

76

Archer, Jerome W., and
A. Schwartz.
A Reader for Writers.

1971
Published

1976 NY

Removed from the Island Trees Union Free School District High School library in 1976 along with nine other titles because they were considered "immoral, anti-American, anti-Christian, or just plain filthy." Returned to the library after the U.S. Supreme Court ruling on June 25, 1982 in Board of Education, *Island Trees Union Free School District No. 26 et al. v. Pico et al.*, 457 U.S. 853 (1982).
Source: 11, Nov. 1982, p. 197.

77

Aristophanes.
Lysistrata.

411 B.C.
Published

1930

U.S. Customs lifts ban. In successful challenge to the Comstock Act of 1873, which empowered the Postmaster General to rule on obscenity of literature sent through the mail, Lysistrata was declared mailable.
Source: 4, p. 2.

78

Aristotle.
The Metaphysics.

400 B.C.
Published

1210

The bishops of the Provincial Council of Paris, France, forbade the public or private teaching of the natural philosophy and metaphysics of Aristotle. The ban, which applied to instruction of the arts faculty of the University of Paris, was imposed under penalty of excommunication and confirmed in 1215.

1231
Pope Gregory IX in Rome, Italy, prohibited the reading of the works of Aristotle until they were purged of heresy.

Source: 1, p. 205.

79
Arms, Karen, and
Pamela S. Camp.
Biology.

1980 NC
Text was rejected by the superintendent of the city-county school system on the basis that it might violate a school policy forbidding the teaching of specific methods of birth control in Winston-Salem.

1985 TX
Bowing to pressure from opponents of the textbook planned for use in a high school honors course, the Garland Independent School District's central textbook selection committee withdrew its recommendation because the text includes "overly explicit diagrams of sexual organs, intricate discussion of sexual stimulation, and the implication of abortion as a means of birth control."

Source: 11, Nov. 1980, p. 128; July 1985, p. 114.

80
Armstrong, William Howard.
Sounder.

1969
Published

1970
Newbery Medal

1996 NY
Challenged, but retained, in the Rockingham County schools. A parent had problems with the use of the word "nigger" on page twenty-one and a reference to the main character, a black sharecropper, as "boy."

Source: 11, Sept. 1996, p. 169; Nov. 1996, p. 212.

81
Asher, Don.
Blood Summer.

1977
Published

1979 AR
Returned to publisher because it failed to meet literary standards in Little Rock.

Source: 11, Sept. 1979, p. 104.

82
Asimov, Isaac.
In the Beginning: Science Faces God in the Book of Genesis.

1981
Published

1981 CA
Officials of the Christian Research Center requested San Diego school administrators to keep this title out of all high school libraries because Asimov "subjects the *Bible* to merciless and unremitting destructive attack."

Source: 11, Jan. 1982, p. 8.

83
Asturias, Miguel Angel.
The Green Pope.

1954
Published

1967
Nobel Prize for Literature

1954
Banned in Guatemala along with *Strong Wind* (1950) and *The President* (1946) for its exposure of the effects of American imperialism.

Source: 7, pp. 467–68.

84
Atkins, Catherine.
Alt Ed.

2003
Published

2007 OR
Challenged as an optional reading in a bullying unit at the Lake Oswego Junior High School because the novel is "peppered with profanities, ranging from derogatory slang terms to sexual encounters and violence." Students are given a list of book summaries and a letter to take to their parents. Four of the eight optional books offered are labeled as having "mature content/language."

Source: 11, July 2007, p. 149.

85
Atkins, Catherine.
When Jeff Comes Home.

1999
Published

2000
Best Books for Young Adults

2006
TX Restricted to students with parental permission in the Irving schools. The book is about a boy's recovery after being kidnapped and sexually abused by a man. The publisher recommends the book for readers thirteen and older, while *School Library Journal* suggested it for readers in grades ten and above.

Source: 11, Mar. 2006, pp. 72–73.

86
Atwood, Margaret.
The Handmaid's Tale.

1985
Published

1985
Governor General's Award for English-language Fiction

1986
Best Books for Young Adults

1987
Arthur C. Clarke Award

1990 CA
Challenged as a book assignment at the Rancho Cotati High School in Rohnert Park because it is too explicit for students.

1992 IA
Challenged in the Waterloo schools because of profanity, lurid passages about sex, and statements defamatory to minorities, God, women, and the disabled. The book was eventually retained.

1993 MA
Removed from the Chicopee High School English class reading list because it contains profanity and sex.

1998 WA
Challenged for use in the Richland high school English classes along with six other titles because the "books are poor-quality literature and stress suicide, illicit sex, violence, and hopelessness."

1999 FL
Challenged because of graphic sex, but retained on the advanced placement English list at Chamberlain High School in Tampa.

2000 PA
Downgraded from "required" to "optional" on the summer reading list for eleventh graders in the Upper Moreland School District due to "age-inappropriate" subject matter.

2001 TX
Challenged, but retained, in the Dripping Springs senior Advanced Placement English courses as an optional reading assignment. Some parents were offended by the book's descriptions of sexual encounters.

2006 TX
The Judson school district board overruled Superintendent Ed Lyman's ban of the novel from an Advanced Placement English curriculum. Lyman had banned the book after a parent complained it was sexually explicit and offensive to Christians. In doing so, he overruled the recommendation of a committee of teachers, students, and parents. The committee appealed the decision to the school board.

2012 NC
Challenged as required reading for a Page High School International Baccalaureate class and as optional reading for Advanced Placement reading courses at Grimsley High School because the book is "sexually explicit, violently graphic and morally corrupt." Some parents thought the book is "detrimental to Christian values." The novel was nominated for the 1986 Nebula Award, the 1986 Booker Prize, and the 1987 Prometheus Award. It has been adapted for the cinema, radio, opera, and stage.
Source: 11, Jan. 1991, p. 15; July 1992, p. 126; May 1993, p. 73; Mar. 1999, p. 40; Sept. 1999, p. 121; Nov. 1999, p. 173; Sept. 2000, p. 145; July 2001, p. 174; May 2006, pp. 154-55; Jan. 2013, p. 11.

87
Auel, Jean.
Clan of the Cave Bear.

1980
Published

1980
Best Books for Young Adults

1988 MI
Challenged at the Berrien Springs High School for use in classrooms and libraries because the novel is "vulgar, profane, and sexually explicit."

1992 OR
Banned from the Cascade Middle School library in Eugene after a parent complained about a rape scene.

1993 CA
Challenged, but retained, on the Moorpark High School recommended reading list in Simi Valley despite objections that it contains "hard-core graphic sexual content."
Source: 11, Jan. 1989, p. 28; July 1992, p. 107; Jan. 1994, p. 14; Mar. 1994, p. 70; May 1994, p. 99.

88
Auel, Jean.
The Mammoth Hunters.

1985
Published

1993 CA
Challenged, but retained, from the Moorpark High School recommended reading list in Simi Valley despite objections that it contains "hard-core graphic sexual content."
Source: 11, Mar. 1994, p. 70; May 1994, p. 99.

89
Auel, Jean.
Plains of Passage.

1990
Published

1993 CA
Challenged, but retained, from the Moorpark High School recommended reading list in Simi Valley despite objections that it contains "hard-core graphic sexual content."
Source: 11, Mar. 1994, p. 70; May 1994, p. 99.

90
Auel, Jean.
Valley of the Horses.

1982
Published

1985 PA
Banned from the Stroudsburg High School library because it was "blatantly graphic, pornographic, and wholly unacceptable for a high school library."

1985 TX
Challenged at the Bastrop Public Library because "the book violates Texas obscenity laws."

1993 CA
Challenged, but retained, on the Moorpark High School recommended reading list in Simi Valley despite objections that it contains "hard-core graphic sexual content."
Source: 11, May 1985, pp. 75, 79; Mar. 1986, pp. 33, 64; Jan. 1994, p. 145; Mar. 1994, p. 70; May 1994, p. 99.

91
Avent, Sue.
Spells, Chants and Potions.

1977
Published

1992 VA
Pulled, but later placed on reserve to children with parental permission at the Forrest Elementary School library in Newport News.

1997 PA
Challenged at the Muncy school library because of the book's "magical thinking."
Source: 11, July 1992, p. 108; Sept. 1992, p. 139; May 1997, p. 61.

92
Averroes (Ibn Rushd).
Commentaries.

1168-90
Published

1210
The ban applied to instruction at the University of Paris, France.

1210
Church authorities in Rome, Italy, banned his writings on the works of Aristotle between 1210 and 1277 for proposing that philosophy could claim truth outside established religious source. In 1231, Pope Gregory IX prohibited the reading of the works of Aristotle until they were purged of heresy.

1231
Pope Gregory IX prohibited the reading of the works of Aristotle until they were purged of heresy.
Source: 1, pp. 50–51.

93

Avi.

The Fighting Ground.

1984
Published

1984
Best Books for Young Adults

2000 NH
Retained as part of the John Fuller School curriculum in Conway, despite a complaint by a resident calling himself a concerned Christian.

2008 FL
Banned from the Bay District school's library shelves in Panama City after a parent noted several profanities uttered by some soldiers. The award-winning book, intended for the fourth-grade reading level, is about a twenty-four-hour period in the life of a thirteen-year-old boy during the Revolutionary War.

Source: 11, Jan. 2001, p. 37; Mar. 2001, p. 75; July 2008, p. 140.

94

Aylesworth, Thomas G.
Servants of the Devil: A History of Witchcraft.

1970
Published

1989 OK
Removed from the Cleveland middle school libraries because witchcraft is a "religion" and that the First Amendment bars the teaching of religion in schools.

Source: 11, July 1989, p. 128.

95

Aylisli, Akram.
Stone Dreams.

2013
Published

2013
Novella published in *Druzhba Narodov* (Friendship of the Peoples). Burned at various locations around Azerbaijan. The novella is sympathetic to Armenians and recounts Azeri atrocities in the war between Azerbaijan and Armenia twenty years ago. Azerbaijani President Ilham Aliyev stripped the author of his title of "People's Writer" and the pension that goes with it. A progovernment political party in Baku, Azerbaijan, announced that it will pay $12,700 to anyone who cuts off the ear of the 75-year-old novelist for portraying Azerbaijanis as savages.

Source: 11, May 2013, pp. 108-9.

96

Babbitt, Natalie.
The Devil's Storybook.

1974
Published

1975
National Book Award for Young People's Literature

1986 TN
Returned to the Claxton Elementary School library shelves. The complaint against the book objected to "the total theme of the book," which makes "hell and the devil innocent and alluring."

2004 PA
Challenged at the Chestnut Ridge Middle School in Washington Township. The complainants wanted the school district to seek parental approval before elementary- and middle-school students could check out books related to the occult.

Source: 11, Mar. 1987, p. 50; May 2004, pp. 117–18.

97

Babbitt, Natalie.
The Imp in the Basket.

1981
Published

1991 PA
Challenged as required reading in the Annville-Cleona School District because of the story's references to demon possession.

Source: 11, July 1990, p. 147; July 1991, p. 130.

98

Babinski, Edward T.
Leaving the Fold: Testimonials of Former Fundamentalists.

1995
Published

1995 SC
Challenged, but retained, at the Anderson County Library, because the book presented fundamentalism in a negative light.

Source: 11, Jan. 1996, p. 30.

99

Bach, Alice.
When the Sky Began to Roar.

1984
Published

1987 NE
Removed from the East Junior-Senior High School library in Lincoln because the book "creates despair, disrespect for parents, and a sense of hopelessness."

1988 NE
Challenged at the Seward Public Library because it is "obscene."

Source: 11, May 1987, p. 87; May 1988, p. 85.

100

Bacon, Francis.
Advancement of Learning.

1605
Published

1640
All works by Bacon were banned by the Inquisition in Spain and placed on the Sotomayor's Index.

1948
Book IX of Bacon's work, dedicated to the king, was placed on the *Index Librorum Prohibitorum* (List of Prohibited Books) in Rome, Italy, where it remained in the 1948 edition of the list.

Source: 1, p. 5; 4, p. 17.

101

Bailey, Jacqui, and Jan McCafferty.
Sex, Puberty, and All That Stuff: A Guide to Growing Up.

2004
Published

2008 CT
Retained in the Windsor Library after being challenged as inappropriate for its descriptions of sexual development. The book is designed for students from grades five through ten.

Source: 11, Nov. 2008, pp. 253-54.

102
Bailey, Thomas A., and David M. Kennedy.
The American Pageant: A History of the Republic.

1956
Published

1966 MD
The John Birch Society's chapter in Glen Burnie condemned the textbook and demanded that it be banned in the Anne Arundel County public schools.

1981 MS
Removed from the Mississippi state-approved textbook list.

1984 WI
Returned to the Racine Unified School District curriculum just one week after the school board voted to ban it. Opponents of the book on the board charged that the social studies volumes contained "judgmental writing" and, in the words of one board member, "a lot more funny pictures of Republicans and nicer pictures of Democrats." Opponents also said that one text did not present an adequate analysis of the Vietnam War.
Source: 7, pp. 34–36; 11, May 1981, p. 67; July 1981, p. 93; Sept. 1984, p. 158.

103
Baker, Keith.
Who Is the Beast?

1990
Published

1994 PA
Temporarily removed from the Marple schools following a verbal request from a parent who said its message offended his family's religious beliefs.
Source: 11, July 1994, p. 116.

104
Baker, Larry.
The Flamingo Rising.

1997
Published

2010 IL
Challenged on the Stevenson High School, Lincolnshire summer reading list because a parent complained that "a sexual encounter depicted in the novel was definitely something you could consider X-rated."
Source: 11, Mar. 2011, p. 53.

105
Baldwin, James.
Another Country.

1962
Published

1963 LA
Considered obscene, the book was banned from the New Orleans Public Library. After a year of litigation, it was restored.
Source: 4, p. 97; 8, pp. 406–7.

106
Baldwin, James.
Blues for Mr. Charlie.

1964
Published

1980 SD
Challenged in Sioux Falls because it's "pornographic" and it "tears down Christian principles."
Source: 11, May 1980, p. 61.

107
Baldwin, James.
Go Tell It on the Mountain.

1953
Published

1994 NY
Challenged as required reading in the Hudson Falls schools because the book has recurring themes of rape, masturbation, violence, and degrading treatment of women.

1998 VA
Challenged as a ninth-grade summer reading option in Prince William County because the book "was rife with profanity and explicit sex."
Source: 11, Nov. 1994, p. 190; Jan. 1995, p. 13; Mar. 1995, p. 55; Nov. 1998, p. 183.

108
Baldwin, James.
If Beale Street Could Talk.

1974
Published

1974
Best Books for Young Adults

1989 OR
Removed from the St. Paul High School library because the book contains obscene language and explicit descriptions of sexual activity.
Source: 11, July 1989, p. 128.

109
Baldwin, James.
Tell Me How Long the Train's Been Gone.

1968
Published

1983 AL
Four members of the Alabama State Textbook Committee called for its rejection because Baldwin's work preaches "bitterness and hatred against whites."
Source: 11, Mar. 1983, p. 39.

110
Balian, Lorna.
Humbug Potion: An A-B-Cipher.

1984
Published

1991 OR
Challenged for promoting satanism and witchcraft, but retained, at the Multnomah County Library.
Source: 11, Jan. 1992, p. 6.

111
Balzac, Honoré de.
Droll Stories.

1832-37
Published

1850
All works banned in Russia.

1914
Banned by Canadian Customs.

1930
U.S. Customs lifts ban. U.S. declares the Concord Book Catalog as obscene because it features *Droll Stories.*

1953
Banned in Ireland until 1967. The novel attracted the attention of censors for its excretory references and graphic sexual descriptions.

Source: 4, p. 39; 6, p. 411; 12, p. 140; 13, pp. 62–63.

112

Banks, Lynne Reid.
The Indian in the Cupboard.

1980
Published

1993 FL
The school librarian at the Suwannee County Elementary School routinely erased words from books deemed objectionable. In this instance, the words "heck" and "hell" were removed.

1995 MN
Removed from the Bemidji school district voluntary reading list and from the school library shelves because it contains subtle stereotypes inconsistent with district diversity goals.

Source: 11, May 1993, pp. 69–70; Nov. 1995, p. 183.

113

Banks, Lynne Reid.
Return of the Indian.

1985
Published

1995 MN
Removed from the Bemidji school district voluntary reading list and from the school library shelves because it contains subtle stereotypes inconsistent with district diversity goals.

Source: 11, Nov. 1995, p. 183.

114

Bannerman, Helen.
Little Black Sambo.

1899
Published

1956
Removed from classrooms and school library shelves by the Toronto, Ontario, Canada, board of education after the board received complaints from several groups that "the popular book was a cause of mental suffering to Negroes in particular and children in general."

1959 NY
Removed from a school library in New York City after a black resident challenged the book as racially derogatory. The book was eventually restored to library shelves.

1964 NE
Removed from the open shelves of the Lincoln school system on the orders of the School Superintendent because of the inherent racism of the book. The superintendent relocated the book on the "Reserved" shelves, with a note explaining that while it was not "a part of the instructional program, it will be available to those who want to read it as optional material."

1971 AL
Banned in Montgomery schools because the book is "inappropriate" and "not in keeping with good human relations."

1972
Attacked in English schools and libraries because it symbolized "the kind of dangerous and obsolete books that must go."

1972
In Hamilton, Ontario, Canada, teachers ordered students to tear from school readers the pages that contained the story.

1972
The Montreal-based Canadian National Black Coalition mobilized efforts to remove the book from school and library shelves.

1972
The book was banned entirely in New Brunswick, Canada.

1972 TX
Removed from the Dallas school libraries because it "distorts a child's view of black people."

Source: 3, p. 328; 11, Apr. 1956, pp. 3–4; July 1963, p. 51; Jan. 1965, p. 12; 14, pp. 212–14.

115

Banville, John.
The Untouchable.

1997
Published

1998 CT
Challenged at the Bristol Public Library because of references to sexual relations between men and boys.

Source: 11, May 1998, p. 69.

116

Baraka, Imamu Amiri.
The Toilet.

1964
Published

1969
Expurgated at Eastern High School to eliminate all "four-letter words or vernacular."

Source: 11, May 1969, p. 51.

117

Bargar, Gary W.
What Happened to Mr. Foster?

1981
Published

1982 SC
Challenged at the Greenville County Library because the novel's principal character is a homosexual.

Source: 11, Jan. 1983, p. 9.

118

Barker, Clive.
Tapping the Vein, Book 2.

1989
Published

1991 OR
Removed from the Multnomah County Library because of its graphic violence, language, and sexual content.

Source: 11, Jan. 1992, p. 6.

119

Barnes, Derrick.
The Making of Dr. Truelove.

2006
Published

2007 VA
Removed from the Liberty High School in Bedford County because of "sexually explicit content." Administrators pulled the book from the shelf after a parental complaint. While the school system's general policy on content challenges calls for a formal committee's review of the book, that policy was not followed.

Source: 11, Jan. 2008, pp. 14, 35.

120
Barnes, Djuna.
Ryder.

1981
Published

1984
Seized by the British Customs Office as "indecent and obscene."
Source: 11, Jan. 1985, p. 16.

121
Barron, T. A.
The Great Tree of Avalon: Child of the Dark Prophecy.

2003
Published

2008 NY
Restored by the Lackawanna School Board along with several other books following accusations of censorship by some parents and teachers. The books were pulled from the middle school library recommended list because of concerns that the books deal with the occult.
Source: 11, May 2008, pp. 115-16.

122
Barth, Edna.
Witches, Pumpkins and Grinning Ghosts.

1972
Published

1992 AZ
Challenged at the Neely Elementary School in Gilbert because the book "interests little minds into accepting the devil with all of his evil works."

1992 OR
Challenged in the Salem-Keizer school libraries because it would encourage children to experiment with witchcraft.
Source: 11, May 1992, p. 78; July 1992, pp. 124–25.

123
Baskin, Julia, Lindsey Newman, Sophie Pollitt-Cohen, and Courtney Toombs.
The Notebook Girls.

2006
Published

2006 NJ
Challenged, but retained, at the Cape May County Library. The book is comprised of the entries four New York City high-school students made in a shared journal in the aftermath of the September 11 terrorist attacks.

2011 IA
Reclassified from the young adult section to the adult nonfiction section at the Waukee Public Library because of a complaint citing "foul language" and "cussing." The book includes frank discussions about adolescent sex, drinking, and drug use. Body image, sexual orientation, and the 9/11 terrorist attacks are also addressed.
Source: 11, Jan. 2007, p. 29; Jan. 2011, p. 7.

124
Bass, Herbert J.
Our American Heritage.

1979
Published

1987 AL
Removed from Alabama's list of approved texts—and from the state's classrooms— because the book promotes the "religion of secular humanism." U.S. District Court Judge W. Brevard Hand ruled on March 4, 1987, that thirty-nine history and social studies texts used in Alabama's 129 school systems "discriminate against the very concept of religion and theistic religions in particular, by omissions so serious that a student learning history from them would not be apprised of relevant facts about America's history.... References to religion are isolated and the integration of religion in the history of American society is ignored." Other texts removed included: *History of a Free People,* by Henry W. Bragdon; *Teen Guide,* by Valerie Chamberlain; *America Is,* by Frank Freidel; *Today's Teen,* by Joan Kelly; *A History of Our American Republic,* by Glenn M. Linden; *Caring, Deciding and Growing,* by Helen McGinley; *Homemaking: Skills for Everyday Living,* by Frances Baynor Parnell; *People and Our Country,* by Norman K. Risjord; *Contemporary Living,* by Verdene Ryder; *Exploring Our Nation's History,* by Sidney Schwartz; *These United States,* by James P. Shenton; *The American Dream,* by Lew Smith; Social Studies Series published by Scott, Foresman; and *The Rise of the American Nation,* by Lewis

Paul Todd. On August 26, 1987, the U.S. Court of Appeals for the Eleventh Circuit unanimously overturned Judge Hand's decision by ruling that the information in the book was "essentially neutral in its religious content." The fact that the texts omitted references to religion was not "an advancement of secular humanism or an active hostility toward theistic religion."
Source: 11, Jan. 1987, p. 6; May 1987, pp. 75, 104–7; Sept. 1987, pp. 166-67; Nov. 1987, pp. 217–18; Jan. 1988, p. 17; Mar. 1988, p. 40.

125
Baudelaire, Charles.
The Flowers of Evil.

1857
Published

1857
The author, publisher, and printer were prosecuted under the Second Empire, for an "affront to public decency." Baudelaire was arrested and fined 300 francs.

1949
Ban lifted in France.
Source: 4, p. 46; 13, pp. 74–75.

126
Bauer, Marion Dane, ed.
Am I Blue?: Coming Out from the Silence.

1994
Published

1995
Best Books for Young Adults

2000 IA
Challenged, but retained, at the Fairfield Middle School and High School libraries despite objections to sexually explicit passages, including a sexual encounter between two girls.
Source: 11, Mar. 2000, p. 62; May 2000, p. 91.

127
Bauer, Marion Dane.
On My Honor.

1986
Published

1987
Newbery Honor Book

1989
William Allen White Children's Book Award

1989 IA
Retained at the Orchard Hill Elementary School in Cedar Falls after being challenged because the book contained "two swear words and one vulgarity."

1992 TX
Challenged at the Alamo Heights School District Elementary School because the book uses the words "hell," "damn," and "frigging."

1995 PA
Challenged in fourth to sixth grade reading classes in Grove City because it was "depressing." The criteria used to select the book along with a list of other books that focus on "divorce, death, suicide and defeat," was contested.
Source: 11, Mar. 1990, p. 47; May 1990, p. 107; Jan. 1993, p. 13; Sept. 1995, p. 137.

128
Bauman, Robert.
The Gentleman from Maryland: The Conscience of a Gay Conservative.

1986
Published

1993 OR
Challenged at the Deschutes County Library in Bend because it "encourages and condones" homosexuality.
Source: 11, Sept. 1993, pp. 158–59.

129
Bayle, Pierre.
Historical and Critical Dictionary.

1697
Published

1754
Burned in France.

1757
Placed by the Vatican on the *Index Librorum Prohibitorum* (Index of Prohibited Books) in Rome, Italy, where it remained through the first two-thirds of the twentieth century.
Source: 1, pp. 135–36.

130
Beard, Charles.
Rise of American Civilization.

1927
Published

1937 LA
Seized and destroyed by New Orleans police.
Source: 15, Vol. III, p. 650.

131
Beaumarchais, Pierre Augustin Caron de.
Barber of Seville.

1773
Published

1773
For two years, forbidden to be performed in France.
Source: 4, p. 32.

132
Beaumarchais, Pierre Augustin Caron de.
Marriage of Figaro.

1778
Published

1778
Suppressed for six years by Louis XVI at court in Paris, France, and in public performances on the ground of profound immorality. The author was imprisoned in St. Lazare.
Source: 4, p. 32.

133
Bechdel, Alison.
Fun Home: A Family Tragi-comic.

2006
Published

2006 MO
Challenged, but retained, in the adult fiction section of the Marshall Public Library despite being deemed "pornographic" by some members of the community.
Source: 11, Nov. 2006, p. 289; Jan. 2007, pp. 9-10; May 2007, p. 115; July 2007, pp. 163-64.

134
Beck, Robert E., ed.
Literature of the Supernatural.

1975
Published

1986 CO
Challenged at the Jefferson County school libraries in Lakewood because parents objected to many of the stories because they "promoted the occult, sexual promiscuity, and anti-Americanism, and that they attacked other traditional American values." The textbook is a collection of stories written by such authors as Edgar Allen Poe, O. Henry, Ray Bradbury, Dante, and Shakespeare. The Jefferson County School Board refused to ban the book.
Source: 11, May 1986, p. 82; Sept. 1986, p. 173; Nov. 1986, p. 224.

135
Behan, Brendan.
Borstal Boy.

1958
Published

1958
Banned by the Irish Republic's Censorship of Publications Board. The Irish Censorship Board was not required to give any public explanation for its decisions, but it was generally assumed that the book was banned because of its treatment of adolescent sexuality and its extensive use of expletives. In fact, Behan does not write graphically about sex and his characters discuss the topic more than they practice it. There can be little doubt that the book was banned essentially because of its attempted subversion of Irish power structures religious, social, and political.

1959
Banned in Australia.

1959
Banned in New Zealand.
Source: 6, pp. 203–4.

136
Beiderwell, Bruce, and Jeffrey M. Wheeler, eds.
The Literary Experience.

2007
Published

2007 MI
Retained in the Grand Rapids Advanced Placement English classes despite considerations of returning the 1,846 page anthology to its publisher or clipping out about seventy pages with objectionable material, including a drama, "Topdog/Underdog" by Suzan-Lori Parks that contained profanity and descriptions of sexual activity.
Source: 11, Jan. 2008, p. 29.

137
Beisner, Monika.
Secret Spells and Curious Charms.

1985
Published

1992 OR
Retained by the Salem-Keizer School Board after complaints that the book was a how-to book for satanism.
Source: 11, May 1992, p. 94.

138
Belair, Richard L.
Double Take.

1979
Published

1982 LA
Challenged in Livingston due to "objectionable" language.
Source: 11, May 1982, p. 83.

139
Bell, Alan P., and Martin S. Weinberg.
Homosexualities: A Study of Diversity among Men and Women.

1979
Published

1993 OR
Challenged at the Deschutes County Library in Bend because it "encourages and condones" homosexuality.
Source: 11, Sept. 1993, pp. 158–59.

140
Bellairs, John.
The Figure in the Shadows.

1975
Published

1990 AZ
Restricted at the Dysart Unified School District libraries in El Mirage because of two uses of profanity and because of its link to magic.
Source: 11, Jan. 1991, p. 11.

141
Belpré, Pura, and Carlos Sanchez.
Pérez and Martina.

1939
Published

1988 OR
Challenged at the Multnomah County Library in Portland because the death of a mouse in the story could upset children.
Source: 11, Jan. 1989, p. 3.

142
Benchley, Peter.
Jaws.

1974
Published

1978 KS
Removed from all school libraries in Gardner due to a sexually explicit section.

1979 UT
Challenged at the Ogden School District and placed in a restricted circulation category.

1980 NC
Removed from all elementary and middle school libraries in Clinton due to "objectionable" language.

1986 GA
Challenged in the Gwinnett County public schools because of "obscene language."
Source: 11, May 1978, p. 56; May 1979, p. 49; Sept. 1980, p. 99; Mar. 1987, p. 65.

143
Benjamin, Carol Lea.
The Wicked Stepdog.

1982
Published

1994 MT
Challenged by a parent at Newman Elementary School in Billings because of objectionable language including the words "boobs," "ass," and "smoldering kisses." Despite an appeal from parents at

a meeting where the offending words were emblazoned on pickets in the audience, two trustees upheld a decision not to remove the book from the district's library shelves.
Source: 11, July 1994, p. 110; Sept. 1994, p. 166.

144
Bennett, James.
Blue Star Rapture.

1998
Published

1999 IL
Challenged, but retained, on the Downers Grove High School reading lists despite parents' complaints that the book is "obscene" and "vulgar."
Source: 11, Jan. 2000, p. 28.

145
Bentham, Jeremy.
An Introduction to the Principles of Morals and Legislation.

1789
Published

1819
Placed on the *Index Librorum Prohibitorum* (Index of Prohibited Books) in Rome, Italy, by the Catholic Church, remaining listed through its last edition in effect until 1966.
Source: 1, pp. 166–67.

146
Berendt, John.
Midnight in the Garden of Good and Evil: A Savannah Story.

1994
Published

1995
Boeke Prize

1995
Pulitzer Prize Finalist for Nonfiction

2008 ND
Banned for just four days from the Beulah High School library. Two school employees followed school policy to request removing the book after their son brought it home from an accelerated–reading program, in which students pick from a couple of hundred titles. The parents said the 1994

runaway nonfiction best seller was too pornographic and at odds with student behavior promoted in the school handbook. The board reversed its decision at the encouragement of the board president, who said the board moved too fast and unleashed a possible court case it would never win. He said there might be more palatable alternatives, like creating a list of restricted books that parents have to approve before their children can check them out. A decision to review school policies and investigate less–restrictive means to control library books was approved by the school board.

Source: 11, Mar. 2009, pp. 55-56.

147
Berger, John.
To the Wedding.

1995
Published

2011 CA
Challenged as assigned reading for juniors in the International Baccalaureate program at Murrieta Valley High School because some parents said students shouldn't be exposed to the mature content, which includes, on at least three occasions, the use of the f-word to describe sexual relations that take place.

Source: 11, Mar. 2012, p. 59.

148
Berger, Melvin.
The Supernatural: From ESP to UFOs.

1977
Published

1993 TN
Challenged, but retained, at the Cleveland Public Library along with seventeen other books, most of which are on sex education, AIDS awareness, and some titles on the supernatural.

Source: 11, Sept. 1993, p. 146.

149
Berger, Thomas.
Little Big Man.

1964
Published

1986 WA
Retained on a list of supplementary texts for honor history classes at Juanita High School in Bellevue despite claims that the book is "full of sexual material and questionable messages and should be banned."

Source: 11, Sept. 1986, p. 173.

150
Bergson, Henri.
Creative Evolution.

1907
Published

1907
The Vatican condemned "modernist" views, and in 1914, it placed Bergson's work on the *Index Librorum Prohibitorum* (Index of Prohibited Books) in Rome, Italy where it remained through the last edition, published until 1966.

Source: 1, pp. 62–63.

151
Berkeley, George.
Alciphron, or the Minute Philosopher.

1732
Published

1897
Placed on the *Index Librorum Prohibitorum* (Index of Prohibited Books) in Rome, Italy. It was retained on the Index of Pope Leo XII in 1897 and remained listed through the last edition, compiled in 1948 and in print until 1996.

Source: 1, p. 11.

152
Betancourt, Jeanne.
Sweet Sixteen and Never…

1987
Published

1991 MD
Challenged in the Howard County schools because of the book's graphic depiction of teenage romance.

Source: 11, Mar. 1992, p. 40.

153
Bhagavad Gita.

1968
Published

2012
A Russian court has dismissed a call to ban an edition of the Hindu holy book, in a case that triggered protests in India. The commentary, not the text itself, was the cause for scrutiny, according to prosecutors in the Siberian city of Tomsk who wanted the edition to be ruled "extremist." The Russian translation of the book was at risk of being placed on the Federal List of Extremist Materials, which bans more than 1,000 texts, including *Mein Kampf* and publications by the Jehovah's Witness and Scientology movements.

Source: 11, Mar. 2012, p. 82

154
The Bible.

1624
Martin Luther's translation of 1534 was burned by Papal authority in Germany.

1926
Soviet officials stated, "The section [in libraries] on religion must contain solely anti-religious books," and the Bible was not published again in the USSR until 1956.

1978
Banned in Ethiopia as "contradictory to the ongoing revolution."

1986
Translations of the Old and New Testament were banned in Turkey.

1992 MN
In 1952 and 1953, Fundamentalists in the U.S. attacked the Revised Standard Version because of changes in terminology. Challenged by an atheist "seeking to turn the tables on the religious right," but retained, at the Brooklyn Center Independent School District. The challenger stated "the lewd, indecent, and violent contents of that book are hardly suitable for young students."

1993 AK
Challenged as "obscene and pornographic," but retained, at the Noel Wien Library in Fairbanks.

1993 PA

Challenged, but retained, in the West Shore schools near Harrisburg despite objections that it "contains language and stories that are inappropriate for children of any age, including tales of incest and murder. There are more than three hundred examples of 'obscenities' in the book."

2001 FL

Challenged, but retained, in the Marion-Levy Public Library System in Ocala.

Source: 4, pp. 3–5; 5, Sept. /Oct. 1978, p. 66; July/Aug. 1986, p. 46; 6, pp. 229–32; 8, pp. 208–12; 11, Jan. 1993, p. 8; Mar. 1993, p. 55; Mar. 1993, p. 55; July 1993, p. 123; Jan. 1994, p. 36; May 2001, p. 123.

155

Billington, Ray.
Limericks: Historical and Hysterical.

1981
Published

1988 CA

Removed, but later returned to the Tokay High School library in Lodi because it was "really inappropriate and there ought to be better books on limericks available."

Source: 11, May 1989, p. 75.

156

Bing, Leon.
Do or Die.

1991
Published

1992
Best Books for Young Adults

1993 WY

Challenged at the Sweetwater County Library in Green River because the book tells young people how to become involved in a gang. The book was retained.

Source: 11, Jan. 1994, p. 14; Mar. 1994, p. 70.

157

Bird, Malcolm.
The Witch's Handbook.

1988
Published

1991 OR

Challenged for promoting witchcraft, but retained, at the Multnomah County Library.

Source: 11, Jan. 1992, p. 6.

158

Birdseye, Tom.
Attack of the Mutant Underwear.

2003
Published

2006 FL

Removed from the Pinellas school district's Battle of the Books program because officials found it unsuitable for younger readers. The book is on the Sunshine State Young Reader's Award list of books for third, fourth, and fifth-graders.

Source: 11, Nov. 2006, pp. 290-91.

159

Bishop, Claire Huchet.
The Five Chinese Brothers.

1938
Published

1994 WA

Challenged at the Spokane School District library because it is too violent.

1998 CA

Challenged, but retained, at the Colton elementary schools despite a parent's protest that it contains descriptions of violent plots to execute five brothers. Other books have been unsuccessfully challenged in recent years in the Colton School District, including John Steinbeck's *Of Mice and Men* for its use of profanity and Stephen King's *Misery* for violence.

Source: 11, Jan. 1995, p. 9; Mar. 1999, p. 47.

160

Blank, Joani.
A Kid's First Book about Sex.

1983
Published

1986 IN

Challenged at the Hammond Public Library because "the book promotes immorality and promiscuity. It promotes no moral values whatsoever."

Source: 11, Jan. 1987, p. 30.

161

Blank, Joani.
Laugh Lines.

1982
Published

1990 CA

Removed from the McKinleyville Elementary School library for its "demeaning manner" toward individuals who read the riddles and cannot figure out the answers, rather than for its political or sexual content.

Source: 11, Mar. 1991, p. 42.

162

Blatty, William P.
The Exorcist.

1971
Published

1975 IA

Challenged at the Grinnell-Newburg school system as "vulgar and obscene by most religious standards."

1976 CO

Banned for use in Aurora High School English classes on the grounds of "immorality."

Source: 11, Mar. 1975, p. 41; May 1975, p. 87; May 1976, p. 70; May 1977, p. 79.

163

Block, Francesca Lia, and Suza Scalora.
The Rose and the Beast: Fairy Tales Retold.

2000
Published

2002 VA

Challenged, along with seventeen other titles in the Fairfax County elementary and secondary libraries, by a group called Parents Against Bad Books in Schools. The group contends the books "contain profanity and descriptions of drug abuse, sexually explicit conduct, and torture."

Source: 11, Jan. 2003, p. 10.

164
Block, Francesca Lia.
Baby Be-Bop.

1995
Published

1996
Best Books for Young Adults

1998 WI
Removed from the Barron School District because of the book's use of vulgar language and sexually explicit passages. The ACLU of Wisconsin filed suit against the school district on Feb. 16, 1999. The books were then returned to the library while a federal court considered the lawsuit. On October 8, 1999, it was agreed that the novel will remain available to students as part of the school district's settlement of the federal lawsuit.

2000 CA
Removed from the mandatory reading program at the Norman L. Sullivan Middle School in Bonsall due to sexually explicit language.

2009 WI
Four Wisconsin men belonging to the Christian Civil Liberties Union (CCLU) sought $30,000 apiece for emotional distress they suffered from the West Bend Community Memorial Library for displaying a copy of the book. The claim states that, "specific words used in the book are derogatory and slanderous to all males" and "the words can permeate violence and put one's life in possible jeopardy, adults and children alike." The CCLU called for the public burning of this title. Four months later, the library board unanimously voted 9–0 to maintain, "without removing, relocating, labeling, or otherwise restricting access," this and other challenged books in the young adult section at the West Bend Community Memorial Library.

Source: 8, pp. 415–16; 11, Jan. 1999, p. 9; Mar. 1999, p. 37; May 1999, p. 68; Jan. 2000, p. 28; May 2000, p. 76; July 2009, pp. 128, 132, 134; Sept. 2009, pp. 169–70.

165
Block, Francesca Lia.
Girl Goddess #9: Nine Stories.

1996
Published

2002 VA
Challenged, along with seventeen other titles in the Fairfax County elementary and secondary libraries, by a group called Parents Against Bad Books in Schools. The group contends the books "contain profanity and descriptions of drug abuse, sexually explicit conduct, and torture."

Source: 11, Jan. 2003, p. 10.

166
Block, Francesca Lia.
I Was a Teenage Fairy.

1995
Published

2002 VA
Challenged, along with seventeen other titles in the Fairfax County elementary and secondary libraries, by a group called Parents Against Bad Books in Schools. The group contends the books "contain profanity and descriptions of drug abuse, sexually explicit conduct, and torture."

Source: 11, Jan. 2003, p. 10.

167
Block, Francesca Lia.
Witch Baby.

1991
Published

2002 VA
Challenged, along with seventeen other titles in the Fairfax County elementary and secondary libraries, by a group called Parents Against Bad Books in Schools. The group contends the books "contain profanity and descriptions of drug abuse, sexually explicit conduct, and torture." On March 10, 2003, the school board determined the book is suitable for elementary- and middle-school collections and placed a young-adult sticker on its spine.

Source: 11, Jan. 2003, p. 10; May 2003, p. 117.

168
Bloom, Harold, ed.
Modern Critical Views: James Baldwin.

1986
Published

2000 PA
Removed in the Southern Columbia School District in Elysburg because of concerns about sexual references and foul language in a single passage.

Source: 11, July 2000, p. 104.

169
Blumberg, Rhoda.
Devils and Demons.

1982
Published

1988 OR
Challenged at the Newberg Public Library because the book was too graphic and the topic was negative and degrading.

Source: 11, Jan. 1990, pp. 4–5.

170
Blume, Judy.
Are You There God? It's Me, Margaret.

1970
Published

1980 AZ
Challenged in many libraries but removed from the Gilbert elementary school libraries, and ordered that parental consent be required for students to check out this title from the junior high school library.

1982 AL
Challenged in the Tuscaloosa school system.

1982 MN
Restricted in Zimmerman to students who have written permission from their parents.

1982 WI
Challenged in the Fond du Lac school systems because the book is "sexually offensive and amoral."

1983 MN
After the Minnesota Civil Liberties Union sued the Elk River School Board, the Board reversed its decision to restrict this title to students who have written permission from their parents.

1983 OH
Challenged at the Xenia school libraries because the book "is built around just two themes: sex and anti-Christian behavior."

1985 MT
Challenged as profane, immoral, and offensive, but retained, in the Bozeman school libraries.

Source: 9; 11, Jan. 1981, p. 9; Sept. 1982, pp. 155–56; Mar. 1983, pp. 34, 39; May 1983, p. 71; Sept. 1983, pp. 139, 153; Nov. 1983, p. 197; July 1985, p. 112.

171
Blume, Judy.
Blubber.

1974
Published

1980 MD
Removed from all library shelves in the Montgomery County elementary schools.

1981 AZ
Temporarily banned in Sunizona.

1983 IA
Challenged in the Des Moines schools due to "objectionable" subject matter.

1983 OH
Challenged at the Xenia school libraries because the book "undermines authority since the word 'bitch' is used in connection with a teacher."

1983 OH
Challenged at the Akron School District libraries.

1983 TX
Challenged at the Smith Elementary School in Del Valle because it contained the words "damn" and "bitch" and showed children cruelly teasing a classmate.

1984 IL
Banned, but later restricted to students with parental permission at the Peoria School District libraries because of its strong sexual content and language, and alleged lack of social or literary value.

1984 NJ
Restricted at the Lindenwold elementary school libraries because of "a problem with language."

1984 PA
Removed from the Hanover School District's elementary and secondary libraries, but later placed on a "restricted shelf" at middle school libraries because the book was "indecent and inappropriate."

1984 WY
Challenged at the Casper school libraries.

1985 MT
Challenged as profane, immoral, and offensive, but retained, in the Bozeman school libraries.

1986 WI
Challenged at the Muskego Elementary School because "the characters curse and the leader of the taunting (of an overweight girl) is never punished for her cruelty."

1991 OH
Challenged at the Perry Township elementary school libraries because in the book, "bad is never punished. Good never comes to the fore. Evil is triumphant."

1998 AL
Banned at Clements High School in Athens because of objections to two uses of the word "damn" and "bitch" in the novel. The decision was later reversed.

1999 TX
Removed from an elementary school in Arlington because educators objected to "verbal, physical, and sexual abuse of student upon student."

Source: 9; 11, May 1980, p. 51; Mar. 1982, p. 57; May 1982, p. 84; July 1982, pp. 124, 142; May 1983, pp. 73, 85–86; July 1983, p. 121; Sept. 1983, pp. 139, 153; Nov. 1983, p. 197; Nov. 1984, p. 185; Jan. 1985, pp. 8–9; Mar. 1985, pp. 33, 42, 58; July 1985, p. 112; Jan. 1987, p. 31; Mar. 1992, p. 41; July 1992, p. 124; Mar. 1999, p. 35; May 1999, p. 83; Jan. 2000, p. 8.

172
Blume, Judy.
Deenie.

1973
Published

1980 AZ
Removed from the Gilbert elementary school libraries, and ordered that parental consent be required for students to check out this title from the junior high school library.

1980 UT
Removed from the Utah State Library bookmobile because the book contains "the vilest sexual descriptions" and if given to "the wrong kid at the wrong time (would) ruin his life."

1982 CA
Challenged in the Cotati-Rohnert Park School District because the novel allegedly undermines parental moral values.

1982 FL
Challenged in Orlando.

1983 MN
After the Minnesota Civil Liberties Union sued the Elk River School Board, the Board reversed its decision to restrict this title to students who have written permission from their parents.

1984 IL
Banned, but later restricted to students with parental permission at the Peoria School District libraries because of its strong sexual content and language, and alleged lack of social or literary value.

1984 PA
Removed from the Hanover School District's elementary and secondary libraries, but later placed on a "restricted shelf" at middle school libraries because the book was "indecent and inappropriate."

1984 WY
Challenged at the Casper school libraries.

1985 GA
Banned from district elementary school libraries in Gwinnett County as "inappropriate."

1985 GA
Returned to the elementary and junior high school library shelves in Clayton County after school officials determined that the book is appropriate for young readers.

1985 MT
Challenged as profane, immoral, and offensive, but retained, in the Bozeman school libraries.

1996 NC
Challenged by a parent in the Cornelius Elementary School library in Charlotte due to the novel's sexual content.

2003 FL
Challenged by a parent in the Spring Hill Elementary School District in Hernando County due to passages that talk frankly about masturbation. The board decided to retain the title but require students to have written parental permission to access the novel.

Source: 9; 11, Nov. 1980, p. 128; Jan. 1981, p. 9; July 1982, p. 125; Sept. 1982, pp. 155–56; Jan. 1983, p. 21; May 1983, p. 71; Sept. 1983, p. 153; Jan. 1985, pp. 8–9; Mar. 1985, pp. 33, 42, 58; July 1985, p. 112; Sept. 1985, p. 151; Nov. 1985, p. 193; Jan. 1986, pp. 8–9, 21; May 1996, p. 83; Jan. 2003, pp. 8–9; Mar. 2004, pp. 48–49; May 2004, pp. 95–96.

173
Blume, Judy.
Forever.

1975
Published

1996
Margaret A. Edwards Award for Lifetime Achievement

1982 FL
Challenged at the Orlando schools.

1982 MO
Challenged at the Park Hill South Junior High School library where it was housed on restricted shelves because the book promotes "the stranglehold of humanism on life in America."

1982 PA
Challenged at the Midvalley Junior-Senior High School in Scranton because it contains "four letter words and talked about masturbation, birth control, and disobedience to parents."

1983 OH
Challenged at the Akron School District libraries.

1983 WI
Challenged at the Howard-Suamico High School because "it demoralizes marital sex."

1984 IA
Challenged at the Cedar Rapids Public Library because it is "pornography and explores areas God didn't intend to explore outside of marriage."

1984 NE
Challenged and eventually moved from the Holdrege Public Library young adult section to the adult section because the "book is pornographic and does not promote the sanctity of life, family life."

1986 VA
Placed on a restricted shelf at Patrick County School Board.

1986 WY
Challenged at the Campbell County school libraries because it is "pornographic" and would encourage young readers "to experiment with sexual encounters."

1987 CA
Challenged at the Moreno Valley Unified School District libraries because it "contains profanity, sexual situations, and themes that allegedly encourage disrespectful behavior."

1987 ME
Challenged at the Marshwood Junior High School classroom library in Eliot because the "book does not paint a responsible role of parents;" its "cast of sex-minded teenagers is not typical of high schoolers today;" and the "pornographic sexual

exploits (in the book) are unsuitable for junior high school role models."

1988 FL
West Hernando Middle School principal recommended that Blume's novel be removed from school library shelves because it is "inappropriate."

1992 IL
Placed on reserve at the Herrin Junior High School library and can be checked out only with a parent's written permission because the novel is "sexually provocative reading."

1993 IL
Removed from the Frost Junior High School library in Schaumburg because "it's basically a sexual 'how-to-do' book for junior high students. It glamorizes [sex] and puts ideas in their heads."

1993 WI
Placed on the "parental permission shelf" at the Rib Lake high school libraries after Superintendent Ray Parks filed a "request for reconsideration" because he found the book "sexually explicit." It was subsequently confiscated by the high school principal. A federal jury in Madison, awarded $394,560 to a former Rib Lake High School guidance counselor after finding that his contract was not renewed in retaliation for speaking out against the district's material selection policy. The counselor criticized the decision of the Rib Lake High School principal to restrict student access to the novel.

1994 IA
Removed from Mediapolis School District libraries because it "does not promote abstinence and monogamous relationships [and] lacks any aesthetic, literary, or social value." Returned to the shelves a month later but accessible only to high school students.

1995 FL
Removed from the Fort Clarke Middle School library in Gainesville after a science teacher objected to its sexually explicit content and a reference to marijuana.

1995 IN
Restricted to a reserve section of the Delta High School Library in Muncie. Parents must give their permission in writing before their children can check out the book.

1996 IA
Challenged at the Wilton School District for junior and senior high school students because of its sexual content.

1997 IL
Banned from middle school libraries in the Elgin School District U46 because of sex scenes. The decision was upheld in June 1999 after an hour of emotional school board discussion. After a four-year absence, the book was returned in 2002 to the shelves of the district's middle school libraries.

2005 AR
Challenged in the Fayetteville Middle and Junior High School libraries. The complainant also submitted a list of more than fifty books, citing the books as too sexually explicit and promoting homosexuality.

Source: 8, pp. 334–35; 9; 11, July 1982, pp. 124, 142; May 1982, p. 84; May 1983, pp. 85–86; Mar. 1984, p. 39; May 1984, p. 69; Mar. 1985, p. 59; Sept. 1985, p. 167; Mar. 1986, p. 39; Mar. 1987, pp. 66–67; July 1987, p. 125; Nov. 1987, p. 239; Mar. 1988, p. 45; May 1992, p. 80; May 1993, p. 70; July 1993, pp. 98, 104–5; Sept. 1993, pp. 146–47; May 1994, pp. 83, 86; July 1994, p. 109; Mar. 1995, p. 56; July 1995, p. 93; Nov. 1995, p. 183; May 1996, p. 97; May 1997, pp. 60–61; Sept. 1999, p. 119; Mar. 2002, p. 105; May 2002, pp. 135–36; Sept. 2005, p. 215.

174
Blume, Judy.
Here's to You, Rachel Robinson.

1993
Published

1994
Best Books for Young Adults

1999 NY
Challenged, but retained, at the Granville School library in Catskill despite a parent's objection to three words.
Source: 11, Sept. 1999, p. 131.

175
Blume, Judy.
Iggie's House.

1970
Published

1984 WY
Challenged at the Casper school libraries.
Source: 11, Mar. 1985, p. 42.

176
Blume, Judy.
It's Not the End of the World.

1972
Published

1984 NJ
Restricted at the Lindenwold elementary school libraries because of "a problem with language."

1984 PA
Removed from the Hanover School District's elementary and secondary libraries, but later placed on a "restricted shelf" at middle school libraries because the book was "indecent and inappropriate."

1984 WY
Challenged at the Casper school libraries.

1985 MN
Challenged at the Orchard Lake Elementary School library in Burnsville.

1998 GA
Restricted to fourth- and fifth-graders at W. C. Britt Elementary School in Gwinnett County due to concerns about profanity.
Source: 11, Nov. 1984, p. 185; Jan. 1985, p. 9; Mar. 1985, p. 42; Nov. 1985, p. 203; May 1998, pp. 69–70.

177
Blume, Judy.
The One in the Middle Is the Green Kangaroo.

1969
Published

1984 WY
Challenged at the Casper school libraries.
Source: 11, Mar. 1985, p. 42.

178
Blume, Judy.
Otherwise Known as Sheila the Great.

1972
Published

1984 WY
Challenged at the Casper school libraries.
Source: 11, Mar. 1985, p. 42.

179
Blume, Judy.
Starring Sally J. Freedman as Herself.

1977
Published

1984 PA
Removed from the Hanover School District's elementary and secondary libraries, but later placed on a "restricted shelf" at middle school libraries because the book was "indecent and inappropriate."

1984 WY
Challenged at the Casper school libraries.

1985 MT
Challenged as profane, immoral, and offensive, but retained, in the Bozeman school libraries.
Source: 11, Jan. 1985, p. 9; Mar. 1985, p. 42; July 1985, p. 112.

180
Blume, Judy.
Superfudge.

1980
Published

1984 WY
Challenged at the Casper school libraries.

1985 MT
Challenged as profane, immoral, and offensive, but retained, in the Bozeman school libraries.
Source: 11, Mar. 1985, p. 42; July 1985, p. 112.

181
Blume, Judy.
Then Again, Maybe I Won't.

1971
Published

1980 AZ
Challenged in many libraries but removed from the Gilbert elementary school libraries, and ordered that parental consent be required for students to check out this title from the junior high school library.

1982 AL
Challenged in Tuscaloosa because the book is "sexually offensive and amoral."

1982 FL
Challenged in Orlando.

1982 MD
Challenged in the Harford County school systems.

1983 MN
After the Minnesota Civil Liberties Union sued the Elk River School Board, the Board reversed its decision to restrict this title to students who have written permission from their parents.

1984 IL
Banned, but later restricted to students with parental permission at the Peoria School District libraries because of its strong sexual content and language, and alleged lack of social or literary value.

1984 LA
Removed from all school library collections in St. Tammany Parish because its "treatment of immorality and voyeurism do not provide for the growth of desirable attitudes," but later reinstated.

1984 WY
Challenged at the Casper school libraries.

1985 MT
Challenged as profane, immoral, and offensive, but retained, in the Bozeman school libraries.

1988 IA
Challenged in the Des Moines elementary schools because of sexual content.

1989 OR
Challenged at the Salem-Keizer School District because it is a "dismal tale of a young boy's inability to cope and his very inappropriate responses to the changes taking place in his life."

1990 PA
Challenged at the elementary library in Tyrone because the book deals with masturbation and erections, and explains how to drink whiskey, vodka, and gin.
Source: 9; 11, July 1982, p. 124; Sept. 1982, pp. 155–56; May 1983, p. 71; Sept. 1983, p. 153; May 1984, p. 69; July 1984, p. 121; Jan. 1985, p. 8; Mar. 1985, pp. 33, 42, 58; July 1985, p. 112; Jan. 1990, pp. 4–5; July 1990, p. 127; Mar. 1991, p. 62.

182
Blume, Judy.
Tiger Eyes.

1981
Published

1981
Best Books for Young Adults

1981
National Book Award for Children's Books

1984 IN
Challenged at the Daleville Elementary School library due to alleged sexual innuendo in the book.

1984 PA
Removed from the Hanover School District's elementary and secondary libraries, but later placed on a "restricted shelf" at middle school libraries because the book was "indecent and inappropriate."

1984 WY
Challenged at the Casper school libraries.

1999 LA
Pulled from the Many Junior High library shelves because of descriptions of a girl's sexual encounters, getting drunk at school, and the use of profanities.
Source: 11, Jan. 1985, p. 9; Mar. 1985, pp. 42, 59; Jan. 2000, p. 11.

183
Boccaccio, Giovanni.
The Decameron.

1353
Published

1497
Burned and prohibited in Italy also in 1559.

1800s
Banned in France.

1906 OH
Declared to be an "obscene, lewd and lascivious book of indecent character" by a jury in Cincinnati.

1926
Banned in U.S. until 1931.

1934 MI
Seized by Detroit police.

1935 MA
Still banned in Boston.

1950s
Attempts to get the work destroyed, some of them successful, continued until the 1950s.
Source: 6, pp. 257–58; 8, pp. 327–29; 9, p. 7; 10, p. 140.

184
Bode, Janet, and Stan Mack.
Heartbreak and Roses: Real Life Stories of Troubled Love.

1994
Published

1995
Best Books for Young Adults

1996 LA
Pulled from the Ouachita Parish School library in Monroe because of sexual content. The Louisiana chapter of the ACLU filed a lawsuit in the federal courts on October 3, 1996, claiming that the principal and the school superintendent violated First Amendment free speech rights and also failed to follow established procedure when they removed the book. The three-year-old school library censorship case headed to court after the Ouachita Parish School Board made no decision to seek a settlement at a special meeting April 12, 1999. On August 17, 1999, the Ouachita Parish School Board agreed to return the book to the library and to develop a new book-selection policy that follows state guidelines for school media programs.
Source: 11, Sept. 1996, pp. 151–52; Jan. 1997, p. 7; July 1999, p. 93; Jan. 2000, p. 27.

185
Bode, Janet.
View from Another Closet.

1976
Published

1982 MI
Challenged at the Niles Community Library because the book is "a devious attempt to recruit our young people into the homosexual lifestyle."
Source: 11, Jan. 1983, p. 8.

186
Bogart, Bonnie.
Ewoks Join the Fight.

1983
Published

1987 CA
Challenged at the La Costa Public Library because "every page except for three has some sort of violence — somebody gets knocked down or the Death Star is destroyed."
Source: 11, July 1987, p. 125.

187
Bonner, Cindy.
Lily.

1992
Published

1993
Best Books for Young Adults

1994 PA
Removed temporarily from the Richland Middle School Library while a "Parental Guidance" program that gives parents more control over what their children read in school is explored. A local parent complained that it was "sexually explicit" and had "no moral guidance."
Source: 11, Jan. 1995, p. 8; Mar. 1995, p. 41.

188
Booth, Jack.
Impressions series.

1984
Published

1987 WA
Challenged in the Oak Harbor school system because it "undermines parental authority, is filled with morbid, frightening imagery and involves children in witchcraft and sorcery." In addition, opponents claimed, "the series promotes Eastern and other religions to the exclusion of Christianity."

1988 OR
Challenged at the Talent Elementary School in Phoenix because it "promotes witchcraft and secular humanism and lacks Christian values."

1989 CA
Temporarily banned at the Hacienda La Puente Unified School District in Hacienda Heights because of morbid imagery.

1989 CA
Removed from the East Whittier School District because parents complained that some stories were evil and morbid.

1989 ID
Challenged in the Coeur d'Alene elementary schools.

1990 AK
Challenged in the Fairbanks schools.

1990 CA
Challenged in the Stockton schools.

1990 CA
Challenged in the Redondo Beach schools.

1990 CA
Challenged in the Yucaipa schools.

1990 CA
Challenged in the Winters schools.

1990 CA
Challenged in the Shingletown schools.

1990 CA
Challenged in the Campbell schools.

1990 CA
Challenged in the Saratoga schools.

1990 ID
Challenged in the Boise schools.

1990 IL
Challenged in the Wheaton schools. U.S. District Court Judge James B. Moran dismissed a lawsuit filed against Wheaton-Warrenville School District by parents who claimed school officials failed to implement rules allowing their children to be excluded from using the series.

1990 IL
Challenged in the Palatine schools.

1990 IL
Challenged in the Barrington schools.

1990 IL
Challenged in the Arlington Heights schools.

1990 NM
Challenged in the Albuquerque schools.

1990 NM
Challenged in the Santa Fe schools.

1990 NY
Challenged in the Lakewood schools.

1990 SD
Challenged in the Box Elder schools.

1990 TN
Challenged in the Nashville schools.

1991 CA
Challenged in the Eureka schools.

1991 CA
Challenged in the Grass Valley schools. U.S. District Court Judge William Shubb dismissed a lawsuit in California alleging that the series violated the state and federal constitutions by promoting the "religion of witchcraft and neo-paganism."

1991 ME
Challenged in the Gardiner schools.

1991 OH
Challenged in the Willard schools because the series of readers "undermines absolute truth and value, teaches situational ethics and a lack of respect for authority, and curiosity in the occult." The first editions of the series were challenged because there was too much of a Canadian emphasis.

1991 OR
Challenged in the Newport schools.

1991 OR
Removed in the North Marion School District in Aurora.

1992 IL
U.S. District Court Judge James B. Moran dismissed a lawsuit filed against Wheaton-Warrenville School District by parents who claimed school officials failed to implement rules allowing their children to be excluded from using the series.

1992 MD
Challenged in Frederick County schools.

Source: 11, Jan. 1988, p. 13; Jan. 1989, p. 3; Jan. 1990, p. 11; Mar. 1990, p. 46; May 1990, pp. 85-86; Sept. 1990, pp. 160–61; Nov. 1990, p. 210; Jan. 1991, pp. 14, 16, 17, 29; Mar. 1991, pp. 46–48; July 1991, pp. 107, 131–32; Sept. 1991, pp. 178 79; Jan. 1992, p. 9; Mar. 1992, pp. 32, 45, July 1992, pp. 110–11, 117; Sept. 1992, p. 163; Jan. 1993, pp. 11, 18.

189
Bopp, Joseph B.
Herbie Capleenies.

1978
Published

1982 OR
Removed from the Hermiston Elementary School library because of the main character's activities, which included machine-gunning his boring friends and making naked snow women.
Source: 11, July 1982, p. 124.

190
Borland, Hal.
When the Legends Die.

1963
Published

1995 WY
Removed from the Lincoln County High School curriculum because of "considerable obscenities." The parent

complained that there were 57 swear words in 40 consecutive pages.
Source: 11, July 1995, p. 100.

191
Borten, Helen.
Halloween.

1965
Published

1992 AZ
Challenged at the Neely Elementary School in Gilbert because the book shows the dark side of religion through the occult, the devil, and satanism.
Source: 11, May 1992, p. 78; July 1992, p. 124.

192
Bossert, Jill.
Humor 2.

1988
Published

1992 WA
Challenged at the Sno-Isle Regional Library System in Marysville because the jokes in the book deal with adult subjects.
Source: 11, Nov. 1992, p. 185.

193
Boston Women's Health Book Collective.
Our Bodies, Ourselves.

1973
Published

1975 FL
Removed from high school libraries in Pinellas County.

1975 VT
Removed from high school libraries in Townshend.

1976
Best Books for Young Adults

1977 WV
Removed from high school libraries in Morgantown.

1978 MT
Removed from high school libraries in Helena.

1982 MI
Challenged in Three Rivers Public Library because it "promotes homosexuality and perversion."

1982 WI
Challenged in Amherst due to its "pornographic" nature.

1984 MO
Challenged at the William Chrisman High School in Independence because the book is "filthy." The controversial feminist health manual was on a bookshelf in the classroom and was the personal property of the teacher.
Source: 9; 11, July 1975, p. 105; Sept. 1975, p. 138; July 1977, p. 100; Mar. 1979, p. 27; May 1982, p. 100; Mar. 1983, p. 29; July 1984, p. 106; 15, Vol. IV, p. 714.

194
Boswell, Robert.
Mystery Ride.

1993
Published

1994 OR
Expurgated by an apparent self-appointed censor at the Coquille Public Library along with several other books. Most were mysteries and romances in which single words and sexually explicit passages were whited out by a vandal who left either dots or solid ink pen lines where the words had been.
Source: 11, Sept. 1994, p. 148.

195
Bowden, Mark.
Black Hawk Down: A Story of Modern War.

1999
Published

2008 LA
Removed from a classroom at Central Lafourche High School in Raceland for violating the district policy on cursing. The book is the story of a failed Special Forces mission in Somalia.
Source: 11, Jan. 2009, pp. 9-10.

196
Bower, William Clayton.
The Living Bible.

1969
Published

1981 NC
Burned in Gastonia because it is "a perverted commentary of the King James Version."
Source: 11, July 1981, p. 105.

197
Boyle, T. Coraghessan.
The Tortilla Curtain.

1995
Published

2010 CA
Challenged on the Santa Rosa High School reading list. A review committee approved the continued use of the book with the following guidelines: "The teacher must appropriately prepare students for parts of the book that may be considered provocative; limit the book to juniors and seniors; should a parent object to the book, board policy is currently in place that allows a student to be excused from the book assignment, and provides for an alternative assignment without penalty to the student."
Source: 11, Mar. 2010, pp. 55-56.

198
Bradbury, Ray.
Fahrenheit 451.

1953
Published

1984
Prometheus Award

1992 CA
Expurgated at the Venado Middle School in Irvine. Students received copies of the book with scores of words—mostly "hells" and "damns"—blacked out. The novel is about book-burning and censorship. After receiving complaints from parents and being contacted by reporters, school officials said the censored copies would no longer be used.

2006 TX
Challenged at the Conroe Independent School District because of the following: "discussion of being drunk, smoking cigarettes, violence, 'dirty talk,' references to the *Bible*, and using God's name in vain." The novel went against the complainants' "religious beliefs."
Source: 6, p. 279; 8, pp. 446-47; 11, July 1992, pp. 108-9; Nov. 2006, p. 293.

199
Bradbury, Ray.
The Martian Chronicles.

1950
Published

1982 FL
Challenged at the Haines City High School due to several instances of profanity and the use of God's name in vain in the work.

1987 NC
Challenged at the Newton-Conover High School as a supplemental reading due to profanity.

1993 TN
Challenged as required reading at the Gatlinburg-Pittman High School due to profanity.

1998 NJ
Pulled and replaced with a newer version at the Herbert Hoover Middle School in Edison because a chapter contains the words "the niggers are coming." The new abridged edition of the book omits the inflammatory story, titled "Way Up in the Air."
Source: 11, Jan. 1983, p. 22; May 1987, p. 103; Sept. 1993, p. 149; May 1998, pp. 71–72; July 1998, p. 109.

200
Bradbury, Ray.
The Veldt.

1951
Published

2006 OR
Retained on the Beaverton School District's reading list. The short story was challenged by a middle-school parent who thought its language and plot were inappropriate for students. Her biggest concern is that the story offers no consequences for the children's actions. The short story is part of Bradbury's *The Illustrated Man* anthology. It is twenty pages long and was published in 1951 as the first in the collection of eighteen science fiction stories.
Source: 11, Nov. 2006, p. 319.

201
Bradford, Richard.
Red Sky at Morning.

1968
Published

1968
Best Books for Young Adults

1979 WA
Challenged in Omak due to "profane language."

1987 MT
Challenged at the Big Sky High School in Missoula because the "language was inappropriate for freshman."

2007 MT
Challenged, but retained, on the reading list for freshman English classes in Billings School District 2 despite concerns that the book contains excessive profanity and includes sexually suggestive passages that the complainant thought were not appropriate for fourteen-year-olds. The book has been used in the district for more than twenty years.

Source: 11, July 1979, p. 75; July 1987, p. 150; July 2007, pp. 164-65.

202
Brancato, Robin F.
Winning.

1977
Published

1977
Best Books for Young Adults

1986 CO
Challenged at the Greeley-Evans School District in Greeley because the book contained "obscenities, allusions to sexual references, and promoted contempt for parents and acceptance of drug use."

Source: 11, Sept. 1986, p. 171.

203
Brannen, Sarah.
Uncle Bobby's Wedding.

2008
Published

2008 CO
Challenged at the Douglas County Libraries in Castle Rock because "some material may be inappropriate for young children." The children's book features two gay guinea pigs. A resident requested that the book be removed from the library and placed in a special area or labeled "some material may be inappropriate for young children."

2012 MO
Challenged, but retained, at the Brentwood Public Library despite a resident who did not like the book's subject matter. The picture book involves a young guinea pig and her beloved uncle, who is going to marry his male partner.

Source: 11, Sept. 2008, pp. 183-84; Jan. 2013, p. 33.

204
Brashares, Ann.
Forever in Blue, the Fourth Summer of the Sisterhood.

2007
Published

2010 WI
Challenged at the Theisen Middle School in Fond du Lac by a parent who believes that the book has inappropriate subject matter for children. "Some (of the characters in the book) are sexually active, and alcohol is part of their recreation."

Source: 11, July 2010, pp. 156, 176.

205
Brashler, Anne.
Getting Jesus in the Mood.

1991
Published

1992 MD
Challenged at the Carroll County Public Library in Westminster because the widely praised short story collection is "smutty" and contains pornography aimed at Jesus Christ.

Source: 11, Sept. 1992, pp, 137–38.

206
Brautigan, Richard.
The Abortion: An Historical Romance.

1966
Published

1978 CA
Removed from high school library in Redding due to "unsuitable obscene and sexual references." A California state appeals court ruled in 1989 in *Wexner v. Anderson Union High School District Board of Trustees* that the school board acted improperly when it banned this book.

Source: 11, Jan. 1979, p. 11; Mar. 1989, p. 52.

207
Brautigan, Richard.
A Confederate General from Big Sur.

1964
Published

1978 CA
Removed from high school library in Redding due to "unsuitable obscene and sexual references." A California state appeals court ruled in 1989 in *Wexner v. Anderson Union High School District Board of Trustees* that the school board acted improperly when it banned this book.

Source: 11, Jan. 1979, p. 11; Mar. 1989, p. 52.

208
Brautigan, Richard.
The Pill vs. the Springhill Mine Disaster.

1969
Published

1978 CA
Removed from high school library in Redding due to "unsuitable obscene and sexual references." A California state appeals court ruled in 1989 in *Wexner v. Anderson Union High School District Board of Trustees* that the school board acted improperly when it banned this book.

1988 GA
Removed from the shelves of the Southeast Whitfield High School library because it includes four poems that use "inappropriate" language or have sexual connotations.

Source: 11, Jan. 1979, p. 11; Jan. 1989, p. 7; Mar. 1989, p. 52.

209
Brautigan, Richard.
The Revenge of the Lawn.

1971
Published

1978 CA
Removed from high school library in Redding due to "unsuitable obscene and sexual references." A California state appeals court ruled in 1989 in *Wexner v. Anderson Union High School District Board of Trustees* that the school board acted improperly when it banned this book.

Source: 11, Jan. 1979, p. 11; Mar. 1989, p. 52.

210

Brautigan, Richard.
Rommel Drives on Deep into Egypt.

1970
Published

1978 CA
Removed from high school library in Redding due to "unsuitable obscene and sexual references." A California state appeals court ruled in 1989 in *Wexner v. Anderson Union High School District Board of Trustees* that the school board acted improperly when it banned this book.
Source: 11, Jan. 1979, p. 11; Mar. 1989, p. 52.

211

Brautigan, Richard.
Trout Fishing in America.

1967
Published

1978 CA
Removed from high school library in Redding due to "unsuitable obscene and sexual references." A California state appeals court ruled in 1989 in *Wexner v. Anderson Union High School District Board of Trustees* that the school board acted improperly when it banned this book.
Source: 11, Jan. 1979, p. 11; Mar. 1989, p. 52.

212

Bredes, Don.
Hard Feelings.

1977
Published
1977
Best Books for Young Adults

1981 WI
Removed from the Montello High School library.

1982 MI
Challenged in Flat Rock because of "objectionable" language.
Source: 11, Sept. 1981, p. 126; Sept. 1982, p. 156.

213

Briggs, Raymond.
Father Christmas.

1973
Published

1979 MI
Removed from all elementary classrooms in Holland after several parents complained that the work portrays Santa Claus as having a negative attitude toward Christmas.

1988 OR
Challenged at the Albany Public Library because it contains cursing, drinking, and a negative image of Santa Claus.
Source: 9; 11, Jan. 1980, p. 7; Jan. 1989, p. 3.

214

Brink, Andre.
A Dry White Season.

1979
Published

1979
Banned in South Africa in Sept. 1979. The ban was lifted in Nov. 1979, but Brink was branded a "malicious writer."
Source: 5, Feb. 1980, p. 73.

215

Bronstein, Leo.
El Greco.

1967
Published

1994 AZ
Retained at Maldonado Elementary School in Tucson after being challenged by parents who objected to nudity and "pornographic," "perverted," and "morbid" themes.
Source: 11, July 1994, p. 112.

216

Brooks, Bruce.
The Moves Make the Man.

1984
Published

1985
Best Books for Young Adults

1985
Newbery Honor Book

1992 CA
Removed from a San Lorenzo High School reading list after a parent complained that racist terms in the dialogue were offensive to black students.
Source: 11, Sept. 1992, pp. 140–41.

217

Brown, Claude.
Manchild in the Promised Land.

1965
Published

1974 WI
Removed from high school libraries in Waukesha.

1976 FL
Removed from high school libraries in Plant City.

1977 LA
Removed from classroom use and placed on the restricted shelf in the Baton Rouge school library after Concerned Citizens and Taxpayers for Decent Books listed the book along with 64 other "offensive" works.

1980 OH
Removed from high school libraries in North Jackson due to "filth and obscenity."

1987 OR
Challenged at the Parkrose High School because the content is "violent, the language offensive, and women are degraded." The protestors also questioned its relevance, claiming that Parkrose students have no need to understand life in a black ghetto.
Source: 8, pp. 469–70; 9; 11, May 1980, p. 51; Sept. 1987, p. 176; Nov. 1987, p. 240.

218

Brown, Dan.
The Da Vinci Code.

2003
Published

2006
Banned in Egypt. The culture minister told parliament, "We ban any book that insults any religion. We will confiscate this book." Parliament was debating the book at the request of several Coptic Christian members who demanded a ban because, "It's based on Zionist myth, and it contains insults towards Christ, and it insults the Christian religion and Islam."

2006
Banned in Iran.
Source: 11, Sept. 2006, p. 232; Jan. 2007, p. 35.

219

Brown, Dee.
Bury My Heart at Wounded Knee.

1970
Published

1971
Best Books for Young Adults

1974 WI
Removed in Wild Rose by a district administrator because the book was "slanted" and "if there's a possibility that something might be controversial, then why not eliminate it."
Source: 11, Nov. 1974, p. 145.

220

Brown, Laurene Krasny, and Marc Brown.
Dinosaurs Divorce.

1986
Published

1995 GA
Challenged at the Rebecca Minor Elementary School in Gwinnett County because the book could offend children whose parents are going through a divorce and create fears and anxiety in children from stable families.
Source: 11, Sept. 1995, p. 157.

221

Brown, Laurie Krasny, and Marc Brown.
What's the Big Secret? Talking about Sex with Girls and Boys.

1997
Published

2011 WA
Challenged, but retained, at the Oak Harbor School District No. 201 despite a parent's concern that the book discusses sex and "it's completely too graphic."
Source: 11, July 2011, p. 137.

222

Brown, Marc Tolon.
Buster's Sugartime.

2006
Published

2009 OK
Challenged, but retained, at the Union district elementary school libraries despite a parent's complaint that the book features two same-sex couples and their children.
Source: 11, Mar. 2010, pp. 53-54.

223

Browne, Sir Thomas.
Religio Medici.

1643
Published

1645
The Catholic Church placed it on the *Index Librorum Prohibitorum* (Index of Prohibited Books) in Rome, Italy, for its skeptical, rationalist perspective, and its allegiance to the Anglican Church. The book remained listed until 1966.
Source: 1, pp. 282–83.

224

Browning, Elizabeth Barrett.
Aurora Leigh.

1857
Published

1857 MA
Condemned in Boston as "the hysterical indecencies of an erotic mind."
Source: 4, p. 42.

225

Bruno, Giordano.
On the Infinite Universe and Worlds.

1584
Published

1592
Author imprisoned, tried on charges of blasphemy, immoral conduct, and heresy, and executed in Rome, Italy, on February 17, 1600. Placed on the *Index Librorum Prohibitorum* (Index of Prohibited Books) in 1603, where it remained through the last edition of the Index, in effect until 1966.
Source: 8, pp. 273–75.

226

Bryant, Sara Cone.
Epaminondas and His Auntie.

1907
Published

1989 SC
Retained, but moved from the children's section to the folk life section at the Spartanburg County Library because "the book's drawings were stereotypical and demeaning to black people."
Source: 11, Nov. 1989, pp. 236–37.

227

Budbill, David.
Bones on Black Spruce Mountain.

1978
Published

1988 VT
Challenged at the Bennington School District because of inappropriate language.

1993 PA
Challenged in the Gettysburg public schools because of offensive language.
Source: 11, Mar. 1989, p. 61; Mar. 1994, p. 55.

228

Bunch, Robert.
Invisible Marijuana and Psychedelic Mushroom Gardens.

1998
Published

2000 IL
Challenged at the Warrenville Public Library because "it provides a step-by-step manual for circumventing the law."
Source: 11, Mar. 2000, p. 48.

229

Bunn, Scott.
Just Hold On.

1982
Published

1988 WA
Banned at the Covington Junior High School in Vancouver because the book is devoid of hope and positive role models.
Source: 11, Mar. 1989, p. 61; May 1989, p. 79.

230

Bunting, Eve.
Karen Kepplewhite Is the World's Best Kisser.

1983
Published

1989 OR
Challenged at the Little Butte Intermediate School in Eagle Point because the book was too mature for the elementary class students.
Source: 11, Jan. 1990, pp. 4–5.

231
Burgess, Anthony.
A Clockwork Orange.

1962
Published

2008
Prometheus Award

1973 UT
A book seller in Orem was arrested for selling the novel. Charges were later dropped, but the book seller was forced to close the store and relocate to another city.

1976 CO
Removed from Aurora high school due to "objectionable" language.

1977 MA
Removed from high school classrooms in Westport because of "objectionable" language.

1982 AL
Removed from two Anniston high school libraries, but later reinstated on a restricted basis.
Source: 8, pp. 440–41; 11, May 1976, p. 70; Jan. 1977, p. 8; Mar. 1983, p. 37.

232
Burgess, Melvin.
Doing It.

2004
Published

2005
Best Books for Young Adults

2005 AR
Challenged in the Fayetteville High School library. The complainant also submitted a list of more than fifty books, citing the books as too sexually explicit and promoting homosexuality.
Source: 11, Sept. 2005, p. 215.

233
Burroughs, Augusten.
Running with Scissors.

2003
Published

2007 MI
Challenged in the Howell High School because of the book's strong sexual content. In response to a request from the president of the Livingston Organization for Values in Education, or LOVE, the county's top law enforcement official reviewed the books to see whether laws against distribution of sexually explicit materials to minors had been broken. "After reading the books in question, it is clear that the explicit passages illustrated a larger literary, artistic or political message and were not included solely to appeal to the prurient interests of minors," the Livingston County prosecutor wrote. "Whether these materials are appropriate for minors is a decision to be made by the school board, but I find that they are not in violation of the criminal laws."

2010 FL
Challenged as a suggested reading in a class where juniors and seniors earn college credit in Hillsborough County. Four high schools—Plant, Middleton, Hillsborough, and Bloomingdale—voted to keep the book and place a "Mature Reader" label on the front cover. Three high schools—Sickles, Robinson, and Lennard—will require parental consent. Gaither High School and Riverview High School voted to ban the book. The book was banned at Riverview because, "This book has extremely inappropriate content for a high school media center collection. The book contained explicit homosexual and heterosexual situations, profanity, underage drinking and smoking, extreme moral shortcomings, child molesters, graphic pedophile situations and total lack of negative consequences throughout the book."
Source: 11, May 2007, p. 116; May 2010, pp. 103-4.

234
Burroughs, Edgar Rice.
Tarzan.

1912
Published

1929 CA
Removed from the Los Angeles Public Library because Tarzan was allegedly living in sin with Jane.
Source: 10, p. 130.

235
Burroughs, William, and Allen Ginsberg.
The Yage Letters.

1963
Published

1976 CO
Banned from use in Aurora High School English classes on the grounds of "immorality."
Source: 11, May 1976, p. 70; May 1977, p. 79.

236
Burroughs, William.
Naked Lunch.

1959
Published

1965 MA
Found obscene in Boston Superior Court. The finding was reversed by the State Supreme Court the following year.
Source: 4, p. 89; 6, pp. 388–89; 8, p. 472.

237
Buss, Fran Leeper, and Daisy Cubias.
Journey of the Sparrows.

1991
Published

1992
Best Books for Young Adults

1994 IN
Challenged at the Carmel Junior High School because a parent objected to profanity and language dealing with urination, rape, violence, and sex. The parent also objected to the depiction of illegal immigration. The book was retained.
Source: 11, Mar. 1995, p. 43; July 1995, p. 111.

238
Butler, Dori Hillestad.
My Mom's Having a Baby.

2005
Published

2011 FL
Retained at the Hillsborough County Public Library System. The book tells of a little girl named Elizabeth who is curious about childbirth and how her mother

became pregnant. Throughout the book's thirty pages, little Elizabeth learns about these topics in great detail.

2011 TX
Challenged in the Carrollton Library because it is inappropriate for children. The book won an Editor's Choice award from *Booklist* in 2005 and was named a Top Ten Sci-Tech book for Youth by *Booklist*.
Source: 11, May 2011, pp. 95, 116.

239
Butler, William.
The Butterfly Revolution.

1961
Published

1987 KS
Challenged as a supplemental reading list at the Fort Scott High School library because the book "suggested dislike of the *Bible*, belief in atheism, vile social habits, obscene language, and plots against adult authority."
Source: 11, May 1987, p. 90.

240
Butz, Arthur R.
The Hoax of the Twentieth Century.

1976
Published

1984
Removed from the shelves of the University of Calgary library by the Royal Canadian Mounted Police. Import of the book was banned, after the university bought its copy, under a Canadian law barring import of materials considered seditious, treasonable, immoral, or indecent.

1995
Seized from the Didsbury, Alberta, Canada Public Library and shredded.
Source: 8, pp. 82–85; 11, Jan. 1985, p. 15.

241
Cabell, James Branch.
Jurgen: A Comedy of Justice.

1919
Published

1920 NY
The New York Society for the Suppression of Vice seized all plates and copies of the book and editor was charged with violating the anti-obscenity provisions of the New York State Penal Code.

1953
Banned in Ireland.
Source: 4, p. 64; 13, pp. 126–27; 15, Vol. III, pp. 412–13.

242
Cain, James M.
Serenade.

1937
Published

1949 MA
After receiving complaints from patrons of the Free Public Library in Worcester, the state attorney general ordered that copies of the novel be removed from library shelves. The case appeared before the Superior Court of Suffolk County, Massachusetts, which judged the book "not obscene." The attorney general filed an appeal with the Supreme Judicial Court where, in September 1950, the novel was cleared again in a 4-3 decision in *Attorney General v. Books Named "Serenade,"* 326 Mass. 324, 94 N.E.2d 259 (1950). In presenting the majority decision, Judge Spalding write that the sexual episodes were "not portrayed in a manner that would have a 'substantial tendency to deprave or corrupt readers by inciting lascivious thoughts or arousing lustful desires.'"
Source: 13, p. 210.

243
Calderone, Mary Steichen, and James W. Ramey.
Talking with Your Child about Sex: Questions and Answers for Children from Birth to Puberty.

1982
Published

1986 GA
The Gainesville Public Library prohibits young readers from checking out this book along with forty other books. The books, on subjects ranging from hypnosis to drug abuse to breast-feeding and sexual dysfunction, are kept in a locked room.
Source: 11, July 1986, p. 117; Sept. 1986, pp. 151–52; Nov. 1986, p. 207.

244
Caldwell, Erskine.
God's Little Acre.

1933
Published

1933 MA
Sued for obscenity but acquitted.

1947 CO
Banned in the $.25 edition to keep the book out of hands of teenage children.

1948
Banned in Ireland.

1948 PA
Seized in Philadelphia mass bookstore raid by the police and later exonerated.

1950 MA
Banned as indecent, obscene, and impure.

1960
Banned in Australia.
Source: 2, p. 148; 4, p. 83; 15, Vol. III, p. 643, Vol. IV, p. 701.

245
Caldwell, Erskine.
Tobacco Road.

1932
Published

1941
Banned from the mails.

1953
Banned in Ireland.
Source: 4, pp. 83 84.

246
Caldwell, Erskine.
Tragic Ground.

1944
Published

1944 MA
Boston Watch and Ward Society lodged a complaint with the police, claiming the novel was "obscene" and dealt with "low life matters." Miss. E. Margaret Anderson of the Dartmouth Book Stall in Boston was arrested for her "distributing obscene material." In delivering a ruling, Judge Adlow observed to the police, "It's not for me or for you to try to establish literary tastes of the community." He stated that he found the novel to be "dull," but concluded that "the judges of the Municipal Court and the members of the Police Department were not qualified to pass on the literary value of books."
Source: 13, pp. 252–53.

247
Califia-Rice, Patrick.
Sapphistry: The Book of Lesbian Sexuality.

1980
Published

1982 CA
Challenged as an "inappropriate" recommended text for college students at Long Beach State University.

1984
Seized and shredded by the British customs office.
Source: 11, Sept. 1982, p. 158; Jan. 1985, p. 16.

248
Callen, Larry.
Just-Right Family: Cabbage Patch Kids series.

1984
Published

1987 NC
Challenged at the Rutherford County Elementary School library because the book used ungrammatical writing.
Source: 11, Nov. 1987, p. 239.

249
Calvin, John.
Civil and Canonical Law.

1542
Published

1542
Forbidden by the Sorbonne in Paris, France, as containing "false doctrine against the Catholic faith."

1555
Banned in England for "containing false doctrine against the Catholic faith."

1559
Listed as heresy in the *Index Librorum Prohibitorum* (List of Prohibited Books) in Rome, Italy.
Source: 4, p. 14.

250
Cameron, Paul.
Exposing the AIDS Scandal.

1988
Published

1990 IL
Challenged at the Downers Grove Public Library because it is factually inaccurate and promotes common fallacies related to the disease.
Source: 11, Mar. 1991, p. 61.

251
Canaday, John.
The Artist as Visionary.

1958
Published

1994 AZ
Retained at Maldonado Elementary School in Tucson after being challenged by parents who objected to nudity and "pornographic," "perverted," and "morbid" themes.
Source: 11, July 1994, p. 112.

252
Canaday, John.
Painting in Transition: Precursors of Modern Art.

1959
Published

1994 AZ
Retained at Maldonado Elementary School in Tucson after being challenged by parents who objected to nudity and "pornographic," "perverted," and "morbid" themes.
Source: 11, July 1994, p. 112.

253
Capote, Truman.
In Cold Blood: A True Account of a Multiple Murder and Its Consequences.

1966
Published

2000 GA
Banned, but later reinstated after community protests at the Windsor Forest High School in Savannah. The controversy began in early 1999 when a parent complained about sex, violence, and profanity in the book that was part of an Advanced Placement English class.

2011 CA
Some Glendale Unified School District officials and parents attempted to block a request by a high school English teacher to add the text to the district's advanced English curriculum because the nonfiction book was "too violent for a young audience;" the school board voted 4-0 to approve the book for Advanced Placement students. Since its publication in 1965, it has been widely recognized as a seminal work in American literature, frequently appearing on high school and college reading lists.
Source: 11, Mar. 2001, p. 76; Nov. 2011, p. 204; Jan. 2012, pp. 35-36.

254
Card, Orson Scott.
Ender's Game.

1985
Published

1985
Best Books for Young Adults

1985
Nebula Award for Best Novel

1986
Hugo Award for Best Novel

2012 SC
A teacher at Schofield Middle School in Aiken will not face criminal charges for reading to his students from the science-fiction book. In addition to the Card novel, which has won several science-fiction awards and is listed on numerous children's literary review websites as appropriate for children twelve and older, the teacher read excerpts from an Agatha Christie novel and a young adult novel set in the Old West, officials said. The incident came to light after the materials were characterized by one student and one parent as pornographic, according to a press release issued by the school district.
Source: 11, May 2012, p. 107.

255
Carle, Eric.
Draw Me a Star.

1992
Published

1996 WA
This children's book dealing with the creation story was challenged in the elementary school libraries in the Edmonds School District because the book is illustrated with highly stylized representations of a naked woman and man.

1999 NY
Challenged, but retained, in the Dorothy B. Bunce Elementary School library in Pavilion despite a parent's objection to a collage picture of a naked man and woman representing Adam and Eve.

Source: 11, Nov. 1996, pp. 211–12; May 1999, pp. 83–84.

256
Carpenter, Edward.
Iolaus: An Anthology of Friendship.

1902
Published

1984
Seized by the British Customs Office as "indecent and obscene." When first published in London, England, the book was not suppressed.

Source: 11, Jan. 1985, p. 16.

257
Carroll, Jim.
The Basketball Diaries.

1978
Published

1998 GA
Challenged, but retained, at the Gwinnett County Library after the county solicitor declined to give a legal opinion on whether the book is harmful to minors. The library board had voted 2-1 to ban the book if the solicitor found the book meets the state's legal definition of harmful to minors.

Source: 11, Sept. 1998, pp. 139–40; Nov. 1998, p. 191; Jan. 1999, p. 19.

258
Carroll, Lewis.
Alice's Adventures in Wonderland.

1865
Published

1931
Banned in China on the ground that "Animals should not use human language, and that it was disastrous to put animals and human beings on the same level."

Source: 4, p. 49.

259
Cart, Michael.
My Father's Scar.

1996
Published

1997
Best Books for Young Adults

2004 TX
Challenged at the Montgomery County Memorial Library System along with fifteen other young-adult books with gay-positive themes. The objections were posted at the Library Patrons of Texas website. The language describing the books is similar to that posted at the website of the Fairfax County, Virginia-based Parents Against Bad Books in Schools, to which Library Patrons of Texas links.

Source: 11, Nov. 2004, pp. 231–32.

260
Carter, Alden R.
Sheila's Dying.

1987
Published

1987
Best Books for Young Adults

1992 NJ
Restricted to those in the eighth grade or above at the Pitman Middle School library because the book promotes teenage stealing, drinking, profanity, and premarital sex.

Source: 11, July 1992, p. 106; Jan. 1993, p. 27.

261
Carter, Forrest.
The Education of Little Tree.

1976
Published

1995 OR
Challenged, but retained, at the Astoria Elementary School. The complainants wanted the book removed because it includes profanity, mentions sex, and portrays Christians as "liars, cheats and child molesters."

Source: 11, Jan. 1996, p. 17; Mar. 1996, p. 64.

262
Carter, Jimmy.
Keeping Faith: Memoirs of a President.

1982
Published

1983
Banned from the 1983 Moscow, Russia International Book Fair along with more than fifty other books because it is "anti-Soviet."

Source: 11, Nov. 1983, p. 201.

263
Carter, Judy.
The Homo Handbook: Getting in Touch with Your Inner Homo.

1996
Published

2005 AR
Challenged in the Fayetteville High School library. The complainant also submitted a list of more than fifty books, citing the books as too sexually explicit and promoting homosexuality.

Source: 11, Sept. 2005, p. 215.

264
Carus, Marianne.
What Joy Awaits You.

1977
Published

1988 UT
The Utah State Textbook Commission declined to remove this elementary school book from its list of approved texts. The book contains essays by Plymouth settler John Smith and early American writer Washington Irving which refer to Indians as "savages" and "bloodthirsty" and was branded as racist and demeaning to contemporary Indian people.

Source: 11, May 1988, p. 104.

265
Casanova de Seingalt, Giovanni Giacomo.
Mémoires (History of My Life).

1826-38
Published

1820
Original manuscript confined to the German publisher's safe and never published in unexpurgated form until the twentieth century.

1834
Placed on the *Index Librorum Prohibitorum*

(Index of Prohibited Books) in Rome, Italy.

1863
Condemned in France.

1933
Banned in Ireland.

1935
Banned by Mussolini in Italy.

1943 MI
Seized by police in Detroit.
Source: 4, p. 31.

266
Casey, Bernie.
Look at the People.

1969
Published

1980 NC
Removed from the Southport school libraries due to inappropriate words and ideas.
Source: 11, Sept. 1980, p. 100.

267
Cashdan, Linda.
It's Only Love.

1992
Published

1994 OR
Expurgated by an apparent self-appointed censor at the Coquille Public Library along with several other books. Most were mysteries and romances in which single words and sexually explicit passages were whited out by a vandal who left either dots or solid ink pen lines where the words had been.
Source: 11, Sept. 1994, p. 148.

268
Cast, P. C., and Kristin Cast.
House of Night series.

2007
Published

2009 TX
Banned at Henderson Junior High School in the Stephenville Independent School District. The entire teen vampire series was banned for sexual content and nudity. Since the series has not been completed, "Stephenville ISD actually banned books that have not yet been published and

perhaps even books that have yet to be written. There is no way the district could know the content of these books, and yet they have been banned."
Source: 11, Nov. 2009, pp. 197-98, 225.

269
Cast, P.C., and Kristin Cast.
Betrayed.

2007
Published

2011 AK
Challenged in the North Star Borough School District, Fairbanks high school libraries because, "It simply causes kids to think even more of things sexual." The teenage vampire novel is part two of the "House of Night" series.
Source: 11, May 2011, p. 93

270
Cavendish, Richard, ed.
Man, Myth and Magic: Illustrated Encyclopedia of Mythology, Religion and the Unknown.

1970
Published

1986 CA
Challenged by the "God Squad," a group of three students and their parents, at the El Camino High School in Oceanside because the book "glorified the devil and the occult." The debate evoked interest in witchcraft books in other Oceanside school libraries.
Source: 11, Sept. 1986, p. 151; Nov. 1986, p. 224; Jan. 1987, p. 9.

271
Cervantes Saavedra, Miguel de.
Don Quixote.

1605-16
Published

1640
Placed on the Index in Madrid, Spain, for one sentence: "Works of charity negligently performed are of no worth."

1981
The Chilean military junta banned the novel for supporting individual freedom and attacking authority.
Source: 1, pp. 83–84; 4, p. 16

272
Chamberlain, Wilt.
Wilt.

1973
Published

1975 MI
Banned from the Gaylord Middle School library because pupils "are more interested in learning how to dribble and shoot" than in his off-court activities.
Source: 9; 11, Sept. 1975, p. 138.

273
Chambers, Aidan.
Dance on My Grave: A Life and Death in Four Parts.

1982
Published

1983
Best Books for Young Adults

1993 OR
Challenged at the Deschutes County Library in Bend because it "encourages and condones" homosexuality.

2004 TX
Challenged at the Montgomery County Memorial Library System along with fifteen other young-adult books with gay-positive themes. The objections were posted at the Library Patrons of Texas website. The language describing the books is similar to that posted at the website of the Fairfax County, Virginia-based Parents Against Bad Books in Schools, to which Library Patrons of Texas links.
Source: 11, Sept. 1993, pp. 158–59; Nov. 2004, pp. 231–32.

274
Chapman, Robert L.
New Dictionary of American Slang.

1986
Published

1994 MI
Labeled and restricted at the Walled Lake School District in Commerce Township because "This book contains words which might be offensive to the reader."
Source: 11, Sept. 1994, pp. 146–47.

275

Charyn, Jerome.
Billy Budd, KGB.

1991
Published

1992 AK

Challenged at the Noel Wien Library in Fairbanks because it was too sexually explicit and violent.

Source: 11, Sept. 1992, p. 161; Nov. 1992, p. 196.

276

Chaucer, Geoffrey.
Canterbury Tales.

1387-1400
Published

1908

"Expurgated almost from its first appearance in America, and was still being subjected to revisions as late as 1928. Even editions available today and considered otherwise acceptable avoid some four-letter words."

1995 IL

Removed from a senior college preparatory literature course at the Eureka High School because some parents thought the sexual content of some of the tales was not appropriate for the students.

Source: 8, pp. 426–28; 11, Nov. 1995, p. 185; Jan. 1996 p. 14; 15, Vol. II, p. 617.

277

Chbosky, Stephen.
The Perks of Being a Wallflower.

1999
Published

2000
Best Books for Young Adults

2002 VA

Challenged, along with seventeen other titles in the Fairfax County elementary and secondary libraries, by a group called Parents Against Bad Books in Schools. The group contends the books "contain profanity and descriptions of drug abuse, sexually explicit conduct, and torture."

2003 NY

Removed as a reading assignment in an elective sociology course at the Massapequa High School because of its "offensive" content.

2004 TX

Challenged at the Montgomery County Memorial Library System along with fifteen other young-adult books with gay-positive themes. The objections were posted at the Library Patrons of Texas website. The language describing the books is similar to that posted at the website of the Fairfax County, Virginia-based Parents Against Bad Books in Schools, to which Library Patrons of Texas links.

2005 AZ

Arizona Superintendent of Public Instruction sent a letter to charter schools and public school principals and district superintendents asking them to make sure that the book is no longer available to minors or any other students. The book contains numerous sexual references, including a scene where a girl is forced to have oral sex with a boy during a party.

2005 WI

Retained in the Arrowhead High School curriculum in Merton. Reading the book was optional and parents could choose to have their children read something else.

2006 IL

Retained on the Northwest Suburban High School District 214 reading list in Arlington Heights, along with eight other challenged titles. A board member, elected amid promises to bring her Christian beliefs into all board decision-making, raised the controversy based on excerpts from the books she'd found on the Internet. Chbosky's novel, which contains references to masturbation, homosexuality, and bestiality, got the bulk of the criticism.

2007 NY

Challenged on the Commack High School summer reading list because the novel contains a two-page date rape scene. Educators in Commack revamped their reading list after finding students weren't interested in the choices and Chbosky's novel was added to attract "reluctant readers."

2008 IN

Removed from Portage High School classrooms for topics such as homosexuality, drug use, and sexual behavior. The novel chronicles the freshman year of high school of a young man struggling with awkwardness and the changing world around him.

2009 OH

Challenged on Wyoming high school district's suggested reading list. The book contains frank and sometimes explicit descriptions of sex, drugs, suicide, and masturbation.

2009 VA

Restricted at the William Byrd and Hidden Valley high schools in Roanoke to juniors and seniors. Freshmen and sophomores, however, will need parental permission to check out the book.

2009 WI

Challenged at the West Bend Community Memorial Library as being "obscene or child pornography" in a section designated "Young Adults." The library board unanimously voted 9–0 to maintain, "without removing, relocating, labeling, or otherwise restricting access," the book in the young adult section at the West Bend Community Memorial Library. The vote was a rejection of a four-month campaign conducted by the citizen's group West Bend Citizens for Safe Libraries to move fiction and nonfiction books with sexually explicit passages from the young-adult section to the adult section and label them as containing sexual material.

2011 NY

Challenged, but retained, at the Clarkstown North High School despite a parent's complaint about the teen coming-of-age novel, which deals graphically with teenage sex, homosexuality, and bestiality.

2012 OH

Challenged as an assigned reading at the Grandview Heights High School because the book deals with drugs, alcohol, sex, homosexuality, and abuse.

2013 FL

Challenged on a summer reading list for incoming freshmen at Wharton High School in Tampa because "it deals with sexual situations and drug use."

2013 IL

Removed from eighth-grade classrooms at Hadley Junior High School in Glen Ellyn because of concerns about sexually explicit content and language. In June, the Glen Ellyn Elementary District 41 School Board overturned the decision and returned the book to the library shelves. Most board members were willing to reinstate the book after assurances from district administrators that a revised parental notification letter would be sent at the start of each school year warning parents that their children could be getting access to sometimes mature content in classroom libraries. The coming-of-age tale is about an introspective fifteen-year-old high school freshman who writes letters to an anonymous friend. Intelligent beyond his years, he is an unconventional thinker; yet, as the story begins, Charlie is also shy and unpopular. In 2012, a film adaptation of the novel was released to positive critical response and commercial success. The film won numerous awards.

Source: 11, Jan. 2003, p. 10; Jan. 2004, pp. 12–13; Nov. 2004, pp. 231–32; Jan. 2005, p. 11; May 2005, pp. 111–12; Jan. 2006, p. 9; July 2006, pp. 210–11; Sept. 2007, pp. 184-85; Jan. 2009, pp. 8-9; May 2009, pp. 80-81; Sept. 2009, pp. 169-70; Nov. 2009, pp. 202-3; Jan. 2010, pp. 13-14; May 2011, pp. 97-98; July 2011, p. 161; Jan. 2013, pp. 11-12; July 2013, pp. 143-44; Sept. 2013, pp. 184, 201.

278
Chelminski, Rudolph.
Paris.

1977
Published

1981 FL
Nine pages, depicting Parisian nightlife and showing pictures of nude dancers, were removed by the Indian River County school superintendent.

Source: 9; 11, Mar. 1982, p. 43.

279
Chevalier, Tracy.
Girl with a Pearl Earring.

1999
Published

2001
Alex Award

2001
Best Books for Young Adults

2006
Banned in Iran. "The new government intends to take positive steps for reviving neglected values and considering religious teachings in the cultural field." *The New York Times* bestselling novel was made into an Oscar-nominated film.

Source: 11, Jan. 2007, p. 35.

280
Chick, Jack T.
Big Betrayal.

1981
Published

1981
Banned in Canada.

1981 NJ
Challenged in New Jersey as immoral and indecent anti-Catholic literature.

Source: 11, Jan. 1982, pp. 24–25.

281
Chick, Jack T.
Double-Cross.

1981
Published

1981
Banned in Canada.

1981 NJ
Challenged in New Jersey as immoral and indecent anti-Catholic literature.

Source: 11, Jan. 1982, pp. 24-25.

282
Childress, Alice.
A Hero Ain't Nothin' but a Sandwich.

1973
Published

1973
Best Books for Young Adults

1974
Coretta Scott King Author Honor Book

1974
National Book Award for Young People's Literature

1976 NY
Removed from Island Trees School Union Free District High School library in 1976 along with nine other titles because they were considered "immoral, anti-American, anti-Christian, or just plain filthy." Returned to the library after the U.S. Supreme Court ruling on June 25, 1982, in *Board of Education, Island Trees Union Free School District No. 26 et al. v. Pico et al.*, 457 U.S. 853 (1982).

1978 GA
Removed from the Savannah school libraries due to "objectionable" language.

1978 TX
Removed from the San Antonio high school libraries due to "objectionable" passages, but later reinstated after teachers filed a grievance in protest.

1994 MD
Challenged at the Aberdeen High School in Bel Air because the novel is "racist and vulgar."

1994 SC
Challenged at the Lamar Elementary School library in Darlington by a parent who stated that "offensive language in the book makes it unsuitable for any children."

Source: 11, Sept. 1978, p. 123; Nov. 1982, p. 197; July 1978, p. 87; May 1994, p. 85; Jan. 1995, p. 12.

283
Childress, Alice.
Rainbow Jordan.

1981
Published

1981
Best Books for Young Adults

1982
Coretta Scott King Author Honor Book

1986 GA
Challenged at the Gwinnett County public schools because of "foul language and sexual references."

1986 WA
Banned from Spokane middle schools because the book's storyline about a prostitute's daughter was "too mature."

Source: 11, Mar. 1987, p. 65; July 1998, p. 110.

284
Chomsky, Noam, and Edward S. Herman.
Manufacturing Consent: The Political Economy of the Mass Media.

1988
Published

2006
The Turkish Chief Public Prosecution Office in Ankara decided to prosecute two publishers that released the book because it "degrades the Turkish identity and the Turkish Republic, and fuels hatred and discrimination among the people." The publishers could face up to six years in prison if found guilty.

Source: 11, Sept. 2006, p. 234.

285
Chopin, Kate.
The Awakening.

1899
Published

2006 IL
Retained on the Northwest Suburban High School District 214 reading list in Arlington Heights, along with eight other challenged titles. A board member, elected amid promises to bring her Christian beliefs into all board decision-making, raised the controversy based on excerpts from the books she'd found on the Internet. First published in 1899, this novel so disturbed critics and the public that it was banished for decades afterward.

2011 GA
Challenged at the Oconee County Library because the cover of the book—a novel about a woman whose desires run against the family structure of the 1890s—shows a painting of a woman's bare chest and upset the patron.
Source: 11, July 2006, pp. 210-11; Jan. 2011, p. 7.

286
Christelow, Eileen.
Jerome and the Witchcraft Kids.

1988
Published

1991 KS
Challenged, but retained, in the Wichita public schools because it promotes witchcraft.
Source: 11, Jan. 1992, p. 26.

287
Christensen, James C., Renwick St. James, and Alan Dean Foster.
Voyage of the Basset.

1996
Published

2006 UT
Retained in the Davis County Library. The complainant objected to the book after her five-year-old son borrowed it from the children's section and showed her the illustrations it contains of topless mermaids and other partially clothed mythical creatures. The author is a retired Brigham Young University art professor and cochair of the Mormon Arts Foundation.
Source: 11, Nov. 2006, p. 319.

288
Christopher, John.
The Prince in Waiting.

1970
Published

1988 OR
Challenged at the Canby junior high school library because it promotes "positive attitudes toward the occult and ridicule toward Christianity."
Source: 11, May 1989, p. 78.

289
Christopher, Matt.
The Kid Who Only Hit Homers.

1972
Published

1989 OR
Challenged at the Beaverton School District because the book mentions the occult, witchcraft, and astrology.
Source: 11, Jan. 1990, pp. 4–5.

290
Chute, Carolyn.
The Beans of Egypt.

1985
Published

1996 ME
Challenged at the Oxford Hills High School in Paris. A parent stated that "teachers are not qualified to explore the issues of rape, incest, suicide and mental illness contained in Chute's novel."
Source: 11, Nov. 1996, p. 212.

291
Clancy, Tom.
The Hunt for Red October.

1984
Published

1997 WV
Removed from the Jackson County school libraries along with sixteen other titles.
Source: 11, Jan. 1998, p. 13.

292
Clapp, Patricia.
Witches' Children: A Story of Salem.

1982
Published

1982
Best Books for Young Adults

1990 MD
Challenged at Cannon Road Elementary School library in Silver Spring because students who read it will be encouraged "to dabble with the occult."

1991 MD
Challenged at the Howard County schools because the book was "not appropriate positive pleasurable reading for the young age group."
Source: 11, Mar. 1991, p. 43; Mar. 1992, p. 40.

293
Clark, Mary Higgins.
I'll Be Seeing You.

1993
Published

1994 PA
Challenged at the Big Spring School in Carlisle.
Source: 11, Mar. 1995, p. 56.

294
Clark, Walter Van Tilburg.
The Ox-Bow Incident.

1940
Published

1980 IL
Challenged in Johnston City "because of the profanity and the use of God's name in vain."
Source: 11, Sept. 1980, p. 107.

295
Clauser, Suzanne.
A Girl Named Sooner.

1972
Published

1988 CO
Removed from the Stott Elementary School library in Arvada after a parent complained that its graphic sex scenes make it inappropriate for children.

1991 OR
Removed by decision of the school board

from the library at the Jefferson Middle School because of its explicit sexual content.

Source: 11, July 1988, p. 119; July 1992, p. 103.

296
Clavell, James.
Shogun.

1975
Published

2002 VA
Challenged, along with seventeen other titles in the Fairfax County elementary and secondary libraries, by a group called Parents Against Bad Books in Schools. The group contends the books "contain profanity and descriptions of drug abuse, sexually explicit conduct, and torture."

Source: 11, Jan. 2003, p. 10.

297
Cleaver, Eldridge.
Soul on Ice.

1968
Published

1968
Best Books for Young Adults

1969 CA
Barred from elective courses on black studies by California Superintendent of Instruction.

1973 CT
Challenged, but retained, in the Ridgefiled senior high school ethnic studies class.

1975 CT
Challenged at the Greenwich High School library because the book is "crime provoking and anti-American as well as obscene and pornographic."

1976 NY
Removed from Island Trees Union Free School District High School library in 1976 along with nine other titles because they were considered "immoral, anti-American, anti-Christian, or just plain filthy." Returned to the library after the U.S. Supreme Court ruling on June 25, 1982, in *Board of Education, Island Trees Union Free School District No. 26 et al. v. Pico et al.,* 457 U.S. 853 (1982).

1979 WA
Challenged at Omak due to "profane language."

Source: 4, p. 100; 11, May 1975, p. 87; July 1979, p. 75; Nov. 1982, p. 197; 14, pp. 260–61.

298
Cleland, John.
Fanny Hill.

1748
Published

1749
Author imprisoned on the orders of the British secretary of state on a charge of "corrupting the King's subjects."

1821 MA
Banned in Massachusetts in the first known U.S. obscenity case.

1963 NJ
The highest court in New Jersey declared it obscene.

1965
Seized and burned in Japan.

1965
Seized in Berlin, Germany.

1965
Burned in Manchester.

Source: 4, p. 29; 6, pp. 533-34; 8, pp. 330-32; 15, Vol. I, pp. 561–62, Vol. II, p. 610.

299
Clerc, Charles, and Louis Leiter, ed.
Seven Contemporary Short Novels.

1969
Published

1999 OR
Removed from the Baker City High School language arts program because of two selections in the book. *The Bluest Eye,* by Toni Morrison, includes a description of a father raping his eleven-year-old daughter. *Being There,* by Jerzy Kosinski, includes descriptions of sexual relations.

Source: 11, May 1999, p. 70.

300
Clinton, Cathryn.
A Stone in My Hand.

2002
Published

2003 FL
Challenged, but retained, in the Marion County Public Library System in Ocala despite a complaint that the subject matter was too mature and the book "was written one-sidedly, specifically showing one party to be fully wrong." Reviewers noted that the book is told from a Muslim perspective and that it can be taken to be anti-Israel. An Ocala resident noted that "this book will help further hatred of Jews, anti-Semitism, and hatred of Israel, on the part of children, the target audience."

Source: 11, Nov. 2003, pp. 227–28; Jan. 2004, pp. 7–8; Mar. 2004, pp. 47–48.

301
Close, Robert S.
Love Me Sailor.

1945
Published

1945
Politicians, churchmen, and civic leaders denounced the book as likely to corrupt the morals of young; and librarians publicly burned copies in Australia.

Source: 6, p. 535.

302
Clunis, D. Merilee, and G. Dorsey Green.
Lesbian Couple.

1988
Published

1990 IA
Challenged at the Muscatine Public Library because it is "wrong to promote immorality."

Source: 11, Nov. 1990, p. 225.

303
Clutton-Brock, Juliet.
Horse.

1992
Published

2004 MT
Challenged, but retained, at the Smith Elementary School in Helena despite a parent's concern that it "promotes evolution."

Source: 11, May 2004, p. 97; July 2004, p. 157.

304

Cody, Robin.
Ricochet River.

1992
Published

2000 OR
Retained by the West Linn-Wilsonville School Board in Wilsonville despite objections that the book contains explicit depictions of teenage sexual encounters without explanation of the consequences.
Source: 11, Jan. 2001, p. 36.

305

Cohen, Barbara.
Unicorns in the Rain.

1980
Published

1980
Best Books for Young Adults

1986 CO
Challenged at the Jefferson County school library because the book "puts too much emphasis on drugs and sex."
Source: 11, Jan. 1987, p. 10; Mar. 1987, p. 49.

306

Cohen, Daniel.
Curses, Hexes and Spells.

1974
Published

1986 TN
Placed on restricted status at the Claxton Elementary School library because the book "contains satanic themes."

1989 OK
Removed from the Cleveland middle school libraries because witchcraft is a "religion" and the First Amendment bars the teaching of religion in schools.

1990 MD
Removed from elementary school libraries in Howard County because it is virtual "how-to" manual on demon worship.

1997 TX
Removed from the Kirby Junior High School in Wichita Falls because of "Satanic" themes.
Source: 11, Mar. 1987, p. 50; July 1989, p. 128; Jan. 1991, pp. 11–12; July 1997, p. 95.

307

Cohen, Daniel.
Ghostly Warnings.

1996
Published

1999 NE
Challenged, but retained, at the Hastings Public Library along with forty other books on the topics of witches, magic, the zodiac, fortune telling, and ghost stories (most of the Dewey Decimal category 133.47). The books were called "demonic" and unsuitable for young children.
Source: 11, May 1999, p. 66; July 1999, p. 104.

308

Cohen, Daniel.
The Headless Roommate and Other Tales of Terror.

1980
Published

1993 NJ
Restricted from fourth and fifth graders at the Old Turnpike School in Tewksbury Township because of its violence.
Source: 11, July 1993, p. 100.

309

Cohen, Daniel.
Phantom Animals.

1991
Published

1999 NE
Challenged, but retained, at the Hastings Public Library along with forty other books on the topics of witches, magic, the zodiac, fortune telling, and ghost stories (most of the Dewey Decimal category 133.47). The books were called "demonic" and unsuitable for young children.
Source: 11, May 1999, p. 66; July 1999, p. 104.

310

Cohen, Daniel.
The Restless Dead: Ghostly Tales from Around the World.

1984
Published

1989 OR
Challenged at the Ochoco Elementary School in Prineville because the book is "totally preoccupied with the macabre, occult, and demonic activity."
Source: 11, Jan. 1990, pp. 4–5.

311

Cohen, Daniel.
Southern Fried Rat and Other Gruesome Tales.

1983
Published

1991 MD
Challenged at the Matthew Henson Middle School in Waldorf because the collection of folktales contains stories involving unusual violence and humorous anecdotes of drug use in school and ways for students to cheat on exams.
Source: 11, July 1991, p. 129.

312

Cohen, Daniel.
The World's Most Famous Ghosts.

1978
Published

2002 KY
Proposed for removal, along with more than fifty other books, from the high school library in Russell Springs by a teachers' prayer group.
Source: 11, May 2002, p. 116.

313

Cohen, Susan, and Daniel Cohen.
When Someone You Know Is Gay.

1989
Published

1990
Best Books for Young Adults

1998 WI
Removed from the Barron School District because the 1992 data is outdated. The ACLU of Wisconsin filed suit against the school district on February 16, 1999. The books were then returned to the library while a federal court considered the lawsuit. On October 8, 1999, it was agreed that the book will remain available to students as part of the school district's settlement of the federal lawsuit.
Source: 11, Jan. 1999, p. 9; Mar. 1999, p. 37; May 1999, p. 68; Jan. 2000, p. 28.

314
Colasanti, Susane.
When It Happens.

2008
Published

2013 IL
Challenged, but retained, in the teen section of the Helen Matthes Library in Effingham despite concerns that the content is too explicit.

Source: 11, Mar. 2013, p. 79.

315
Cole, Babette.
Mommy Laid an Egg.

1994
Published

1998 MO
Moved from the children's section to the adult section of the Camden County Library because the book explains the birth process from conception to delivery.

Source: 11, Mar. 1998, p. 40.

316
Cole, Brock.
The Goats.

1987
Published

1987
Best Books for Young Adults

1992 WA
Removed from the Housel Middle School library in Prosser because it contains a passage describing the rescue of a naked girl.

1994 NH
Challenged at the Timberland Regional Middle School in Plaistow because parents said it contained "offensive and inappropriate" language for seventh graders.

1997 IN
Challenged in the Vigo County School District classrooms and libraries because the book is "morally offensive and inappropriate for middle school students." In November 1997, the Vigo County School Corporation committee affirmed that the novel is appropriate for use by middle and high school students in classrooms and libraries.

2000 NH
Challenged in the Londonderry schools because "it's sexuality that drive the book." The book was eventually returned to the library and curriculum.

Source: 8, pp. 340–41; 11, Mar. 1993, p. 43; Jan. 1995, p. 25; Jan. 1998, p. 11; Mar. 1998, p. 55.

317
Cole, Joanna.
Asking about Sex and Growing Up.

1988
Published

1994 AK
Challenged, but retained, in Anchorage School District elementary school libraries after the school board voted to "retain the book despite complaints that it is inappropriate for elementary school children and teaches values opposed to those of the majority of parents."

Source: 11, May 1994, p. 97.

318
Cole, Joanna.
Bony-Legs.

1983
Published

1986 CO
Challenged at the Jefferson County school library because the book deals with subjects such as "witchcraft, cannibalism, and white magic."

Source: 11, Mar. 1987, p. 49.

319
Cole, Joanna.
How You Were Born.

1984
Published

1987 WA
Placed on restricted shelves at the Evergreen School District elementary school libraries in Vancouver in accordance with the school board policy to restrict student access to sex education books in elementary school libraries.

Source: 11, May 1987, p. 87.

320
Cole, Joanna.
I'm Mad at You.

1978
Published

1988 MO
Placed on "restricted access" at the North Kansas City elementary schools because "some children might not understand the book's use of humor and sarcasm."

Source: 11, July 1988, p. 121; Sept. 1988, pp. 151–52.

321
Cole, Joanna.
A Snake's Body.

1981
Published

1988 OR
Challenged at the Multnomah County Library in Portland because the photographs of a python crushing and eating a chick would upset and sadden children.

Source: 11, Jan. 1990, pp. 4–5.

322
Cole, William.
Oh, That's Ridiculous!

1972
Published

1990 OH
Challenged as inappropriate for children and kept off the Mansfield school library shelves for over a year after a complaint against it got lost in the shuffle of a school system reorganization. It was returned to open access in January when the Board of Education voted to retain the title.

Source: 11, May 1990, p. 106.

323
Colfer, Eoin.
The Supernaturalist.

2004
Published

2008 NY
Restored by the Lackawanna School Board along with several other books following accusations of censorship by some parents and teachers. The books were pulled from the middle school

library recommended list because of concerns that the books deal with the occult.

Source: 11, May 2008, pp. 115-16.

324
Collen, Lindsey.
The Rape of Sita.

1993
Published

1993
Banned by the Mauritian government and temporarily withdrawn by its publisher after protests by Hindu fundamentalists. Won a 1994 Commonwealth Writers Prize for the best book from Africa.

Source: 1, pp. 277–78.

325
Collier, James Lincoln, and Christopher Collier.
Jump Ship to Freedom.

1981
Published

1993 VA
Removed from the Fairfax County elementary school libraries because its young black hero, a slave, questions his own intelligence, refers to himself as a "nigger," and is called that by other characters.

1996 IL
Challenged at the Nathan Hale Middle School in Crestwood because it "was damaging to the self-esteem of young black students."

Source: 11, July 1993, pp. 102–3; Sept. 1993, p. 146; Jan. 1994, p. 13; Mar. 1997, p. 39.

326
Collier, James Lincoln, and Christopher Collier.
My Brother Sam Is Dead.

1974
Published

1975
National Book Award for Young People's Literature

1975
Newbery Honor Book

1984 GA
Challenged at the Gwinnett County school libraries because some of its characters

use profanity. An abridged version with the profanity deleted has been substituted in the elementary school libraries.

1989 OH
Removed from the curriculum of fifth grade classes in New Richmond because the book contained the words "bastard," "goddamn," and "hell" and did not represent "acceptable ethical standards for fifth graders."

1991 SC
Challenged in the Greenville County Schools because the book uses the name of God and Jesus in a "vain and profane manner along with inappropriate sexual references."

1993 KS
Challenged at the Walnut Elementary School in Emporia by parents who said that it contained profanity and graphic violence.

1994 CA
Removed from fifth grade classes at Bryant Ranch Elementary School in the Placentia-Yorba Linda Unified School District because "the book is not G-rated. Offensive language is offensive language. Graphic violence is graphic violence, no matter what the context."

1994 PA
Challenged, but retained, at the Palmyra area schools due to profanity and violence.

1996 CA
Retained in the Antioch elementary school libraries after a parent complained about the novel's profanity and violence.

1996 CO
Challenged in the Jefferson County Public Schools in Lakewood because of "the persistent usage of profanity" in the book, as well as references to rape, drinking, and battlefield violence.

1998 VA
Challenged at the McSwain Elementary School in Staunton because of "bad language."

1998 VA
Challenged as a gifted fifth-grade student assignment in Tucker-Capps Elementary School in Hampton because the book uses vulgar and profane language and contains scenes of graphic violence.

2000 IL
Challenged in the fifth-grade Oak Brook Butler District 53 curriculum because of violence and inappropriate language.

2009 GA
Retained in all Muscogee County elementary school libraries, despite a parent's concerns about profanity in the book.

Source: 8, pp. 136–37; 11, Sept. 1983, p. 139; Mar. 1990, p. 48; July 1991, p. 129; July 1993, pp. 126–27; Sept. 1994, p. 149; Nov. 1994, p. 190; Jan. 1995, p. 26; July 1996, p. 121; Jan. 1997, p. 25; July 1998, p. 110; Mar. 1999, p. 40; Mar. 2000, p. 49; May 2009, p. 93.

327
Collier, James Lincoln, and Christopher Collier.
War Comes to Willy Freeman.

1983
Published

1994 MN
Removed from the Nettleton Math and Science Magnet School in Duluth because of objections to the book's portrayal of African American characters as demeaning and claims that use of the word "nigger" in the text led students to use it outside the classroom.

1996 IL
Pulled from two classes at Western Avenue School in Flossmoor after a parent complained that the book "represents totally poor judgment, a complete lack of racial sensitivity and is totally inappropriate for fifth-graders. This book is an education in racism, a primer for developing prejudice."

Source: 11, Sept. 1994, pp. 150-51; Jan. 1997, p. 9.

328
Collier, James Lincoln, and Christopher Collier.
With Every Drop of Blood.

1994
Published

1997 SC
Challenged at the Lonnie B. Nelson Elementary School in Columbia because passages considered racist were "inappropriate for fifth grade."

2000 IL
Challenged in the fifth-grade Oak Brook Butler District 53 curriculum because the book contains racial slurs.

Source: 11, July 1997, p. 94; Mar. 2000, p. 49.

329
Collignon, Jeff.
Her Monster.

1992
Published

1997 SC
Removed from the Lakeview Middle School library in Greenville by the school district administrator because the book's sexual content "is inappropriate for middle school students."
Source: 11, May 1997, pp. 61–62.

330
Collins, Jackie.
Lovers and Gamblers.

1977
Published

1988
Destroyed in Beijing, China, and legal authorities threatened to bring criminal charges against the publishers.
Source: 11, Jan. 1989, p. 15.

331
Collins, Jim.
Unidentified Flying Objects.

1977
Published

1984 FL
Challenged at the Escambia County School District because the complainant claimed the book indicated that "Ezekiel had seen a UFO when he spoke in the Bible about seeing something that looked like a wheel in the sky."
Source: 11, Sept. 1984, p. 156.

332
Collins, Suzanne.
The Hunger Games.

2008
Published

2009
Best Books for Young Adults

2010 NH
Challenged and presented to the Goffstown school board by a parent claiming that it gave her eleven-year-old nightmares and could numb other students to the effects of violence.
Source: 11, Jan. 2011, pp. 10–11.

333
Colman, Hila.
Diary of a Frantic Kid Sister.

1973
Published

1982 TX
Removed from the Hurst-Euless-Bedford School District libraries because the book uses the word "intercourse."
Source: 9; 11, May 1982, p. 84.

334
Coman, Carolyn.
Tell Me Everything.

1993
Published

1997 WV
Removed from the Jackson County school libraries along with sixteen other titles.
Source: 11, Jan. 1998, p. 13.

335
Comfort, Alex, and Jane Comfort.
The Facts of Love.

1980
Published

1981 KS
Challenged in Great Bend Public Library.

1982 ID
Challenged at the Boise Public Library.
Source: 11, Nov. 1981, p. 169; Sept. 1982, p. 155.

336
Comfort, Alex.
The Joy of Sex: The Cordon Bleu Guide to Lovemaking.

1987
Published

1996 NJ
Removed from the Clifton Public Library and replaced with a dummy book made of styrofoam. The library's new policy restricts to adults any material containing "patently offensive graphic illustrations or photographs of sexual or excretory activities or contact as measured by contemporary community standards for minors."
Source: 11, July 1996, pp. 118–19.

337
Comfort, Alex.
Joy of Sex.

1972
Published

1978 KY
Confiscated from three bookstores by police in Lexington.

1979 AL
Removed from the Fairhope Public Library.

1987
Banned in Ireland to protect the young.

1994 CT
Challenged at the Guilford Free Library, but the Board of Directors voted to reaffirm the library's circulation and book selection policies, which allow all patrons access to all library materials.

2009 KS
Restricted minors' access in the Topeka and Shawnee County Public Library because Kansans for Common Sense Policy contended that the material is "harmful to minors under state law." Later the board voted 6-3 in favor of adopting a staff recommendation to keep the books where they are currently located on the shelves in the library's Health Information Neighborhood section.
Source: 4, p. 93; 11, July 1979, p. 93; May 1987, p. 110; Sept. 1994, p. 165; May 2009, pp. 77-78; July 2009, p. 139.

338
Comfort, Alex.
More Joy of Sex.

1975
Published

1978 KY
Confiscated from three bookstores by police in Lexington.

1979 AL
Removed from the Fairhope Public Library.

1996 NJ
Restricted to patrons over eighteen years of age at the Main Memorial Library in Clifton. The book is hidden behind the checkout counter and on the shelves is a dummy book jacket. The book was described as hard-core pornography by the complainant.
Source: 4, p. 93; 11, July 1979, p. 93; Mar. 1996, p. 63; May 1996, p. 83.

339
Comfort, Alex.
The New Joy of Sex.

1992
Published

2005 ID
Challenged at the Nampa Public Library along with seven other books because "they are very pornographic in nature and they have very explicit and detailed illustrations and photographs which we feel don't belong in a library." The library board approved policy changes that restrict children's access to any holdings that may fall under the state's harmful to minors statute and barred the library from buying movies rated NC-17 or X. The book was relocated to the director's office in 2008 and it was eventually restored to the collection in 2008.
Source: 11, May 2008, pp. 96-97; July 2008, pp. 140-41; Nov. 2008, pp. 254-55.

340
Comte, Auguste.
The Course of Positive Philosophy.

1830-42
Published

1869
The Catholic Church placed the third edition on the *Index Librorum Prohibitorum* (Index of Prohibited Books) in Rome, Italy. It was still prohibited when the last Index was compiled in 1948.
Source: 1, pp. 60–61.

341
Confucius.
Analects.

Third-fourth century
Published

250 B.C.
The first ruler of the Chin Dynasty, wishing to abolish the feudal system, consigned to the flames all books relating to the teaching of Confucius; he also buried alive hundreds of his disciples.

191 B.C.
The rulers of the Han Dynasty rescinded the book-burning edict. Because the teachings of Confucius were handed down orally from master to disciple, scholars were able to reconstruct the texts from memory and from hidden manuscripts that escaped destruction.

1966
In the twentieth century, the Analects and the Confucian canon were again attacked. During the Great Proletarian Cultural Revolution of 1966-74, Mao Zedong and the leaders of the Communist Party called for a comprehensive attack on the "four old" elements within Chinese society—culture, thinking, habits, and customs. During 1973-74, the Communist Party criticized Confucian thinking as promoting an ideology of exploitation, elitism, social hierarchy, and preservation of the status quo.
Source: 4, p. 1; 8, pp. 205–6.

342
Conly, Jane Leslie.
Crazy Lady!

1993
Published

1994
Best Books for Young Adults

1994
Newbery Honor Book

1996 IL
Challenged at the Prospect Heights school libraries because of "swear words."

1997 CA
Parental notification is required at the San Jose Unified School District for the use of the book as a supplemental reading assignment because of objectionable language. The book uses the words "damn," "hell," and "bitch" five times.
Source: 11, Mar. 1996, p. 46; Mar. 1998, p. 55.

343
Connell, Richard Edward.
The Most Dangerous Game.

1924
Published

2012 CO
Challenged at the Bromley East Charter School in Brighton because the 1924 short story "only serves to encourage school violence." English teachers have used it for decades to teach literary concepts like symbols and motifs.
Source: 11, Jan. 2013, pp. 9-10.

344
Connell, Vivian.
The Chinese Room.

1942
Published

1950 MA
Removed from sale, along with thirteen other books, in Fall River as "indecent, obscene or impure, or manifestly tend to corrupt the morals of youth."

1950 NJ
Middlesex County prosecutor Matthew Melko collaborated with the local Committee on Objectionable Literature to produce a list of objectionable publications. Bantam Books then sued Melko in *Bantam Books v. Melko, Prosecutor of Middlesex County*, 25 N.J. Super. 292, 96 A.2d 47 (1953) for banning the book. Ultimately, the New Jersey Supreme Court granted county prosecutors the right to ban the distribution and sale of publications they found objectionable or obscene, and the court further condoned the creation of censorship committees to aid prosecutors in such actions. The decision of the high court agreed that Connell's novel was not obscene.
Source: 13, pp. 45–46.

345
Connell, Vivian.
September in Quinze.

1952
Published

1952
Banned in Ireland after the Irish Board of Censors found the novel "obscene" and "indecent."

1954
The novel became the subject of litigation after the British Treasury Counsel examined the novel and determined it was "obscene." Hutchinson Publishing and its director, Katherine Webb, were each fined 500 pounds.
Source: 13, pp. 208–09.

346
Conner, Macet Al, and Gerry Contreras.
You and Your Family.

1982 PA
Challenged and nearly banned from the Allentown schools because the book asked questions about the students' families, e.g., "Every family has rules. Who makes rules in your family?"
Source: 11, Mar. 1983, p. 52.

347
Conniff, Richard.
The Devil's Book of Verse.

1983
Published

1983 TN
Publication canceled by Dodd, Mead & Company because of language in the book considered "objectionable" by Thomas Nelson, Inc., of Nashville—Dodd, Mead's parent company.
Source: 11, Nov. 1983, p. 188.

348
Conrad, Joseph.
The Nigger of the Narcissus.

1897
Published

1984 IL
Challenged in the Waukegan School District because Conrad's work uses the word "nigger."
Source: 11, July 1984, p. 105.

349
Conrad, Pam.
Holding Me Here.

1986
Published

1991 VA
Challenged at the Lynchburg school libraries because the book contains "cursing and profane language and uses God's name" in a slanderous manner.
Source: 11, Sept. 1991, p. 178.

350
Conran, Shirley.
Lace.

1982
Published

1984 LA
Challenged at the Covington Public Library as "pornographic." The complainant checked the book out after watching the TV series and found that while the TV program had been tastefully done, in the book "pornographic styling [was] unnecessary."
Source: 11, July 1984, p. 103.

351
Conroy, Pat.
Beach Music.

1995
Published

2007 WV
Suspended from the Nitro High, Kanawha County honors English and Advanced Placement literature classes after parents complained about the book's scenes of violence, sexual assault, child rape, suicide, and more. A Kanawha County Board of Education member suggested the institution of a book rating system. Eventually, the book was approved for return to the classroom, as long as students are offered alternative texts.
Source: 11, Jan. 2008, p. 42; Mar. 2008, p. 80.

352
Conroy, Pat.
The Great Santini.

1976
Published

1992 MN
Removed from the Eagan High School classroom in Burnsville.

1993 CA
Challenged as "obscene and pornographic," but retained, in the Anaheim Union High School District.

1993 NY
Challenged, but retained, on the Guilderland High School's list of approved reading materials. A student filed the complaint stating that it was offensive and inappropriate for students his age.
Source: 11, Mar. 1993, p. 56; Sept. 1993, p. 160; Nov. 1993, pp. 192–93; Jan. 1994, p. 14.

353
Conroy, Pat.
The Lords of Discipline.

1980
Published

1992 GA
Challenged in the Cobb County schools because of passages that include profane language and describe sadomasochistic acts.

1992 MN
Removed from an elective English course by the Westonka School Board after parents complained about bad language and sex in the story.

1999 GA
Banned, but later reinstated after community protests at the Windsor Forest High School in Savannah. The controversy began when a parent complained about sex, violence, and profanity in the book that was part of an Advanced Placement English class.
Source: 11, July 1992, p. 110; Mar. 1993, p. 44; Mar. 2000, p. 63; Mar. 2001, p. 76.

354
Conroy, Pat.
The Prince of Tides.

1986
Published

1988 SC
Removed as a reading assignment for an advanced English class at the St. Andres Parish Public School because it is "trashy pulp pornography." Following the challenge, the school board passed a resolution urging teachers to "use professional judgement and discretion in selecting works…which…contain passages which most people would find abhorrent."

2007 WV
Suspended from the Nitro High School honors English and Advanced Placement literature classes after parents complained about the book's scenes of violence, sexual assault, child rape, suicide, and more. A Kanawha County Board of Education member suggested the institution of a book rating system. Eventually, the book was returned to the classroom, as long as students are offered alternative texts.
Source: 11, May 1988, p. 89; Jan. 2008, p. 42; Mar. 2008, p. 80.

355
Conroy, Pat.
The Water Is Wide.

1987
Published

1991 SC

Challenged in the Greenville County schools because the book uses the name of God and Jesus in a "vain and profane manner along with inappropriate sexual references."

Source: 11, July 1991, p. 130.

356
Cook, Robin.
Coma.

1977
Published

1978
Best Books for Young Adults

1992 PA

Removed from Big Spring High School English classes in Newville, but retained, in the library. The decision came in response to complaints that the book is obscene and encourages the maltreatment of women and "radical feminism."

Source: 11, Jan. 1993, p. 13; Mar. 1993, p. 44.

357
Cooke, John Peyton.
The Lake.

1989
Published

1991 OR

Challenged for having too much violence, but retained, at the Multnomah County Library.

Source: 11, Jan. 1992, p. 6.

358
Cooney, Caroline.
The Terrorist.

1997
Published

2000 IA

Challenged, but retained, at the Franklin Middle School in Cedar Rapids despite objections that the book negatively portrays the Islamic religion and Arabs. The book is on the Iowa Teen Award list.

2000 MD

Retained in Rockville on Montgomery County middle school reading lists, over objections that the book is anti-Arab.

Source: 11, May 2000, p. 77; Jan. 2001, p. 35.

359
Cooney, Nancy H.
Sex, Sexuality and You: A Handbook for Growing Christians.

1980
Published

1985 MA

Because of its approach to abortion, the book was removed from the library shelves of the Roman Catholic chancery of Worcester, dropped from their sex education program, and is no longer used as a reference source.

Source: 11, Mar. 1986, pp. 38–39.

360
Copernicus, Nicolaus.
On the Revolution of Heavenly Spheres.

1543
Published

1616

Copernicus was the first person to propose the theory that the earth moves around the sun, and the Catholic Church viewed the Copernican theory as a challenge to orthodoxy. In 1616, the book was placed on the *Index Librorum Prohibitorum* (Index of Prohibited Books) in Rome, Italy. The general prohibition against Copernicus's theories remained in effect until 1753, and his name was not removed from the Index until 1835.

Source: 1, p. 248.

361
Cormier, Robert.
After the First Death.

1979
Published

1979
Best Books for Young Adults

1989 OR

Challenged as an assigned ninth-grade reading in the Troutdale schools because of the book's portrayal of teen suicide as well as the way the U.S. Army and the Palestine Liberation Organization were depicted.

2000 CT

Challenged, but retained, in the Manchester curriculum despite charges that the book is "offensively graphic in its descriptions of violence, terrorism, and suicidal thoughts."

2000 VA

Challenged, but retained, on the Liberty High School ninth-grade gifted and talented reading list in Fauquier. Opponents of the book charged that it was too violent and treated suicide in a cavalier manner. Other parents cited inappropriate sexual content or gender stereotyping.

Source: 11, Mar. 1990, p. 63; May 2000, p. 92; Sept. 2000, p. 145.

362
Cormier, Robert.
Beyond the Chocolate War.

1985
Published

2000 PA

Retained as optional reading for eighth graders at Rice Avenue Middle School in Girard. A grandmother found the book offensive and didn't want her granddaughters reading it.

Source: 11, May 2000, p. 92.

363
Cormier, Robert.
The Chocolate War.

1974
Published

1974
Best Books for Young Adults

1981 MI

Challenged and temporarily removed from the English curriculum in two Lapeer high schools because of "offensive language and explicit descriptions of sexual situations in the book."

1982 MD

Removed from the Liberty High School in Westminster due to the book's "foul language," portrayal of violence, and degradation of schools and teachers.

1983 RI

Challenged at the Richmond High School because the book was deemed "pornographic" and "repulsive."

1984 AZ

Removed from the Lake Havasu High School freshman reading list. The school district board charged the Havasu teachers with failing to set good examples for students, fostering disrespect in the classroom, and failing to support the board.

1984 SC
Banned from the Richland Two School District middle school libraries in Columbia due to "language problems," but later reinstated for eighth graders only.

1985 NY
Challenged at the Cornwall High School because the novel is "humanistic and destructive of religious and moral beliefs and of national spirit."

1985 PA
Banned from the Stroudsburg High School library because it was "blatantly graphic, pornographic and wholly unacceptable for a high school library."

1986 FL
Removed from the Panama City school classrooms and libraries because of "offensive" language.

1986 MA
Challenged at Barnstable High School in Hyannis because of the novel's profanity, "obscene references to masturbation and sexual fantasies," and "ultimately because of its pessimistic ending." The novel, complainants said, fostered negative impressions of authority, of school systems, and of religious schools.

1987 CA
Challenged at the Moreno Valley Unified School District libraries because it "contains profanity, sexual situations, and themes that allegedly encourage disrespectful behavior."

1988 FL
West Hernando Middle School principal recommended that Cormier's novel be removed from the school library shelves because it is "inappropriate."

1990 CT
Challenged as suitable curriculum material in the Harwinton schools because it contained profanity and subject matter that set bad examples and gave students negative views of life.

1990 CT
Challenged as suitable curriculum material in the Burlington schools because it contained profanity and subject matter that set bad examples and gave students negative views of life.

1990 NH
Suspended from classroom use, pending review, at the Woodsville High School in Haverhill because the novel contains expletives, references to masturbation and sexual fantasies, and derogatory characterizations of a teacher and of religious ceremonies.

1992 CT
Challenged at the New Milford schools because the novel contains language, sexual references, violence, subjectivity, and negativism that are harmful to students.

1993 AZ
Challenged in the Kyrene elementary schools because of a masturbation scene.

1994 GA
Returned to the Hephzibah High School tenth-grade reading list in Augusta after the complainant said, "I don't see anything educational about that book. If they ever send a book like that home with one of my daughters again I will personally burn it and throw the ashes on the principal's desk."

1994 NY
Challenged as required reading in the Hudson Falls schools because the book has recurring themes of rape, masturbation, violence, and degrading treatment of women.

1995 MA
Challenged at the Nauset Regional Middle School in Orleans due to profanity and sexually explicit language.

1995 PA
Challenged in the Stroudsburg school system on the grounds that the will "foster more disobedience."

1996 CA
Removed from the middle school libraries in the Riverside Unified School District as inappropriate for seventh- and eighth-graders to read without class discussion due to mature themes, sexual situations, and smoking.

1996 PA
Removed from the East Stroudsburg ninth-grade curriculum after complaints about the novel's language and content.

1998 OK
Banned from the Broken Arrow schools because it is the "antithesis of the district's character development curriculum." The board of education is considering forming a parent committee to review all books listed on the district's electronic bookshelf and to design a ratings system for more than four hundred titles found there.

1998 TX
Removed from the Greenville Intermediate School library because "it contained blasphemy, profanity, and graphic sexual passages."

1999 NY
Challenged on the required reading list for ninth graders at Colton schools due to references to masturbation, profanity, disrespect of women, and sexual innuendo.

2000 CO
Challenged as part of the Silverheels Middle School's supplemental reading material in South Park because parents objected to sexually suggestive language in the book.

2000 MA
Challenged on the eighth-grade reading list of the Lancaster School District, due to the book's language and content.

2000 OH
Challenged at the Maple Heights School because "the book teaches immorality."

2000 PA
Retained as optional reading for eighth graders at Rice Avenue Middle School in Girard. A grandmother found the book offensive and didn't want her granddaughters reading it.

2000 VA
Challenged in York County due to sexually explicit language.

2001 FL
Challenged, but retained, at the Dunedin Highland Middle School in St. Petersburg despite objections to profanity, scenes about masturbation and sexual fantasy, and segments of the book that were considered denigrating to girls.

2001 OH
Challenged at a Beaver Local Board of Education meeting in Lisbon as a "pornographic" book that should be removed from high school English classes.

2002 VA
Challenged, along with seventeen other titles in the Fairfax County elementary and secondary libraries, by a group called Parents Against Bad Books in Schools. The group contends the books "contain profanity and descriptions of drug abuse, sexually explicit conduct, and torture."

2006 CT

Challenged, but retained, in the West Hartford schools. Parents of a King Philip Middle School eighth-grader thought the language, sexual content, and violence make the book PG-13.

2006 NC

Challenged in the Wake County schools because the book has "vulgar and sexually explicit language." Parents are getting help from Called2Action, a Christian group that says its mission is to "promote and defend our shared family and social values."

2007 ID

Challenged in the Coeur d'Alene School District. Some parents say the book, along with five others, should require parental permission for students to read them.

2007 IL

Challenged as required reading for seventh-grade students at the John H. Kinzie Elementary School in Chicago.

2007 MD

Removed from the Harford County High School curriculum because its message on the dangers of bullying is overshadowed by instances of vulgar language, including homophobic slurs. In November 2007, the Harford County's school superintendent reversed her decision to bar Cormier's novel and returned it to the classroom. Teachers now have the option of using the novel in a course that deals with harassment and decision making, but must get permission from all parents of students in the class.

2007 OH

Challenged at the Northridge School District in Johnstown because, "if these books were a movie, they would be rated R. Why should we be encouraging them to read these books?"

2007 OR

Challenged as an optional reading in a bullying unit at the Lake Oswego Junior High School because the novel is "peppered with profanities, ranging from derogatory slang terms to sexual encounters and violence." Students are given a list of book summaries and a letter to take to their parents. Four of the eight optional books offered are labeled as having "mature content/language."

Source: 9; 11, Mar. 1981, p. 48; Sept. 1982, p. 156; Sept. 1983, p. 152; Sept. 1984, p. 138; Jan. 1985, p. 10; Mar. 1985, p. 45; May 1985, p. 79; May 1986, p. 79; Nov. 1986, p. 209; July 1987, pp. 125, 126–28; Sept. 1987, pp.

168–69, Mar. 1988, p. 45; May 1990, p. 87; Mar. 1991, p. 44; May 1991, p. 90; May 1992, pp. 96–97; Jan. 1994, p. 34; July 1994, p. 130; Nov. 1994, p. 190; Jan. 1995, p. 13; Mar. 1995, p. 55; May 1995, p. 70; July 1995, p. 94; Nov. 1995, p. 184; May 1996, p. 99; July 1996, p. 82; Nov. 1996, p. 198; July 1998, p. 106; Sept. 1998, pp. 140–41; Sept. 1999, p. 122; Jan. 2000, p. 16; Mar. 2000, pp. 49, 51–52; May 2000, pp. 78, 92; Sept. 2000, pp. 144–45; Mar. 2001, pp. 43, 57; Jan. 2002, pp. 49-50; Jan. 2003, p. 10; July 2006, pp. 184–85, 187; Sept. 2006, p. 231; July 2007, pp. 147-49; Sept. 2007, p. 181; Nov. 2007, pp. 242-43; Jan. 2008, pp. 28-29.

364

Cormier, Robert.
Fade.

1988
Published

1988
Best Books for Young Adults

1990 WY
Challenged in the Campbell County junior high schools because of sexual and violent themes.

Source: 11, Jan. 1991, p. 13; Mar. 1991, p. 62.

365

Cormier, Robert.
Heroes.

1998
Published

1999
Best Books for Young Adults

2002 VA
Challenged, along with seventeen other titles in the Fairfax County elementary and secondary libraries, by a group called Parents Against Bad Books in Schools. The group contends the books "contain profanity and descriptions of drug abuse, sexually explicit conduct, and torture."

Source: 11, Jan. 2003, p. 10.

366

Cormier, Robert.
I Am the Cheese.

1977
Published

1977
Best Books for Young Adults

1985 NY
Challenged at the Cornwall High School because the novel is "humanistic and destructive of religious and moral beliefs and of national spirit."

1986 FL

Banned from the Bay County's four middle schools and three high schools in Panama City because of "offensive" language. The controversy snowballed further on May 7, 1987, when 64 works of literature were banned from classroom teaching at Bay and Mosley High Schools by the Bay County school superintendent. After 44 parents filed a suit against the district claiming that its instructional aids policy denies constitutional rights, the Bay County School Board reinstated the books. "Banned" from Bay High School: *A Farewell to Arms*, by Ernest Hemingway; *The Great Gatsby*, by F. Scott Fitzgerald; *Intruder in the Dust*, by William Faulkner; *Lost Horizon*, by James Hilton; *Oedipus Rex*, by Sophocles; *The Red Badge of Courage*, by Stephen Crane; *A Separate Peace*, by John Knowles; *Shane*, by Jack Shaefer; *Three Comedies of American Life*, edited by Joseph Mersand. "Banned" from Mosley High School: *Adventures in English Literature*, by Patrick Murray; *After the First Death*, by Robert Cormier; *Alas, Babylon*, by Pat Frank; *Animal Farm*, by George Orwell; *Arrangement in Literature*, by Edmund J. Farrell; *The Autobiography of Benjamin Franklin*; *Best Short Stories*, edited by Raymond Harris; *Brave New World*, by Aldous Huxley; *The Call of the Wild*, by Jack London; *The Canterbury Tales*, by Geoffrey Chaucer; *The Crucible*, by Arthur Miller; *Death Be Not Proud*, by John Gunther; *Deathwatch*, by Robb White; *Desire under the Elms, The Emperor Jones*, and *Long Day's Journey into Night*, by Eugene O'Neill; *Exploring Life through Literature*, by Edmund J. Farrell; *Fahrenheit 451*, by Ray Bradbury; *The Fixer*, by Bernard Malamud; *Miss Julie*, by August Strindberg; *The Glass Menagerie*, by Tennessee Williams; *Great Expectations*, by Charles Dickens; *The Great Gatsby*, by F. Scott Fitzgerald; *Growing Up by Russell Baker; Hamlet, King Lear, The Merchant of Venice*, and *Twelfth Night*, by William Shakespeare; *Hippolytus*, by Euripides; *In Cold Blood*, by Truman Capote; *The Inferno*, by Dante; *The Little Foxes*, by Lillian Hellman; *Lord of the Flies*, by William Golding; *Major British Writers*, by G. B. Harrison; *The Man Who Came to Dinner*, by George S. Kaufman and Moss Hart; *The Mayor of Casterbridge*, by Thomas Hardy; *McTeague*, by Frank Norris;

Mister Roberts, by Thomas O. Heggen; *The Oedipus Plays of Sophocles*; *Of Mice and Men* and *The Pearl*, by John Steinbeck; *The Old Man and the Sea*, by Ernest Hemingway; *On Baile's Strand*, by W. B. Yeats; *The Outsiders*, by S. E. Hinton; *Player Piano*, by Kurt Vonnegut; *The Prince and the Pauper*, by Mark Twain; *Prometheus Unbound*, by Percy Bysshe Shelley; *Tale Blazer Library* and *A Raisin in the Sun*, by Lorraine Hansberry; *To Kill a Mockingbird*, by Harper Lee; *Watership Down*, by Richard Adams; *Winterset*, by Maxwell Anderson; *Wuthering Heights*, by Charlotte Bronte; *The Red Badge of Courage*, by Stephen Crane; *A Separate Peace*, by John Knowles.

2004 NV

Challenged on the seventh-grade honors English reading list at Elko Junior High School because of the book's sexual content.

Source: 8, pp. 88–93; 11, Mar. 1985, p. 45; Nov. 1986, p. 209; Mar. 1987, p. 52; July 1987, pp. 126–28; Sept. 1987, pp. 168–69; Nov. 1987, p. 224; Jan. 2005, pp. 9–10.

367
Cormier, Robert.
Tenderness.

1998
Published

1998
Best Books for Young Adults

2002 VA

Challenged, along with seventeen other titles in the Fairfax County elementary and secondary libraries, by a group called Parents Against Bad Books in Schools. The group contends the books "contain profanity and descriptions of drug abuse, sexually explicit conduct, and torture."

Source: 11, Jan. 2003, p. 10.

368
Cormier, Robert.
We All Fall Down.

1991
Published

1992
Best Books for Young Adults

1994 CA
Pulled from elementary and junior high school libraries in Stockton after parents complained that it glorifies alcoholism and violence, contains a violent rape scene, and its characters use too much profanity.

2000 FL
Removed from the Carver Middle School library in Leesburg after parents complained about the book's content and language.

2000 TX
Restricted in Arlington middle and high schools to students who have written parental permission, due to concerns over violent content.

2001 PA
Challenged in the Tamaqua Area School District because the book "might not be appropriate for younger schoolmates." The school board is considering the establishment of a restrictedmaterials section in the district's middle-school library for books deemed objectionable. Students would need parental permission to access any title placed there.

2003 KS
Pulled from a Baldwin ninth grade class by the school district superintendent because "it was clear to him it wasn't fit for his own daughter or granddaughter." The original complaint objected to fifty passages that contained profanity and sexual content.

2005 NJ
Challenged at the Cherry Hill Public Library's young adult section by a parent claiming its "deplorable" content was unfit for young minds. The book was retained.

Source: 11, Mar. 1995, p. 39; May 2000, p. 75; July 2000, p. 103; Mar. 2001, p. 54; July 2001, p. 145; Nov. 2003, p. 229; Jan. 2004, p. 12; Nov. 2005, p. 296.

369
Corsaro, Maria, and Carole Korzeniowsky.
Woman's Guide to a Safe Abortion.

1983
Published

1984 MA
Challenged at the Walpole Public Library because the book is "inaccurate factually, because it is deliberately misleading and deceitful, and because its avowed purpose is to promote a behavior—killing unborn babies…By maintaining and displaying this material at public expense, to the public, and in particular to pregnant women who are vulnerable and may be in need of real guidance, the Walpole

Public Library is promoting and abetting abortion."

Source: 11, Nov. 1984, p. 184.

370
Cory, Donald Webster.
Homosexuality in America.

1951
Published

1989 SC
Returned to shelves of the Horry County School District middle school libraries in Conway after an attorney advised that the 1988 state health education law did not prohibit books on homosexuality and abortion. Other titles temporarily removed include: *The Abortion Controversy in America*, by Carol Emmens; *Kids Having Kids*, by Janet Bode; and *Who They Are: The Right-to-Lifers*, by C. Paige.

Source: 11, July 1989, p. 143.

371
Cottrell, Randall.
Wellness: Stress Management.

1992
Published

1992 OR
Rejected as a supplemental health book in the Eagle Point schools because three women complained that the book cited yoga and Transcendental Meditation as ways to reduce stress, but failed to mention Christian prayer.

Source: 11, Jan. 1993, p. 12.

372
Coupe, Peter.
The Beginner's Guide to Drawing Cartoons.

1996
Published

1999 WA
Removed from the Meadow Ridge Elementary School library in Spokane after a mother complained that nude cartoon characters of Adam and Eve were a bad influence on children.

Source: 11, May 1999, p. 68.

373

Courtenay, Bryce.
The Power of One.

1989
Published

1996 TX
Retained on the Round Rock Independent High School reading list after a challenge that the book was too violent.

Source: 11, May 1996, p. 99.

374

Coville, Bruce.
"Am I Blue?"

1988
Published

2004 IA
Challenged in the Solon eighth-grade language arts class because the short fictional story explores a boy's confusion with his sexual identity and the gay fairy godfather who helps him overcome homophobia at school. The short story, published in *Am I Blue?: Coming out from the Silence* edited by Marion Dane Bauer, was eventually retained.

Source: 11, Jan. 2005, p. 8.

375

Coville, Bruce.
The Dragonslayers.

1994
Published

1995 SC
Challenged in the Berkeley County School District because of the "witchcraft" and "deception" and because a "main character openly disobeys his parents."

Source: 11, Mar. 1996, p. 63.

376

Coville, Bruce.
Jeremy Thatcher, Dragon Hatcher.

1991
Published

1993 IA
Returned to the shelves of the Carroll Middle School library after an "avalanche" of appeals overturned a Reconsideration of Instructional Materials Committee decision that the book be removed because it "was not forthright with the message it intended to present."

1993 IA
Returned to the shelves of the Fairview Elementary library after an "avalanche" of appeals overturned a Reconsideration of Instructional Materials Committee decision that the book be removed because it "was not forthright with the message it intended to present."

Source: 11, Nov. 1993, p. 191.

377

Coville, Bruce.
My Teacher Glows in the Dark.

1991
Published

1995 CA
Contested in the classrooms and school libraries in Palmdale because the book includes the words "armpit farts" and "farting."

Source: 11, Mar. 1996, p. 45.

378

Coville, Bruce.
My Teacher Is an Alien.

1990
Published

1994 PA
Challenged in the Elizabethtown schools because it demeans teachers and parents as dumb and portrays the main character as handling a problem on her own, rather than relying on the help of others.

Source: 11, Mar. 1995, p. 44.

379

Coward, Noel.
Blithe Spirit.

1941
Published

1989 OR
Challenged in the Springfield schools because the play encourages occult activities.

Source: 11, Mar. 1990, p. 63.

380

Cox, Elizabeth.
Night Talk.

1997
Published

2008 GA
Challenged at the South Gwinnett High School's library because the story, which portrays the friendship of a white girl and a black girl during the Civil Rights era, contains "graphic sex scenes that read like a how-to guide." A school committee, comprising of three teachers and four parents, denied the request to restrict the book's use or have it removed from the media center.

Source: 11, Mar. 2009, pp. 37-38.

381

Cox, R. David.
Student Critic.

1974
Published

1979 IN
Expurgated in Warsaw to remove four pages of a story entitled "A Chip off the Old Block" because the story contains the words "damn" and "hell."

Source: 11, May 1979, p. 64.

382

Cranmer, Thomas, and Others.
The Book of Common Prayer.

1549
Published

1553
Cranmer was responsible for the writing of most of the first Book of Common Prayer in 1549, brought into compulsory use in the Church of England by act of Parliament, and for the 1552 revision of the book. In 1553, the Catholic Queen Mary banned the use of the Prayer Book. Crammer was convicted of treason and heresy and executed.

Source: 1, p. 31.

383

Crawford, Brent.
Carter Finally Gets It.

2009
Published

2012 OK
Challenged, but retained, in the Broken Arrow middle school libraries despite a parent's complaint that it is "vulgar, vulgar, vulgar." The book was recognized by the Young Adult Library Services Association as one of 2010's Amazing Audiobooks.

Source: 11, July 2012, p. 179.

384
Crichton, Michael.
Congo.

1980
Published

1995 CA
Challenged as an optional text in an Yerba Buena High School interdisciplinary course by the father of two black students who said it is part of racially discriminatory practices. The parent has filed an $8 million civil rights suit against the school district.
Source: 11, Jan. 1996, p. 13.

385
Crowley, Aleister.
Magick in Theory and Practice.

1929
Published

1988 OR
Challenged at the Dalles-Wasco County Public Library because the book promotes criminal activity in its depiction of human and animal sacrifice.
Source: 11, Jan. 1989, p. 15.

386
Crumb, R.
The R. Crumb Coffee Table Art Book.

1997
Published

1999 IN
Challenged at the Alexandrian Public Library in Mount Vernon.
Source: 11, Nov. 1999, p. 171.

387
Cruse, Howard.
Stuck Rubber Baby.

1995
Published

2004 TX
Challenged at the Montgomery County Memorial Library System along with fifteen other titles. The objections to the books, which contain young-adult fiction with gay-positive themes, were posted at the Library Patrons of Texas website. The language describing the books is similar to that posted at the website of the Fairfax County, Virginia-based Parents Against Bad Books in Schools, to which Library Patrons of Texas links.
Source: 11, Nov. 2004, pp. 231–32.

388
Crutcher, Chris.
Athletic Shorts.

1991
Published

1992
Best Books for Young Adults

1995 SC
Challenged at the Charleston County School library because the books deals with divorce, violence, AIDS, and homosexuality.

1999 AK
Pulled from the elementary school collections, but retained, at the middle school libraries in Anchorage. A parent challenged the book of short stories because of the book's lack of respect for parents and God, its treatment of homosexuality, and its bad language.
Source: 11, July 1995, p. 94; May 1999, p. 65.

389
Crutcher, Chris.
Chinese Handcuffs.

1989
Published

1990
Best Books for Young Adults

1998 WI
Challenged, but retained, at the Lincoln High School in Wisconsin Rapids. A parent complained about "the book's depiction of incest, rape, animal torture, teen drug use, breaking and entering, illegal use of a video camera, profanity directed to a school principal, and graphic sexual references."

2009 IN
Retained in Delphi Community High School's curriculum despite claims of inappropriate sexual content and graphic language.
Source: 11, May 1998, p. 89; May 2009, p. 94.

390
Crutcher, Chris.
Deadline.

2007
Published

2009 KY
Withdrawn from classroom use and the approved curriculum at the Montgomery County High School, but available at the high school library and student book club. Some parents have complained about five novels containing foul language and covering topics—including sex, child abuse, suicide, and drug abuse—unsuited for discussion in coed high school classes. They also contend that the books don't provide the intellectual challenge and rigor that students need in college preparatory classes. The titles appeared on suggested book lists compiled by the Young Adult Library Services Association, a division of the American Library Association, for twelve- to eighteen-year-olds who are "reluctant readers." The superintendent removed the book because it wasn't on the pre-approved curriculum list and couldn't be added by teachers in the middle of a school year without permission.
Source: 11, Jan. 2010, pp. 16-17; Mar. 2010, p. 56.

391
Crutcher, Chris.
"In the Time I Get."

1991
Published

2004 IA
Challenged in the Solon eighth-grade language arts class because the short story is about a man who befriends a young man dying of AIDS. The short story, published in *Athletic Shorts*, by Chris Crutcher, was eventually retained.
Source: 11, Jan. 2005, p. 8.

392
Crutcher, Chris.
Running Loose.

1983
Published

1983
Best Books for Young Adults

1986 GA
Challenged at the Gwinnett County public schools because of its discussion of sex.
Source: 11, Mar. 1987, p. 65.

393
Crutcher, Chris.
Staying Fat for Sarah Byrnes.

1993
Published

1994
Best Books for Young Adults

2011 WI
The Belleville School Board decided to keep a book that's required reading for high school freshmen in the curriculum despite a parent's complaint that the book was "pornography" and its language was "pervasively vulgar." The novel had been read by ninth-grade students at Belleville High School for eight years. The book deals with topics of abortion, sexuality, and the power of religion.
Source: 11, Jan. 2011, p. 13; Mar. 2011, p. 75.

394
Crutcher, Chris.
Stotan!

1986
Published

1986
Best Books for Young Adults

1997 WV
Removed from the Jackson County school libraries along with sixteen other titles.
Source: 11, Jan. 1998, p. 13.

395
Crutcher, Chris.
Whale Talk.

2001
Published

2002
Best Books for Young Adults

2005 AL
Removed from all five Limestone County high school libraries because of the book's use of profanity.

2005 MI
Challenged at the Grand Ledge High School.

2005 SC
Removed from the suggested reading list for a pilot English-literature curriculum by the superintendent of the South Carolina Board of Education.

2007 IA
Challenged at the Missouri Valley High School because the book uses racial slurs and profanity.
Source: 11, May 2005, p. 107; July 2005, pp. 153–54; May 2007, p. 98; July 2007, p. 149; 14, pp. 295–97.

396
Cunningham, Antonia, ed.
Guinness Book of World Records.

2002 WI
Retained in the Waukesha elementary schools despite a challenge that the book was sexually explicit.
Source: 11, May 2002, p. 136.

397
Currie, Ian.
You Cannot Die: The Incredible Findings of a Century of Research on Death.

1978
Published

1987 MI
Challenged at the Plymouth-Canton school system in Canton because the book is "not only offensive to our faith, but it is a dangerous teaching to children today when the suicide rate is so high."
Source: 11, May 1987, p. 110.

398
Curry, Hayden, and Denis Clifford.
A Legal Guide for Lesbian and Gay Couples.

1980
Published

1993 OR
Challenged at the Deschutes County Library in Bend because it "encourages and condones" homosexuality.
Source: 11, Sept. 1993, pp. 158–59.

399
Curtis, Christopher Paul.
The Watsons Go to Birmingham—1963.

1995
Published

1996
Best Books for Young Adults

1996
Coretta Scott King Author Honor Book

1996
Newbery Honor Book

2002 VA
Challenged in the Stafford County middle schools because a parent was offended.
Source: 11, July 2002, pp. 154–55.

400
Curtis, Helena.
Biology.

1968
Published

1982 CA
San Diego school system was threatened with a lawsuit unless the book was removed because "it treats the topic of evolution in a dogmatic manner."
Source: 11, Mar. 1983, p. 40.

401
Cusack, Isabel Langis.
Mr. Wheatfield's Loft.

1981
Published

1988 OR
Challenged at the Springfield Public Library because of profanity and the appearance of the subject of prostitution.
Source: 11, Jan. 1990, pp. 4–5.

402
Cushman, Karen.
The Midwife's Apprentice.

1995
Published

1996
Best Books for Young Adults

1996
Newbery Medal

1998 KS
Challenged in the Newton schools and public library because a parent thought the book was "not appropriate for middle school students."
Source: 11, July 1998, pp. 108–9.

403
Dacey, John S.
Adolescents Today.

1979
Published

1985 PA
The Norwin School Board decided to retain the textbook used in the district's tenth-grade health classes despite accusations that it is amoral, anti-family, and has a Marxist bent. A group of nineteen parents filed a federal lawsuit in March 1987. The suit charged that in the book abstaining from sex until marriage is portrayed unfavorably, birth control techniques are evaluated, and homosexuality is taught as a natural stage of sexual development.
Source: 11, July 1985, p. 135; July 1987, p. 131.

404
Dahl, Roald.
The BFG.

1982
Published

1987 IA
Challenged at the Amana first-grade curriculum because the book was "too sophisticated and did not teach moral values."
Source: 11, Sept. 1987, pp. 194–95.

405
Dahl, Roald.
Charlie and the Chocolate Factory.

1964
Published

1988 CO
Removed from a locked reference collection at the Boulder Public Library. The book was originally locked away because the librarian thought the book espouses a poor philosophy of life.
Source: 11, Jan. 1989, p. 27.

406
Dahl, Roald.
The Enormous Crocodile.

1978
Published

1988 OR
Challenged at the Multnomah County Library in Portland because of the book's sinister nature and the negative action of animals.
Source: 11, Jan. 1989, p. 3.

407
Dahl, Roald.
George's Marvelous Medicine.

1981
Published

1995 VA
Challenged at the Stafford County Schools because the book "posed a safety threat because the boy in the story warms household items, such as paint thinner and soap, to make a potion."
Source: 11, Sept. 1995, pp. 159–60.

408
Dahl, Roald.
James and the Giant Peach.

1961
Published

1991 FL
Challenged at the Deep Creek Elementary School in Charlotte Harbor because it is "not appropriate reading material for young children."

1991 WI
Challenged at the Pederson Elementary School in Altoona because the book uses the word "ass" and parts of the book deal with wine, tobacco, and snuff.

1992 FL
Challenged at the Morton Elementary School library in Brooksville because the book contains a foul word and promotes drugs and whiskey.

1995 VA
Challenged at the Stafford County Schools because the tale contains crude language and encourages children to disobey their parents and other adults. The book was removed from the classrooms and placed in the library, where access was restricted.

1999 TX
Banned from an elementary school in Lufkin because it contains the word "ass."
Source: 11, July 1991, p. 108; Mar. 1992, p. 65; Jan. 1993, p. 27; Sept. 1995, p. 160; Jan. 2000, p. 8.

409
Dahl, Roald.
Matilda.

1988
Published

1993 MI
Retained on the shelves in the Grand Rapids school libraries, but not allowed to be read in the elementary classrooms. Ten parents complained about the book, calling it offensive and "appalling in its disrespect for adult figures and children."

1994 ME
Challenged, but retained, in the Margaret Chase Smith School library in Skowhegan after the complainant came to understand that attaching a warning label also would amount to censorship.

1995 VA
Challenged at the Stafford County Schools because the tale contains crude language and encourages children to disobey their parents and other adults. The book was removed from the classrooms and placed in the library, where access was restricted.
Source: 11, Nov. 1993, p. 179; May 1994, p. 98; Sept. 1995, p. 160.

410
Dahl, Roald.
The Minipins.

1991
Published

1995 VA
Challenged at the Stafford County Schools because the tale contains crude language and encourages children to disobey their parents and other adults. The book was removed from the classrooms and placed in the library, where access was restricted.
Source: 11, Sept. 1995, p. 160.

411
Dahl, Roald.
Revolting Rhymes.

1982
Published

1990 IA
Challenged at the Northeast High School in Goose Lake because of its alleged violence, the use of the word "slut," and the subject of witches.

1992 MA
Banned in the Rockland elementary schools after a parent complained that the book of fractured fairy tales was offensive and inappropriate for children.

1995 VA
Challenged at the Stafford County Schools because the book spoofs nursery rhymes.
Source: 11, May 1990, p. 105; Jan. 1993, p. 8; Sept. 1995, pp. 159–60.

412
Dahl, Roald.
Rhyme Stew.

1989
Published

1990 DE
Moved from the children's section to the adult section at the Dover Public Library. The complainant called for the establishment of a national rating system similar to that of the motion picture industry that would classify books according to local community standards.
Source: 11, Mar. 1991, p. 42.

413
Dahl, Roald.
The Witches.

1983
Published

1987 IA
Challenged at the Amana first-grade curriculum because the book was "too sophisticated and did not teach moral values."

1990 IA
Challenged at the Goose Lake Elementary School because of its alleged violence, the use of the word "slut," the subject of witches, and the fact that "the boy who is turned into a mouse by the witches will have to stay a mouse for the rest of his life."

1991 OR
Challenged at the Dallas Elementary School library because the book entices impressionable or emotionally disturbed children into becoming involved in witchcraft or the occult.

1992 CA
Placed on a library restricted list by the Escondido Union Elementary School District after four parents filed complaints that it promoted the occult and was too frightening. Returned to the shelves of the Escondido Union School District school libraries after the school board lifted a partial ban. A complaint was filed by four parents who stated the book promoted satanism. The district still retains bans on four books, including *Halloween ABC*, which some parents charged with promoting the occult.

1992 CA
Challenged at the La Mesa-Spring Valley School District because it includes horrifying depictions of witches as ordinary-looking women, against whom there is no defense. Other opponents added that it promotes the religion of Wicca, or witchcraft.

1993 PA
Challenged at Pine Forge Elementary School in the Boyertown area.

1993 WI
Challenged in the Spencer schools because it desensitizes children to crimes related to witchcraft.

1994 MI
Challenged, but retained, at the Battle Creek Elementary School library despite the protests from a parent who said the book is satanic.

1995 VA
Challenged at the Stafford County Schools because the tale contains crude language and encourages children to disobey their parents and other adults. The book was to be removed from the classrooms and placed in the library, where access could be restricted.

1998 OH
Challenged, but retained, at the Dublin school district despite objections that the book is "derogatory toward children and conflicts with family religious and moral beliefs."
Source: 11, Sept. 1987, pp. 194–95; May 1990, p. 105; Jan. 1992, p. 26; May 1992, pp. 78–79; Nov. 1992, pp. 196–97; July 1993, p. 127; Sept. 1993, p. 157; May 1994, p. 85; Nov. 1994, p. 200; Sept. 1995, p. 160; Sept. 1998, p. 156.

414
Dahrendorf, Ralf.
Class and Class Conflict in Industrial Society.

1959
Published

1985
Banned in South Korea.
Source: 5, Apr. 1986, pp. 30–33.

415
Dakin, Edwin Franden.
Mrs. Eddy: The Biography of a Virginal Mind.

1929
Published

1929
The Christian Science Church attempted to suppress this biography of Mary Baker Eddy, the Church's founder, by demanding its withdrawal from sale.
Source: 15, Vol. III, p. 418.

416
Daldry, Jeremy.
The Teenage Guy's Survival Guide.

1999
Published

2005 AR
Restricted, but later returned to general circulation shelves with some limits on student access, based on a review committee's recommendations, at the Holt Middle School parent library in Fayetteville despite a parent's complaint that it was sexually explicit.
Source: 11, May 2005, p. 135; Sept. 2005, p. 215; Nov. 2005, pp. 295–96.

417
Dalrymple, Douglas J., and Leonard J. Parsons.
Marketing Management: Text and Cases.

1976
Published

1981 NE
Seven pages of this book were expurgated at the University of Nebraska-Omaha because they contain a case study dealing with a firm that sells contraceptive devices.
Source: 11, Jan. 1982, p. 19.

418
Dalrymple, Willard.
Sex Is for Real.

1969
Published

1977 MI
Banned from the Brighton High School library along with all the other sex education materials.
Source: 11, Sept. 1977, p. 133.

419
Dandicat, Edwidge.
Krik! Krak!

1996
Published

2004 WI
Challenged by a parent at the Arrowhead High School in Merton as an elective reading list assignment because the book contains "sexually explicit and inappropriate material."
Source: 11, Jan. 2005, p. 11.

420
Dante Alighieri.
The Divine Comedy.

1302-21
Published

1497
Burned in Florence, Italy.

1581
Prohibited by church authorities in Lisbon, Portugal, until all copies were delivered to the Inquisition for correction.

1978
Banned in Ethiopia.
Source: 4, p. 6; 5, Sept./Oct. 1978, p. 66.

421
Dante Alighieri.
On Monarchy.

1310-13
Published

1329
Dante argued against papal control over secular authority and the Pope condemned the book in Rome, Italy.

1329
Publicly burned in the marketplace of Bologna, Italy.

1500
In the sixteenth century, the Spanish Inquisition banned it, and it was listed on the Catholic Church's first *Index Librorum Prohibitorum* (Index of Prohibited Books), where it remained until the nineteenth century.
Source: 1, p. 234.

422
Darwin, Charles B.
On the Origin of Species.

1859
Published

1859
Banned from Trinity College in Cambridge, England.

1925 TN
Tennessee passed a law prohibiting teachers from teaching the theory of evolution in state supported schools. John T. Scopes, a science teacher in Dayton, volunteered to be the test case for Tennessee's anti-evolution law. The Scopes "monkey trial," eventually, was thrown out on a technicality.

1935
Banned in Yugoslavia.

1937
Banned in Greece.

1968 AR
The U.S. Supreme Court considered a case similar to Scopes. Susan Epperson, a high school biology teacher, challenged the constitutionality of the Arkansas Anti-Evolution Statute of 1928, which provided that teachers who used a textbook that included Darwin's theory of evolution could lose their jobs. The Supreme Court ruled that the law was unconstitutional and conflicted with the First and Fourteenth Amendments. Government power could not be used to advance religious beliefs. In the early 1980s, Arkansas state board of education required the teaching of both creationism and evolution in public schools. This law was ruled unconstitutional in 1987 by the U.S. Supreme Court in *Edwards v. Aguillard* as advocating a religious doctrine and violating the establishment clause of the First Amendment.

1980 LA
In the early 1980s, Arkansas and Louisiana state boards of education required the teaching of both creationism and evolution in public schools. These laws were ruled unconstitutional in 1987 by the U.S. Supreme Court in *Edwards v. Aguillard* as advocating a religious doctrine and violating the establishment clause of the First Amendment. Battles about the teaching of evolution, however, still rage on, especially at the local school board level.
Source: 4, pp. 42-43; 8, pp. 276–79.

423
Darwin, Erasmus.
Zoonomia.

1794-96
Published

1817
Sixty-five years before his grandson Charles Darwin revolutionized biological science, Darwin formulated an evolutionary system in this treatise on animal life. Placed on the Catholic Church's *Index Librorum Prohibitorum* (Index of Prohibited Books) in Rome, Italy, where it remained listed until 1966.
Source: 1, pp. 359–60.

424
Davis, Deborah.
My Brother Has AIDS.

1994
Published

2004 TX
Challenged at the Montgomery County Memorial Library System along with fifteen other young-adult books with gay-positive themes. The objections were posted at the Library Patrons of Texas website. The language describing the books is similar to that posted at the website of the Fairfax County, Virginia-based Parents Against Bad Books in Schools, to which Library Patrons of Texas links.
Source: 11, Nov. 2004, pp. 231–32.

425
Davis, Jenny.
Sex Education.

1988
Published

1993 ND
Challenged at Hughes Junior High School in Bismarck because it is "offensive."
Source: 11, Sept. 1993, p. 145.

426

Davis, Jim.
Garfield: His Nine Lives.

1984
Published

1989 MI
Moved to the adult section of the Public Libraries of Saginaw after patrons requested that children be denied access.
Source: 11, May 1989, p. 77.

427

Davis, Kathryn.
The Dakotas: At the Wind's Edge.

1983
Published

1983 ND
Banned from sale in all Medora bookstores because some Medora residents did not approve of some of Davis's fictional embellishments to the history of their town.
Source: 11, July 1983, p. 123.

428

Davis, Lindsey.
Silver Pigs.

1989
Published

1990
Best Books for Young Adults

2002 VA
Challenged, along with seventeen other titles in the Fairfax County elementary and secondary libraries, by a group called Parents Against Bad Books in Schools. The group contends the books "contain profanity and descriptions of drug abuse, sexually explicit conduct, and torture."
Source: 11, Jan. 2003, p. 10.

429

Davis, Terry.
Vision Quest.

1979
Published

1979
Best Books for Young Adults

1984 WA
Challenged at the Mead School District.

1984 WI
Placed on a restricted reading list by the New Berlin School Board because it is "vulgar and not educational."

1984 WI
Challenged at the West Milwaukee High School library because it is "obscene."

1986 WI
Banned from the West Allis-West Milwaukee school libraries because of its profanities.

1993 ND
Moved from the Hughes Junior High School in Bismarck to the high school because a parent considered some passages obscene, pornographic, or inappropriate for junior high students.
Source: 11, July 1984, p. 101; Sept. 1984, pp. 139–40; Nov. 1984, pp. 186, 196; Jan. 1985, p. 10; Mar. 1986, p. 39; Mar. 1987, p. 51; Sept. 1993, p. 145; Nov. 1993, pp. 178–79; Jan. 1994, p. 38.

430

Day, Doris.
Doris Day: Her Own Story.

1976
Published

1982 AL
Removed from two Anniston high school libraries due to the book's "shocking" contents particularly "in light of Miss Day's All-American image," but later reinstated on a restricted basis.
Source: 11, Mar. 1983, p. 37.

431

Day, Susan, and Elizabeth McMahan.
The Writer's Resource: Readings for Composition.

1983
Published

1991 MO
Banned from the Jasper schools because a character in a story used profanity and slang.
Source: 11, Jan. 1992, p. 8.

432

DeClements, Barthes.
No Place for Me.

1987
Published

1991 CO
Challenged in the Douglas County school libraries in Castle Rock because it introduces children to witchcraft.
Source: 11, May 1991, p. 89.

433

de Haan, Linda, and Stern Nijland.
King & King.

2002
Published

2004 IN
Moved from the children's section to the adult section at the Shelbyville-Shelby County Public Library because the book's homosexual story was considered inappropriate by a parent.

2004 NC
Restricted to adults at the Freeman Elementary School in Wilmington, the children's book is about a prince whose true love turns out to be another prince.

2005 OK
Challenged by seventy Oklahoma state legislators calling for the book to be removed from the children's section and placed in the adult section of the Metropolitan Library System in Oklahoma City.

2006 MA
Parents of a Lexington second-grader protested that their son's teacher read the fairy tale about gay marriage to the class without warning parents first. The book was used as part of a lesson about different types of weddings. "By presenting this kind of issue at such a young age, they're trying to indoctrinate our children," stated the parent. The incident renewed the efforts of Waltham-based Parents' Rights Coalition to rid the state's schools of books and lessons that advance the "homosexual agenda" in public schools. U.S. District Court Judge Mark Wolf ruled February 23, 2007, that public schools are "entitled to teach anything that is reasonably related to the goals of preparing students to become engaged and productive citizens in our democracy." Wolf said the courts had decided in other cases that parents' rights to exercise their religious beliefs were not violated when their children were exposed to contrary ideas in school. The parents appealed to the U.S. Court of Appeals for the First Circuit, which dismissed the case on January 31, 2008. The courts said, "There is no evidence of systemic indoctrination. There is no allegation that the student was asked to

affirm gay marriage. Requiring a student to read a particular book is generally not coercive of free exercise rights. Public schools are not obligated to shield individual students from ideas which potentially are religiously offensive, particularly when the school imposes no requirement that the student agree with or affirm those ideas, or even participate in discussions about them." The parents plan to appeal to the U.S. Supreme Court claiming the curriculum violated their right to religious freedom.

2007 PA
Retained at the Lower Macungie Library. The donated book was challenged because, "let them be kids... and not worry about homosexuality, race, religion. Just let them live freely as kids."

2008
Withdrawn from two Bristol, England, primary schools following objections from parents who claimed the book was unsuitable for children and that they had not been consulted on their opinions.
Source: 11, May 2004, p. 97; July 2004, pp. 137-38; May 2005, pp. 108-9; July 2006, pp. 186-87; May 2007, pp. 105-6; Jan. 2008, pp. 25-26; Mar. 2008, p. 79; July 2008, pp. 146, 166; Sept. 2008, pp. 194-95.

434
de Jenkins, Lyll Becerra.
The Honorable Prison.

1988
Published

1992 WA
Challenged at the Commodore Middle School in Bainbridge Island as inappropriate by three parents because of violence, sexual scenes, and "lack of family values."
Source: 11, May 1992, p. 84.

435
de Schweinitz, Karl.
Growing Up: How We Become Alive, Are Born and Grow.

1965
Published

1987 WA
Placed on restricted shelves at the Evergreen School District elementary school libraries in Vancouver in accordance with the school board policy

to restrict student access to sex education books in elementary school libraries.
Source: 11, May 1987, p. 87.

436
De Veaux, Alexis.
Na-ni.

1973
Published

1988 VA
Removed from open shelves to students in grades K-2 at South Accomack Elementary Schools after the county school board agreed that it contains vulgar words ("dog turd") and improper punctuation.
Source: 11, May 1988, p. 87.

437
Dean, Roger.
Album Cover Album.

1977
Published

1987 WA
Challenged at the Evergreen School District Junior High School library in Vancouver because "of the way some of the covers represented women" citing one album cover depicting the "Statue of Liberty with bare breasts as exemplary of several photos that were pretty raw toward women."
Source: 11, May 1987, p. 102.

438
Defoe, Daniel.
Adventures of Robinson Crusoe.

1719
Published

1720
Placed on the Spanish Index.
Source: 4, p. 25.

439
Defoe, Daniel.
Moll Flanders.

1721
Published

1930
U.S. Customs raised its ban.
Source: 4, p. 25; 8, pp. 367-68.

440
Defoe, Daniel.
Political History of the Devil.

1743
Published

1743
Listed on the *Index Librorum Prohibitorum* (List of Prohibited Books) in Rome, Italy.
Source: 4, p. 25.

441
Defoe, Daniel.
Roxana.

1724
Published

1930
U.S. Customs raised its ban.
Source: 4, p. 25.

442
Defoe, Daniel.
The Shortest Way with the Dissenters.

1702
Published

1703
Burned and the author fined, imprisoned, and pilloried in London, England.
Source: 4, p. 25.

443
Del Vecchio, John M.
The 13th Valley: A Novel.

1982
Published

1993 IL
Banned from the Amundsen High School classrooms in Chicago because of "explicit sexual content."
Source: 11, Sept. 1993, pp. 147-48.

444
DeLillo, Don.
Americana.

1971
Published

1980 UT
Removed from the Davis County Library.
Source: 11, Nov. 1980, p. 127.

445
Dell, Floyd.
Janet March.

1923
Published

1923 MA
Banned in Boston.

1923 NY
New York Society for the Suppression of Vice lodged a formal complaint with the New York City district attorney, charging the book was "obscene." Instead of fighting the threat, the publisher, Alfred A. Knopf, promised to cease printing future copies of the book and withdrew the book.
Source: 13, pp. 122–23

446
DeMille, Nelson.
The Charm School.

1988
Published

1999 MA
Removed from the Waltham High School summer reading list because of two sexually graphic passages.
Source: 11, Jan. 2000, p. 14.

447
Dengler, Marianna.
A Pebble in Newcomb's Pond.

1979
Published

1984 CA
Judged unacceptable at the Thompson Junior High School in Bakersfield.
Source: 11, July 1984, p. 105.

448
Denneny, Michelle; Charles Ortlieb; and Thomas Steele.
First Love/Last Love: New Fiction from Christopher Street.

1985
Published

1993 OR
Challenged at the Deschutes County Library in Bend because it "encourages and condones" homosexuality.
Source: 11, Sept. 1993, pp. 158–59.

449
Descartes, Rene.
Discourse on Method.

1637
Published

1640
Prohibited at the University of Leiden in Netherlands because it was considered anti-Protestant. Calvinists persuaded the University of Leiden to ban Cartesian doctrine from all lectures and writings.

1640
Prohibited at the University of Utrecht in Netherlands because it was considered anti-Protestant.

1663
Placed on the *Index Librorum Prohibitorum* (Index of Prohibited Books) in Rome, Italy, fourteen years after his death.

1926
Banned in the USSR.

1948
Descartes remained on the Index.
Source: 6, pp. 665–66.

450
Dessen, Sarah.
Just Listen.

2006
Published

2007
Best Books for Young Adults

2007 FL
Challenged in the Hillsborough County school system because it was considered too intense for teens.
Source: 11, Mar. 2008, p. 59.

451
Deuker, Carl.
On the Devil's Court.

1988
Published

1990
Best Books for Young Adults

1999 VA
Challenged, but retained, at the Virginia Run Elementary School in Centreville despite a parent's claim that the book espouses "pro-Satanism."
Source: 11, Nov. 1999, pp. 172–73.

452
Deveraux, Jude.
A Knight in Shining Armor.

1989
Published

1993 CA
Retained at the Lassen Union High School in Quincy. The book was checked out from a recreational reading library provided by the English instructor. Parents called the romance novel "obscene."
Source: 11, Nov. 1993, p. 193.

453
Diagram Group.
Man's Body: An Owner's Manual.

1976
Published

1979 OR
Banned from the Monroe High School when parents complained that the reference book's portrayals of male and female anatomies were too explicit.
Source: 9; 11, May 1979, p. 51.

454
Diagram Group.
Woman's Body: An Owner's Manual.

1977
Published

1979 OR
Banned from the Monroe High School when parents complained that the reference book's portrayals of male and female anatomies were too explicit.

1987 WI
Challenged at the Evansville High School library because the book is "filth" and it is "sick," even though it is on a restricted shelf behind the librarian's desk.
Source: 9; 11, May 1979, p. 51; May 1987, p. 102.

455
Dickens, Charles.
Oliver Twist.

1837
Published

1949 NY
A group of Jewish parents in Brooklyn went to court claiming that the assignment of Dickens's novel to senior high school literature classes violated the rights of their children to receive an education free of religious bias in *Rosenberg v. Board of Education of the City of New York*, 196 Misc. 542, 92 N.Y. Supp. 2d 344.
Source: 8, pp. 271–73; 12, pp. 23, 230.

456
Dickens, Frank.
Albert Herbert Hawkins: The Naughtiest Boy in the World.

1971
Published

1985 CO
Relegated to an adult shelf at the Castle Rock elementary school libraries because it "advocates defiance of adult authority by showing misbehavior for which the protagonist goes unpunished." The Douglas County Board of Education reversed its ruling seven months later and decided the book could go back into general circulation.
Source: 11, May 1985, p. 76; Sept. 1985, p. 151; Nov. 1985, p. 203.

457
Dickens, Frank.
Albert Herbert Hawkins and the Space Rocket.

1978
Published

1985 CO
Relegated to an adult shelf at the Castle Rock elementary school libraries because it "advocates defiance of adult authority by showing misbehavior for which the protagonist goes unpunished," the Douglas County Board of Education reversed its ruling seven months later and decided the book could go back into general circulation.
Source: 11, May 1985, p. 76; Sept. 1985, p. 151; Nov. 1985, p. 203.

458
Dickey, Eric Jerome.
The Other Woman.

2003
Published

2005 AR
Challenged in the Fayetteville High School library. The complainant also submitted a list of more than fifty books, citing the books as too sexually explicit and promoting homosexuality.
Source: 11, Sept. 2005, p. 215.

459
Dickey, James.
Deliverance.

1970
Published

1973 ND
Burned in Drake, but U.S. District Court ruled that teachers should be allowed to use this title in eleventh- and twelfth-grade English classes.

1974 MD
Challenged in Montgomery County on the grounds that it employs "gutter language" and depicts "perverted acts."

1993 ND
Moved from the Hughes Junior High School in Bismarck to the High School because a parent considered some passages obscene, pornographic, or inappropriate for junior high students.

1998 CT
Challenged, but retained, in the Sheehan High School English curriculum in Wallingford because the book was too "graphic and contained explicit language." After two hundred people attended a special board meeting and after listening to the teachers and "articulate" students, the board denied that request for removal.
Source: 11, July 1975, p. 118; Nov. 1975, p. 174; Sept. 1993, p. 145; Nov. 1993, pp. 178–79; Jan. 1994, p. 38; July 1998, p. 120.

460
Diderot, Denis, and Jean Le Rond d'Alembert.
Encyclopédie.

1751-52
Published

1759
Censored repeatedly during the twenty-one years of its publication. In 1759, the Catholic Church placed the first seven volumes, and in 1804, the entire work on the *Index Librorum Prohibitorum* (Index of Prohibited Books) in Rome, Italy, where it remained until 1966.
Source: 1, pp. 91–94.

461
Dieckman, Ed, Jr.
The Secret of Jonestown: The Reason Why.

1981
Published

1990 IL
Challenged at the La Grange Public Library because it promotes "hate" for the Jewish people. "It is a Nazi book and it doesn't belong in La Grange."
Source: 11, May 1990, p. 84.

462
Diehl, William.
Sharky's Machine.

1978
Published

1982 LA
Challenged at the Northside High School Library in Lafayette due to "the book's treatment of drugs, prostitution, and race."
Source: 11, May 1982, p. 83.

463
Doig, Ivan.
Dancing at the Rascal Fair.

1987
Published

2007 ID
Challenged in the Coeur d'Alene School District because sexual descriptions in the book were not appropriate. Some parents say the book, along with five others, should require parental permission for students to read them.
Source: 11, Sept. 2007, p. 181.

464
Donleavy, John P.
The Ginger Man.

1955
Published

1955
Originally published by Girodias in Paris. Author expurgated that text himself to permit publication in England.
Source: 4, p. 97.

465

Dorner, Marjorie.
Nightmare.

1987
Published

1995 MN
Pulled from the Winona Middle School media center and classroom libraries because of language and violence in the book.
Source: 11, Jan. 1996, p. 11.

466

Dorris, Michael.
A Yellow Raft in Blue Water.

1987
Published

1987
Best Books for Young Adults

1997 TX
Challenged as required reading for freshmen in the Advanced Placement Honors English Class at Clear Lake High School in Houston. A parent described the contents as "not suggestive, not explicit, but pornographic, and in the guise of multi-cultural reading."

1999 GA
Challenged at the Pebblebrook High School in Marietta because of the book's profanity and explicit sexual language.
Source: 11, Mar. 1998, p. 42; May 1999, p. 66.

467

Dorson, Richard M.
America in Legend: Folklore from the Colonial Period to the Present.

1973
Published

1977 GA
Removed from a library in Cobb County because the book "condones draft dodging" and contains the song "Casey Jones," which includes several stanzas describing the fabled railroad engineer's sexual prowess.
Source: 11, Sept. 1977, p. 133.

468

Doyle, Robert P.
Banned Books.

1998
Published

1999 VA
Banned from a display at Spotswood High School in Harrisonburg after a parent determined that some materials listed in the publication were inappropriate for students. Students were not required to read or even look at the publication, nor were they required to read any of the books listed in the publication.
Source: 11, Jan. 2000, p. 16; Mar. 2000, pp. 39, 45.

469

Doyle, Sir Arthur Conan.
The Adventures of Sherlock Holmes.

1892
Published

1929
Banned in the USSR because of its references to occultism and spiritualism.
Source: 4, p. 56.

470

Doyle, Sir Arthur Conan.
A Study in Scarlet.

1886
Published

2011 VA
Removed from the Albemarle County School sixth-grade required reading list because the book casts Mormonism in a negative light. The complaint cited the novel's reference to Mormons as "murderous" and "intolerant," as reason to remove the work. The complaint also alleged that the work unfairly characterized Mormons as murderous kidnappers. The classic novel was the first to present the character of the brilliant sleuth Sherlock Holmes and his friend, Dr. Watson. Doyle wrote the novel in three weeks.
Source: 11, Sept. 2011, pp. 177, 200–01; Nov. 2011, p. 205–6.

471

Dozois, Gardner, ed.
Isaac Asimov's Skin Deep.

1995
Published

1995 OH
Challenged in the Fairfield County District Library because it includes profanity and explicit sex scenes.
Source: 11, Nov. 1995, p. 184; Jan. 1996, p. 29.

472

Dragnich, Alex N.
Serbs and Croats: The Struggle in Yugoslavia.

1992
Published

1994 IL
Challenged at the Lincolnwood Public Library because the book is "pro-Serbian and anti-Croatian."
Source: 11, Mar. 1995, p. 53.

473

Dragonwagon, Crescent, and Paul Zindel.
To Take a Dare.

1982
Published

1982
Best Books for Young Adults

1989 OR
Challenged at the Crook County Middle School library because of "excessive use of profanity."
Source: 11, May 1989, p. 93.

474

Dramer, Dan.
Monsters.

1985
Published

1986 CO
Challenged at the Jefferson County school libraries in Lakewood. The book is a junior high text of monster stories including several Greek myths on the Cyclops, the Minotaur, and Medusa, as well as stories of several modern monsters such as King Kong, Dracula, and Frankenstein's monster. The Jefferson County School Board refused to ban the book.
Source: 11, May 1986, p. 82; Sept. 1986, p. 173; Nov. 1986, p. 224.

475
Draper, John William.
History of the Conflict between Religion and Science.

1874
Published

1876
First American book to be listed on the *Index Librorum Prohibitorum* (Index of Prohibited Books) in Rome, Italy. In the last twenty years of his life, Draper sought to apply Charles Darwin's theories of biological evolution to human history and politics.
Source: 1, pp. 137-38.

476
Draper, Sharon M., and Adam Lowenbein.
Romiette and Julio.

2001
Published

2006 VA
Challenged in the Albemarle County schools, spurring a debate over the age-appropriateness of material with sexual innuendo and fictional online chat room chatter. The school board determined to move the book from the supplemental summer reading list after fifth grade to the sixth-grade second semester curriculum.
Source: 11, Jan. 2007, pp. 15-16.

477
Dreiser, Theodore.
An American Tragedy.

1925
Published

1927 MA
Banned in Boston.

1933
Burned by the Nazis in Germany because it "deals with low love affairs."

1935 IN
The librarian of the Angola Public Library was ordered to "collect and burn every one of Dreiser's books."
Source: 2, p. 133; 3, pp. 13-15; 4, p. 61; 6, p. 690; 8, p. 315; 15, Vol. III, pp. 404, 407.

478
Dreiser, Theodore.
Dawn.

1931
Published

1932
Banned in Ireland.
Source: 4, p. 61.

479
Dreiser, Theodore.
Genius.

1915
Published

1916 NY
Suppressed by the New York Society for the Suppression of Vice.

1933
Burned by the Nazis in Germany because it "deals with low love affairs."
Source: 2, p. 100; 4, p. 61; 6, p. 690; 13, pp. 84–85; 15, Vol. II, pp. 631–32.

480
Dreiser, Theodore.
Sister Carrie.

1900
Published

1900 NY
Suppressed in New York City.

1958 VT
Banned in Vermont.
Source: 4, p. 61; 9, p. 141.

481
Driggs, John, and Stephen Finn.
Intimacy between Men.

1990
Published

1991 AR
Challenged, but retained, at the Rogers-Hough Memorial Library, because "we're headed down the road to another San Francisco community."
Source: 11, Sept. 1991, pp. 151, 177.

482
Drill, Esther.
Deal with It! A Whole New Approach to Your Body, Brain, and Life as a gURL.

1999
Published

2001 FL
Challenged, but retained, at the Marion-Levy Public Library System in Ocala.

2004 TX
Challenged at the Montgomery County Memorial Library System along with fifteen other young-adult books with gay-positive themes. The objections were posted at the Library Patrons of Texas website. The language describing the books is similar to that posted at the website of the Fairfax County, Virginia-based Parents Against Bad Books in Schools, to which Library Patrons of Texas links.

2005 AR
Challenged, but retained, in the Fayetteville Public school libraries. The complainant also submitted a list of more than fifty books, citing the books as too sexually explicit and promoting homosexuality.

2009 WI
Challenged at the West Bend Community Memorial Library as being "pornographic and worse than an R-rated movie." The library board unanimously voted 9–0 to maintain, "without removing, relocating, labeling, or otherwise restricting access," the books in the young adult category at the West Bend Community Memorial Library. The vote was a rejection of a four month campaign conducted by the citizen's group West Bend Citizens for Safe Libraries to move fiction and nonfiction books with sexually explicit passages from the young adult section to the adult section and label them as containing sexual material.
Source: 11, Nov. 2001, p. 246; Nov. 2004, pp. 231–32; Jan. 2005, pp. 5–6; May 2005, p. 135; Sept. 2005, p. 215; Nov. 2005, pp. 295–96; May 2009, pp. 80-81; Sept. 2009, pp. 169-70.

483

Dubberley, Emily.
Sex for Busy People: The Art of the Quickie for Lovers on the Go.

2006
Published

2009 KS
Restricted minors' access in the Topeka and Shawnee County Public Library because Kansans for Common Sense contended that the material is "harmful to minors under state law." Later the board organization voted 6-3 in favor of adopting a staff recommendation to keep the books where they are currently located on the shelves in the library's Health Information Neighborhood section.
Source: 11, May 2009, pp. 77-78; July 2009, p. 139.

484

Dumas, Alexandre.
Camille.

1848
Published

1850
Banned in England.

1852
Banned in France.

1863
Banned in Italy.

1958
Ban lifted in USSR.
Source: 4, p. 48; 14, p. 74.

485

Duncan, Lois.
Daughters of Eve.

1979
Published

1997 WV
Removed from the Jackson County school libraries along with sixteen other titles.

2000 VA
Removed from the Fairfax County middle school libraries and classrooms because "it promotes risky behavior and violence and also seeks to prejudice young vulnerable minds on several issues."

2005 IN
Challenged at the Lowell Middle

School because of the book's profanity and sexual content.
Source: 11, Jan. 1998, p. 13; July 2000, p. 105; May 2005, pp. 109–10.

486

Duncan, Lois.
Don't Look Behind You.

1989
Published

1990
Best Books for Young Adults

1993 IN
Challenged at the Charlestown Middle School library because of graphic passages, sexual references, and alleged immorality in the book.
Source: 11, July 1993, p. 124.

487

Duncan, Lois.
Killing Mr. Griffin.

1978
Published

1978
Best Books for Young Adults

1988 CA
Challenged at the Sinnott Elementary School in Milpitas because the book contained "needlessly foul" language and had no "redeeming qualities."

1992 CA
Pulled from a Bonsall Middle School eighth-grade reading list because of disgusting violence and profanity.

1995 PA
Challenged in the Shenandoah Valley Junior-Senior High School curriculum because of violence, strong language, and unflattering references to God.

2000 PA
Challenged in a Bristol Borough middle school for violence and language.
Source: 11, July 1988, pp. 122–23; Sept. 1988, p. 179; Mar. 1993, p. 43; July 1995, p. 99; May 2000, p. 78.

488

Duong, Thu Huong.
Novel without a Name.

1990
Published

1991
Forbidden in Vietnam. Duong was

arrested and imprisoned without trial. She was charged with having contacts with "reactionary" foreign organizations and with having smuggled "secret documents" out of the country.
Source: 6, p. 702; 8, pp. 146–47.

489

Duong, Thu Huong.
Paradise of the Blind.

1988
Published

1988
Banned in Vietnam. The novel outraged Vietnamese leaders, particularly the sections describing the 1953-56 land reform campaign—its excesses and its management, its destructive effects. Party Secretary Nguyen Van Linh publicly denounced Duong as "a whore;" he issued a second banning order. The depictions of these situations and their repercussions established her leadership of the dissident movement, leading to her arrest and the banning of her works.
Source: 8, pp. 151–52.

490

Durack, Mary, and Elizabeth Durack.
Kookanoo and the Kangaroo.

1966
Published

1978 MD
Removed from Howard County because, "it would be hard for primary youngsters to make the distinction between the aborigines in Australia and black children in the U.S."
Source: 11, Mar. 1978, p. 30.

491

Durang, Christopher.
Laughing Wild.

1987
Published

1998 FL
Challenged at the Manatee County School District in Bradenton Beach because the play contains references to Dr. Ruth Westheimer and uses several slang words for sexual acts.
Source: 11, May 1998, p. 71.

492

Durant, Penny Raife.
When Heroes Die.

1992
Published

1993 OR
Challenged at the Seaside Public Library for promoting homosexuality.
Source: 11, Jan. 1994, p. 36.

493

Durrell, Lawrence.
The Black Book.

1938
Published

1961
Seized by the U.S. Customs Bureau.
Source: 4, p. 88.

494

Earth Science.

1987 MI
Challenged at the Plymouth-Canton school system in Canton because this book "teaches the theory of evolution exclusively. It completely avoids any mention of Creationism… The evolutionary propaganda also underminds [sic] the parental guidance and teaching the children are receiving at home and from the pulpits."
Source: 11, Nov. 1981, pp. 162–63; May 1987, p. 109.

495

Eban, Abba.
My People: The History of the Jews.

1978
Published

1983
Banned from the 1983 Moscow, Russia, International Book Fair along with more than fifty other books because it is "anti-Soviet."
Source: 11, Nov. 1983, p. 201.

496

Ebert, Alan.
The Homosexuals.

1977
Published

1982 MI
Challenged at the Niles Community Library because, "it belongs on the shelves of a porno-shop."
Source: 11, Jan. 1983, p. 8.

497

Edgerton, Clyde.
The Floatplane Notebooks.

1988
Published

1988
Best Books for Young Adults

1992 VA
Challenged at the Carroll County High School in Hillsville because "it was wishy-washy" and "could warp a child's mind." The complainants circulated a petition demanding the firing of an English teacher and the dismissal of all school officials connected with the decision to use the novel.
Source: 11, May 1992, p. 84; Sept. 1992, p. 143.

498

Edgerton, Clyde.
Walking Across Egypt.

1987
Published

1997 VA
Removed from a Clover Hill High School class in Richmond because the book refers to African-Americans as "niggers," is punctuated with profanity, and is "unacceptable and unnecessary."
Source: 11, May 1997, p. 67.

499

Ehrenreich, Barbara.
Nickel and Dimed: On (Not) Getting By in America.

2001
Published

2002
Alex Award

2003 NC
Criticized as the book chosen for the University of North Carolina at Chapel Hill summer reading program by Republican state lawmakers, citing a "pattern" of the university being anti-Christian. In 2002, three freshmen sued the university over its choice of *Approaching the Qur'an: The Early Revelations*, by Michael A. Sells. The federal lawsuit was filed on the students' behalf by the Family Policy Network, a Christian group based in Virginia. Court later rejected the argument that the reading requirement violated the U.S. Constitution.

2010 NH
Removed from the Bedford School District's required Personal Finance course after two parents complained about the "book's profanity, offensive references to Christianity, and biased portrayal of capitalism." The nonfiction account is about Ehrenreich's struggles to make a living on multiple minimum-wage jobs in America. A checklist has been proposed that Bedford school officials would use to rate books and other instructional materials.

2012 PA
Challenged, but retained, on the Easton Area High School's Advanced Placement English reading list despite several residents and persons from outside the district calling the book "faddish," of "no moral value," and even "obscene."
Source: 11, Sept. 2003, p. 182; May 2010, p. 107; Mar. 2011, pp. 53-54; May 2011, pp. 96-97; May 2012, pp. 128-29; July 2012, pp. 179-80.

500

Ehrlich, Max.
The Reincarnation of Peter Proud.

1973
Published

1976 CO
Banned from use in Aurora High School English classes on the grounds of "immorality."
Source: 11, May 1976, p. 70; May 1977, p. 79.

501

Ehrlich, May.
Where It Stops, Nobody Knows.

1988
Published

1998 SC
Removed from the Cayce-West Columbia School District's Congaree Elementary School library because of a blasphemy and slang term for sex.
Source: 11, Mar. 1999, p. 36.

502

El Saadawi, Nawal.
*The Hidden Face of Eve:
Women in the Arab World.*

1977
Published

1980
Prohibited from entry to many
Arab countries including Egypt, where
Egyptian customs and excise authorities
barred it under the Importing of Foreign
Goods Act. The author was imprisoned in
1981 under the Sadat regime, blacklisted
from Egyptian television and radio, and
the target of numerous death threats by
Muslim fundamentalists. In 1993, she left
Egypt, fearing for her life, and moved to
the United States.

1980
Burned in Tehran, Iran, along with the
publishing house.
Source: 8, pp. 245–47.

503

Eleveld, Mark, ed.
*The Spoken Word Revolution:
Slam, Hip Hop & the Poetry
of a New Generation.*

2003
Published

2006 WA
Challenged, but retained, in the Sequim
School District despite complaints
that the book contains "profanity and
references to sex, drugs, and mistreatment
of women that are inappropriate for
young teens."
Source: 11, Sept. 2006, p. 257.

504

Eliot, George.
Adam Bede.

1859
Published

1859
Attacked as "the vile outpourings of a
lewd woman's mind" and withdrawn from
the British circulating libraries.
Source: 4, p. 45.

505

Eliot, George.
Silas Marner.

1861
Published

1978 CA
Banned from the Anaheim Union
High School District English classrooms
according to the Anaheim Secondary
Teachers Association.
Source: 11, Jan. 1979, p. 6.

506

Eliot, John.
The Christian Commonwealth.

1659
Published

1661 MA
Banned in Massachusetts for stating that
even royal authorities owed their power to
higher source. Any Massachusetts citizen
who owned copies of the banned work
had to "cancel or deface" them and bring
them to local judges, who would then
dispose of them.
Source: 1, pp. 37–38.

507

Elish, Dan.
*Born Too Short:
The Confessions of an
Eighth-Grade Basket Case.*

2002
Published

2005 MD
Banned in Carroll County schools.
No reason stated.
Source: 11, Mar. 2006, pp. 70–71.

508

Elliot, David.
An Alphabet for Rotten Kids.

1991
Published

1999 WA
Pulled from the Spokane School District
libraries after a parent complained its
depictions of children hitting animals and
destroying property gave her
second-grader the wrong message.
Source: 11, May 1999, p. 68.

509

Ellis, Bret Easton.
American Psycho.

1991
Published

1991 MO
The Carthage public librarian was directed
first "to take the book off the shelf and
keep it under the circulation desk" and
then "lose it." The incident involving the
novel "snowballed" and was one of the
reasons why, under protest, the librarian
submitted her resignation.
Source: 11, Nov. 1991, p. 195.

510

Ellis, Elisabeth Gaynor,
and Anthony Esler.
World History.

2007
Published

2013 FL
Challenged, but retained, in the Volusia
County high schools despite a thirty-two-
page chapter on "Muslim Civilizations" that
covers the rise of Islam and the building
of a Muslim empire. Protesters believe the
Volusia high schools are using the world
history textbook to "indoctrinate" students
into the Islamic religion and recommend
student volunteers tear the chapter out
of the 1,000-page book.
Source: 11, Jan. 2014, pp. 9-10.

511

Ellis, Havelock.
Studies in the Psychology of Sex.

1897-10
Published

1898
Condemned as "lewd, wicked,
bawdy, scandalous and obscene" and
burned in England.

1941
Banned from the mail by the U.S. Post
Office Department unless addressed
to a doctor.

1953
Banned in Ireland.
Source: 4, pp. 56–57; 6, pp. 732–33.

512

Ellison, Ralph.
Invisible Man.

1952
Published

1953
National Book Award for Fiction

1975 PA
Excerpts banned in Butler.

1975 WI
Removed from the high school English reading list in St. Francis.

1994 WA
Retained in the Yakima schools after a five-month dispute over what advanced high school students should read in the classroom. Two parents raised concerns about profanity and images of violence and sexuality in the book and requested that it be removed from the reading list.

2013 NC
Challenged, but retained, on the shelves of the Randolph County high school libraries despite the book's strong language. In 1998, the Modern Library ranked the novel nineteenth on its list of the 100 best English-language novels of the twentieth century. *TIME* magazine included the novel in its 100 Best English-language Novels from 1923 to 2005.
Source: 11, July 1975, p. 105; Nov. 1994, pp. 202–3; Nov. 2013, pp. 242-43.

513

Elson, Robert T.
Prelude to World War II.

1976
Published

1989 OR
Challenged at the Douglas County Library in Roseburg because the book contains nudity and violent photos harmful to children researching the war.
Source: 11, Jan. 1990, pp. 4–5.

514

Elwell, Walter A., ed.
Evangelical Commentary on the Bible.

1989
Published

1991 OR
Challenged, but retained, at the Multnomah County Library by a patron who believed public funds should not be expended on religious books.
Source: 11, Jan. 1992, p. 6.

515

Emerson, Zack.
Echo Company.

1991
Published

1993 AZ
Restricted access at the Marana Unified School District because of complaints about profanity.
Source: 11, Sept. 1993, p. 143.

516

Encyclopaedia Britannica.

1986
Banned and then pulped in Turkey because it was a "means of separatist propaganda."
Source: 3, p. 579.

517

The Endless Quest.

1982
Published

1985 IA
Challenged in Newton because the books in the series contain excessive violence, destruction, witchcraft, and the occult. The titles in the series include: *The Hero of Washington Square, The King's Quest, Light on Quest Mountain, Spell of the Winter Wizard,* and *Under the Dragon's Wing.*
Source: 11, Mar. 1986, p. 38.

518

Enger, Eldon D., et al.
Concepts in Biology.

1979
Published

1980 MA
Two pages removed from the Waltham High School text due to their explicit nature.
Source: 11, Jan. 1981, p. 10.

519

Erasmus, Desiderius.
Colloquies.

1518-33
Published

1526
Condemned, along with *The Praise of Folly*, by the Sorbonne and the Parlement of Paris, France, for allegedly heretical sympathies with Lutheranism. All of Erasmus's works were listed in the first *Index Librorum Prohibitorum* (Index of Prohibited Books) established in 1559, a ban that remained until the 1930s.
Source: 1, pp. 48–49.

520

Erdoes, Richard, and Alfonso Ortiz.
American Indian Myths and Legends.

1989
Published

1997 AK
Removed from the Anchorage school library shelves that are accessible to students. The anthology, which contains some sexually explicit tales, was placed in special resource collections available only to teachers.
Source: 11, Mar. 1998, p. 39; May 1998, pp. 70–71.

521

Erlbach, Arlene.
The Middle School Survival Guide.

2003
Published

2013 NJ
Removed from the Walnut Street School library in Delanco because "the book provided too much information about sexual issues for middle school students."
Source: 11, July 2013, p. 141.

522

Escher, M. C.
The Graphic Work of M. C. Escher.

1961
Published

1994 AZ
Retained at Maldonado Elementary School in Tucson after being challenged by parents who objected to nudity and "pornographic," "perverted," and "morbid" themes.
Source: 11, July 1994, p. 112.

523

Escoffier, Jeffrey.
John Maynard Keynes.

1995
Published

2000 CA
Removed from the Anaheim school district because school officials said the book is too difficult for middle school students and that it could cause harassment against students seen with it. The American Civil Liberties Union (ACLU) of Southern California filed suit in *Doe v. Anaheim Union High School District* alleging that the removal is "a pretext for viewpoint-based censorship." The ACLU claims no other books have been removed from the junior high library for similar reasons, even though several, such as works by Shakespeare and Dickens, are more difficult reading. The ACLU contends that the school officials engaged in unconstitutional viewpoint discrimination by removing the book because it contains gay and lesbian material. In March 2001, the school board approved a settlement that restored the book to the high school shelves and amended the district's policy to prohibit the removal of books for subject matter involving sexual orientation, but the book will not be returned to the middle school.
Source: 11, Mar. 2001, p. 53; May 2001, p. 95; July 2001, p. 173.

524

Esquivel, Laura.
Like Water for Chocolate: A Novel in Monthly Installments, with Recipes, Romances, and Home Remedies.

1989
Published

1989
Best Books for Young Adults

2004 WI
Challenged at the Arrowhead High School in Merton as an elective reading

list assignment by a parent because the book contains "sexually explicit and inappropriate material."

2012 ID
Removed from the reading list at Nampa High School because it was considered too racy for sophomores. The book has been considered a contemporary classic in Latin American literature.
Source: 11, Jan. 2005, p. 11; Nov. 2012, pp. 237-38.

525

Etchison, Dennis.
Cutting Edge.

1986
Published

1988 OR
Challenged at the Eugene Public Library for its language, sexual nature, and "perversity."
Source: 11, Jan. 1989, p. 3.

526

Evans, Tabor.
Longarm in Virginia City.

1984
Published

1985 IN
Challenged at the Allen County Public Library in Fort Wayne as "pornographic and objectionable."

1988 OR
Removed from the Jordan Valley Union High School because it was "too sexually graphic."

2001 AR
Challenged, but retained, at the Springdale Public Library along with all other "western" novels because the writings include "pornographic, sexual encounters."
Source: 11, July 1985, pp. 111-12; Jan. 1989, p. 3; Nov. 2001, p. 277.

527

Evertts, Eldonna L.
Holt Basic Readings.

1983
Published

1983 TN
Challenged at the Hawkins County school system in Church Hill by the Citizens Organized for Better Schools

because they claim the reading series indoctrinates students in "secular humanist" beliefs. Over 400 specific objections were filed against the reading series including specific complaints against the following works included in the series: *Rumpelstiltskin; Cinderella; The Wizard of Oz,* by L. Frank Baum; Shakespeare's *Macbeth; Anne Frank: The Diary of a Young Girl*; readings from anthropologist Margaret Mead; science fiction writer Isaac Asimov; and fairy tale creator Hans Christian Andersen. On October 24, 1986, U.S. District Court Judge Thomas G. Hull ruled in favor of the citizens' group and that the school's use of the textbook series "burdened" the plaintiffs' First Amendment rights to exercise freedom of religion. He ordered the Hawkins County public schools to excuse fundamentalist children from reading class. On August 24, 1987, a three-judge panel of the U.S. Court of Appeals for the Sixth Circuit reversed Judge Hull's decision by ruling unanimously that public school students can be required to read and discuss the disputed books, even though parts of those books might conflict with their beliefs. The court further ruled that there was no evidence that "the conduct required of the students was forbidden by their religion." On February 22, 1988, the U.S. Supreme Court declined to consider the appeal. The denial of certiorari in the case of *Mozert v. Hawkins County* left standing the August decision by the U.S. Court of Appeals for the Sixth Circuit.
Source: 11, Jan. 1984, p. 11; Mar. 1984, p. 40; May 1984, p. 79; July 1984, pp. 112-13; Jan. 1987, pp. 1, 36–38; May 1987, pp. 75, 104–7; Sept. 1987, pp. 166–67; Nov. 1987, pp. 217–18; Mar. 1988, pp. 40–41, 58; May 1988, pp. 94–95.

528

Evslin, Bernard.
Cerberus.

1987
Published

1990 MO
Removed from the elementary school library shelves, but retained, in the junior and senior high school libraries in the Francis Howell School District in St. Peters. Allegedly, the book's story line is too graphic, its titles too gruesome, and its illustrations "pornographic." (The illustrations are drawings by

Michelangelo and other Old Masters.) The book was said to "encourage satanism."

Source: 11, May 1990, p. 84; July 1990, pp. 126–27; Sept. 1990, p. 159.

529
Eyerly, Jeannette.
Someone to Love Me.

1987
Published

1997 WV
Removed from the Jackson County school libraries along with sixteen other titles.

Source: 11, Jan. 1998, p. 13.

530
Fanon, Frantz.
The Wretched of the Earth.

1961
Published

1985
Banned in South Korea.

Source: 5, Apr. 1986, pp. 30–33.

531
Farmer, Philip J.
Image of the Beast.

1968
Published

1981 WV
Challenged at the Chapmanville Public Library because the book puts "mental pictures in the mind [that] have no place in the library."

Source: 11, Mar. 1981, p. 41.

532
Farrell, James T.
Studs Lonigan: A Trilogy.

1932-35
Published

1942
Young Lonigan was published in 1932 with the notice that it was "limited to physicians, social workers, teachers, and other persons having a professional interest in the psychology of adolescence." Banned in Canada.

1948 PA
Seized in Philadelphia.

1953
Banned in Ireland.

1953
Banned in overseas libraries controlled by the U.S. Information Agency.

1953 MN
Banned in St. Cloud.

Source: 2, p. 148; 4, p. 85.

533
Farrell, James T.
A World I Never Made.

1936
Published

1937
John S. Sumner and the Society for the Suppression of Vice took Vanguard Press to court, claiming that the novel was "obscene" and "pornographic." The court determined the book was not pornographic and dismissed the case.

1948 PA
The novel was one of nine novels identified as obscene in criminal proceedings in the Court of Quarter in Philadelphia County. The court ruled the novels were not obscene.

1957
The U.S. Information Agency banned all of Farrell's novels from overseas libraries under its control.

1957 MN
Banned in St. Cloud.

1957 WI
Banned in Milwaukee.

Source: 2, p. 159; 14, pp. 301–2; 15, Vol. III, pp. 648, 650.

534
Fassbender, William.
You and Your Health.

1977
Published

1987 WA
Challenged in the Seattle school system because of its views on substance abuse and morality, as well as promiscuity.

Source: 11, July 1987, p. 131.

535
Fast, Howard.
Citizen Tom Paine.

1943
Published

1947 NY
Banned from high school libraries in New York City because it was allegedly written by a spokesman of a totalitarian movement and because it contains incidents and expressions not desirable for children and was improper and indecent.

1953
Withdrawn from U.S. Information Agency libraries overseas.

Source: 4, p. 89; 7, pp. 111–12; 15, Vol. IV, p. 700.

536
Fast, Howard.
The Immigrants.

1977
Published

1982 NC
Restricted to high school students with parental permission at the Governor Morehead School in Raleigh due to the explicit sexual scenes and vulgarities.

Source: 11, Nov. 1982, p. 205.

537
Fast, Howard.
Second Generation.

1978
Published

1982 NC
Restricted to high school students with parental permission at the Governor Morehead School in Raleigh due to the explicit sexual scenes and vulgarities.

Source: 11, Nov. 1982, p. 205.

538
Faulkner, William.
As I Lay Dying.

1930
Published

1949
Nobel Prize in Literature

1986 KY

Banned in the Graves County School District in Mayfield because it contained "offensive and obscene passages referring to abortion and used God's name in vain." The decision was reversed a week later after intense pressure from the ACLU and considerable negative publicity.

1987 KY

Challenged as a required reading assignment in an advanced English class of Pulaski County High School in Somerset because the book contains "profanity and a segment about masturbation."

1991 MD

Challenged, but retained, in the Carroll County schools. Two school board members were concerned about the book's coarse language and dialect.

1994 KY

Banned at Central High School in Louisville temporarily because the book uses profanity and questions the existence of God.

Source: 11, Nov. 1986, p. 208; May 1987, p. 90; Mar. 1992, p. 64; Nov. 1994, p. 189.

539
Faulkner, William.
The Hamlet.

1940
Published

1954
Banned in Ireland.
Source: 4, p. 77.

540
Faulkner, William.
Mosquitoes.

1927
Published

1948 PA
Seized in raid in Philadelphia.

1954
Banned in Ireland.
Source: 4, p. 78.

541
Faulkner, William.
Pylon.

1935
Published

1954
Blacklisted by the National Organization of Decent Literature; condemned by local censorship groups; banned in Ireland.
Source: 4, p. 78.

542
Faulkner, William.
A Rose for Emily.

1930
Published

1996 AZ

Challenged as required reading in an honors English class at the McClintock High School in Tempe by a teacher on behalf of her daughter and other African-American students at the school. In May 1996, a class-action lawsuit was filed in U.S. District Court in Phoenix, alleging that the district deprived minority students of educational opportunities by requiring racially offensive literature as part of class assignments. In January 1997, a federal judge dismissed the lawsuit stating he realized that "language in the novel was offensive and hurtful to the plaintiff," but that the suit failed to prove the district violated students' civil rights or that the works were assigned with discriminatory intent. The U.S. Court of Appeals for the Ninth Circuit in San Francisco ruled that requiring public school students to read literary works that some find racially offensive is not discrimination prohibited by the equal protection clause or Title VI of the 1964 Civil Rights Act. The ruling came in the case *Monteiro v. Tempe Union High School District.*
Source: 11, May 1997, p. 72; Jan. 1999, pp. 13–15.

543
Faulkner, William.
Sanctuary.

1931
Published

1948 PA
The novel along with eight other novels were identified as obscene in criminal proceedings in the Court of Quarter sessions in Philadelphia County. Indictments were brought by the state district attorney against five booksellers who were charged with possessing and intending to sell the books. In *Commonwealth v. Gordon*, 66 D. & C. 101 (1949), the court determined that the novel is not obscene. Faulkner was awarded the Nobel Prize for literature in 1950. Although the novel did not go to court again, by 1954, it was again condemned as obscene by numerous local censorship groups throughout the U.S., and the National Organization of Decent Literature placed it on the disapproval list.

1954
Ireland banned the novel, along with most of the author's other works, because of the language such as "son of a bitch," "whore," "slut," and "bastard" combined with the brutal violence of the story. Irish and U.S. Censors also objected to the character Ruby, who prostituted herself to obtain money to free her common-law husband from jail, to obtain legal fees, and to pay their expenses.
Source: 4, p. 78; 8, pp. 378–79.

544
Faulkner, William.
Soldier's Pay.

1926
Published

1954
Banned in Ireland.

1954
Blacklisted by the National Organization of Decent Literature; condemned by local censorship groups.
Source: 4, p. 78.

545
Faulkner, William.
Wild Palms.

1939
Published

1948 PA
Seized in raid in Philadelphia.

1954
Banned in Ireland.
Source: 4, p. 77.

546

Federico, Ronald C.
Sociology.

1975
Published

1982 FL
Removed from the Florida list of approved textbooks because, as the Pro-Family Forum argued, the textbook attacks religion and promotes nudity and profanity.
Source: 11, July 1982, p. 125.

547

Feelings, Muriel L.
Jambo Means Hello: The Swahili Alphabet.

1974
Published

1975
Caldecott Honor Book

1994 NY
Challenged by a school board member in the Queens school libraries because it "denigrate[s] white American culture, 'promotes racial separation, and discourages assimilation.'" The rest of the school board voted to retain the book.
Source: 11, July 1994, pp. 110–11; Sept. 1994, p. 166.

548

Feitelson, Rose, and George Salomon.
The Many Faces of Anti-Semitism.

1978
Published

1983
Banned from the 1983 Moscow, Russia, International Book Fair along with more than fifty other books because it is "anti-Soviet."
Source: 11, Nov. 1983, p. 201.

549

Ferguson, Alane.
Show Me the Evidence.

1989
Published

1993 IN
Challenged at the Charlestown Middle School library because of graphic passages, sexual references, and alleged immorality in the book.
Source: 11, July 1993, p. 124.

550

Ferlinghetti, Lawrence.
Coney Island of the Mind.

1958
Published

1976 CO
Banned for use in Aurora High School English classes on the grounds of "immorality."
Source: 11, May 1976, p. 70; May 1977, p. 79; 12, pp. 128–32, 238.

551

Ferlinghetti, Lawrence.
Starting from San Francisco.

1961
Published

1976 CO
Banned for use in Aurora High School English classes on the grounds of "immorality."
Source: 11, May 1976, p. 70; May 1977, p. 79; 12, pp. 128–32, 238.

552

Ferris, Jean.
Eight Seconds.

2000
Published

2002
Best Books for Young Adults

2004 TX
Challenged at the Montgomery County Memorial Library System along with fifteen other young-adult books with gay-positive themes. The objections were posted at the Library Patrons of Texas website. The language describing the books is similar to that posted at the website of the Fairfax County, Virginia-based Parents Against Bad Books in Schools, to which Library Patrons of Texas links.
Source: 11, Nov. 2004, pp. 231–32.

553

Fielding, Henry.
Tom Jones.

1749
Published

1749
Banned in France.
Source: 4, p. 29.

554

Fierstein, Harvey.
The Sissy Duckling.

2002
Published

2004 TX
Challenged at the Montgomery County Memorial Library System along with fifteen other young-adult books with gay-positive themes. The objections were posted at the Library Patrons of Texas Web site. The language describing the books is similar to that posted at the web site of the Fairfax County, Virginia-based Parents Against Bad Books in Schools, to which Library Patrons of Texas links.
Source: 11, Nov. 2004, pp. 231–32.

555

Findley, Timothy.
The Wars.

1977
Published

1977
Governor General's Award for English-language Fiction.

2011
Challenged, but retained, in the Bluewater, Ont., Canada, classrooms despite requests to ban the book because it "includes a number of very explicit and detailed descriptions of sexual encounters, most of them exploitive and violent." Several parents "objected especially to details about the hero's visit to a 'whorehouse' and to a vivid description of the young Canadian soldier's gang rape by fellow soldiers." The book is not compulsory and is on the list of books that can be used in the Grade Twelve curriculum, the final year of secondary school in Canada with students being seventeen or eighteen years old.
Source: 11, July 2011, p. 139; Jan. 2012, p. 36.

556
Fitzgerald, F. Scott.
The Great Gatsby.

1925
Published

1987 SC
Challenged at the Baptist College in Charleston because of "language and sexual references in the book."
Source: 11, July 1987, p. 133.

557
Fitzgerald, Frances.
Cities on a Hill: A Journey through Contemporary American Cultures.

1987
Published

1993 OR
Challenged at the Deschutes County Library in Bend because it "encourages and condones" homosexuality.
Source: 11, Sept. 1993, pp. 158–59.

558
Fitzgerald, John Dennis.
The Great Brain.

1972
Published

1992 NY
Removed from a list of supplemental reading material for fourth graders at the Port Jervis schools because the novel contains a discussion of suicide.
Source: 11, Nov. 1992, pp. 186–87.

559
Fitzhugh, Louise.
Harriet the Spy.

1964
Published

1983 OH
Challenged in the Xenia school libraries because the book "teaches children to lie, spy, backtalk, and curse."
Source: 6, pp. 832–33; 9; 11, Sept. 1983, p. 139; Nov. 1983, p. 197.

560
Fitzhugh, Louise.
The Long Secret.

1965
Published

1993 MT
Challenged in the Eagle Cliffs Elementary School library in Billings because the book is "demented" and pokes fun at religion.
Source: 11, Jan. 1994, p. 36.

561
Fitzhugh, Louise.
Sport.

1979
Published

1998 IA
Challenged at the Madison Elementary School in Cedar Rapids due to "cuss words" and other harsh language.
Source: 11, May 1998, pp. 87–88.

562
Flaubert, Gustave.
Madame Bovary.

1856
Published

1857
Flaubert was brought to trial in 1857 for the novel under a French law, first passed in May 1819, which aimed to suppress the exhibition, distribution, or sale of any printed matter constituting an "outrage to public and religious morality and to public decency."

1864
Placed on the *Index Librorum Prohibitorum* (List of Prohibited Books) in Rome, Italy.

1954
Banned by the National Organization of Decent Literature.
Source: 4, p. 47; 6, pp. 834–35; 8, pp. 362–63; 10, p. 142.

563
Flaubert, Gustave.
Novembre.

1842
Published

1935 NY
The New York Society for the Suppression of Vice charged a bookseller with selling an obscene book. The City Magistrates Court of New York City, Fourth District, Borough of Manhattan dismissed the complaint and discharged the defendant, after noting that there was not sufficient cause to hold the defendant for trial.
Source: 13, pp. 174–75.

564
Flora, James.
Grandpa's Ghost Stories.

1978
Published

1994 MT
Challenged as inappropriate at the Broadwater Elementary School Library in Billings because "[children] don't need to be allowed to read anything they want."
Source: 11, May 1994, p. 84.

565
Foer, Jonathan Safran.
Extremely Loud and Incredibly Close.

2005
Published

2010 WA
Challenged in the Richland School District. Used in a tenth-grade honors language arts class at Hanford High, the book tells the story of Oskar Schell, a young boy whose father died in the 9/11 World Trade Center attacks. The book contains profanity, sex, and descriptions of violence.
Source: 11, July 2010, pp. 156-57.

566
Fogelin, Adrian.
My Brother's Hero.

2002
Published

2006 FL
Removed from the Hillsborough County fourth-grade reading list, although the book is on the Sunshine State Young Reader's Award list of books for third, fourth, and fifth-graders.
Source: 11, Nov. 2006, pp. 290-91.

567
Follett, Ken.
Eye of the Needle.

1978
Published

1979
Edgar Award

1993 KS
Banned from the Marysville high school and junior high school libraries along with five other Follett novels—*The Key to Rebecca, Lie Down with Lions, Night Over Water, The Pillars of the Earth,* and *Triple*—because the books were "pornographic." Later, however, the board decided to reconsider its vote, follow an established review procedure, and retain the six books.
Source: 11, May 1993, pp. 70–71; Nov. 1993, p. 177; Jan. 1994, p. 35.

568
Follett, Ken.
The Hammer of Eden.

1998
Published

2000 MT
Challenged at the Great Falls High School library. Parents called for the review of all library books and the adoption of stricter rules to keep "obscenity" off library shelves.
Source: 11, Mar. 2001, p. 54.

569
Follett, Ken.
Night Over Water.

1991
Published

1993 OH
Returned to the open shelves at the Medina High School library despite some sexually explicit passages. The complainant then filed a police complaint against the Medina city schools, claiming the district is pandering obscenity to its students.
Source: 11, May 1993, p. 86; July 1993, p. 101.

570
Follett, Ken.
Pillars of the Earth.

1989
Published

1994 KS
Moved to a new "reserve" section of the Chanute school library. The book came under fire because of some use of obscenity and graphic violence.

2009 TX
Removed from a Cleburne summer reading list for a dual credit, high school English class because the novel contains a rape scene and passages of explicit sex.

2013 PA
Pulled from a senior English honors class in the Troy Area School District after parent objections. The objections concerned material of a sexual nature in the book that the parents deemed inappropriate. The historical novel, set in the middle of the twelfth century, is about the building of a cathedral in the town of Kingsbridge, England. The book was selected for Oprah's Book Club in 2007.
Source: 11, Sept. 1994, p. 146; Mar. 1995, p. 40; May 2009, pp. 107-8; Nov. 2013, pp. 219-20.

571
Ford, Michael Thomas.
One Hundred Questions and Answers about AIDS.

1992
Published

1993
Best Books for Young Adults

1993 WI
Challenged because it encourages sexual activity, but retained, in the Eau Claire public school libraries.

1997 WV
Removed from the Jackson County school libraries along with sixteen other titles.
Source: 11, July 1993, p. 104; Sept. 1993, p. 159; Jan. 1998, p. 13.

572
Forrest, Katherine.
Beverly Malibu.

1989
Published

1991 IL
Challenged, but retained, at the Oak Lawn Public Library because the sleuth in the mystery is a lesbian.
Source: 11, Nov. 1991, p. 209.

573
Forster, E. M.
Maurice.

1971
Published

1995 NH
Banned from the Mascenic Regional High School in New Ipswich because it is about gays and lesbians. An English teacher was fired for refusing to remove the book. An arbitrator ruled in April 1996 that she can return to work in September without a year's back pay. The Mascenic Regional School Board is appealing the ruling. The teacher was eventually reinstated after a decision by the state's Public Employee Labor Relations Board.
Source: 11, Sept. 1995, p. 166; Jan. 1996, p. 15; July 1996, pp. 130–31; Jan. 1997, p. 27.

574
Forsyth, Frederick.
The Devil's Alternative.

1979
Published

1983 WA
Removed from the Evergreen School District of Vancouver along with twenty-nine other titles. The American Civil Liberties Union of Washington filed suit contending that the removals constitute censorship, a violation of plaintiff's rights to free speech and due process, and a violation of the state Open Meetings Act because the removal decisions were made behind closed doors.
Source: 11, Nov. 1983, pp. 185–86.

575
Fossey, Dian.
Gorillas in the Mist.

1983
Published

1993 PA
Teachers at the Westlake Middle School in Erie using felt-tip pens, blacked out passages pertaining to masturbation and mating.
Source: 11, July 1993, p. 109.

576
Fox, Mem.
Guess What?

1990
Published

1991 IL
Challenged at the Cook Memorial Library in Libertyville because it features witches, boiling cauldrons, names of punk rockers, and a reference that could be interpreted as meaning "God is dead."
Source: 11, Sept. 1991, p. 153.

577
Fox, Paula.
The Slave Dancer.

1973
Published

1974
Newbery Medal

1996 GA
Challenged, but retained, by the Fayette County school system. The book is about a thirteen-year-old boy who is snatched from the docks of New Orleans and put on a slave ship bound for Africa. The book was considered objectionable because of language that is "insensitive and degrading."

1998 PA
Challenged as part of the curriculum at the North Bedford County School District in Loysburg because of the book's graphic detail and derogatory racial references.

2005 KY
Challenged at the Shelbyville East Middle School because the book is a too-graphic depiction of the slave trade.
Source: 11, May 1996, p. 99; Mar. 1999, p. 40; May 2005, pp. 110–11.

578
France, Anatole
(Jacques-Anatole Thibault).
Penguin Island.

1908
Published

1921
Nobel Prize in Literature

1922
Placed on the Catholic Church's *Index Librorum Prohibitorum* (Index of Prohibited Books) in Rome, Italy, along with all of his works. They remained on the Index until 1966. Anatole France received Nobel Prize in literature in 1921.
Source: 1, p. 252.

579
Franco, Betsy, ed.
You Hear Me?: Poems and Writings by Teenage Boys.

2000
Published

2001
Best Books for Young Adults

2002 GA
Challenged in the Houston County public schools by a parent concerned about the book's language and topics.
Source: 11, Sept. 2002, pp. 195–96.

580
Frank, Anne.
Anne Frank: The Diary of a Young Girl.

1947
Published

1982 VA
Challenged in Wise County due to protests of several parents who complained the book contains sexually offensive passages.

1983 AL
Four members of the Alabama State Text-book Committee called for the rejection of this title because it is a "real downer."

1998 TX
Removed for two months from the Baker Middle School in Corpus Christi after two parents charged that the book was pornographic. The book was returned after students waged a letterwriting campaign to keep it and a review committee recommended the book's retention.

2010 VA
Challenged at the Culpeper County public schools by a parent requesting that her daughter not be required to read the book aloud. Initially, it was reported that officials decided to stop assigning a version of Anne Frank's diary, one of the most enduring symbols of the atrocities of the Nazi regime, due to the complaint that the book includes sexual material and homosexual themes.

The director of instruction announced the edition published on the fiftieth anniversary of Frank's death in a concentration camp will not be used in the future despite the fact the school system did not follow its own policy for handling complaints. The remarks set off a hailstorm of criticism online and brought international attention to the 7,600-student school system in rural Virginia. The superintendent said, however, that the book will remain a part of English classes, although it may be taught at a different grade level.

2013 MI
Challenged, but retained, in the Northville middle schools despite anatomical descriptions in the book. Before the school district's vote, ten free speech organizations signed a letter urging the Northville School District to keep the book. The letter, which was sent to the superintendent and board of education members, "emphasized the power and relatability of Frank's diary for middle school students. Frank's honest writings about her body and the changes she was undergoing during her two-year period of hiding from the Nazis in Amsterdam can serve as an excellent resource for students themselves undergoing these changes." The diary has now been published in more than sixty different languages and is on several lists of the top books of the twentieth century.
Source: 8, pp. 402–3; 11, Mar. 1983, p. 39; July 1998, pp. 119–20; Mar. 2010, pp. 57–58; May 2010, p. 107; July 2013, p. 163.

581
Frank, E. R.
America.

2003
Published

2003
Best Books for Young Adults

2007 OH
Challenged in the Ravenna schools because, "What we kept finding and going over was sexual content and profanity," said the complainant. The novel has received several awards including *The New York Times* Notable Book Award. It also was a Garden State Teen Book Award nominee.
Source: 11, May 2007, p. 93.

582
Frank, E. R.
Life Is Funny.

2002
Published

2005 CA
Pulled from the shelves of two Merced middle-school libraries because of an "X-rated" passage describing two teens' first experience with sexual intercourse.
Source: 11, May 2005, p. 107.

583
Frank, Mel, and Ed Rosenthal.
Marijuana Grower's Guide.

1978
Published

2004 WY
Challenged at the Teton County Public Library in Jackson because "tax dollars are being used to purchase a how-to crime manual."
Source: 11, May 2004, p. 98.

584
Frank, Pat.
Alas, Babylon.

1959
Published

1987 IL
Challenged at the Taylorville Junior High School because it "contains profane language."
Source: 11, Sept. 1987, p. 194.

585
Franklin, Benjamin.
The Autobiography of Benjamin Franklin.

1791
Published

1791
"The expurgation of Benjamin Franklin seems to have increased over the years until he became in the early twentieth century one of the most censored and yet at the same time one of the most widely reprinted writers in American history. Two essays, in particular, are frequently expurgated, 'Advice on the Choice of a Mistress' and the 'Letters to the Royal Academy of Brussels.'"

1957
As Chief Judge Clarke noted in *Roth v. United States*, 345 U.S. 476, the discussed works by Franklin "which a jury could reasonably find 'obscene,' according to the judge's instructions in the case at bar" would also have subjected a person to prosecution if sent through the mails in 1957 and "to punishment under the federal obscenity statute."
Source: 8, pp. 411–12; 10, p. 134; 15, Vol. II, p. 616.

586
Freedom Writers.
The Freedom Writers Diary: How a Teacher and 150 Teens Used Writing to Change Themselves and the World Around Them.

1999
Published

2007 MI
Challenged in the Howell High School along with several other books because of strong sexual content. In response to a request from the president of the Livingston Organization for Values in Education, or LOVE, the county's top law enforcement official reviewed the books to see whether laws against distribution of sexually explicit materials to minors had been broken. "After reading the books in question, it is clear that the explicit passages illustrated a larger literary, artistic, or political message and were not included solely to appeal to the prurient interests of minors," the Livingston County prosecutor wrote. "Whether these materials are appropriate for minors is a decision to be made by the school board, but I find that they are not in violation of the criminal laws." The best-selling book has achieved national acclaim and was made into a recent hit movie.
Source: 11, Mar. 2007, pp. 51-52; May 2007, p. 118.

587
Freud, Sigmund.
Introductory Lectures on Psychoanalysis.

1933
Published

1930
Freud's works were banned from bookstores and libraries under Stalin in the Soviet Union as bourgeois ideology.

They circulated in bootleg editions until the mid-1980s.

1934
Pope Pius XI published a statement in Rome, Italy, criticizing psychoanalysis and Freud's ideas on religious belief. Freud's writings were considered off-limits to Catholics as dangerous to faith and morals according to canon law.

1939
Burned by the Nazis.
Source: 1, pp. 169–70.

588
Freymann-Weyr, Garret.
My Heartbeat.

2002
Published

2003
Best Books for Young Adults

2004 TX
Challenged at the Montgomery County Memorial Library System along with fifteen other young-adult books with gay-positive themes. The objections were posted at the Library Patrons of Texas website. The language describing the books is similar to that posted at the website of the Fairfax County, Virginia-based Parents Against Bad Books in Schools, to which Library Patrons of Texas links.
Source: 11, Nov. 2004, pp. 231–32.

589
Friday, Nancy.
Men in Love.

1980
Published

1981 IL
Temporarily placed in storage on the second floor of the Alpha Park Library and restricted to patrons over eighteen years old unless they have written parental consent because several area residents objected to its "vulgarity."
Source: 11, Jan. 1982, p. 9; May 1982, p. 100.

590
Friday, Nancy.
Women on Top: How Real Life Has Changed Women's Fantasies.

1991
Published

1994 GA

Removed from the Chestatee Regional Library System in Gainesville because the book on women's sexual fantasies is "pornographic and obscene" and lacks "literary merit." After months of protest and maneuvering, the library's only copy was destroyed when the child of a patron accidentally dropped it into a dishpan full of water. The book is out of print and the library does not plan to replace it.

1996 PA

Challenged at the Chester County Library at Charlestown because of graphic details about sex acts and fantasies.

1997

Winnipeg, Manitoba, Canada, police seized the novel from the public library.

1997 GA

Pulled from the Gwinnett County Public Library shelves after two residents complained about its sexually explicit content. Following four years of controversy over keeping adult-themed books from children, the board approved two new policies. One policy creates a "parental advisory" shelf of non-fiction sex and health books that extensively and explicitly depict human sex acts, either visually or verbally, or books the library staff deems are appropriate only for adults. The other policy allows parents to decide—with electronic designations on new library cards—whether their child can check out books on the parental advisory shelf. Parents also can restrict further what types of books the child can get from the library.

Source: 6, p. 415; 11, Nov. 1994, p. 187; Mar. 1995, p. 39; May 1995, p. 65; Nov. 1996, p. 194; Jan. 1997, p. 8; Mar. 1997, p. 49; May 1997, p. 60; Nov. 1997, p. 165.

591
Fritz, Jean.
Around the World in a Hundred Years: From Henry the Navigator to Magellan.

1994
Published

1995 MD

Removed from the Carroll County schools because a passage on the burning of the library in Alexandria during the fourth century said that "Christians did not believe in scholarship" and mentioned intellectual suppression by Christians. "It's a sweeping generalization and it's definitely anti-Christian."

Source: 11, Nov. 1995, p. 186.

592
Fuentes, Carlos.
Aura.

1962
Published

2009 PR

Banned from the curriculum in Puerto Rican public high schools along with four other books because of coarse language. Written by one of Latin America's most prominent contemporary writers, the novel contains a brief romantic encounter beneath a crucifix. It is a scene that prompted Mexico's former interior secretary to try to have the book dropped from a reading list at his daughter's private school, without success. Fuentes said that the attempt boosted sales. The other titles banned were: *Antologia Personal*, by José Luis González; *Mejor te lo Cuento: Antologia Personal, 1978-2005*, by Juan Antonio Ramos; *Reunión de Espejos*, by José Luis Vega; and *El Entierro de Cortijo: 6 de Octubre de 1982*, by Edgardo Rodriguez Juliá.

Source: 11, Nov. 2009, p. 204.

593
Fuentes, Carlos.
The Death of Artemio Cruz.

1964
Published

1994 WA

Retained in the Yakima schools after a five-month dispute over what advanced high school students should read in the classroom. Two parents had raised concerns about profanity and images of violence and sexuality in the book and requested that it be removed from the reading list.

Source: 11, Nov. 1994, pp. 202–3.

594
Fuentes, Carlos.
The Old Gringo.

1985
Published

1996 NC

Retained in the Guilford County school media centers after a parent wanted the book removed because of its explicit language.

Source: 11, Jan. 1997, p. 25.

595
Fugard, Athol.
Master Harold and the Boys.

1982
Published

1982
Drama Desk Award for Outstanding Play

1982
Tony Award for Best Play

1983
London Critic's Circle Theatre Award for Best Play

1982

A South African order banning printed copies of the play was imposed in December 1982, but was lifted temporarily a week later.

Source: 5, Mar. 1983, p. 47.

596
Gaiman, Neil.
Neverwhere.

1996
Published

2013 NM

Temporarily removed from the Alamogordo High School library and curriculum because of what one parent calls "inappropriate content." The British author wrote in *The Guardian*: "Well-meaning adults can easily destroy a child's love of reading. Stop them reading what they enjoy or give them worthy-but-dull books that you like—the twenty-first-century equivalents of Victorian 'improving' literature—you'll wind up with a generation convinced that reading is uncool and, worse, unpleasant."

Source: 11, Nov. 2013, pp. 217-18.

597
Gaines, Ernest J.
The Autobiography of Miss Jane Pittman.

1971
Published

1971
Best Books for Young Adults

1995 TX
Pulled from a seventh-grade class in Conroe after complaints about racial slurs in the book. School officials later reinstated it.

2006 WA
Challenged as an eighth-grade district-wide reading assignment in the Puyallup schools because "racial slurs and stereotyping are used throughout the book, as well as scenes of sex, rape, and implied incest." The Puyallup School Board voted to uphold an earlier decision by a district committee requiring eighth-graders to read the novel. In explaining their vote, each board member recounted the difficulty of balancing valid concerns on each side of the debate. "It wasn't a sole issue of dealing with racism or the "n-word." "But it is our hope by giving them an explanation of the word and where it came from they'll understand it's inappropriate to use it in the future."
Source: 11, Mar. 1995, p. 46; May 1995, p. 84; Jan. 2007, pp. 11-12; Mar. 2007, pp. 74-75.

598
Gaines, Ernest.
A Lesson Before Dying.

1993
Published

1993
National Book Critics Award

1994
Best Books for Young Adults

1999 GA
Banned, but later reinstated after community protests at the Windsor Forest High School in Savannah. The controversy began in early 1999 when a parent complained about sex, violence, and profanity in the book that was part of an Advanced Placement English class.

2004 LA
Removed from the college book store at Louisiana College, Pineville, by the college president because a love scene described in the book clashes with the school's Christian values.
Source: 11, Mar. 2000, p. 63; Mar. 2001, p. 76; Mar. 2004, pp. 53-54.

599
Galbraith, John Kenneth.
The Affluent Society.

1958
Published

1972 NJ
Removed from the Roselle high school library list along with *The Age of Keynes,* by Robert Lekachman, *The Struggle for Peace,* by Leonard Beaton, and *Today's Isms: Communism, Fascism, Capitalism, Socialism,* by William Ebenstein. The president of the board said, "The books were too liberal and I disagree with their points of view." Months later, after considerable public protest, the superintendent of schools placed a rush order for the books and said that they would be on the library bookshelves.
Source: 7, pp. 5-7.

600
Galdone, Joanna.
The Tailypo: A Ghost Tale.

1977
Published

1988 LA
Challenged at the Jefferson Terrace Elementary School library in East Baton Rouge because "it is too scary" and gave the complainant's "child a nightmare."
Source: 11, May 1988, p. 87.

601
Gale, Jay.
A Young Man's Guide to Sex.

1984
Published

1984
Best Books for Young Adults

1993 AK
Removed from the Kenai Peninsula Borough School District libraries in Homer because it was thought to have "outdated material that could be harmful to student health."

1993 TN
Challenged, but retained, at the Cleveland Public Library along with seventeen other books, most of which are on sex education, AIDS awareness, and some titles on the supernatural.
Source: 11, Sept. 1993, p. 146; Jan. 1994, p. 33.

602
Galileo, Galilei.
Dialogue Concerning the Two Chief World Systems.

1632
Published

1633
Banned by Pope Urban VIII in Rome, Italy, for heresy and breach of good faith and sentenced to prison for an indefinite period. It was not until 1824, when Canon Settele, a Roman astronomy professor, published a work on modern scientific theories, that the Roman Catholic Church finally announced its acceptance of "general opinion of modern astronomers." In the papal Index of 1835, the names of Galileo, Copernicus, and Kepler were removed. On October 31, 1992, Pope John Paul II formally rehabilitated Galileo—359 years, four months, and nine days after Galileo had been forced to recant his heresy that the earth moved around the sun.
Source: 4, p. 17; 8, pp. 231-33.

603
Gallagher, I. J.
The Case of the Ancient Astronauts.

1977
Published

1984 FL
Challenged at the Escambia County school district because the complainant claimed the book indicated that "Ezekiel had seen a UFO when he spoke in the Bible about seeing something that looked like a wheel in the sky."
Source: 11, Sept. 1984, p. 156.

604
Gao Xingjian.
Fugitives.

1989
Published

2000
Nobel Prize in Literature

1989
All works by Gao Xingjian banned in China. The Chinese government denounced the awarding of the 2000 Nobel Prize in Literature to Gao, accusing the Nobel committee of being politically motivated.
Source: 7, p. 184.

605
García Márquez, Gabriel.
Love in the Time of Cholera.

1985
Published

1982
Nobel Prize in Literature

1998 MD
Challenged, but retained, on the Montgomery County reading lists and school library shelves. A parent had complained that the book should be removed from all county schools because it contained "perverse sexual acts, adults having sex with children, and rape."
Source: 11, May 1998, p. 70; July 1998, p. 119.

606
García Márquez, Gabriel.
One Hundred Years of Solitude.

1967
Published

1982
Nobel Prize in Literature

1986 CA
Purged from the book list for use at the Wasco Union High School because the book was "garbage being passed off as literature."

1990 SC
Removed from the Advanced Placement English reading list at St. Johns High School in Darlington because of profane language.

1997 VA
Challenged for sexual explicitness, but retained, on the Stonewall Jackson High School's academically advanced reading list in Brentsville.

1998 MD
Challenged on the Montgomery County reading lists and school library shelves.
Source: 11, July 1986, p. 119; May 1989, p. 78; Jan. 1991, p. 18; Nov. 1997, pp. 169–70; Jan. 1998, p. 29; May 1998, p. 70.

607
Garden, Nancy.
Annie on My Mind.

1982
Published

1982
Best Books for Young Adults

2003
Margaret A. Edwards Award for Lifetime Achievement

1988 OR
Challenged at the Cedar Mill Community Library in Portland because the book portrays lesbian love and sex as normal.

1990 ME
Challenged in Sedgwick by a parent when she learned that the novel was included in the seventh- and eighth-grade library. The parent objected to the lesbian relationship portrayed. The book was retained.

1992 TX
Challenged in the Colony Public Library because "it promotes and encourages the gay lifestyle."

1993 KS
Removed at the Olathe East High School. In response, the American Civil Liberties Union joined several families and a teacher and sued the school district for removing the book. Two years later in September 1995, the case went to trial. In November 1995, U.S. District Court justice Thomas Van Bebber ruled that while a school district is not obligated to purchase any book, it cannot remove a book from library shelves unless that book is deemed educationally unsuitable. He ruled Garden's book to be educationally suitable, and called its removal an unconstitutional attempt to "prescribe what shall be orthodox in politics, nationalism, religion, or other matters of opinion." On December 29, 1999, the school district announced it would not appeal the court's decision, and restored the novel to library shelves. The entire proceeding had cost the district more than $160,000.

1993 KS
The Kansas City school district donated the book to the city's public library.

1993 MI
Challenged, but retained, at the Lapeer West High School library.

1993 MO
Challenged at several Kansas City area schools after the books were donated by a national group that seeks to give young adults "fair, accurate, and inclusive images of lesbians and gay men." Protesters burned copies of the book but the Kansas City School District kept Garden's novel on the high school shelves.

1993 MO
The book was returned to general circulation at the Shawnee Mission School District.

1993 MO
Removed by the Lee's Summit superintendent from the schools. The federal district court in Kansas, later found the removal of the book unconstitutional and ordered it restored to the school district's libraries.

1993 OR
Challenged because it "encourages and condones" homosexuality, but retained, at the Bend High School.

1994 KS
Removed from shelves of the Chanute High School Library and access to them limited to only those students with written parental permission because of concerns about its content.

1994 KS
Students and parents sued in *Stevana Case v. Unified School District No. 233, Johnson County Kansas.* Judge G. T. Van Bebber ruled on December 29, 1995, in favor of the plaintiffs, ordering the books to be returned to the school libraries.

1994 MO
Challenged, but retained, at the Liberty High School library.
Source: 3, pp. 16-17; 8, pp. 404–6; 11, Jan. 1990, pp. 4-5; July 1992, pp. 125–26; Sept. 1993, pp. 158–59; Nov. 1993, pp. 191–92; Jan. 1994, p. 13; Mar. 1994, pp. 51–52; May 1994 p. 84; July 1994, p. 129; Sept. 1994, pp. 140–41; Mar. 1995, p. 40; Mar. 1996, p. 54.

608
Garden, Nancy.
Good Moon Rising.

1996
Published

2004 TX
Challenged at the Montgomery County Memorial Library System along with fifteen other young-adult books with gay-positive themes. The objections were posted at the Library Patrons of Texas website. The language describing the books is similar to that posted at the website of the Fairfax County, Virginia-based Parents Against Bad Books in Schools, to which Library Patrons of Texas links.
Source: 11, Nov. 2004, pp. 231–32.

609
Garden, Nancy.
Holly's Secret.

2000
Published

2004 TX
Challenged at the Montgomery County Memorial Library System along with fifteen other young-adult books with gay-positive themes. The objections were posted at the Library Patrons of Texas website. The language describing the books is similar to that posted at the website of the Fairfax County, Virginia-based Parents Against Bad Books in Schools, to which Library Patrons of Texas links.
Source: 11, Nov. 2004, pp. 231–32.

610
Garden, Nancy.
Witches.

1975
Published

1986 CA
Challenged by the "God Squad," a group of three students and their parents, at the El Camino High School in Oceanside because the book "contains a lot of information on witch covens. This information can be easily used to form a coven."

1997 KS
Removed from the Kirby Junior High School in Wichita Falls because of "Satanic" themes.
Source: 11, Sept. 1986, p. 151; Nov. 1986, p. 224;

611
Gardner, Benjamin Franklin.
Black.

1933
Published

1976 OH
Removed from the Dayton schools after complaints that the work contained "hard-core pornography."
Source: 11, Jan. 1977, p. 7.

612
Gardner, John C.
Grendel.

1971
Published

1972
Mythopoeic Award for Best Novel

1978 MD
Challenged at the Frederick County school system because the novel is "anti-Christian, antimoral, full of vulgarity."

1986 CA
Placed on a restricted list at the Wasco High School which prohibits the novel's use in the classroom until every student in the class receives parental permission. The novel is the only book on the restricted list, and an objection by the high school principal to the "profane" nature of the novel was the catalyst that generated the restricted list policy.

1986 IN
Challenged in the Indianapolis schools as an accelerated English class assignment.

1991 UT
Challenged at the Viewmont High School in Farmington because the book "was obscene and should not be required reading."

1992 NJ
Challenged, but retained, as part of the Pinelands Regional High School's English curriculum in Bass River Township because of obscenities.

1993 GA
Challenged in the Clayton County School District's supplemental reading list for advanced English students in Jonesboro because the book was too violent and graphic.

1997 CO
Challenged, but retained, on the Douglas County high school reading list. Parents complained that the novel was too obscene and violent for high school students. The school board also declined to create a rating system for books.

2008 OR
Retained in the Sherwood School District sophomore honors English reading list after concerns were expressed about some of the novel's scenes describing torture and mutilation.
Source: 11, Mar. 1978, p. 39; May 1978, p. 58; May 1986, pp. 81–82; July 1986, p. 119; Jan. 1987, p. 32; May 1989, p. 87; May 1991, p. 92; Jan. 1993, p. 11; Mar. 1993, p. 56; May 1993, p. 87; May 1997, p. 78; Jan. 2009, p. 23.

613
Garrigue, Sheila.
Between Friends.
1978
Published

1983 IA
Challenged in the Des Moines schools due to the use of the word "damn."
Source: 11, May 1983, p. 73.

614
Garrison, Eric Marlowe.
Mastering Multiple Position Sex.

2009
Published

2009 OH
Challenged, but retained, at the Pataskala Public Library. The library decided to implement a new juvenile library card. A parent or guardian will be able to sign off on the card, thereby restricting his or her child's borrowing rights to juvenile materials.
Source: 11, Jan. 2010, pp. 12-13; Mar. 2010, p. 53.

615
Gassner, John, and Clive Barnes, eds.
Best American Plays: Sixth Series, 1963–1967.

1971
Published

1984 OK
Challenged at the Miami High School library because the anthology contains "The Toilet," by Leroi Jones [Imamu Amiri Baraka].
Source: 11, May 1984, p. 87.

616
Gates, Doris.
Two Queens of Heaven.

1974
Published

1979 AZ
Placed on restricted shelves in the libraries of Prescott elementary schools because it contains two illustrations of a bare-breasted goddess.
Source: 11, Jan. 1980, p. 6.

617
Gautier, Théophile.
Mademoiselle de Maupin.

1835
Published

1835
Banned until 1853 by Nicholas I in Russia.

1917 NY
Challenged in New York City and finally
cleared in 1921 after a long court fight.
Source: 4, p. 43; 15, Vol. III, p. 413.

618
Genet, Jean.
Our Lady of the Flowers.

1942
Published

1957
Seized from the Birmingham, England,
Public Library.

1958
Banned in France.
Source: 4, p. 88; 13, pp. 178–79.

619
Genet, Jean.
The Thief's Journal.

1954
Published

1961
Banned in Ireland. The Irish Board of
Censors found the novel "obscene" and
"indecent," objecting particularly to
the author's handling of the theme of
homosexuality and the poetic treatment
of crime.
Source: 13, p. 246.

620
George, Jean Craighead.
Julie of the Wolves.

1972
Published

1973
Newbery Medal

1982 MO
Challenged in Mexico because of the
book's "socialist, communist, evolutionary,
and anti-family themes."

1989 CO
Challenged in Littleton school libraries
because "the subject matter was better
suited to older students, not sixth graders."

1994 AZ
Challenged at the Erie Elementary School
in Chandler because the book includes
a passage that some parents found
inappropriate in which a man forcibly
kisses his wife. The book, depicting

the experiences of an Eskimo girl, was
chosen by the teacher of a third-, fourth-,
and fifth-grade class for the Antarctic
unit she was teaching.

1995 CA
Challenged in the classrooms and
school libraries in Palmdale because the
book describes a rape.

1996 CA
Challenged at the Hanson Lane
Elementary School in Ramona because
the book includes an attempted rape
of a thirteen-year-old girl.

1996 PA
Removed from the sixth-grade curriculum
of the New Brighton Area School District
in Pulaski Township because of a graphic
marital rape scene.
Source: 11, Nov. 1982, p. 215; Sept. 1989, p. 186; Jan. 1995,
p. 9; Mar. 1996, p. 45; May 1996, p. 88; Jan. 1997, p. 9.

621
Gettings, Fred.
Dictionary of Demons.

1988
Published

2000 OH
Moved out of the circulating collection
of the Norwood High School library
because of concerns that the book
promotes the occult.
Source: 11, May 2000, p. 75.

622
Gibbon, Edward.
*History of the Decline and Fall
of the Roman Empire.*

1776-88
Published

1783
Placed on the *Index Librorum
Prohibitorum* (List of Prohibited Books)
in Rome, Italy, because it contradicted
official church history.
Source: 4, p. 33.

623
Gibran, Kahlil.
Spirits Rebellious.

1908
Published

1908
The collection of short stories protesting
religious and political tyranny was
publicly burned in the Beirut, Lebanon,
marketplace. Gibran was exiled from
Lebanon and excommunicated from the
Maronite Church.

1908
Suppressed by the Syrian government.
Source: 1, pp. 320–21.

624
Gibson, Walter Brown, and
Litzka R. Gibson.
*Complete Illustrated Book
of Divination and Prophecy.*

1973
Published

1987 MI
Challenged at the Plymouth-Canton
school system in Canton because the
book deals with witchcraft.
Source: 11, May 1987, p. 110; Jan. 1988, p. 11.

625
Gide, André.
If It Die.

1926
Published

1947
Nobel Prize in Literature

1935 NY
The owner of the Gotham Book Mart was
arrested by a patrolman who considered
the work obscene. In 1936, Magistrate
Nathan D. Perlman said in his decision
that the author had "unveiled the darker
corners of life," but he held that "the book
as a complete entity was not obscene"
and dismissed the case.

1938
Banned in Soviet Union.

1952
Placed on the *Index Librorum Prohibitorum*
(List of Prohibited Books) in Rome, Italy.

1953
Banned in Ireland.
Source: 4, p. 59; 13, p. 114; 15, Vol. III, p. 648.

626

Giles, Gail.
Shattering Glass.

2002
Published

2003
Best Books for Young Adults

2007 OR
Challenged as an optional reading in a bullying unit at the Lake Oswego Junior High School because the novel is "peppered with profanities, ranging from derogatory slang terms to sexual encounters and violence." Students are given a list of book summaries and a letter to take to their parents. Four of the eight optional books offered are labeled as having "mature content/language."
Source: 11, July 2007, p. 149.

627

Gilstrap, John.
Nathan's Run.

1996
Published

1997
Best Books for Young Adults

1998 PA
Removed from the Annville-Cleona Middle-High School library because "the obscene/profane language and violence in this book are of a degree that it [was] concluded to be inappropriate for a middle/high school library collection."

2000 WA
Challenged in the Everett School District due to sexual explicitness and violence.
Source: 11, Sept. 1998, p. 141; Mar. 1999, p. 40; Sept. 2000, p. 144.

628

Ginsberg, Allen.
Collected Poetry, 1947-1980.

1984
Published

1989 GA
Removed from the Murray County High School library in Chatsworth because "it was really gutter stuff."

1989 IN
Challenged at the North Central High School library in Indianapolis because explicit descriptions of homosexual acts were deemed inappropriate subject matter for high school students.
Source: 11, July 1989, p. 128; Jan. 1990, p. 9; Mar. 1990, pp. 61–62.

629

Ginsberg, Allen.
Howl and Other Poems.

1956
Published

1957 CA
Seized by U.S. Customs officials in San Francisco.

2000 FL
Prohibited in the Jacksonville Forrest High School Advanced Placement English class because of descriptions of homosexual acts. The class syllabus warns students and parents that some people might find the reading objectionable and offers an alternative assignment. The prohibition led to the review of all materials taught in the class.
Source: 4, p. 97; 6, pp. 955–56; 7, pp. 459–60; 11, Jan. 2001, p. 12.

630

Ginsberg, Allen.
Kaddish and Other Poems.

1961
Published

1976 CO
Banned for use in Aurora High School English classes on the grounds of "immorality."
Source: 11, May 1976, p. 70; May 1977, p. 79; 12, pp. 128–32, 238.

631

Giovanni, Nikki.
My House: Poems.

1972
Published

1973
Best Books for Young Adults

1975 WI
Banned from the Waukesha public school libraries.

1990 NY
Challenged at the West Gennessee High School in Syracuse because the book contains obscenities.

1992 FL
Challenged at the Duval County public school libraries because it contains the word "nigger" and was accused of vulgarity, racism, and sex.
Source: 11, July 1975, p. 104; July 1990, p. 127; July 1992, p. 105.

632

Glasser, Ronald J.
365 Days.

1971
Published

1982 ME
Banned, but later reinstated by a U.S. District Court ruling in Baileyville. The class-action suit was filed by the Maine Civil Liberties Union on behalf of Michael Sheck, a former Woodland High School student, and four other students and their parents. The book was hailed by literary critics at the time of its publication for its honest portrayal of the soldiers and the war. The book was ordered removed from the high school library by the school committee after the parents of one student complained about the expletives and four-letter words it contained.
Source: 11, Mar. 1982, p. 33.

633

Glenn, Mel.
Who Killed Mr. Chippendale?: A Mystery in Poems.

1996
Published

1997
Best Books for Young Adults

1999 AL
Removed from the Central School library in Hunstville as inappropriate for fourth graders. After the book's removal, the complainant called for the formation of a group of parents to go through all the library's books, as well as monitor new books. The school's principal stated, "If a book is sexual, if it is racial, if it's violent, we'll pull it off the shelves."
Source: 11, July 1999, p. 93.

634

Godchaux, Elma.
Stubborn Roots.

1936
Published

1937 LA
Seized and destroyed by
New Orleans police.
Source: 15, Vol. III, p. 650.

635

Goethe, Johann Wolfgang von.
Faust.

1790
Published

1808
Production suppressed in Berlin,
Germany until certain dangerous passages
concerning freedom were deleted.

1939
Franco purged Spanish libraries of
all of Goethe's writings.
Source: 4, p. 35.

636

Goethe, Johann Wolfgang von.
The Sorrows of Werther.

1774
Published

1776
Prohibited in Denmark.

1939
Purged from Spanish libraries by Spanish
dictator Francisco Franco.
Source: 4, p. 35; 8, pp. 298–99.

637

Going, K. L.
Fat Kid Rules the World.

2003
Published

2004
Best Books for Young Adults

2004
Michael L. Printz Award

2007 IL
Challenged as a suggested summer
reading at the Alsip Prairie Junior High
because the book is "laced with profanity
and other mature content." The District
126 superintendent plans to retain the
selection as one of the many titles offered
to students to read, preferably from the
recommended summer reading list,
before school begins.

2007 SC
Removed from the Pickens County
middle- and high-school library shelves
because "the language, the sexual
references, and drug use are not appropriate
for middle-school students."
Source: 11, May 2007, pp. 93-94; Nov. 2007, pp. 242-43.

638

Gold, Robert S., ed.
Point of Departure.

1973
Published

1983 WA
Removed from the required reading list at
the North Thurston High School because
of the book's "alleged strong language and
allusions to sexual conduct." The decision
was later reversed.
Source: 11, July 1983, p. 109; Nov. 1983, p. 187.

639

Goldfarb, Mace.
*Fighters, Refugees, Immigrants:
A Tale of the Hmong.*

1982
Published

1988 IA
Restricted to teachers only at the
Des Moines elementary schools because
the book "could lead students to form a
derogatory image of Southeast Asians if
they are not mature enough."
Source: 11, Mar. 1988, p. 46.

640

Golding, William.
Lord of the Flies.

1954
Published

1983
Nobel Prize in Literature

1974 TX
Challenged at the Dallas Independent
School District High School libraries.

1981 NC
Challenged at Owen High School because
the book is "demoralizing inasmuch
as it implies that man is little more than
an animal."

1981 SD
Challenged at the Sully Buttes High school.

1983 AZ
Challenged at the Marana High School
as an inappropriate reading assignment.

1984 TX
Challenged at the Olney Independent
School District because of "excessive vio-
lence and bad language."

1988
A committee of the Toronto, Ontario,
Canada, Board of Education ruled on
June 23, 1988, that the novel is "racist and
recommended that it be removed from all
schools." Parents and members of the
black community complained about a
reference to "niggers" in the book and said
it denigrates blacks.

1992 IA
Challenged in the Waterloo schools
because of profanity; lurid passages
about sex; and statements defamatory
to minorities, God, women, and
the disabled.

2000 NY
Challenged, but retained, on the ninth-
grade accelerated English reading list in
Bloomfield. The board was still set to review *Catcher in the Rye,* by J. D. Salinger,
and *A Death in the Family,* by James Agee.
Source: 11, Jan. 1975, p. 6; July 1981, p. 103; Jan. 1982
p. 17; Jan. 1984, pp. 25-26; July 1984, p. 122; Sept. 1988,
p. 152; July 1992, p. 126; Mar. 2000, p. 64.

641

Goode, Erich, and Richard
Troiden, eds.
*Sexual Deviance and Sexual
Deviants.*

1974
Published

1977 PA
Destroyed by the St. Mary's Public
Library Board.
Source: 11, Sept. 1977, p. 100.

642

Goodwin, June.
*Cry Amandla!: South
African Women and the
Question of Power.*

1984
Published

1984
Banned by the Directorate of Publications in Cape Town, South Africa. Without giving a reason, the Directorate declared "it will be an offense to import or distribute" the work.
Source: 11, Nov. 1984, p. 197.

643
Gordimer, Nadine.
Burger's Daughter.

1979
Published

1991
Nobel Prize in Literature

1979
Banned on July 5, 1979, in South Africa. The decision was lifted in Oct. 1979 when the government's Publication Appeal Board overruled the earlier decision of a censorship committee. Two previous novels by Gordimer also were banned but later reinstated. In 1980, Gordimer was awarded the CNA Prize, one of South Africa's highest literary awards, for the novel.
Source: 5, Nov./Dec. 1979, p. 69; Apr. 1980, p. 73; 8, pp. 31–32.

644
Gordimer, Nadine.
July's People.

1981
Published

1993 PA
Challenged in the honors and academic English classes in the Carlisle schools. Teachers must send parents a letter warning about the work's content and explaining that their children may read alternate selections.

1994 WA
Retained in the Yakima schools after a five-month dispute over what advanced high school students should read in the classroom. Two parents raised concerns about profanity and images of violence and sexuality in the book and requested that it be removed from the reading list.
Source: 11, July 1993, p. 127; Nov. 1994, pp. 202–3.

645
Gordon, Sharon.
Cuba.

2003
Published

2006 FL
Removed from all Miami-Dade County school libraries because of a parent's complaint that the book does not depict an accurate life in Cuba. The American Civil Liberties Union (ACLU) of Florida filed a lawsuit challenging the decision to remove this book and the twenty-three other titles in the same series from the district school libraries. In granting a preliminary injunction in July 2006 against the removal, Judge Alan S. Gold of U.S. District Court in Miami characterized the matter as a "First Amendment issue" and ruled in favor of the ACLU of Florida, which argued that the books were generally factual and that the board should add to its collection, rather than remove books it disagreed with. When the district court entered a preliminary injunction ordering the school district immediately to replace the entire series on library shelves, the Miami-Dade School Board appealed the decision to the Eleventh Circuit Court in Atlanta. In a February 5, 2009, two to one decision, the U.S. Court of Appeals for the Eleventh Circuit said the board did not breach the First Amendment, and ordered a Miami federal judge to lift a preliminary injunction that had allowed the book to be checked out from school libraries. But the three-judge panel's opinion—not unlike the School Board's initial vote—was so fraught with political rhetoric such as "book banning" that further appeals seem inevitable. On November 13, 2010, the U.S. Supreme Court declined to take up the case. The action let stand a 2-1 ruling by the U.S. Court of Appeals for the Eleventh Circuit that the school board's decision to remove the book was not censorship in violation of the First Amendment.
Source: 11, May 2007, pp. 91–92.

646
Gordon, Sol.
Facts about Sex: A Basic Guide.

1970
Published

1984 AR
Challenged and recommended for a "parents only" section at the Concord school library because the book "has in it terms that would be considered vulgar by any thoughtful person."
Source: 11, Jan. 1985, p. 7; May 1985, p. 75; Jan. 1986, pp. 7–8.

647
Gordon, Sol.
The Teenage Survival Book.

1981
Published

1982 TX
Removed from the Hurst-Euless-Bedford School District libraries.
Source: 9; 11, May 1982, p. 84.

648
Gould, Lois.
Necessary Objects.

1972
Published

1976 KS
Removed from the Hutchinson High School library due to its explicit sexual content.
Source: 11, Jan. 1977, p. 7.

649
Gould, Lois.
Such Good Friends.

1970
Published

1976 KS
Removed from the Hutchinson High School library due to its explicit sexual content.
Source: 11, Jan. 1977, p. 7.

650
Gould, Steven C.
Jumper.

1992
Published

1993
Best Books for Young Adults

1995 NY
Challenged at the Plattsburgh schools because of vulgarity, sex, and excessive violence.

1995 OR
Challenged at the West Linn-Wilsonville School District because according to the complainant "it was inappropriate for school children to read" because of a violent scene when the book's main character escapes from a sexual attack by a group of male truck drivers.
Source: 11, July 1995, p. 110; Jan. 1996, p. 16.

651

Gramick, Jeannine, and Pat Furey.
The Vatican and Homosexuality: Reactions to the "Letter to the Bishops of the Catholic Church on the Pastoral Care of Homosexual Persons."

1988
Published

1993 OR
Challenged at the Deschutes County Library in Bend because it "encourages and condones" homosexuality.
Source: 11, Sept. 1993, pp. 158–59.

652

Graves, Robert.
I, Claudius.

1934
Published

1955
Banned in South Africa under the Customs Act of 1955.
Source: 4, p. 76.

653

Gravett, Paul.
Manga: 60 Years of Japanese Comics.

2004
Published

2006 CA
Removed from all branches of the San Bernardino County Library because "there are a couple of pretty graphic scenes, especially one showing sex with a big hamster, that are not especially endearing to our community standards."
Source: 11, July 2006, pp. 181-82.

654

Grawunder, Ralph, and Marion Steinmann.
Life and Health.

1980
Published

1980 CO
Banned from the Boulder Valley Board of Education's health and sex education classes attended only by students with parental permission.

1985 OH
Challenged in the Parma classrooms because "it preaches a religion of moral indifference."
Source: 11, Jan. 1981, p. 9; Mar. 1986, p. 42.

655

Gray, Heather M., and Samantha Phillips.
Real Girl/Real World: Tools for Finding Your True Self.

1998
Published

2006 NJ
Challenged, but retained, at the Cape May County Library. The book explores issues such as body image, emerging sexuality, and feminism.
Source: 11, Jan. 2007, p. 29.

656

Green, John.
Looking for Alaska.

2006
Published

2006
Best Books for Young Adults

2006
Michael L. Printz Award

2008 NY
Challenged, but retained, for the eleventh-grade Regents English classes in Depew despite concerns about graphic language and sexual content. The school sent parents a letter requesting permission to use the novel, and only three students were denied permission to read the book.

2012 TN
Challenged as required reading for Knox County High Schools' Honors and as Advanced Placement outside readings for English II because of "inappropriate language." School Superintendent Dr. James P. McIntyre, Jr., said that a parent identified this as an issue and the book was removed from the required reading list. He didn't say whether the book was still in the schools.

2012 TN
Banned as required reading for Sumner County schools because of "inappropriate language."

2013 NJ
Challenged in the Verona High School curriculum because a parent found the sexual nature of the story inappropriate.
Source: 11, May 2008, p. 11; May 2012, pp. 107-8; July 2012, pp. 158-59; Nov. 2013, pp. 218-19.

657

Green, Jonathon, comp.
Cassell Dictionary of Slang.

2000
Published

2006 NC
Banned in the Wake County schools under pressure from one of a growing number of conservative Christian groups using the Internet to encourage schoolbook bans.
Source: 11, Sept. 2006, p. 231.

658

Greenberg, Jerrold S., and Robert Gold.
Holt Health.

1993 OH
Challenged in the Garrettsville school system because it "condones" homosexuality.
Source: 11, Nov. 1993, pp. 179–80.

659

Greenburg, David.
Slugs.

1983
Published

1984 WA
Challenged at the Evergreen School District libraries because of its graphic

descriptions of "slugs being dissected with scissors" and its verses describing the roasting, toasting, stewing, and chewing of the creatures were potentially frightening to young children.

1985 CA
Banned from the Escondido Elementary School District libraries as "unsuitable and should not have been allowed in the libraries in the first place."
Source: 11, Sept. 1984, p. 155; July 1985, p. 111.

660
Greene, Bette.
The Drowning of Stephan Jones.

1991
Published

1993 TX
Removed from the curriculum and school library shelves in Boling because the book "teaches anti-Christian beliefs and condones illegal activity." The story is about two gay men who are the objects of prejudice and violence, resulting in the drowning death of one of them.

1995 NH
Banned from the Mascenic Regional High School in New Ipswich because it is about gays and lesbians. An English teacher was fired for refusing to remove the book.

1998 WI
Removed from the Barron School District because of the book's homosexual theme. The ACLU of Wisconsin filed suit against the school district on February 16, 1999. The books were then returned to the library while a federal court considered the lawsuit. On October 8, 1999, it was agreed that the book will remain available to students as part of the school district's settlement of the federal lawsuit.

2002 SC
Banned in the Horry County School District Board middle school libraries because the book is "educationally unsuitable and contains unacceptable language."

2004 TX
Challenged at the Montgomery County Memorial Library System along with fifteen other young-adult books with gay-positive themes. The objections were

posted at the Library Patrons of Texas website. The language describing the books is similar to that posted at the website of the Fairfax County, Virginia-based Parents Against Bad Books in Schools, to which Library Patrons of Texas links.
Source: 8, pp. 445–46; 11, Mar. 1994, p. 53; Sept. 1996, p. 166; Jan. 1996, p. 15; Jan. 1999, p. 9; Mar. 1999, p. 37; May 1999, p. 68; Jan. 2000, p. 28; Nov. 2004, pp. 231–32.

661
Greene, Bette.
Summer of My German Soldier.

1973
Published

1974
National Book Award for Young People's Literature

1990 CT
Challenged as suitable curriculum material in the Burlington and Hawinton schools because it contains profanity and subject matter that set bad examples and gives students negative views of life.

1996 NJ
Temporarily removed from an eighth-grade supplemental reading list in Cinnaminson because it contains offensive racial stereotypes.
Source: 11, Mar. 1991, p. 44; May 1991, p. 90; Jan. 1997, p. 10.

662
Greene, Constance C.
Al(Exandra) the Great.

1982
Published

1984 NJ
Restricted at the Lindenwold elementary school libraries because of "a problem with language."
Source: 11, Nov. 1984, p. 185.

663
Greene, Constance C.
Beat the Turtle Drum.

1976
Published

1985 MN
Challenged at the Orchard Lake Elementary School library in Burnsville.
Source: 11, Nov. 1985, p. 203.

664
Greene, Constance C.
I Know You, Al.

1975
Published

1984 WA
Removed from the Hockinson Middle School library because the book did not uphold the principles of the United States, which were "established on the moral principles of the *Bible.*"

1989 OR
Challenged at the Multnomah County Library in Portland because of sexual references, the presentation of divorce as a fact of life, and derogatory remarks about friends.
Source: 11, Sept. 1984, p. 139; Jan. 1990, pp. 4–5.

665
Greene, Gael.
Doctor Love.

1982
Published

1983 AR
Challenged at the White County Public Library in Searcy because, "it's the filthiest thing I've ever seen."
Source: 11, Nov. 1983, p. 185; Jan. 1984, p. 25.

666
Greene, Graham.
J'Accuse: Nice, the Dark Side.

1982
Published

1982
A French court ordered the seizure of all copies of this exposé of alleged corruption in Nice, France. The author was also ordered to pay 100 francs for each copy seized to a building developer, Daniel Guy, who is the main figure in the book. Greene told the press that the court had made no attempt to give him or his publishers advance warning about the seizure.
Source: 5, Oct. 1982, p. 34.

667

Greene, Sheppard M.
The Boy Who Drank Too Much.

1979
Published

1991 MN
Removed from an eighth-grade literature class in the Underwood schools because of the book's alleged sexism and its seeming toleration of alcohol consumption by minors.

Source: 11, Mar. 1992, p. 44.

668

Griffin, John Howard.
Black Like Me.

1961
Published

1966 WI
A Wisconsin man sued the local school board, claiming that the book contained obscene language for any age level. He further charged that his child was damaged by having read the book as an assignment in English class. The court dismissed the case.

1967 AZ
The parent of an Arizona high school student challenged the use of the book in the classroom because of its obscene and vulgar language and the situations depicted. The school board removed the book from the classroom.

1977 PA
Language, particularly "four-letter words," was the charge leveled by a Pennsylvania parent and a clergyman, but the challenge was denied.

1982 IL
An objection to the subject matter was similarly denied in a challenge in Illinois.

1982 MO
The book was placed on a closed shelf when a parent challenged the book on the grounds that it was obscene and vulgar and "because of black people being in the book."

Source: 8, pp. 421–22.

669

Griffin, John Howard.
The Devil Rides Outside.

1952
Published

1954 MI
Bookseller Alfred E. Butler was found guilty and fined for selling the novel to an undercover police officer in Detroit. Butler appealed to the U.S. Supreme Court, which reversed the lower court's decision. In *Butler v. Michigan*, 352 U.S. 380 (1957), the court ruled unconstitutional the standards for defining obscenity that had been used for more than seventy years by U.S. federal and state censors. It declared the view that whatever corrupted the morals of youth was obscene to be an undue restriction on the freedom of speech.

Source: 13, pp. 57–59.

670

Grimm, Jacob, and Wilhelm K. Grimm.
The Complete Fairy Tales of the Brothers Grimm.

1987
Published

1994 AZ
Restricted to sixth- through eighth-grade classrooms at the Kyrene elementary schools due to its excessive violence, negative portrayals of female characters, and anti-Semitic references.

Source: 11, Jan. 1994, p. 34; Sept. 1994, p. 149.

671

Grimm, Jacob, and Wilhelm K. Grimm.
Hansel and Gretel.

1812
Published

1992 CA
Challenged at the Mount Diablo School District because it teaches children that it is acceptable to kill witches and paints witches as child-eating monsters.

Source: 11, July 1992, p. 108.

672

Grimm, Jacob, and Wilhelm K. Grimm.
Little Red Riding Hood.

1812
Published

1990 CA
Banned by two California school districts—Culver City and Empire—because an illustration shows Little Red Riding Hood's basket with a bottle of wine as well as fresh bread and butter. The wine could be seen as condoning the use of alcohol.

1990 FL
The presence of the wine bottle in the book's illustration motivated challenges by parents of students in the fifth and sixth grades in Clay County Elementary School.

1991 FL
A Bradford County teacher initiated a complaint that the book was violent because of the actions of the wolf. The teacher questioned the appropriateness of the little girl taking wine to her grandmother and her grandmother later drinking the wine.

1991 FL
Two teachers in Levy County challenged the storybook.

Source: 11, July 1990, p. 128; 14, pp. 217–18.

673

Grimm, Jacob, and Wilhelm K. Grimm.
Snow White.

1812
Published

1992 FL
Restricted to students with parental permission at the Duval County public school libraries because of its graphic violence: a hunter kills a wild boar, and a wicked witch orders Snow White's heart torn out.

Source: 11, July 1992, pp. 105–6.

674
Grisham, John.
The Client.

1993
Published

1996 NJ
Challenged in a sixth-grade high-level reading class in Hillsborough because of its violence and use of "curse words."

1997 WV
Removed from the Jackson County school libraries along with sixteen other titles.
Source: 11, July 1996, p. 122; Sept. 1996, p. 155; Jan. 1998, p. 13.

675
Grisham, John.
The Firm.

1991
Published

1997 WV
Removed from the Jackson County school libraries along with sixteen other titles.
Source: 11, Jan. 1998, p. 13.

676
Grisham, John.
The Pelican Brief.

1992
Published

1993
Best Books for Young Adults

1997 WV
Removed from the Jackson County school libraries along with sixteen other titles.
Source: 11, Jan. 1998, p. 13.

677
Grisham, John.
A Time to Kill.

1989
Published

2005 ND
Challenged, but retained, in the Fargo North High School advanced English classes despite complaints about the novel's graphic rape and murder scenes.
Source: 11, July 2005, p. 161; Sept. 2005, p. 239; Jan. 2006, pp. 14–15.

678
Groening, Matt.
The Big Book of Hell.

1990
Published

1995 PA
Challenged at the Hershey Public Library because "the entire book teaches conduct contrary to wishes of parents" and is "trash" with "no morals." A request was made to "destroy all books of a similar nature."
Source: 11, Sept. 1995, p. 158.

679
Groom, Winston.
Forrest Gump.

1986
Published

1999 FL
Challenged at the Bay Point School in South Dade County because the novel "pokes fun at blacks, makes numerous references to sex, and uses foul language inappropriate for tenth graders." First-year teacher Michael Weiss was fired over the incident because the book was not on the district's approved list and another instructor was placed on probation.
Source: 11, July 1999, p. 95.

680
Grotius, Hugo.
On the Law of War and Peace.

1625
Published

1642
The Spanish Inquisition condemned all of his books.

1662
The States-General of Netherlands banned the book.

1700
In the eighteenth century his complete works were placed on the *Index Librorum Prohibitorum* (Index of Prohibited Books) in Rome, Italy, where they remained until 1966.
Source: 1, pp. 239–40.

681
Grove, Vicki.
The Starplace.

1999
Published

2008 FL
Challenged at the Turner Elementary School in New Tampa because the novel contains a racial epithet. The book about an interracial middle-school friendship in 1960s Oklahoma was highly recommended by *Children's Literature Review*.
Source: 11, May 2008, p. 96.

682
Gruen, Sara.
Water for Elephants.

2006
Published

2007
Alex Award

2010 NH
Removed from a spring break elective course at the Bedford School District after a parent complained about the novel's sexual content. The complainant further suggested that the school only allow "youth versions" of particular books or organize a parental review system over the summer that would look at books that students need parental permission to read. A checklist has been proposed that Bedford school officials would use to rate books and other instructional materials.
Source: 11, May 2011, pp. 96–97.

683
Gruenberg, Sidonie Matsner.
The Wonderful Story of How You Were Born.

1952
Published

1982 FL
Moved from the children's room of the Tampa-Hillsborough County Public Library to the adult section.
Source: 11, Jan. 1982, pp. 4–5.

684
Grumbach, Jane, and Robert Emerson, eds.
Monologues: Women II.

1988
Published

1990 CO
Removed from a suggested reading list at Adams City High School after a parent complained about obscene language in the book.
Source: 11, Jan. 1991, p. 15.

685
Guare, John.
Landscape of the Body.

1978
Published

1998 FL
Challenged at the Manatee County School District in Bradenton Beach because the play includes a paragraph in which a woman describes being in a pornographic movie.
Source: 11, May 1998, p. 71.

686
Guest, Judith.
Ordinary People.

1976
Published

1976
Best Books for Young Adults

1981 OH
Temporarily banned in Enon from junior and senior English classrooms.

1982 NH
Challenged at the Merrimack High School after a parent found the novel obscene and depressing.

1985 NY
Challenged in North Salem as an optional summer reading book because of profanity and graphic sex scenes and because its topic—teenage suicide—was too intense for tenth graders.

1993 CA
Challenged because it is "degrading to Christians," but retained, at the Anaheim Union High School District.

1994 IN
No longer required reading at Delta High School in Delaware due to profanity and descriptions of sexual situations in the novel.

1994 SD
Removed from the Faulkton district classrooms.

1996 NY
Temporarily pulled from the Lancaster High School curriculum because two parents contended it contains foul language, graphic references to sex, and inappropriate handling of the subject of suicide. A Lancaster student took the matter to the New York Civil Liberties Union, which sent a letter to the school board saying that it was "greatly dismayed" with the board's action.

1999 OH
Removed, but later returned to the English classrooms and library shelves at the Fostoria High School despite complaints about the novel's obscene language and sexual innuendos.
Source: 11, Jan. 1982, p. 77; Sept. 1982, p. 170; Sept. 1985, p. 168; May 1993, pp. 86–87; Nov. 1993, pp. 192–93; Jan. 1994, p. 14; Sept. 1994, pp. 150, 152; Sept. 1996, pp. 155–56; Nov. 1996, p. 197; July 1999, p. 104.

687
Guest, Judith.
Second Heaven.

1983
Published

1991 SC
Challenged in the Greenville County schools because the book uses the name of God and Jesus in a "vain and profane manner along with inappropriate sexual references."
Source: 11, July 1991, p. 130.

688
Gunther, John.
Death Be Not Proud.

1949
Published

1995 NC
Retained by the Edgecombe County Board of Education in Tarboro after complaints that the "book has words in it that even unsaved people would have spanked their children for saying."
Source: 11, May 1995, p. 84.

689
Gunther, John.
Inside Russia Today.

1958
Published

1970 IA
Removed from the Glenwood school library shelves along with eight other titles—*The Catcher in the Rye,* by J. D. Salinger; *Who's Afraid of Virginia Woolf,* by Edward Albee; *Looking Backward,* by Edward Bellamy; *The Liberal Hour,* by John Kenneth Galbraith; *Black Like Me,* by John H. Griffin; *Black Power,* by Stokley Carmichael; and an unknown title. After considerable controversy, the banned books were returned to the library shelves.
Source: 7, pp. 234–35.

690
Guterson, David.
Snow Falling on Cedars.

1994
Published

1995
PEN/Faulkner Award

1997 WA
Challenged in the Snohomish School District by parents who acknowledged the book's literary value, but complained that its descriptions of sexual intercourse, masturbation, and use of obscene language make it inappropriate for high school students. The book was named 1995 Book of the Year by the American Booksellers Association.

1999 TX
Pulled from the Boerne Independent High School library and barred from the curriculum after several parents and students complained about its racial epithets and sexually graphic passages. The book was later returned to the library.

2000 WA
Restricted by the South Kitsap School District board after critics complained about the book's sexual content and profanity. After being approved by committees at the high school and district levels, the book was being considered for the district's approved reading list for high school students. Students are not required to read listed books of which they or their parents disapprove.

2003 CA
Challenged, but retained, in the advanced English classes in Modesto. The seven-member Modesto City School Board said administrators should instead give parents more information about the books their children read, including annotations of each text. Parents can opt their children out of any assignment they find objectionable.

2007 ID
Challenged in the Coeur d'Alene School District. Some parents say the book, along with five others, should require parental permission for students to read them.

2011 WA
Retained in college-level classes at Richland high schools. Teachers said the book was selected for the curriculum twelve years ago because it deals with prejudice against Japanese-Americans in the Pacific Northwest during and shortly after World War II.
Source: 8, pp. 381–85; 11, Sept. 1997, p. 129; Nov. 1999, p. 163; Jan. 1999, pp. 8, 12; July 2000, p. 106; Jan. 2004, pp. 27–28; Sept. 2007, p. 181; Mar. 2011, p. 74.

691
Guthrie, Alfred B., Jr.
The Big Sky.

1947
Published

1962 TX
Banned in Amarillo.

1991 MT
Challenged in the Big Timber schools because the book is filled with explicit, vulgar language.
Source: 4, p. 82; 11, Mar. 1992, p. 44.

692
Guthrie, Alfred B., Jr.
The Way West.

1949
Published

1950
Pulitzer Prize for Fiction

1962 TX
Banned in Amarillo.
Source: 4, p. 82.

693
Guy, Rosa.
Edith Jackson.

1978
Published

1978
Best Books for Young Adults

1984 LA
Removed from all school libraries collections in St. Tammany Parish because its "treatment of immorality and voyeurism does not provide for the growth of desirable attitudes," but later reinstated.
Source: 11, May 1984, p. 69; July 1984, p. 121.

694
Guy, Rosa.
The Music of Summer.

1992
Published

1993
Best Books for Young Adults

1994 GA
Removed from Adamson Middle School shelves, and Clayton public libraries and placed in the young adult section for eighth graders and up because of a "really gross" sex scene.
Source: 11, July 1994, p. 109.

695
Haas, Ben.
Daisy Canfield.

1973
Published

1984 LA
Challenged at the Covington Public Library because it "had objectionable language throughout."
Source: 11, July 1984, p. 103.

696
Haddix, Margaret Peterson.
Don't You Dare Read This, Mrs. Dunphrey.

1996
Published

1997
Best Books for Young Adults

2003 CA
Banned from the Galt Joint Union Elementary School District classrooms in Sacramento and restricted to students with parental permission in the middle school libraries. The novel discusses parental neglect, sexual harassment at an after-school job, and other stresses experienced by the young-adult fictional character.
Source: 11, Mar. 2004, p. 52; May 2004, p. 98.

697
Haddon, Mark.
The Curious Incident of the Dog in the Night-Time.

2003
Published

2003
Whitbread Book of the Year Award

2004
Alex Award

2004
Best Books for Young Adults

2004
Boeke Prize

2006 TX
Challenged at the Galveston County Reads Day because the book could "pollute" young minds.

2010 MI
Removed from the Lake Fenton summer reading program after parents complained about its "foul language." The book is about an autistic child who investigates the death of a neighborhood dog.
Source: 11, Mar. 2006, pp. 71–72; Sept. 2010, p. 200.

698
Hahn, Mary Downing.
The Dead Man in Indian Creek.

1990
Published

2010 OR
Challenged at the Salem-Keizer School District elementary schools because of the drugs and drug smuggling activities in the book. The book was previously challenged in 1994 in the same school district because of graphic violence, examples of inappropriate parenting, and because it was too frightening for elementary students. The book has won awards from the International Reading Association, the Children's Book Council, and the American Library Association.
Source: 11, May 2010, pp. 105-6.

699

Hahn, Mary Downing.
Wait Till Helen Comes.

1986
Published

1996 KS
Challenged in the Lawrence School District curriculum because the book presents suicide as a viable, "even attractive way of dealing with family problems. Ghosts, poltergeists and other supernatural phenomena are presented as documented reality and these are capable of deadly harm to children."
Source: 11, May 1996, pp. 87–88.

700

Haislip, Barbara.
Stars, Spells, Secrets and Sorcery.

1976
Published

1993 WI
Challenged at Nashotah school library because the book "promotes satanism."
Source: 11, May 1993, p. 86.

701

Haldeman, Joe.
War Year.

1972
Published

1981 AK
Removed from the Soldotna Junior High School library because of its raw language and graphic descriptions of battlefield violence.
Source: 11, July 1981, p. 91.

702

Haley, Gail E.
Go Away, Stay Away.

1977
Published

1994 MN
Challenged, but retained, in the Echo Park Elementary School media center in Apple Valley. A parent filed the complaint because the story "was frightening subject matter and [I] didn't see a good lesson in [it]."
Source: 11, July 1994, p. 129.

703

Hall, Elizabeth.
Possible Impossibilities.

1977
Published

1977
Best Books for Young Adults

1985 FL
Challenged at the Sikes Elementary School media center in Lakeland because the book "would lead children to believe ideas contrary to the teachings of the *Bible*."
Source: 11, July 1985, p. 133.

704

Hall, Radclyffe.
The Well of Loneliness.

1928
Published

1928
Suppressed in England as obscene. The *London Sunday Express* denounced it as "an challenge to every instinct of social sanity and moral decency which distinguishes Christian civilization from the corruptions of paganism."

1929 NY
Publisher arrested in New York City.

1939 NY
The book was finally cleared. The case was significant because the judge sought to inject an element into the obscenity law in declaring the subject matter, rather than words or phrases, "offensive to decency."
Source: 4, p. 71; 6, pp. 1,019–21; 15, Vol. III, pp. 416–17.

705

Halle, Louis J.
Men and Nations.

1972
Published

1982 KY
Challenged in the Jefferson County School District because the book is a "soft sell of communism."
Source: 11, Mar. 1983, p. 41.

706

Halpern, Julie.
Get Well Soon.

2007
Published

2010 WI
Challenged at the Theisen Middle School in Fond du Lac by a parent who believes that the book contains inappropriate subject matter for children.
Source: 11, May 2010, p. 127; July 2010, pp. 156, 176.

707

Hamilton, David.
Age of Innocence.

1995
Published

1998 GA
Despite pressure from protestors demanding that Barnes & Noble face child pornography charges, a prosecutor in Cobb County declined to take the nation's largest bookstore chain to court for carrying Hamilton's book. Activists from Operation Rescue claimed the book contains children in sexually suggestive positions and should be deemed illegal. Barnes & Noble officials noted that the decision follows similar rulings by prosecutors in Texas, Maryland, Kansas, and Wisconsin.

1998 KS
Barnes & Noble officials noted that the decision follows similar rulings by prosecutors in Kansas.

1998 MD
Barnes & Noble officials noted that the decision follows similar rulings by prosecutors in Maryland.

1998 TX
Barnes & Noble officials noted that the decision follows similar rulings by prosecutors in Texas.

1998 WI
Barnes & Noble officials noted that the decision follows similar rulings by prosecutors in Wisconsin.
Source: 11, Jan. 1999, p. 20.

708

Hamlin, Liz.
I Remember Valentine.

1987
Published

1987
Best Books for Young Adults

1990 TX
Challenged at the Commerce High School library because of "pornographic" material in the book. The complainant asked that all "romance" books be removed.
Source: 11, Mar. 1991, p. 43.

709

Hanckel, Frances, and John Cunningham.
A Way of Love, A Way of Life: A Young Person's Introduction to What It Means to Be Gay.

1979
Published

1979
Best Books for Young Adults

1982 AL
Removed from two Anniston high school libraries, but later reinstated on a restrictive basis.

1982 IA
Challenged in Atlantic because it is a "morally corrupting force."

1984 AK
Challenged at the Fairbanks North Star Borough School District libraries because schools should teach the basics, "not how to become queer dope users."

1998 WI
Challenged at the Barron School District because the book is about homosexuality.
Source: 11, May 1982, p. 82; Mar. 1983, p. 37; Sept. 1984, pp. 137, 149–50; Jan. 1999, p. 9; Mar. 1999, p. 37.

710

Handford, Martin.
Where's Waldo?

1987
Published

1989 MI
Challenged at the Public Libraries of Saginaw because "on some of the pages there are dirty things."

1993 NY
Removed from the Springs Public School library in East Hampton because there is a tiny drawing of a woman lying on the beach wearing a bikini bottom but no top.
Source: 11, May 1989, p. 78; July 1993, p. 100.

711

Hanigan, James P.
Homosexuality: The Test Case for Christian Sexual Ethics.

1988
Published

1993 OR
Challenged at the Deschutes County Library in Bend because it "encourages and condones" homosexuality.
Source: 11, Sept. 1993, pp. 158–59.

712

Haning, Peter.
The Satanists.

1969
Published

1986 CA
Challenged by the "God Squad," a group of three students and their parents, at the El Camino High School in Oceanside because the book "glorified the devil and the occult."
Source: 11, Sept. 1986, p. 151; Nov. 1986, p. 224; Jan. 1987, p. 9.

713

Hanley, James.
Boy.

1931
Published

1934
Police seized the book from a lending library in Manchester and charged the librarian with distributing an "obscene publication." Impounded under British obscenity law for its graphic violence and brutal sexuality.
Source: 13, pp. 29–30.

714

Hansberry, Lorraine.
A Raisin in the Sun.

1959
Published

1979 UT
Responding to criticisms from an anti-pornography organization, the Ogden School District restricted circulation of Hansberry's play.

2004 IL
Challenged, but retained, in the Normal Community High School sophomore literature class despite objections that the play is degrading to African Americans.
Source: 11, May 1979, p. 49; Sept. 2004, pp. 177–78.

715

Harcourt, J. M. [John Mewton].
Upsurge.

1934
Published

1934
Banned throughout Australia on November 20, 1934, when the Trade and Custom Department released its report, concluding: "This book is not without merit, though somewhat crude. But it is disfigured by some grossly indecent passages, without any excuse of being necessary."
Source: 6, pp. 1,028–29.

716

Hardin, Garrett James.
Population, Evolution and Birth Control.

1964
Published

1977 MI
The Brighton School Board voted to remove all sex education books from the high school library.
Source: 11, Sept. 1977, p. 133.

717

Harding, Kat.
Lesbian Kama Sutra.

2005
Published

2009 KS
Restricted minors' access in the Topeka and Shawnee County Public Library because the organization Kansans for Common Sense contended that the material is "harmful to minors under state law." Later the board voted 6-3 in favor of adopting a staff recommendation to keep the books where they are currently located on the shelves in the library's Health Information Neighborhood section.
Source: 11, May 2009, pp. 77–78; July 2009, p. 139.

718

Hardy, Thomas.
Jude the Obscure.

1895
Published

1896
Banned by Bristol, England, circulating libraries.
Source: 4, p. 51; 8, pp. 349–51.

719
Hardy, Thomas.
Tess of the D'Urbervilles.

1891
Published

1891 MA
Banned by Mudie's and Smith's circulating libraries. The novel was also the object of banning by the Watch and Ward Society in Boston, which charged that the novel contained illicit sexuality and immorality. The society forced Boston booksellers to agree that they would not advertise or sell the novel, and most adhered to the request.

1896
Banned by Bristol, England, circulating libraries.
Source: 4, p. 51; 13, pp. 242–43.

720
Harington, Donald.
Lightning Bug.

1970
Published

1991 AR
Challenged at the Rogers-Hough Memorial Library because the book uses language "very descriptive of. . . perverted sex."
Source: 11, Sept. 1991, p. 151.

721
Harkness, Jon L., and David M. Helgren, eds.
Populations.

1993
Published

1994 NJ
Removed from the Palmyra School District's science curriculum after nearly three hours of passionate debate between parents who believed the book presented only one side of how world overpopulation should be addressed and teachers who found it an integral part of the class curriculum.
Source: 11, Mar. 1995, p. 45.

722
Harlan, Elizabeth.
Footfalls.

1983
Published

1988 OR
Challenged at the Obsidian Junior High School in Redmond for its profanity and sexual content.
Source: 11, Jan. 1989, p. 3.

723
Harris, E. Lynn.
And This Too Shall Pass.

1997
Published

1998 KY
Challenged, but retained, at the Central High School in Louisville despite claims the book describes homosexual acts in a positive light.
Source: 11, Mar. 1998, p. 55; May 1998, p. 71.

724
Harris, E. Lynn.
Invisible Life.

1991
Published

1998 KY
Challenged, but retained, at the Central High School in Louisville despite claims the book is pornographic and a recruitment tool for the gay community.
Source: 11, Mar. 1998, p. 55; May 1998, p. 71.

725
Harris, E. Lynn.
Just As I Am.

1995
Published

1998 KY
Challenged, but retained, at the Central High School in Louisville despite claims the book describes homosexual acts in a positive light.
Source: 11, Mar. 1998, p. 55; May 1998, p. 71.

726
Harris, Frank.
My Life and Loves.

1922
Published

1922
Banned in England. Not published in that country until 1938.

1922 AL
Imports banned in the U.S. and frequently destroyed by U.S. Customs from 1922 to 1956.
Source: 4, p. 54; 13, pp. 170–71; 15, Vol. III, p. 415.

727
Harris, Raymond, ed.
Best Short Stories, Middle Level.

1983
Published

1993 NE
Challenged, but retained, in a sixth-grade literature class at Hichborn Middle School in Howland. The challenge was directed at the Ray Bradbury story, "A Sound of Thunder," which contains "offensive" language.
Source: 11, Sept. 1993, p. 160.

728
Harris, Raymond, ed.
Best-Selling Chapters.

1982
Published

1993 NE
Challenged, but retained, in a sixth-grade literature class at Hichborn Middle School in Howland. The challenge was directed at the Ray Bradbury story, "A Sound of Thunder," which contains "offensive" language.

1993 NH
Challenged in the Keene Middle School because of some of the language and subject matter in the textbook, specifically in passages from John Steinbeck's *Of Mice and Men; To Kill a Mockingbird,* by Harper Lee; and *A Day No Pigs Would Die,* by Robert Newton Peck. The complainant objected to expressions such as "crazy bastard," "hell" and "damn," "Jesus Christ," and "God Almighty."
Source: 11, Sept. 1993, p. 160; Jan. 1994, p. 15.

729

Harris, Robie H.
*It's Perfectly Normal:
A Book about Changing
Bodies, Growing Up, Sex,
and Sexual Health.*

1994
Published

1996 PA
Challenged at the Chester County Library because the "book is an act of encouragement for children to begin desiring sexual gratification…and is a clear example of child pornography."

1996 UT
Challenged at the Provo Library because it contains discussions of intercourse, masturbation, and homosexuality.

1996 WA
Removed from the Clover Park School District library shelves because parents charged that it was too graphic and could foster more questions than it answers.

1997 MO
Challenged, but retained, in the children's section of the Mexico-Audrain County Library. A Baptist minister complained not only about this title, but also about other "material concerning family sensitive issues, such as sexuality, the death of a loved one, or the birth process."

1997 ND
Challenged, but retained, at the Fargo Public Library. The statement requesting the book's removal cited the book as "too explicit, pornographic, and too easily accessible to children."

1999 CA
Challenged, but retained, at the Auburn-Placer County Library because of sexually explicit material.

2000 MA
Challenged in the Holland Public Library due to its sexually explicit content. The book was moved from the children's to the adult section of the library.

2001 AK
Restricted to elementary school pupils with parental permission at the Anchorage due to objections to the book's "value statements" and because "marriage is mentioned once in the whole book,

while homosexual relationships are allocated an entire section."

2001 FL
Challenged at the Marion County Public Library. Critics called the book pornographic and demanded it be permanently removed from the library or placed in a special restricted-access area.

2002 TX
Challenged, but retained, in the Montgomery County library system after a conservative Christian group, the Republican Leadership Council, characterized the book as "vulgar" and trying "to minimize or even negate that homosexuality is a problem."

2003 TX
Relocated from the young adult to the adult section of the Fort Bend County Libraries in Richmond. The same title was recently moved to the restricted section of the Fort Bend School District's media centers after a resident sent an e-mail message to the superintendent expressing concern about the book's content. The Spirit of Freedom Republican Women's Club petitioned the superintendent to have it, along with *It's So Amazing*, moved because they contain "frontal nudity and discussion of homosexual relationships and abortion."

2005 AR
Challenged, but retained, at the Holt Middle School parent library in Fayetteville despite a parent's complaint that it was sexually explicit.

2007 ME
A Lewiston patron refused to return the acclaimed sex education book from the Auburn public library because she was "sufficiently horrified by the illustrations and sexually graphic, amoral, abnormal contents." A police investigation found the library did not violate the town ordinance against obscenity, and the patron who removed the book from the library will stand trial for theft. The book was retained and other patrons donated four copies of the book, which remains in circulation at the library.

2011 FL
Challenged, but retained, at the Lee County libraries despite the book's explicit illustrations.

Source: 8, pp. 346–48; 11, Sept. 1996, p. 152; Jan. 1997, p. 8; Mar. 1997, p. 49; Nov. 1997, p. 181; Jan. 1998, p. 27; Nov. 1999, p. 171; Sept. 2000, p. 143; Mar. 2001, p. 54; Nov. 2001, pp. 247, 278; Jan. 2002, p. 13; Nov. 2002, pp. 256–57; Jan. 2003, p. 33; Jan. 2004, p. 9; May 2005, p. 135; Sept. 2005, p. 215; Nov. 2005, pp. 295–96; Nov. 2007, p. 240; Jan. 2008, p. 13; Mar. 2008, p. 78; Nov. 2008, p. 255; Nov. 2011, p. 218.

730

Harris, Robie H.
It's So Amazing.

1999
Published

2003 FL
Relocated from the young adult to the adult section of the Fort Bend County Libraries in Richmond. The same title was recently moved to the restricted section of the Fort Bend School District's media centers after a resident sent an e-mail message to the superintendent expressing concern about the book's content. The Spirit of Freedom Republican Women's Club petitioned the superintendent to have it, along with *It's Perfectly Normal: A Book about Changing Bodies, Growing Up, Sex, and Sexual Health,* moved because they contain "frontal nudity and discussion of homosexual relationships and abortion."

2005 WI
Relocated to the reference section of the Northern Hills Elementary school media center in Onalaska because a parent complained about its frank yet kid-friendly discussion of reproduction topics, including sexual intercourse, masturbation, abortion, and homosexuality.

Source: 11, Jan. 2004, p. 9; May 2005, p. 135; Sept. 2005, p. 215; Nov. 2005, pp. 281-82, 295–96.

731

Hart, Jack.
*Gay Sex: Manual for Men
Who Love Men.*

1991
Published

1993 WA
Challenged at the Fort Vancouver Regional Library when a group of citizens asked the Goldendale City Council to establish more restrictive criteria for sexually explicit material.

Source: 11, July 1993, p. 103.

732

Hartinger, Brent.
Geography Club.

2003
Published

2005 WA
Withdrawn from Curtis Junior
High and Curtis Senior High school
libraries after a University Place couple
with children in both schools filed a
written complaint. They wrote that the
book could result in a "casual and loose
approach to sex," encourage use of
Internet porn, and the physical meeting
of people through chat rooms.

2009 WI
Challenged at the West Bend Community
Memorial Library as being "obscene
or child pornography" in a section
designated "Young Adults." The library
board unanimously voted 9-0 to maintain,
"without removing, relocating, labeling, or
otherwise restricting access," the books in
the young adult category at the West Bend
Community Memorial Library. The vote
was a rejection of a four-month campaign
conducted by the citizen's group West
Bend Citizens for Safe Libraries to move
fiction and nonfiction books with
sexually explicit passages from the young
adult section to the adult section and
label them as containing sexual material.
Source: 11, Jan. 2006, pp. 12–13; Mar. 2006, p. 73;
May 2009, pp. 80-81; Sept. 2009, pp. 169-70.

733

Hartley, William H., and
William S. Vincent.
American Civics.

1970
Published

1976 NJ
Challenged in Mahwah by several
local residents and a school trustee who
argued that it "promotes socialized
medicine and considers government a
big machine with the people having no
voice." The deciding vote on the issue
was split, 4-4, in effect denying the use
of the textbook for ninth grade.
Source: 7, p. 30.

734

Harwood, Richard.
Did Six Million Really Die?

1974
Published

1985
In Toronto, Ontario, Canadian law
bars the import of materials considered
seditious, treasonable, immoral, or
indecent; so-called hate crime is included
in these categories. Ernest Zundel, the
publisher, was charged under S.181 of
Canada's Criminal Code with "publishing
false news" and was tried in 1985 for
publishing a booklet that denies the
official accounts of Nazis exterminating
Jews in wartime prison camps. The case
worked its way in the Canadian courts
and in a ruling in 1992 *(R. v. Zundel)*,
the Supreme Court in a 4-3 decision held
that section 181 of the Criminal Code was
indeed unconstitutional as a violation
of the right of freedom of expression
guarantees. The code requires the
expression to be nonviolent; the court
found the novel to be nonviolent. Thus,
Zundel was acquitted.

1991
Publishing or distributing neo-Nazi or
Holocaust-denial literature is illegal in
Germany. Zundel was convicted during
the 1991 visit to Germany for inciting
racial hatred.
Source: 7, pp. 149–50.

735

Haskins, Jim.
Voodoo and Hoodoo.

1990
Published

1992 LA
Banned at the Clearwood Junior High
School library in Slidell because the book
included "recipes" for spells. U.S. District
Court Judge Patrick Carr ruled on October
6, 1994, that the St. Tammany Parish
School Board cannot ban the book solely
because members do not approve of
its content. A week later, the board voted
8-5 to appeal the judgment. The school
board appealed the decision to the U.S.

Court of Appeals for the Fifth Circuit.
On April 1, 1996, the St. Tammany Parish
School Board, however, ended the
four-year attempt to ban the book by
returning it to the library. Under the
agreement, it will be available only with
written parental permission to students
in eighth grade or above. Momentum
for a settlement occurred after two board
members who fought to ban the book
left the board in 1994. Additionally, the
board's insurer indicated that it might not
foot the bill if the board continued to
fight the suit.
Source: 11, July 1992, p. 106; Sept. 1992, p. 137;
Jan. 1993, p. 23; Mar. 1993, p. 41; Jan. 1995, pp. 19–20;
Sept. 1995, p. 153; July 1996, p. 134.

736

Hastings, Selina.
*Sir Gawain and the Loathly
Lady.*

1985
Published

1989 MI
Challenged at the public libraries of
Saginaw. The complainant requested the
library to "white out the swearing"
which appears on page 16 of the book.
The objectionable words were "God
Damn You."

1992 WI
Challenged at the elementary school
libraries in Antigo because a parent
objected to a reference to the Loathly Lady
as a "hell-hag" and to another passage in
which the Black Knight suggests that
King Arthur "roast in hell."
Source: 11, May 1989, p. 77; Jan. 1993, p. 28.

737

Haugaard, Erick Christian.
The Samurai's Tale.

1984
Published

1995 CA
Challenged at the Wilsona School
District in Lake Los Angeles because of
violence and references to Buddha and
ritual suicide.
Source: 11, Jan. 1996, p. 13.

738

Hautzig, Deborah.
Hey Dollface.

1978
Published

1978
Best Books for Young Adults

1993 OR
Challenged at the Bend High School because it "encourages and condones" homosexuality.

2004 TX
Challenged at the Montgomery County Memorial Library System along with fifteen other young-adult books with gay-positive themes. The objections were posted at the Library Patrons of Texas website. The language describing the books is similar to that posted at the website of the Fairfax County, Virginia-based Parents Against Bad Books in Schools, to which Library Patrons of Texas links.

Source: 11, Sept. 1993, pp. 158–59; Nov. 2004, pp. 231–32.

739

Hawes, Hampton, and Don Asher.
Raise Up Off Me.

1974
Published

1989 TX
Challenged at the King High School in Corpus Christi because the book contains "vulgar language and descriptions of abnormal sexual activity."

Source: 11, Jan. 1990, p. 32.

740

Hawthorne, Nathaniel.
The Scarlet Letter.

1850
Published

1852
Banned in Russia by Czar Nicholas I. The ban was lifted four years later when Czar Alexander II came into power.

1852 MA
Subject of savage attacks by moralists in 1852. The main complaint of those who wanted to ban the novel was that Hawthorne sided with Hester and condemned her husband's revenge. Strict morality required that Hester suffer in more painful and obvious ways than Hawthorne provided. The citizens of Salem were so incensed by Hawthorne's novel that he moved his family out of the city to a farmhouse in the Berkshires.

1925
The National Board of Censorship forced the producers of the film version to change a few things; for one, Hester had to get married.

1961 MI
Challenged in Michigan high school English classes by parents claiming that it was "pornographic and obscene." They demanded that the book be taken out of the curriculum, but the request was denied.

1977 MI
Challenged again by a Michigan parent and principal objecting to the inclusion of the novel in the high school curriculum because it dealt with a clergyman's "involvement in fornication." The book was removed from the classroom use and from the recommended reading list.

1977 MO
That same year, a parent in Missouri condemned the book for its use of "4-letter words" and "other undesirable content" and demanded its removal from the high school library. The school librarian recognized that the parent had not read the book because no obscenities appeared in the novel, and she convinced the parent of his error. The book was retained.

1996 TX
Banned from the Lindale Advanced Placement English reading list because the book "conflicted with the values of the community."

1999 PA
Challenged, but retained, in the sophomore curriculum at West Middlesex High School.

Source: 8, pp. 480–81; 9, p. 142; 11, Nov. 1996, p. 199; July 1999, p. 105; 15, Vol. I, p. 562.

741

Hawthorne, Nathaniel.
Young Goodman Brown and Other Short Stories.

1835
Published

1992 NY
Challenged at the Copenhagen Central School because the story may give children the wrong message about witchcraft.

Source: 11, Jan. 1993, p. 12.

742

Hayden, Penny.
Confidence.

1992
Published

1994 OR
Expurgated by an apparent self-appointed censor at the Coquille Public Library along with several other books. Most were mysteries and romances in which single words and sexually explicit passages were whited out by a vandal who left either dots or solid ink pen lines where the words had been.

Source: 11, Sept. 1994, p. 148.

743

Hedayat, Sadegh.
The Blind Owl.

1937
Published

2006
The widely acclaimed Iranian classic, written in the 1930s, was banned in Iran. "The new government intends to take positive steps for reviving neglected values and considering religious teachings in the cultural field."

Source: 11, Jan. 2007, p. 35.

744

Hedderwick, Mairi.
Katie Morag and the Tiresome Ted.

1986
Published

1989 MI
Challenged at the public libraries of Saginaw because on the last page of the story "the mother's sweater is open to fully expose her breast." The library was asked to cover the drawing with a marker.
Source: 11, May 1989, p. 77.

745
Hedges, Peter.
What's Eating Gilbert Grape.

1991
Published

2006 IA
Banned by the superintendent at the Carroll High School because of parental concerns about an oral sex scene. In response, students started an Internet protest on the social network Facebook. Hundreds joined the group — "Un-ban Gilbert Grape! Censorship is Wrong"— and organizers say they plan to collect signatures calling for a formal review. "Parents were already notified of its content, and had to sign a permission slip for their child to read it." Later, the Carroll school board voted to overturn Superintendent Rob Cordes' decision to ban the book from the high school's literature-to-film class. The author said, "The district shouldn't let those larger themes be obscured by the relatively few pages with sexual content that he intended to drive plot."
Source: 11, Jan. 2007, pp. 12-13; Mar. 2007, p. 73.

746
Hegi, Ursula.
Stones from the River.

1994
Published

2000 GA
Banned, but later reinstated after community protests at the Windsor Forest High School in Savannah. The controversy began in early 1999 when a parent complained about sex, violence, and profanity in the book that was part of an Advanced Placement English class.
Source: 11, Mar. 2000, p. 63; Mar. 2001, p. 76.

747
Heidish, Marcy.
Woman Called Moses.

1976
Published

1992 NC
Removed by a patron at the Wilmington school library because of strong language.
Source: 11, July 1992, p. 107.

748
Heinlein, Robert A.
The Day After Tomorrow.

1941
Published

2008 IL
Removed from the Beardstown High School library. A parent requested its removal. A committee determined the novel "rather very adult in nature" and, because the library already had a large selection of other valuable science fiction and spy literature, elected to remove the book from the high school's circulation and donate it to the public library.
Source: 11, Nov. 2008, pp. 229-30.

749
Heinlein, Robert.
Stranger in a Strange Land.

1961
Published

1962
Hugo Award for Best Novel

2003 TX
Challenged, but retained, in the South Texas Independent School District in Mercedes. Parents objected to the adult themes—sexuality, drugs, and suicide. Heinlein's book was part of the summer Science Academy curriculum. The board voted to give parents more control over their childrens' choices by requiring principals to automatically offer an alternative to a challenged book.
Source: 11, Nov. 2003, pp. 249–50.

750
Heller, Joseph.
Catch-22.

1961
Published

1972 OH
Banned in Strongsville, but school board's action was overturned in 1976 by a U.S. District Court in *Minarcini v. Strongsville City School District,* 541 F 2d 577 (6th Cir. 1976).

1974 TX
Challenged at the Dallas Independent School District high school libraries.

1979 WA
Challenged in Snoqualmie because of its several references to women as "whores."
Source: 4, p. 96; 8, pp. 433–34; 11, Jan. 1975, p. 6; July 1979, p. 85; 12, pp. 145–48.

751
Heller, Joseph.
Good as Gold.

1979
Published

1979
Banned on June 28, 1979, in South Africa. The government's censorship authorities gave no reason.
Source: 5, Nov. /Dec. 1979, p. 69.

752
Heller, Joseph.
Something Happened.

1974
Published

1974
Banned in South Africa. The government's censorship authorities gave no reason.
Source: 5, Nov. /Dec. 1979, p. 69.

753
Helms, Tom.
Against All Odds.

1978
Published

1979
Best Books for Young Adults

1983 WA
Removed from the Evergreen School District of Vancouver along with twenty-nine other titles. The American Civil Liberties Union of Washington filed suit contending that the removals constitute censorship, a violation of plaintiff's rights to free speech and due process, and a violation of the state Open Meetings Act because the removal decisions were made behind closed doors.
Source: 11, Nov. 1983, pp. 185–86.

754
Helper, Hinton Rowan.
The Impending Crisis of the South: How to Meet It.

1857
Published

1857 NC
Banned in most Southern states because the author suggested the elimination of slavery. In North Carolina, the Reverend Daniel Worth had to stand trial for owning the text, and in Arkansas three men were hanged for owning the book.
Source: 10, p. 131.

755
Helvétius, Claude-Adrien.
De l'esprit.

1758
Published

1758
Condemned in Paris, France, as atheistic, materialistic, sacrilegious, immoral, and subversive, the epitome of all the dangerous philosophical trends of the age. Banned by the archbishop of Paris in 1758, the Parlement of Paris in 1759, and the Sorbonne in 1759, the book became an underground best seller.

1759
Banned by the Pope in Rome, Italy.
Source: 1, pp. 71–72.

756
Hemingway, Ernest.
Across the River and into the Trees.

1950
Published

1953
Banned in Ireland.

1954
Nobel Prize in Literature

1956
Banned in South Africa as "objectionable and obscene."
Source: 4, p. 80.

757
Hemingway, Ernest.
A Farewell to Arms.

1929
Published

1929
Banned in Italy because of its painfully accurate account of the Italian retreat from Caporetto, Italy.

1929 MA
The June 1929 issue of *Scribner's Magazine,* which ran Hemingway's novel, was banned in Boston.

1933
Burned by the Nazis in Germany.

1939
Banned in Ireland.

1974 TX
Challenged at the Dallas Independent School District high school libraries.

1980 NY
Challenged at the Vernon-Verona-Sherill School District as a "sex novel."
Source: 2, p. 137; 4, pp. 79–80; 11, Jan. 1975, pp. 6-7; May 1980, p. 62.

758
Hemingway, Ernest.
For Whom the Bell Tolls.

1940
Published

1940
Declared nonmailable by the U.S. Post Office.

1973
On February 21, 1973, eleven Turkish book publishers went on trial before an Istanbul martial law tribunal on charges of publishing, possessing, and selling books in violation of an order of the Istanbul martial law command. They faced possible sentences of between one month's and six month's imprisonment "for spreading propaganda unfavorable to the state" and the confiscation of their books. Eight booksellers also were on trial with the publishers on the same charge involving *For Whom the Bell Tolls.*
Source: 4, p. 80; 5, Summer 1973, xii.

759
Hemingway, Ernest.
"Hills Like White Elephants"

1927
Published

2009 NH
Pulled from a Litchfield Campbell High School elective course classroom after parents voiced their concerns about a short-stories unit called "Love/Gender/Family Unit" that dealt with subject matters including abortion, cannibalism, homosexuality, and drug use. The parents said the stories promoted bad behavior and a "political agenda" and shouldn't be incorporated into classroom teachings. The Campbell High School English curriculum adviser eventually resigned.
Source: 11, Sept. 2009, p. 154.

760
Hemingway, Ernest.
The Killers.

1927
Published

1995 CT
Challenged, but retained, in the Bridgeport public schools. The short story repeatedly uses the word "nigger." It was not part of the curriculum, but was chosen by a teacher as part of a unit on violence in literature.
Source: 11, Jan. 1996, p. 30.

761
Hemingway, Ernest.
The Sun Also Rises.

1926
Published

1930 MA
Banned in Boston.

1933
Burned in Nazi bonfires in Germany.

1953
Banned in Ireland.

1960 CA
Banned in Riverside.

1960 CA
Banned in San Jose.
Source: 4, pp. 79–80; 14, pp. 272–73.

762
Hemingway, Ernest.
To Have and Have Not.

1937
Published

1938 MI
Banned in Detroit and barred from sale by the Prosecutor of Wayne County on complaint of Catholic organizations

1938 NY
Distribution forbidden in Queens.
Source: 4, pp. 79–80; 14, pp. 274–75; 15, Vol. III, p. 652.

763
Hendrix, Harville.
Keeping the Love You Find: A Guide for Singles.

1992
Published

1995 MN
Pulled from the Staples-Motley High School health classes because its sexual subject matter was deemed inappropriate for freshmen and sophomores. The book was not a textbook or required reading, but a resource.
Source: 11, May 1995, p. 70.

764
Henege, Thomas.
Skim.

1984
Published

1983 TN
Publication canceled by Dodd, Mead & Company because of language in the book considered "objectionable" by Thomas Nelson, Inc., of Nashville—Dodd, Mead's parent company.
Source: 11, Nov. 1983, p. 188.

765
Hentoff, Nat.
The Day They Came to Arrest the Book.

1982
Published

1990 VA
Challenged in the Albemarle County schools in Charlottesville because it offers an inflammatory challenge to authoritarian roles.
Source: 11, Jan. 1991, p. 18.

766
Herbert, Frank.
Soul Catcher.

1972
Published

1972
Best Books for Young Adults

1993 WA
Challenged, but retained, at the Lake Washington School District in Kirkland despite objections there is "a very explicit sex scene," it is "a mockery of Christianity," and "very much anti-God."
Source: 11, Jan. 1994, p. 16; Mar. 1994, p. 71.

767
Hergé. [Georges Prosper Remi].
Tintin in America.

1932
Published

1995 WA
Removed from the Spokane School District libraries as racially demeaning and insulting.
Source: 11, Jan. 1996, p. 12.

768
Hergé. [Georges Prosper Remi].
Tintin in the Congo.

1946
Published

2012
A Belgian court rejected a five-year-old bid by a Congolese student to have the 1946 edition of Hergé's book banned because of its racist depictions. "It is clear that neither the story, nor the fact that it has been put on sale, has a goal to... create an intimidating, hostile, degrading or humiliating environment," the court said in its judgment. Bienvenu Mbutu Mondondo, who launched the campaign in 2007 to ban the book, plans to appeal.
Source: 11, Jan. 2012, pp. 17-18; May 2012, p. 130.

769
Herman, Victor.
Coming Out of the Ice.

1979
Published

1998 WA
Restricted to seniors at the Mount Baker High School in Bellingham. In addition, before the book is assigned, parents will get a summary of its plot, along with a description of the graphic passages that led one parent to ask that the book be pulled from the high school's curriculum.
Source: 11, July 1998, p. 110.

770
Hermes, Patricia.
Solitary Secret.

1985
Published

1985
Best Books for Young Adults

1988 CO
Moved from the library at Parker Junior High School to the senior high school because of its graphic detail of sex.
Source: 11, Mar. 1988, p. 45.

771
Heron, Ann.
How Would You Feel If Your Dad Was Gay?

1991
Published

1993 AZ
Challenged at the Mesa Public Library because it "is vile, sick and goes against every law and constitution."

1993 OH
Retained at the Dayton and Montgomery County Public Library.

1994 MA
Challenged, but retained, in the Oak Bluffs school library. Though the parent leading the protest stated that, "The subject matter... is obscene and vulgar and the message is that homosexuality is okay," the selection review committee voted unanimously to keep the book.
Source: 11, Jan. 1994, p. 34; Mar. 1994, p. 69; May 1994, p. 98.

772

Heron, Ann.
One Teenager in Ten: Testimony by Gay and Lesbian Youth.

1983
Published

1993 OR
Challenged at the Deschutes County Library in Bend because it "encourages and condones" homosexuality.

1994 CO
Retained at the Estes Park Public Library after challenges to the book for its graphic content.

Source: 11, Sept. 1993, pp. 158–59; Sept. 1994, p. 165.

773

Heron, Ann.
Two Teenagers in Twenty.

1994
Published

1998 WI
Removed from the Barron School District because of the book's homosexual theme and because it contains outdated information about AIDS. The ACLU of Wisconsin filed suit against the school district on February 16, 1999. The book was then returned to the library while a federal court considered the lawsuit. On October 8, 1999, it was agreed that the book will remain available to students as part of the school district's settlement of the federal lawsuit.

Source: 11, Jan. 1999, p. 9; Mar. 1999, p. 37; May 1999, p. 68; Jan. 2000, p. 28.

774

Herron, Carolivia.
Nappy Hair.

1997
Published

1998 NY
Challenged in Brooklyn because it was considered racially insensitive.

Source: 11, Jan. 1999, p. 10; Mar. 1999, p. 25.

775

Herzberg, Max J.
Myths and Their Meanings.

1984
Published

1992 CO
Challenged in the Woodland Park High School because the stories about mythological figures like Zeus and Apollo threaten Western civilization's foundations.

Source: 11, May 1992, p. 82.

776

Hesse, Hermann.
Steppenwolf.

1927
Published

1946
Nobel Prize in Literature

1943
Forbidden by Hitler in Germany for its "lewd lustfulness."

1982 CO
Challenged at the Glenwood Springs High School library due to book's references to lesbianism, hermaphroditism, sexual perversion, drug use, murder, and insanity.

Source: 9; 11, Sept. 1982, p. 169; 14, pp. 263–64.

777

Hewitt, Kathryn.
Two by Two: The Untold Story.

1984
Published

1991 OH
Challenged at the Hubbard Public Library because the book alters the story of Noah's Ark, making it secular and confusing to children.

Source: 11, Sept. 1991, p. 153.

778

Hill, Douglas Arthur.
Witches and Magic-Makers.

1984
Published

1999 NE
Challenged, but retained, at the Hastings Public Library along with forty other books on the topics of witches, magic, the zodiac, fortune telling, and ghost stories (most of the Dewey Decimal category 133.47). The books were called "demonic" and unsuitable for young children.

Source: 11, May 1999, p. 66; July 1999, p. 104.

779

Hinton, S. E.
The Outsiders.

1967
Published

1986 WI
Challenged on an eighth-grade reading list in the South Milwaukee schools because "drug and alcohol abuse was common" in the novel and "virtually all the characters were from broken homes."

1992 IA
Challenged at the Boone School District because the book glamorizes smoking and drinking and uses excessive violence and obscenities.

2000 WV
Challenged at the George Washington Middle School in Eleanor due to objections to the focus on gangs and gang fights.

Source: 11, Jan. 1987, p. 13; Nov. 1992, p. 199; July 2000, p. 106.

780

Hinton, S. E.
Rumble Fish.

1975
Published

1975
Best Books for Young Adults

1991 WV
Challenged at the Poca Middle School in Charleston because the book is "too frank."

Source: 11, Jan. 1992, p. 9.

781

Hinton, S. E.
Tex.

1979
Published

1979
Best Books for Young Adults

1995 FL
Challenged due to foul language and violence, but retained, at Campbell Middle School in Daytona Beach.

2000 PA
Restricted by the Central Dauphin school board in Harrisburg due to graphic language.

Source: 11, May 1995, pp. 69–70; July 1995, pp. 110–11; Sept. 2000, p. 144.

782
Hinton, S. E.
That Was Then, This Is Now.

1971
Published

1971
Best Books for Young Adults

1983 CO
Challenged at the Pagosa Springs schools because a parent objected to the "graphic language, subject matter, 'immoral tone,' and lack of literary quality."

1986 WI
Challenged on an eighth-grade reading list in the South Milwaukee schools because "drug and alcohol abuse was common" and "virtually all the characters were from broken homes."

1991 WV
Challenged at the Poca Middle School in Charleston because the book is "too frank."
Source: 9; 11, Mar. 1984, p. 53; Jan. 1987, p. 13; Jan. 1992, p. 9.

783
Hitchcock, Alfred.
Alfred Hitchcock's Witch's Brew.

1977
Published

1982 WI
Challenged at the Fond du Lac school system because the anthology contains stories about magic, witchcraft, and the supernatural.
Source: 11, Mar. 1983, p. 39.

784
Hite, Shere.
The Hite Report on Male Sexuality.

1981
Published

1983 NC
Challenged at the Southern Pine Public Library because it is inappropriate "for the development of moral character in children or anyone for that matter."
Source: 11, May 1983, p. 85.

785
Hitler, Adolf.
Mein Kampf.

1925-27
Published

1932
Banned in Czechoslovakia for its fierce militaristic doctrines.

1933
Banned by a court in Warsaw, Poland, for being "insulting."

1933 NY
The American Hebrew and Jewish Tribune, along with other Jewish organizations and individuals, attempted to prevent the first U.S. publication of the book.

1937
Banned in Palestine.

1945
Banned in occupied Germany, ban continued by the Federal Republic of Germany. Today, it is only available to the public in excerpted, commented versions.

1989
Banned from the 158 Stars and Stripes bookstores in West Germany. Since all Nazi literature has been banned in West Germany for decades, the circulation manager for the U.S. government chain stated, "we're guests in Germany, and I think we should show certain respect to our hosts."

1992
The ban was removed, then re-applied after public protests in Poland.

1993
Romanian president Ion Iliescu called for a ban, but the government's chief attorney would not comply.

1995
Seized by police in Latvia.

1996
In Hungary sales were suspended in 1996, and a full ban followed in 1997.

1997
Sales were blocked in Sweden, ostensibly because of copyright issues. The Bavarian state government is the copyright holder, and does not allow any copying or printing in German. It opposes copying or printing in other countries, as well.

1998
In Portugal sales were blocked for a similar reason as Sweden.

2001
The publisher of the first unabridged Czech edition received a three-year suspended sentence for promoting Nazism. Czech police seized some 300 copies of the book.

2009
Plans by German scholars to reprint as an academic treatise were rejected by the state copyright holders, who said a new edition of the book could fuel support for far-right groups. The Bavarian authorities reaffirmed a sixty-four-year-old ban on the book after the Munich-based Institute of Contemporary History, or IFZ, applied for permission to reprint the work.
Source: 4, p. 72; 6, p. 1382; 8, pp. 130–34; 11, Jan. 1989, p. 14; Mar. 2001, p. 62; Sept. 2009, pp. 155-56.

786
Hobbes, Thomas.
Leviathan.

1651
Published

1661
The House of Commons discussed the revival of the fifteenth-century writ that sentenced heretics to burnings. The bill failed. Hobbes was forbidden thereafter by the English government from publishing his philosophic opinion and turned to the writing of history.

1703
Banned in Holland because of its frank materialism.

1703
Placed on the Catholic Church's *Index Librorum Prohibitorum* (Index of Prohibited Books) in Rome, Italy, and remained listed through the last edition of the Index published until 1966.
Source: 1, pp. 187–88.

787
Hobson, Laura Z.
Gentleman's Agreement.

1947
Published

1948 NY
Banned from reading lists at DeWitt

Clinton High School, Bronx by the high school principal "on the grounds that it makes light of extramarital relations." After considerable protest, the board of superintendents reversed the ban eight months later.

Source: 14, pp. 154–55.

788
Hodges, Hollis.
Don't Tell Me Your Name.

1978
Published

1985 WA
Relegated to the restricted shelf at the Covington Junior High School library in Vancouver. The Evergreen School Board reversed its earlier ruling and decided to keep the novel despite parents' contention it is sexually explicit and inappropriate for junior high readers.

Source: 11, July 1985, p. 133; Nov. 1985, pp. 203–4; July 1986, p. 118.

789
Hogan, William.
The Quartzsite Trip.

1980
Published

1980
Best Books for Young Adults

1985 WA
Challenged at Vancouver Pacific Junior High School library because "the subject matter was too adult for junior high school students."

1987 NE
Placed in a collection for teacher use only in the Lincoln East High School library after a complaint was filed by a teacher.

Source: 11, May 1985, p. 91; July 1985, p. 134; Nov. 1987, p. 225.

790
Hoke, Helen.
Witches, Witches, Witches.

1976
Published

1988 NV
Challenged at the Smith Valley school libraries because the book "is replete with scenes of intrusion, oppression, cannibalism, abduction, transformation, incantations, deceptions, threats, and sexism."

Source: 11, July 1988, pp. 121–22; Sept. 1988, p. 178.

791
Holland, Margaret, and Craig McKee.
The Unicorn Who Had No Horn.

1985
Published

1991 WI
Challenged at the Cornell Elementary School library because it allegedly promotes "New Age religion" and includes content related to witchcraft and the occult.

Source: 11, Jan. 1992, p. 6; Mar. 1992, p. 63.

792
Holliday, Laurel.
Children in the Holocaust and World War II: Their Secret Diaries.

1995
Published

1999 OH
Limited to students in the seventh grade or higher at the Canal Winchester Middle School in Columbus because of references to sex, a self-induced abortion, and drug use.

Source: 11, July 1999, p. 94; Nov. 1999, pp. 171–72.

793
Holmes, Melisa, and Trish Hutchison.
Hang-ups, Hook-ups, and Holding Out: Stuff You Need to Know about Your Body, Sex, and Dating.

2007
Published

2008 NY
Retained in the Galway Public Library after complaints about the book's "factual errors, philosophy, and perceived bias." A review of the book by the library determined that the book received excellent reviews and contained no factual errors.

Source: 11, Jan. 2009, p. 22.

794
Homer.
The Odyssey.

8th century B.C.
Published

35 A.D.
Caligula tried to suppress it because it expressed Greek ideals of freedom—dangerous in autocratic Rome.

387 B.C.
Plato suggested expurgating Homer for immature readers.

Source: 4, p. 1.

795
Homes, A. M.
Jack.

1989
Published

1990
Best Books for Young Adults

1996 NC
Placed on the Spindale school library's reserve shelf. This meant parental permission was required for a student to check it out. A parent did not find the novel "proper to be in the library due to the language."

1998 WI
Challenged in the Barron School District.

Source: 11, Nov. 1996, pp. 193–94; Jan. 1999, p. 9.

796
Hoobler, Dorothy, and Thomas Hoobler.
Nelson and Winnie Mandela.

1987
Published

1988 OR
Challenged at the Hillsboro Public Library by a patron who charged that the Mandelas and the African National Congress are Communist-backed and advocate violence. After being reviewed, the book was retained in the library's collection.

Source: 7, p. 361; 11, Jan. 1989, p. 3.

797
Horowitz, Anthony.
Snakehead.

2007
Published

2011 FL
Challenged at the Westside Elementary School library in Brooksville because

"drug andweapons smuggling and gang violence is too much for any child to have access to at that age."
Source: 11, Mar. 2011, p. 52.

798
Hosseini, Khaled.
The Kite Runner.

2003
Published

2004
Alex Award

2004
Boeke Prize

2008 FL
Retained in the Jackson County School District in Marianna after being removed from the required reading list for one class. The school board voted to retain the book in the library by a vote of five to two.

2008 IL
Removed from the reading list at Centennial High School in Champaign due to objections from a parent whose child was assigned the book for summer reading.

2008 NC
Challenged as appropriate study in tenth-grade honors English class at Freedom High School in Morganton because the novel depicts a sodomy rape in graphic detail and uses vulgar language.

2008 NC
Challenged in Burke County schools in Morgantown by parents concerned about the violence and sexual situations portrayed in the book.

2011 AR
Challenged, but retained, as part of Senior Advanced Placement English at the Valley View High School in Jonesboro. The issue arose after two patrons disapproved of the novel because of a scene depicting male-on-male rape, sexual innuendo, and vulgar language, as well as religious content throughout the book.

2012 PA
Challenged as optional reading in the tenth-grade honors class at Troy area schools because the novel depicts a rape in graphic detail and uses vulgar language.
Source: 11, May 2008, pp. 97-98; Nov. 2008, pp. 256-57; Jan. 2009, pp. 8, 10; Mar. 2012, p. 79; May 2012, pp. 106-7.

799
Hotze, Sollace.
A Circle Unbroken.

1988
Published

1988
Best Books for Young Adults

1994 IL
Challenged at Cary Junior High School because references in the book to sex are too explicit for seventh and eighth graders; retained by school board vote.
Source: 11, May 1994, p. 83; July 1994, pp. 128–29.

800
Howe, James.
Totally Joe.

2005
Published

2007 VA
Removed from the Jefferson Elementary School in Bedford County because of "inappropriate content." Administrators pulled the book from the shelf after a parental complaint. While the school system's general policy on content challenges calls for a formal committee's review of the book, that policy was not followed. Rather, officials decided the book was not appropriate for elementary-school students, but did not decide whether to allow the book in middle or high schools.

2012 UT
Marked for removal in the Davis School District because parents might find it objectionable. The title character, a thirteen-year-old boy, writes an alphabiography—his life from A to Z—and explores issues of friendship, family, school, and the challenges of being a gay teenager.
Source: 11, Jan. 2008, pp. 14, 35; July 2012, p. 156.

801
Howe, Norma.
God, the Universe and Hot Fudge Sundaes.

1984
Published

1988 OR
Challenged at the Canby Junior High School library because the book "pushes several items of the humanist agenda:

death education, anti-God, pro-evolution, anti-Bible, anti-Christian, and logic over faith."
Source: 11, May 1989, p. 78.

802
Hoyt, Olga.
Demons, Devils and Djinn.

1974
Published

1990 KY
Challenged at Elkhorn Middle School in Frankfort because "it describes devil worship."
Source: 11, May 1990, p. 84; July 1990, p. 145.

803
Hubbard, L. Ron.
Mission Earth.

1985
Published

1990 GA
Challenged at the Dalton Regional Library System because of "repeated passages involving chronic masochism, child abuse, homosexuality, necromancy, bloody murder, and other things that are anti-social, perverted, and anti-everything."
Source: 11, July 1990, p. 125.

804
Huegel, Kelly.
GLBTQ: The Survival Guide for Queer and Questioning Teens.

2003
Published

2005 AR
Challenged in the Fayetteville High School library. The complainant also submitted a list of more than fifty books, citing the books as too sexually explicit and promoting homosexuality.
Source: 11, Sept. 2005, p. 215.

805
Hughes, Langston.
The Best Short Stories by Negro Writers.

1967
Published

1976 NY
Removed from the Island Trees Union Free District High School library in 1976 along with nine other titles because they were considered "immoral, anti-American, anti-Christian, or just plain filthy"; returned to the library after the U.S. Supreme Court ruling on June 25, 1982, in *Board of Education, Island Trees Union Free School District No. 26 et al. v. Pico et al.*, 457 U.S. 853 (1982).
Source: 11, Nov. 1982, p. 197.

806
Hughes, Tracy, ed.
Everything You Need to Know about Teen Pregnancy.

1988
Published

1993 TN
Challenged, but retained, at the Cleveland Public Library along with seventeen other books, most of which are on sex education, AIDS awareness, and some titles on the supernatural.
Source: 11, Sept. 1993, p. 146.

807
Hugo, Victor.
Hernani.

1830
Published

1850
Banned by Nicholas I in Russia.
Source: 4, p. 41.

808
Hugo, Victor.
Les Miserables.

1862
Published

1864
Listed in the *Index Librorum Prohibitorum* (List of Prohibited Books) in Rome, Italy, from 1864-1959.

1904 PA
Voted out of a library by a Philadelphia school committee because it mentioned a grisette, a young woman combining part-time prostitution with some other occupation.
Source: 2, p. 92; 4, p. 41.

809
Hugo, Victor.
Notre Dame de Paris.

1831
Published

1850
Banned by Nicholas I in Russia.

1864
Listed in the *Index Librorum Prohibitorum* (List of Prohibited Books) in Rome, Italy, from 1864-1959.
Source: 4, p. 41.

810
Hull, Eleanor Means.
Alice with the Golden Hair.

1982
Published

1990 PA
Removed, but later reinstated at the Pine Middle School library in Gibsonia because of its adult language.
Source: 11, Nov. 1990, pp. 209–10; Jan. 1991, pp. 28–29.

811
Hume, David.
On Religion.

1779
Published

1827
All of his historical and philosophical works were placed on the *Index Librorum Prohibitorum* (Index of Prohibited Books) in Rome, Italy, where they remained until 1966.

1986
Banned in Turkey.
Source: 1, pp. 77–78; 5, July/Aug. 1986, p. 46.

812
Humphrey, Derek.
Final Exit.

1991
Published

1991 IL
Challenged at the Cook Memorial Library in Libertyville because the book "diminishes the value of the elderly and encourages breaking the law by assisting homicide and drug abuse."

1992
Banned in Australia. After an appeal by the book distributors, in June 1992, the Australian Film and Literature Board of Review reversed the decision of the censors and classified the Book as Category 1—Restricted. Under this designation, the book must be sealed in plastic and cannot be sold to anyone under the age of eighteen.

1992
Publishers will not publish the work because assisted suicide is against the law in England.

1992
New Zealand custom officials were ordered to seize all copies of the book coming into the country and to hold them until the Office of Indecent Publications could review the suitability of the work. After careful review, the censors determined that the book would be permitted unrestricted entry.
Source: 8, p. 454; 11, Jan. 1992, p. 25.

813
Hunter, Evan.
The Chisholms.

1976
Published

1981 CA
A Livermore Valley Unified School District book selection committee voted to remove this title from the Granada High School library due to poor literary quality, gratuitous violence, and explicitly sexual passages.
Source: 11, Jan. 1982, p. 8.

814
Hurston, Zora Neale.
Their Eyes Were Watching God.

1937
Published

1997 VA
Challenged for sexual explicitness, but retained, on the Stonewall Jackson High School's academically advanced reading list in Brentsville. A parent objected to the novel's language and sexual explicitness.
Source: 11, Nov. 1997, pp. 169–70; Jan. 1998, p. 29.

815
Hurwin, Davida Wills.
Time for Dancing.

1995
Published

1996
Best Books for Young Adults

2002 VA
Challenged, along with seventeen other titles in the Fairfax County elementary and secondary libraries, by a group called Parents Against Bad Books in Schools. The group contends the books "contain profanity and descriptions of drug abuse, sexually explicit conduct, and torture."
Source: 11, Jan. 2003, p. 10.

816
Hus, Jan.
De Ecclesia: The Church.

1413
Published

1415
His work denied the pope's infallibility and proposed that the state should supervise the church. Put on trail at the church Council of Constance, Germany, he was convicted of heresy. His books were destroyed, and he was burned at the stake.
Source: 1, pp. 66–67.

817
Hutchins, Maude.
A Diary of Love.

1950
Published

1950 IL
Banned by the Chicago Police Bureau of Censorship because the book was "so candidly filthy in spots as to constitute a menace to public morals."
Source: 15, Vol. IV, p. 710.

818
Huxley, Aldous.
Antic Hay.

1923
Published

1930 MA
Banned on grounds of obscenity in Boston.

1952 MD
A Baltimore teacher was dismissed for assigning Huxley's novel to his senior literature class. The teacher's unsuccessful quest for vindication is reported in *Parker v. Board of Education*, 237 F. Supp. 222 (D. Md.).
Source: 4, p. 75; 12, pp. 23, 230.

819
Huxley, Aldous.
Brave New World.

1932
Published

1932
Banned in Ireland.

1980 MO
Removed from classroom in Miller and challenged frequently throughout the U.S.

1988 OK
Challenged as required reading at the Yukon High School because of "the book's language and moral content."

1993 CA
Challenged as required reading in the Corona and Norco Unified School Districts because it is "centered around negative activity." The book was retained, and teachers selected alternatives if students object to Huxley's novel.

2000 AL
Removed from the Foley High School library pending review because a parent complained that its characters showed contempt for religion, marriage, and the family. The parent complained to the school and to Alabama Governor Don Siegelman.

2003 TX
Challenged, but retained, in the South Texas Independent School District in Mercedes. Parents objected to the adult themes—sexuality, drugs, and suicide—found in the novel. Huxley's book was part of the summer Science Academy curriculum. The board voted to give parents more control over their childrens' choices by requiring principals to automatically offer an alternative to a challenged book.

2008 ID
Retained in the Coeur D'Alene School District despite objections that the book has too many references to sex and drug use.

2010 MD
Challenged at North County High School in Glen Burnie by a small group of parents who circulated a petition to have the book removed from use by county schools over concerns about explicit sexual content. The 1932 novel depicts a dystopian future where science and technology have run amok resulting in a morally bankrupt society.

2011 WA
Retained on the list of approved materials that Seattle high school teachers may use in their language arts curriculum. A parent had complained that the book has a "high volume of racially offensive derogatory language and misinformation on Native Americans. In addition to the inaccurate imagery, and stereotype views, the text lacks literary value which is relevant to today's contemporary multicultural society."
Source: 4, p. 75; 5; 8, pp. 424–25; 11, May 1980, p. 52; July 1988, p. 140; Jan. 1994, p. 14; Mar. 1994, p. 70; Nov. 2000, p. 193; Jan. 2001, p. 11; Nov. 2003, pp. 249–50; Jan. 2009, pp. 7–8; Jan. 2011, pp. 10, 12–13; Mar. 2011, pp. 74–75.

820
Huxley, Aldous.
The Doors of Perception.

1954
Published

1980 WI
Challenged at the Oconto Unified School District because it "glorifies the use of drugs."
Source: 11, Mar. 1981, p. 41.

821
Huxley, Aldous.
Eyeless in Gaza.

1936
Published

1936
Banned in Ireland until 1953.
Source: 4, p. 75.

822
Huxley, Aldous.
Point Counter Point.

1928
Published

1930
Banned in Ireland on the grounds of offending public morals. The ban was not revoked until 1970.

Source: 4, p. 75; 13, p. 194.

823
Hyde, Margaret O., and Elizabeth Forsyth.
Know about AIDS.

1987
Published

1993 TN
Challenged, but retained, at the Cleveland Public Library along with seventeen other books, most of which are on sex education, AIDS awareness, and some titles on the supernatural.

Source: 11, Sept. 1993, p. 146.

824
Ibsen, Henrik.
A Doll's House.

1879
Published

1983 AL
Four members of the Alabama State Textbook Committee called for the rejection of Ibsen's work because it propagates feminist views.

Source: 11, Mar. 1983, p. 39.

825
Ibsen, Henrik.
An Enemy of the People.

1882
Published

1939
Works purged by Franco government in Spain.

1958
Works formerly banned reported to be extremely popular in USSR.

Source: 4, p. 48.

826
Ibsen, Henrik.
Four Great Plays by Ibsen.

1959
Published

1991 MD
Challenged, but retained, in the Carroll County schools. Two school board members were concerned about the play, *Ghosts,* which deals with venereal disease, incest, and suicide.

Source: 11, Mar. 1992, p. 64.

827
Ibsen, Henrik.
Ghosts.

1881
Published

1892
Banned in England.

1939
Purged by the Franco government in Spain.

1958
Ban lifted in USSR.

Source: 4, p. 48.

828
Ignatow, Amy.
The Popularity Papers.

2010
Published

2013 WA
Challenged, but retained, at two Prosser elementary school libraries. Only available to fifth graders, the book is about two girls who want to unlock the secrets to being popular in middle school. One of the girls has two fathers; the other has only a mother. The American Library Association's Rainbow Project selected it as a top-ten title for 2011. It was a 2010 National Parenting Publications Association Gold Award winner and selected by the Chicago Public Library as one of the 2011 "Best of the Best" books.

Source: 11, May 2013, p. 124.

829
Illustrated Encyclopedia of Family Health.

1983
Published

1986 WY
Removed from the library at Sage Valley Junior High School in Gillettt after a resident said the book contained photographs that were "very nude and very explicit."

1991 OR
Challenged in an intermediate school library in Beaverton because of explicit line drawings of sexual intercourse positions and removed from the library, but maintained for staff use only.

Source: 11, July 1986, p. 118; July 1992, p. 103.

830
Irving, John.
A Prayer for Owen Meany.

1989
Published

1992 PA
Pulled from the Boiling Springs High School senior literature class in Carlisle after several complaints from parents about its content and language.

2000 WV
Challenged in the Kanawha County high schools as "pornographic, offensive and vulgar." The novel is on the county book list for suggested reading material for the eleventh and twelfth grades.

2009 MA
Removed from the Pelham school district recommended summer reading list after a parent complained about the novel's objectionable language and sexuality.

Source: 11, July 1992, p. 112; Sept. 1992, p. 142; July 2000, p. 10; Sept. 2009, pp. 153-54.

831
Isay, Richard.
Being Homosexual: Gay Men and Their Development.

1984
Published

1993 OR
Challenged at the Deschutes County Library in Bend because it "encourages and condones" homosexuality.
Source: 11, Sept. 1993, pp. 158–59.

832
Isensee, Rick.
Love Between Men.

1990
Published

1996 PA
Challenged at the Chester County Library at Charlestown because it was "pornographic and smutty."
Source: 11, Nov. 1996, p. 194.

833
Ives, Vernon.
Russia.

1943
Published

1955 NY
Removed from library shelves at Proctor high schools on the advice of a textbook commission of the New York Education Department. According to the commission, the book, while not seditious or disloyal, contained passages "that are either untrue or almost certain to evoke untrue inferences."

1955 NY
Removed from library shelves at New Hartford high schools on the advice of a textbook commission of the New York Education Department. According to the commission, the book, while not seditious or disloyal, contained passages "that are either untrue or almost certain to evoke untrue inferences."

1966 LA
Banned by the Avoyelles Parish school board in Marksville because the book was "pro-Russian in comparing Russia to the United States."
Source: 7, pp. 435–36.

834
Izzi, John.
Metrication, American Style.

1974
Published

1985 RI
Banned at the Toll Gate High School in

Warwick because it is "discriminatory toward women."
Source: 11, July 1985, p. 114.

835
Jackson, Jesse.
Call Me Charley.

1945
Published

1979 MI
Parents of a black fourth-grade student filed suit against Grand Blanc school officials after a teacher read this title to their son's class. The work includes a white character who calls a black youth "Sambo," "nigger," and "coon."
Source: 11, Mar. 1979, p. 38.

836
Jackson, Jon A.
Dead Folks.

1996
Published

2009 MT
Challenged in the Big Sky High School in Missoula because the local author's work was viewed as too graphic in its discussion of sex.
Source: 11, May 2009, pp. 82–84.

837
Jackson, Shirley.
The Lottery.

1948
Published

1981 MN
The film version of Jackson's short story was banned in Forest Lake but reinstated by U.S. District Court judge.
Source: 9; 11, July 1981, p. 88.

838
Jacobs, Anita.
Where Has Deedie Wooster Been All These Years?

1981
Published

1981
Best Books for Young Adults

1984 WA
Removed from the Hockinson Middle School library because it is "garbage"

and the novel's discussion of a young girl's first menstrual cycle is particularly objectionable.
Source: 11, Sept. 1984, p. 138.

839
Jagendorf, Moritz A.
Tales of Mystery: Folk Tales from Around the World.

1979
Published

1992 NE
Removed to a locked closet in the superintendent's office in Banner County because the book "has to do with a lot of negative things and might not be good for someone with low self-esteem or suicide tendencies."
Source: 11, May 1992, p. 80.

840
Jahn-Clough, Lisa.
Me, Penelope.

2007
Published

2008 FL
Challenged in the middle school library in Tavares. The book is part of a collection that requires permission from the school librarian to check out. Objections centered on the book's depiction of a sixteen-year-old who is dealing with the death of her brother and reference to sexual experimentation.
Source: 11, Jan. 2009, pp. 5–6.

841
Jaivin, Linda.
Eat Me.

1996
Published

2003 FL
Removed from the Marion County Public Library in Ocala. The library director noted that the Australian best-seller was removed because the library lacks a designated erotica collection, and the novel met only three of seventeen criteria used to evaluate books for acquisition. The Marion County Public Library Advisory Board recommended that the library director retain the novel. The board's vote was only a suggestion and the final

decision went back to the library director. In February 2004, the director reversed her earlier decision, reinstated the novel, and stated that her personal dislike for the book overshadowed her objectivity and adherence to policy.

Source: 11, Jan. 2004, pp. 7–8; Mar. 2004, pp. 47–48; May 2004, pp. 115–16; Sept. 2004, pp. 175–76.

842
Jakes, John.
Bastard.

1974
Published

1976 PA
Removed from the Montour High School library.

Source: 11, Nov. 1976, pp. 143–44.

843
James, E. L.
Fifty Shades of Grey.

2011
Published

2012 FL
Pulled, but later returned to the Brevard County public libraries' shelves "in response to public demand." The racy romance trilogy is particularly popular among middle-aged women. Despite overwhelming demand and long wait lists for library copies, some other libraries across the country are refusing to acquire the book.

Source: 11, July 2012, pp. 145, 147–48.

844
James, Henry.
Turn of the Screw.

1898
Published

1995 FL
Challenged at the St. Johns County Schools in St. Augustine.

Source: 11, Jan. 1996, p. 14.

845
James, Norah Cordner.
Sleeveless Errand.

1929
Published

1929
Police in England seized copies at the premises of Scholaris Press and the director of public prosecution cited the "obscene" language used by the characters as evidence of its "shocking depravity." The magistrate ruled in favor of the prosecution and granted the destruction order, stating that the novel suggested "thoughts of the most impure character" to readers of all ages.

Source: 13, p. 223.

846
Jameson, Jenna, and Neil Strauss.
How to Make Love Like A Porn Star: A Cautionary Tale.

2004
Published

2005 TX
Houston mayor ordered city librarians to keep the book behind the counter. After committee review, the best seller was returned to the open shelves.

Source: 11, Mar. 2005, pp. 55–56; May 2005, pp. 131–32.

847
Jay, Carla, and Allen Young.
The Gay Report.

1979
Published

1982 MI
Challenged at the Niles Community Library.

Source: 11, Jan. 1983, p. 8.

848
Jefferson, Thomas.
A Summary View of the Rights of British America.

1774
Published

1833
Banned for political reasons in Russia under Czar Nicholas I.

Source: 7, p. 476.

849
Jenness, Aylette.
Families: A Celebration of Diversity, Commitment and Love.

1990
Published

1990 IL
Temporarily removed, but later reinstated, at the Winfield Public Library because of objections to two of the stories. One involves a gay couple who adopted a baby at birth and the other involves a lesbian couple who raise one of the couple's children.

Source: 11, Mar. 1991, p. 61.

850
Jennings, Gary.
Black Magic, White Magic.

1964
Published

1989 TX
Retained at the Ector County school library after being challenged because the book might lure children into the occult.

Source: 11, Jan. 1990, p. 9; May 1990, p. 107.

851
Jennings, Kevin, ed.
Becoming Visible: A Reader in Gay and Lesbian History for High School and College Students.

1994
Published

1996 MO
Banned from the two high school libraries in Mehlville by order of the superintendent. The donated book was removed because it "does not meet the needs of the curriculum."

Source: 11, May 1996, pp. 82–83.

852
Jeschke, Susan.
The Devil Did It.

1975
Published

1990 MD
Challenged at the elementary school libraries in Howard County because it shows the devil as "a benign or friendly force."
Source: 11, Jan. 1991, p. 12.

853
Jewkes, Wilfred Thomas.
The Perilous Journey.

1973
Published

1989 MD
Pulled from the curriculum of the Baltimore County school system because a three-page retelling of an African-American folk legend was considered racially insensitive. The offensive story was "All God's Chillen Had Wings."
Source: 11, Jan. 1990, p. 11.

854
Jiménez de Aberásturi, Juan Carlos and Luis Maria.
Euskadi at War.

1978
Published

1988
The European Court of Human Rights ruled against France's 1988 banning the book, which recounts the history, culture, social situation, and political context of the Basque country. Guilty of violating the freedom of speech principle, France was ordered to compensate the publishing group.
Source: 3, p. 185.

855
Jimenez, Carlos M.
The Mexican-American Heritage.

1994
Published

1996 CA
Challenged in the Santa Barbara schools because the book promotes "Mexican nationalism."
Source: 11, May 1996, p. 98.

856
Johnson, Earvin (Magic).
What You Can Do to Avoid AIDS.

1992
Published

1993
Best Books for Young Adults

1996 NY
Removed from the Horace Greeley High School in Chappaqua because a group of parents complained that the basketball player's written description of oral and anal sex were inappropriate for fourteen- and fifteen-year-olds. Johnson's book is endorsed by the American Medical Association and the Children's Defense Fund.
Source: 11, May 1996, p. 88; July 1996, p. 119.

857
Johnson, Eric W.
Love and Sex and Growing Up.

1990
Published

1993 TN
Challenged, but retained, at the Cleveland Public Library along with seventeen other books, most of which are on sex education, AIDS awareness, and some titles on the supernatural.
Source: 11, Sept. 1993, p. 146.

858
Johnson, Eric W.
Love and Sex in Plain Language.

1965
Published

1982 FL
Moved from the children's room of the Tampa-Hillsborough County Public Library.

1988 PA
Challenged in the Williamsport schools because of allegedly inaccurate and misleading information in the book.
Source: 11, Jan. 1982, pp. 4–5; May 1988, p. 104.

859
Johnson, Eric W.
Sex: Telling It Straight.

1970
Published

1987 WA
Placed on restricted shelves at the Evergreen School District elementary school libraries in Vancouver in accordance with the school board policy to restrict student access to sex education books in elementary school libraries.
Source: 11, May 1987, p. 87.

860
Johnson, Maureen.
The Bermudez Triangle.

2004
Published

2009 PA
Challenged at the Leesburg Public Library because of sexual innuendo, drug references, and other adult topics.
Source: 11, July 2009, p. 131.

861
Johnson, Sam, et al.
Beavis and Butt-Head Ensucklopedia.

1994
Published

1995 UT
Challenged at the Salt Lake County Public Library by a parent because it has "no literary value whatsoever. It was totally perverse garbage, trash. I consider it pornography." The complainant requested the removal of all Beavis and Butt-Head materials, including seven cassettes, seven CDs, and two copies of MTV's *Beavis and Butt-Head Experience.*
Source: 11, May 1995, pp. 67–68.

862
Johnston, Julie.
Adam and Eve and Pinch-me.

1994
Published

1997 SC
Challenged at the Greenville middle school libraries because the book uses objectionable language like "damn" and "jerk-ass."
Source: 11, Sept. 1997, p. 126.

863
Jonas, Ann.
Aardvarks Disembark.

1990
Published

1991 OH
Challenged at the Hubbard Public Library because the book alters the story of Noah's Ark, making it secular and confusing to children.
Source: 11, Sept. 1991, p. 153.

864
Jones, Clinton R.
Understanding Gay Relatives and Friends.

1978
Published

1982 IN
Challenged at the Elkhart Public Library because it attempts to "get people to accept the homosexual lifestyle, like there is nothing wrong with it."
Source: 11, Mar. 1983, p. 56.

865
Jones, James.
From Here to Eternity.

1951
Published

1952
National Book Award for Fiction

1951 CO
Banned in Denver.

1951 MA
Banned in Springfield.

1951 MA
Banned in Holyoke.

1955 NY
Banned from the mails by the New York City post office.

1956 MI
The prosecuting attorney in Port Huron, St. Clair County, ordered booksellers and distributors to cease displaying and selling all books that appeared on the disapproved list of the National Organization for Decent Literature, a Catholic censorship group founded in 1938.
Source: 4, p. 94; 13, pp. 82–83.

866
Jong, Erica.
Fear of Flying.

1973
Published

1982 IN
Challenged in Terre Haute as optional reading in an elective course for junior and senior high school students.
Source: 11, May 1982, p. 86.

867
Jordan, June.
Living Room.

1985
Published

1990 MI
Banned from the Baldwin High School library because it contains profanity and racial slurs.
Source: 11, Jan. 1991, p. 12.

868
Josephs, Rebecca.
Early Disorders.

1980
Published

1988 WI
Challenged at the Mukwonago High School because the book's "portrayal of anorexia nervosa was not factual and the account of a girl's life, thoughts, and emotions used pornographic language and made fun of religion."
Source: 11, May 1988, p. 104.

869
Joyce, James.
Dubliners.

1912
Published

1912
Destroyed by printer because he found passages objectionable.
Source: 4, p. 65.

870
Joyce, James.
Exiles.

1918
Published

1986
Banned in Turkey.
Source: 5, July/Aug. 1986, p. 46.

871
Joyce, James.
Ulysses.

1918
Published

1918
Burned in U.S.

1922
Burned in Ireland.

1922
Burned in Canada.

1929
Banned and burned in England.
Source: 4, pp. 65–66; 6, p. 412; 8, pp. 391–92; 15, Vol. III, pp. 411–12, 557–58, 645.

872
Jukes, Mavis.
The Guy Book: An Owner's Manual.

2002
Published

2006 MT
Challenged in the Lockwood Middle School library by parents who objected to what they believe to be misleading, sexually explicit material in the book. The book was retained. The challenge came on the heels of a December decision by the board to pull three books from the middleschool library. Those books were *The Vanishing Hitchhiker: American Urban Legends,* by Jan Brunvand, and *Urban Legends* and *Alligators in the Sewer,* both by Thomas Craughwell. The same parent brought those titles—and their content—to the attention of the librarian and superintendent.
Source: 11, May 2006, pp. 129-30.

873

Jukes, Mavis.
It's a Girl Thing: How to Stay Healthy, Safe and in Charge.

1996
Published

1999 FL
Written parental permission is required to see the book at the Palm Beach elementary and middle schools because of concerns that the book—written for preteen girls—is more explicit than some parents would find acceptable.
Source: 11, May 1999, p. 66.

874

Julian, Cloyd J., and Nancy S. Simon.
Family Life and Human Sexuality.

1987 NE
Challenged as a supplemental text in an elective course in the Omaha School District because the book promotes "Planned Parenthood, abortion, and artificial methods of birth control." The book was adopted after the course's previous text, *Finding My Way,* by Andrew Riker, was replaced because it was considered too controversial.
Source: 11, Nov. 1987, p. 225.

875

Juster, Norton.
The Phantom Tollbooth.

1961
Published

1988 CO
Removed from a locked reference collection at the Boulder Public Library. The book was originally locked away because the librarian considered it a poor fantasy.
Source: 11, Jan. 1989, p. 27.

876

Kallen, Stuart A.
Ghastly Ghost Stories.

1991
Published

1992 IL
Challenged, but retained, in the Warrensburg-Latham school library because the series of seven books are "possibly harmful to a child's psychological development."
Source: 11, Jan. 1993, p. 7; Mar. 1993, p. 41.

877

Kallen, Stuart A.
Vampires, Werewolves and Zombies.

1991
Published

1993 TN
Challenged, but retained, at the Cleveland Public Library along with seventeen other books, most of which are on sex education, AIDS awareness, and some titles on the supernatural.
Source: 11, Sept. 1993, p. 146.

878

Kane, William M., and Mary Bronson Merki.
Human Sexuality: Relationships and Responsibilities.

1989
Published

1992 WA
Challenged at the Bremerton schools because it allegedly is "based on fraudulent research, stresses homosexuality, and is inappropriate for teenagers."
Source: 11, July 1992, p. 112.

879

Kane, William; Peggy Blake; and Robert Frye.
Understanding Health.

1982
Published

1983 KY
Challenged in Jefferson County because it contains a chapter on sex education, which includes slang sexual terminology.

1983 OH
Banned from the curriculum at the Oak Hills High School because the book discusses abortion, premarital sex, and euthanasia.
Source: 11, Sept. 1983, p. 142; Nov. 1983, p. 186; July 1984, p. 107; Sept. 1984, p. 157.

880

Kant, Immanuel.
The Critique of Pure Reason.

1781
Published

1827
Placed on the *Index Librorum Prohibitorum* (List of Prohibited Books) in Rome, Italy, until the 20th century.

1928
Purged from Soviet Union libraries.

1939
Purged from Spain's libraries.
Source: 3, p. 308; 4, p. 31; 8, p. 288.

881

Kant, Immanuel.
Religion within the Boundaries of Pure Reason.

1793
Published

1794
Banned by the Lutheran church because, "Our sacred person you have with your so-called philosophy attempted to bring into contempt…and you have at the same time assailed the truth of the Scriptures and the foundations of Creed beliefs… We order that henceforth you shall employ your talents to better purpose and that you shall keep silence on matters which are outside of your proper functions."

1928
Prohibited in the Soviet Union along with all of Kant's writings, presumably because the metaphysical and transcendental themes of Kant's works were thought to conflict with Marxist-Leninist ideology.

1939
All of Kant's works were purged from libraries of Spain under the Franco dictatorship.
Source: 3, p. 308; 8, pp. 286–88.

882

Kantor, MacKinlay.
Andersonville.

1955
Published

1956
Pulitzer Prize for Fiction

1962 TX
Banned from the four Amarillo High schools and at Amarillo College because its political ideas and because its author was cited by the House Un-American Activities Committee.

1963 MI
Withdrawn from the eleventh grade reading list at the Whitehall High School because the book "wasn't fit for high school students."

1967 OH
Challenged, but retained, in Amherst high school despite claims the book is "filth."

1969 WI
Challenged in Rock County.

1973 NC
Challenged, but retained, in the Buncombe County schools despite claims the book was unsuitable for school libraries because it contains objectionable language.
Source: 4, p. 85; 8, pp. 10–12.

883
Kauffmann, Stanley.
The Philanderer.

1952
Published

1953
Condemned by legal authorities on the Isle of Man after police received a complaint that a person could obtain the book at Boots' Library. The novel's trial was influential in changing the obscenity law in England, a change motivated largely by the summation of Mr. Justice Sable, who presided over the trial in the Queen's Bench Division in the Old Bailey. Sable warned that if criminal law were to be driven too far in the desire to stamp out the "bawdy muck," there existed a risk of a revolt, "a demand for a change in the law, so that the pendulum may swing to far the other way and allow to creep in things that at the moment we can keep out." The decision was not binding on future cases because it was not a court of appeal judgment, and Customs and postal authorities continued to seize books in transit; but this case set the stage for change in English obscenity laws.
Source: 13, pp. 190–91.

884
Kaufman, Joe.
How We Are Born, How We Grow, How Our Bodies Work, and How We Learn.

1975
Published

1991 FL
Removed from circulation collection, and now available only as a reference book, at the Old Kings Elementary School in Bunnell because two pages on the reproductive process were found objectionable.
Source: 11, Mar. 1992, p. 40.

885
Kaufman, Sue.
Falling Bodies.

1974
Published

1982 IN
Challenged in Terre Haute as optional reading in an elective course for junior and senior high school students.
Source: 11, May 1982, p. 86.

886
Kaysen, Susanna.
Girl, Interrupted.

1993
Published

1994
Best Books for Young Adults

2006 ME
Removed temporarily from the curriculum, pending its review, from the Orono High School after a parent complained about strong language and vivid descriptions. Movie stars Angelina Jolie and Winona Ryder brought the book into the limelight when they starred in the 2000 film version.

2008 NY
The New Rochelle Board of Education announced that it would replace all fifty copies of Susanna Kaysen's memoir after school officials tore pages from the book deemed "inappropriate" due to sexual content and strong language. Removed was a scene where the rebellious Lisa encourages Susanna to circumvent hospital rules against sexual intercourse by engaging in oral sex instead.
The incident was a hot topic across the blogosphere, transcending political ideology. It was featured on the left-leaning *Boing Boing,* the most widely read blog in the world, as well as the top conservative site, *Hot Air,* which is owned by Michelle Malkin of Fox News. *The New Yorker* magazine and *The Atlantic* also picked up the story as well as dozens of blog sites focused on literary and free speech issues.
Source: 11, Mar. 2006, pp. 73–74; Mar. 2009, pp. 56-57.

887
Kazan, Elia.
Acts of Love.

1978
Published

1980 UT
Removed from the Utah State Library bookmobile.
Source: 11, Nov. 1980, p. 128.

888
Kazantzakis, Nikos.
The Last Temptation of Christ.

1951
Published

1954
The novel was placed on the Roman Catholic Church's *Index Librorum Prohibitorum* (List of Prohibited Books) in Rome, Italy.

1954
The author was excommunicated in 1954 from the Eastern Orthodox Church in Constantinople, Turkey.

1962 CA
Challenged in Long Beach from 1962 to 1965.

1988
Banned in Singapore as a result of pressure from fundamentalist Christians.

1998 NJ
Challenged, but retained, at the Sussex County Community College in Newton despite an employee's charges that the book is "totally offensive" and "an outrage and insult to every Christian in the world."
Source: 4, p. 68; 8, pp. 260–61; 11, Mar. 1999, p. 47.

889
Keable, Robert.
Simon Called Peter.

1921
Published

1922 MA
The Boston Watch and Ward Society brought charges against Edith Law of Arlington, Massachusetts, the owner of a Boston rental library, who was convicted in the Cambridge District Court in October 1922 and fined $100 for stocking the novel in her rental library. In an appeal, Judge Stone suspended the fine but warned Law that she faced a jail sentence if she were ever again convicted in an obscenity case. The case drew particular attention because the novel had been a best seller for more than a year.

1922 NY
The New York Society for the Suppression of Vice tried without success to have the book banned, but the courts refused to hear the complaint.
Source: 13, pp. 219–20.

890
Keefer, Edward C., ed.
Foreign Relations of the United States 1964-68, Volume XXVI, Indonesia, Malaysia-Singapore, Philippines.

2000
Published

2001
The U.S. government recalled all copies of this U.S. State Department history book from hundreds of libraries in the U.S. and abroad because it details the U.S. role in Indonesia's deadly purge of communists in the 1960s. The prestigious series, which began in 1861, is often embattled. For example, the history dealing with Greece, Cyprus, and Turkey was printed in February 2000, but is locked up at the Government Printing Office under the label: "Embargo: This publication cannot be released." Officials declined to say why.
Source: 11, Nov. 2001, pp. 245–46.

891
Keehn, Sally.
I Am Regina.

1991
Published

1996 IL
Challenged as optional fifth-grade reading at the Orland Park School District 135 because the book uses unflattering stereotypes to depict Native Americans and uses the word "squaw," which was offensive.
Source: 11, Jan. 1997, p. 10.

892
Keeping, Charles.
Through the Window.

1970
Published

1985 IA
Challenged at the Cedar Rapids Public Library because "the harsh realities of life it depicts are not suitable for young readers."
Source: 11, Sept. 1985, p. 167.

893
Kehret, Peg.
Abduction!

2004
Published

2006 MN
Challenged, but retained, at the two Apple Valley middle- and eight elementary-school libraries despite the complaint that the book was too violent.
Source: 11, July 2006, p. 208.

894
Kehret, Peg.
Stolen Children.

2008
Published

2011 PA
Challenged, but retained, at the Central York School District despite a parental concern that the book "was too violent." The book centers on the kidnapping of thirteen-year-old Amy and her three-year-old babysitting charge. The kidnappers videotape the pair and send the DVDs to their parents for ransom. Amy works to send clues through the videos to help police find them.
Source: 11, Mar. 2011, p. 52; May 2011, p. 114.

895
Kellerman, Faye.
Milk and Honey.

1990
Published

1991 AR
Challenged at the Rogers-Hough Memorial Library because of "sacrilegious language."
Source: 11, Sept. 1991, p. 151.

896
Kelley, Leo P.
Night of Fire and Blood.

1979
Published

1984 CO
Found unsuitable for younger children in Aurora because it deals with "violence and self-mutilation."
Source: 11, May 1984, p. 69.

897
Kellogg, Marjorie.
Tell Me That You Love Me, Junie Moon.

1968
Published

1968
Best Books for Young Adults

1978 MD
Challenged at the Frederick County school system because it teaches that "it's all right to do things against society's rules."
Source: 11, Mar. 1978, p. 39; May 1978, p. 58.

898
Kellogg, Steven.
Pinkerton, Behave!

1979
Published

1979
National Book Award for Young People's Literature

2000 AR
Challenged, but retained, at the Elm Tree Elementary School library in Benton despite the objections to a character in the book holding a gun.

2004 IL
Challenged, but retained, at the Evanston Public Library despite complaints that the image of a masked burglar pointing a gun at woman is too violent for young readers.
Source: 11, Jan. 2001, p. 35; July 2004, p. 157; Nov. 2004, pp. 255–56.

899
Kenan, Randall.
James Baldwin.

1994
Published

2000 CA
Removed from the Anaheim school district because school officials said the book is too difficult for middle school students and that it could cause harassment against students seen with it. The American Civil Liberties Union (ACLU) of Southern California filed suit in *Doe v. Anaheim Union High School District* alleging that the removal is "a pretext for viewpoint-based censorship." The ACLU claims no other books have been removed from the junior high library for similar reasons, even though several, such as works by Shakespeare and Dickens, are more difficult reading. The ACLU contends that the school officials engaged in unconstitutional viewpoint discrimination by removing the book because it contains gay and lesbian material. In March 2001, the school board approved a settlement that restored the book to the high school shelves and amended the district's policy to prohibit the removal of books for subject matter involving sexual orientation, but the book will not be returned to the middle school.
Source: 11, Mar. 2001, p. 53; May 2001, p. 95; July 2001, p. 173.

900
Kennedy, X. J.
Literature: Introduction to Fiction, Poetry and Drama.

1976
Published

1993 CA
Challenged in the Ojai schools because selections contained foul language and blasphemy, and they glamorize sexual misconduct.
Source: 11, Jan. 1994, p. 37.

901
Kepler, Johannes.
The New Astronomy.

1609
Published

1619
Banned by the Vatican in Rome, Italy, under a general prohibition on reading or teaching heliocentric theory. The ban on his theories remained in effect until 1753.
Source: 1, pp. 212–13.

902
Kerr, M. E.
Dinky Hocker Shoots Smack.

1972
Published

1977 WA
Removed from Kent elementary school libraries because of complaints about "vulgarity" and "defamation of the word of God in the work."

1998 FL
Challenged, but retained, at the Merritt Brown Middle School library in Panama City despite a parent's concern that passages are "sacrilegious and morally subversive."
Source: 9; 11, Mar. 1977, p. 36; Sept. 1998, p. 139.

903
Kerr, M. E.
Gentlehands.

1978
Published

1978
Best Books for Young Adults

1983 VA
Challenged at the Lake Braddock Secondary School because the book is "anti-Semitic" and "glamorizes drug abuse and makes drugs 'tempting' to teenagers."
Source: 11, July 1983, p. 109; Nov. 1983, p. 187; Mar. 1984, p. 53.

904
Kesey, Ken.
One Flew Over the Cuckoo's Nest.

1962
Published

1971 CO
Challenged in the Greeley public school district as a non-required American Culture reading.

1974 OH
Five residents of Strongsville sued the board of education to remove the novel. Labeling it "pornographic," they charged the the novel "glorifies criminal activity, has a tendency to corrupt juveniles and contains descriptions of bestiality, bizarre violence, and torture, dismemberment, death, and human elimination."

1975 NY
Removed from public school libraries in Randolph.

1975 OK
Removed from public school libraries in Alton.

1977 MA
Removed from the required reading list in Westport.

1978 ID
Banned from the St. Anthony Freemont High School classrooms and the instructor fired—*Fogarty v. Atchley.*

1982 NH
Challenged at the Merrimack High School.

1986 WA
Challenged as part of the curriculum in an Aberdeen High School honors English class because the book promotes "secular humanism." The school board voted to retain the title.

2000 CA
Challenged in the Placentia-Yorba Linda Unified School District after complaints by parents stated that teachers "can choose the best books, but they keep choosing this garbage over and over again."
Source: 8, pp. 478–79; 11, Jan. 1977, p. 8; May 1978, p. 57; July 1978, pp. 96, 100; Sept. 1982, p. 170; 12, pp. 104–11, 229; Nov. 1986, p. 225; Mar. 2001, p. 55; 15, Vol. IV, p. 714.

905
Kesey, Ken.
Sometimes a Great Notion.

1964
Published

1998 WA
Challenged for use in Richland high school English classes along with six other titles because the "books are poor-quality literature and stress suicide, illicit sex, violence, and hopelessness."
Source: 11, Mar. 1999, p. 40.

906
Kessel, Joyce K.
Halloween.

1980
Published

1992 AZ
Challenged at the Neely Elementary School in Gilbert because the book shows the dark side of religion through the occult, the devil, and satanism.
Source: 11, May 1992, p. 78; July 1992, p. 124.

907
Keyes, Daniel.
Flowers for Algernon.

1966
Published

1967
Nebula Award for Best Novel

1976 FL
Banned from the Plant City public schools because of references to sex.

1977 PA
Banned from the Emporium public schools because of references to sex.

1981 AR
Banned from the Glen Rose High School library.

1983 OH
Challenged at the Oberlin High School because several pages of the novel detail a sexual encounter of the protagonist.

1984 WY
Challenged as a required reading at the Glenrock High School because several "explicit love scenes were distasteful."

1986 NC
Challenged at the Charlotte-Mecklenburg schools as a tenth-grade supplemental reading because it is "pornographic."

1996 VA
Challenged, but retained, in the Yorktown schools. A parent complained about the profanity and references to sex and drinking in the novel.

1997 GA
Removed from the ninth-grade curriculum by the Rabun County Board of Education because it was "inappropriate" for the ninth grade.
Source: 11, July 1976, p. 85; May 1977, p. 73; July 1981, p. 91; Jan. 1984, p. 26; July 1984, p. 122; Jan. 1987, p. 12; Mar. 1987, p. 54; May 1987, p. 103; July 1987, p. 150; May 1996, p. 100; July 1997, p. 97.

908
Kidd, Flora.
Between Pride and Passion.

1982
Published

1984 OR
More than fifty Harlequin romances donated by Glide residents were threatened with removal from the high school library because "teenagers already have trouble with their emotions without being stimulated by poorly written books."
Source: 11, July 1984, p. 104.

909
Kilgore, Kathleen.
The Wolfman of Beacon Hill.

1982
Published

1989 OR
Challenged at the Pilot Butte Junior High School in Bend because the material does not enlighten, uplift, or encourage character-building traits.
Source: 11, Jan. 1990, pp. 4–5.

910
Killingsworth, Monte.
Eli's Songs.

1991
Published

1992 OR
Challenged in the Rural Dell School District in Molalla because the book is "anti-local," has "logger-bashing" sentiments and an "ecological slant."
Source: 11, July 1992, pp. 124–25.

911
Kincaid, Jamaica.
Lucy.

1990
Published

1994 PA
Challenged at the West Chester schools as "most pornographic." The book was changed from required to optional reading.
Source: 11, Jan. 1995, p. 25; Mar. 1995, p. 45; May 1995, p. 71.

912
Kincaid, James Russell.
Erotic Innocence: The Culture of Child Molesting.

1998
Published

2002 TX
Challenged, but retained, in the Montgomery County library system after a conservative Christian group, the Republican Leadership Council, characterized the book as "helping to lay the groundwork for a culture of child molesters and homosexuals."
Source: 11, Jan. 2003, p. 33.

913
King, Frederick M.; Herbert C. Rudman; and Doris Leavell.
Understanding the Social Sciences Program.

1981
Published

1987 AL
Removed from Alabama's list of approved texts—and from the state's classrooms—because the book promotes the "religion of secular humanism." U.S. District Court Judge W. Brevard Hand ruled on March 4, 1987, that thirty-nine history and social studies texts used in Alabama's 129 school systems "discriminate against the very concept of religion and theistic religions in particular, by omissions so serious that a student learning history from them would not be apprised of relevant facts about America's history... References to religion are isolated and the integration of religion in the history of American society is ignored." The series includes: *Understanding People; Understanding Families; Understanding Communities; Understanding Religions of the World; Understanding Our Country;* and *Understanding the World.* On August 26, 1987, the U.S. Court of Appeals for the Eleventh Circuit unanimously overturned Judge

Hand's decision by ruling that the information in the book was "essentially neutral in its religious content." The fact that the texts omitted references to religion was not "an advancement of secular humanism or an active hostility toward theistic religion."

Source: 11, Jan. 1987, p. 6; May 1987, pp. 75, 104–7; Sept. 1987, pp. 166-67; Nov. 1987, pp. 217–18; Jan. 1988, p. 17; Mar. 1988, p. 40.

914
King, Larry.
Tell It to the King.

1988
Published

1989 MI
Challenged at the Public Libraries of Saginaw because it is "an insult to one's intelligence" and contains foul language.
Source: 11, May 1989, p. 77.

915
King, Stephen.
The Bachman Books.

1977
Published

1987 IA
Removed from the West Lyon Community School library in Larchwood because "it does not meet the standards of the community."
Source: 11, May 1987, p. 86; July 1987, p. 125.

916
King, Stephen.
Carrie.

1973
Published

1975 NV
Challenged at the Clark High School library in Las Vegas because it is "trash."

1978 VT
Placed in special closed shelf at the Vergennes Union High School library because it could "harm" students, particularly "younger girls."

1987 IA
Removed from the West Lyon Community School library in Larchwood because "it does not meet the standards of the community."

1991 NY
Banned from the Altmar-Parish-Williamstown district libraries.

1994 ND
Challenged, along with eight other Stephen King novels, in Bismarck by a local minister and a school board member, because of "age appropriateness."

1994 PA
Challenged by a parent at the Boyertown Junior High East library. The parent "objected to the book's language, its violence, and its sexual descriptions, as well as what she described as a 'Satanic killing' sequence."
Source: 11, Jan. 1979, p. 6; May 1987, p. 86; July 1987, p. 125; Mar. 1992, p. 40; May 1994, pp. 84–85.

917
King, Stephen.
Christine.

1983
Published

1985 AL
The Washington County Board of Education voted unanimously to ban the novel from all county school libraries because the book contains "unacceptable language" and is "pornographic."

1987 IA
Removed from the West Lyon Community School library in Larchwood because "it does not meet the standards of the community."

1989 CT
Removed from the Washington Middle School library in Meriden after a parent complained about offensive passages.

1990 MT
Removed from the Livingston Middle School library because it was deemed not "suitable for intended audience," owing to violence, explicit sex, and inappropriate language.

1993 IL
Challenged at the Webber Township High School library in Bluford along with all other King novels.

1994 ND
Challenged, along with eight other Stephen King novels, in Bismarck by a local minister and a school board member, because of "age appropriateness."
Source: 11, Jan. 1986, p. 7; May 1987, p. 86; July 1987, p. 125; May 1989, p. 75; Jan. 1991, p. 12; July 1993, p. 124; May 1994, pp. 84–85.

918
King, Stephen.
Cujo.

1982
Published

1982
British Fantasy Society Award

1984 MS
Challenged at the Rankin County School District because it is "profane and sexually objectionable."

1985 AL
The Washington County Board of Education voted unanimously to ban the novel from all county school libraries because the book contains "unacceptable language" and is "pornographic."

1985 CA
Rejected for purchase by the Hayward school trustees because of "rough language" and "explicit sex scenes."

1985 NY
Removed from the shelves of the Bradford school library "because it was a bunch of garbage."

1987 WI
Removed from a high school library in Durand pending review by a nine-member panel of school personnel and community members.

1992 IL
Challenged from Sparta schools. The school board honored the parents' request to bar their children from using the book, but refused to ban the book.

1992 ME
Challenged, but retained, at a South Portland middle school despite complaints of "profanity" and sexual references.

1994 ND
Challenged, along with eight other Stephen King novels, in Bismarck by a local minister and a school board member, because of "age appropriateness."

1998 FL
Challenged at the West Hernando Middle School in Brooksville because of the book's sexually explicit scenes and language.

1998 OR
Removed at the Crook County High School in Prineville because it contains "profanity, sexual content, and other factors." The parent also requested that all books by Stephen King be removed from the school because, "I object to any book written by Stephen King as he writes horror fiction, which has no value." Three other King books are under review: *The Running Man, Bachman Books,* and *The Green Mile, Part 1.*

Source: 8, pp. 442–44; 11, May 1984, p. 69; Jan. 1985, p. 8; May 1985, pp. 75, 77; July 1985, p. 111; Jan. 1986, p. 7; Nov. 1987, p. 226; May 1994, pp. 84–85; July 1998, p. 110; Jan. 1999, p. 7.

919
King, Stephen.
The Dark Half.

1989
Published

1994 OR
Retained in the Roseburg High School library despite a parent's complaint that the book contains "extreme, bloodthirsty violence."

1998 WI
Banned, but later reinstated in the Stanley-Boyd School District high school library despite a parent's objection to the "profane" language in the first chapter. The school board enacted a new policy that allows parents to call the school librarian and restrict their children's access to certain books or authors.

Source: 11, Sept. 1994, pp. 166–67; Jan. 1999, p. 9; Mar. 1999, p. 37.

920
King, Stephen.
The Dead Zone.

1979
Published

1987 IA
Removed from the West Lyon Community School library in Larchwood because "it does not meet the standards of the community."

1992 FL
Restricted to high school students with parental permission at the Duval County school system because of "filthy language" in the book.

1992 IN
Banned in the Peru school system along with *Cujo* and *Christine* because the books are "filthy."

1994 ND
Challenged, along with eight other Stephen King novels, in Bismarck by a local minister and a school board member, because of "age appropriateness."

Source: 11, May 1987, p. 86; July 1987, p. 125; May 1992, pp. 79, 80; July 1992, pp. 105, 106; May 1994, pp. 84–85.

921
King, Stephen.
Different Seasons.

1982
Published

1987 IA
Removed from the West Lyon Community School library in Larchwood because "it does not meet the standards of the community."

1989 CT
Removed from the Washington Middle School library in Meriden after a parent complained about offensive passages.

1992 MN
Challenged at the Eagan High School in Burnsville.

2001 FL
Accessible to West Hernando Middle School library students in Brooksville only if they have a signed and verified permission slip from their parents. A student was offended by references to oral sex and prison rape scenes in the short story "Rita Hayworth and Shawshank Redemption," the basis for the 1994 movie *The Shawshank Redemption.*

2012 CA
Challenged, but retained, at the Rocklin High School library despite a parent's complaint that the book contained a graphic rape scene.

Source: 11, May 1987, p. 86; July 1987, p. 125; May 1989, p. 75; Mar. 1993, p. 56; Jan. 2002, p. 15; Jan. 2013, p. 33.

922
King, Stephen.
The Drawing of the Three.

1987
Published

1994 ND
Challenged, along with eight other Stephen King novels, in Bismarck by a local minister and a school board member, because of "age appropriateness."

Source: 11, May 1994, pp. 84–85.

923
King, Stephen.
The Eyes of the Dragon.

1987
Published

1994 ND
Challenged, along with eight other Stephen King novels, in Bismarck by a local minister and a school board member, because of "age appropriateness."

Source: 11, May 1994, pp. 84–85.

924
King, Stephen.
Firestarter.

1980
Published

1980
Best Books for Young Adults

1983 WY
Challenged at the Campbell County School System because of its alleged "graphic descriptions of sexual acts, vulgar language, and violence."

1989 CT
Removed from the Washington Middle School library in Meriden after a parent complained about offensive passages.

Source: 11, Mar. 1984, p. 39; May 1989, p. 75.

925
King, Stephen.
Four Past Midnight.

1990
Published

1990
Bram Stoker Award

1992 IL
Challenged at the Sparta High School library, along with all other King novels, due to violence, sex, and explicit language.
Source: 11, July 1992, p. 106.

926
King, Stephen.
Gerald's Game.

1993
Published

1998 FL
Removed from Columbia High School in Lake City because of the book's portrayal of graphic violence and lewd sexual conduct. A parent threatened to take legal action against the school system if the school did not decide to remove all "offensive" library books.
Source: 11, Jan. 1999, pp. 7–8.

927
King, Stephen.
It.

1987
Published

1987 NE
Challenged in the Lincoln school libraries because of the novel's "corruptive, obscene nature."

1992 NY
Placed on a "closed shelf" at the Franklinville Central High School library because of explicit sexual acts, violence, and profane language. Students will need parental permission to check it out.
Source: 11, Nov. 1987, p. 225; Mar. 1993, p. 41.

928
King, Stephen.
Night Shift.

1980
Published

1980
Best Books for Young Adults

1980
Balrog Award

1987 IA
Removed from the West Lyon Community School library in Larchwood because "it does not meet the standards of the community."

1988 WI
Removed from the Green Bay School District classrooms because the book contains a short story entitled "Children of the Corn," which "teaches about the occult and rebellion by children and makes a mockery of Christianity." The book was returned, however, after questions were raised by school board members about the administrative decision to ban the book.
Source: 11, May 1987, p. 86; July 1987, p. 125; Jan. 1989, p. 11; Mar. 1989, p. 44.

929
King, Stephen.
Pet Sematary.

1983
Published

1994 ND
Challenged, along with eight other Stephen King novels, in Bismarck by a local minister and a school board member, because of "age appropriateness."
Source: 11, May 1994, pp. 84–85.

930
King, Stephen.
Salem's Lot.

1978
Published

1986 TX
Banned from the Cleveland Independent High School English classes overruling a review committee's recommendation, even after teachers already had inked out objectionable words with a felt-tip marker. A single copy is available in the restricted section of the high school library to students who have a permission slip signed by their parents.

1988 VT
Banned from the Goochland High School library because of sexually explicit language.
Source: 11, Jan. 1987, p. 12; Mar. 1987, pp. 54–55; Sept. 1988, p. 152.

931
King, Stephen.
The Shining.

1977
Published

1983 WY
Challenged at the Campbell County School System because "the story contains violence, demonic possession and ridicules the Christian religion." The novel is now available to all students in grades seven through twelve, at the discretion of district librarians.

1986 WA
Removed from the Evergreen School District's four junior high school libraries in Vancouver because the book's "descriptive foul language" made it unsuitable for teenagers.

1990 MT
Removed from the Livingston Middle School library because it was deemed not "suitable for intended audience," owing to violence, explicit sex, and inappropriate language.

1994 ND
Challenged, along with eight other Stephen King novels, in Bismarck by a local minister and a school board member, because of "age appropriateness."
Source: 11, Jan. 1984, p. 10; Mar. 1984, p. 39; May 1986, p. 81; July 1987, p. 125; Jan. 1991, p. 12; May 1994, pp. 84–85.

932
King, Stephen.
The Skeleton Crew.

1986
Published

1993 ID
Challenged at the Salmon High School library because of graphic street language about homosexuality, among other reasons.
Source: 11, July 1993, p. 124.

933

King, Stephen.
The Stand.

1978
Published

1989 OR
Restricted to ninth grade students with parental consent at the Whitford Intermediate School in Beaverton because of "sexual language, casual sex, and violence."
Source: 11, Jan. 1990, pp. 4–5.

934

King, Stephen.
Survivor Type: A Short Story from Skeleton Crew.

1986
Published

2009 NH
Pulled from a Litchfield Campbell High School elective course classroom after parents voiced their concerns about a short-stories unit called "Love/Gender/Family Unit" that dealt with subject matters including abortion, cannibalism, homosexuality, and drug use. The parents said the stories promoted bad behavior and a "political agenda" and they shouldn't be incorporated into classroom teachings. The Campbell High School English curriculum adviser eventually resigned.
Source: 11, Sept. 2009, p. 154.

935

King, Stephen.
The Talisman.

1984
Published

1993 ID
Challenged at the Salmon High School library because of graphic street language about homosexuality, among other reasons.
Source: 11, July 1993, p. 124.

936

King, Stephen.
Thinner.

1984
Published

1994 ND
Challenged, along with eight other Stephen King novels, in Bismarck by a local minister and a school board member, because of "age appropriateness."
Source: 11, May 1994, pp. 84–85.

937

King, Stephen.
The Tommyknockers.

1987
Published

1992 FL
Restricted to high school students with parental permission at the Duval County school system because of "filthy language" in the book and "it's extremely graphic."
Source: 11, May 1992, p. 79; July 1992, p. 105.

938

Kingsolver, Barbara.
Animal Dreams.

1990
Published

1991
Best Books for Young Adults

2007 PA
Challenged in the Manheim Township schools due to sexual references. The book was moved from the ninth-grade English curriculum to the eleventh-grade curriculum.
Source: 11, July 2007, pp. 149-50.

939

Kingsolver, Barbara.
The Bean Trees.

1988
Published

1989
Best Books for Young Adults

1998
New York Times Notable Books

1998 IL
Temporarily restricted in the Yorkville schools because it is "obscene, coarse, disgusting, and irreverent."

2009 CA
Challenged at the William S. Hart Union High School District in Saugus as required summer reading for the honors English program because the novel includes sexual scenes and vulgar language. Students have

the option of alternative assignments that still meet objectives and teaching goals.
Source: 11, July 1998, p. 108; Sept. 1998, p. 156; Jan. 2010, pp. 15–16.

940

Kingston, Jeremy.
Witches and Witchcraft.

1976
Published

1987 KY
Removed from the Duerson-Oldham County Public Library in LaGrange because "young or immature minds may become intrigued by Satan as a result of reading the book."
Source: 11, Sept. 1987, p. 174.

941

Kinsey, Alfred.
Sexual Behavior in the Human Female.

1953
Published

1953
Banned in South Africa.

1953
Banned in Ireland.

1953
Banned in U.S. Army post exchanges in Europe as having "no worthwhile interest for soldiers."
Source: 4, p. 75.

942

Kinsey, Alfred.
Sexual Behavior in the Human Male.

1948
Published

1953
Banned in South Africa.

1953
Banned in Ireland.

1953
Banned in U.S. Army post exchanges in Europe as having "no worthwhile interest for soldiers."
Source: 4, p. 75.

943

Kipling, Rudyard.
Drums of the Fore and Aft.

1898
Published

1907
Nobel Prize in Literature

1899 IN
Removed from the Sunday school library of the Crawfordsville First Methodist Episcopal Church because a parishioner complained that it was "fairly reeking with profanity, and the most outrageous slang."
Source: 15, Vol. II, p. 624.

944

Kipling, Rudyard.
The Elephant's Child.

1902
Published

1993 IA
Challenged in the Davenport Community School District because the book is "99 percent" violent. Throughout the book, when the main character, an elephant child, asks a question, he receives a spanking instead of answers.
Source: 11, July 1993, p. 99.

945

Kipling, Rudyard.
Just So Stories.

1902
Published

1990 NC
Challenged at the Hardin Park Elementary School library in Watauga County because the word "nigger" appears in the story "How the Leopard Got Its Spots."
Source: 11, July 1990, p. 145.

946

Kirk, Marshall, and Hunter Madison.
After the Ball: How America Will Conquer Its Hatred and Fear of Homosexuals in the '90s.

1989
Published

1993 OR
Challenged at the Deschutes County Library in Bend because it "encourages and condones" homosexuality.
Source: 11, Sept. 1993, pp. 158–59.

947

Kirkwood, James.
There Must Be a Pony! A Novel.

1960
Published

1984
Seized by the British customs office as "indecent and obscene."
Source: 11, Jan. 1985, p. 16.

948

Kittredge, Mary.
Teens with AIDS Speak Out.

1991
Published

1993
Best Books for Young Adults

1993 TN
Challenged, but retained, at the Cleveland Public Library along with seventeen other books, most of which are on sex education, AIDS awareness, and some titles on the supernatural.
Source: 11, Sept. 1993, p. 146.

949

Kitzinger, Sheila.
Being Born.

1986
Published

1991 OR
Challenged at the Lakeview school libraries because the complainant's son asked "rather pointed questions" about childbirth.

1993 NV
Challenged, but retained, at the Washoe County Library System in Reno because, "Nobody in their right mind would give a book like that to children on their own, except the library."
Source: 11, Nov. 1991, p. 209; Sept. 1994, p. 147; Nov. 1994, pp. 200–01.

950

Klause, Annette Curtis.
Blood and Chocolate.

1992
Published

1998
Best Books for Young Adults

2001 TX
Temporarily pulled from the LaPorte Independent School District school library shelves until the district can review and possibly amend its selection policies.
Source: 11, Nov. 2001, p. 247.

951

Klausen, Jytte.
The Cartoons That Shook the World.

2009
Published

2009 CT
Yale University Press in New Haven removed twelve cartoons of the Prophet Muhammad from an upcoming book about how they caused outrage across the Muslim world, citing fears of violence. A Danish newspaper originally published the cartoons—including one depicting Muhammad wearing a bomb-shaped turban—in 2005. Other Western publications reprinted them. The following year, the cartoons triggered massive protests from Morocco to Indonesia. Rioters torched Danish and other Western diplomatic missions. Some Muslim countries boycotted Danish products. Islamic law generally opposes any depiction of the prophet, even favorable, for fear it could lead to idolatry.
Source: 11, Nov. 2009, pp. 204-7.

952

Klein, Aaron E.
Science and the Supernatural.

1979
Published

1993 TN
Challenged, but retained, at the Cleveland Public Library along with seventeen other books, most of which are on sex education, AIDS awareness, and some titles on the supernatural.
Source: 11, Sept. 1993, p. 146.

953
Klein, Norma.
Angel Face.

1984
Published

1990 TX
Challenged at the Commerce High School library because of "pornographic" material in the book. The complainant asked that all "romance" books be removed.
Source: 11, Mar. 1991, p. 43.

954
Klein, Norma.
Beginners' Love.

1983
Published

1999 SC
Challenged, but retained, in the Chester High School library with the provision that parents can instruct the school not to let their own children borrow it. The book's graphic description of sex, discussions of abortion, and the character's use of marijuana were considered objectionable by some parents. South Carolina Attorney General Charlie Condon ruled that the school board could reasonably conclude that the novel was "pervasively vulgar" and "educationally unsuitable" and, thus, removal by the board would not violate the First Amendment.
Source: 11, Mar. 1999, p. 36; Nov. 1999, p. 163.

955
Klein, Norma.
Confessions of an Only Child.

1974
Published

1985 GA
Challenged, but retained, in a Gwinnett County Elementary School library because "the use of a profanity by the lead character's father during a single episode destroyed the entire book."
Source: 11, Mar. 1986, p. 57; Mar. 1986, p. 57; July 1986, p. 135.

956
Klein, Norma.
Family Secrets.

1985
Published

1991 MD
Removed from the Howard County middle school media centers because the book's "constant reference to the sex act" and "inappropriate foul language."
Source: 11, Mar. 1992, p. 40.

957
Klein, Norma.
Give Me One Good Reason.

1977
Published

1984 CO
Challenged at the Widefield School District because the book is "filled with promiscuity, homosexuality, abortion, and profanity."
Source: 11, May 1984, p. 69.

958
Klein, Norma.
Honey of a Chimp.

1980
Published

1984 PA
Removed from the Hanover School District's elementary and secondary libraries, but later placed on a "restricted shelf" at middle school libraries, because the book contained "strong sexual content, bias to liberal values and morals, and indecent language. The material condones certain values, attitudes, and behaviors."
Source: 11, Jan. 1985, p. 9.

959
Klein, Norma.
It's Not What You Expect.

1973
Published

1980 MD
Removed from all the Montgomery County elementary school libraries.
Source: 11, May 1980, p. 51.

960
Klein, Norma.
It's OK If You Don't Love Me.

1977
Published

1981 CA
Banned in Hayward County because of the book's sexually explicit passages and "rough language."

1983 CO
Removed from the shelves of the Widefield High School library because it portrays "sex as the only thing on young people's minds."

1984 WA
Removed from the Vancouver School District due to its sexual passages, but later reinstated at the high school level libraries.
Source: 11, Mar. 1982, p. 44; May 1983, p. 71; July 1984, p. 104.

961
Klein, Norma.
Just Friends.

1990
Published

1994 CT
Challenged at the Hamden Middle School because it is "nothing more than pornographic smut."

1998 MO
Banned at, but later returned to, the Cameron High School library after student complaints. The book was initially challenged because it was "too explicit and did not link actions to consequences."

2000 CA
Removed from the mandatory reading program at the Norman L. Sullivan Middle School in Bonsall due to sexually explicit language.
Source: 11, Nov. 1994, p. 189; July 1998, p. 119; May 2000, p. 76.

962
Klein, Norma.
Love Is One of the Choices.

1978
Published

1983 WA
Removed from the Evergreen School District of Vancouver along with twenty-nine other titles. The American Civil Liberties Union of Washington filed suit contending that the removals constitute censorship, a violation of plaintiff's rights to free speech and due process, and a violation of the state Open Meetings Act because the removal decisions were made behind closed doors.
Source: 11, Nov. 1983, pp. 185–86.

963
Klein, Norma.
Mom, the Wolf Man and Me.

1972
Published

1980 FL
Challenged at the Orlando Public Library due to its "objectionable" subject matter.
Source: 11, Mar. 1981, p. 47.

964
Klein, Norma.
My Life as a Body.

1987
Published

1989 OR
Challenged at the Douglas County Library in Roseburg because the book condones homosexuality and premarital sex.

1991 OR
Challenged for being too explicit, but retained at the Multnomah County Library.
Source: 11, Jan. 1990, pp. 4–5; Jan. 1992, p. 6.

965
Klein, Norma.
Naomi in the Middle.

1974
Published

1977 NY
Restricted in Brockport to students with parental permission.

1980 FL
Challenged at the Orlando Public Library due to its "objectionable" subject matter.

980 LA
Banned in Monroe because "it is certainly not our intention to have objectionable materials on library shelves."

1986 NC
Challenged at the Charlotte public library system because the book "is a perfect picture of secular humanism."

1992 CA
Challenged at the Napa City-County Library because of sexually explicit language.

1995 AZ
Challenged at the Mesa Public Libraries because of four pages of inappropriate material describing human sexual anatomy and how babies are conceived.
Source: 11, Nov. 1977, p. 155; July 1980, p. 76; Mar. 1981, p. 47; Jan. 1987, p. 31; July 1992, p. 105; July 1995, p. 109.

966
Klein, Norma.
The Queen of the What Ifs.

1982
Published

1989 CA
Pulled from the Monte Vista Middle School library in Tracy after two parents complained that its sexual content made the book inappropriate for middle school students. About a half dozen other titles also were removed, and the parents have indicated a desire to review all books ordered for the library.
Source: 11, May 1989, p. 75.

967
Klein, Norma.
Sunshine.

1975
Published

1975 LA
Removed from the East Baton Rouge Parish after the parents of a student said they found the language and content of the book offensive.
Source: 11, July 1975, p. 104.

968
Klein, Norma.
That's My Baby.

1987
Published

1998 MO
Banned at, but later returned to, the Cameron High School library after student complaints. The book was initially challenged because it was "too explicit and did not link actions to consequences."
Source: 11, July 1998, p. 119.

969
Klein, Norma.
What It's All About.

1975
Published

1984 IA
Challenged at the Dubuque Community School District because, "it condones and even endorses immoral behavior because it contains profanity, nudity, sexual relationships outside of marriage and an excessive number of people who are divorced."
Source: 11, Sept. 1984, p. 155.

970
Klein, Stanley.
Steck-Vaughn Social Studies.

1983
Published

1987 AL
Removed from Alabama's list of approved texts—and from the state's classrooms—because the book promotes the "religion of secular humanism." U.S. District Court Judge W. Brevard Hand ruled on March 4, 1987, that thirty-nine history and social studies texts used in Alabama's 129 school systems "discriminate against the very concept of religion and theistic religions in particular, by omissions so serious that a student learning history from them would not be apprised of relevant facts about America's history... References to religion are isolated and the integration of religion in the history of American society is ignored." The series includes: *Our Family; Our Neighbors; Our Communities; Our Country Today; Our Country's History;* and *Our World Today.* On August 26, 1987, the U.S. Court of Appeals for the Eleventh Circuit unanimously overturned Judge Hand's decision by ruling that the information in the book was "essentially neutral in its religious content." The fact that the texts omitted references to religion was not

"an advancement of secular humanism or an active hostility toward theistic religion." Source: 11, Jan. 1987, p. 6; May 1987, pp. 75, 104–7; Sept. 1987, pp. 166–67; Nov. 1987, pp. 217–18; Jan. 1988, p. 17; Mar. 1988, p. 40.

971
Knott, Blanche.
Truly Tasteless Jokes.

1983
Published

1988 AZ
Removed from open display at the Casa Grande Public Library and restricted to adult use only with proof of age before checking the book out or even looking at it.
Source: 11, Jan. 1989, p. 7.

972
Knowles, Jo (Johanna Beth).
Lessons from a Dead Girl.

2007
Published

2009 KY
Withdrawn from classroom use and the approved curriculum at the Montgomery County High School, but available at the high school library and student book club. Some parents have complained about five novels containing foul language and that cover topics—including sex, child abuse, suicide, and drug abuse—unsuited for discussion in coed high school classes. They also contend that the books don't provide the intellectual challenge and rigor that students need in college preparatory classes. The titles appeared on suggested book lists compiled by the Young Adult Library Services Association, a division of the American Library Association, for twelve- to eighteen-year-olds who are "reluctant readers." The superintendent removed the book because it wasn't on the pre-approved curriculum list and couldn't be added by teachers in the middle of a school year without permission.
Source: 11, Jan. 2010, pp. 16-17; Mar. 2010, p. 56.

973
Knowles, John.
A Separate Peace.

1959
Published

1980 NY
Challenged in Vernon-Verona-Sherill School District as a "filthy, trashy sex novel."

1985 PA
Challenged at the Fannett-Metal High School in Shippensburg because of its allegedly offensive language.

1989 TN
Challenged as appropriate for high school reading lists in the Shelby County school system because the novel contained "offensive language."

1991 IL
Challenged, but retained, in the Champaign high school English classes despite claims that "unsuitable language" made it inappropriate.

1991 IL
Challenged by the parent of a high school student in Troy citing profanity and negative attitudes. Students were offered alternative assignments while the school board took the matter under advisement, but no further action was taken on the complaint.

1996 NC
Challenged at the McDowell County schools because of "graphic language."
Source: 11, May 1980, p. 62; Nov. 1985, p. 204; Jan. 1990, pp. 11–12; Jan. 1997, p. 11; 14, pp. 256–57.

974
Knowlton, Charles.
Fruits of Philosophy: The Private Companion of Married Couples.

1832
Published

1832 MA
The author was brought to trial in Taunton, Massachusetts, and charged with distributing "obscene material," then filed $50 and court costs.

1832 MA
In December 1832, Knowlton was found guilty of distributing his book and sentenced to three months of hard labor in the Cambridge House of Corrections.

1834 MA
Knowlton appeared in the court of Greenfield three different times, but the case was finally dismissed because the jury in all three trials could not come to a decision.

1876
A bookseller in Bristol, England, was convicted under the obscenity law for selling Knowlton's work. It had been on sale without hindrance in Britain for forty years. The complaint against the book was twofold: "It advocated contraception rather than chastity for the control of pregnancies and, at only 6d (2.5p) a copy, the poor could not afford to buy it." While the defendants were sentenced to six months' imprisonment and a fine, they were released on bail and the convictions were quashed in February 1878 on appeal.
Source: 3, pp. 186-87; 14, pp. 148–50.

975
Knudsen, Eric Alfred.
Teller of Tales.

1987
Published

1992 GA
Challenged in the Columbia County school libraries because the biography of Hans Christian Andersen contains the phrase "go to hell."
Source: 11, Nov. 1992, p. 197.

976
Koertge, Ronald.
The Arizona Kid.

1988
Published

1988
Best Books for Young Adults

1993 OR
Challenged because it "encourages and condones" homosexuality, but retained, at the Bend High School.

1994 MN
Pulled from and later restored to the seventh-grade English classroom at Minnetonka Middle School West after a parent found the content inappropriate for twelve- and thirteen-year-olds.
Source: 11, Sept. 1993, pp. 158–59; Nov. 1993, p. 192; July 1994, p. 114; Sept. 1994, p. 166.

977
Koertge, Ronald.
The Brimstone Journals.

2001
Published

2002
Best Books for Young Adults

2007 MO
Challenged, but retained, at the William Chrisman High School library in Independence. A parent was concerned about profanity as well as some of the subjects discussed in the book.
Source: 11, Sept. 2007, p. 205.

978
Koertge, Ronald.
Where the Kissing Never Stops.

1986
Published

1986
Best Books for Young Adults

2000 PA
Retained as optional reading for eighth graders at Rice Avenue Middle School in Girard. A grandmother found the book offensive and didn't want her granddaughters reading it.
Source: 11, May 2000, p. 92.

979
Koontz, Dean R.
Funhouse.

1980
Published

1995 NC
Removed from the South Brunswick Middle School Library in Boiling Spring Lakes by a patron because the book "contains material on orgies, rape, and lesbianism. There is also blasphemy and the book promotes domestic violence and alcohol abuse." The book was donated by the Lions Club in a book drive.
Source: 11, Nov. 1995, pp. 183–84; Jan. 1996, p. 11.

980
Koontz, Dean R.
Night Chills.

1976
Published

1992 OR
Challenged at the Mountain View High School in Bend because it contains "explicit" sexual incidents.
Source: 11, Jan. 1993, p. 9.

981
Koontz, Dean R.
The Voice of the Night.

1980
Published

2000 ME
Challenged as extra reading material at Westcott Junior High School in Westbrook because the novel describes people having sex and the mutilation of animals and people.
Source: 11, Mar. 2000, p. 50.

982
Koontz, Dean R.
Watchers.

1987
Published

1987
Best Books for Young Adults

1996 PA
Removed from the Hickory High School curriculum in Sharon by the superintendent because the language was offensive.
Source: 11, Mar. 1997, p. 50.

983
Kopay, David, and Perry D. Young.
The David Kopay Story: An Extraordinary Self-Revelation.

1977
Published

1977
Best Books for Young Adults

1993 OR
Challenged because it "encourages and condones" homosexuality, but retained, at the Bend High School.
Source: 11, Sept. 1993, pp. 158–59; Nov. 1993, p. 192.

984
The Koran.

600s A.D.
Published

1530
First Arabic edition published in Europe (Venice) ordered to be burned by the Pope in Rome, Italy.

1790
Ban lifted by the Spanish Index.

1926
Restricted to students of history in USSR.

1960
During the Chinese Cultural Revolution of the 1960s and 1970s, study of the *Koran* was forbidden and its reading in mosques prohibited.

1986
Under the socialist military government in Ethiopia, it was reported that copies of the *Koran* were destroyed or confiscated by the army, Koranic schools and mosques were closed or razed, Muslims were prohibited from praying and some were ordered to Christianity and burn the *Koran*.

1995
A Malay translation was banned by the government of Malaysia. The banning was part of an official policy aimed at outlawing "deviant" Islamic sects.

2011 FL
Burned by Evangelical pastor Terry Jones at his Gainesville, Florida, church, the Dove World Outreach Center. In response, thousands of protesters overran the United Nations compound in Mazar-I-Sharif, Afghanistan, killing at least twelve people.
Source: 1, p. 172; 4, p. 5; 8, pp. 251–53; 11, July 2011, p. 131.

985
Korman, Gordon.
Jake, Reinvented.

2003
Published

2004
Best Books for Young Adults

2007 AZ
Challenged in the Higley Unified School District in Gilbert because the novel contains themes of teen drinking, sex, and violence.
Source: 11, Jan. 2008, p. 36.

986
Kornblum, William, and
Joseph Julian.
Social Problems.

1983
Published

1993 OK
Reinstated at the Anadarko Public
Schools after a textbook review committee
recommendation. The text was challenged
by a minister who complained about
the book's references to homosexuality,
lesbians, and child molesters.
Source: 11, Sept. 1993, p. 160.

987
Kosinski, Jerzy.
Being There.

1971
Published

1989 NE
Challenged as a reading assignment
for an eleventh-grade English class at
Crete High School.

1989 PA
Reinstated after being removed from
the Mifflinburg High School because the
book's main character has a homosexual
experience.

1993 IA
Challenged as required reading in a
senior advanced English course in
Davenport because of a description
of masturbation.

1995 CT
Challenged on the curricular reading list
at Pomperaug High School in Southbury
because sexually explicit passages are not
appropriate high school reading.
Source: 11, May 1989, pp. 79, 93; July 1993, p. 105;
July 1995, p. 98.

988
Kotzwinkle, William, and
Glenn Murray.
Walter the Farting Dog.

2001
Published

2004 WI
Challenged, but retained, on the library
shelves of the West Salem Elementary
School despite the book's use of the word
"fart" and "farting" twenty-four times.
Source: 11, May 2004, p. 118; July 2004, p. 138.

989
Kotzwinkle, William.
Nightbook.

1974
Published

1980 SD
Challenged at the Huron Public Library
because "there's not a page in [the book]
fit to be read by anyone."
Source: 11, July 1980, p. 84.

990
Kovic, Ron.
Born on the Fourth of July.

1976
Published

1976
Best Books for Young Adults

1982 MD
Placed on a closed shelf in Maryland
after a parent objected to the book as
un-American, finding fault also with its
language and its display of sex.
Source: 7, 64.

991
Krantz, Judith.
Mistral's Daughter.

1983
Published

1985 PA
Banned from the Stroudsburg High
School library because it was "blatantly
graphic, pornographic, and wholly
unacceptable for a high school library."
Source: 11, May 1985, p. 79.

992
Kroeker, Gary.
The Magi at Christmas.

1997
Published

993
Kroll, Ken.
*Enabling Romance: A Guide
to Love, Sex and Relationships
for the Disabled.*

1998 CA
Banned at the Los Altos High School in
Hacienda Heights because the novel was
"too racy." The author is an English
teacher at the school.
Source: 11, July 1998, p. 104; Mar. 1999, p. 35.

1992
Published

1996 NJ
Removed from the Clifton Public Library
and replaced with a dummy book made
of styrofoam. The library's new policy
restricts to adults any material containing
"patently offensive graphic illustrations
or photographs of sexual or excretory
activities or contact as measured by
contemporary community standards
for minors."
Source: 11, July 1996, pp. 118–19.

994
Kropp, Paul.
Wilted.

1980
Published

1983 WA
Banned from the Evergreen School
District libraries in Vancouver because
the "sexual scenes were a bit much for
elementary schools."
Source: 11, Sept. 1983, p. 139.

995
Kung, Hans.
Infallible?: An Inquiry.

1971
Published

1979
The Vatican in Rome, Italy, withdrew
the Swiss priest and prominent Catholic
theologian, barred him from teaching in
the name of the church, and prohibited
Catholic institutions from employing him.
Source: 8, pp. 249–50.

996
Kushner, Ellen.
Mystery of the Secret Room.

1986
Published

1992 SC
Challenged at the Berkeley County school libraries because the book teaches witchcraft.
Source: 11, July 1992, p. 108.

997
Kuskin, Karla.
The Dallas Titans Get Ready for Bed.

1986
Published

1989 OR
Challenged at the Douglas County Library in Roseburg because children are not ready for illustrations and conversation about jockstraps.
Source: 11, Jan. 1990, pp. 4–5.

998
LaCour, Nina.
Hold Still.

2009
Published

2010
Best Books for Young Adults

2011 MO
Pulled from the Blue Springs School District library and classrooms because the book is "riddled with obscenities." The novel is about a young girl coping with the suicide of her best friend. The book, according to parents, was read as part of an extra credit assignment in a freshman English class. The local chapter of the ACLU is threatening to get involved if the book is permanently removed.
Source: 11, Jan. 2012, pp. 9-10.

999
Lader, Lawrence.
Foolproof Birth Control.

1972
Published

1977 MI
Banned from the Brighton High School library along with all other sex education materials.
Source: 11, Sept. 1977, p. 133.

1000
Laine, James W.
Shivaji: Hindu King in Islamic India.

2003
Published

2003
Hindu fundamentalists, contending that he had insulted the reputation of Shivaji, the seventeenth century century Hindu king and warrior, ransacked the institute in Pune, India, where he had conducted research for his book. The book was banned in Maharashtra State in India, which brought criminal charges against Laine and his publisher and threatened to extradite him to India. A high court in Bombay stayed the criminal charges against him.
Source: 1, pp. 303–5.

1001
Laing, Frederick.
Tales from Scandinavia.

1979
Published

1992 NE
Removed to a locked closet in the superintendent's office in Banner County because the book "has to do with a lot of negative things and might not be good for someone with low self-esteem or suicide tendencies."
Source: 11, May 1992, p. 80.

1002
Landis, James David.
The Sisters Impossible.

1979
Published

1985 OK
Removed from the Sallisaw school libraries due to offensive language. Later, returned to the shelves of the Eastside Elementary School library in Sallisaw after the school board agreed to an out-of-court settlement with a group of parents who filed a suit to reverse the board's 1985 decision to ban the book. The book was originally banned because it uses "hell" seven times and the words "fart" and "bullshit" once each in its 169 pages.

1988 AK
Challenged in the Fairbanks school libraries because of "the language in the book and to a scene in which aspiring young ballerinas danced naked in a dressing room before class."

1997 GA
Challenged because of objectionable language, but retained, at the J. G. Dyer Elementary School library in Gwinnett County.
Source: 11, July 1985, p. 112; Mar. 1986, pp. 60, 65–66; July 1986, p. 136; Mar. 1988, p. 71; July 1997, p. 109; Sept. 1997, p. 148.

1003
Langley, Andrew.
100 Greatest Tyrants.

1997
Published

2006
Challenged at the Mount Isa, Queensland, Australia, high school by a legislator who described the book as offensive and inappropriate for history studies in any Australian school. The school principal refused to remove the book from the library, describing it as a useful resource for generating debate and critical-thinking skills among students.
Source: 11, Jan. 2007, pp. 33-34.

1004
Langton, Jane.
The Fragile Flag.

1984
Published

1986 CO
Challenged at the Jefferson County school library because the book portrays the U.S. government as "shallow" and "manipulative," and "lacking in intelligence and responsibility."
Source: 11, Jan. 1987, p. 29; Mar. 1987, p. 49.

1005
LaPlace, John.
Health.

1972
Published

1981 NY
Banned from senior high school classrooms in the Diocese of Buffalo.

1984 NJ
Challenged at the Randolph High School by a group of parents and clergy who say "the textbook is too liberal and should be replaced or supplemented by a more traditional book."
Source: 11, Jan. 1981, p. 10; July 1984, p. 106.

1006
Larrick, Nancy, and Eve Merriam.
Male and Female under 18.

1973
Published

1977 MA
Banned by the Chelsea School Board from the high school library because of objections to one poem by a teenage girl. The banning was reversed by a U.S. District Court ruling in *Right to Read Defense Committee v. School Committee of the City of Chelsea*, 454 F. Supp. 703 (D. Mass. 1978).
Source: 4, p. 104; 12, pp. 12–14, 148–53, 229, 239.

1007
Larson, Rodger.
What I Know Now.

1997
Published

2004 TX
Challenged at the Montgomery County Memorial Library System along with fifteen other young-adult books with gay-positive themes. The objections were posted at the Library Patrons of Texas web-site. The language describing the books is similar to that posted at the website of the Fairfax County, Virginia-based Parents Against Bad Books in Schools, to which Library Patrons of Texas links.
Source: 11, Nov. 2004, pp. 231–32

1008
Laurence, Margaret.
Christmas Birthday Story.

1980
Published

1982 ME
Challenged at the York school system.
Source: 11, July 1982, p. 124.

1009
Laurence, Margaret.
A Jest of God.

1966
Published

1966
Governor General's Award for English-language Fiction

1984
Challenged at the Peterborough, Ontario, Canada, County schools after a resolution from the nearby Burleigh-Anstruther municipal council asked that the books be reviewed for their moral content.
Source: 11, Mar. 1985, p. 45.

1010
Laurence, Margaret.
The Stone Angel.

1964
Published

1984
Challenged at the Peterborough, Ontario, Canada, County schools after a resolution from the nearby Burleigh-Anstruther municipal council asked that the books be reviewed for their moral content.
Source: 11, Mar. 1985, p. 45.

1011
Lawrence, D. H.
Collected Paintings.

1929
Published

1929
Banned by U.S. Customs.
Source: 10, p. 142; 15, Vol. III, p. 414.

1012
Lawrence, D. H.
Lady Chatterley's Lover.

1928
Published

1929
Banned by U.S. Customs.

1932
Banned in Ireland.

1932
Banned in Poland.

1959
Banned in Australia.

1959
Banned in Japan.

1959
Banned in India.

1960
Banned in Canada until 1962.

1987
Dissemination of Lawrence's novel has been stopped in China because the book "will corrupt the minds of young people and is also against the Chinese tradition."
Source: 2, p. 137; 4, pp. 69–70; 6, pp. 1,382–86; 8, pp. 354–57; 11, July 1987, pp. 135–36; 15, Vol. III, pp. 407, 414.

1013
Lawrence, D. H.
Paintings of D. H. Lawrence.

1929
Published

1929
Barred by U.S. Customs.
Source: 4, p. 69.

1014
Lawrence, D. H.
Pansies.

1929
Published

1928
Seized by postal authorities in England and was substantially altered prior to its republication in 1929.
Source: 3, p. 170; 322, pp. 184–85.

1015
Lawrence, D. H.
The Rainbow.

1915
Published

1915
Ordered destroyed by the British magistrate's court.

Source: 2, p. 100; 4, p. 69; 13, pp. 198–99.

1016
Lawrence, D. H.
Sons and Lovers.

1913
Published

1961 OK
An Oklahoma City group called Mothers United for Decency hired a trailer, dubbed it "smutmobile," and displayed books deemed objectionable, including Lawrence's novel.

Source: 4, p. 119.

1017
Lawrence, D. H.
Women in Love.

1920
Published

1922 NY
Seized by John Summers of the New York Society for the Suppression of Vice and declared obscene.

Source: 8, p. 394; 11, p. 142; 15, Vol. III, p. 415.

1018
Lawrence, Jerome, and Robert E. Lee.
Inherit the Wind.

1955
Published

1997 OH
Challenged, but retained, at the Lakewood High School. The book was challenged by parents who objected to what they called the play's allegedly anti-religious nature.

Source: 11, May 1997, p. 79.

1019
Lawrence, Margaret.
The Diviners.

1974
Published

1984
Challenged at the Peterborough, Ontario, Canada, County schools after a resolution from the nearby Burleigh-Anstruther municipal council asked that the books be reviewed for their moral content.

1997 NJ
Removed from the summer reading list for the Clark School District's seventh graders because of detailed descriptions of sexual intercourse. A group called Parents Against Pornographic Adult Literature was formed to ensure reading lists are correctly oriented and reviewed for Clark students.

Source: 11, Mar. 1985, p. 45; Nov. 1997, p. 169.

1020
Lawson, Robert.
They Were Strong and Good.

1940
Published

1941
Caldecott Medal

1991 OR
Challenged because the novel "glorifies slavery and racism," but retained, at the Multnomah County Library.

Source: 11, Jan. 1992, p. 6.

1021
Leach, Maria.
Whistle in the Graveyard: Folktales to Chill Your Bones.

1974
Published

1992 AZ
Challenged at the Neely Elementary School in Gilbert because the book shows the dark side of religion through the occult, the devil, and satanism.

Source: 11, May 1992, p. 78; July 1992, p. 124.

1022
Lebert, Benjamin.
Crazy.

2000
Published

2001
Best Books for Young Adults

2003 TX
Removed from the Canyon Vista Middle School in Round Rock by the principal who decided a parent was correct in being concerned about the book's availability. The parent called the book "vulgar; it talked about parts of the body." There was free use of the "F-word" and several "C-words." The book was taken off the shelf at the district's other junior high school library.

Source: 11, Nov. 2003, p. 229.

1023
Lederer, William J., and Eugene Burdick.
The Ugly American.

1958
Published

1958
Immediately after the novel's 1958 publication, it was temporarily censored by George A. Allen, director of the U.S. Information Agency, the federal agency responsible for U.S. overseas libraries, because the book "would not be in the interest of the United States." In December 1958, Allen changed his mind. Senator J. W. Fullbright criticized the novel from the Senate floor in 1959. He was upset by the portrayal of American overseas as "boobs or worse," while Russian diplomats were portrayed as "talented, dedicated servants of communism."

1963 WI
In a 1963 survey by the Wisconsin English Department chairpersons and school administrators, a Wisconsin teacher and a group of parents objected to the novel because of its critical pictures of Americans abroad. Others have been critical of the novel based on its "filthy language and reference to sex" and its profane and vile language.

Source: 8, pp. 180–81.

1024

Lee, Harper.
To Kill a Mockingbird.

1960
Published

1961
Pulitzer Prize for Fiction

1977 MN
Challenged in Eden Valley and
temporarily banned due to
words "damn" and "whore lady"
used in the novel.

1980 NY
Challenged in the Vernon-Verona-Sherill
School District as a "filthy, trashy novel."

1981 IN
Challenged at the Warren Township
schools because the book does
"psychological damage to the positive
integration process" and "represents
institutionalized racism under the guise
of 'good literature.'" After unsuccessfully
banning Lee's novel, three black parents
resigned from the township human
relations advisory council.

1984 IL
Challenged in the Waukegan School
District because the novel uses the
word "nigger."

1985 AZ
Retained on a supplemental eighth-
grade reading list in the Casa Grande
Elementary School District, despite the
protests by black parents and the
National Association for the Advancement
of Colored People who charged the book
was unfit for junior high use.

1985 MO
Challenged in the Kansas City junior
high schools.

1985 MO
Challenged at the Park Hill Junior
High School because the novel "contains
profanity and racial slurs."

1995 CA
Challenged at the Santa Cruz Schools
because of its racial themes.

1995 LA
Removed from the Southwood High
School Library in Caddo Parish because
the book's language and content
were objectionable.

1996 MS
Challenged at the Moss Point School
District because the novel contains a
racial epithet.

1996 TX
Banned from the Lindale Advanced
Placement English reading list because
the book "conflicted with the values
of the community."

2001 GA
Challenged by a Glynn County School
Board member because of profanity.
The novel was retained.

2001 OK
Returned to the freshmen reading list at
Muskogee High School despite complaints
over the years from black students and
parents about racial slurs in the text.

2004 IL
Challenged, but retained, in the Normal
Community High School sophomore
literature class despite concerns the novel
is degrading to African Americans.

2004 NC
Challenged at the Stanford Middle
School in Durham because the novel
uses the word "nigger."

2006 TN
Challenged at the Brentwood Middle
School because the book contains
"profanity" and "contains adult themes
such as sexual intercourse, rape, and incest."
The complainants also contend that the
book's use of racial slurs promotes "racial
hatred, racial division, racial separation,
and promotes white supremacy."

2007 NJ
Retained in the English curriculum
by the Cherry Hill Board of Education.
A resident had objected to the novel's
depiction of how blacks are treated by
members of a racist white community in
an Alabama town during the Depression.
The resident feared the book would
upset black children reading it.

2009
Removed from the St. Edmund Campion
Secondary School classrooms in Brampton,
Ontario, Canada, because a parent
objected to language used in the novel,
including the word "nigger."

Source: 8, p. 483; 11, Mar. 1978, p. 31; May 1980, p. 62;
Mar. 1982, p. 47; July 1984, p. 105; May 1985, p. 80; July
1985, p. 134; Mar. 1986, pp. 57–58; May 1995, p. 68; Nov.
1995, p. 183; Nov. 1996, pp. 196–97, 199; Nov. 2001, pp.
277–78; Jan. 2002, p. 50; Jan. 2004, p. 11; May 2004, pp.
98–99; Mar. 2006, p. 74; Mar. 2008, p. 80; May 2008,
pp. 117-18; Nov. 2009, pp. 203-4.

1025

Lee, Joanna.
I Want to Keep My Baby.

1977
Published

1994 NC
Removed from the Morehead High School
library in Rockingham County because
of "antireligious sentiments—the
girl's comment that her boyfriend was
'her God'—and sexual situations." After a
three-hour public debate, the Rockingham
County School Board later reversed its
previous ban against the book.

Source: 11, Sept. 1994, p. 148; Nov. 1994, p. 201.

1026

Legman, Gershon, ed.
*The Limerick: 1,700 Examples
with Notes, Variants and Index.*

1969
Published

1991 IL
Challenged at the Oak Lawn Public
Library because the book contains bawdy
limericks with explicit sexual references.

Source: 11, Nov. 1991, p. 209; Jan. 1992, p. 26.

1027

Le Guin, Ursula K.
A Fisherman of the Inland Sea.

1994
Published

2006 TX
Removed from the West Brazoria Junior
High School library because of inappropriate language. Books on "sensitive topics
such as death, suicide, physical or sexual
abuse, and teenage dating relationships"
were moved to a restricted "young-adult"
section from which students can borrow
only with written parental permission.

Source: 11, Nov. 2006, pp. 289-90.

1028
LeGuin, Ursula K.
Lathe of Heaven.

1971
Published

1984 WA
Challenged on a Washougal High School reading list because it contained "profuse profanity."
Source: 11, Sept. 1984, p. 157.

1029
Lehrman, Robert.
Juggling.

1982
Published

1982
Best Books for Young Adults

1990 MN
Challenged at Woodbury Library. The book is about the life and sexual encounters of a teenage soccer player.
Source: 11, July 1990, p. 145.

1030
Lelyveld, Joseph.
Great Soul: Mahatma Gandhi and His Struggle With India.

2011
Published

2011
Banned in parts of India.

2011 CA
A Santa Cruz educational organization, Foundation for Excellence, canceled an event planned in honor of the Pulitzer Prize-winning author. The foundation provides scholarships for students in India and canceled the event after the biography hinted a homosexual relationship between Gandhi and a German named Hermann Kallenbach. The foundation "didn't want to be involved with any controversy."
Source: 11, July 2011, pp. 141-42.

1031
L'Engle, Madeleine C.
Many Waters.

1986
Published

1987
Best Books for Young Adults

1991 OH
Challenged at the Hubbard Library because the book alters the story of Noah's Ark, making it secular and confusing to children.
Source: 11, Sept. 1991, p. 153.

1032
L'Engle, Madeleine C.
A Wrinkle in Time.

1962
Published

1963
Newbery Medal

1985 FL
Challenged, but retained, on the media center shelves of the Polk City Elementary School. A student's parent filed the complaint, contending the story promoted witchcraft, crystal balls, and demons.

1990 AL
Challenged in the Anniston schools because the book sends a mixed signal to children about good and evil. The complainant also objected to listing the name of Jesus Christ together with the names of great artists, philosophers, scientists, and religious leaders when referring to defenders of Earth against evil.

1996 NC
Challenged, but retained, by the Catawba County School Board in Newton. A parent requested the book be pulled from the school libraries because it allegedly undermines religious beliefs.
Source: 11, July 1985, p. 133; Mar. 1991, p. 62; May 1996, pp. 97-98.

1033
Lenin, Vladimir I.
The State and Revolution.

1917
Published

1927
Seized as subversive in Hungary.

1927 MA
Seized as obscene in Boston.

1933
Burned In Munich, Germany, by the Nazi government.

1940 OK
In Oklahoma City a vigilante group raided a bookstore owned by Robert Wood, who was also the state secretary of the Communist Party. They seized copies of the book along with other Communist literature, various works of fiction, books on economics, and copies of the U.S. Constitution and the Declaration of Independence. Mr. and Mrs. Wood, along with several other people who happened to be in the store, were arrested on charges of "criminal syndicalism" and held incommunicado. Six people including the Woods were sentenced to ten years in prison. A court of appeals overturned the convictions in 1943.

1954 RI
Seized by Providence postal authorities attempting to withhold from delivery to Brown University 75 copies of this "subversive" title.

1989
Banned in Grenada along with eighty-five other titles.
Source: 4, p. 60; 7, pp. 461-63.

1034
Letts, Billie.
Where the Heart Is.

1995
Published

2001 PA
Challenged in the Tamaqua Area School District because the book "might not be appropriate for younger schoolmates." The school board is considering the establishment of a restricted materials section in the district's middle-school library for books deemed objectionable. Students would need parental permission to access any title placed there.

2002 WY
Retained in the Natrona County School District after being challenged for graphic violence, obscene language, and drug use.
Source: 11, Mar. 2001, p. 54; July 2001, p. 145; Sept. 2002, p. 223.

1035
Levenkron, Steven.
The Best Little Girl in the World.

1978
Published

1978
Best Books for Young Adults

2000 PA
Retained as optional reading for eighth graders at Rice Avenue Middle School in Girard. A grandmother found the book offensive and didn't want her granddaughters reading it.
Source: 11, May 2000, p. 92.

1036
Levin, Ira.
Rosemary's Baby.

1967
Published

1976 CO
Banned from use in Aurora High School English classes on the grounds of "immorality."

1977 MA
Removed from the required reading list in Westport.
Source: 11, Jan. 1977, p. 8; May 1977, p. 79.

1037
Levin, Ira.
Stepford Wives.

1972
Published

1979 IN
Prohibited for use in the Warsaw schools because of its "questionable nature" and because it might offend someone in the community.
Source: 11, Mar. 1980, p. 40.

1038
Levine, Ellen.
I Hate English.

1989
Published

1994 NY
Challenged by a school board member in the Queens school libraries because, "The book says what a burden it is they have to learn English. They should just learn English and don't complain about it." The rest of the school board voted to retain the book.
Source: 11, July 1994, pp. 110–11; Sept. 1994, p. 166.

1039
Levitt, Steven D., and Stephen J. Dubner.
Freakonomics: A Rogue Economist Explores the Hidden Side of Everything.

2005
Published

2006 IL
Retained on the Northwest Suburban High School District 214 reading list in Arlington Heights, along with eight other challenged titles. A board member, elected amid promises to bring her Christian beliefs into all board decision-making, raised the controversy based on excerpts from the books she'd found on the Internet.
Source: 11, July 2006, pp. 210–11.

1040
Levoy, Myron.
Alan and Naomi.

1977
Published

1977
National Book Award for Young People's Literature

1981 GA
Challenged in Gwinnett County because of objections to the book's language ("hell" and "damn") and mature subject matter.

1991 MD
Challenged, but retained, in the Carroll County schools. Two school board members were concerned about the "sad ending" and "poor" portrayal of Jews.
Source: 11, Nov. 1981, p. 168; Mar. 1992, p. 64.

1041
Levy, Edward.
Came a Spider.

1978
Published

1986 WA
Removed and later returned to the shelves of the Freeman High School library in Spokane because it contained a two-page description of teenagers engaged in sexual intercourse.
Source: 11, May 1986, pp. 80–81.

1042
Lewin, Albert E., and Esther Lewin.
Random House Thesaurus of Slang.

1988
Published

1992 OR
Placed on a limited access shelf at the Floyd Light Middle School library in Portland.
Source: 11, May 1992, p. 81.

1043
Lewis, C. S.
The Lion, the Witch and the Wardrobe.

1950
Published

1990 MD
Challenged in the Howard County school system because it depicts "graphic violence, mysticism, and gore."
Source: 11, Jan. 1991, p. 28.

1044
Lewis, Richard, comp.
There Are Two Lives: Poems by Children of Japan.

1970
Published

1999 PA
Despite being on the library's open shelves for twenty-five years, this book is now restricted to students with parental permission at the Annville-Cleona Elementary School library because an anonymous parent "objected to the entire book."
Source: 11, May 1999, pp. 66–67.

1045
Lewis, Sinclair.
Cass Timberlane.

1945
Published

1930
Nobel Prize in Literature

1953
Banned in Ireland.

1954
Banned in East Berlin, Germany.
Source: 4, pp. 70-71.

1046

Lewis, Sinclair.
Elmer Gantry.

1927
Published

1927
Banned in Glasgow, Scotland.

1927 MA
Banned in Boston because a religious hero was depicted as obscene. The publishers defended the suit and expressed their amazement at the discretionary powers invested in local officials.

1927 NJ
Banned in Camden.

1931
U.S. Post Office banned any catalog listing of this title.

1931
Banned in Ireland as offensive to public morals.
Source: 2, p. 133; 4, pp. 70–71; 14, pp. 126–27; 15, Vol. III, pp. 404–5.

1047

Lewis, Sinclair.
It Can't Happen Here.

1935
Published

1937
Banned in Germany. In 1954, all of Sinclair Lewis's books were banned in East Berlin.
Source: 7, pp. 266–67.

1048

Lewis, Sinclair.
Kingsblood Royal.

1947
Published

1947 NY
In New York City, the Society for the Suppression of Vice sought to prevent sales of the book after complaints arose about the suggested sexual content of the novel. The society's efforts to bring charges against the book were fruitless, and only a few booksellers agreed to remove the novel from their stock.

1953
Banned in Ireland for the use of the term nigger and the "suggestive sexuality."

1953 IL
Removed from Illinois libraries on a mother's complaint that her daughter had borrowed a book that was offensive.
Source: 4, p. 71; 14, pp. 203–204.

1049

Leyland, Winston, ed.
My Deep Dark Pain Is Love: A Collection of Latin American Gay Fiction.

1983
Published

1984
Seized and shredded by the British Customs Office.
Source: 11, Jan. 1985, p. 16.

1050

Leyland, Winston, ed.
Now the Volcano: An Anthology of Latin American Gay Literature.

1979
Published

1984
Seized and shredded by the British Customs Office.
Source: 11, Jan. 1985, p. 16.

1051

Li, Hongzhi.
Zhuan Falun: The Complete Teachings of Falun Gong.

1994
Published

1996
The Chinese government's Press and Publications Administration issued a notice banning five Falun Gong publications for propagating ignorance and superstition. On July 22, 1999, the government declared that Falun Gong, as an "evil cult" that advocated superstition and jeopardized social stability, was now an illegal organization. It was prohibited "to distribute books, video/audio tapes or any other materials that propagate Falun Dafa (Falun Gong)" and thousands of people were sent to labor camps, psychiatric wards, or prisons.
Source: 8, pp. 308–10.

1052

Lieberman, E. Jones, and Ellen Peck.
Sex and Birth Control: A Guide for the Young.

1973
Published

1973
Best Books for Young Adults

1993 TN
Challenged at the Cleveland Public Library along with seventeen other books, most of which are on sex education, AIDS awareness, and some titles on the supernatural.
Source: 11, Sept. 1993, p. 146.

1053

Lightner, A. M.
Gods or Demons?

1973
Published

1988 OR
Challenged at the Canby Junior High School library because the book "promotes a secularhumanistic belief in evolution and portrays the '*Bible* as myth.'"
Source: 11, May 1989, p. 78.

1054

Lindgren, Astrid.
The Children on Troublemaker Street.

1964
Published

1992 WY
Challenged at the Sweetwater County Library in Green River because of concerns about how it depicts the "almost swearing of a four-year-old child."
Source: 11, July 1992, p. 126.

1055

Lindgren, Astrid.
The Runaway Sleigh Ride.

1984
Published

1995 IN
Challenged in the Kokomo-Howard County Public Library because it makes "light of a drinking situation." The book is by the author of the Pippi Longstocking series.

1999 CT
Removed, but later returned to the
Enfield elementary school libraries
despite a parent's objection to passages in
which characters sing songs praising
drinking.
Source: 11, Mar. 1996, p. 46; May 1999, pp. 65–66;
July 1999, p. 104.

1056
Lingeman, Richard R.
*Drugs from A to Z:
A Dictionary.*

1969
Published

1986 IA
Challenged, but retained, in the Des
Moines school libraries because the book
"not only gives definitions of drugs
but also tells how and what to use to get
a cheap high—which could be lethal."
Source: 11, July 1986, p. 135.

1057
Lion, Elizabeth M.
*Human Sexuality in
Nursing Process.*

1982
Published

1982
President of the National Black Nurses
Association called on nursing schools to
boycott this text because it contains
material that is "offensive and insensitive"
to blacks.
Source: 11, Jan. 1983, p. 23.

1058
Lionni, Leo.
In the Rabbit's Garden.

1975
Published

1986 OR
Challenged at the Naas Elementary
School library in Boring because the story
about two rabbits living in a lush garden
paradise made a mockery of the *Bible's*
tale of Adam and Eve. Unlike the story of
Adam and Eve, Lionni rewards his bunnies
for eating the forbidden fruit by allowing
them to live happily ever after.
Source: 11, Mar. 1987, p. 66.

1059
Lipke, Jean Coryllel.
Conception and Contraception.

1971
Published

1977 MI
The Brighton School Board voted to
remove all sex education books from
the high school library.
Source: 11, Sept. 1977, p. 133.

1060
Lippman, Laura.
*The Crack Cocaine Diet:
A Short Story from Hardly
Knew Her.*

2005
Published

2009 NH
Pulled from a Litchfield Campbell High
School elective course classroom after
parents voiced their concerns about a
short-stories unit called "Love/Gender/
Family Unit" that dealt with subject
matters including abortion, cannibalism,
homosexuality, and drug use. The parents
said the stories promoted bad behavior
and a "political agenda" and they
shouldn't be incorporated into classroom
teachings. The Campbell High School
English curriculum said the short story
was not intended to glorify bad behavior,
rather, it was chosen for its tone and point
of view and to show the often devastating
consequences of drug use. The English
curriculum adviser eventually resigned.
Source: 11, Sept. 2009, p. 154.

1061
Lipsyte, Robert.
The Contender.

1967
Published

1989 TN
Challenged as a summer youth program
reading assignment in Chattanooga because "it sounds like pretty explicit stuff."
Source: 11, Nov. 1989, p. 162.

1062
Lipsyte, Robert.
One Fat Summer.

1977
Published

1997 NY
Removed from the required reading
list at the Jonas E. Salk Middle School in
Levittown because it was "sexually explicit
and full of violence." The book was a
New York Times Outstanding Children's
Book of 1977.

1997 SC
Challenged at the Greenville middle
school libraries because the book includes
a passage on masturbation.

1999 FL
Pulled from Rock Crusher Elementary
School in Crystal River after a
parent complained that it contains
derogatory terms for African-Americans,
Jews, and Italians and describes
a male character masturbating.

2004 CT
Pulled from the Ansonia Public Library
local schools' display following a parental
complaint about a paragraph describing
the masturbation fantasy of a teenage boy.
Source: 11, Sept. 1997, pp. 126–28; Jan. 2000, p. 11;
Nov. 2004, p. 229.

1063
Llywelyn, Morgan.
Druids.

1991
Published

2001 VA
Removed from middle school libraries
in Fairfax County due to its depictions of
oral sex and rape.
Source: 11, Sept. 2000, pp. 145–46; May 2001, p. 96.

1064
Locke, John.
*An Essay Concerning
Human Understanding.*

1690
Published

1683

Locke's theory of civil, religious, and philosophical liberty was too radical. He escaped to Holland, the asylum of exiles such as Decartes, Erasmus, Grotius, and Spinoza, in search of liberty of thought. King Charles II deprived him of his studentship at Oxford, thereby closing the university to him.

1700

Placed on the *Index Librorum Prohibitorum* (List of Prohibited Books) in Rome, Italy.

1701

Prohibited reading at Oxford in London, England. A Latin version was permitted only on the proviso that "no tutors were to read with their students this essential investigation into the basis of knowledge."
Source: 1, pp. 96–97; 3, p. 329; 4, p. 24.

1065
Locker, Sari.
Sari Says: The Real Dirt on Everything from Sex to School.

2001
Published

2002 IA
Removed from the shelves at the James Kennedy Public Library in Dyersville because it deals with sexual issues.
Source: 11, Sept. 2002, p. 196; Nov. 2002, pp. 255–56.

1066
Lockhart, E.
The Boy Book: A Study of Habits and Behaviors, Plus Techniques for Taming Them.

2006
Published

2009 TX
Challenged in the Keller Independent School District because some say it is "too adult for young eyes."
Source: 11, May 2009, pp. 79-80.

1067
Lockridge, Ross, Jr.
Raintree County.

1948
Published

1953 NY
Attacked in New York City as "1066 pages of rank obscenity, blasphemy and sacrilege...inimical to faith and morals [and] within the prohibition of the Catholic Index."
Source: 15, Vol. IV, p. 709.

1068
Loewen, James W., and Charles Sallis, eds.
Mississippi: Conflict and Change.

1974
Published

1980 MS
Rejected from use in the Mississippi public schools because the textbook stressed black history too much. A U.S. District Court ruled that the criteria used for rejecting this text were not justifiable in *Loewen v. Turnipsend,* 488 F. Supp. 1138 (N. D. Miss. 1980).
Source: 11, July 1980, p. 86; 12, pp. 167–71, 239.

1069
Lofting, Hugh John.
The Story of Doctor Dolittle.

1920
Published

1988
Expurgated in the 1960s by J. B. Lippincott Company in the effort to make the books conform to the changing sensibilities of a world that was beginning "to coalesce into one international, multiracial society." The 1988 version of the *Doctor Dolittle* books, published by Dell Publishing, was the result of radical censoring by two editors at Dell and by Christopher Lofting, the author's son.
Source: 14, pp. 111–12.

1070
Logan, Daniel.
America Bewitched: The Rise of Black Magic and Spiritism.

1974
Published

1986 CA
Challenged by the "God Squad," a group of three students and their parents, at the El Camino High School in Oceanside because the book "glorified the devil and the occult."
Source: 11, Sept. 1986, p. 151; Nov. 1986, p. 224; Jan. 1987, p. 9.

1071
Logan, Jake.
Slocum series.

1975
Published

2001 AR
Challenged, but retained, at the Springdale Public Library along with all other "western" novels because the writings include "pornographic, sexual encounters."
Source: 11, Nov. 2001, p. 277.

1072
London, Jack.
The Call of the Wild.

1903
Published

1929
Banned in Italy.

1929
Banned in Yugoslavia.

1933
Burned in Nazi bonfires in Germany.
Source: 4, p. 63.

1073
Longstreet, Stephen, ed.
The Drawings of Renoir.

1965
Published

1994 AZ
Retained at Maldonado Elementary School in Tucson after being challenged by parents who objected to nudity and "pornographic," "perverted," and "morbid" themes.
Source: 11, July 1994, p. 112.

1074
Lopez, Tiffany Ana.
*Growing Up Chicana/o:
An Anthology.*

1993
Published

2002 VA
Challenged, along with seventeen other titles in the Fairfax County elementary and secondary libraries, by a group called Parents Against Bad Books in Schools. The group contends the books "contain profanity and descriptions of drug abuse, sexually explicit conduct, and torture."
Source: 11, Jan. 2003, p. 10.

1075
Lott, Bret.
The Hunt Club.

1998
Published

2011 SC
Challenged as one option for the required summer reading at Wando High School in Mount Pleasant because it "uses foul language, degrades women, and people of color." The novel is set in the South Carolina low country and tells the story of a teenage boy and his uncle who find a dead body and have to figure out what happened.
Source: 11, Nov. 2011, pp. 204-5.

1076
Loux, Matthew.
SideScrollers.

2006
Published

2012 CT
Removed as an option on the Enfield school district's ninth-grade summer reading list after a parent complained of profanity and sexual references. The graphic novel was chosen as one of the Young Adult Library Services Association's Great Graphic Novels for Teens in 2008.
Source: 11, Nov. 2012, p. 237.

1077
Louys, Pierre.
Aphrodite.

1896
Published

1929
Banned by U.S. Customs Department as lascivious, corrupting, and obscene. In 1930, a New York book dealer, E. B. Marks, was fined $250 for possessing a copy of *Aphrodite* in contravention of the state laws on obscene publications. In 1935, an attempt was made to import the publication into America. This was banned, although the authorities overlooked a 49-cent edition, openly advertised in *The New York Times Book Review* and apparently, despite postal regulations, available through the mail.
Source: 3, p. 176; 4, pp. 332-33.

1078
Louys, Pierre.
The Songs of Bilitis.

1896
Published

1929
Banned by U.S. Customs Department as lascivious, corrupting, and obscene.
Source: 4, p. 60.

1079
Louys, Pierre.
The Twilight of the Nymphs.

1903
Published

1929
Banned by U.S. Customs Department as lascivious, corrupting, and obscene.
Source: 4, p. 60.

1080
Lowen, Paul.
Butterfly.

1988
Published

1988 OR
Challenged at the Tigard Public Library because of explicit sex and extreme physical and psychological cruelty.
Source: 11, Jan. 1990, pp. 4-5.

1081
Lowry, Lois.
Anastasia Again!

1981
Published

1981
National Book Award for Children's Books

2005 FL
Removed from the Lake Wales elementary school library because of a complaint that the book's references to beer, *Playboy* magazine, and Anastasia making light of wanting to kill herself were inappropriate for children.
Source: 11, May 2005, p. 107.

1082
Lowry, Lois.
Anastasia at Your Service.

1982
Published

1984 WY
Challenged at the Casper school libraries.
Source: 11, Mar. 1985, p. 42.

1083
Lowry, Lois.
Anastasia Krupnik.

1981
Published

1986 CA
Removed by the school's principal, and later returned to the Roosevelt Elementary School library in Tulare with the word "shit" whited out.

1991 KS
Challenged, but retained, in the Wichita public schools because it was offensive.

1992 WI
Removed from, but later returned to, the Stevens Point Area School elementary recommended reading list due to the book's profanity and occasional references to underage drinking.

1998 SC
Removed from the Cayce-West Columbia School District's Congaree Elementary School library because of Lowry's use of a vulgarity for human waste, as well as the use of a slang term for sex.
Source: 11, Mar. 1987, p. 49; Jan. 1992, p. 26; Mar. 1993, p. 45; May 1993, p. 87; Mar. 1999, p. 36.

1084
Lowry, Lois.
Autumn Street.

1980
Published

1984 WY
Challenged at the Casper school libraries.
Source: 11, Mar. 1985, p. 42.

1085
Lowry, Lois.
Find a Stranger, Say Goodbye.

1978
Published

1984 WY
Challenged at the Casper school libraries.
Source: 11, Mar. 1985, p. 42.

1086
Lowry, Lois.
The Giver.

1993
Published

1994
Best Books for Young Adults

1994
Newbery Medal

1994 CA
Temporarily banned from classes by the Bonita Unified School District in La Verne and San Dimas after four parents complained that violent and sexual passages were inappropriate for children.

1995 MT
Restricted to students with parental permission at the Columbia Falls school system because of the book's treatment of themes of infanticide and euthanasia.

1996 OH
Challenged at the Lakota High School in Cincinnati.

1999 FL
Challenged, but retained, at a Lake Butler public middle school. A parent complained because the issues of infanticide and sexual awakening are discussed in the book.

1999 OH
Challenged at the Troy Intermediate School in Avon Lake as an "optional" reading choice for sixth-grade students. A pastor objected to the books "mature themes"—suicide, sexuality, and euthanasia.

2003 MO
Challenged as a suggested reading for eighth-grade students in Blue Springs. Parents called the book "lewd" and "twisted" and pleaded for it to be tossed out of the district. The book was reviewed by two committees and recommended for retention, but the controversy continues in 2005.

2006 KS
Challenged, but retained, at the Seaman Unified School District 345 elementary school library.

2007 CA
Appalled by descriptions of adolescent pill-popping, suicide, and lethal injections given to babies and the elderly, two parents demanded that the Mt. Diablo School District, headquartered in Concord, eliminate the controversial but award-winning book from the school reading lists and libraries.
Source: 11, Mar. 1995, p. 42; Jan. 1996, p. 11; Nov. 1996, p. 198; May 1999, p. 70; Jan. 2000, p. 13; Mar. 2005, pp. 57–58; May 2006, p. 153; Jan. 2008, p. 8.

1087
Lowry, Lois.
The One Hundredth Thing About Caroline.

1983
Published

1984 WY
Challenged at the Casper school libraries.
Source: 11, Mar. 1985, p. 42.

1088
Lowry, Lois.
A Summer to Die.

1977
Published

1984 WY
Challenged at the Casper school libraries.
Source: 11, Mar. 1985, p. 42.

1089
Lowry, Lois.
Taking Care of Terrific.

1983
Published

1984 WY
Challenged at the Casper school libraries.
Source: 11, Mar. 1985, p. 42.

1090
Ludlum, Robert.
The Matarese Circle.

1979
Published

1983 NE
Restricted at the Pierce High School to students with parental consent because the book contains unnecessarily rough language and sexual descriptions.
Source: 11, May 1983, p. 72.

1091
Ludwig, Coy L.
Maxfield Parrish.

1993
Published

1994 AZ
Retained at Maldonado Elementary School in Tucson after being challenged by parents who objected to nudity and "pornographic," "perverted," and "morbid" themes.
Source: 11, July 1994, p. 112.

1092
Lund, Doris Herold.
Eric.

1974
Published

1994 NC
Pulled from Lexington Middle School classrooms because of the intense way in which it addresses death.
Source: 11, July 1994, p. 115.

1093
Luther, Martin.
Address to the German Nobility.

1520
Published

1520
Luther's books were burned in Liege, Belgium, in October 1520.

1520
Luther's books were burned in Louvain, Belgium, in October 1520.

1520
Luther's books were burned in Cologne, Germany, in late 1520.

1520
Luther's books were burned in Mainz, Germany, in late 1520.

1521
Luther was excommunicated by Pope Leo X in Rome, Italy, in 1521. Luther's works remained on the Vatican's *Index Librorum Prohibitorum* (Index of Prohibited Books) until 1930. They were still prohibited, however, according to the church's canon law barring Catholics under penalty of mortal sin from reading books "which propound or defend heresy or schism."

1521
Charles V issued an edict in Germany against Luther and ordered his books seized. At the same time he sent him a safe conduct to appear before the Diet of Worms. The Diet issued an edict against him, and threatened to exterminate his followers.

1522
Following the Diet of Worms, Luther's works and those of his disciples were destroyed and banned in England.

1522
Following the Diet of Worms, Luther's works and those of his disciples were destroyed and banned in France.

1522
Following the Diet of Worms, Luther's works and those of his disciples were destroyed and banned in the Netherlands.

1522
Following the Diet of Worms, Luther's works and those of his disciples were destroyed and banned in Spain.

Source: 4, pp. 11-12; 8, pp. 267–69.

1094
Luther, Martin.
Ninety-five Theses.

1517
Published

1520
Luther's books were burned in Liege, Belgium, in October 1520.

1520
Luther's books were burned in Louvain, Belgium, in October 1520.

1520
Luther's books were burned in Cologne, Germany, in late 1520.

1520
Luther's books were burned in Mainz, Germany, in late 1520.

1521
Luther was excommunicated by Pope Leo X in Rome, Italy, in 1521. Luther's works remained on the Vatican's *Index Librorum Prohibitorum* (Index of Prohibited Books) until 1930. They were still prohibited, however, according to the church's canon law barring Catholics under penalty of mortal sin from reading books "which propound or defend heresy or schism."

1521
Charles V issued an edict in Germany against Luther and ordered his books seized. At the same time he sent him a safe conduct to appear before the Diet of Worms. The Diet issued an edict against him, and threatened to exterminate his followers.

1522
Following the Diet of Worms, Luther's works and those of his disciples were destroyed and banned in England.

1522
Following the Diet of Worms, Luther's works and those of his disciples were destroyed and banned in France.

1522
Following the Diet of Worms, Luther's works and those of his disciples were destroyed and banned in Spain.

1522
Following the Diet of Worms, Luther's works and those of his disciples were destroyed and banned in the Netherlands.

Source: 4, pp. 11–12; 8, pp. 267–69.

1095
Lyga, Barry.
I Hunt Killers.

2012
Published

2013 KY
Challenged on the Lexington Henry Clay High School reading list because it is too violent for teens. The book is listed on the Kentucky Bluegrass Awards for ninth through twelfth grades.

Source: 11, Jan. 2014, p. 10.

1096
Lynch, Chris.
Extreme Elvin.

1999
Published

2003 GA
Removed from the Crawford County Middle School library because the book deals with complex issues teenagers confront.

Source: 11, Jan. 2004, p. 9.

1097
Lynch, Chris.
The Iceman.

1994
Published

1995
Best Books for Young Adults

1995 TX
Removed from the Carroll Middle School Library in Southlake because of "profanity" and because it "was not highly recommended for its literary value."

1996 KS
Challenged at the Haysville Middle School library when a parent counted thirty-six places where profanity was used in the book.

1998 CT

Challenged on the summer reading list at the Windsor Locks Middle School because of the book's language and the main character's violent behavior. The superintendent proposed a plan to segregate "controversial" materials in the library and require parental permission to read them.

1999 WI

Removed from the Medford Middle School library because of foul language and the opinion that it was not "inspiring."

Source: 11, May 1995, p. 67; Mar. 1997, p. 49; Jan. 1999, p. 7; May 1999, p. 69.

1098

Maas, Peter.
Serpico.

1973
Published

1973
Best Books for Young Adults

1982 MN

Challenged in the Zimmerman School District high school libraries. Maas's book was available to students under eighteen only with parental permission.

Source: 11, Sept. 1982, p. 156.

1099

Maas, Peter.
The Valachi Papers.

1968
Published

1966

U.S. Department of Justice sued author to restrain the book's publication. Grounds were that it would hamper law enforcement and be inconsistent with the Bureau of Prisons rule against publishing prisoners' manuscripts that dealt with their lives in crime.

1968

Suit settled, book published by Putnam.

Source: 4, p. 99.

1100

Machiavelli, Niccolo.
Discourses.

1503
Published

1555

Placed in the *Index Librorum Prohibitorum* (List of Prohibited Books) in Rome, Italy.

Source: 4, p. 9.

1101

Machiavelli, Niccolo.
The Prince.

1513
Published

1555

Placed in the *Index Librorum Prohibitorum* (List of Prohibited Books) in Rome, Italy.

Source: 4, pp. 9–10; 8, pp. 156–57.

1102

Mackler, Carolyn.
The Earth, My Butt, and Other Big Round Things.

2003
Published

2004
Best Books for Young Adults

2004
Michael L. Printz Award

2006 MD

Banned by the Carroll County Superintendent in Westminster, but after protests from students, librarians, national organizations, and the publisher, the book was returned to the high school libraries, but not middle schools. The superintendent objected to the book's use of profanity and its sexual references. The book was named the International Reading Association's 2005 Young Adults' Choice, among other accolades.

Source: 11, Mar. 2006, pp. 70–71.

1103

Mackler, Carolyn.
Love and Other Four Letter Words.

2000
Published

2001 IL

Removed from the Lincoln Junior High School in Naperville because in addition to swear words and discussions about "getting wasted," the book contains graphic passages about masturbation and sexual intercourse.

Source: 11, Jan. 2002, pp. 15–16.

1104

Mackler, Carolyn.
Tangled.

2010
Published

2011 TX

Banned from the Borger Independent School District intermediate and middle school library and removed from class reading lists because of concerns over sexual content and profanity.

Source: 11, Nov. 2011, pp. 203-4.

1105

Mackler, Carolyn.
Vegan Virgin Valentine.

2004
Published

2007 FL

Challenged in the Mandarin High School library in Jacksonville because of inappropriate language.

2011 TX

Challenged at the Quitman Junior High library by a parent who described one scene as "on the verge of pornography."

Source: 11, May 2007, p. 91; Jan. 2011, p. 8.

1106

Madaras, Lynda, and Dane Saavedra.
What's Happening to My Body? Book for Boys: A Growing-up Guide for Parents & Sons.

1984
Published

1986 IL

Challenged at the Mt. Morris School District seventh grade class because it is written from a "permissive point of view."

1993 AK

Challenged in the Kenai Peninsula Borough schools in Homer because of objections to the way masturbation and homosexuality were presented and to slang words used to describe sexual methods as well as the male anatomy.

1993 TN
Challenged, but retained, at the Cleveland Public Library along with seventeen other books, most of which are on sex education, AIDS awareness, and some titles on the supernatural.

1994 NV
Challenged, but retained, at the Washoe County Library System in Reno because "nobody in their right mind would give a book like that to children on their own, except the library."

1994 WI
Missing from the Northside Intermediate School library in Milton after a parent complained, "I don't think my ten-year-old son, or anyone's, needs to know that stuff."

1997 FL
Removed from the media center at Denn John Junior Middle School in Kissimmee because it describes inappropriate subjects like group masturbation. The book is accessible to parents only through the guidance office.

2011 TX
Banned from twenty-one school libraries in Buda after a parent's complaint. The book includes definitions of rape, incest, sexual assault, and intercourse.

Source: 11, Mar. 1987, p. 53; July 1987, pp. 149–50; Sept. 1993, p. 146; Jan. 1994, p. 33; July 1994, pp. 111–12; Sept. 1994, p. 147; Nov. 1994, pp. 200–201; Nov. 1997, p. 167; Jan. 2011, p. 8.

1107
Madaras, Lynda, and Area Madaras.
What's Happening to My Body? Book for Girls: A Growing-up Guide for Parents & Daughters.

1983
Published

1983
Best Books for Young Adults

1986 IL
Challenged at the Mt. Morris School District seventh grade class because it is written from a "permissive point of view."

1993 TN
Challenged, but retained, at the Cleveland Public Library along with seventeen other books, most of which are on sex education, AIDS awareness, and some titles on the supernatural.

1997 FL
Removed from the media center at the Denn Junior Middle School in Kissimmee because it describes inappropriate subjects like group masturbation. The book is accessible to parents only through the guidance office.

1998 WA
Challenged at the Crescent Harbor Elementary School library in Oak Harbor because of the book's frankness and use of slang terminology for body parts and sexual acts. H. W. Wilson's *Children's Catalogue* recommends the book for children from nine to fifteen, and the book is also featured on Disney's "Parent Express" website.

Source: 11, Mar. 1987, p. 53; July 1987, pp. 149–50; Sept. 1993, p. 146; Nov. 1997, p. 167; Sept. 1998, pp. 141–42.

1108
Madaras, Lynda.
Lynda Madaras Talks to Teens about AIDS: An Essential Guide for Parents, Teachers & Young People.

1988
Published

1989
Best Books for Young Adults

1993 TN
Challenged, but retained, at the Cleveland Public Library along with seventeen other books, most of which are on sex education, AIDS awareness, and some titles on the supernatural.

Source: 11, Sept. 1993, p. 146.

1109
Madden, David.
The Suicide's Wife.

1978
Published

1984 LA
Challenged at the Covington Public Library because it was "just too immorally written all the way through."

Source: 11, July 1984, p. 103.

1110
Madonna.
Sex.

1992
Published

1992
Banned in Ireland.

1992 AZ
In Mesa, the mayor ordered the library not to shelve the book.

1992 CO
The Pikes Peak Library in Colorado Springs cancelled the library's order after citizen protest.

1992 CT
Challenged at the Manchester Public Library.

1992 IA
Challenged at the Des Moines Public Library.

1992 IL
Challenged at the Champaign Public Library.

1992 IN
Challenged at South Bend Public Library.

1992 KS
Challenged at Topeka and Shawnee County Public Library.

1992 MI
Ingham County library board declined to ban the controversial book.

1992 MO
The St. Louis Public Library cancelled the library's order after citizen protest.

1992 NE
The Omaha Public Library did not plan to buy the book, but six of seven City Council members asked the library to remove it from any potential acquisitions list.

1992 TX
The mylar-wrapped, spiral-bound book of photographs of the exhibitionist pop star Madonna in revealing and erotic poses raised challenges across the country soon after its release in October.

1992.
In several cities political leaders exerted pressure on libraries not to acquire or to restrict circulation of the book. In Houston, a group called Citizens Against Pornography (CAP) mobilized efforts to have the book removed. The public library agreed to keep the book, but not allow it to circulate and to restrict in-library access to adults only.

1992 TX
In Austin, the county attorney told the library that to make the book available to minors in any way was illegal.

1993 IL
Retained at the Downers Grove Public Library.

1993 IL
Excluded at the Naperville Public Library.

1993 MI
Challenged, but retained, at the Monroe County Library System following a three-and-half meeting that at times degenerated into a screaming match.

1993 WA
Challenged at Spokane Public Library.

1993 WI
Challenged at the Beloit Public Library, along with other adult literature, after complaints that minors were perusing the book's photographs of erotic poses and skimpy outfits.

Source: 6, p. 1,211; 11, Jan. 1993, pp. 1, 31–33; Mar. 1993, pp. 37–38; May 1993, pp. 65–66; July 1993, p. 104; Nov. 1993, p. 179.

1111
Magnus, Erica.
The Boy and the Devil.

1986
Published

1987 KY
Challenged at the Science Hill Elementary School library because the book "hints of a satanic cult" since "there's no way a person can outwit the devil without God's help and nowhere is God mentioned in the book."

Source: 11, May 1987, p. 86; July 1987, pp. 147–48.

1112
Maguire, Gregory.
Wicked: The Life and Times of the Wicked Witch of the West.

2007
Published

2008 NY
Retained in the tenth-grade honors program of the Canandaigua Academy in Ontario County despite concerns about the sexual content on a few pages of the book. The district will offer alternative reading for anyone who objects to the book.

Source: 11, Jan. 2009, p. 23.

1113
Mah, Adeline Yen.
A Thousand Pieces of Gold: My Discovery of China's Character in the History and Meaning of Its Proverbs.

2002
Published

2002 VA
Challenged, along with seventeen other titles in the Fairfax County elementary and secondary libraries, by a group called Parents Against Bad Books in Schools. The group contends the books "contain profanity and descriptions of drug abuse, sexually explicit conduct, and torture."

Source: 11, Jan. 2003, p. 10.

1114
Mahfouz, Naguib.
Children of the Alley.

1959
Published

1988
Nobel Prize in Literature

1959
Banned by Cairo, Egypt's Al-Azhar University condemning it as "blasphemous," and calling the author a heretic for causing offense to the prophets of Islam and for misrepresenting the character of Muhammad. In 1988, Mahfouz won the Nobel Prize and fundamentalists renewed their attacks, fearing that the prize would be used as a pretext to remove the book from the proscribed list. In October 1994, Mahfouz was stabbed several times in the neck as he sat in a car outside his Cairo home. A few weeks after the attack, the novel was published in the Egyptian press for the first time in thirty-five years. As of mid-1997, however, the novel had not been published in book form in Egypt.

Source: 8, pp. 219–20.

1115
Mailer, Norman.
Ancient Evenings.

1983
Published

1985 CA
Rejected for purchase by the Hayward school trustees because of "rough language" and "explicit sex scenes."

Source: 11, July 1985, p. 111.

1116
Mailer, Norman.
The Naked and the Dead.

1948
Published

1949
Banned in Canada.

1949
Banned in Australia.

Source: 4, p. 96; 6, p. 412.

1117
Mailer, Norman.
Why Are We in Vietnam?

1967
Published

1987 AL
The Huntsville assistant city attorney requested that the novel be removed from the public library shelves. After considerable controversy, the book was eventually returned to the public library shelves.

Source: 7, pp. 529–30.

1118
Maimonides.
The Guide for the Perplexed.

1197
Published

1200
Condemned by his orthodox opponents as heresy. Copies of the publication were burned when discovered, it was barred from Jewish homes, and anyone reading it was excommunicated; the work was still facing bans in the 19th century. Orthodox Jewish opponents objected to Maimonides's sympathy for Aristotelian thought, which was considered fundamentally incompatible with Hebrew tradition. Maimonides was probably the first Jewish author to have his works burned.

Source: 3, p. 62; 8, pp. 237–38.

1119
Malamud, Bernard.
The Fixer.

1966
Published

1967
National Book Award for Fiction

1967
Pulitzer Prize for Fiction

1976 CO
Banned from use in Aurora High School English classes.

1976 NY
Removed from the Island Trees Union Free School District High School library in 1976 along with nine other titles because they were considered "immoral, anti-American, anti-Christian, or just plain filthy." Returned to the library after the U.S. Supreme Court ruling on June 25, 1982, in *Board of Education, Island Trees Union Free School District No. 26 et al. v. Pico et al.*, 457 U.S. 853 (1982).
Source: 11, May 1977, p. 79; Nov. 1982, p. 197.

1120
Malcolm X, and Alex Haley.
The Autobiography of Malcolm X.

1965
Published

1993 FL
Challenged in the Duval County public schools because the slain Black Muslim leader advocated anti-white racism and violence.

1994 FL
Restricted at the Jacksonville middle school libraries because it presents a racist view of white people and is a "how-to manual" for crime.
Source: 11, Sept. 1993, p. 147; May 1994, p. 83.

1121
Maloney, Ray.
The Impact Zone.

1987
Published

1989 OR
Challenged at the Multnomah County Library in Portland because of profanity and sexual references.
Source: 11, Jan. 1990, pp. 4–5.

1122
Malory, Sir Thomas.
Le Morte D'Arthur.

1485
Published

1987 KY
Challenged as a required reading assignment at the Pulaski County High School in Somerset because it is "junk."
Source: 11, May 1987, p. 90.

1123
Manchester, William Raymond.
The Glory and the Dream: A Narrative History of America, 1932-1972.

1974
Published

1989 AR
Challenged at the Conway High School as having inappropriate sexual and racial content.
Source: 11, July 1989, p. 129; Sept. 1989, p. 186.

1124
Mandela, Nelson.
The Struggle Is My Life.

1978
Published

1988
Confiscated in Grenada.

1990
Banned in South Africa until Mandela was released from prison in 1990.
Source: 7, pp. 471–72.

1125
Mandeville, Bernard.
The Fable of the Bees.

1714
Published

1723–28
Presented twice by a Middlesex, England, grand jury for blasphemy.

1740
Burned in France.

1745
The Vatican listed it on the *Index Librorum Prohibitorum* (Index of Prohibited Books) in Rome, Italy, where it remained until 1966.
Source: 1, pp. 104–6.

1126
Manes, Stephen.
Slim Down Camp.

1981
Published

1992 IL
Challenged at the Des Plaines Public Library because it contains "repeated profanity and immoral situations."
Source: 11, May 1992, p. 79.

1127
Manet, Edouard.
Manet.

1983
Published

1994 AZ
Retained at Maldonado Elementary School in Tucson after being challenged by parents who objected to nudity and "pornographic," "perverted," and "morbid" themes.
Source: 11, July 1994, p. 112.

1128
Manji, Irshad.
Allah, Liberty, and Love.

2011
Published

2012
Banned because officials in Malaysia said it went against Islamic teachings and led to a raid on a bookstore in the country. Activists and others said they believe Manji's book was banned because she is a lesbian.
Source: 11, July 2012, pp. 183-84; Sept. 2012, pp. 203-4.

1129
Mann, Patrick.
Dog Day Afternoon.

1975
Published

1978 VT
Placed in a special closed shelf at the Vergennes Union High School library. Decision upheld in *Bicknell v. Vergennes Union High School Board*, 475 F. Supp. 615 (D. Vt. 1979), 638 F. 2d 438 (2d Cir. 1980).
Source: 11, Jan. 1979, p. 6; 12, pp. 151, 239; 14, pp. 113–15; 15, Vol IV, p. 715.

1130
Manson, Marilyn.
The Long, Hard Road Out of Hell.

1998
Published

1998 IL
Challenged because of explicit references to sex, violence, and the occult, but retained, at the West Chicago Public Library.
Source: 11, Jan. 1999, p. 19.

1131
Maple, Eric.
Devils and Demons.

1981
Published

1988 FL
Challenged at the Essrig Elementary School in Carrollwood because the book contains a pledge to Satan.
Source: 11, Jan. 1989, p. 7.

1132
Mapplethorpe, Robert.
Mapplethorpe.

1987
Published

1998
Seized by police from the University of Central England library in Birmingham, England. Lawyers acting for the Crown Prosecution Service decided parts of it were likely to "deprave or corrupt" under the 1959 Obscene Publications Act, and advised the police that they had grounds to ask the university to destroy it. The university and publisher have refused to destroy the book. The Crown Prosecution Service concluded that there was insufficient evidence to expect a conviction.
Source: 11, May 1998, p. 75; Mar. 1999, p. 48.

1133
Maraini, Fosco.
Tokyo.

1976
Published

1983 WV
Challenged at the Cherry River Elementary School library in Richwood because the book includes a photograph of the backsides of nude Japanese men in a public bath.
Source: 11, July 1983, p. 122.

1134
Marchetti, Victor, and John D. Marks.
The CIA and the Cult of Intelligence.

1974
Published

1972
Announcement of this book by the publisher led the Central Intelligence Agency to obtain a U.S. court injunction against its publication. Toward the close of its 1974-1975 term the U.S. Supreme Court declined for the second time to review an appeal by the authors, thus upholding the CIA's right to enforce its secrecy agreement with Marchetti, a former employee, and required him to submit material before publication.

1974
The book was published with 168 passages deleted out of 339 deletions originally demanded by the CIA.

1977
The author asked the U.S. Department of Justice to get the injunction lifted, and asked the CIA to permit the restoration of most deletions because they were capricious, arbitrary, or confined to information since published elsewhere. The Fourth Circuit Court of Appeals held in favor of the agency.
Source: 4, p. 100; 5, Spring 1976, pp. 88–89.

1135
Marcus, Eric.
Is It a Choice? Answers to Three Hundred of the Most Frequently Asked Questions about Gays and Lesbians.

1993
Published

1993 IA
Challenged at the Indianola Public Library because it was not "of much concern to the Christian believing people of this community."
Source: 11, Jan. 1994, p. 35.

1136
Marcus, Eric.
The Male Couple's Guide to Living Together: What Gay Men Should Know about Living with Each Other and Coping in a Straight World.

1988
Published

1990 IA
Challenged at the Muscatine Public Library because it is "wrong to promote immorality."
Source: 11, Nov. 1990, p. 225.

1137
Marianna.
Miss Flora McFlimsey's Easter Bonnet.

1951
Published

1991 MI
Challenged at the Troy Public Library because it contained an offensive and unflattering illustration of a black doll.
Source: 11, Jan. 1992, p. 26.

1138
Marieb, Elaine Nicpon.
Human Anatomy and Physiology.

1998
Published

1998 FL
Challenged, but retained, in the Escambia County schools because of pictures showing a vaginal birth, vaginal warts caused by herpes, and a self-examination for breast cancer.
Source: 11, July 1998, p. 107.

1139
Marsden, John.
Letters from the Inside.

1992
Published

1995
Best Books for Young Adults

1997 OH
Challenged, but retained, as required reading for the Youngstown, Ohio State University English Festival because the book contains the "F-word."
Source: 11, May 1997, p. 66.

1140
Martin, Michael.
Kurt Cobain.

2004
Published

2009 MN
Removed from all elementary and middle Farmington school library because the book was "very dark and violent and made references to the use of Ritalin as being a precursor to the use of illicit drugs. It also covered topics such as mental illness and suicide."
Source: 11, Jan. 2010, p. 11.

1141
Martin, Tony.
The Jewish Onslaught: Despatches from the Wellesley Battlefront.

1993
Published

1994 MD
Criticized at the Enoch Pratt Free Library in Baltimore because the book accuses Jews of masterminding the slave trade and blocking the advance of African Americans. "There's no reason for our public library to spend shrinking public funds to promote the circulation of such hatred."
Source: 11, Sept. 1994, p. 146.

1142
Martin, W. K.
Marlene Dietrich.

1995
Published

2000 CA
Removed from the Anaheim school district because school officials said the book is too difficult for middle school students and that it could cause harassment against students seen with it. The American Civil Liberties Union (ACLU) of Southern California filed suit in *Doe v. Anaheim Union High School District* alleging that the removal is "a pretext for viewpoint-based censorship." The ACLU claims no other books have been removed from the junior high library for similar reasons, even though several, such as works by Shakespeare and Dickens, are more difficult reading. The ACLU contends that the school officials engaged in unconstitutional viewpoint discrimination by removing the book because it contains gay and lesbian material. In March 2001, the school board approved a settlement that restored the book to the high school shelves and amended the district's policy to prohibit the removal of books for subject matter involving sexual orientation, but the book will not be returned to the middle school.
Source: 11, Mar. 2001, p. 53; May 2001, p. 95; July 2001, p. 173.

1143
Martinac, Paula.
k. d. lang.

1996
Published

2000 CA
Removed from the Anaheim school district because school officials said the book is too difficult for middle school students and that it could cause harassment against students seen with it. The American Civil Liberties Union (ACLU) of Southern California filed suit in *Doe v. Anaheim Union High School District* alleging that the removal is "a pretext for viewpoint-based censorship." The ACLU claims no other books have been removed from the junior high library for similar reasons, even though several, such as works by Shakespeare and Dickens, are more difficult reading. The ACLU contends that the school officials engaged in unconstitutional viewpoint discrimination by removing the book because it contains gay and lesbian material. In March 2001, the school board approved a settlement that restored the book to the high school shelves and amended the district's policy to prohibit the removal of books for subject matter involving sexual orientation, but the book will not be returned to the middle school.
Source: 11, Mar. 2001, p. 53; May 2001, p. 95; July 2001, p. 173.

1144
Martinez, Elizabeth.
500 Years of Chicano History in Pictures.

1991
Published

2012 AZ
Banned from the Tucson Unified School District along with *Critical Race Theory,* by Richard Delgado; *Message to Aztlan,* by Rodolfo Corky Gonzales; *Chicano! The History of the Mexican Civil Rights Movement,* by Arturo Rosales; *Pedagogy of the Oppressed,* by Paulo Freire; *Rethinking Columbus: The Next 500 Years,* edited by Bill Bigelow and Bob Peterson; and *Occupied America: A History of Chicanos,* by Rodolfo Acuña. In a district with over sixty percent of the students coming from Mexican-American backgrounds, the school board "dismantled its Mexican-American Studies program, packed away its offending books, shuttled its students into other classes," according to a January 21, 2012, *New York Times* editorial because "it was blackmailed into doing so." The *Times* referred to measures taken by Arizona Superintendent of Public Instruction John Huppenthal, who threatened to withhold millions of dollars if the school district didn't terminate the nationally acclaimed program immediately. The superintendent has spent years crusading against ethnic-studies programs that he claims are "brainwashing" children into thinking that Latinos have been victims of white oppression. On March 8, 2013, a federal court upheld most provisions of an Arizona state law used to prohibit the controversial Mexican-American Studies curriculum in Tucson. Activists plan to appeal the ruling to the U.S. Court of Appeals for the Ninth Circuit.
Source: 11, Mar. 2012, pp. 49, 51, 82-84; May 2012, pp. 102-3; May 2013, pp. 114-15.

1145
Marx, Karl, and
Friedrich Engels.
German Ideology.

1846
Published

1953
East Germany rewrote or expurgated
all of Marx's writing.

1974
Marx's texts were included on the South
African Index of Objectionable Literature.
Marx's works were removed from the
list in 1991.

1985
Banned in South Korea.
Source: 5, Apr. 1986, pp. 30–33; 7, pp. 127–29.

1146
Marx, Karl.
Capital.

1867-95
Published

1894
Reprinting was forbidden in Russia.
Ban lifted in 1897.

1929
Prohibited reading in China.

1939
Banned by the Nazi government
from 1939 to 1945 in Germany and
German-occupied countries.

1940 OK
Banned in Oklahoma City. Bookstore
owners were sentenced to ten years in
prison and fined $5,000,000 for selling
Marx's work.

1950 MA
Challenged at the Boston Public Library
from 1950 to 1953 because of the book's
communistic message.

1953
East Germany rewrote or expurgated all
of Marx's writing.

1953 WI
Restricted at Marquette University in
Milwaukee. Instructors submitted the
names of students who borrowed the
book; the list was subsequently turned
over to the archbishop.

1974
Marx's texts were included on the South
African Index of Objectionable Literature.
Marx's works were removed from the list
in 1991.

1987
In South Korea, where communism is
illegal, the government sued the
publisher in court, charging a violation of
South Korea's National Security Law.
Source: 4, pp. 44–45; 7, pp. 127–29.

1147
Marx, Karl.
The Communist Manifesto.

1847
Published

1878
Prohibited in Germany.

1929
Prohibited in China.

1950 MA
Challenged at the Boston Public
Library until 1953 because of the book's
communistic message.

1974
Marx's texts were included on the
South African Index of Objectionable
Literature. Marx's works were removed
from the list in 1991.

1987
In South Korea, where communism is
illegal, the government sued the
publisher in court, charging a violation of
South Korea's National Security Law.
Source: 4, pp. 44–45; 7, pp. 127–29; 8, pp. 122–25.

1148
Masland, Robert P. Jr., ed., and
David Estridge, ex. ed.
*What Teenagers Want to
Know About Sex: Questions
and Answers.*

1988
Published

1993 AK
Challenged in the Kenai Peninsula
Borough schools in Homer because it
presents "sexual relations in an
amoral light."
Source: 11, Jan. 1994, pp. 33–34.

1149
Mason, Bobbie Ann.
In Country.

1985
Published

1985
Best Books for Young Adults

1994 GA
Recalled as supplemental reading in two
college preparatory English classes at the
Charlton County High School in Folkston.
All of the parents of the forty-eight students
in the classes had given permission
for their children to read the book. But it
was removed from their hands in May
after one of those parents complained it
included profanity.

1994 PA
Challenged at the West Chester schools as
"most pornographic."

2009 IN
Retained in Delphi Community High
School's curriculum despite claims of
inappropriate sexual content and
graphic language.
Source: 11, Sept. 1994, p. 150; Jan. 1995, p. 25; Mar. 1995,
p. 45; July 1995, p. 99; May 2009, p. 94.

1150
Masters, Edgar Lee.
Spoon River Anthology.

1915
Published

1974 OH
Several students brought suit against the
Scioto-Darby School District in Willard
for removing two pages because the poems
were "inappropriate" and their language
might be offensive to some. The case was
dismissed in *Kramer v. Scioto-Darby City
School District,* Civil Action 72-406,
Southern District of Ohio, Mar. 8, 1974.
Source: 12, pp. 133–34, 238

1151
Mathabane, Mark.
*Kaffir Boy: The True Story of
a Black Youth's Coming of Age
in Apartheid South Africa.*

1986
Published

1993 CA
Challenged at the Amador High School in Sutter Creek.

1993 NJ
Challenged at the Manasquan schools because of a brief but graphic passage involving homosexuality.

1996 CT
Challenged as part of the sophomore curriculum at the Lewis S. Mills High School in Burlington because of brutal and graphic language.

1996 NC
Temporarily pulled from the Greensboro high school libraries after a resident sent letters to school board members and some administrators charging that the book could encourage young people to sexually assault children.

1997 CA
Challenged, but retained, on a core reading list for high school sophomores, at the Lincoln Unified School District in Stockton. Some parents referred to the book as "pornographic and racially insensitive."

1999 OH
Removed from a Federal Hocking High School English class in Athens because it contains a sexually graphic passage that some have deemed offensive.

2000 CA
Removed from sophomore reading list at Armijo High School in Fairfield due to its sexual content.

2000 MI
Kearsley school officials deleted six sentences describing a homosexual molestation scene in the book after some parents found it offensive.

2006 CA
Retained at the East Union High School in Manteca senior English class. The controversial autobiography was challenged as inappropriate because a passage uses the words "penis" and "anus" to describe a scene in which a group of young boys are about to prostitute themselves to a group of men for food.

2007 CA
Banned from the Burlingame Intermediate School. The book has been challenged frequently since its

publication in 1986 because of two graphic paragraphs describing men preparing to engage in anal sex with young boys. It earned the 1987 Christopher Award for literature, "affirming the highest values of the human spirit." It was also a finalist for the Robert F. Kennedy Award for books representing "concern for the poor and the powerless."

2010 CA
Challenged, but retained, at the San Luis Obispo High School despite containing a passage that graphically details sexual assault. The book had been taught at the school for more than a decade without controversy.
Source: 11, Jan. 1994, pp. 15, 38; July 1996, p. 119; Mar. 1997, p. 38; May 1997, p. 62; July 1997, pp. 109-10; May 1999, p. 70; Mar. 2000, p. 50; Nov. 2000, p. 195; July 2006, pp. 209-10; July 2007, pp. 145-46; Jan. 2011, p. 29.

1152
Matthiessen, Peter.
In the Spirit of Crazy Horse.

1983
Published

1983 SD
South Dakota Governor William J. Janklow named three South Dakota bookstores in a $20-million libel suit because the bookstores refused to stop selling Matthiessen's book. A Sioux Falls judge ruled on June 18, 1984, that Matthiessen's work is not defamatory and threw out the case.
Source: 6, pp. 1,555 56; 8, pp. 100-105; 11, July 1983, p. 112; Jan. 1984, p. 18; May 1984, p. 75; July 1984, p. 116; Sept. 1984, p. 148.

1153
May, Julian.
A New Baby Comes.

1970
Published

1987 WA
Placed on restricted shelves at the Evergreen School District elementary school libraries in Vancouver in accordance with the school board policy to restrict student access to sex education books in elementary school libraries.
Source: 11, May 1987, p. 87.

1154
Mayer, Mercer.
Liza Lou and the Yeller Belly Swamp.

1976
Published

1988 OR
Challenged at the Douglas County Library in Roseburg because of scary pictures and references to boiling children.
Source: 11, Jan. 1990, pp. 4–5.

1155
Mayer, Mercer.
A Special Trick.

1976
Published

1992 OR
Challenged at the Coburg Elementary School in Eugene for allegedly satanic art. The book was retained, but an accompanying audiotape that encourages children to look closely at the art work was removed by the school principal.
Source: 11, July 1992, p. 103.

1156
Mayle, Peter.
What's Happening to Me? The Answers to Some of the World's Most Embarrassing Questions.

1975
Published

1983 NV
Challenged and eventually moved from the Henderson Public Library children's section to the adult shelves because the book is "too sexually explicit and unsuitable for children."

1993 TN
Challenged, but retained, at the Cleveland Public Library along with seventeen other books, most of which are on sex education, AIDS awareness, and some titles on the supernatural.
Source: 11, Mar. 1984, p. 39; May 1984, p. 71; Sept. 1993, p. 146.

1157
Mayle, Peter.
Where Did I Come From?

1973
Published

1980 CT
Banned from elementary classrooms in Hamden because it was judged not appropriate.

1994 NV
Challenged at the Washoe County Library System in Reno because, "Nobody in their right mind would give a book like that to children on their own, except a library."
Source: 11, Mar. 1980, p. 32; Sept. 1994, p. 147.

1158
Mazer, Harry.
I Love You, Stupid!

1981
Published

1981
Best Books for Young Adults

1982 IA
Banned from Des Moines junior high school libraries after a parent's complaint that the book was "morally inappropriate."

1983 WA
Removed from the Evergreen School District of Vancouver along with twenty-nine other titles. The American Civil Liberties Union of Washington has filed suit contending that the removals constitute censorship, a violation of plaintiff's rights to free speech and due process, and a violation of the state Open Meetings Act because the removal decisions were made behind closed doors.
Source: 11, Sept. 1982, p. 155; Nov. 1983, pp. 185–86.

1159
Mazer, Harry.
The Last Mission.

1979
Published

1979
Best Books for Young Adults

1984 NJ
Challenged at the Pequannock Valley Middle School in Pompton Plains because of its "language."

1986 WI
Moved from the Alexander Middle School library to the Nekoosa High School library because of "profanity" in the book.

1995 TX
Banned, but later reinstated, in the Carroll Middle School Library in Southlake. In the original complaint, a parent requested its removal because of excessive profanity.

1999 CA
Challenged, but retained, at the Auburn-Placer County Library because of sexually explicit material.
Source: 11, Nov. 1984, p. 185; Mar. 1985, p. 59; Jan. 1987, p. 10; May 1995, p. 67; July 1995, p. 95; Sept. 1995, p. 159; Nov. 1999, p. 171.

1160
Mazer, Harry.
Snow Bound.

1973
Published

1987 WI
Challenged at the Stoughton Middle School reading program because the book includes "several profane oaths invoking the deity, two four-letter words for bodily wastes, and the term 'crazy bitch' and 'stupid female.'"
Source: 11, May 1987, p. 103.

1161
Mazer, Norma Fox.
Out of Control.

1993
Published

1994
Best Books for Young Adults

1995 OK
Banned at the Cooper Middle School Library in Putnam City because of language "inappropriate for that age level."

1995 OK
Challenged at the Oklahoma City Metropolitan Library System, but retained.
Source: 11, July 1995, p. 94.

1162
Mazer, Norma Fox.
Saturday, the Twelfth of October.

1975
Published

1977 VT
Removed from the seventh-grade classroom in Chester after a parent described the book as "filthy."
Source: 11, Mar. 1978, p. 31.

1163
Mazer, Norma Fox.
Up in Seth's Room: A Love Story.

1979
Published

1979
Best Books for Young Adults

1982 WY
Removed from the Campbell County School District libraries and classrooms. After complaints of three district media specialists about the "illegitimately constituted" review committee, however, the book was reinstated.
Source: 11, Mar. 1983, p. 51.

1164
McAlpine, Helen, and William McAlpine.
Japanese Tales and Legends.

1959
Published

1995 CA
Challenged at the Wilsona School District in Lake Los Angeles because of depictions of violence and references to Buddha and ritual suicide.
Source: 11, Jan. 1996, p. 13.

1165
McBain, Ed.
Alice in Jeopardy.

2005
Published

2006 WA
Challenged at the Sno-Isle Libraries in Arlington because of "curse words and graphic sex scenes."
Source: 11, Jan. 2007, p. 11.

1166
McBride, Will, and Helga Fleischhauer-Hardt.
Show Me!

1975
Published

1975 MA
Publisher prosecuted on obscenity charges in Massachusetts. The judge ruled as a matter of law that the title was not obscene.

1976

Publisher prosecuted on obscenity charges in Toronto, Ontario, Canada. The judge ruled as a matter of law that the title was not obscene.

1976 IL

Challenged at the Oak Lawn Public Library because the book was "vulgar, obscene. . . and a threat to community," a spokesperson asserted. "In the final analysis, I see the destruction of marriage and I see a country destroyed." The book was eventually restricted to parents' shelf. The conflict resulted in the introduction of two bills in the Illinois General Assembly that would in effect remove the "affirmative defense" feature from the Harmful to Minor Statutes that exempted libraries from prosecution when providing harmful materials to persons under 18 years of age; both were defeated.

1976 NH

Publisher prosecuted on obscenity charges in New Hampshire. The judge ruled as a matter of law that the title was not obscene.

1976 OK

Publisher prosecuted on obscenity charges in Oklahoma. The judge ruled as a matter of law that the title was not obscene.

1984 CA

Frequently challenged in libraries across the country, e.g., at the Stanislaus County library.

1984 CA

Challenged at the San Jose library because the book "condones child molestation or child pornography." Less than two weeks later, the copy of the book was reported lost by the borrower, a member of the Turlock Action Committee, which organized the movement to ban the book.

1985 WA

Challenged at the Seattle Public Library because "it is inappropriate for the library collection."

1986 CA

Challenged at the Alameda County Library because "we are giving the pedophile a platform on which to stand" and placed on restrictive shelves in three branches.

1986 NY

Challenged at the Steele Memorial Library in Elmira because it "promotes masturbation, sex between young people, and incest."

Source: 11, Nov. 1984, pp. 183, 195; Jan. 1985, pp. 7, 27; May 1985, p. 79; July 1985, pp. 112–13; Mar. 1986, p. 37; May 1986, p. 97; Jan. 1987, pp. 29–31.

1167
McCall, Don.
Jack the Bear.

1974
Published

1978 IA

Removed from the Monticello school library due to "objectionable" language.

Source: 11, May 1978, p. 56.

1168
McCammon, Robert R.
Boy's Life.

1991
Published

1992
Best Books for Young Adults

1994 NY

Challenged as required reading in the Hudson Falls schools because the book has recurring themes of rape, masturbation, violence, and degrading treatment of women.

Source: 11, Nov. 1994, p. 190; Jan. 1995, p. 13; Mar. 1995, p. 55.

1169
McCammon, Robert R.
Mystery Walk.

1983
Published

1992 OR

Challenged in the Salem-Keizer school libraries because, "it is full of violence and profanity."

Source: 11, July 1992, p. 125.

1170
McCarthy, Cormac.
Child of God.

1984
Published

2007 TX

Removed as an appropriate pre-Advanced English Placement reading at the Jim Ned High School in Tuscola.

Source: 11, Jan. 2008, pp. 41-42.

1171
McCarthy, Mary.
The Group.

1963
Published

1964

Placed on its "Publication Restricted or Prohibited" list by New Zealand Customs. Faced with public disapproval, the comptroller of Customs lifted the prohibition.

1964

Banned in Ireland on January 21, 1964. The Irish Board of Censors found the work "obscene" and "indecent," objecting particularly to the author's handling of the characters' sexuality, suggestions of homosexuality and "promiscuity." The work was officially banned from sale in Ireland until 1967.

1982 IN

Challenged in Terre Haute as an optional reading in an elective English course for junior and senior high school students.

Source: 8, pp. 343–44; 11, May 1982, p. 86.

1172
McCoy, Kathy, and Charles Wibbelsman.
The New Teenage Body Book.

1987
Published

1990 MA

Withdrawn as a textbook, but retained, as a "classroom resource," in the ninth-grade health classes in Pembroke because it is "obscene." Parents have asked that the abstinence-based sex education program Sex Respect be substituted. Complainant wants school officials indicted for distributing obscene materials to children.

Source: 11, Jan. 1991, p. 17; Mar. 1991, p. 44; Jan. 1992, p. 8.

1173
McCuen, Gary E., and David L. Bender.
The Sexual Revolution.

1972
Published

1977 MI

Banned from the Brighton High School library along with all other sex education materials.

Source: 11, Sept. 1977, p. 133.

1174
McCullers, Carson.
Member of the Wedding.

1946
Published

2001 PA

Challenged in the Tamaqua Area School District because the book "might not be appropriate for younger schoolmates." The school board is considering the establishment of a restricted materials section in the district's middle-school library for books deemed objectionable. Students would need parental permission to access any title placed there.

Source: 11, Mar. 2001, p. 54; July 2001, p. 145.

1175
McCunn, Ruthanne Lum.
Thousand Pieces of Gold.

1981
Published

1984 CA

Removed from elementary school library shelves in Sonoma County because certain passages were too "sexually explicit."

1992 WA

Challenged at the Commodore Middle School in Bainbridge Island as inappropriate by three parents because of violence, sexual scenes, and "lack of family values."

1994 CA

Rejected as an addition to a core literature list by the Amador County Unified School District because "it makes America look bad."

Source: 11, Sept. 1984, p. 137; May 1992, p. 84; July 1994, p. 109.

1176
McDermott, Beverly Brodsky.
The Golem: A Jewish Legend.

1976
Published

1977
Caldecott Honor Book

1993 NY

A first grade teacher asked the Newburgh school officials to ban this children's book about the persecution of Jews in sixteenth-century Prague. The teacher objected to the strong language and threatening artwork that children might not understand.

Source: 11, Nov. 1993, p. 178.

1177
McDonald, Brian.
In the Middle of the Night: The Shocking True Story of a Family Killed in Cold Blood.

2009
Published

2009 CT

Challenged at the Cheshire Public Library. McDonald's book revisits 2007, when Joshua Komisarjevsky and Steven Hayes allegedly invaded the Cheshire home of Dr. William Petit, beating him with a baseball bat and raping, torturing, and murdering his wife and two daughters. Complainants want the book kept off the library shelves until the men accused of the crime have been tried.

Source: 11, Jan. 2010, pp. 7-8; Mar. 2010, p. 51.

1178
McFarland, Philip James, et al.
Themes in World Literature.

1972
Published

1995 AZ

Challenged at the Tempe Union High School District in Mesa. The story, "A Rose for Emily," by William Faulkner was objectionable because it uses the word "nigger" six times as well as other demeaning phrases.

Source: 11, Jan. 1996, p. 13; May 1996, p. 98.

1179
McGahern, John.
The Dark.

1965
Published

1965

Banned in Ireland. No detailed official statement was required to be made available for the historical record, but it was assumed the novel was banned on the basis of several passages that dealt with the central character's discovery of his sexuality.

Source: 6, pp. 1,480–81.

1180
McHargue, Georgess.
Meet the Werewolf.

1976
Published

1983 WA

Challenged at the Evergreen School District in Vancouver because the book was "full of comments about becoming a werewolf, use of opium, and pacts with the devil."

1985 FL

Challenged because the book would lead children to believe ideas contrary to the teachings of the Bible, but retained, by the Sikes Elementary School media center in Lakeland.

1992 NY

Challenged at the Barringer Road Elementary School in Ilion because the book's passages on the occult were objectionable.

Source: 11, Sept. 1983, p. 139; July 1985, p. 133; Jan. 1993, p. 9.

1181
McHugh, Vincent.
The Blue Hen's Chicken.

1947
Published

1947 NY

Confiscated in New York City because the poetry book contained a part titled "Suite from Catullus," eight short poems that were variations on a theme of the Roman poet.

Source: 15, Vol. IV, p. 699.

1182
McKay, Susan.
Living Law.

1981 MS

Removed from the Mississippi state-approved textbook list because of complaints that the book "undermines" the values parents teach at home.

Source: 11, May 1981, p. 67; July 1981, p. 93.

1183
McKissack, Fredrick, Jr.
Shooting Star.

2009
Published

2010 OK
Retained in the Broken Arrow Sequoyah Middle School library despite a parent's concern about several swear words in the text. The book is about a high school football player who, after becoming discouraged about his size, starts using steroids to bulk up, resulting in negative effects on his life and personality.
Source: 11, Nov. 2010, p. 257.

1184
McKissack, Patricia C.
Mirandy and Brother Wind.

1988
Published

1989
Caldecott Honor Book

1989
Coretta Scott King Book Award

1991 FL
Challenged at the Glen Springs Elementary School in Gainesville because of the book's use of black dialect.
Source: 11, July 1991, p. 129.

1185
McMillan, Rosalyn.
Knowing.

1996
Published

1999 NC
Challenged, but retained, at the Cumberland County Library in Fayetteville despite a complaint that the book contains profanity. In addition, the complainant suggested that the library move sexually explicit materials, as well as ones about homosexuality, into an adult section and establish a review committee to screen materials.
Source: 11, July 1999, p. 94; Jan. 2000, pp. 27–28.

1186
McNally, John, ed.
When I Was a Loser: True Stories of (Barely) Surviving High School by Today's Top Writers.

2007
Published

2007 RI
Challenged as a Cumberland high school reading assignment because the entire compilation is filled with essays that are "lewd, contain profanity, and references to bestiality."
Source: 11, Jan. 2008, pp. 38-39.

1187
Mead, Richelle.
Vampire Academy series.

2007
Published

2009 TX
Banned at Henderson Junior High School in the Stephenville, Texas, Independent School District (ISD). The entire teen vampire series was banned for sexual content or nudity. Since the series has not been completed, "Stephenville ISD actually banned books that have not yet been published and perhaps even books that have yet to be written. There is no way the district could know the content of these books, and yet they have been banned."
Source: 11, Nov. 2009, pp. 197-98, 225.

1188
Medved, Michael.
Hollywood vs. America: Popular Culture and the War on Traditional Values.

1992
Published

1997 IN
Withdrawn from the freshman curriculum at Greencastle High School because of the graphic language in Medved's work, especially the chapter devoted to popular music.
Source: 11, July 1997, p. 98.

1189
Meeks, Linda, and Philip Heit.
Your Relationship.

1990
Published

1990 IL
Challenged in the Barrington School District because the book has a chapter on incest that creates "ugly imagery for innocent minds."
Source: 11, Jan. 1991, p. 29.

1190
Melville, Herman.
Moby-Dick.

1851
Published

1996 TX
Banned from the Advanced Placement English reading list at the Lindale schools because it "conflicts with the values of the community."
Source: 11, Nov. 1996, p. 199.

1191
Mercado, Nancy E., ed.
Tripping over the Lunch Lady and Other Short Stories.

2004
Published

2007 VA
After a challenge and three appeals, the York County School Board chose to keep the collection of short stories in the Magruder Elementary School library in Williamsburg despite claims that it is offensive to children with loved ones serving in the military and inappropriate for elementary school students. A parent wanted the book removed because one of the short stories contained references to war, bombs, and soldier casualties.
Source: 11, Jan. 2008, p. 27.

1192
Meretzky, Eric.
Zork: The Malifestro Quest.

1983
Published

1990 MI
Challenged at the Jeffers Elementary School in Spring Lake because it "is a disgrace to the Lord and to the Spring Lake school system."
Source: 11, May 1990, p. 84; July 1990, p. 145.

1193
Meriwether, Louise.
Daddy Was a Number Runner.

1970
Published

1970
Best Books for Young Adults

1977 CA
Removed from all Oakland junior high school libraries and its use restricted in senior high schools, following a complaint about the book's explicit depiction of ghetto life.
Source: 11, May 1977, p. 71.

1194
Mernissi, Fatima.
The Veil and the Male Elite: A Feminist Interpretation of Women's Rights in Islam.

1991
Published

1991
Banned in Morocco. Authorities regarded as particularly threatening Mernissi's contention that the sacred texts were manipulated as political weapons and that commonly accepted hadith are based on falsehood. Saudia Arabia is ruled by Muslim religious law, or sharia, which encompasses the hadith. Moroccan legal family codes at the time were also based on sharia.

1991
Banned in Saudia Arabia.

1991
Banned in Syria.

2003
The book was translated for the first time into Farsi and published in Tehran, Iran, by Ney Publications. In August 2003, its translator, publisher, and the Iranian official who authorized the book's publication were convicted by the Criminal Court of Tehran, Iran, of "insulting and undermining the holy tenets of Islam," "sullying the person of the Prophet Muhammad," and "distorting Islamic history" by "publishing false, slanderous, and fabricated texts." The court also ordered that copies of Mernissi's book be shredded.
Source: 8, pp. 305–6.

1195
Merriam-Webster Collegiate Dictionary.

1982 NM
Removed from classrooms in Carlsbad schools because the dictionary defines "obscene" words.

1989 NJ
Challenged in the Upper Pittsgrove Township schools because the definition of sexual intercourse was objectionable.

1993 NV
Challenged, but the 1,100 copies of the dictionary were returned to the Sparks Elementary School classrooms. A sixth-grade teacher objected to the book because it includes obscene words.

2010 CA
Pulled from the Menifee Union School District because a parent complained when a child came across the term "oral sex." Officials said the district is forming a committee to consider a permanent classroom ban of the dictionary.
Source: 11, Nov. 1982, p. 206; Jan. 1990, p. 11; Jan. 1994, p. 37; Mar. 2010, p. 55.

1196
Merriam, Eve.
Halloween ABC.

1987
Published

1989 OR
Challenged at the Douglas County Library in Roseburg because the book encourages devil worshipping.

1991 KS
Challenged in the Wichita public schools because it is "satanic and disgusting."

1991 MD
Challenged at the Howard County school libraries because "there should be an effort to tone down Halloween and there should not be books about it in the schools."

1992 CO
Challenged at the Acres Green Elementary School in Douglas County.

1992 WA
Challenged and retained, but will be shelved with other works generally available only to older students and won't be used in future Halloween displays at the Federal Way School District in Seattle. The compromise was for a group of parents who objected to the book's satanic references.

1993 TX
Challenged, but retained, at the Ennis Public Library.

1993 WA
Challenged, but retained, in the Othello elementary school libraries because the book "promotes violent criminal and deviant behavior."

1993 WI
Challenged in the Cameron Elementary School library in Rice Lake because the "poems promote satanism, murder, and suicide." The book was retained.

1994 WA
Challenged in the Spokane School District library by a father who found the poems morbid and satanic. In particular, the parent disapproved of one poem which "appears to be a chant calling forth the Devil."

1995 MA
Challenged in the Sandwich Public Library because it is "too violent for young children."

2000 NY
Challenged, but retained, in the Wellsville elementary school library despite complaints the book promotes violence.
Source: 11, Jan. 1990, pp. 4–5; Sept. 1991, p. 178; Jan. 1992, p. 26; May 1992, p. 94; Mar. 1993, p. 43; July 1993, pp. 103–4; Sept. 1993, p. 159; Jan. 1994, pp. 13–14; Mar. 1994, pp. 69–70; Jan. 1995, p. 9; Mar. 1995, p. 41; Sept. 1995, p. 158; Mar. 2001, p. 75.

1197

Merriam, Eve.
The Inner City Mother Goose.

1969
Published

1972 CA
Challenged in San Francisco.

1972 MD
Challenged in Baltimore.

1972 MN
Challenged in Minneapolis.

1972 NY
An Erie County judge called for a grand jury investigation of this satirical book of adult nursery rhymes, alleging it taught crime.

2000 NY
Removed from the Whitney Point middle school library after a parent complained about its language and content.
Source: 4, p. 91; 11, July 2000, p. 104.

1198

Merrick, Gordon.
One for the Gods.

1971
Published

1984
Seized by the British Customs Office.
Source: 11, Jan. 1985, p. 26.

1199

Metalious, Grace.
Peyton Place.

1956
Published

1957 TN
The city of Knoxville activated a city ordinance that permitted the Knoxville City Board of Review to suppress any publication that it considered to be obscene. The target was Metalious' novel; local dealers were forbidden to sell it. When one indignant newsstand owner tested the ordinance, it was ruled unconstitutional.

1958
Banned in Ireland from 1958 until the introduction of the Censorship of Publications Bill in 1967.

1958
Temporary ban lifted in Canada.

1959 RI
The Rhode Island Commission to Encourage Morality in Youth brought action against Bantam and three other New York paperback publishers. The Rhode Island Superior Court upheld the decision, which was later reversed by the U.S. Supreme Court in *Bantam Books, Inc. et al., v. Joseph A. Sullivan, et al.*
Source: 4, p. 97; 8, pp. 373–74.

1200

Meyer, Michael, ed.
Bedford Introduction to Literature.

1987
Published

2000 FL
The principal of Paxon School for Advanced Studies in Jacksonville authorized teachers to cut out the play *Angels in America* from the textbook. The Duval County School Board first banned the play three years earlier after learning that it was being used in a class at Douglas Anderson School of the Arts. The play is the first half of Tony Kushner's work depicting the United States in the 1980s as the AIDS epidemic began to spread. It won the 1993 Pulitzer Prize for drama and several Tony awards, including best play.
Source: 11, Mar. 2001, p. 56.

1201

Meyer, Stephenie H.
Twilight series.

2005
Published

2006
Best Books for Young Adults

2008
British Children's Book of the Year

2009
Kid's Choice Award for Favorite Book

2008 CA
Removed from and later reinstated in the middle school libraries of the Capistrano Unified School District. The books were initially ordered removed by the district's instructional materials specialist, who ordered that the books be moved from middle school to high school collections. That order was rescinded and the books remain in the middle school libraries.

2009
Banned in Australia for primary school students because the series is too racy. Librarians have stripped the books from shelves in some junior schools because they believe the content is too sexual and goes against religious beliefs. They even have asked parents not to let kids bring their own copies of Stephenie Meyer's smash hit novels—which explore the stormy love affair between a teenage girl and a vampire—to school.

2009 UT
Challenged at the Brockbank Junior High in Magna by a parent over the sexual content in the Mormon author's fourth novel, *Breaking Dawn*.
Source: 11, Nov. 2008, p. 253; Jan. 2009, p. 5; May 2009, p. 80; Nov. 2009, pp. 207-8.

1202

Mezrich, Ben.
Bringing Down the House: The Inside Story of Six M.I.T. Students Who Took Vegas for Millions.

2002
Published

2004 OR
Challenged in the Beaverton schools as supplemental reading because it contains profanity and abundant references to prostitution and gambling. In 2004, the book was number eighteen on *The New York Times'* paperback nonfiction best-seller list.
Source: 11, Mar. 2005, pp. 58–59.

1203

Mill, John Stuart.
Social Philosophy.

1848
Published

1856
Listed on the *Index Librorum Prohibitorum* (List of Prohibited Books) in Rome, Italy.
Source: 4, p. 42.

1204

Mill, John Stuart.
System of Logic.

1843
Published

1856
Listed on the *Index Librorum Prohibitorum*
(List of Prohibited Books) in Rome, Italy.
Source: 4, p. 42.

1205

Millard, Anne, and
Patricia Vanags.
*The Usborne Book of
World History.*

1985
Published

1998 GA
Restricted to teachers only in the
Gwinnett County schools after objections
to nude drawings depicting life in ancient
civilizations. Complainants also
objected to *The Usborne Time Traveler
Books (Pharaohs and Pyramids),*
by Tony Allan.
Source: 11, Sept. 1998, pp. 143–44.

1206

Miller, Arthur.
The Crucible.

1952
Published

1953
Tony Award for Best Play

1982 PA
Challenged at the Cumberland Valley High
School, Harrisburg because the play
contains "sick words from the mouths of
demon-possessed people. It should be
wiped out of the schools or the school board
should use them to fuel the fire of hell."

1987 KY
Challenged as a required reading
assignment at the Pulaski County High
School in Somerset because it is "junk."

1999 PA
Challenged, but retained, in the sopho-
more curriculum at West Middlesex
High School.
Source: 11, Mar. 1983, pp. 52–53; May 1987, p. 90;
July 1999, p. 105.

1207

Miller, Arthur.
Death of a Salesman.

1949
Published

1949
Pulitzer Prize for Drama

1949
Tony Award for Best Play

1974 TX
Challenged at the Dallas Independent
School District high school libraries.

1981 IN
Banned from English classes at Spring
Valley Community High School in French
Lick because the play contains the words
"goddamn," "son of a bitch," and "bastard."

1987 KY
Challenged as a required reading
assignment at the Pulaski County High
School in Sinking Valley because
it is "junk."

1997 IL
Challenged, but retained, at Egyptian
High School in Tamms. The play was
considered offensive by some because
of "profanity."
Source: 11, July 1975, pp. 6–7; May 1981, p. 68;
May 1987, p. 90; May 1997, p. 78.

1208

Miller, Deborah A., and
Alex Waigandt.
*Coping with Your Sexual
Orientation.*

1990
Published

1994 NJ
Moved from the Chestnut Ridge Middle
School library in Washington Township
because school administrators have
been accused of "indoctrinating children
in the gay lifestyle."
Source: 11, Sept. 1994, p. 148.

1209

Miller, Henry.
Opus Pistorum.

1983
Published

1993 NC
Removed from the Cumberland
County library system because it lacks
"serious literary or artistic merit for
this library's collection."
Source: 11, Mar. 1993, p. 42.

1210

Miller, Henry.
Sexus.

1949
Published

1950
Banned in France.

1956
Banned in Norway.
Source: 4, p. 74.

1211

Miller, Henry.
Tropic of Cancer.

1934
Published

1934
Banned by the U.S. and also
Canadian Customs.

1964
U.S. Supreme Court found the book
was not obscene.

1986
Banned in Turkey.
Source: 4, p. 74; 5, July/Aug. 1986, p. 46; 6,
pp. 1,597–98; 8, pp. 387–89.

1212

Miller, Henry.
Tropic of Capricorn.

1939
Published

1953 CA
Ban upheld by U.S. Court of Appeals
in San Francisco.

1989
An appeals court in Istanbul,
Turkey, authorized a public burning of
Miller's novel as sexually exploitative.
Source: 4, p. 74; 6, pp. 1,597–98; 8, pp. 387–89; 11,
May 1989, p. 90.

1213

Miller, Jim, ed.
The Rolling Stone Illustrated History of Rock and Roll.

1976
Published

1977
Best Books for Young Adults

1982 KY
Challenged in Jefferson County because it "will cause our children to become immoral and indecent."
Source: 11, Mar. 1983, p. 41.

1214

Milton, John.
Paradise Lost.

1667
Published

1758
Listed on the *Index Librorum Prohibitorum* (List of Prohibited Books) in Rome, Italy.
Source: 4, p. 22.

1215

Mishima, Yukio.
The Sound of Waves.

1956
Published

1993 WA
Challenged, but retained, at the Lake Washington School District in Kirkland despite objections that it is "crude, vulgar, degrading to women, seductive, enticing, and suggestive."

2001 CA
Challenged in the Newark Unified School District because the book is sexually explicit.
Source: 11, Jan. 1994, p. 16; Mar. 1994, p. 71; Mar. 2001, p. 55.

1216

Mitchell, Margaret.
Gone with the Wind.

1936
Published

1937
Pulitzer Prize for Fiction

1978 CA
Banned from the Anaheim Union High School District English classrooms according to the Anaheim Secondary Teachers Association.

1984 IL
Challenged in the Waukegan School District because the novel uses the word "nigger."
Source: 11, Jan. 1979, p. 6; July 1984, p. 105.

1217

Mitchell, Stephen.
Gilgamesh: A New English Version.

2004
Published

2006 NJ
Challenged in the Clearview Regional High School in Harrison Township because the modern translation of one of the oldest known pieces of literature was considered sexually descriptive and unnecessarily explicit. The work itself dates back to about 1700 B.C., some one thousand years before the writings of Homer.
Source: 11, Jan. 2007, p. 10.

1218

Mochizuki, Ken.
Baseball Saved Us.

1995
Published

2006 CT
Challenged, but retained, on the second-grade reading list in the New Milford schools despite the fact the word "Jap" is used to taunt the main character in the book. The children's story is about the World War II Japanese-American internment.
Source: 11, July 2006, pp. 183–84.

1219

Moe, Barbara A.
Everything You Need to Know about Sexual Abstinence.

1996
Published

1996 LA
Pulled from the Ouachita Parish School library in Monroe because of sexual content. The Louisiana chapter of the ACLU filed a lawsuit in the federal courts on October 3, 1996, claiming that the principal and the school superintendent violated First Amendment free speech rights and also failed to follow established procedure when they removed the book. The three-year-old school library censorship case headed to court after the Ouachita Parish School Board made no decision to seek a settlement at a special meeting April 12, 1999. On August 17, 1999, the Ouachita Parish School Board agreed to return the book to the library and to develop a new book-selection policy that follows state guidelines for school media programs.
Source: 11, Sept. 1996, pp. 151–52; Jan. 1997, p. 7; July 1999, p. 93; Jan. 2000, p. 27.

1220

Mohr, Richard D.
A More Perfect Union: Why Straight America Must Stand Up for Gay Rights.

1994
Published

1996 ME
Challenged, but retained, at the Belfast Free Library because "homosexuality destroys marriages and families; it destroys the good health of the individual and the innocent are infected by it."
Source: 11, May 1996, p. 97.

1221

Momaday, N. Scott.
House Made of Dawn.

1977
Published

1969
Pulitzer Prize for Fiction

1989 OR
Challenged at the Reynolds High School in Troutdale because two pages were sexually explicit.

1996 TX
Retained on the Round Rock Independent High School reading list after a challenge that the book was too violent.
Source: 11, Jan. 1990, p. 32; May 1996, p. 99.

1222

Monette, Paul.
*Selected from
Borrowed Time:
An AIDS Memoir.*

1992
Published

2011 TN
Pulled from circulation at the Cheatham Middle School. The selection from Paul Monette's *Borrowed Time: An AIDS Memoir,* chronicles how Monette coped with a lover's death from AIDS. The book talks frankly about past promiscuity and uses profanity. School policy was changed after the complaint. The previous policy kept challenged books available in the library until two weeks after the review process was complete. Now the book is removed and a decision is made within forty-eight hours.
Source: 11, May 2011, p. 95.

1223

Montaigne, Michel de.
Essays.

1580
Published

1595
Sections banned in France.

1676
Listed on the *Index Librorum Prohibitorum* (List of Prohibited Books) in Rome, Italy.
Source: 1, pp. 98–100; 4, p. 15; 8, pp. 234–36.

1224

Moore, Alan.
*The League of Extraordinary
Gentlemen: Black Dossier.*

2002
Published

2009 KY
Challenged at the Jessamine County Public Library in Nicholasville. A petition with 950 signatures was presented to the board to overturn its collection policy. The petition specifically asked for the removal of four works on the grounds that they "offended me in that they depict sexual acts and/or describe such acts in a way that in my opinion are contrary to the Jessamine County public opinion" of what should be in a public, taxpayer-supported collection. The petition concluded the works constituted a public safety issue in that they encourage sexual predators. In addition to Moore's graphic novel, the other works challenged were *Snuff,* by Chuck Palahniuk; *Choke,* a DVD based on a novel by Palahniuk; and the DVD *Ron White: You Can't Fix Stupid.* The graphic novel eventually got two employees fired for breaching library policies; the library director was threatened with physical harm; and the book was recataloged, along with other graphic novels with mature trends, to a separate but unrestricted graphic novels section of the library.
Source: 11, Jan. 2010, pp. 8–9; Mar. 2010, p. 52.

1225

Moore, Alan.
Neonomicon.

2010
Published

2012 SC
Banned at the Greenville County Public Library after a patron's teenage daughter checked it out of the library's adult section. The teenage girl was given an adult library card, which allowed her to check out adult-themed books. The head of the library system overturned an internal review committee's decision to retain the graphic novel because the pictures gave her pause.
Source: 11, Sept. 2012, p. 201; Mar. 2013, pp. 48-49.

1226

Moore, George.
Esther Waters.

1894
Published

1894
Excluded from British circulating libraries, as both Mudie's Library and Smith's Library refused to stock it, viewing it as too risqué because the main character suffers as the result of her one sexual indiscretion, but does not die, and because of the candid manner in which her situation is presented.
Source: 14, pp. 132–33.

1227

Moore, Patrick.
*Tweaked: A Crystal Meth
Memoir.*

2006
Published

2010 MA
Removed from the North Middlessex Regional High School because the book contains "'F' words and instructions on how to make certain types of illegal drugs."
Source: 11, Nov. 2010, p. 243.

1228

Morris, Desmond.
The Naked Ape.

1967
Published

1976 NY
Removed from the Island Trees Union Free School District High School library in 1976 along with nine other titles because they were considered "immoral, anti-American, anti-Christian, or just plain filthy." Returned to the library after the U.S. Supreme Court ruling on June 25, 1982, in *Board of Education, Island Trees Union Free School District No. 26 et al. v. Pico et al.,* 457 U.S. 853 (1982).

1989 PA
Reinstated after being removed from the Mifflinburg High School because the book includes material on human sexuality that is "explicit, almost manual description of what some would refer to as deviant sexual relations."
Source: 11, Nov. 1982, p. 197; May 1989, p. 93.

1229

Morrison, Lillian.
*Remember Me When
This You See.*

1961
Published

2005
Coretta Scott King
Author Award

1986 GA
Challenged at the Gwinnett County Elementary School library because a line from the poetry book—"Don't make love in a potato field/Potatoes have eyes"—was objectionable.
Source: 11, Mar. 1987, p. 65.

1230
Morrison, Toni.
Beloved.

1987
Published

1987
National Book Critics Circle Fiction Finalist

1988
American Book Award

1988
Pulitzer Prize for Fiction

1993
Nobel Prize in Literature

1995 FL
Challenged at the St. Johns County Schools in St. Augustine.

1996 TX
Retained on the Round Rock Independent High School reading list after a challenge that the book was too violent.

1997 ME
Challenged by a member of the Madawaska School Committee because of the book's language. The novel has been required reading for the Advanced Placement English class for six years.

1998 FL
Challenged in the Sarasota County schools because of sexual material.

2006 IL
Retained on the Northwest Suburban High School District 214 reading list in Arlington Heights, along with eight other challenged titles. A board member, elected amid promises to bring her Christian beliefs into all board decision-making, raised the controversy based on excerpts from the books she'd found on the Internet.

2007 ID
Challenged in the Coeur d'Alene School District. Some parents say the book, along with five others, should require parental permission for students to read them.

2007 KY
Pulled from the senior Advanced Placement (AP) English class at Eastern High School in Louisville because two parents complained that the novel about antebellum slavery depicted the inappropriate topics of bestiality, racism, and sex. The principal ordered teachers to start over with the *The Scarlet Letter,* by Nathaniel Hawthorne in preparation for upcoming AP exams.

2012 MI
Challenged, but retained, as a text in Salem High School Advanced Placement English courses. The complainants cited the allegedly obscene nature of some passages in the book and asked that it be removed from the curriculum. District officials determined the novel was appropriate for the age and maturity level of Advanced Placement students. In reviewing the novel, the committee also considered the accuracy of the material, the objectivity of the material, and the necessity of using the material in light of the curriculum.

2013 VA
Challenged at the Fairfax County schools because a parent complained that the book "depicts scenes of bestiality, gang rape, and an infant's gruesome murder."
Source: 11, Jan. 1996, p. 14; May 1996, p. 99; Jan. 1998, p. 14; July 1998, p. 120; July 2006, pp. 210–11; May 2007, pp. 98-99; July 2007, p. 147; Sept. 2007, p. 181; Mar. 2012, pp. 79-80; May 2012, pp. 127-28; Mar. 2013, pp. 50-51.

1231
Morrison, Toni.
The Bluest Eye.

1970
Published

1994 AK
Pulled from an eleventh grade classroom at Lathrop High School in Fairbanks by school administrators because "It was a very controversial book; it contains lots of very graphic descriptions and lots of disturbing language."

1994 PA
Challenged at the West Chester schools as "most pornographic."

1994 PA
Banned from the Morrisville Borough High School English curriculum after complaints about its sexual content and objectionable language.

1995 FL
Challenged at the St. Johns County Schools in St. Augustine.

1995 MA
Challenged on the optional summer reading list at the Lynn schools because of the book's sexual content.

1998 MD
Challenged on Montgomery County reading lists and school library shelves.

1999 NH
Removed from the reading list for ninth- and tenth-graders at Stevens High School in Claremont because of a parent's complaint about the book's sexual content.

2003 CA
Challenged, but retained, at the Kern High School District in Bakersfield despite complaints of the book's sexually explicit material.

2005 CO
Banned from the Littleton curriculum and library shelves after complaints about its explicit sex, including the rape of an eleven-year-old girl by her father.

2007 MI
Challenged in the Howell High School along with several other books because of strong sexual content. In response to a request from the president of the Livingston Organization for Values in Education, or LOVE, the county's top law enforcement official reviewed the books to see whether laws against distribution of sexually explicit materials to minors had been broken. "After reading the books in question, it is clear that the explicit passages illustrated a larger literary, artistic, or political message and were not included solely to appeal to the prurient interests of minors," the Livingston County prosecutor wrote. "Whether these materials are appropriate for minors is a decision to be made by the school board, but I find that they are not in violation of the criminal laws."

2009 IN
Retained in Delphi Community High School's curriculum despite claims of inappropriate sexual content and graphic language.

2011 CT
Challenged in the Brookfield High School curriculum because of sex scenes, profanity, and age appropriateness of the book. Students in the high school have been reading Morrison's book since 1995.

2013 CO
Challenged in Legacy High School's Advanced Placement English classes in Adams County because it was a "bad book." A notice was sent home to let parents and students know what they would be reading and why and an alternate assignment was offered to those who wanted it. Half a dozen students of about 150 opted to read one of the alternative texts and received instruction on those works outside of class time.

2013 OH
Challenged on a suggested reading list for Columbus high school students by the school board president because it is inappropriate for the school board to "even be associated with it." A fellow board member described the book as having "an underlying socialist-communist agenda." Morrison is an Ohio native, Pulitzer Prize-winning author, and Nobel laureate.

Source: 8, p. 321; 11, May 1994, p. 86; Jan. 1995, p. 25; Mar. 1995, pp. 44–45; May 1995, p. 71; July 1995, p. 98; Jan. 1996, p. 14; May 1998, p. 70; Sept. 1999, pp. 121–22; Mar. 2004, pp. 50–51; May 2004, pp. 118–19; Jan. 2006, p. 13; Mar. 2007, pp. 51-52; May 2007, pp. 117-18; May 2009, p. 24; Jan. 2012, pp. 11-12; Sept. 2013, p. 184; Nov. 2013, p. 219.

1232
Morrison, Toni.
Song of Solomon.

1977
Published

1977
National Book Critics Circle Award for Fiction

1993 OH
Challenged, but retained, in the Columbus schools. The complainant believed that the book contains language degrading to blacks and is sexually explicit.

1994 GA
Removed from required reading lists and library shelves in the Richmond County School District after a parent complained that passages from the book were "filthy and inappropriate."

1995 FL
Challenged at the St. Johns County Schools in St. Augustine.

1998 MD
Removed from the St. Mary's County schools' approved text list by the school superintendent overruling a faculty committee recommendation. Complainants referred to the novel as "filth," "trash," and "repulsive."

2009 MI
Reinstated in the Shelby school Advanced Placement English curriculum, but parents are to be informed in writing and at a meeting about the book's content. Students not wanting to read the book can choose an alternative without academic penalty. The superintendent had suspended the book from the curriculum.

2010 IN
Retained in the Franklin Central High School's Advanced Placement English curriculum in Indianapolis, despite some parents' concerns about the novel's language and sexual content.

Source: 11, July 1993, p. 108; Sept. 1993, p. 160; May 1994, p. 86; Jan. 1996, p. 14; Mar. 1998, p. 42; July 2009, pp. 140-41; July 2010, p. 177.

1233
Morrison, Toni.
Sula.

1974
Published

2000 MD
Challenged on the Poolesville High School reading list because of the book's sexual content and language. On October 5, 2000, Montgomery County Circuit Court Judge Paul McGuckian dismissed the bid to ban the work from the curriculum. The school, however, decided to remove the book from the summer reading list.

Source: 11, Nov. 2000, p. 196; Jan. 2001, pp. 36–37.

1234
Mosca, Frank.
All-American Boys.

1983
Published

1993 KS
Challenged in the Kansas City school district, which donated the book to the city's public library.

1993 MO
Challenged at several Kansas City area schools after the books were donated by a national group that seeks to give young adults "fair, accurate and inclusive images of lesbians and gay men." At the Shawnee Mission School District the book was returned to general circulation; at the Olathe East High School the book was removed; protesters burned copies of the book, but the Kansas City School District kept Mosca's novel on the high school shelves.

1993 MO
The school superintendent removed the book in Lee's Summit.

Source: 11, Mar. 1994, pp. 51–52; May 1994, p. 84.

1235
Mother Goose: Old Nursery Rhymes.

1983 FL
Challenged at the Dade County Public Library by a Miami Metro Commissioner because the anthology of nursery rhymes contains the following anti-Semitic verse: "Jack sold his gold egg/to a rogue of a Jew/ who cheated him out of/half of his due."

Source: 11, July 1983, p. 107; Jan. 1984, p. 25.

1236
Mowat, Farley.
And No Birds Sang.

1979
Published

1994 OH
Challenged in the Northwestern Middle School library, Springfield, because of "improper language."

Source: 11, July 1994, p. 111.

1237
Mowat, Farley.
Never Cry Wolf.

1963
Published

1987 FL
Removed from the Panama City school classrooms and libraries because of "offensive" language.

Source: 11, July 1987, pp. 126–28; Sept. 1987, pp. 168–69.

1238

Mowat, Farley.
Woman in the Mists: The Story of Dian Fossey & the Mountain Gorillas of Africa.

1987
Published

1991 NE
Removed from a required reading list in the Omaha public schools because the book has racial slurs, passages degrading to women, profanity, and a long discussion of the aftermath of Fossey's abortion.
Source: 11, Mar. 1992, p. 44.

1239

Muller, Gilbert H., and Harvey S. Wiener, comps.
The Short Prose Reader.

1982
Published

1994 MD
Challenged at the Cecil County Board of Education in Elkton. Many deemed the text controversial because it included essays dealing with issues of abortion, gay rights, alcohol, and sex education.
Source: 11, Mar. 1995, p. 55.

1240

Mungo, Raymond.
Liberace.

1995
Published

2000 CA
Removed from the Anaheim school district because school officials said the book is too difficult for middle school students and that it could cause harassment against students seen with it. The American Civil Liberties Union (ACLU) of Southern California filed suit in *Doe v. Anaheim Union High School District* alleging that the removal is "a pretext for viewpoint-based censorship." The ACLU claims no other books have been removed from the junior high library for similar reasons, even though several, such as works by Shakespeare and Dickens, are more difficult reading. The ACLU contends that the school officials engaged in unconstitutional

viewpoint discrimination by removing the book because it contains gay and lesbian material. In March 2001, the school board approved a settlement that restored the book to the high school shelves and amended the district's policy to prohibit the removal of books for subject matter involving sexual orientation, but the book will not be returned to the middle school.
Source: 11, Mar. 2001, p. 53; May 2001, p. 95; July 2001, p. 173.

1241

Murakami, Haruki.
Norwegian Wood.

1987
Published

2011 NJ
Pulled from the required summer reading list for middle school and high school students at the Monroe Township Schools in Williamstown after parents complained about a gay sex scene.
Source: 11, Nov. 2011, p. 204.

1242

Murdoch, Iris.
The Nice and the Good.

1968
Published

1977
Banned in South Africa.
Source: 5, Nov./Dec. 1977, p. 68.

1243

Murphy, Barbara Beasley.
Home Free.

1970
Published

1988 NJ
Retained at the Hillcrest School library in East Ramapo, but the book will not be lent to a fourth or fifth grader who is not deemed an "advanced reader or critical thinker" by a parent, teacher, or librarian. The book contains the word "nigger."
Source: 11, May 1988, p. 86.

1244

Murphy, Barbara Beasley.
No Place to Run.

1977
Published

1982 AL
Removed from two Anniston high school libraries due to "the curse words and using the Lord's name in vain," but later reinstated on a restricted basis.
Source: 11, Mar. 1983, p. 37.

1245

Murray, William.
Tip on a Dead Crab.

1984-1985
Published

1983 TN
Publication canceled by Dodd, Mead & Company because of language in the book considered "objectionable" by Thomas Nelson, Inc. of Nashville—Dodd, Mead's parent company.
Source: 11, Nov. 1983, p. 188.

1246

Myers, Lawrence W.
Improvised Radio Jamming Techniques.

1989
Published

1991 OR
Challenged for promoting illegal actions, but retained, at the Multnomah County Library.
Source: 11, Jan. 1992, p. 6.

1247

Myers, Walter Dean.
Fallen Angels.

1988
Published

1988
Best Books for Young Adults

1988
Best Book of 1988 by *School Library Journal*

1989
Coretta Scott King Author Award

1990 OH
Challenged in the Bluffton schools because of its use of profane language.

1992 GA
Restricted as supplemental classroom reading material at the Jackson County High School because of undesirable language and sensitive material.

1994 PA
Challenged at the West Chester schools.

1995 OH
Removed from a twelfth-grade English class in Middleburg Heights after a parent complained of its sexually explicit language.

1997 OH
Challenged, but retained, at the Lakewood High School. The book was challenged by parents who objected to the novel's violence and vulgar language.

1999 CA
Removed from the Laton Unified School District because the novel about the Vietnam War contains violence and profanity.

1999 MI
Removed as required reading in the Livonia public schools because it contains "too many swear words."

2000 TX
Challenged, but retained, in the Arlington school district's junior high school libraries despite a parent's complaint that the book's content was too strong for younger students.

2002 MS
Banned from the George County schools because of profanity.

2002 VA
Challenged, along with seventeen other titles in the Fairfax County elementary and secondary libraries, by a group called Parents Against Bad Books in Schools. The group contends the books "contain profanity and descriptions of drug abuse, sexually explicit conduct, and torture."

2003 IN
Banned at the Franklin Central High School in Indianapolis because of concerns about the book's profanity. The book was assigned in English classes for sophomores.

2005 KS
The book was assigned in English classes for sophomores. Removed from the Blue Valley School District's high school curriculum in Overland Park.

2006 IL
The book was challenged by parents and community members along with thirteen other titles. Retained on the Northwest Suburban High School District 214 reading list in Arlington Heights, along with eight other challenged titles. A board member, elected amid promises to bring her Christian beliefs into all board decision-making, raised the controversy based on excerpts from the books she'd found on the Internet.

2007 ID
Challenged in the Coeur d'Alene School District. Some parents say the book, along with five others, should require parental permission for students to read them.

2008 NC
Challenged on the accelerated reading list at Chinquapin Elementary School in Duplin County because the book is littered with hundreds of expletives, including racial epithets and slang terms for homosexuals.

2013 OH
Challenged on the Danbury Middle School reading list in Toledo because of inappropriate language. The book depicts the reality of the Vietnam War, with sometimes gruesome descriptions of combat and frequent foul language from soldiers.
Source: 8, pp. 451–53; 11, Nov. 1990, p. 211; Sept. 1992, p. 142; Jan. 1995, p. 25; Mar. 1996, p. 49; May 1996, p. 79; Nov. 1999, pp. 164-65; Jan. 2001, p. 36; Jan. 2003, p. 10; Mar. 2003, p. 55; Jan. 2004, pp. 11-12; Nov. 2005, pp. 282–83; July 2006, pp. 210-11; Sept. 2007, p. 181; May 2008, p. 97; May 2013, p. 104.

1248
Myers, Walter Dean.
Fast Sam, Cool Clyde and Stuff.

1975
Published

1976
Coretta Scott King Author Honor Book

1983 OH
Challenged by an elementary school administrator in Akron.
Source: 9; 11, May 1983, p. 86.

1249
Myers, Walter Dean.
Hoops.

1981
Published

1981
Best Books for Young Adults

1989 CO
Challenged in Littleton school libraries because the book "endorses" drinking, stealing, and homosexuality, uses offensive words, and contains a sex scene.

2000 OH
Challenged, but retained, in Vanlue High School English classes despite objections that the book is evil and depicts drugs, alcohol, and sex.

2009 IA
Challenged in the Council Bluffs schools because it contains "derogatory remarks, racial slurs, and sexual content."
Source: 11, Sept. 1989, p. 186; July 2000, p. 125; May 2009, p. 77.

1250
Myers, Walter Dean.
Young Martin's Promise.

1993
Published

1994 NY
Challenged by a school board member in the Queens school libraries because King "was a leftist hoodlum with significant Communist ties. King was a hypocritical adulterer." The rest of the school board voted to retain the book.
Source: 11, July 1994, pp. 110–11; Sept. 1994, p. 166.

1251
Myracle, Lauren.
ttfn.

2006
Published

2008 OK
Removed from the Marietta Middle School library due to descriptions of sex and drug use. The book, which is recommended for older students, depicts online conversations between three eleventh-grade girls.
Source: 11, Nov. 2008, p. 232; May 2010, p. 127.

1252
Myracle, Lauren.
ttyl.

2004
Published

2007 NY
Challenged at the William Floyd Middle School library in Mastic because the book

includes "curse words, crude references to the male and female anatomy, sex acts and adult situations like drinking alcohol and flirtation with a teacher that almost goes too far." A spokesman for the William Floyd School District said the book will remain in the library, and that the book is very popular with students across the country. The spokesperson also said unlike many books that young people read, the book deals with controversial subjects without glorifying negative behaviors. It is the first book written entirely in the format of instant messaging— the title itself is a shorthand reference to "talk to you later."

2008 TX
Challenged in the Round Rock Independent School District middle school library due to the book's descriptions of sex, porn, alcohol, and inappropriate teacher-student relationships. The school offers parents the ability to tell the school if they do not want their children to check out particular books at the library.

2009 WI
Challenged, but retained, at the John Muir Middle School library in Wausau despite a parent's request that the book be removed because of sexually explicit content. The author said, "The book's dialogue about sex and alcohol is frank but the characters criticize those who engage in those behaviors."

2010 CT
Retained in the Ponus Ridge Middle School library in Norwalk. While some critics decry its style as "grammatically incorrect," most who take exception point to its "foul language," sexual content, and questionable sexual behavior. It is the first book written entirely in the format of instant messaging—the title itself is a shorthand reference to "talk to you later."
Source: 11, May 2007, p. 92; Nov. 2008, pp. 232-33; Jan. 2009, pp. 6-7; July 2009, p. 140; May 2010, p. 127.

1253
Myrer, Anton.
A Green Desire.

1981
Published

1985 PA
Banned from the Stroudsburg High School library because it was "blatantly

graphic, pornographic and wholly unacceptable for a high school library."
Source: 11, May 1985, p. 79.

1254
Nabokov, Vladimir.
Lolita.

1955
Published

1955
Banned as obscene in England from 1955 to 1959.

1956
Banned as obscene in France from 1956 to 1959.

1959
Banned as obscene in Argentina.

1960
Banned as obscene in New Zealand.

1982
The South African Directorate of Publications announced on November 27, 1982, that *Lolita* had been taken off the banned list, eight years after a request for permission to market the novel in paperback had been refused.

2006 FL
Challenged at the Marion-Levy Public Library System in Ocala. The Marion County commissioners voted to have the county attorney review the novel that addresses the themes of pedophilia and incest, to determine if it meets the state law's definition of "unsuitable for minors."
Source: 4, p. 81; 5, Apr. 1983, p. 47; 8, pp. 359-60; 11, Mar. 2006, pp. 69-70; Nov. 2006, p. 317.

1255
Nasrin, Taslima.
Lajja (Shame).

1993
Published

1993
Banned in Bangladesh on the grounds that it had "created misunderstanding among communities." A fatwa, or death decree, was issued by a mullah, or Muslim cleric, of the Council of Soldiers of Islam, a militant group based in Sylhet, Bangladesh. The author fled to Stockholm, Sweden, and remained in exile in Europe and the United States.

2012
The head teacher at the K.C. Technical and Business Management College in Dhaka, Bangladesh, was arrested after the book, considered blasphemous by some Muslims, was found in the school's library. The teacher could face up to three years in jail if he is found guilty of authorizing the book's inclusion in the library. The *Prothom Alo* newspaper said the teacher denied having the book and said he was the victim of a conspiracy. The novel was banned a year after its publication in 1993, and Nasrin was forced to flee Bangladesh to escape death threats from radical Muslims who considered it blasphemous for advocating secularism.
Source: 8, pp. 255–58; 11, Mar. 2012, p. 63.

1256
National Register Publishing Co. Official Catholic Directory.

1991 OR
Challenged by a patron who believed public funds should not be expended on religious books, but retained, at the Multnomah County Library.
Source: 11, Jan. 1992, p. 6.

1257
Naylor, Phyllis Reynolds.
Achingly Alice.

1998
Published

2002 MO
Banned from the Webb City school library because the book promotes homosexuality and discusses issues "best left to parents."
Source: 11, Nov. 2002, p. 256.

1258
Naylor, Phyllis Reynolds.
The Agony of Alice.

1985
Published

2000 VA
Challenged, but retained, at the Franklin Sherman Elementary School library and on the Fairfax County approved reading list. The book, however, is limited in its classroom use to small discussion groups for girls only.
Source: 11, Mar. 2000, p. 62.

1259
Naylor, Phyllis Reynolds.
Alice in Lace.

1996
Published

2002 MO
Banned from the Webb City school library because the book promotes homosexuality and discusses issues "best left to parents."
Source: 11, Nov. 2002, p. 256.

1260
Naylor, Phyllis Reynolds.
Alice In-Between.

1994
Published

1998 CT
Removed from the Monroe sixth-grade required reading list after some parents called attention to the book's sexual content. The series of books by the Newbery Award-winning children's author includes *The Agony of Alice* and *Outrageously Alice.*
Source: 11, Nov. 1998, p. 182.

1261
Naylor, Phyllis Reynolds.
Alice on Her Way.

2005
Published

2008 WA
Restricted to students who have parental consent at the Icicle River Middle School library in Leavenworth due to its depiction of sexuality. One other book, Gary Paulsen's *Harris and Me,* has been similarly restricted at the school for almost a decade. Parents challenged the book's use during classroom reading because of "two cuss words."
Source: 11, May 2008, p. 97.

1262
Naylor, Phyllis Reynolds.
Alice on the Outside.

1999
Published

2005 KY
Available with parental permission in the librarian's office at Shelbyville East Middle School because the book is "too sexually explicit" for middle-school students.
Source: 11, May 2005, p. 108; July 2005, pp. 185–86.

1263
Naylor, Phyllis Reynolds.
Alice the Brave.

1995
Published

2004 TX
Challenged in the Mesquite Pirrung Elementary School library due to sexual references.
Source: 11, Nov. 2004, p. 231.

1264
Naylor, Phyllis Reynolds.
All But Alice.

1992
Published

1997 ME
Restricted to students with parental permission at the Monroe Elementary School library in Thorndike.

1997 MN
Removed from the elementary school libraries in the Rosemount-Apple Valley-Eagan Independent School District # 196 because of a brief passage in which the seventh-grade heroine discusses sexually oriented rock lyrics with her father and older brother; the school board considered the book inappropriate for the ages of the students.
Source: 11, Sept. 1997, pp. 126, 148; Nov. 1997, p. 166.

1265
Naylor, Phyllis Reynolds.
The Fear Place.

1994
Published

1998 IA
Challenged at the Madison Elementary School in Cedar Rapids. A review committee asked that the book carry a warning about objectionable language and that teachers consider notifying parents if they are going to use the book in class.
Source: 11, May 1998, pp. 87–88.

1266
Naylor, Phyllis Reynolds.
The Grooming of Alice.

2000
Published

2002 MO
Banned from the Webb City school library because the book promotes homosexuality and discusses issues "best left to parents."
Source: 11, Nov. 2002, p. 256.

1267
Naylor, Phyllis Reynolds.
Intensely Alice.

2009
Published

2013 MO
Challenged, but retained, in the Buffalo middle school despite the principal's formal complaint against several "very questionable pages" featuring a safe sex scene.
Source: 11, May 2013, pp. 123-24.

1268
Naylor, Phyllis Reynolds.
Lovingly Alice.

2004
Published

2011 AZ
Removed from the Quail Run Elementary library in the Paradise Valley Unified School District after the mother of an eight-year-old student complained about its sexual content.
Source: 11, July 2011, pp. 136-37.

1269
Naylor, Phyllis Reynolds.
Reluctantly Alice.

1991
Published

2006 NC
Challenged in the Wake County schools. Parents are getting help from Called2Action, a Christian group that says its mission is to "promote and defend our shared family and social values."
Source: 11, Sept. 2006, p. 231.

1270
Naylor, Phyllis Reynolds.
Send No Blessings.

1990
Published

1991
Best Books for Young Adults

1993 WA
Challenged at the Cedar Valley Elementary School in Kent because parents claimed the book condones child molestation and promiscuity.
Source: 11, Mar. 1993, p. 55.

1271
Naylor, Phyllis Reynolds.
Witch Herself.

1978
Published

1989 TX
Retained at the Ector County school library after being challenged because the book might lure children into the occult.
Source: 11, Jan. 1990, p. 9; May 1990, p. 107.

1272
Naylor, Phyllis Reynolds.
Witch Water.

1977
Published

1989 TX
Retained at the Ector County school library after being challenged because the book might lure children into the occult.
Source: 11, Jan. 1990, p. 9; May 1990, p. 107.

1273
Naylor, Phyllis Reynolds.
Witch's Sister.

1975
Published

1988 OR
Challenged at the Multnomah County Library in Portland because the occult topic could be frightening and traumatic for children.

1989 TX
Retained at the Ector County school library after being challenged because the book might lure children into the occult.
Source: 11, Jan. 1989, p. 3; Jan. 1990, p. 9; May 1990, p. 107.

1274
Nehring, James.
Why Do We Gotta Do This Stuff, Mr. Nehring?

1989
Published

1994 ID
Challenged, but retained, by the Pocatello Library Board, which refused to remove or label books that contain obscene language.
Source: 11, May 1994, pp. 97–98.

1275
Nelson, O. T.
The Girl Who Owned a City.

1975
Published

2000 ME
Challenged in the Fort Fairfield schools because the book promotes violence, including explaining how to make a Molotov cocktail.
Source: 11, July 2000, p. 104.

1276
Nelson, Theresa.
Earthshine.

1994
Published

1995
Best Books for Young Adults

1997 AK
Challenged, but retained, in the Anchorage school libraries. Parents of a student wanted the book removed from all public school libraries because "it contains profanity and deals with subjects like homosexuality, abortion, and children running away from home."
Source: 11, May 1997, p. 77.

1277
Neufeld, John.
Freddy's Book.

1973
Published

1977 IL
Removed from the elementary school library in Spring Valley after a parent complained about the book's theme.

1989 MI
Challenged, but retained, at the Lake Fenton Elementary School library because of the book's descriptions of male and female genitalia, menstruation, erections, sexual intercourse, and wet dreams. The book was, however, placed on a restricted shelf and requires parents to check the book out. Partly as a result of the controversy, all of the district's library books were slated to be reviewed by a four-member committee consisting of a parent, teacher, librarian, and district administrator.
Source: 11, Jan. 1978, p. 6; Jan. 1990, p. 9.

1278
Neville, Henry.
Isle of Pines.

1668
Published

1668 MA
Banned the year of its publication after authorities in the Massachusetts colony discovered it while searching for unlicensed material on the premises of the only two printers in the colony.
Source: 13, p. 116.

1279
Newman, Felice.
The Whole Lesbian Sex Book.

1999
Published

2007 AR
The father of two teenage boys asked city officials to fine the Bentonville Public Library for keeping the book on open shelves. He wanted the city to pay him $10,000 per child, the maximum allowed under Arkansas obscenity law. After receiving the original complaint, the library advisory committee board voted to remove the book from circulation and look for a similar, less graphic resource for the open stacks. The library director said she disagreed with the complainant's conclusion that having Newman's book in the library follows an "immoral social agenda."
Source: 11, July 2007, p. 143.

1280
Newman, Leslea.
Gloria Goes to Gay Pride.

1991
Published

1992 NY
Removed from the Brooklyn School District's curriculum because the school board objected to words that were "age inappropriate."

1993 OH
Retained at the Dayton and Montgomery County Public Library.

1994 AZ
Challenged at the Chandler Public Library because the book is a "skillful presentation to the young child about lesbianism/homosexuality."

Source: 11, May 1992, p. 83; Mar. 1994, p. 69; July 1994, p. 128; Nov. 1994, p. 187.

1281
Newman, Leslea.
Heather Has Two Mommies.

1989
Published

1992 NC
Challenged, but retained, at the Cumberland County Library. Opponents argued the book promoted a dangerous and ungodly lifestyle from which children must be protected.

1992 NY
Removed from the Brooklyn School District's curriculum because the school board objected to words that were "age inappropriate."

1993 AZ
Challenged at the Mesa Public Library because it "is vile, sick, and goes against every law and constitution."

1993 GA
Moved from the children's section to the young adult section at the Chestatee Regional Library System in Gainesville. Three area legislators wanted the book removed and said, "We could put together a resolution to amend the Georgia state constitution to say that tax dollars cannot be used to promote homosexuality, pedophilia, or sado-masochism."

1993 MD
Challenged at the Wicomico County Free Library in Salisbury.

1993 NC
Moved from the children's section to the adult section in Elizabethtown library because it "promotes a dangerous and ungodly lifestyle from which children must be protected."

1993 NJ
Moved from the children's section to the adult section at the Mercer County Library System in Lawrence.

1993 NJ
Challenged at the North Brunswick Public Library.

1993 OH
Retained at the Dayton and Montgomery County Public Library.

1994 AZ
Challenged at the Chandler Public Library because the book is a "skillful presentation to the young child about lesbianism/homosexuality."

1994 MA
Challenged, but retained, in the Oak Bluffs school library. Though the parent leading the protest stated "The subject matter… is obscene and vulgar and the message is that homosexuality is okay," the selection review committee voted unanimously to keep the book.

1994 OR
Removed by officials at the Cottage Grove Lane County Head Start Center.

1998 TX
Challenged at the Wichita Falls Public Library. The deacon body of the First Baptist Church requested that any literature that promotes or sanctions a homosexual lifestyle be removed. The Wichita Falls City Council established a policy that allows library card holders who collect 300 signatures to have children's books moved to an adult portion of the library. U.S. District Court Judge Jerry Buchmeyer struck down the library resolution as unconstitutional and the books were returned.

1999 ID
Challenged, but retained, in the juvenile non-fiction section of the Nampa Public Library.

Source: 11, May 1992, p. 83; Jan. 1993, pp. 9, 28; May 1993, p. 71; July 1993, pp. 100–101, 126; Sept. 1993, pp. 143–44; Nov. 1993, pp. 177–78; Jan. 1994, pp. 13, 34-35; Mar. 1994, p. 69; May 1994, p. 98; July 1994, pp. 110, 115; Sept. 1994, pp. 147 –48, 166; Nov. 1994, p. 187; July 1998, pp. 106–7; Jan. 1999, pp. 8–9; Mar. 1999, p. 36; May 1999, p. 67; Sept. 1999, p. 131; Nov. 1999, p. 172; Nov. 2000, pp. 201–2.

1282
Newton, Michael.
The Encyclopedia of Serial Killers.

1992
Published

2002 FL
Challenged and retained in the Hillsborough County School District over a parent's objections to the book's "gruesome details."

Source: 11, July 2002, p. 179.

1283
Nichols, John.
The Milagro Beanfield War.

1974
Published

1999 OH
Pulled from a junior English class at the Shawnee High School in Lima because it contained offensive material, including sex and violence.

Source: 11, July 1999, p. 97.

1284
Nix, Garth.
Shade's Children.

1997
Published

1997
Best Books for Young Adults

2001 NY
Challenged, but retained, at the Transit Middle School library in Williamsville after objections that the book "is vulgar, obscene, and educationally unsuitable."

Source: 11, May 2001, p. 124.

1285
Nixon, Joan Lowery.
Whispers from the Dead.

1989
Published

2008 NY
Restored by the Lackawanna School Board along with several other books following accusations of censorship by some parents and teachers. The books were pulled from the middle school library recommended list because of concerns that the books deal with the occult.
Source: 11, May 2008, p. 116.

1286
Noel, Janet.
The Human Body.

1973
Published

1982 ME
The York Middle School review committee voted unanimously to remove the book from the library "because of the inappropriateness of written and pictorial material." After a backlash from anti-censorship parents, the book was moved from the middle school library to the junior high library for use by seventh and eighth graders.
Source: 11, July 1982, pp. 123–24.

1287
Norstog, Knut J., and Andrew J. Meyerriecks.
Biology.

1983
Published

1986 OK
A Sallisaw Senior High School biology teacher removed pages 467–76 from the textbook because they were "irrelevant" to the school's curriculum requirements. The pages contained information on reproduction and birth control. The teacher said he was "trying to circumvent a problem, rather than create one, when students were forced to take the books parents might find objectionable into their homes."
Source: 11, July 1986, p. 121.

1288
Norton, Jim.
Happy Endings: The Tales of a Meaty-Breasted Zilch.

2007
Published

2007 MS
Available upon request, but not placed in general circulation at the Jackson-George Regional Library System in Pascagoula after complaints that the comedian's best-selling book is "garbage that doesn't belong in a library."
Source: 11, Nov. 2007, p. 263.

1289
Nunokawa, Jeff.
Oscar Wilde.

1995
Published

2000 CA
Removed from the Anaheim school district because school officials said the book is too difficult for middle school students and that it could cause harassment against students seen with it. The American Civil Liberties Union (ACLU) of Southern California filed suit in *Doe v. Anaheim Union High School District* alleging that the removal is "a pretext for viewpoint-based censorship." The ACLU claims no other books have been removed from the junior high library for similar reasons, even though several, such as works by Shakespeare and Dickens, are more difficult reading. The ACLU contends that the school officials engaged in unconstitutional viewpoint discrimination by removing the book because it contains gay and lesbian material. In March 2001, the school board approved a settlement that restored the book to the high school shelves and amended the district's policy to prohibit the removal of books for subject matter involving sexual orientation, but the book will not be returned to the middle school.
Source: 11, Mar. 2001, p. 53; May 2001, p. 95; July 2001, p. 173.

1290
Nye, Robert.
Beowulf, a New Telling.

1968
Published

1998 OR
Challenged, but retained, in the Hood River County schools. A parent complained that the book was "inappropriate for middle school students because of the evil intentions of its characters, graphic descriptions of gore and mutilations, and descriptions of monstrous characters."
Source: 11, July 1998, p. 121.

1291
Oates, Joyce Carol.
Sexy.

2005
Published

2007 MT
Retained at Jefferson High School in Boulder despite objections to "inappropriate" language and sexually explicit passages in the novel.
Source: 11, Jan. 2008, p. 25.

1292
Oates, Joyce Carol.
Where Are You Going, Where Have You Been?

1966
Published

1990 PA
Challenged in the Tyrone schools because of its use of profane language.
Source: 11, Mar. 1991, pp. 61–62.

1293
Oates, Stephen.
Portrait of America, Vol. II.

1973
Published

1984 WI
Returned to the Racine Unified School District curriculum just one week after the school board voted to ban it. Opponents of the books on the board charged that the social studies volumes contained "judgmental writing" and, in the words of one board member, "a lot more funny pictures of Republicans and nicer pictures of Democrats." Opponents also said that one text did not present an adequate analysis of the Vietnam War.
Source: 11, Sept. 1984, p. 158.

1294
O'Brien, Edna.
August Is a Wicked Month.

1965
Published

1960

All novels published by Edna O'Brien during the 1960s were banned in Ireland by the Censorship of Publications Board: *The Country Girls* (1960); *The Lonely Girl* (1962) and its reprint *Girl with Green Eyes* (1964); *Girls in Their Married Bliss* (1964); and *August Is a Wicked Month* (1965). O'Brien's work gained notoriety in Ireland in the 1960s because of its detailed exploration of female sexuality.

1965

Banned in Australia.

1965

Banned in Rhodesia.

1965

Banned in South Africa.

Source: 6, pp. 1,749–50.

1295
O'Brien, Kate.
The Land of the Spices.

1941

Published

1941

Banned in Ireland by the Censorship of Publications Board. The impact of the banning was considerable. In the short term, it drew attention to the extremes to which the Censorship Board went in recommending books to be banned, particularly those by Irish authors. In the long term, the 1942 Irish Senate debate initiated the discussions that led to the creation of a Censorship of Publications Appeal Board in 1946.

Source: 6, pp. 1,750–51.

1296
O'Brien, Sharon.
Willa Cather.

1995

Published

2000 CA

Removed from the Anaheim school district because school officials said the book is too difficult for middle school students and that it could cause harassment against students seen with it. The American Civil Liberties Union (ACLU) of Southern California filed suit in *Doe v. Anaheim Union High School District* alleging that the removal is "a pretext for viewpoint-based censorship." The ACLU claims no other books have been removed from the junior high library for similar reasons, even though several, such as works by Shakespeare and Dickens, are more difficult reading. The ACLU contends that the school officials engaged in unconstitutional viewpoint discrimination by removing the book because it contains gay and lesbian material. In March 2001, the school board approved a settlement that restored the book to the high school shelves and amended the district's policy to prohibit the removal of books for subject matter involving sexual orientation, but the book will not be returned to the middle school.

Source: 11, Mar. 2001, p. 53; May 2001, p. 95; July 2001, p. 173.

1297
O'Brien, Tim.
In the Lake of the Woods.

1994

Published

1998 WA

Challenged for use in the Richland high school English classes along with six other titles because the "books are poor-quality literature and stress suicide, illicit sex, violence, and hopelessness."

Source: 11, Mar. 1999, p. 40.

1298
O'Brien, Tim.
The Things They Carried.

1990

Published

1990

Best Books for Young Adults

1990

National Book Critics Circle Fiction Finalist

1990

Prix du Meilleur Livre Etranger

1991

Pulitzer Prize for Fiction

1992 WI

Determined unsuitable for classroom reading in Waukesha because of "anti-American attitudes, offensive language, political bias, and disturbing fiction."

2000 PA

Challenged, but retained, at the Pennridge high school despite a protest of the book's strong language.

2002 MS

Banned from the George County schools because of profanity.

2006 IL

Retained on the Northwest Suburban High School District 214 reading list in Arlington Heights, along with eight other challenged titles. A board member, elected amid promises to bring her Christian beliefs into all board decision-making, raised the controversy based on excerpts from the books she'd found on the Internet.

Source: 11, Jan. 2001, p. 37; Mar. 2003, p. 55; July 2006, pp. 210-11.

1299
Ockler, Sarah.
Twenty Boy Summer.

2009

Published

2010 MO

Removed from Republic High School, but later returned and stored in a secure section of the library only accessible to parents. Teachers cannot require the book nor read it aloud in school. A Republic resident filed a complaint about the appropriateness of the book because it sensationalizes "sexual promiscuity, questionable language, drunkenness, lying to parents, and a lack of remorse by the characters."

Source: 11, Nov. 2010, pp. 243-44; Sept. 2011, p. 175; Nov. 2011, p. 203.

1300
O'Connor, Flannery.
The Complete Stories.

1971

Published

1972

National Book Award for Fiction

2000 LA

Prohibited at the Opelousas Catholic High School by Bishop Edward J. O'Donnell of Lafayette along with any "similar book." Some parents protested when they saw the word "nigger" in the collection of short stories assigned for summer reading.

Source: 11, Jan. 2001, p. 13.

1301
O'Connor, Frank.
Dutch Interior.

1940
Published

1940
Banned in Ireland. The Irish Republic's Censorship Board was not required to state publicly why it banned individual books as "indecent or obscene," but it was widely believed that O'Connor's novel and short stories were so treated primarily because of their critique of the Irish Catholic middle class.
Source: 6, pp. 1,757–58.

1302
O'Connor, Jane.
Just Good Friends.

1983
Published

1988 OR
Removed from the Jefferson Magnet Arts Library and transferred to a middle school in Eugene because of the book's sexual references.
Source: 11, Jan. 1989, p. 3.

1303
O'Connor, Jane.
Lu Lu and the Witch Baby.

1986
Published

1991 IL
Challenged at the Dakota Primary School because it "promotes lying and witchcraft."
Source: 11, May 1991, p. 89.

1304
O'Donnell, E. P.
Green Margins.

1936
Published

1937 LA
Seized and destroyed by New Orleans police.
Source: 15, Vol. III, p. 650.

1305
O'Faolain, Sean.
Midsummer Night Madness and Other Stories.

1932
Published

1932
Banned in Ireland.
Source: 6, pp. 1,761–62.

1306
Oh, Minya.
Bling Bling: Hip Hop's Crown Jewels.

2005
Published

2008 WI
Retained with limited access at the Maplewood Middle School Library in Menasha. The book for reluctant readers contains photographs and interviews with rap artists and focuses on how hiphop taste for flashy jewelry typifies their musical and cultural evolution of the last twenty-five years. In addition to retaining the book, board members voted unanimously to adopt procedures intended to secure and record parental consent before limited access books are released to students.
Source: 11, July 2008, p. 164.

1307
O'Hara, Frank.
Lunch Poems.

1964
Published

1976 CO
Banned for use in Aurora High School English classes on the grounds of "immorality."
Source: 11, May 1977, p. 79.

1308
O'Hara, John.
Appointment in Samarra.

1934
Published

1941
Declared not mailable by the U.S. Post Office Department because of "obscene language." The novel remained on the U.S. Post Office's index of banned books through the mid-1950s. The novel also attracted the attention of the National Organization for Decent Literature (NODL), a Roman Catholic organization that identified "objectionable" literature and advised members against reading "offensive" and "objectionable" novels. In 1953, NODL found the novel to be "objectionable" and placed it on their list of blacklisted books. The list was then sent to cooperating book dealers who agreed to remove the book from their racks.

1941 MI
Banned from sale in Port Huron.

1941 MI
Banned from sale in Detroit.

1950 MN
Banned from sale in St. Cloud during the 1950s. Sales were limited in numerous other cities, through the efforts of local chapters of the NODL, until the demise of the organization in the late 1950s.
Source: 4, p. 86; 8, pp. 409–10.

1309
O'Hara, John.
Ten North Frederick.

1955
Published

1956
National Book Award for Fiction

1957 MI
Banned by Police Commissioner in Detroit, a series of local bans and seizures spread over a two-year period from 1957 to 1958.
Source: 4, pp. 86–87.

1310
O'Hara, Mary.
My Friend Flicka.

1941
Published

1990 FL
Pulled from fifth- and sixth-grade optional reading lists in Clay County schools because the book uses the word "bitch" to refer to a female dog, as well as the word "damn."
Source: 11, Jan. 1991, p. 16.

1311
O'Huigin, Sean.
Scary Poems for Rotten Kids.

1989
Published

1990 MI
Challenged in the Livonia schools because the poems frightened first-grade children.
Source: 11, Mar. 1991, p. 62.

1312
O'Keeffe, Georgia.
Georgia O'Keeffe.

1993
Published

1994 AZ
Retained at Maldonado Elementary School in Tucson after being challenged by parents who objected to nudity and "pornographic," "perverted," and "morbid" themes.
Source: 11, July 1994, p. 112.

1313
The Old Farmer's Almanac.

1941
During World War II, according to Robb Sagendorph, the U.S. Army temporarily banned the publication on the grounds that its weather forecasts aided the enemy.
Source: 6, p. 45.

1314
O'Malley, Kevin, illus.
Froggy Went A-Courtin'.

1992
Published

1996 MD
This version of the folk song was restricted at the Baltimore County school libraries because of Froggy's nefarious activities including burning money, and speeding away from the cat police, as well as robbery and smoking. The book is to be kept in restricted areas of the libraries where only parents and teachers will be allowed to check it out and read it to children.
Source: 11, Jan. 1997, p. 7; Mar. 1997, p. 36.

1315
Opie, Iona Archibald, and Peter Opie, eds.
I Saw Esau: The Schoolchild's Pocket Book.

2000
Published

2007 TN
Challenged at the Cedar Grove Elementary School in Murfreesboro. The complainant stated, "I understand that it is a book of poetry, but there is a fine line between poetry art and porn and this book's illustrations are absolutely offensive in every way." The book is a collection of schoolyard jokes, riddles, insults, and jump-rope rhymes and is illustrated by Maurice Sendak.
Source: 11, May 2007, p. 94.

1316
Oppenheim, Irene.
Living Today.

1981
Published

1984 WI
Returned to the Racine Unified School District curriculum just one week after the school board voted to ban it. The home economics text was criticized for encouraging premarital sex and advocating that unmarried couples live together.
Source: 11, Sept. 1984, p. 158.

1317
Orenstein, Peggy.
Schoolgirls: Young Women, Self-esteem and the Confidence Gap.

1994
Published

1996 OH
Challenged in Courtland High School because of its "rotten, filthy language." The teacher offered the parents a black marker with which to delete offending passages, but the parents wanted it banned. The school board voted to continue the book.
Source: 11, Mar. 1997, p. 50.

1318
Orgel, Doris.
The Devil in Vienna.

1988
Published

2000 IA
Challenged, but retained, at the Grant Wood Elementary School media center in Cedar Rapids despite objections to the book's inclusion of a brief incident of an old man exposing himself to a six-year-old girl.
Source: 11, Mar. 2000, p. 61.

1319
Ortiz, Victoria.
The Land and People of Cuba.

1973
Published

1974 FL
Removed from the Rockaway Junior High School school library in Miami by the principal because the book "was anti-American propaganda favoring the pro-Castro viewpoint."

1974 FL
Rejected by Dade County's public libraries.
Source: 7, pp. 294–95.

1320
Orwell, George.
1984.

1949
Published

1981 FL
Challenged in the Jackson County School Board because Orwell's novel is "pro-communist and contained explicit sexual matter."
Source: 8, pp. 141–42; 9; 11, May 1981, p. 73.

1321
Orwell, George.
Animal Farm.

1945
Published

1963 WI
A Wisconsin survey revealed that the John Birch Society had challenged the novel's use; it objected to the words "masses will revolt."

1968 NY
The New York State English Council's Committee on Defenses Against Censorship conducted a comparable study in New York State English classrooms. Its findings identified the novel on its list of "problem books;" the reason cited was that "Orwell was a communist."

1977
Suppressed from being displayed at the Moscow, Russia, International Book Fair.

1982 GA
A survey of censorship challenges in the schools, conducted in DeKalb County for the period 1979 to 1982, revealed that the novel had been objected to for its political theories.

1987 FL
Banned from Bay County's four middle schools and three high schools in Panama City by the Bay County school superintendent. After 44 parents filed a suit against the district claiming that its instructional aids policy denies constitutional rights, the Bay County School Board reinstated the book, along with sixty-four others banned.

2002
Banned from schools in the United Arab Emirates, along with 125 others. The Ministry of Education banned it on the grounds that it contained written or illustrated material that contradicts Islamic and Arab values—in this text, pictures of alcoholic drinks, pigs, and other "indecent images."
Source: 8, pp. 15–16.

1322
Ostrovsky, Victor, and Claire Hoy.
By Way of Deception: The Making and Unmaking of a Mossad Officer.

1990
Published

1990
The government of Israel initiated the challenges through lawsuits seeking to block publication.

1990
The Israelis won a court order in Toronto, Ontario, Canada, that blocked publication. Israel's request was based on its claim that the book "would disseminate confidential information and that this information could endanger the lives of various people in the employ of the State of Israel and would be detrimental to the State of Israel."

1990 NY
The New York Supreme Court found the Israeli claims of endangered lives "groundless" and that the "heavy presumption against a prior restraint on publication" had not been overcome. Following this ruling, the Israeli government withdrew its lawsuit in Canada.
Source: 7, p. 84.

1323
Othman, Norani, ed.
Muslim Women and the Challenges of Islamic Extremism.

2005
Published

2008
Banned by the Malaysian Ministry of Home Affairs on the grounds that it was "prejudicial to public order" and that it could confuse Muslims, particularly Muslim women. The Malaysian High Court overturned the ban on January 25, 2010; and on March 14, 2013, the Federal Court threw out the government's appeal to reinstate the ban.
Source: 11, May 2013, pp. 125-26.

1324
Ovid.
The Art of Love.

1 B.C.
Published

8 A.D.
Emperor Augustus banished the author.

1497
Burned in Florence, Italy.

1599
Proscribed in the Tridentine Index of 1564, and in England in 1599 a translation

by the poet Christopher Marlowe was burned at Stationer's Hall on the orders of the archbishop of Canterbury, on account of its immorality.

1929
Barred by U.S. Customs.
Source: 3, p. 415; 4, p. 2; 6, pp. 1,787–88; 8, p. 320.

1325
Ovid.
Elegies.

16 B.C.
Published

1497
Burned in Florence, Italy.

1599
Burned in England.
Source: 4, p. 2.

1326
Oxenbury, Helen.
Tiny Tim: Verses for Children.

1981
Published

1987 NJ
Challenged at the Cherry Hill Elementary School because the book is too violent. One rhyme reads: "I had a little brother, his name is Tiny Tim. I put him in the bathtub to teach him how to swim. He drank up all the water. He ate up all the soap. He died last night with a bubble in his throat." In another rhyme, a man "who had a face made out of cake" was baked in an oven and exploded.
Source: 11, July 1987, p. 149.

1327
Packer, Kenneth L., and Jeannine Bower.
Let's Talk about Health.

1980
Published

1986 OR
Challenged at the Salem-Keizer School District because of the book's handling of issues such as dating, premarital sex, homosexuality, and masturbation.
Source: 11, May 1986, p. 84.

1328
Paine, Thomas.
The Age of Reason.

1793
Published

1792

Author and publisher imprisoned in France because of his hostility to the Jacobins.

1797

Prosecuted in England, and Richard Carlile was prosecuted for publishing the works of Paine, was fined 1,000 pounds and imprisoned for two years in 1819. But because Paine never hesitated to speak his mind, by the end of his life he had become an outcast in America, England, and France. Although he spent his final years in America, he was ostracized and shunned as an atheist and as a traitor to the cause of freedom. He survived a murder attempt, was stripped of his right to vote, and labeled a blasphemer.

1812

Publisher Daniel Isaac Eaton was prosecuted and found guilty of the crime of blasphemy; he was sentenced to stand in the pillory and to serve eighteen months in Newgate Prison, London, England. Publisher Richard Carlisle served more than nine years between 1817 and 1835; his wife, his sister, and more than twenty of his workers were also prosecuted and imprisoned.

Source: 2, p. 7; 3, pp. 7-8; 4, pp. 33-34; 8, pp. 202-3.

1329
Paine, Thomas.
The Rights of Man.

1791-92
Published

1792

Author and publisher imprisoned in France because of his hostility to the Jacobins.

1797

Prosecuted in England, and Richard Carlile was prosecuted for publishing the works of Paine, was fined 1,000 pounds and imprisoned for two years in England (1819). But because Paine never hesitated to speak his mind, by the end of his life

he had become an outcast in America, England, and France. Although he spent his final years in America, he was ostracized and shunned as an atheist and as a traitor to the cause of freedom. He survived a murder attempt, was stripped of his right to vote, and labeled a blasphemer.

Source: 4, pp. 33-34; 8, pp. 160-62.

1330
Palahniuk, Chuck.
Choke: A Novel.

2001
Published

2005 AR

Challenged in the Fayetteville High School library. The complainant also submitted a list of more than fifty books, citing the books as too sexually explicit and promoting homosexuality.

Source: 11, Sept. 2005, p. 215.

1331
Palahniuk, Chuck.
Fight Club.

1996
Published

2012 TX

Removed from the Katy Independent School District required reading list following parental complaints about the book's violent nature and explicit undertones.

Source: 11, Mar. 2013, p. 50.

1332
Parish, James Robert.
Whoopi Goldberg: Her Journey from Poverty to Mega-Stardom.

1997
Published

2000 WI

Challenged in the Muskego-Norway School District because it contains vulgar language.

Source: 11, July 2000, p. 105; Nov. 2000, p. 216.

1333
Park, Barbara.
Junie B. Jones and Some Sneaky, Peeky Spying.

1994
Published

2006 NC

Challenged in the Wake County schools. Parents are getting help from Called2Action, a Christian group that says its mission is to "promote and defend our shared family and social values."

Source: 11, Sept. 2006, p. 231.

1334
Park, Barbara.
Junie B. Jones and the Stupid Smelly Bus.

1992
Published

1998 NJ

Challenged, but retained, in the second-grade reading curriculum at the Harmony Township school. A parent complained that the book sends a message to children that extreme emotions such as hate are fine, and that the book never resolves any of the issues it raises or points out that there are ways to handle negative emotions constructively.

Source: 11, Nov. 1998, pp. 191-92.

1335
Park, Barbara.
Mick Harte Was Here.

1995
Published

1998 SC

Challenged, but retained, at the Liberty Middle School Library in Seneca after a seventh grader's grandmother complained to school officials.

2004 ND

Challenged, but retained, at the Centennial Elementary School library in Fargo after parents complained to school officials that the book contains themes and language inappropriate for elementary students.

Source: 11, May 1998, p. 70; Nov. 2004, pp. 229-30; Jan. 2005, p. 27; May 2005, p. 131.

1336

Parker, Stephen.
Life Before Birth: The Story of the First Nine Months.

1979
Published

1987 WA
Placed on restricted shelves at the Evergreen School District elementary school libraries in Vancouver in accordance with the school board policy to restrict student access to sex education books in elementary school libraries.
Source: 11, May 1987, p. 87.

1337

Parks, Gordon.
The Learning Tree.

1964
Published

1976 WY
Temporarily banned from the junior high school in Cheyenne.

1978 MD
Citizens United for Responsible Education demanded that Park's novel be removed from the Montgomery County school system.

1979 RI
Challenged at the Westerly High School.

1982 WA
Subject of a court challenge by the Moral Majority of Washington State in Mead because it includes "objectionable material, swearing, obscene language, explicit detail of premarital sexual intercourse, other lewd behavior, specific blasphemies against Jesus Christ and excessive violence and murder." The case was dismissed by U.S. District Court Judge Robert McNichols.

1991 FL
Removed from, and then restored to, a Suwannee High School library because the book is "indecent."

1992 MN
Challenged at Eagan High School on the grounds that it contains vulgar and sexually explicit language and descriptions of violent acts.

2006 AL
Challenged on the summer reading list at LeFlore High School in Mobile because the author frequently used inappropriate words, such as "nigga," "bitch," "bastard," and "ass."
Source: 9; 11, July 1976, p. 68; Sept. 1978, p. 123; May 1979, p. 59; Nov. 1982, p. 212; Jan. 1992, p. 25; Mar. 1993, p. 56; Nov. 2006, p. 290.

1338

Parr, Todd.
The Family Book.

2003
Published

2012 IL
Banned from an Erie elementary school's shelves because of a line that reads, "some families have two moms or two dads." The district also banned everything furnished by GLSEN (Gay, Lesbian and Straight Education Network), including learning materials and various programs aimed at preventing bullying.
Source: 11, July 2012, p. 157; Sept. 2012, pp. 202-3.

1339

Parsipur, Shahrnush.
Touba and the Meaning of Night.

1989
Published

1989
Banned in Iran because of the novel's controversial depiction of women. The main character's exploration of orthodox religion, Sufism, nationalism, and other forms of thoughts did not sit comfortably with the Islamic Republic. In addition to the novel's content, Parsipur's writing style blurs the boundaries between reality and fiction. Imprisoned both by the shah's security agency and later the Islamic Republic, the author sought political refugee status and moved to the United States in 1994. A critically acclaimed bestseller in Iran, the novel, like all of the author's books of fiction and memoir, remains banned.
Source: 1, pp. 353-54.

1340

Parsipur, Shahrnush.
Women Without Men: A Novel of Modern Iran.

1989
Published

1989
Banned in Iran as "un-Islamic" because of its treatment of the themes of virginity, rape, prostitution, failed marriage, and references to Western culture. The novella proved to be far too radical in its critique of male patriarchy, and while it brought Parsipur success, it also prompted the government to arrest her. Mohammad Reza Aslani, the publisher and owner of Noghreh Publishing, was also arrested, and his publishing house was immediately closed down. In 1994, Parsipur sought political refugee status and moved to the United States.
Source: 1, pp. 353-54.

1341

Parsons, Alexander.
Leaving Disneyland.

2001
Published

2005 MD
Banned in Carroll County schools. No reason stated.
Source: 11, Mar. 2006, pp. 70-71.

1342

Partridge, Eric.
Dictionary of Slang and Unconventional English.

1937
Published

1973 FL
Challenged in Pinellas County due to profanity.
Source: 11, Mar. 1974, p. 32.

1343

Pascal, Blaise.
Pensées.

1670
Published

1789
Placed on the *Index Librorum Prohibitorum* (List of Prohibited Books) in Rome, Italy.
Source: 4, p. 24.

1344
Pascal, Blaise.
The Provincial Letters.

1656-1657
Published

1657
Burned in France for its alleged anti-religiosity. Louis XIV ordered in 1660 that it "be torn up and burned… at the hands of the High Executioner, fulfillment of which is to be certified to His Majesty within the week; and that meanwhile all printers, booksellers, vendors and others, of whatever rank and station, are explicitly prohibited from printing selling, and distributing, and even from having in their possession the said book… under the pain of public, exemplary punishment."

1664
First placed on the *Index Librorum Prohibitorum* (List of Prohibited Books) in Rome, Italy. Pascal's works remained there until the 20th century.
Source: 3, p. 427.

1345
Pascal, Francine.
Hanging Out with Cici.

1977
Published

1986 CO
Challenged at the Greeley-Evans School District in Greeley because the book contained "obscenities, allusions to sexual references, and promoted contempt for parents and acceptance of drug use."
Source: 11, Sept. 1986, p. 171.

1346
Pasternak, Boris Leonidovich.
Doctor Zhivago.

1958
Published

1958
Nobel Prize in Literature

1958
Moscow, Russia, condemned the book, refused to publish it, and vilified the author.

1961
A year after Pasternak's death his friend and collaborator Olga Ivinskaya was arrested for allegedly receiving foreign royalties for Pasternak's works. She was sentenced to eight years imprisonment and hard labor in Siberia, and her daughter received three years for alleged complicity.
Source: 4, p. 73; 6, pp. 1,823–24; 8, pp. 44–45.

1347
Paterson, Katherine.
Bridge to Terabithia.

1977
Published

1978
Newbery Medal

1986 NE
Challenged as sixth-grade recommended reading in the Lincoln schools because it contains "profanity" including the phrase "Oh, Lord" and "Lord" used as an expletive.

1990 CT
Challenged as suitable curriculum material in the Harwinton and Burlington schools because it contains language and subject matter that set bad examples and give students negative views of life.

1992 CA
Challenged at the Apple Valley Unified School District because of vulgar language.

1992 PA
Challenged at the Mechanicsburg Area School District because of profanity and references to witchcraft.

1992 TX
Challenged and retained in the libraries, but will not be required reading, at the Cleburne Independent School district because of profane language.

1993 KS
A challenge to this book in Oskaloosa led to the enactment of a new policy that requires teachers to examine their required material for profanities. Teachers will list each profanity and the number of times it was used in the book, and forward the list to parents, who will be asked to give written permission for their children to read the material.

1993 PA
Challenged in the Gettysburg public schools because of offensive language.

1995 ME
Challenged at the Medway schools because the book uses "swear words."

1996 PA
Removed from the fifth-grade classrooms of the New Brighton Area School District in Pulaski Township due to "profanity, disrespect of adults, and an elaborate fantasy world they felt might lead to confusion."

2002 CT
Challenged in the middle school curriculum in Cromwell due to concern that it promotes witchcraft and violence.
Source: 11, Mar. 1987, p. 67; Mar. 1991, p. 44; May 1992, p. 95; Sept. 1992, pp. 162–63; Nov. 1992, p. 198; Mar. 1993, p. 45; July 1993, pp. 105-6; Mar. 1994, p. 55; July 1995, p. 97; May 1996, p. 88; Sept. 2002, p. 197; Nov. 2002, pp. 257–58.

1348
Paterson, Katherine.
The Great Gilly Hopkins.

1978
Published

1979
National Book Award for Children's Literature

1979
Newbery Honor Book

1983 KS
Challenged at the Lowell Elementary School in Salina because the book used the words "God," "damn," and "hell" offensively.

1985 MN
Challenged at the Orchard Lake Elementary School library in Burnsville because "the book took the Lord's name in vain" and had "over forty instances of profanity."

1988 CO
Challenged at the Jefferson County elementary schools because "Gilly's friends lie and steal, and there are no repercussions. Christians are portrayed as being dumb and stupid."

1991 CT
Pulled from, but later restored to, the language arts curriculum at four Cheshire elementary schools because the book is "filled with profanity, blasphemy and obscenities, and gutter language."

1992 TX
Challenged at the Alamo Heights School District elementary schools because it contains the words "hell" and "damn."

1993 KS
Challenged at the Walnut Elementary School in Emporia by parents who said that it contains profanity and graphic violence.

1997 NV
Challenged due to explicit language, but retained, in the Lander County School District.
Source: 11, July 1983, p. 121; Nov. 1985, p. 203; Mar. 1988, p. 45; Mar. 1992, p. 42; May 1992, p. 96; July 1992, pp. 109–10; Jan. 1993, p. 13; July 1993, pp. 126–27; Mar. 1998, p. 56.

1349
Paterson, Katherine.
Jacob Have I Loved.

1980
Published

1980
Best Books for Young Adults

1981
National Book Award for Young People's Literature

1981
Newbery Medal

1989 NJ
Challenged at the Bernardsville schools as unsuitable for a sixth-grade reading class. The book was offensive to several parents on moral and religious grounds.

1993 PA
Challenged in the Gettysburg public schools because of offensive language.
Source: 11, Jan. 1990, p. 33; Mar. 1994, p. 55.

1350
Paterson, Thomas.
American Foreign Policy, Vol. II.

1984 WI
Returned to the Racine Unified School District curriculum just one week after the school board voted to ban it. Opponents of the books on the board charged that the social studies volumes contained "judgmental writing" and, in the words of one board member, "a lot more funny pictures of Republicans and nicer pictures of Democrats." Opponents also said that one text did not present an adequate analysis of the Vietnam War.
Source: 11, Sept. 1984, p. 158.

1351
Patrick, John J., and Carol Berkin.
The History of the American Nation.

1986
Published

1987 MA
Challenged at the Amherst-Pelham Regional Junior High School by a group of parents who charge that, among other things, it is sexist and distorts the history of minorities.
Source: 11, Jan. 1988, p. 11.

1352
Patterson, James.
Cradle and All.

2000
Published

2007 NY
Removed from the Westhampton Beach High School's ninth-grade reading list because of "inappropriate sexual content." The reading list contains more than three hundred books from which ninth-graders must choose to read for course credit.
Source: 11, Jan. 2008, pp. 37-38; Mar. 2008, p. 63.

1353
Patterson, Lillie.
Halloween.

1963
Published

1992 AZ
Challenged at the Neely Elementary School in Gilbert because the book shows the dark side of religion through the occult, the devil, and satanism.
Source: 11, May 1992, p. 78; July 1992, p. 124.

1354
Paulsen, Gary.
The Foxman.

1977
Published

1994 IL
Challenged at Cary Junior High School because references in the book to sex are too explicit for seventh and eighth graders; retained by a school board vote.
Source: 11, May 1994, p. 83; July 1994, pp. 128–29.

1355
Paulsen, Gary.
Harris and Me.

1993
Published

1993
Best Books for Young Adults

1997 NV
Challenged due to explicit language, but retained, in the Lander County School District.
Source: 11, Mar. 1998, p. 56.

1356
Paulsen, Gary.
Nightjohn.

1993
Published

1993
Best Books for Young Adults

1998 VA
Challenged as a seventh-grade summer reading option in Prince William County because the book "was rife with profanity and explicit sex."
Source: 11, Nov. 1998, p. 183.

1357
Paulsen, Gary.
Zero to Sixty: The Motorcycle Journey of a Lifetime.

1999
Published

2006 TX
Removed from the West Brazoria Junior High School library because of depictions of sex acts and profanity. Books on "sensitive topics such as death, suicide, physical or sexual abuse, and teenage dating relationships" were moved to a restricted "young-adult" section from which students can borrow only with written parental permission.
Source: 11, Nov. 2006, pp. 289-90.

1358
Peck, M. Scott.
The Road Less Traveled.

1978
Published

2003 LA
Removed from the college bookstore at Louisiana College, Pineville, by the college president because "profane language in the book clashes with the school's Christian values."
Source: 11, Mar. 2004, pp. 53–54.

1359
Peck, Robert Newton.
A Day No Pigs Would Die.

1972
Published

1972
Best Books for Young Adults

1988 CO
Challenged in Jefferson County school libraries because "it is bigoted against Baptists and women and depicts violence, hatred, animal cruelty, and murder."

1990 CT
Challenged as suitable curriculum material in the Burlington and Harwinton schools because it contains language and subject matter that set bad examples and give students negative views of life.

1993 FL
Challenged at the Sherwood Elementary School in Melbourne because the book could give the "impression that rape and violence are acceptable." The comment was made in reference to a descriptive passage about a boar mating a sow in the barnyard.

1994 UT
Removed from seventh-grade classes at Payson Middle School after several parents "had problems with language, with animal breeding, and with a scene that involves an infant grave exhumation."

1994 WI
Challenged, but retained, on the shelves at Waupaca school libraries after a parent "objected to graphic passages dealing with sexuality in the book."

1995 OK
Challenged at the Pawhuska Middle School because the book uses bad language, gives "gory" details of mating, and lacks religious values.

1995 SC
Pulled from an Anderson middle school library because of the "gory" descriptions of two pigs mating, a pig being slaughtered, and a cow giving birth.

1996 MO
Challenged at the Anderson Junior High School because of its content.

1997 MI
Banned from the St. Lawrence School in Utica because of a passage involving pig breeding. The teacher quit her job over the banning of the novel.
Source: 11, May 1988, p. 85; July 1988, pp. 119–20, 139; Sept. 1988, pp. 151, 177; Mar. 1991, p. 44; May 1991, p. 90; July 1993, pp. 97–98; May 1994, pp. 98–99; July 1994, pp. 117, 129; July 1995, p. 98; Mar. 1996, p. 46; Jan. 1997, p. 10; May 1997, p. 64.

1360
Peck, Robert Newton.
Soup.

1974
Published

1992 NJ
Challenged as a fourth-grade reading assignment at the Woodbridge schools because of objectionable language and because "it teaches children how to lie, manipulate, steal, and cheat."
Source: 11, Jan. 1993, p. 12.

1361
Peck, Robert Newton.
Trig.

1977
Published

1985 WI
Challenged at the Cunningham Elementary School in Beloit because the book "encourages disrespectful language."
Source: 11, July 1985, p. 134.

1362
Pell, Derek.
Doktor Bey's Suicide Guidebook.

1977
Published

1986 IA
Placed "on reserve" at the Prairie High School library in Cedar Rapids because the book "could push a classmate contemplating suicide over the edge."
Source: 11, Sept. 1986, p. 152.

1363
Pelzer, Dave.
A Child Called It.

1995
Published

2000 DE
Removed from the Sussex Central Middle School until the committee completes its review because of the book's profanity and violence.

2013 WA
Challenged at the Housel Middle School in Prosser because the autobiography provides graphic depiction of child abuse. Middle-school students had to have parental permission to check out the book.
Source: 11, July 2000, p. 105; Mar. 2013, p. 49.

1364
Penney, Alexandra.
How to Make Love to a Man...Safely.

1982
Published

1995 TX
Former Weslaco librarian filed a federal lawsuit charging that she was fired for publicly discussing that city's efforts to ban Penney's work from the library.
Source: 11, Sept. 1995, p. 155.

1365
Perkins, Al.
Don and Donna Go to Bat.

1966
Published

1987 VT
Returned to Shaftsbury Elementary School library. The complainant stated that children should not be exposed to "sexist attitudes in the story."
Source: 11, Sept. 1987, p. 194.

1366
Perry, Shawn, ed.
Words of Conscience: Religious Statements of Conscientious Objectors.

1980
Published

1982 WI
Access restricted in Coleman due to the book's alleged political overtones.
Source: 11, July 1982, p. 126.

1367
Perry, Troy.
The Lord Is My Shepherd and He Knows I'm Gay.

1972
Published

1982 MI
Challenged at the Niles Community Library because of the book's "pornographic" nature.
Source: 11, Jan. 1983, p. 8.

1368
Peters, Lisa Westberg.
Our Family Tree: An Evolution Story.

2003
Published

2006 KS
Retained in the Seaman Unified School District 345 elementary school library. Objections were raised because the book is about the scientific theory of evolution.
Source: 11, May 2006, p. 153.

1369
Petronius, Gaius.
Satyricon.

Late 1st Century
Published

1934
Ordered destroyed by the police

court of the City of Westminster in London, England.
Source: 4, p. 3; 13, pp. 206–7.

1370
Pettit, Mark.
A Need to Kill.

1990
Published

1998 NE
Challenged in the Lincoln middle school libraries. The book is about an executed child-killer and contains passages concerning murder, masturbation, and perverse sex, considered inappropriate for junior high.
Source: 11, July 1998, p. 106.

1371
Pfeiffer, Susan Beth.
About David.

1980
Published

1980
Best Books for Young Adults

1986 FL
Challenged at the Bay County's four middle schools and three high schools in Panama City because it contains "profanity and sexual explicit passages."
Source: 11, Nov. 1986, p. 209.

1372
Picoult, Jodi.
My Sister's Keeper.

2004
Published

2005
Alex Award

2008 MI
Pulled from classrooms in Clawson as too racy for middle school students. The novel is the story of a young girl who sues her parents because they want her to donate a kidney to her sister.
Source: 11, Mar. 2009, p. 40.

1373
Picoult, Jodi.
Nineteen Minutes.

2007
Published

2008 IL
Restricted to high school students with parental permission at the Beardstown High School library because the novel "describes sex, uses foul language, and contains other 'R-rated' content."
Source: 11, Sept. 2008, pp. 229-30.

1374
Picoult, Jodi.
The Tenth Circle.

2006
Published

2007 NY
Removed from the Westhampton Beach High School's ninth-grade reading list because of "inappropriate sexual content." The reading list contains more than three hundred books from which ninth-graders must choose to read for course credit.
Source: 11, Jan. 2008, pp. 37-38; Mar. 2008, p. 63.

1375
Pierce, Ruth I.
Single and Pregnant.

1970
Published

1970
Best Books for Young Adults

1984 AR
Challenged and recommended for a "parents only" section at the Concord school library because the author had "little to say that would discourage premarital sex."
Source: 11, Jan. 1985, p. 7; May 1985, p. 75; Jan. 1986, pp. 7–8.

1376
Pierce, Tamora.
Alanna: Song of the Lioness, Book One.

1983
Published

1989 OR
Removed by a library staff member, but later returned to the shelves of the David Hill Elementary School in Hillsboro because of sexual references and the use of an amulet to prevent pregnancy.
Source: 11, Jan. 1990, pp. 4–5.

1377

Pierce, Tamora.
*In the Hand of the Goddess:
Song of the Lioness, Book Two.*

1984
Published

1989 OR
Removed by a library staff member, but later returned to the shelves of the David Hill Elementary School in Hillsboro because of sexual references and use of an amulet to prevent pregnancy.

Source: 11, Jan. 1990, pp. 4–5.

1378

Pierce, Tamora.
*The Woman Who Rides
Like a Man: Song of
the Lioness, Book Three.*

1986
Published

1989 OR
Removed by a library staff member, but later returned to the shelves of the David Hill Elementary School in Hillsboro because of sexual references and the use of an amulet to prevent pregnancy.

Source: 11, Jan. 1990, pp. 4–5.

1379

Pike, Christopher.
Bury Me Deep.

1991
Published

2000 ID
Removed from the Nampa West Middle School due to its violence and sexual content.

Source: 11, May 2000, p. 74.

1380

Pike, Christopher.
Chain Letter 2: The Ancient Evil.

1992
Published

2000 ID
Removed from the Nampa West Middle School due to its violence and sexual content.

Source: 11, May 2000, p. 74.

1381

Pike, Christopher.
Die Softly.

1991
Published

1999 CA
Removed from Escondido middle school libraries along with 24 other novels by the best-selling author. Passages deemed offensive made references to whiskey drinking, bribery, sex, and a nightmare about dismemberment.

Source: 11, July 1998, p. 104; Nov. 1999, p. 161.

1382

Pike, Christopher.
Final Friends: The Party.

1988
Published

1998 CA
Recommended for removal from Escondido middle school libraries because the book is "vulgar and unsuitable."

Source: 11, July 1998, p. 104.

1383

Pike, Christopher.
*Final Friends:
The Graduation.*

1989
Published

1992 PA
Challenged at the Weatherly Area Middle School library because parents were upset by passages in the book dealing with depression, suicide, and contraception.

Source: 11, May 1992, p. 81; July 1992, p. 125.

1384

Pike, Christopher.
Last Act.

1988
Published

2000 ID
Removed from the Nampa South Middle School due to its violence and sexual content.

Source: 11, May 2000, p. 74.

1385

Pike, Christopher.
The Listeners.

1995
Published

2000 ID
Removed from the Nampa West Middle School due to its violence and sexual content.

Source: 11, May 2000, p. 74.

1386

Pike, Christopher.
The Lost Mind.

1995
Published

2000 ID
Removed from the Nampa West Middle School due to its violence and sexual content.

Source: 11, May 2000, p. 74.

1387

Pike, Christopher.
The Midnight Club.

1994
Published

2000 ID
Removed from the Nampa West Middle School due to its violence and sexual content.

Source: 11, May 2000, p. 74.

1388

Pike, Christopher.
Remember Me.

1989
Published

1998 SC
Removed from the Liberty Middle School library in Seneca after a seventh-grader's grandmother complained to school officials.

Source: 11, May 1998, p. 70.

1389

Pike, Christopher.
Remember Me 3: The Last Story.

1995
Published

2000 ID
Removed from the Nampa West Middle School due to its violence and sexual content.
Source: 11, May 2000, p. 74.

1390

Pike, Christopher.
Road to Nowhere.

1993
Published

1998 CA
Recommended for removal from Escondido middle school libraries because the book is "vulgar and unsuitable."
Source: 11, July 1998, p. 104.

1391

Pike, Christopher.
The Star Group.

1997
Published

2000 ID
Removed from the Nampa West Middle School due to its violence and sexual content.
Source: 11, May 2000, p. 74.

1392

Pike, Christopher.
Witch.

1990
Published

2000 ID
Removed from the Nampa West Middle School due to its violence and sexual content.
Source: 11, May 2000, p. 74.

1393

Pilkey, Dav.
Adventures of Captain Underpants.

1997
Published

2000 CT
Removed from the Maple Hill School in Naugatuck due to concerns that it caused unruly behavior among children.
Source: 8, p. 430; 11, May 2000, p. 73.

1394

Pilkey, Dav.
The Adventures of Super Diaper Baby.

2002
Published

2003 CA
Challenged, but retained, in the Riverside Unified School District classrooms and libraries, despite a complaint of the book's "inappropriate" scatological storyline.

2011 TX
Banned from the Channelview Independent School District because it contained the phrase "poo poo head."
Source: 8, p. 431; 11, Sept. 2003, p. 201; Sept. 2011, p. 176.

1395

Pilkey, Dav.
Captain Underpants and the Invasion of the Incredibly Naughty Cafeteria Ladies from Outer Space (and the Subsequent Assault of Equally Evil Lunchroom Zombie Nerds).

1999
Published

2000 WI
Challenged, but retained, at the Orfordville Elementary School library. A parent charged that the book taught students to be disrespectful, not to obey authority, not to obey the law, including God's law, improper spelling, to make excuses and lie to escape responsibility, to make fun of what people wear, and poor nutrition.
Source: 11, Mar. 2000, p. 62.

1396

Pilkey, Dav.
Captain Underpants and the Perilous Plot of Professor Poopypants.

2000
Published

2002 TX
Removed from the Page Consolidated School District because a parent "didn't care for the language. I didn't care for the innuendo." The board approved a policy requiring that the consolidated school board approve all library purchases and allowing them to reject materials "that label or characterize undeserving individuals in a derogatory manner."
Source: 8, p. 430.

1397

Pinkwater, Daniel.
The Devil in the Drain.

1984
Published

1987 WI
Challenged in the Galesville-Ettrick School District.
Source: 11, Nov. 1987, p. 226.

1398

Pipher, Mary.
Reviving Ophelia.

1994
Published

1998 WA
Challenged for use in the Richland high school English classes along with six other titles because the "books are poor-quality literature and stress suicide, illicit sex, violence, and hopelessness."
Source: 11, Mar. 1999, p. 40.

1399

Plante, David.
The Catholic.

1986
Published

1986
Banned in South Africa.
Source: 5, June 1986, p. 41.

1400

Plath, Sylvia.
The Bell Jar.

1963
Published

1971
Best Books for Young Adults

1979 IN
Prohibited for use in the Warsaw schools.

1981 IL
Challenged in Edwardsville when three hundred residents signed a petition against Plath's novel because it contains sexual material and advocates an "objectionable" philosophy of life.

1998 WA
Challenged for use in the Richland high school English classes along with six other titles because the "books are poor-quality literature and stress suicide, illicit sex, violence, and hopelessness."

Source: 8, pp. 418-19; 11, Mar. 1980, p. 40; July 1981, p. 102; Mar. 1999, p. 40.

1401
Platt, Kin.
Headman.

1975
Published

1975
Best Books for Young Adults

1982 MO
The Anaconda School Board handed school principal Patrick Meloy a list of thirty-four restricted titles including Platt's book and gave him authority to censor or destroy any book he believes is "pornographic."

1983 IA
Challenged at the Elkader Central High School library because the book's description of the Los Angeles ghetto by a youth gang leader contains "street talk and four-letter words offensive to Elkader residents."

1984 MS
Challenged at the Rankin County School District because it is "profane and sexually objectionable."

Source: 11, Mar. 1983, p. 41; July 1983, p. 121; May 1984, p. 70; Jan. 1985, p. 8.

1402
Plum-Ucci, Carol.
The Body of Christopher Creed.

2000
Published

2001
Best Books for Young Adults

2010 WI
Challenged, but retained, in the Appleton Area School District despite the book's references to suicide and sex. Other titles also considered inappropriate by the local parent group, Valley School Watch, include *The Catcher in the Rye* and *The House on Mango Street*. The reading list for the group's ideal alternate class would contain books with no profanity, obscenity, or sexual material.

Source: 11, Jan. 2011, pp. 30-31; July 2012, p. 180.

1403
Polacco, Patricia.
In Our Mothers' House.

2009
Published

2012 UT
Removed from the shelves of elementary school libraries in Davis County after a group of parents raised objections about the suitability of the story. It remained available only if a student presented a permission slip from a parent to check out the book. A parent then sued the Davis School District in November 2012 alleging her children's First Amendment rights were violated by the book's removal. On January 15, 2013, the book was reinstated without restrictions and the school district agreed to pay $15,000 in attorneys' fees for the lawsuit brought by the American Civil Liberties Union (ACLU).

Source: 11, July 2012, pp. 155-57; Sept. 2012, pp. 201-2; Jan. 2013, pp. 7-8; Mar. 2013, p. 80.

1404
Pollan, Michael.
The Botany of Desire: A Plant's-Eye View of the World.

2001
Published

2006 IL
Retained on the Buffalo Grove High School, along with eight other challenged titles. A board member, elected amid promises to bring her Christian beliefs into all board decision-making, raised the controversy based on excerpts from the books she'd found on the Internet.

Source: 11, July 2006, pp. 210-11.

1405
Pomeroy, Wardell B.
Boys and Sex.

1968
Published

1983 NM
Challenged at the Santa Fe High School library by a school librarian because of its "sordid, suggestive, permissive type of approach."

1988 NY
Removed from two Greece middle school libraries because the book "promotes prostitution, promiscuity, homosexuality, and bestiality."

1990 WI
Pulled from the Black River Falls Middle School library because the book "dealt with bestiality, masturbation and homosexuality, and endorsed pre-adolescent and premarital sex."

1994 CO
Pulled from the Rangely Middle School library shelves.

2000 NC
Challenged in the Charlotte Public Library because of its sexual content.

Source: 11, May 1983, p. 85; July 1988, p. 121; Sept. 1988, p. 178; May 1991, p. 75; May 1994, p. 83; Sept. 2000, p. 143.

1406
Pomeroy, Wardell B.
Girls and Sex.

1970
Published

1983 NM
Challenged at the Santa Fe High School library by a school librarian because of its "sordid, suggestive, permissive type of approach."

1990 WI
Pulled from the Black River Falls Middle School library because the book "dealt with bestiality, masturbation and homosexuality, and endorsed pre-adolescent and premarital sex."

1994 CO
Pulled from the Rangely Middle School library shelves.

2000 NC
Challenged in the Charlotte Public Library because of its sexual content.
Source: 11, May 1983, p. 85; May 1991, p. 75; May 1994, p. 83; Sept. 2000, p. 143.

1407
Ponce, Charles.
The Game of Wizards.

1975
Published

1986 CA
Challenged by the "God Squad," a group of three students and their parents, at the El Camino High School in Oceanside because the Chinese yin and yang symbol is drawn on page 95. The complainant wrote, "This is the symbol of Confucianism and represents reincarnation. This book also deals with transcendental meditation."
Source: 11, Sept. 1986, p. 151; Nov. 1986, p. 224; Jan. 1987, p. 9.

1408
Portal, Colette.
The Beauty of Birth.

1971
Published

1982 FL
Moved from the children's room of the Tampa-Hillsborough County Public Library to the adult section.
Source: 11, Jan. 1982, pp. 4–5.

1409
Potok, Chaim.
My Name Is Asher Lev.

1972
Published

1972
Best Books for Young Adults

1983
Banned from the 1983 Moscow, Russia, International Book Fair along with more than fifty other books because it is "anti-Soviet."
Source: 11, Nov. 1983, p. 201.

1410
Prelutsky, Jack.
The Headless Horseman Rides Tonight and Other Poems to Trouble Your Sleep.

1980
Published

1982 NY
Challenged at the Victor Elementary School media center in Rochester because it "was too frightening for young children to read."
Source: 11, July 1982, p. 142.

1411
Prelutsky, Jack.
Nightmares: Poems to Trouble Your Sleep.

1976
Published

1979 WA
Placed in the professional reading section of the Kirkland district libraries where it would be unavailable to students without a teacher's permission.

1987 NV
Challenged at the Paul E. Culley Elementary School in Las Vegas because the poems were too frightening for small children.

1988 OR
Placed in a "reserved" section at Little Butte Intermediate School in Eagle Point because the book could "disturb a child's sleep and offered no learning experience."

1993 SC
Removed from the Berkeley County schools that include fourth graders and younger children due to violent passages.

1993 WI
Removed from the Eau Claire elementary school libraries because the poems "graphically describe violent acts against children that would be criminal activity if acted out."
Source: 11, Sept. 1979, p. 104; Jan. 1988, p. 32; Jan. 1989, p. 3; Sept. 1993, pp. 148–49; Mar. 1994, p. 53.

1412
Prelutsky, Jack.
Rolling Harvey Down the Hill.

1980
Published

1989 CT
Challenged at the Consolidated School library in New Fairfield because the book of children's verses is "repulsive" and against the country's "moral fiber."
Source: 11, July 1989, p. 127.

1413
Pressfield, Steven.
Gates of Fire.

1988
Published

2002 VA
Retained in the Fairfax County Public Schools after being challenged for "too much profanity."
Source: 11, July 2002, p. 179.

1414
Preston, Richard.
The Hot Zone.

1994
Published

1996
Best Books for Young Adults

1998 WA
Challenged for use in the Richland high school English classes along with six other titles because the "books are poor-quality literature and stress suicide, illicit sex, violence, and hopelessness."
Source: 11, Mar. 1999, p. 40.

1415
Price, Richard.
Bloodbrothers.

1976
Published

1985 PA
Banned from the Stroudsburg High School library because it was "blatantly graphic, pornographic, and wholly unacceptable for a high school library."
Source: 11, May 1985, p. 79.

1416
Price, Richard.
Wanderers.

1974
Published

1978 VT
Banned from the Vergennes Union High School library. Decision upheld in *Bicknell v. Vergennes Union High School Board,* 475 F. Supp. 615 (D. Vt. 1979), 638 F. 2d 438 (2d Cir. 1980).
Source: 11, Jan. 1979, p. 6; 12, pp. 151, 239; 15, Vol. IV, p. 715.

1417
Price, Susan.
The Devil's Piper.

1973
Published

1988 OR
Challenged at the Canby Junior High School library because it "could encourage young minds to pursue occult, suicide, or adopt ill attitudes."
Source: 11, May 1989, p. 78.

1418
Proulx, Annie.
Brokeback Mountain.

1997
Published

2005 TX
Retained at St. Andrew's Episcopal School in Austin. The private school returned a three million dollar donation rather than submit to the donor's request that the novella be removed from the school's list of optional reading for twelfth graders.
Source: 11, Jan. 2006, p. 37.

1419
Pullman, Philip.
The Broken Bridge.

1992
Published

1993
Best Books for Young Adults

1997 WV
Removed from the Jackson County school libraries along with sixteen other titles.
Source: 11, Jan. 1998, p. 13.

1420
Pullman, Philip.
The Golden Compass.

1995
Published

1997
Best Books for Young Adults

2007
Removed, but later returned to the library shelves at dozens of schools in the publicly funded Halton, Ontario, Canada, Catholic school district despite a challenge that the books were "written by an atheist where the characters and text are anti-God, anti-Catholic, and anti-religion." The book and two other Pullman titles from the *Dark Materials* trilogy were pulled from public display for review, but are available to students upon request.

2007
The publicly funded Calgary, Alberta, Canada, Catholic school district returned the book to its library shelves two months after ordering its removal. Detractors accused the book of having anti-religious content. Similar concerns prompted the Catholic League, a Roman-Catholic anti-defamation organization in the U.S., to urge parents to boycott a movie version of the book that was released in December 2007.

2007 CO
Pulled from the library shelves at Ortega Middle School in Alamosa for what critics regard as the book's anti-religious views. District officials later returned the book to circulation.

2007 KY
Challenged at the Conkwright Middle School in Winchester because the main character drinks wine and ingests poppy with her meals, and the book presents an anti-Christian doctrine.

2007 TX
Challenged at the Shallowater Middle School in Lubbock because of the book's "anti-religious messages."

2007 WI
Pulled from the St. John Neumann Middle School and Lourdes High School in Oshkosh because of concerns about what critics call its "anti-Christian message."

2008
Retained by the publicly funded Dufferin-Peel Catholic School District in Mississauga, Ontario, Canada, with a sticker on the inside cover telling readers "representations of the church in this novel are purely fictional," and are not reflective of the real Roman Catholic Church or the Gospel of Jesus Christ.
Source: 11, Jan. 2008, pp. 13-14, 36; Mar. 2008, pp. 61, 63, 77-78; May 2008, p. 116.

1421
Purdy, Candace, and Stan Kendziorski.
Understanding Your Sexuality.

1980
Published

1982 ME
Challenged at the York school system.

1984 PA
Challenged at the Chambersburg Area Senior High School health class because "the Christian child must go to school and be subjected to the immoral teachings of this book."
Source: 11, July 1982, p. 124; Jan. 1985, pp. 11–12.

1422
Puzo, Mario.
The Godfather.

1969
Published

1975 IA
Challenged at the Grinnell-Newburg school system because the book is "vulgar and obscene by most religious standards."
Source: 9; 11, Mar. 1975, p. 41; May 1975, p. 87.

1423
Pyle, Howard.
King Stork.

1973
Published

1993
Boston Globe-Horn Book Award

1989 MI
Challenged at the public libraries of Saginaw because it "would encourage boys beating girls when the drummer beats the enchantress with a switch until she becomes a 'good' princess."

1993 MT
Unavailable to children unless they have written permission from their parents to check out the book or to read it in the library at the Sandstone Elementary School library in Billings. The objections to the near hundred-year-old story included a scene in which a husband beat his witchy wife into submission and illustrations from the 1973 edition of a princess in revealing clothing.
Source: 11, May 1989, p. 77; July 1993, p. 99.

1424
Pynchon, William.
The Meritorius Price of Our Redemption.

1650
Published

1650 MA
First publicly burned in the United States, where it was destroyed by the Massachusetts Colony authorities. Although Pynchon was one of the founders of the colony, and a signatory to its charter, his book proved so contentious in its criticism of the puritan orthodoxy that dominated the theological attitudes of the colony, that after it had been read by the General Council, it was condemned to be burned by the common executioner in the market place. Pynchon himself was publicly censured and escaped further punishment only by sailing back to England.
Source: 3, pp. 462.

1425
Qaradadwi, Yusuf.
The Permitted and Forbidden in Islam.

1992
Published

1995
Banned in France because it could "endanger public order through its clearly anti-Western tone." According to French Muslims, the work lacks overt political content, its purpose being to offer a code of conduct for religious.
Source: 3, p. 185.

1426
Quammen, David.
To Walk the Line.

1970
Published

1974 OK
Banned from all libraries in the Enid public school system libraries.
Source: 11, Mar. 1975, p. 41.

1427
Quinlan, Patricia.
Tiger Flowers.

1999 TX
Challenged, but retained, on the library shelves of a Dallas-Fort Worth-area elementary school. The children's book is about a boy whose uncle dies from AIDS.
Source: 11, Nov. 1999, p. 172.

1428
Rabelais, François.
Gargantua & Pantagruel.

1533 & 1535
Published

1533
Blacklisted in Paris, France, by French Parliament; censored by the Sorbonne in 1552.

1554
Banned by Henry II in England.

1664
Listed on the *Index Librorum Prohibitorum* (List of Prohibited Books) in Rome, Italy.

1930
U.S. Customs Department lifted ban.

1938
Banned in South Africa.

1951 IA
City and county law enforcement officers obtained a warrant and raided the Dubuque Public Library, where they seized the novel as obscene. The book was later returned to library shelves as "restricted" material.
Source: 4, p. 14; 6, pp. 2,003-4; 14, pp. 151–52.

1429
Radishchev, Alkeksandr Nikolaevich.
A Journey from St. Petersburg to Moscow.

1790
Published

1790
Catherine the Great issued orders for the book to be confiscated and the whole edition destroyed because the book "is trying in every possible way to break down respect for authority and for the authorities, to stir up in the people indignation against their superiors and against the government." Radishchev was quickly arrested and condemned to death; his sentence was later commuted to an exile in Siberia. After almost six years in exile, Catherine having died, her successor Paul I issued orders for many in disfavor during his mother's reign, including Radishchev to be released. Alexander I, the next czar, granted him full pardon in 1801.
Source: 7, pp. 275–77.

1430
Radlauer, Ruth, and Ed Radlauer.
Chopper Cycle.

1972
Published

1982 MI
Challenged at the Morrish Elementary School in Swartz Creek because of its negative approach to law enforcement.
Source: 11, Nov. 1982, p. 215.

1431
Rampling, Anne.
Belinda.

1986
Published

1988 OR
Challenged at the Multnomah County Library in Portland because of its sexual nature.
Source: 11, Jan. 1989, p. 3.

1432
Randal, Jonathan C.
After Such Knowledge, What Forgiveness?—My Encounters with Kurdistan.

1998
Published

2002
Confiscated by order of a Turkish state security court. The Istanbul State Security Court sentenced the publisher to six months in jail but converted the sentence to a fine of $500. The book remained banned after the trial. The International Freedom to Publish Committee selected the publisher as the 2005 recipient of the Jeri Laber International Freedom to Publish Award. He was recognized for his long commitment to Kurdish writings in the face of great political obstacles—and personal peril—over the past decades.
Source: 7, pp. 13–14.

1433
Randall, Dudley, ed.
Black Poets.

1971
Published

1982 IL
Banned for use in English classrooms at the Tinley Park High School because the book "extols murder, rape, theft, incest, sodomy, and other acts."
Source: 11, Mar. 1983, p. 40.

1434
Randolph, Vance, comp.
Pissing in the Snow and Other Ozark Folktales.

1976
Published

1988 AR
Challenged at the Rogers-Hough Memorial Library because the book is "vulgar and obscene."
Source: 11, July 1988, p. 119.

1435
Rapp, Adam.
The Buffalo Tree.

1990
Published

2005 PA
Banned from the Muhlenberg High School. Several months later the board reversed that decision and determined that a reading list be made available to parents including a rating system, plot summaries of all assigned books, and the identification of any potentially objectionable content.
Source: 11, July 2005, pp. 161-62; 13, pp. 32–34.

1436
Raucher, Herman.
Summer of '42.

1971
Published

1975 IA
Challenged at the Grinnell-Newburg school system as "vulgar and obscene by most religious standards."

1978 KY
Removed from the reading list of an elective English course at Pulaski County High School after a parent complained about "four-letter language" in the work.
Source: 9; 11, Mar. 1975, p. 41; May 1975, p. 87; Mar. 1979, p. 27.

1437
Ray, Ronald D.
Gays In or Out: The U.S. Military & Homosexuals: A Soucebook.

1993
Published

1996 LA
Pulled from the Ouachita Parish School library in Monroe because of sexual content. The Louisiana chapter of the ACLU filed a lawsuit in the federal courts on October 3, 1996, claiming that the principal and the school superintendent violated First Amendment free speech rights and also failed to follow established procedure when they removed the book. The three-year-old school library censorship case headed to court after the Ouachita Parish School Board made no decision to seek a settlement at a special meeting on April 12, 1999. On August 17, 1999, the Ouachita Parish School Board agreed to return the book to the library and to develop a new book-selection policy that follows state guidelines for school media programs.
Source: 11, Sept. 1996, pp. 151–52; Jan. 1997, p. 7; July 1999, p. 93; Jan. 2000, p. 27.

1438
Reavin, Sam.
The Hunters Are Coming.

1973
Published

1999 ME
Challenged at the Cousens Memorial School library in Lyman because the book portrays hunters in a negative light.
Source: 11, May 1999, p. 83.

1439
Reddin, Keith.
Life and Limb.

1984
Published

1998 FL
Challenged at the Manatee County school district in Bradenton Beach because the play contains references to pornographic magazines, most of them fictional.
Source: 11, May 1998, p. 71.

1440
Reed, Rick.
Obsessed.

1990
Published

1996 GA
Permanently removed from the East Coweta County High School library because of several sexually and violently graphic passages.
Source: 11, Jan. 1997, p. 7; Mar. 1997, p. 35.

1441
Reiss, Johanna.
The Upstairs Room.

1972
Published

1973
Newbery Honor Book

1993 IN
Removed from the required reading list for fourth graders at Liberty Elementary School. The book about a girl in Holland hiding from the Nazis during World War II was investigated because of profanity.

1996 ME
Challenged as assigned reading for sixth-grade students in Sanford because of profanity.
Source: 11, July 1993, p. 105; July 1996, p. 118.

1442
Remarque, Erich Maria.
All Quiet on the Western Front.

1929
Published

1929
Austrian soldiers were forbidden to read it.

1929
Barred from Czech military libraries by the war department.

1929 IL
Seized by U.S. Customs in Chicago.

1929 MA
Banned in Boston on grounds of obscenity.

1930
Banned in Thuringia, Germany, and consigned to the Nazi bonfires.

1933
Banned in Italy because of the book's anti-war propaganda.
Source: 2, pp. 137, 139; 3, pp. 10-12; 4, pp. 6-7; 15, Vol. III, pp. 417–18.

1443
Remarque, Erich Maria.
The Road Back.

1931
Published

1931
Banned in Ireland.
Source: 4, p. 81.

1444
Renan, Ernest.
Life of Jesus.

1863
Published

1897
Condemned by the Catholic Church and placed on the *Index Librorum Prohibitorum* (Index of Prohibited Books) in Rome, Italy, along with nineteen other works by Renan, and remained listed until 1966. The biography was the first to use modern historical methods to recount the life of Jesus.
Source: 1, pp. 190–92.

1445
Rench, Janice E.
Understanding Sexual Identity: A Book for Gay Teens & Their Friends.

1990
Published

1994 CO
Pulled from the Rangely Middle School library shelves.

1994 NJ
Moved from the Chestnut Ridge Middle

School library to the guidance center in Washington Township because school administrators have been accused of "indoctrinating children in the gay lifestyle."

1997 PA
Restricted to students with parental permission at the Brownsville Area High School District library because a parent complained the book contains references to gays and lesbians. The controversy prompted the Greater Pittsburgh chapter of the ACLU to write to the school district saying it would challenge in court any effort to ban the book from the high school library because of its references to homosexuality. The book's author offered to donate three copies to the high school, since the library's copy was never returned.
Source: 11, May 1994, p. 83; Sept. 1994, p. 148; Sept. 1997, p. 126; Nov. 1997, p. 181; Jan. 1998, p. 11.

1446
Rennison, Louise.
Angus, Thongs and Full-Frontal Snogging: Confessions of Georgia Nicolson.

2000
Published

2001
Best Books for Young Adults

2008 WI
Retained with limited access at the Maplewood Middle School Library in Menasha. The coming-of-age novel, which has sexual content, was found offensive by a parent. In addition to retaining the book, board members voted unanimously to adopt procedures intended to secure and record parental consent before limited access books are released to students.
Source: 11, July 2008, p. 164.

1447
Rennison, Louise.
Knocked Out by My Nunga-Nungas: Further, Further Confessions of Georgia Nicolson.

2002
Published

2002 WI
Challenged at the Oregon Middle School by a parent who was particularly offended by a passage in which a boy touches a girl's breast.
Source: 11, Jan. 2003, p. 10.

1448
Rennison, Louise.
On the Bright Side, I'm Now the Girlfriend of a Sex God: Further Confessions of Georgia Nicolson.

2000
Published

2005 MT
Retained in the Bozeman School District's middle-school libraries despite a complaint that an unstable person seeing a girl reading the book might think from the title that the girl is promiscuous and stalk her.
Source: 11, Mar. 2005, p. 74.

1449
Reuben, David.
Everything You Always Wanted to Know about Sex (*but Were Afraid to Ask).*

1969
Published

1984 MO
Challenged at the William Chrisman High School in Independence because the book is "filthy." Reuben's work was on a bookshelf in the classroom and was the personal property of the teacher.
Source: 11, July 1984, p. 106.

1450
Revesz, Therese Ruth.
Witches.

1977
Published

1992 VA
Pulled, but later placed on reserve to children with parental permission at the Forrest Elementary School library in Hampton.
Source: 11, July 1992, p. 108; Sept. 1992, p. 139.

1451
Reynolds, Marilyn.
Detour for Emmy.

1993
Published

1994
Best Books for Young Adults

2000 AZ
Removed from Dysart Unified School District libraries for its portrayal of teenage pregnancy.

2005 TX
Challenged in the Action Middle School library in Granbury because it "talks very vividly about sexual encounters of a fifteen-year-old."
Source: 11, May 2000, p. 73; Nov. 2005, pp. 280–81; Jan. 2006, pp. 10–11.

1452

Rhyne, Nancy.
Murder in the Carolinas.

1990
Published

1992 SC
Removed from the Berkeley County elementary and middle school libraries because the book—real-life stories of South Carolina murders based on newspaper accounts—contained descriptions of actual murders that were too graphic for young readers.
Source: 11, July 1992, pp. 107–8.

1453

Richards, Arlene Kramer, and Irene Willis.
What to Do If You or Someone You Know Is Under 18 and Pregnant.

1983
Published

1983
Best Books for Young Adults

1991 WI
Challenged at the Racine Unified School District libraries because the book uses street language to describe sexual intercourse and contraceptives, contains "sexually suggestive and provocative" language, and "promotes teenage sexual promiscuity."
Source: 11, Jan. 1992, p. 27.

1454

Richardson, Justin, and Peter Parnell.
And Tango Makes Three.

2005
Published

2006 IL
Challenged at the Shiloh Elementary School library. A committee of school employees and a parent suggested the book be moved to a separate shelf, requiring parent permission before checkout. The school's superintendent, however, rejected the proposal and the book remained on the library shelf.

2006 MO
Moved from the children's fiction section to children's nonfiction at two Rolling Hills Consolidated Library's branches in Savannah and St. Joseph after parents complained it had homosexual undertones. The illustrated book is based on a true story of two male penguins that adopted an abandoned egg at New York City's Central Park in the late 1990s.

2007 CA
Challenged at the Lodi Public Library by a resident deriding what she called its "homosexual story line that has been sugarcoated with cute penguins."

2007 NC
Pulled from four elementary-school libraries in the Charlotte-Mecklenburg after a few parents and Mecklenburg County Commissioner Bill James questioned the controversial but true story. The books were returned after the local paper questioned the ban. There was no formal request for the book's removal.

2008
Withdrawn from two Bristol, England primary schools following objections, from parents who claimed the book was unsuitable for children and that they had not been consulted on their opinions.

2008 CA
Retained in the Chico Unified School District, over complaints that the book is inappropriate for elementary school students. The district review committee determined that the book meets library selection standards and district policy.

2008 IA
Challenged in the elementary school library in Ankeny by parents who do not want their children to read the story of two male penguin parents in the Central Park Zoo due to concerns that it promotes homosexuality. On December 15, 2008, the Ankeny school board members voted six to one to keep the book.

2008 MD
Retained by the Calvert County Library in Prince Frederick after requests that the book be removed from the children's section and shelved in a labeled alternative section.

2008 OH
Challenged, but retained, at the Eli Pinney Elementary School in Dublin despite a parent's concerns that the book "is based on one of those subjects that is best left to be discovered by students at another time or in another place."

2008 VA
Returned to the general circulation shelves in the sixteen elementary school libraries in Loudoun County despite a complaint about its subject matter.

2009 MN
Retained in the Meadowview Elementary School in Farmington despite a parent's concern that "a topic such as sexual preference does not belong in a library where it can be obtained by young elementary students."

2009 MO
Challenged, but retained, in the North Kansas City schools despite a parent's concern that the book wasn't age-appropriate, didn't follow the district's policy on human sexuality education, and tries to indoctrinate children about homosexuality. In subsequent discussions, the schools appear to be headed towards segregating elementary school libraries according to "age appropriateness." Students might be restricted to view or check out materials in their own age class or younger.

2011 MN
Pulled from the Gibbs Elementary School in Rochester as inappropriate for elementary school students and removed from school library shelves. This decision was later reversed as a mistake for failing to follow district policy. Eventually, a "temporary resolution" was reached requiring that one of the parents who challenged the book be present when their child checks out books from the school media center in the future.

2012 UT
Marked for removal in the Davis School District because parents might find it objectionable.

Source: 11, May 2006, p. 129; Jan. 2007, p. 9; Mar. 2007, pp. 71–72; July 2007, p. 163; May 2008, pp. 116-17; July 2008, pp. 146, 164, 166; Jan. 2009, pp. 6, 21-22; Mar. 2009, p. 55; May 2009, p. 94; Mar. 2010, pp. 52-53, 73; May 2012, p. 127; July 2012, p. 156.

1455

Richardson, Samuel.
Pamela.

1740
Published

1744
Condemned by the Roman Catholic Church in Rome, Italy, and was prohibited reading for Catholics. It appeared on the *Index Librorum Prohibitorum* (List of Prohibited Books) mainly because it was a novel that related a suggestively romantic relationship. The work appears on the Index of Benedict XIV, issued in 1758, and the Indexes of Pope Leo XIII, issued in 1881 and 1900 and still in force in 1906.

Source: 3, p. 259; 6, pp. 2,039–40; 8, pp. 371–72.

1456

Rigaud, Milo.
Secrets of Voodoo.

1970
Published

1998 IA
Challenged, but retained, at the Madison Elementary School in Cedar Rapids.

Source: 11, May 1998, pp. 87–88.

1457

Riker, Audrey Palm, and Charles Riker.
Finding My Way.

1979
Published

1982 GA
Challenged in Walker County by the Eagle Forum because its "treatment of sexual matters was too explicit and its method of presentation faulty."

1982 IN
Challenged in Tell City.

1987 WY
Challenged at the Laramie Junior High School because the book "doesn't stress saying 'No.'"

1991 OK
Challenged at the Grove High School because it was "too graphic for presentation in the classroom."

Source: 11, May 1982, p. 85; July 1982, p. 142; Sept. 1987, p. 177; Sept. 1991, p. 179.

1458

Riker, Audrey Palm, and Holly E. Brisbane.
Married and Single Life.

1984
Published

1984 WI
Returned to the Racine Unified School District curriculum just one week after the school board voted to ban it. The home economics text was criticized for encouraging premarital sex and advocating that unmarried couples live together.

Source: 11, Sept. 1984, p. 158; Jan. 1985, p. 10.

1459

Riker, Audrey Palm, and Holly E. Brisbane.
Married Life.

1970
Published

1981 IL
Challenged in Collinsville.

1982 KY
Challenged in Jefferson County because it "pushes women's lib which is very degrading to women and will destroy the traditional family."

Source: 11, May 1981, p. 68; Mar. 1983, p. 41.

1460

Riley, Andy.
The Book of Bunny Suicides: Little Fluffy Rabbits Who Just Don't Want to Live Anymore.

2003
Published

2008 OR
Retained at the Central Linn High School library in Halsey. The book depicts cartoon rabbits killing themselves in various ways, from sitting in front of a bobsled run to impaling themselves on Darth Vader's light saber. A parent complained about the book, saying initially she would burn it rather than return it. The story drew national attention and prompted readers to send the school district about twenty-four copies of the book.

Source: 11, Jan. 2009, p. 22; Mar. 2009, p. 56.

1461

Ringgold, Faith.
Tar Beach.

1991
Published

1992
Coretta Scott King Illustrator Honor Book

1994 WA
Challenged in the Spokane elementary school libraries because it stereotypes African Americans as eating fried chicken and watermelon and drinking beer at family picnics. The book is based on memories of its author's family rooftop picnics in 1930s Harlem.

Source: 11, Jan. 1995, p. 9; Mar. 1995, p. 54.

1462

Rivera, Tomás.
And the Earth Did Not Devour Him.

1987
Published

2013 GA
Challenged, but retained, as part of the Clarke County schools class reading list despite "a paragraph in the book full of offensive language." The book is the story of a Mexican boy's life in a migrant family in the 1940s and 1950s, with themes of family life and tensions, getting an education, and growing up. In 1970 Rivera's book won the Premio Quinto Sol literary award, established by a California publisher to encourage and promote Chicano authors.

Source: 11, Sept. 2013, pp. 184-85; Nov. 2013, p. 244.

1463

Robbins, Harold.
The Carpetbaggers.

1961
Published

1961 CT
Sales restricted in Waterbury on the grounds of obscenity.

1961 CT
Sales restricted in Bridgeport.

1961 NY
Sales restricted in Rochester.

1961 RI
Sales restricted in Warwick.

1961 TX
Sales restricted in Mesquite.

1965
Banned in South Africa.

1982
Malaysian police confiscated the works of Robbins because they were considered "prejudicial to the public interest."
Source: 4, p. 88; 5, Jan. 1983, p. 45; 13, p. 40.

1464
Robbins, Harold.
The Lonely Lady.

1976
Published

1980 VA
Challenged in Abingdon because of the book's "pornographic" nature.
Source: 11, Jan. 1981, p. 5.

1465
Robbins, Harold.
Never Love a Stranger.

1948
Published

1949 PA
Identified, along with eight other novels, as obscene in criminal proceedings in the Court of Quarter sessions in Philadelphia County, Pennsylvania. The court refused to declare the novel "obscene" and said that in Robbin's novel, references to sexual activity are brief and general, and the main character's language is important to developing that character.
Source: 14, pp. 236–37.

1466
Robbins, Russell Hope.
Encyclopedia of Witchcraft and Demonology.

1959
Published

1994 MI
Removed from the Detroit public school libraries after a complaint that the book was "obscene, perverse, and immoral."
Source: 11, Mar. 1994, p. 51.

1467
Roberts, J. R.
Ambush Moon.

1994
Published

1995 OH
Challenged, but retained, in the Fairfield County District Library in Lancaster because it includes profanity and explicit sex scenes.
Source: 11, Nov. 1995, p. 184; Jan. 1996, p. 29.

1468
Roberts, J. R.
Hands of the Strangler.

1993
Published

1994 SD
Challenged, but retained, at the Selby Library because of an inappropriate sex scene.
Source: 11, July 1994, p. 129.

1469
Roberts, Willo Davis.
The View from the Cherry Tree.

1993
Published

1995 NV
Retained in Elko County classrooms despite the complaint of an elementary school student. School officials said parents complained that the book contains language inappropriate for sixth-graders, including a cat named S.O.B.
Source: 11, Sept. 1995, p. 160.

1470
Robinson, David.
Herbert Armstrong's Tangled Web.

1980
Published

1981 OK
A suit was filed in Tulsa alleging that the book was based on privileged communications, whose secrecy is protected by law. A restraining order temporarily stopped the release of this book.
Source: 11, Jan. 1982, p. 23.

1471
Rock, Gail.
The House Without a Christmas Tree.

1974
Published

1983 IA
Challenged in the Des Moines schools due to the use of the word "damn."
Source: 11, May 1983, p. 73.

1472
Rockwell, Thomas.
How to Eat Fried Worms.

1973
Published

1988 NJ
Retained in the Middletown elementary school libraries despite a parent's objection that the book contains violence and vulgar language.

1991 IN
Removed from the LaVille Elementary School library in La Paz by a library user because the book contains the word "bastard."
Source: 11, May 1988, p. 103; Sept. 1991, p. 153.

1473
Rodgers, Mary.
Freaky Friday.

1972
Published

2001 FL
Pulled, but later returned to the library shelves of Hernando County schools, after a parent's complaint about the book's references to drinking and smoking, characters who take God's name in vain, and the claim it advocates violence.
Source: 11, Mar. 2001, p. 53; May 2001, p. 123.

1474

Rodriguez, Abraham, Jr.
*The Boy Without a Flag:
Tales of the South Bronx.*

1992
Published

1994 MN
Retained in the Rosemount High School after a complaint about "profane language and promiscuity in the stories."
Source: 11, July 1994, p. 130.

1475

Rodriguez, Luis J.
Always Running.

1993
Published

1996 IL
Challenged as an optional reading at the Guilford High School in Rockford because it is "blatant pornography."

1998 CA
Challenged, but retained, on the San Jose Unified School District optional reading list at district high schools despite complaints that the book is "pornographic and offensive in its stereotyping of Latinos." The book will be kept in libraries, but students must have parental consent to check it out.

1998 CA
Removed from the Santa Rosa high school reading lists.

1998 CA
Removed, pending review, at the Fremont schools.

2003 CA
Challenged, but retained, in three Beyer High School classrooms in Modesto despite complaints that the book is "pornographic." The decision reversed the actions of district administrators who had removed the book in early November 2003. The book won the *Chicago Sun Times* Carl Sandburg Literary Award and was designated as a *New York Times* notable book.

2004 CA
Pulled from the Santa Barbara schools after a parent complained about graphic passages depicting violence and sex.
Source: 11, July 1996, p. 118; Sept. 1998, pp. 142–43; Jan. 2003, pp. 27–28; Mar. 2004, pp. 51–52; Jan. 2005, p. 7; 13, pp. 8–11.

1476

Rojas, Don.
*One People, One Destiny:
The Caribbean and Central
America Today.*

1988
Published

1989
Confiscated by custom officials in Grenada along with *Maurice Bishop Speaks; Thomas Sankara Speaks: The Burkina Faso Revolution, 1983-87,* and other books by Nelson Mandela, Karl Marx, Che Guevara, Fidel Castro, and Malcom X. The books were labeled as "subversive to the peace and security of the country."
Source: 11, Mar. 1989, pp. 49–50; July 1989, pp. 141–42.

1477

Roman, Jo.
Exit House.

1980
Published

1994 AR
Challenged at the Springdale Public Library because it presented suicide as "a rational and sane alternative."
Source: 11, July 1994, p. 128.

1478

Ronan, Margaret, and
Eve Ronan.
*Astrology and Other
Occult Games.*

1972
Published

1982 OH
Challenged in the Akron school system because the book promotes Satan.
Source: 11, Mar. 1983, p. 38.

1479

Roquelaire, A. E. [Anne Rice].
Beauty's Punishment.

1984
Published

1992 GA
Removed from the shelves of the Lake Lanier Regional Library system in Gwinnett County following complaints that centered around sexuality.

1996 OH
Removed from the Columbus Metropolitan Library as hard-core pornography.
Source: 11, Jan. 1993, p. 7; July 1996, pp. 119–20.

1480

Roquelaire, A. E. [Anne Rice].
Beauty's Release.

1985
Published

1992 GA
Removed from the shelves of the Lake Lanier Regional Library system in Gwinnett County following complaints that centered around sexuality.

1996 OH
Removed from the Columbus Metropolitan Library as hard-core pornography.
Source: 11, Jan. 1993, p. 7; July 1996, pp. 119–20.

1481

Roquelaire, A. E. [Anne Rice].
*The Claiming of Sleeping
Beauty.*

1983
Published

1992 GA
Removed from the shelves of the Lake Lanier Regional Library system in Gwinnett County following complaints that centered around sexuality.

1996 OH
Removed from the Columbus Metropolitan Library as hard-core pornography.
Source: 11, Jan. 1993, p. 7; July 1996, pp. 119–20.

1482
Rosen, Lucy.
I Am Bane.

2012
Published

2013 IL
Challenged, but retained, at the Geneva Public Library despite concerns that the images are too scary for young readers. The film *The Dark Knight Rises* inspired the book.
Source: 11, Jan. 2014, p. 25.

1483
Roth, Philip.
Goodbye, Columbus.

1959
Published

1960
National Book Award for Fiction

1980 VA
Challenged in Abingdon because of the book's "pornographic" nature.
Source: 11, Jan. 1981, p. 5.

1484
Roth, Philip.
Portnoy's Complaint.

1969
Published

1969
Many libraries in the U.S. were attacked for carrying this novel, and some librarians' jobs were threatened.
Source: 4, p. 99.

1485
Rounds, Glen.
Wash Day on Noah's Ark.

1991
Published

1991 OH
Challenged at the Hubbard Public Library because the book alters the story of Noah's Ark, making it secular and confusing to children.
Source: 11, Sept. 1991, p. 153.

1486
Rousseau, Jean-Jacques.
Confessions.

1770
Published

1806
Placed on *Index Librorum Prohibitorum* (Index of Prohibited Books) in Rome, Italy, in 1806 by Pope Pius VII. Later, the prohibition was renewed because of the sexual adventures that Rousseau recounted.

1929
Banned by the U.S. Customs Department for being injurious to public morals.

1935
Banned in the USSR.
Source: 4, p. 30; 8, pp. 325–26.

1487
Rousseau, Jean-Jacques.
Emile.

1762
Published

1762
Condemned in Paris, France, by the archbishop and Parlement of Paris, the Sorbonne, and the Inquisition. Rousseau fled France to avoid arrest in 1762.

1763
Banned in Geneva, Switzerland.

1766
Placed on the *Index Librorum Prohibitorum* (Index of Prohibited Books) and remained forbidden to Catholics until 1966.
Source: 1, pp. 88–90.

1488
Rowell, Rainbow.
Eleanor & Park.

2013
Published

2013 MN
Retained, despite a challenge by the chairman of the Anoka-Hennepin School Board because parents of a student objected to the book's content, citing its use of profanity and its treatment of sexuality. The Anoka County Library had scheduled a visit by the author, but the event was cancelled due to the controversy. Set in a poor Omaha neighborhood, the story concerns two outsider teens in the 1980s who find a common bond in music amidst poverty, bullying, abuse, racism, and budding sexuality. Selected by National Public Radio as a 2013 Great Read.
Source: 11, Nov. 2013, pp. 216-17; Jan. 2014, pp. 25-26.

1489
Rowling, J. K.
Harry Potter and the Chamber of Secrets.

1999
Published

1999
British Children's Book Award

2000
Best Books for Young Adults

1999 CA
Parents objected to the book's use in two Moorpark elementary schools.

1999 CO
Parents objected to the book's use in the Douglas County schools.

1999 NY
Parents objected to the book's use in suburban Buffalo, among other districts.

1999 SC
Challenged in South Carolina schools because "the book has a serious tone of death, hate, lack of respect, and sheer evil."

2000
Retained in the Durham School District, Ontario, Canada, after a challenge of the series because of concerns about witchcraft.

2000
Banned from the Christian Outreach College library in Brisbane, Australia, because the book was considered violent and dangerous.

2000 AL
Challenged, but retained, in Arab school libraries and accelerated reader programs over objections that the author "is a member of the occult and the book encourages children to practice witchcraft."

2000 CA
Retained at Orange Grove Elementary School in Whittier; it was challenged for dealing with magic and bad experiences.

2000 CA

Challenged in the Fresno Unified School District classrooms by a religious group voicing concerns about sorcery and witchcraft.

2000 FL

Challenged in six Santa Rosa County schools in Pace for its presentation of witchcraft.

2000 IL

Challenged, but retained, in Frankfort School District 157-C. Parents were concerned that the book contains lying and smart-aleck retorts to adults.

2000 MI

Restricted to fifth- through eighth-graders who have written parental permission in the Zeeland schools. No future installments can be purchased and teachers are prohibited from reading the books aloud in class. The book was considered objectionable because of the intense story line, the violence, the wizardry, and the sucking of animal blood.

2000 MI

Removed from the Bridgeport Township public school because it promotes witchcraft.

2000 NH

Challenged, but retained, in the Newfound Area School District in Bristol despite an objection the book "is scary."

2000 NY

Challenged in the Salamanca elementary school libraries because a family complained about the book's dark themes.

2000 OR

Challenged in Bend at the Three Rivers Elementary School due to references to witchcraft and concerns the book will lead children to hatred and rebellion.

2000 TX

Restricted to students with parental permission in the Santa Fe School District because critics say the book promotes witchcraft.

2001 FL

Challenged, but retained, in the Duval County school libraries despite a complaint about witchcraft depicted in the book.

2001 NM

Burned in Alamogordo outside Christ Community Church because the Potter series is "a masterpiece of satanic deception."

2001 PA

Challenged in the Owen J. Roberts School District classrooms in Bucktown because the "books are telling children over and over again that lying, cheating, and stealing are not only acceptable, but that they're cool and cute."

2002

Challenged in Moscow, Russia, by a Slavic cultural organization that alleged the stories about magic and wizards could draw students into Satanism.

2002 AR

A federal judge overturned restricted access to the Harry Potter book after parents of a Cedarville fourth-grader filed a federal lawsuit challenging the restrictions, which required students to present written permission from a parent to borrow the book. The novel was originally challenged because it characterized authority as "stupid" and portrays "good witches and good magic."

2002 KY

Proposed for removal, along with more than fifty other titles, by a teachers' prayer group at the high school in Russell Springs because the book deals with ghosts, cults, and witchcraft.

2003 CT

Challenged, but retained, in the New Haven schools despite claims the series "makes witchcraft and wizardry alluring to children."

2006 GA

The Gwinnett County school board rejected a parent's pleas to take Harry Potter books out of school libraries, based on the claim they promote witchcraft. The Georgia Board of Education ruled December 14 that the parent had failed to prove her contention that the series "promote[s] the Wicca religion," and therefore that the book's availability in public schools does not constitute advocacy of a religion. On May 29, 2007, Superior Court Judge Ronnie Batchelor upheld the Georgia

Board of Education's decision to support local school officials. County school board members have said the books are good tools to encourage children to read and to spark creativity and imagination.

2007 MA

Removed from the St. Joseph School in Wakefield because the themes of witchcraft and sorcery were inappropriate for a Catholic school.

Source: 11, Jan. 2000, pp. 1, 26; Mar. 2000, pp. 46, 48, 50, 63; May 2000, p. 77; July 2000, p. 124; Sept. 2000, pp. 165–66; Nov. 2000, pp. 193–94, 216; Jan. 2001, pp. 11, 12, 13, 15; Mar. 2001, pp. 43, 62, 75; July 2001, p. 146; Jan. 2002, p. 49; Mar. 2002, p. 61; May 2002, p. 116; Sept. 2002, p. 197; Mar. 2003, p. 77; May 2003, p. 95; July 2003, pp. 137, 159; July 2006, pp. 207-8; Sept. 2006, p. 231; Nov. 2006, p. 289; Mar. 2007, pp. 72-73; July 2007, p. 151; Sept. 2007, pp. 205-6; Jan. 2008, pp. 36-37.

1490

Rowling, J. K.
Harry Potter and the Goblet of Fire.

2000
Published

2001
Hugo Award for Best Novel

2000
Retained in the Durham School District, Ontario, Canada, after a challenge of the series because of concerns about witchcraft.

2000
Banned from the Christian Outreach College library in Queensland, Australia, because the book was considered violent and dangerous.

2000 AL
Challenged, but retained, in Arab school libraries and accelerated reader programs over objections that the author "is a member of the occult and the book encourages children to practice witchcraft."

2000 CA
Challenged in the Fresno Unified School District classrooms by a religious group voicing concerns about sorcery and witchcraft.

2000 FL
Challenged in six Santa Rosa County schools in Pace for its presentation of witchcraft.

2000 NH
Challenged, but retained, in the Newfound Area School District in Bristol despite an objection the book "is scary."

2000 TX
Restricted to students with parental permission in the Santa Fe school district because critics say the book promotes witchcraft.

2001 FL
Challenged, but retained, in the Duval County school libraries despite a complaint about witchcraft depicted in the book.

2001 NM
Burned in Alamogordo outside Christ Community Church because the Potter series is "a masterpiece of satanic deception."

2001 PA
Challenged in the Owen J. Roberts School District classrooms in Bucktown because the "books are telling children over and over again that lying, cheating, and stealing are not only acceptable, but that they're cool and cute."

2002
Challenged in Moscow, Russia, by a Slavic cultural organization that alleged the stories about magic and wizards could draw students into Satanism.

2002 AR
A federal judge overturned restricted access to the Harry Potter book after parents of a Cedarville fourth-grader filed a federal lawsuit challenging the restrictions, which required students to present written permission from a parent to borrow the book. The novel was originally challenged because it character-ized authority as "stupid" and portrays "good witches and good magic."

2002 KY
Proposed for removal, along with more than fifty other titles, by a teachers' prayer group at the high school in Russell Springs because the book deals with ghosts, cults, and witchcraft.

2003 CT
Challenged, but retained, in the New

Haven schools despite claims the series "makes witchcraft and wizardry alluring to children."

2006 GA
The Gwinnett County school board rejected a parent's pleas to take Harry Potter books out of school libraries, based on the claim they promote witchcraft. The Georgia Board of Education ruled December 14 that the parent had failed to prove her contention that the series "promote[s] the Wicca religion," and therefore that the book's availability in public schools does not constitute advocacy of a religion. On May 29, 2007, Superior Court Judge Ronnie Batchelor upheld the Georgia Board of Education's decision to support local school officials. County school board members have said the books are good tools to encourage children to read and to spark creativity and imagination.

2007 MA
Removed from the St. Joseph School in Wakefield because the themes of witchcraft and sorcery were inappropriate for a Catholic school.

Source: 11, Nov. 2000, pp. 193–94, 216; Jan. 2001, pp. 11, 12, 13, 15; Mar. 2001, pp. 43, 62, 75; July 2001, p. 146; Jan. 2002, p. 49; Mar. 2002, p. 61; May 2002, p. 116; Sept. 2002, p. 197; Mar. 2003, p. 77; May 2003, p. 95; July 2003, pp. 137, 159; July 2006, pp. 207-8; Sept. 2006, p. 231; Nov. 2006, p. 289; Mar. 2007, pp. 72-73; July 2007, p. 151; Sept. 2007, pp. 205-6; Jan. 2008, pp. 36-37.

1491
Rowling, J. K.
Harry Potter and the Half-Blood Prince.

2005
Published

2006
Best Books for Young Adults

2006
British Book of the Year

2006 CA
Removed by the Wilsona School District trustees from a list recommended by a parent-teacher committee for the Vista San Gabriel Elementary School library in Palmdale along with twenty-three other books. Trustees said one rejected book contained an unsavory hero who made a bad role model for children; another was about a warlock, which they said was inappropriate; and others were

books with which they were unfamiliar and didn't know whether they promoted good character or conflicted with textbooks. Rejected titles included three bilingual *Clifford the Big Red Dog* books, *Disney's Christmas Storybook*, two books from the Artemis Fowl series, *Beauty is a Beast, California (Welcome to the USA)*, and *The Eye of the Warlock*. The Wilsona School District board approved new library book-selection guidelines in the wake of the trustees' controversial decision. Books now cannot depict drinking alcohol, smoking, drugs, sex, including "negative sexuality, implied or explicit nudity, cursing, violent crime or weapons, gambling, foul humor, and dark content."

2006 GA
The Gwinnett County school board rejected a parent's pleas to take *Harry Potter* books out of school libraries, based on the claim they promote witchcraft. The Georgia Board of Education ruled December 14 that the parent had failed to prove her contention that the series "promote[s] the Wicca religion," and therefore that the book's availability in public schools does not constitute advocacy of a religion. On May 29, 2007, Superior Court Judge Ronnie Batchelor upheld the Georgia Board of Education's decision to support local school officials. County school board members have said the books are good tools to encourage children to read and to spark creativity and imagination.

2007 MA
Removed from the St. Joseph School in Wakefield because the themes of witchcraft and sorcery were inappropriate for a Catholic school.

Source: 11, May 2006, p. 127; July 2006, pp. 207-8; Sept. 2006, pp. 229-31; Nov. 2006, pp. 287-88; Mar. 2007, pp. 72-73; July 2007, p. 151; Sept. 2007, pp. 205-6; Jan. 2008, pp. 36-37.

1492
Rowling, J. K.
Harry Potter and the Prisoner of Azkaban.

1999
Published

1999
Whitbread Book of the Year Award

2000
Best Books for Young Adults

2000
Locus Award for Best Fantasy Novel

1999 CA
Parents objected to the book's use in two Moorpark elementary schools.

1999 CO
Parents objected to the book's use in the Douglas County schools.

1999 NY
Parents objected to the book's use in suburban Buffalo, among other districts.

1999 SC
Challenged in South Carolina schools because "the book has a serious tone of death, hate, lack of respect, and sheer evil."

2000
Retained in the Durham School District, Ontario, Canada, after a challenge of the series because of concerns about witchcraft.

2000
Banned from the Christian Outreach College library in Brisbane, Australia because the book was considered violent and dangerous.

2000 AL
Challenged, but retained, in Arab school libraries and accelerated reader programs over objections that the author "is a member of the occult and the book encourages children to practice witchcraft."

2000 CA
Retained at Orange Grove Elementary School in Whittier; it was challenged for dealing with magic and bad experiences.

2000 CA
Challenged in the Fresno Unified School District classrooms by a religious group voicing concerns about sorcery and witchcraft.

2000 FL
Challenged in six Santa Rosa County schools in Pace for its presentation of witchcraft.

2000 IL
Challenged, but retained, in Frankfort School District 157-C. Parents were concerned that the book contains lying and smart-aleck retorts to adults.

2000 MI
Restricted to fifth- through eighth-graders who have written parental permission in the Zeeland schools. No future installments can be purchased and teachers are prohibited from reading the books aloud in class. The book was considered objectionable because of the intense story line, the violence, the wizardry, and the sucking of animal blood.

2000 MI
Removed from the Bridgeport Township public school because it promotes witchcraft.

2000 NH
Challenged, but retained, in the Newfound Area School District in Bristol despite an objection the book "is scary."

2000 NY
Challenged in the Salamanca elementary school libraries because a family complained about the book's dark themes.

2000 OR
Challenged in Bend at the Three Rivers Elementary School due to references to witchcraft and concerns the book will lead children to hatred and rebellion.

2000 TX
Restricted to students with parental permission in the Santa Fe School District because critics say the book promotes witchcraft.

2001 FL
Challenged, but retained, in the Duval County school libraries despite a complaint about witchcraft depicted in the book.

2001 NM
Burned in Alamogordo outside Christ Community Church because the Potter series is "a masterpiece of satanic deception."

2001 PA
Challenged in the Owen J. Roberts School District classrooms in Bucktown because the "books are telling children over and over again that lying, cheating, and stealing are not only acceptable, but that they're cool and cute."

2002
Challenged in Moscow, Russia, by a Slavic cultural organization that alleged the stories about magic and wizards could draw students into Satanism.

2002 AR
A federal judge overturned restricted access to the Harry Potter book after parents of a Cedarville fourth-grader filed a federal lawsuit challenging the restrictions, which required students to present written permission from a parent to borrow the book. The novel was originally challenged because it characterized authority as "stupid" and portrays "good witches and good magic."

2002 KY
Proposed for removal, along with more than fifty other titles, by a teachers' prayer group at the high school in Russell Springs because the book deals with ghosts, cults, and witchcraft.

2003 CT
Challenged, but retained, in the New Haven schools despite claims the series "makes witchcraft and wizardry alluring to children."

2006 GA
The Gwinnett County school board rejected a parent's pleas to take Harry Potter books out of school libraries, based on the claim they promote witchcraft. The Georgia Board of Education ruled December 14 that the parent had failed to prove her contention that the series "promote[s] the Wicca religion," and therefore that the book's availability in public schools does not constitute advocacy of a religion. On May 29, 2007, Superior Court Judge Ronnie Batchelor upheld the Georgia Board of Education's decision to support local school officials. County school board members have said the books are good tools to encourage children to read and to spark creativity and imagination.

2007 MA
Removed from the St. Joseph School in Wakefield because the themes of witchcraft and sorcery were inappropriate for a Catholic school.

Source: 11, Jan. 2000, pp. 1, 26; Mar. 2000, pp. 46, 48, 50, 63; May 2000, p. 77; July 2000, p. 124; Sept. 2000, pp. 165–66; Nov. 2000, pp. 193–94, 216; Jan. 2001, pp. 11, 12, 13, 15; Mar. 2001, pp. 43, 62, 75; July 2001, p. 146; Jan. 2002, p. 49; Mar. 2002, p. 61; May 2002, p. 116; Sept. 2002, p. 197; Mar. 2003, p. 77; May 2003, p. 95; July 2003, pp. 137, 159; July 2006, pp. 207-8; Mar. 2007, pp. 72-73; July 2007, p. 151; Sept. 2007, pp. 205-6; Jan. 2008, pp. 36-37.

1493
Rowling, J. K.
Harry Potter and the Sorcerer's Stone.

1998
Published

1999
Best Books for Young Adults

1999 CA
Parents objected to the book's use in two Moorpark elementary schools.

1999 CO
Parents objected to the book's use in the Douglas County schools.

1999 NY
Parents objected to the book's use in suburban Buffalo, among other districts.

1999 SC
Challenged in South Carolina schools because "the book has a serious tone of death, hate, lack of respect, and sheer evil."

2000
Retained in the Durham School District, Ontario, Canada, after a challenge of the series because of concerns about witchcraft.

2000
Banned from the Christian Outreach College library in Brisbane, Australia, because the book was considered violent and dangerous.

2000 AL
Challenged, but retained, in Arab school libraries and accelerated reader programs over the objections the author "is a member of the occult and the book encourages children to practice witchcraft."

2000 CA
Challenged, but retained, in the Simi Valley School District. A parent complained that the book was violent, anti-family, had a religious theme, and lacked educational value.

2000 CA
Retained at Orange Grove Elementary School in Whittier. It was challenged for dealing with magic and bad experiences.

2000 CA
Challenged in the Fresno Unified School District classrooms by a religious group voicing concerns about sorcery and witchcraft.

2000 FL
Challenged in six Santa Rosa County schools in Pace for its presentation of witchcraft.

2000 IA
Challenged in the Cedar Rapids school libraries because the book romantically portrays witches, warlocks, wizards, goblins, and sorcerers.

2000 IL
Challenged, but retained, in Frankfort School District 157-C. Parents were concerned that the book contains lying and smart-aleck retorts to adults.

2000 MI
Temporarily restricted to fifth- through eighth-graders who have written parental permission in the Zeeland schools. The Zeeland school superintendent overturned most of the restriction, including that no future installments could be purchased. One restriction remains: teachers are prohibited from reading the books aloud in kindergarten through fifth grade classes. The book was considered objectionable because of the intense story line, the violence, the wizardry, and the sucking of animal blood.

2000 MI
Removed from the Bridgeport Township public school because it promotes witchcraft.

2000 NH
Challenged, but retained, in the Newfound Area School District in Bristol despite an objection that the book "is scary."

2000 NY
Challenged in the Salamanca elementary school libraries because a family complained about the book's dark themes.

2000 OR
Challenged in Bend at the Three Rivers Elementary School due to references to witchcraft and concerns the book will lead children to hatred and rebellion.

2000 TX
Restricted to students with parental permission in the Santa Fe School District because critics say the book promotes witchcraft.

2001 FL
Challenged, but retained, in the Duval County school libraries despite a complaint about witchcraft depicted in the book.

2001 NM
Burned in Alamogordo outside Christ Community Church because the Potter series is "a masterpiece of satanic deception."

2001 PA
Challenged in the Owen J. Roberts School District classrooms in Bucktown because the "books are telling children over and over again that lying, cheating, and stealing are not only acceptable, but that they're cool and cute."

2002
Challenged in Moscow, Russia, by a Slavic cultural organization that alleged the stories about magic and wizards could draw students into Satanism.

2002
In February 2002, board of education officials in the United Arab Emirates banned twenty-six books from the schools, including Rowling's novels because "they have written or illustrated material that contradicts Islamic and Arab values."

2002 AR
A federal judge overturned restricted access to the Harry Potter book after parents of a Cedarville fourth-grader filed a federal lawsuit challenging the restrictions, which required students to present written permission from a parent to borrow the book. The novel was originally challenged because it characterized authority as "stupid" and portrays "good witches and good magic."

2002 KY
Proposed for removal, along with more than fifty other titles, by a teachers' prayer group at the high school in Russell Springs because the book deals with ghosts, cults, and witchcraft.

2003 CT
Challenged, but retained, in the New Haven schools despite claims the series "makes witchcraft and wizardry alluring to children."

2006 GA
The Gwinnett County school board rejected a parent's pleas to take Harry Potter books out of school libraries, based on the claim they promote witchcraft. The Georgia Board of Education ruled December 14 that the parent had failed to prove her contention that the series

"promote[s] the Wicca religion," and therefore that the book's availability in public schools does not constitute advocacy of a religion. On May 29, 2007, Superior Court Judge Ronnie Batchelor upheld the Georgia Board of Education's decision to support local school officials. County school board members have said the books are good tools to encourage children to read and to spark creativity and imagination.

2007 MA
Removed from the St. Joseph School in Wakefield because the themes of witchcraft and sorcery were inappropriate for a Catholic school.

Source: 8, pp. 240–43; 11, Jan. 2000, pp. 1, 26; Mar. 2000, pp. 46, 48, 50, 63; May 2000, p. 77; July 2000, pp. 104, 124; Sept. 2000, pp. 165–66; Nov. 2000, pp. 193–94, 216; Jan. 2001, pp. 11, 12, 13, 15; Mar. 2001, pp. 43, 62, 75; July 2001, p. 146; Jan. 2002, p. 49; Mar. 2002, p. 61; May 2002, p. 116; Sept. 2002, p. 197; Mar. 2003, p. 77; May 2003, p. 95; July 2003, pp. 137, 159; July 2006, pp. 207-8; Nov. 2006, p. 289; Mar. 2007, pp. 72-73; July 2007, p. 151; Sept. 2007, pp. 205-6; Jan. 2008, pp. 36-37.

1494
Royko, Mike.
Boss: Richard J. Daley of Chicago.

1971
Published

1972 CT
Barred from the Ridgefield High School reading list because it "downgrades police departments."

1983 NY
Challenged in the Hannibal High School because the book is "detrimental to students and contributed to social decay because it contains rough language."

Source: 4, p. 99; 5; 11, May 1983, p. 74; July 1983, p. 123.

1495
Ruby, Laura.
Lily's Ghosts.

2003
Published

2006 FL
Removed from the Hillsborough and Pinellas County fourth-grade reading list, although the book is on the Sunshine State Young Reader's Award list of books for third- through fifth-graders.

1496
Ruddell, Robert B., et al.
Person to Person.

1978
Published

1982 KY
Challenged in the Jefferson County School District because the book "confuses sex roles."

1985 WA
The Evergreen School Board in Vancouver banned the textbook because some members said it is too favorable to alternative lifestyles. The controversy centered on a chapter titled "Changing Life Styles," in which the book describes relationships other than the traditional family.

Source: 11, Mar. 1983, p. 41; May 1985, p. 79; July 1985, p. 115.

1497
Rushdie, Salman.
The Satanic Verses.

1988
Published

1988
Banned in Pakistan. In Pakistan five people died in riots against the book. Another man died a day later in Kashmir. Ayatollah Khomeini issued a fatwa or religious edict, stating, "I inform the proud Muslim people of the world that the author of the *Satanic Verses*, which is against Islam, the prophet, and the *Koran*, and all those involved in its publication who were aware of its content, have been sentenced to death."

1989
Banned in Saudi Arabia.

1989
Banned in Egypt.

1989
Banned in Somalia.

1989
Banned in Sudan.

1989
Burned in West Yorkshire, England, and temporarily withdrawn from two bookstores on the advice of police who took threats to staff and property seriously.

1989
Banned in Malaysia.

1989
Banned in Qatar.

1989
Banned in Indonesia.

1989
Banned in South Africa.

1989
Banned in India because of its criticism of Islam.

1989
Banned in Bangladesh.

1989
Owning or reading it was declared a crime under penalty of fifteen months' imprisonment in Venezuela.

1989
The government of Bulgaria restricted its distribution.

1989
The government of Poland restricted its distribution.

1989
Banned under the threat of fines in Japan. In 1991, Hitoshi Igarashi, the Japanese translator was stabbed to death.

1989 KS
Challenged at the Wichita Public Library because the book is "blasphemous to the prophet Mohammed."

1991
The Italian translator, Ettore Capriolo, was seriously wounded.

1993
William Nygaard, the book's Norwegian publisher, was shot and seriously injured.

Source: 3, pp. 492-93; 6, pp. 2,071-75; 8, pp. 291-96; 11, Mar. 1989, p. 47; July 1989, p. 125; Sept. 1989, p. 185.

1498
Russell, Bertrand.
What I Believe.

1925
Published

1950
Nobel Prize in Literature

1929 MA
Banned in Boston.
Source: 4, p. 62.

1499
Russo, Vito.
The Celluloid Closet: Homosexuality in the Movies.

1981
Published

1993 OR
Challenged at the Deschutes County Library in Bend because it "encourages and condones" homosexuality.
Source: 11, Sept. 1993, pp. 158–59.

1500
Sachar, Louis.
The Boy Who Lost His Face.

1989
Published

1991 CA
Challenged at the Thousand Oaks Library because of inappropriate language.

1993 CA
Challenged at the Golden View Elementary school in San Ramon because of its profanity, frequent use of obscene gestures, and other inappropriate subject matter.

1993 IN
Removed from the Jackson Township Elementary School in Clay City due to "unsuitable words."

1993 NY
Removed from the Cuyler Elementary School library in Red Creek because "the age level and use of some swear words may make it inappropriate to younger children."
Source: 11, Mar. 1992, p. 39; May 1993, p. 71; July 1993, p. 97; Sept. 1993, p. 157; Mar. 1994, p. 51.

1501
Sachar, Louis.
Marvin Redpost: Is He a Girl?

1993
Published

2000 AL
Challenged in Chapman Elementary School libraries in Huntsville because it contains a fantasy about kissing your elbow and changing sexes.

2000 IL
Challenged in the New Lenox elementary school because its young hero plays with girls and dreams that he wears a dress to baseball practice.
Source: 11, Mar. 2000, p. 47; July 2000, p. 104.

1502
Sachar, Louis.
Sideways Stories from Wayside Schools.

1978
Published

1992 AZ
Challenged at the Neely Elementary School in Gilbert because the book shows the dark side of religion through the occult, the devil, and satanism.
Source: 11, May 1992, p. 78; July 1992, p. 124.

1503
Sachar, Louis.
There's a Boy in the Girls' Bathroom.

1988
Published

1998 AR
Challenged, but retained, in the fifth-grade Pea Ridge curriculum after objections to "inappropriate language."
Source: 11, May 1998, p. 89.

1504
Sachar, Louis.
Wayside School Is Falling Down.

1989
Published

1995 WI
Removed from the list of suggested readings from the Antigo elementary reading program because the book included passages condoning destruction of school property, disgraceful manners, disrespectful representation of professionals, improper English, and promotion of peer pressure.
Source: 11, July 1995, p. 100.

1505
Sade, Marquis de.
Juliette.

1798
Published

1791
Author imprisoned much of his life in France.

1948
Still on the *Index Librorum Prohibitorum* (List of Prohibited Books) in Rome, Italy.

1962
Seized by British Customs.

1982
Greek police confiscated thousands of books by Marquis de Sade. The publisher, Themis Banousis, was sentenced to two years' imprisonment for violating the laws on indecent literature by translating and publishing the works of de Sade. Forty-seven other publishers were reported arrested in mid-September 1982 for defying the ban.

1982
Malaysian police confiscated the works of de Sade because they were considered "prejudicial to the public interest."
Source: 4, p. 34; 5, Jan. 1983, pp. 44–45.

1506
Sade, Marquis de.
Justine or the Misfortunes of Virtue.

1791
Published

1791
Author imprisoned much of his life in France.

1948
Still on the *Index Librorum Prohibitorum* (List of Prohibited Books) in Rome, Italy.

1962
Seized by British Customs.
Source: 4, p. 34.

1507
Said, Edward W.
The Politics of Dispossession: The Struggle for Palestinian Self-Determination.

1994
Published

1996
Removed from West Bank and Gaza bookstores, the confiscation reportedly having been ordered by the Ministry of Information. The first raid occurred on a small bookstore in central Ramallah. Sales of the book were banned.

Source: 7, p. 411.

1508

Saint-Phalle, Niki de.
AIDS: You Can't Catch It Holding Hands.

1989
Published

1993 KS
Challenged at the Derby Library because "the book didn't say abstinence is the answer and just teach it."

Source: 11, July 1993, p. 124.

1509

Salinger, J. D.
Catcher in the Rye.

1951
Published

1960 OK
Since its publication, this title has been a favorite target of censors. A teacher in Tulsa was fired for assigning the book to an eleventh-grade English class. The teacher appealed and was reinstated by the school board, but the book was removed from use in the school.

1963 OH
A delegation of parents of high school students in Columbus asked the school board to ban the novel for being "anti-white" and "obscene." The school board refused the request.

1975 PA
Removed from the Selinsgrove suggested reading list. Based on parents' objections to the language and content of the book, the school board voted 5-4 to ban the book. The book was later reinstated in the curriculum when the board learned that the vote was illegal because they needed a two-thirds vote for removal of the text.

1977 NJ
Challenged as an assignment in an American literature class in Pittsgrove. After months of controversy, the board ruled that the novel could be read in the Advanced Placement class, but gave parents the right to decide whether or not their children would read it.

1978 WA
Removed from the Issaquah Optional High School reading list.

1979 MI
Removed from the required reading list in Middleville.

1980 OH
Removed from the Jackson-Milton school libraries in North Jackson.

1982
Removed from the school libraries in Morris, Manitoba, Canada, along with two other books because they violate the committee's guidelines covering "excess vulgar language, sexual scenes, things concerning moral issues, excessive violence, and anything dealing with the occult."

1982 AL
Removed from two Anniston high school libraries, but later reinstated on a restrictive basis.

1983 MT
Challenged at the Libby High School due to the "book's contents."

1985 FL
Banned from English classes at the Freeport High School in DeFuniak Springs because it is "unacceptable" and "obscene."

1986 WY
Removed from the required reading list of a Medicine Bow Senior High School English class because of sexual references and profanity in the book.

1987 ND
Banned from a required sophomore English reading list at the Napoleon High School after parents and the local Knights of Columbus chapter complained about its profanity and sexual references.

1988 IN
Challenged at the Linton-Stockton High School because the book is "blasphemous and undermines morality."

1989 CA
Banned from the classrooms in Boron High School because the book contains profanity.

1991 IL
Challenged at the Grayslake Community High School.

1992 FL
Challenged in the Duval County public school libraries because of profanity, lurid passages about sex, and statements defamatory to minorities, God, women, and the disabled.

1992 IA
Challenged in the Waterloo schools.

1992 IL
Challenged at the Jamaica High School in Sidell because the book contains profanities and depicted premarital sex, alcohol abuse, and prostitution.

1992 PA
Challenged at the Cumberland Valley High School in Carlisle because of a parent's objections that it contains profanity and is immoral.

1993 CA
Challenged as required reading in the Corona-Norco Unified School District because it is "centered around negative activity." The book was retained and teachers selected alternatives if students object to Salinger's novel.

1994 NH
Challenged as mandatory reading in the Goffstown schools because of the vulgar words used and the sexual exploits experienced in the book.

1994 WI
Challenged, but retained, at the New Richmond High School for use in some English classes.

1995 FL
Challenged at the St. Johns County Schools in St. Augustine.

1996 ME
Challenged at the Oxford Hills High School in Paris. A parent objected to the use of "the 'F' word."

1997 CA
Removed from the required reading curriculum of the Marysville Joint Unified School District because of profanity and sexual situations. The school superintendent removed it to get it "out of the way so that we didn't have that polarization over a book."

1997 GA
Challenged, but retained, at the Glynn Academy High School in Brunswick. A student objected to the novel's profanity and sexual references.

2000 AL
Challenged, but retained, on the shelves of Limestone County school district despite objections about the book's foul language.

2000 GA
Banned, but later reinstated after community protests at the Windsor Forest High School in Savannah. The controversy began in early 1999 when a parent complained about sex, violence, and profanity in the book that was part of an Advanced Placement English class.

2001 GA
Challenged by a Glynn County school board member because of profanity. The novel was retained.

2001 SC
Removed by a Dorchester District 2 school board member in Summerville because it "is a filthy, filthy book."

2004 ME
Challenged, but retained, as an assigned reading in the Noble High School in North Berwick. Teachers will provide more information to parents about why certain books are studied.

2009 MT
Challenged in the Big Sky High School in Missoula.

2010 FL
Challenged, but retained, in the Martin County School District despite a parent's concern about inappropriate language.

Source: 8, pp. 436–38; 9; 11, Nov. 1978, p. 138; Jan. 1980, pp. 6–7; May 1980, p. 51; Mar. 1983, pp. 37–38; July 1983, p. 122; July 1985, p. 113; Mar. 1987, p. 55; July 1988, p. 123; Jan. 1988, p. 10; Sept. 1988, p. 177; Nov. 1989, pp. 218-19; July 1991, pp. 129-30; May 1992, p. 83; July 1992, pp. 105, 126; Jan. 1993, p. 29; Jan. 1994, p. 14, Mar. 1994, pp. 56, 70; May 1994, p. 100; Jan. 1995, p. 12; Jan. 1996, p. 14; Nov. 1996, p. 212; May 1997, p. 78; July 1997, p. 96; May 2000, p. 91; July 2000, p. 123; Mar. 2001, p. 76; Nov. 2001, pp. 246–47; 277–78; Jan. 2005, pp. 8–9; Mar. 2005, pp. 73–74; May 2009, pp. 82 -84; Nov. 2010, p. 243; Mar. 2011, p. 73.

1510
Salinger, J. D.
Nine Stories.

1953
Published

1987 VA
Removed from the reading list of a writing class at Franklin High School after a parent of one student was offended by some of the language in a story.
Source: 11, July 1987, p. 131.

1511
Salinger, Margaretta M.
Great Paintings of Children.

1956
Published

1994 AZ
Retained at Maldonado Elementary School in Tucson after being challenged by parents who objected to nudity and "pornographic," "perverted," and "morbid" themes.
Source: 11, July 1994, p. 112.

1512
Sams, Ferrol.
Run with the Horsemen.

1984
Published

1995 VA
Challenged in the Rockingham County schools because of sexual content.
Source: 11, Nov. 1995, p. 188; Jan. 1996, p. 18.

1513
Samuels, Gertrude.
Run, Shelley, Run!

1974
Published

1974
Best Books for Young Adults

1977 AR
Removed from the Hot Springs Central Junior High School library and destroyed because of objectionable language.

1979 UT
Challenged at the Ogden School District and placed in a restricted circulation category.

1981 SD
Removed from the Onida High School due to "objectionable" language.

1981 SD
Removed from the Blunt High School due to "objectionable" language.

1982 NC
Removed from the Troutman Middle School library.

1987 NC
Challenged at Alexander Central High School and East Junior High School libraries in Taylorsville because of "foul language."

1995 PA
Removed from the Palmyra middle school classroom because of its language and the portrayal of incidents involving nudity, lesbianism, and prostitution.
Source: 9; 11, Mar. 1977, p. 36; May 1979, p. 49; May 1981, pp. 65–66; Mar. 1982, p. 45; May 1987, p. 87; July 1987, p. 149; July 1995, pp. 98–99; Jan. 1996, p. 17.

1514
Sanchez, Alex.
Rainbow Boys.

2001
Published

2002
Best Books for Young Adults

2004 TX
Challenged at the Montgomery County Memorial Library System along with fifteen other young-adult books with gay-positive themes. The objections were posted at the Library Patrons of Texas website. The language describing the books is similar to that posted at the website of the Fairfax County, Virginia-based Parents Against Bad Books in Schools, to which Library Patrons of Texas links.

2005 AR
Challenged in the Fayetteville High School library. The complainant also submitted a list of more than fifty books, citing the books as too sexually explicit and promoting homosexuality.

2006 NY
Removed from the Webster Central School District summer reading list for high-school students after receiving complaints from parents about explicit sexual content. The book won the International Reading Association's 2003 Young Adults' Choice Award. A year later the book returned to the list after district officials reviewed the process used to select books on the list.

Source: 11, Nov. 2004, pp. 231–32; Nov. 2006, pp. 291-92; July 2007, p. 165.

1515
Sanders, Lawrence.
The Seduction of Peter S.

1983
Published

1985 PA
Banned from the Stroudsburg High School library because it was "blatantly graphic, pornographic, and wholly unacceptable for a high school library."

Source: 11, May 1985, p. 78.

1516
Sanford, John.
Winter Prey.

1993
Published

1994 OR
Expurgated by an apparent self-appointed censor at the Coquille Public Library along with several other books. Most were mysteries and romances in which single words and sexually explicit passages were whited out by a vandal who left either dots or solid ink pen lines where the words had been.

Source: 11, Sept. 1994, p. 148.

1517
Santiago, Esmeralda.
When I Was Puerto Rican.

1994
Published

2001 CA
Challenged in the Newark Unified School District because the book is sexually explicit.

2002 VA
Challenged, along with seventeen other titles by the Fairfax County elementary and secondary libraries, in a group called Parents Against Bad Books in Schools. The group contends the books "contain profanity and descriptions of drug abuse, sexually explicit conduct, and torture."

Source: 11, Mar. 2001, p. 55; Jan. 2003, p. 10.

1518
Sapphire.
Push.

1996
Published

2005 AL
Challenged, but retained, at Fayetteville High School in Fayetteville despite a parent's complaint that it was sexually explicit. The complainant also submitted a list of more than fifty books, citing the books as too sexually explicit and promoting homosexuality.

2011 SC
Challenged on an extracurricular reading list in the Horry County school library. The 1996 novel is based on the story of Precious Jones, an illiterate sixteen-year-old, who grows up in poverty. Precious is raped by her father, battered by her mother, and dismissed by social workers. The story follows Precious, pregnant with a second child by her father, through her journey of learning how to read and be on her own. The novel was made into a critically acclaimed movie, *Precious,* in 2009, which received six Oscar nominations, including Best Picture, for the 82nd Academy Awards and Sundance Film Festival praise.

Source: 11, May 2005, p. 135; Sept. 2005, p. 215; Nov. 2005, pp. 295–96: May 2011, p. 94.

1519
Sarton, May.

The Education of Harriet Hatfield.

1989
Published

1995 NH
Removed from the Mascenic Regional High School in New Ipswich because it is about gays and lesbians. An English teacher was fired for refusing to remove the book.

Source: 11, Sept. 1995, p. 166; Jan. 1996, p. 15.

1520
Sartre, Jean-Paul.
Age of Reason.

1945
Published

1964
Nobel Prize in Literature

1973
On February 21, 1973, eleven Turkish book publishers went on trial before an Istanbul martial law tribunal on charges of publishing, possessing, and selling books in violation of an order of the Istanbul martial law command. They faced possible sentences of between one month's and six months' imprisonment "for spreading propaganda unfavorable to the state" and the confiscation of their books. Eight booksellers also were on trial with the publishers on the same charge involving the *Age of Reason.*

Source: 5, Summer 1973, xii.

1521
Sartre, Jean-Paul.
Saint Genet.

1952
Published

1984
Seized by the British Customs Office as "indecent and obscene."

Source: 11, Jan. 1985, p. 26.

1522
Satrapi, Marjane.
Persepolis: The Story of a Childhood.

2003
Published

2004
Alex Award

2004
Best Books for Young Adults

2013 IL
Removed, via a district directive, from all Chicago public schools due to "graphic illustrations and language" and concerns about "developmental preparedness" and "student readiness." Seventh- and eleventh-grade students study the graphic novel about the author's experience growing up in Iran during the Iranian revolution as part of Chicago Public Schools' Literacy Content Framework.

As the news spread of the directive, students mobilized a media campaign in opposition to "banning a book that's all about the freedom of speech." Students took to their Facebook and Twitter accounts, checked out all library copies of the book, wrote blogs, sent emails, wrote investigative articles for the student newspaper, contacted the author, staged protests, and appeared on local radio and television programs. Eventually, the school issued a letter telling high school principals to disregard the earlier order to pull the book. The book was a *New York Times* Notable Book, a *Time* magazine "Best Comix of the Year," and a *San Francisco Chronicle* and *Los Angeles Times* bestseller. A film version was nominated for Best Animated Feature at the 80th Academy Awards in 2007.
Source: 11, May 2013, pp. 103-4.

1523
Saunders, Richard, and Brian Macne.
Horrorgami.

1990
Published

1993 OR
Removed from the Glendale school libraries in Grants Pass for its alleged "satanic" content. The book is a craft book on origami, but incorporates stories about werewolves and vampires, and is allegedly illustrated with satanic symbols.
Source: 11, July 1993, p. 101.

1524
Savonarola, Girolamo.
Writings.

1495
Published

1498
After a ceremony of degradation, the author was hung on a cross and burned with all his writings, sermons, essays, and pamphlets in Italy.
Source: 1, pp. 53–55; 4, p. 8.

1525
Schechter, Harold, and David Everitt.
The A-Z Encyclopedia of Serial Killers.

1996
Published

2002 FL
Challenged and retained in the Hillsborough County School District because of a parent's objection to the book's "gruesome details."
Source: 11, July 2002, p. 179.

1526
Schniedewind, Nancy.
Open Minds to Equality: A Sourcebook of Learning Activities to Affirm Diversity and Promote Equity.

1983
Published

2007
Challenged at the publicly funded Waterloo, Kitchener, Ontario, Canada, Catholic School District because it presents homosexuality as "morally neutral." The book is used as an optional resource for teachers, and students never see the book. A citizens' organization in Kitchener, Defend Traditional Marriage and Family, objected because the book could lead people "to reject scriptural teaching on homosexual acts."
Source: 11, Nov. 2007, p. 240.

1527
Schnitzler, Arthur.
Casanova's Homecoming.

1918
Published

1930
Simon & Schuster was brought to court for publishing this work.

1939
Banned by Mussolini in Rome, Italy.
Source: 4, p. 57; 13, pp. 42–43; 15, Vol. III, p. 636.

1528
Schnitzler, Arthur.
Reigen.

1900
Published

1929 NY
A bookseller was convicted by the Court of Special Sessions for selling the book. The Appellate Division upheld the conviction, basing their decision more on the "exquisite handling of the licentious" described in the introduction rather than the text. Since the book had been pirated and privately printed, the author was in complete ignorance of the introduction. The conviction was sustained by the highest state court. Shortly afterward the book, which had been studied widely in college and university courses in German literature, was published by Modern Library, and no further attempt was made to suppress it.
Source: 4, p. 57; 15, Vol. III, p. 420.

1529
Schouweiler, Thomas.
The Devil: Opposing Viewpoints.

1992
Published

2004 PA
Challenged at the Chestnut Ridge Middle School in Washington Township. The complainants want the school district to seek parental approval before elementary and middle school students can check out books related to the occult.
Source: 11, May 2004, pp. 117–18.

1530
Schrag, Ariel, ed.
Stuck in the Middle: Seventeen Comics from an Unpleasant Age.

2007
Published

2009 SD
Pulled from the school library collections at two Sioux Falls public middle schools. The book is the work of sixteen cartoonists who recreated true tales from their middle-school years. The book's major themes are bullying and boy-girl awkwardness. Masturbation and marijuana show up in passing, and several of the vignettes include words most parents wouldn't want to hear from their children.

2011 ME
Challenged, but retained, in three Maine towns—Dixfield, Mexico, and Buckfield—at middle school libraries despite "objectionable sexual and language references." The book, however, will be placed in the libraries' professional collection, which means a student may take out the book only if parental permission is granted.

Source: 11, Jan. 2010, p. 13; Mar. 2012, pp. 57-58.

1531

Schreier, Alta.
Vamos a Cuba (A Visit to Cuba).

2001
Published

2006 FL
Removed from all Miami-Dade County school libraries because of a parent's complaint that the book does not depict an accurate life in Cuba. The American Civil Liberties Union (ACLU) of Florida filed a lawsuit challenging the decision to remove this book and the twenty-three other titles in the same series from the district school libraries. In granting a preliminary injunction in July 2006 against the removal, Judge Alan S. Gold of U.S. District Court in Miami characterized the matter as a "First Amendment issue" and ruled in favor of the ACLU of Florida, which argued that the books were generally factual and that the board should add to its collection, rather than remove books it disagreed with. When the district court entered a preliminary injunction ordering the school district immediately to replace the entire series on library shelves, the Miami-Dade School Board appealed the decision to the Eleventh Circuit Court in Atlanta. In a February 5, 2009, 2-1 decision, the U.S. Court of Appeals for the Eleventh Circuit said the board did not breach the First Amendment, and ordered a Miami federal judge to lift a preliminary injunction that had allowed *Vamos a Cuba* to be checked out from school libraries. But the three-judge panel's opinion—not unlike the school board's initial vote—was so fraught with political rhetoric such as "book banning" that further appeals seemed inevitable. On November 13, 2010, the U.S.

Supreme Court declined to take up the case.

Source: 11, July 2006, p. 207; Sept. 2006, pp. 230-31; Nov. 2006, p. 288; Jan. 2007, p. 8; May 2007, pp. 91-92; Mar. 2009, pp. 43-45; Jan. 2010, pp. 25-27

1532

Schusky, Ernest Lester.
Introduction to Social Science.

1981
Published

1985 OR
Challenged in the South Umpqua School District because the book presents a variety of concepts that are "controversial and inappropriate for seventh graders. The book's sections on death education, extrasensory perception, genetic planning, group therapy, and religious values had little to do with the teaching of basic social studies."

Source: 11, Mar. 1986, p. 42.

1533

Schwartz, Alvin.
And the Green Grass Grew All Around.

1992
Published

2000 PA
Removed from elementary and middle school library shelves by the Central Dauphin school board in Harrisburg due to its explicit language.

Source: 11, Sept. 2000, p. 144.

1534

Schwartz, Alvin.
Cross Your Fingers, Spit in Your Hat.

1974
Published

1992 AZ
Challenged at the Neely Elementary School in Gilbert because the book shows the dark side of religion through the occult, the devil, and satanism.

Source: 11, May 1992, p. 78; July 1992, p. 124.

1535

Schwartz, Alvin.
Ghosts! Ghost Stories in Folklore.

1991
Published

1998 WY
Challenged, but retained, in the Campbell County School District despite the claims that "the book misleads the reader—that ghosts are actually possible. . . This book blurs the line between fantasy and reality for younger children."

Source: 11, Mar. 1999, p. 38; May 1999, p. 84.

1536

Schwartz, Alvin.
In a Dark, Dark Room and Other Scary Stories.

1984
Published

1986 CO
Challenged at the Jefferson County school libraries in Lakewood because the book is "too morbid for children." The Jefferson County School Board refused to ban the book.

Source: 11, Sept. 1986, p. 173; Nov. 1986, p. 224.

1537

Schwartz, Alvin.
More Scary Stories to Tell in the Dark.

1984
Published

1988 OR
Challenged at the Dry Hollow Elementary School in The Dalles because it is too scary and violent.

1992 AZ
Challenged at the Neely Elementary School in Gilbert because the book shows the dark side of religion through the occult, the devil, and satanism.

1992 WA
Challenged at the Lake Washington School District in Kirkland as unacceptably violent for children.

1993 AZ
Restricted access at the Marana Unified School District because of complaints about violence and cannibalism.

1994 MT
Challenged, but retained, at the Whittier Elementary School library in Bozeman. The book was challenged because it would cause children to fear the dark, have nightmares, and give them an unrealistic view of death.

1994 WA
Removed from Vancouver School District elementary school libraries after surviving two previous attempts (1991, 1993). Also challenged at neighboring Evergreen School District libraries in 1994 because "This book...is far beyond other scary books."

1995 CA
Challenged in the Tracy school libraries because of the book's violent content and graphic nature.

1995 MI
Challenged as "objectionable" and "disgusting," but retained, on Harper Woods school district reading lists.

2006 KY
Retained in the Greater Clark County elementary-school libraries despite a grandmother's request to ban the *Scary Stories* books written by Alvin Schwartz. She wanted all volumes in the series banned because, she said, they depict cannibalism, murder, witchcraft and ghosts, and include a story about somebody being skinned.
Source: 11, Jan. 1989, p. 3; May 1992, pp. 78, 94-95; July 1992, p. 124; Sept. 1993, p. 143; July 1994, p. 111; Sept. 1994, pp. 148-49, 166; May 1995, p. 65; July 1995, p. 111; Nov. 2006, pp. 317-18.

1538
Schwartz, Alvin.
More Tales to Chill Your Bones.

1991
Published

1992 CT
Challenged at the West Hartford elementary and middle school libraries because of violence and the subject matter.

1992 WA
Challenged at the Lake Washington School District in Kirkland as unacceptably violent for children.

1994 WA
Removed from Vancouver School District elementary school libraries after surviving two previous attempts (1991, 1993). Challenged at neighboring Evergreen School District libraries in 1994 because "This book...is far beyond other scary books."
Source: 11, May 1992, pp. 94–95; Sept. 1992, p. 137; July 1994, p. 111; Sept. 1994, pp. 148–49.

1539
Schwartz, Alvin.
Scary Stories to Tell in the Dark.

1981
Published

1990 MI
Challenged in the Livonia schools because the poems frightened first grade children.

1992 AZ
Challenged at the Neely Elementary School in Gilbert because the book shows the dark side of religion through the occult, the devil and satanism.

1992 CT
Challenged at the West Hartford elementary and middle school libraries because of violence and the subject matter.

1992 IN
Challenged at the elementary school library in Union County.

1992 WA
Challenged at the Lake Washington School District in Kirkland as unacceptably violent for children.

1993 AZ
Restricted access at the Marana Unified School District because of complaints about violence and cannibalism.

1993 KY
Challenged by a parent of a student at Happy Valley Elementary School in Glasgow who thought it was too scary.

1994 WA
Removed from Vancouver School District elementary school libraries after surviving two previous attempts (1991, 1993). Also challenged at neighboring Evergreen

School District libraries in Vancouver because, "This book...is far beyond other scary books."
Source: 11, Mar. 1991, p. 62; May 1992, pp. 78, 94–95; July 1992, p. 124; Sept. 1992, p. 137; Jan. 1993, p. 27; Sept. 1993, pp. 143, 158; July 1994, p. 111; Sept. 1994, pp. 148-49.

1540
Schwartz, Alvin.
Scary Stories.

1981
Published

1993 OH
Challenged in Columbus because children shouldn't be "scared by materials that they read in schools."

1995 CT
Restricted to students in fourth grade or higher in the Enfield elementary schools. The school board was petitioned to remove all "horror" stories from the elementary schools.
Source: 11, May 1993, pp. 85–86; May 1995, p. 69.

1541
Schwartz, Alvin.
Telling Fortunes: Love Magic, Dream Signs, and Other Ways to Learn the Future.

1987
Published

1998 GA
Challenged at Hightower Elementary School in Rockdale because the "book involves instructions and teaches young kids how to tell the future by reading tea leaves, tarot cards, palms, crystal balls, by interpreting dreams, and by looking at an egg."
Source: 11, Mar. 1999, p. 35.

1542
Schwartz, Joel L.
Upchuck Summer.

1982
Published

1988 NJ
Removed from the Winslow Elementary School No. 4 because of "age inappropriateness." The specific problem was the explicitness of scenes in the protagonist recounts a fantasy about two "older kids" kissing while nude.
Source: 11, Jan. 1989, p. 8.

1543

Schwartz, Joel L.,
Aidan Macfarlane, and
Ann McPherson.
*Will the Nurse Make Me Take
My Underwear Off?*

1990
Published

1994 GA
Challenged at the Chestatee Regional
Library in Gainesville.
Source: 11, Nov. 1994, p. 187.

1544

Scoppettone, Sandra.
Happy Endings Are All Alike.

1978
Published

1978
Best Books for Young Adults

1983 WA
Removed from the Evergreen School
District of Vancouver along with twenty-
nine other titles. The American Civil
Liberties Union of Washington filed suit
contending that the removals constitute
censorship, a violation of plaintiff's
rights to free speech and due process, and
a violation of the state Open Meetings
Act because the removal decisions were
made behind closed doors.
Source: 11, Nov. 1983, pp. 185–86

1545

Scott, Elizabeth.
Living Dead Girl.

2008
Published

2009
Best Books for Young Adults

2009 IL
Challenged, but retained, at the
Effingham Helen Matthes Library despite
concerns about its graphic content and
the unsatisfactory ending. The book is
about a fifteen-year-old's perspective of
living with her captor after being forcibly
kidnapped and imprisoned at the age
of ten. The book has received several
accolades from book critics.
Source: 11, Nov. 2009, pp. 219-20.

1546

Sebold, Alice.
The Lovely Bones.

2002
Published

2003
Best Books for Young Adults

2007 CT
Challenged at the Coleytown
Middle School library in Westport.
The school superintendent acknowledged
that the book is "for mature readers"
and also acknowledged "the book is
appropriate to be part of a middle school
library collection serving students
from ages eleven to fourteen, many of
whom possess the maturity level to
read this book."

2008 MA
Moved to the faculty section of the John
W. McDevitt Middle School library in
Waltham because its content was too
frightening for middle school students.
Source: 11, Mar. 2007, p. 71; May 2008, p. 97.

1547

Sedaris, David.
*I Like Guys: A Short Story
from Naked.*

1997
Published

2009 NH
Pulled from a Litchfield Campbell High
School elective course classroom after
parents voiced their concerns about a
short-stories unit called "Love/Gender/
Family Unit" that dealt with subject
matters including abortion, cannibalism,
homosexuality, and drug use. The parents
said the stories promoted bad behavior
and a "political agenda" and shouldn't
be incorporated into classroom teachings.
The Campbell High School English
curriculum adviser said the short story
was selected not only for its tone and
style, but also its message of respect and
acceptance, not for advocating homosexuality. The English curriculum adviser
eventually resigned.
Source: 11, Sept. 2009, p. 154.

1548

Seeley, Robert A.
*A Handbook for
Conscientious Objectors.*

1952
Published

1982 WI
Access restricted in Coleman due to
the book's alleged political overtones.
Source: 11, July 1982, p. 126.

1549

Segel, Elizabeth.
Short Takes.

1986
Published

1994 MD
Challenged at the Cecil County Board of
Education in Elkton. Many deemed
the text controversial because it included
essays dealing with issues of abortion,
gay rights, alcohol, and sex education.
Source: 11, Mar. 1995, p. 55.

1550

Seierstad, Åsne.
The Bookseller of Kabul.

2003
Published

2008 MI
Removed from Roosevelt High School's
library and classrooms in Wyandotte
because it "is too sexually explicit." The
book is a nonfiction account of what life
is like inside an Afghan household.
The school said the book went through
several reviews and was approved for high
school students before being placed
on the assigned reading list for the class.

2009 OH
Challenged, but retained, on Wyoming
high school district's reading list despite
concerns about its sexual content. After a
second challenge to a different title, the
district reviewed all books on reading
lists. Staff members rated each book on its
relationship to the course, its uniqueness,
its appropriateness, and the extent to
which it "could create controversy among
students, parents, and community groups."
Source: 11, Mar. 2009, pp. 40-41; Nov. 2009, pp. 202-3.

1551
Selby, Hubert, Jr.
Last Exit to Brooklyn.

1964
Published

1965 MA
A local city attorney sought an injunction against the book, but Massachusetts Attorney General (later U.S. Senator) Edward W. Brooke directed dismissal of the complaint.

1966
Banned in Italy.

1966
Placed on a restricted list in Russia.

1966
Banned in Ireland.

1966 CT
A circuit court in Connecticut issued a temporary injunction against the book, "as obscene and pornographic." The injunction was overturned, and sales were permitted again.

1967
Judged obscene by jury in England.
Source: 4, pp. 97-98; 6, pp. 2,187-88; 8, pp. 462–63.

1552
Selzer, Adam.
How to Get Suspended and Influence People.

2007
Published

2009 ID
Challenged at the Nampa Public Library by a parent appalled that the cover included an abstract drawing of a nude woman and the back cover contains some profanity. The book explores the theme of censorship through the eyes of a gifted eighth-grader who is suspended after making an avant-garde sex-education video for a class project.
Source: 11, Jan. 2010, p. 8.

1553
Semencic, Carl.
Pit Bulls and Tenacious Guard Dogs.

1991
Published

2011
Banned at the Logan, Australia, West Library because it contains information on restricted dog breeds. In 2001, under Local Law 4 (Animal Management) the Logan City Council placed a ban on, among others, pit bull terriers and American pit bulls. Therefore, Logan City Council libraries do not stock literature on any of the prohibited breeds.
Source: 11, May 2011, p. 118.

1554
Sendak, Maurice.
In the Night Kitchen.

1970
Published

1971
Caldecott Honor Book

1977 IL
Removed from the Norridge school library due to "nudity for no purpose."

1977 MO
Expurgated in Springfield by drawing shorts on the nude boy.

1985 WI
Challenged at the Cunningham Elementary School in Beloit because the book desensitizes "children to nudity."

1988 IL
Challenged at the Robeson Elementary School in Champaign because of "gratuitous" nudity.

1989 NJ
Challenged at the Camden elementary school libraries because of nudity.

1992 MN
Challenged at the Elk River schools because reading the book "could lay the foundation for future use of pornography."

1994 TX
Challenged at the El Paso Public Library because "the little boy pictured did not have any clothes on and it pictured his private area."

2006 NC
Challenged in the Wake County schools. Parents are getting help from Called2Action, a Christian group that says its mission is to "promote and defend our shared family and social values."
Source: 9; 11, May 1977, p. 71; Sept. 1977, p. 134; July 1985, p. 134; Mar. 1989, p. 43; Nov. 1989, p. 217; Mar. 1993, p. 41; Sept. 1994, p. 148; Sept. 2006, p. 231.

1555
Sendak, Maurice.
Some Swell Pup.

1976
Published

1988 OR
Challenged at the Multnomah County Library in Portland because in it a dog urinates on people, and children abuse animals.
Source: 11, Jan. 1989, p. 3.

1556
Servetus, Michael.
Christianity Restored.

1552
Published

1533
The publication in 1531 of *On the Errors of the Trinity* made Servetus notorious and a hunted man, threatened by both the French and Spanish Inquisitions and the Protestants, who banned his book and closed cities to him. In 1532, the Inquisition in Toulouse issued a decree ordering his arrest. He went underground in Paris and assumed a new identity. On October 27, 1553, Servetus was burned at the stake.

1723
Almost two centuries after its first publication, Richard Mead, the physician to the king of England, tried to publish Servetus's work. The government seized and burned the whole printing and imprisoned Mead and his printer.
Source: 8, pp. 221–23.

1557
Seth, Roland.
Witches and Their Craft.

1967
Published

1987 MI
Challenged at the Plymouth-Canton school system in Canton because the book contains information about witches and the devil.
Source: 11, May 1987, p. 110; Jan. 1988, p. 11.

1558

Seuss, Dr.
The Lorax.

1972
Published

1989 CA
Challenged in the Laytonville Unified School District because the book "criminalizes the foresting industry."
Source: 11, Nov. 1989, p. 237; Jan. 1990, pp. 32–33.

1559

Shafak, Elif.
The Bastard of Istanbul.

2006
Published

2006
Prize-winning novelist went on trial in Istanbul, Turkey, accused of belittling Turkishness. The novel had been at the top of Turkish bestseller lists since its publication, but its treatment of the mass murder of Ottoman Armenians in 1915 angered government officials.
Source: 11, Jan. 2007, pp. 35-36.

1560

Shaffer, Paul.
We'll Be Here for the Rest of Our Lives.

2009
Published

2010 SD
Challenged, but retained, at the Mitchell Public Library despite a resident's concern that the book was objectionable with its "too frank depictions and discussions of sex and sexual matters." Written by the longtime leader of David Letterman's band, the book is filled with show business stories and tales of Schaffer's upbringing in Canada.
Source: 11, Sept. 2010, p. 218.

1561

Shahak, Israel.
Jewish History, Jewish Religion.

1994
Published

1995 MA
Challenged at the Milford Library because it is anti-Semitic.
Source: 11, May 1995, p. 66.

1562

Shakespeare, William.
Hamlet.

1603
Published

1978
Banned in Ethiopia.
Source: 5, Sept./Oct. 1978, p. 66.

1563

Shakespeare, William.
King Lear.

1608
Published

1820
Prohibited on the English stage until 1820.
Source: 4, p. 18.

1564

Shakespeare, William.
The Merchant of Venice.

1600
Published

1931 NY
Eliminated from the high school curricula of Manchester.

1931 NY
Eliminated from the high school curricula of Buffalo.

1949 NY
A group of Jewish parents in Brooklyn went to court claiming that the assignment of Shakespeare's play to senior high school literature classes violated the rights of their children to receive an education free of religious bias in *Rosenberg v. Board of Education of the City of New York*, 196 Misc. 542, 92 N.Y. Supp. 2d 344.

1980 MI
Banned from classrooms in Midland.

1986
Banned from the ninth-grade classrooms in Kitchener, Ontario, Canada, until the Ontario Education Ministry or Human Rights Commission rules whether the play is anti-Semitic.

1986
Banned from the ninth-grade classrooms in Waterloo, Ontario, Canada, until the Ontario Education Ministry or Human Rights Commission rules whether the play is anti-Semitic.
Source: 4, p. 19; 11, July 1980, p. 76; Sept. 1986, p. 154; 12, pp. 23, 230.

1565

Shakespeare, William.
Romeo and Juliet
(No Fear Shakespeare).

2003
Published

2012 SC
Some parents in Liberty were furious about the book their kids were reading in middle school. They say it was too mature for their kids because of the sex. The book in question presents the original text of Shakespeare's play side by side with a modern version, with marginal notes and explanations and full descriptions of each character.
Source: 11, May 2012, p. 107.

1566

Shakespeare, William.
Tragedy of King Richard II.

1597
Published

1597
Contains a scene in which the King was deposed and so infuriated Queen Elizabeth in London, England, that she ordered the scene eliminated from all copies.
Source: 4, p. 18.

1567

Shakespeare, William.
Twelfth Night.

1601-02
Published

1996 NH
Removed from a Merrimack high school English class because of a policy that bans any instruction that has "the effect of encouraging or supporting homosexuality as a positive lifestyle alternative."
Source: 11, May 1996, p. 96.

1568
Shannon, George.
Unlived Affections.

1989
Published

1990
Best Books for Young Adults

1993 IL
Removed from the library at the Lundahl Junior High School in Crystal Lake because the book is unfit for sixth grade.
Source: 11, July 1993, p. 98; 14, pp. 281–82.

1569
Shapiro, Amy.
Sun Signs: The Stars in Your Life.

1977
Published

1992 VA
Pulled, but later placed on reserve to children with parental permission, at the Forrest Elementary School library in Hampton.
Source: 11, July 1992, p. 108; Sept. 1992, p. 139.

1570
Sharpe, Jon.
Trailsman series.

1980
Published

2001 AR
Challenged, but retained, at the Springdale Public Library along with all other "western" novels because the writings include "pornographic, sexual encounters."
Source: 11, Nov. 2001, p. 277.

1571
Shaw, George Bernard.
Man and Superman.

1903
Published

1925
Nobel Prize in Literature

1905 NY
The New York Public Library withdrew it from public shelves because books "calculated to make light of dishonesty and criminality were worse than books merely indecent in statement."

1929
Banned from all public libraries in Yugoslavia.
Source: 2, p. 87; 4, p. 55; 15, Vol. II, p. 625.

1572
Shaw, George Bernard.
Mrs. Warren's Profession.

1898
Published

1905
Suppressed in London, England.

1929
Banned from all public libraries in Yugoslavia.
Source: 4, p. 55.

1573
Shaw, Irwin.
Beggarman Thief.

1977
Published

1985 PA
Banned from the Stroudsburg High School library because it was "blatantly graphic, pornographic, and wholly unacceptable for a high school library."
Source: 11, May 1985, p. 79.

1574
Shaw, Irwin.
Nightwork.

1975
Published

1985 PA
Banned from the Stroudsburg High School library because it was "blatantly graphic, pornographic and wholly unacceptable for a high school library."
Source: 11, May 1985, p. 79.

1575
Sheehan, Kathryn, and Mary Waidner.
Earth Child.

1992
Published

1992 OK
Challenged at the Tulsa County schools because the book promotes the Hindu religion and other religious rituals. Opponents also claimed the book is a manual for altering children's minds through psychological games and hypnotic techniques.
Source: 11, Nov. 1992, p. 187.

1576
Sheff, Nic.
Tweak: Growing Up on Methamphetamines.

2007
Published

2011 NJ
Pulled from the required summer reading list for middle school and high school students at the Monroe Township Schools in Williamstown because the book includes "depictions of drug usage and a homosexual orgy."
Source: 11, Nov. 2011, p. 204.

1577
Sheffield, Margaret, and Sheila Bewley.
Where Do Babies Come From?

1972
Published

1981 FL
Moved from the children's section to the adult section of the Tampa-Hillsborough County Public Library by order of the Tampa City Council.

1987 WA
Placed on restricted shelves at the Evergreen School District elementary school libraries in Vancouver in accordance with the school board policy to restrict student access to sex education books in elementary school libraries.
Source: 11, Jan. 1982, p. 4; July 1986, p. 118; Sept. 1986, p. 172; May 1987, p. 87.

1578
Sheldon, Sidney.
Bloodline.

1977
Published

1980 VA
Challenged in Abingdon.

1981 TN
Challenged in Elizabethton.
Source: 11, Jan. 1981, p. 5; May 1981, p. 66.

1579
Shengold, Nina, ed.
The Actor's Book of Contemporary Stage Monologues.

1987
Published

1988 VA
Challenged at the Salem Junior High School in Virginia Beach because it contains racial slurs, profanity, and lewd descriptions.
Source: 11, Mar. 1989, p. 43.

1580
Sherman, Josepha, and T. K. F. Weisskopf.
Greasy Grimy Gopher Guts.

1995
Published

2000
Retained in the collection of the Kingston Frontenac Public Library in Kingston, Ontario, Canada. It had been challenged as unsuitable for children.
Source: 11, Sept. 2000, p. 165.

1581
Shoup, Barbara.
Wish You Were Here.

1994
Published

1995
Best Books for Young Adults

1997 WV
Removed from the Jackson County school libraries along with sixteen other titles.
Source: 11, Jan. 1998, p. 13.

1582
Showers, Paul, and Kay Sperry Showers.
Before You Were a Baby.

1968
Published

1987 WA
Placed on restricted shelves at the Evergreen School District elementary school libraries in Vancouver in accordance with the school board policy to restrict student access to sex education books in elementary school libraries.
Source: 11, May 1987, p. 87.

1583
Showers, Paul.
A Baby Starts to Grow.

1969
Published

1987 WA
Placed on restricted shelves at the Evergreen School District elementary school libraries in Vancouver in accordance with the school board policy to restrict student access to sex education books in elementary school libraries.
Source: 11, May 1987, p. 87.

1584
Shreve, Susan Richards.
Masquerade.

1980
Published

1980
Best Books for Young Adults

1982 OR
Removed from the Grants Pass middle school libraries because of the profanity, violence, and sexual innuendos in the book.
Source: 11, Mar. 1983, p. 39.

1585
Shulman, Irving.
The Amboy Dukes.

1947
Published

1949
Cleared of obscenity charges in Brantford, Ontario, Canada.

1949 MI
Book under fire by local authorities in Detroit.

1949 NJ
Book under fire by local authorities in Newark.

1949 WI
Book under fire by local authorities in Milwaukee.
Source: 4, p. 89.

1586
Shusterman, Neal.
Unwind.

2007
Published

2008
Best Books for Young Adults

2009 KY
Withdrawn from classroom use and the approved curriculum at the Montgomery County High School, but available at the high school library and student book club. Some parents have complained that five novels containing foul language and covering topics—including sex, child abuse, suicide, and drug abuse—are unsuited for discussion in coed high school classes. They also contend that the books don't provide the intellectual challenge and rigor that students need in college preparatory classes. The titles appeared on suggested book lists compiled by the Young Adult Library Services Association, a division of the American Library Association, for twelve- to eighteen-year-olds who are "reluctant readers." The superintendent removed the book because it wasn't on the pre-approved curriculum list and couldn't be added by teachers in the middle of a school year without permission.
Source: 11, Jan. 2010, pp. 16-17; Mar. 2010, p. 56.

1587
Shyer, Marlene Fanta.
Welcome Home, Jellybean.

1978
Published

1991 MD
Challenged, but retained, in the Carroll County schools. Two school board members considered the book depressing.
Source: 11, Mar. 1992, p. 64.

1588
Sidhwa, Bapsi.
Cracking India.

1991
Published

2005 FL
Challenged at Deland High School, near Daytona Beach as part of the school's International Baccalaureate Program, whose curriculum is college-level. In a letter sent home, parents were offered the option of having their children assigned an alternate book. A parent objected to a two-page scene in which the narrator brushes off an older cousin's attempt to trick her into performing oral sex.
Source: 11, Jan. 2006, pp. 13–14.

1589

Sijie, Dai.
Balzac and the Little Chinese Seamstress.

2000
Published

2004 WA
Pulled from the Federal Way's Todd Beamer High School English classes and library by the superintendent, who overruled a committee of educators and parents that unanimously recommended keeping the book. The novel about censorship was considered sexually explicit and inappropriate for high-school students.

Source: 11, July 2004, p. 139.

1590

Silko, Leslie Marmon.
Ceremony.

1997
Published

1995 FL
Removed at the Nease High School in St. Augustine as a required summer reading book for honors English students because of its language, sexual descriptions, and subject matter. The book was recommended for honor students by the National Council of Teachers of English.

1996 TX
Retained on the Round Rock Independent High School reading list after a challenge that the book was too violent.

Source: 11, Nov. 1995, p. 184; Jan. 1996, p. 14; May 1996, p. 99.

1591

Silverstein, Alvin, and Virginia B. Silverstein.
The Reproductive System: How Living Creatures Multiply.

1971
Published

1987 WA
Placed on restricted shelves at the Evergreen School District elementary school libraries in Vancouver in accordance with the school board policy to restrict student access to sex education books in elementary school libraries.

Source: 11, May 1987, p. 87.

1592

Silverstein, Charles, and Edmund White.
The Joy of Gay Sex.

1977
Published

1977 KY
Confiscated from three Lexington bookstores by the local police.

1981 CA
Challenged at the San Jose Public Library.

1984
Seized and shredded by the British Customs Office.

1997 CA
Challenged at the Belmont Public Library because it is "pornographic."

2004 PA
Challenged, but retained, in the Marple Public Library in Broomall along with several sexual instruction manuals including: *Sex Toys 101: A Playfully Uninhibited Guide,* by Rachel Venning; *Great Sex Tips,* by Anne Hooper; *Ultimate Guide to Fellatio,* by Violet Blue; and *The Illustrated Guide to Extended Massive Orgasm,* by Steve Bodansky because the books are "seriously objectionable in text and pictures due to the sexually explicit material."

2005 ID
Challenged at the Nampa Public Library along with seven other books because "they are very pornographic in nature and they have very explicit and detailed illustrations and photographs which we feel don't belong in a library." The library board approved policy changes that restrict children's access to any holdings that may fall under the state's harmful to minors statute and barred the library from buying movies rated NC-17 or X. The book was relocated to the director's office in 2008 and it was eventually restored to the collection in 2008.

2008 MT
Challenged in the Lewis and Clark Library in Helena due to objections over its content. The book has been in the library's collection since 1993. The library director accepted the recommendation of the library's collection review committee that the book be retained in the collection.

2009 KS
Restricted minors' access in the Topeka and Shawnee County Public Library because Kansans for Common Sense contended that the material is "harmful to minors under state law." Later the board organization voted 6-3 in favor of adopting a staff recommendation to keep the books where they are currently located on the shelves in the library's Health Information Neighborhood section.

Source: 11, Mar. 1978, p. 40; Jan. 1982, p. 9; Jan. 1985, p. 26; Sept. 1997, p. 125; Mar. 2004, p. 50; May 2004, p. 117; July 2006, p. 183; May 2008, pp. 96-97; July 2008, pp. 140-41; Nov. 2008, pp. 231-32, 254-55; May 2009, pp. 77-78; July 2009, p.139.

1593

Silverstein, Charles, and Felice Picano.
The New Joy of Gay Sex.

1992
Published

1993 MT
Challenged, but retained, at the Lewis and Clark Library in Helena.

1994 MO
Challenged at the River Bluffs Regional Library in St. Joseph as "pornography." The controversy began after a patron removed a copy of the book from the library and refused to return it, submitting instead a petition with 700 signatures calling for its permanent removal.

1995 MO
Challenged at the Kansas City Public Library. The complainants asked the Jackson County prosecutor's office to ban the book under state's obscenity and sodomy laws.

1996 NJ
Restricted to patrons over eighteen years of age at the Main Memorial Library in Clifton. The book is hidden behind the checkout counter and on the shelves is a dummy book jacket. The book was described as hard-core pornography by the complainant.

Source: 11, July 1993, p. 100; Sept. 1993, p. 158; Nov. 1994, p. 188; Jan. 1995, p. 7; July 1995, p. 94; Mar. 1996, p. 63; May 1996, p. 83.

1594
Silverstein, Charles.
Man to Man.

1982
Published

1986
Seized in London, England, as "indecent or obscene" and "contrary to the prohibition contained in Section 42 of the Customs Consolidation Act, 1876."
Source: 5, May 1986, p. 38.

1595
Silverstein, Shel.
The Giving Tree.

1964
Published

1988 CO
Removed from a locked reference collection at the Boulder Public Library. The book was locked away originally because the librarian considered it sexist.
Source: 11, Jan. 1989, p. 27.

1596
Silverstein, Shel.
A Light in the Attic.

1981
Published

1985 WI
Challenged at the Cunningham Elementary School in Beloit because the book "encourages children to break dishes so they won't have to dry them."

1986 ND
Removed from the shelves of the Minot Public School libraries by the assistant superintendent "in anticipation of a parent's complaint." The superintendent found "suggestive illustrations" on several pages of Silverstein's work. Upon the recommendation of a review committee, the book was returned to the shelves.

1986 NE
Challenged at the elementary schools in the Papillion-LaVista School District in Omaha because the book promotes "behavior abusive to women and children, suicide as a way to manipulate parents, mockery of God, and selfish and disrespectful behavior."

1986 WI
Challenged at the Big Bend Elementary School library in Mukwonago because some of Silverstein's poems "glorified Satan, suicide and cannibalism, and also encouraged children to be disobedient."

1986 WI
Challenged at the West Allis-West Milwaukee school libraries because the book "suggests drug use, the occult, suicide, death, violence, disrespect for truth, disrespect for legitimate authority, rebellion against parents," and because it inspires young people to commit "acts of violence, disbelief, and disrespect."

1987 CA
Challenged at the Moreno Valley Unified School District libraries because it "contains profanity, sexual situations, and themes that allegedly encourage disrespectful behavior."

1987 DE
Challenged at the Appoquinimink schools in Middletown because the book "contains violence, idealizes death, and makes light of manipulative behavior."

1989 IN
Challenged at the South Adams school libraries because the book is "very vile" and "contains subliminal or underlying messages and anti-parent material."

1989 SD
Challenged at the Hot Springs Elementary School as suitable classroom material because of its "objectionable" nature.

1989 TX
The poem "Little Abigail and the Beautiful Pony" from this award-winning children's book was banned from second grade classes in Huffman because a mother protested that it "exposes children to the horrors of suicide."

1992 FL
Restricted to students with parental permission at the Duval County public school libraries because the book features a caricature of a person whose nude behind has been stung by a bee.

1992 PA
Challenged at the West Mifflin schools because the poem "Little Abigail and the Beautiful Pony" is morbid.

1993 FL
Challenged at the Fruitland Park Elementary School library in Lake County because the book "promotes disrespect, horror, and violence."

1996 MO
Challenged, but retained, on the Webb City school library shelves. A parent had protested that the book imparts a "dreary" and "negative" message.
Source: 11, July 1985, p. 134; May 1986, p. 80; Sept. 1986, p. 172; Nov. 1986, p. 224; Jan. 1987, p. 12; Mar. 1987, pp. 51, 67–68; May 1987, p. 101; July 1987, p. 125; May 1989, p. 80; July 1989, p. 129; Jan. 1990, p. 32; July 1992, p. 105; Mar. 1993, p. 45; July 1993, p. 97; Sept. 1993, p. 157; May 1996, p. 97.

1597
Silverstein, Shel.
Where the Sidewalk Ends.

1974
Published

1983 OH
Challenged at the Xenia school libraries because the book is "anti-Christian, against parental and school authorities, and emphasized the use of drugs and sexual activity."

1986 ND
Removed from the shelves of the Minot public school libraries by the assistant superintendent "in anticipation of a parent's complaint." Upon the recommendation of a review committee, the book was returned to the shelves.

1986 WI
Challenged at the Big Bend Elementary School library in Mukwonago because some of Silverstein's poems "glorified Satan, suicide and cannibalism, and also encouraged children to be disobedient."

1986 WI
Challenged at the West Allis-West Milwaukee school libraries because the book "suggests drug use, the occult, suicide, death, violence, disrespect for truth, disrespect for legitimate authority, rebellion against parents," and because it inspires young people to commit "acts of violence, disbelief, and disrespect."

1987 CA
Challenged at the Moreno Valley Unified School District libraries because it "contains profanity, sexual situations, and themes that allegedly encourage disrespectful behavior."

1989 IL
Reversing an earlier decision to remove the poem "Dreadful" from the library's copy of this book in a Riverdale elementary school, the school board retained the book and poem, which was challenged for bad taste.

1990 CA
Retained in the Modesto district libraries and classrooms after being challenged as inappropriate for young readers.

1993 FL
Challenged at the Fruitland Park Elementary School library in Lake County because the book "promotes disrespect, horror, and violence."

1993 PA
Challenged at the Central Columbia School District in Bloomsburg because a poem titled "Dreadful" talks about how "someone ate the baby."
Source: 11, Sept. 1983, p. 139; Nov. 1983, p. 197; May 1986, p. 80; Sept. 1986, p. 172; Nov. 1986, p. 224; Mar. 1987, p. 51; May 1987, p. 101; July 1987, p. 125; Mar. 1990, p. 61; May 1990, p. 105; May 1993, p. 86; July 1993, p. 97; Sept. 1993, p. 157.

1598
Simon, Neil.
Brighton Beach Memoirs.

1983
Published

1983
New York Drama Critics' Circle Best Play

1984
Best Books for Young Adults

1991 IL
Challenged at the Grayslake Community High School.

1996 TX
Removed from the required reading and optional reading lists from the Dallas schools because of passages containing profanity and sexually explicit language.
Source: 11, July 1991, pp. 129-30; May 1996, p. 88.

1599
Simon, Sidney.
Values Clarification.

1972
Published
1979 IN
Burned in Warsaw.
Source: 9; 11, Mar. 1980, p. 40.

1600
Sinclair, April.
Coffee Will Make You Black.

1994
Published

1995
Best Books for Young Adults

1996 IL
Removed from the curriculum at the Julian High School in Chicago because the book was not appropriate for freshman as required reading because of sexually explicit language.
Source: 11, May 1996, p. 87.

1601
Sinclair, Upton.
The Jungle.

1906
Published

1929
Banned from public libraries in Yugoslavia.

1933
Burned in the Nazi bonfires because of Sinclair's socialist views.

1956
Banned in East Germany in 1956 as inimical to Communism.

1985
Banned in South Korea.
Source: 4, p. 63; 5, Apr. 1986, pp. 30–33.

1602
Sinclair, Upton.
Oil!

1927
Published

1927 MA
Forbidden in Boston because of its comments on the Harding Administration—although Harding had died in 1923 and his cronies were long dispersed. Sinclair defended the case himself, at a cost of $2,000, and addressed a crowd of some 2,000 people on Boston Commons, explaining at length the character and intent of his book. The court suppressed nine pages of the book, including a substantial portion of the Biblical "Song of Solomon." The bookseller from whose store the book had been seized was fined $100 and the offending pages were blacked out.

1929
Banned from public libraries in Yugoslavia.

1933
Burned by the Nazi bonfires because of Sinclair's socialist views.

1956
Banned in East Germany in 1956 as inimical to Communism.
Source: 2, p. 133; 3, p. 512; 4, p. 63.

1603
Sinclair, Upton.
Wide Is the Gate.

1943
Published

1953
Banned in Ireland.

1956
Banned in East Germany as inimical to Communism.
Source: 4, p. 63.

1604
Sioux City Community School District.
Sioux City, Past and Present.

1971
Published

1984 IA
Banned from the Sioux City schools because the textbook is "racist and offensive."
Source: 11, Mar. 1985, pp. 43-44.

1605
Sissley, Emily L., and Bertha Harris.
The Joy of Lesbian Sex.

1977
Published

1984
Seized by the British Customs Office.
Source: 11, Jan. 1985, p. 26.

1606
Sittenfeld, Curtis.
Prep: A Novel.

2005
Published

2008 CA
Pulled from the accelerated reading program in the Heritage Oak Private School in Yorba Linda. A parent complained that the book was "pornographic."

2012 PA
Removed from the Emmaus High School ninth-grade summer reading list because the story of a girl from Indiana who goes to a boarding school in New England was "too mature for ninth graders." Instead, it was added to the twelfth-grade Advanced Placement reading list.
Source: 11, May 2008, p. 95.

1607
Sixx, Nikki.
The Heroin Diaries: A Year in the Life of a Shattered Rock Star.

2007
Published

2010 FL
Pulled from an optional, supplemental reading list in an Advanced Placement psychology course in Brooksville Hernando High School because of complaints about explicit language, descriptions of drug use, and photos. Written by the former bassist for the heavy metal band Mötley Crüe, it is a cautionary tale about the dangers of drug use.
Source: 11, Nov. 2010, pp. 242-43.

1608
Skarmeta, Antonio.
Burning Patience.

1987
Published

1995 ME
Challenged as required reading in a freshman English class Orono High School because of the book's sexual content. The book was made into the successful film *The Postman.*
Source: 11, Nov. 1995, p. 186.

1609
Slepian, Jan.
The Alfred Summer.

1980
Published

1981
National Book Award for Young People's Literature

1983 VA
Challenged in Charlotte County due to "objectionable" words in the text.

1991 CT
Pulled, but later restored to the language arts curriculum at four Cheshire elementary schools because the book is "filled with profanity, blasphemy and obscenities, and gutter language."
Source: 11, Nov. 1983, p. 197; Mar. 1992, p. 42; May 1992, p. 96; July 1992, pp. 109–10.

1610
Slier, Deborah, ed.
Make a Joyful Sound.

1991
Published

1992 WA
Challenged at the Deer Park elementary schools because the poetry collection contains the poem, "The Mask," by Dakari Kamaru Hru. A Deer Park parent complained that, "This is religious indoctrination. We in the Western World would refer to it as devil worship. It also smacks of New Age religion."
Source: 11, May 1992, pp. 84–85.

1611
Small, Beatrice.
To Love Again: A Historical Romance.

1993
Published

1993 ID
Challenged at the Pocatello Public Library because a patron considered the romance novel "pornographic."
Source: 11, Mar. 1994, p. 69.

1612
Smiley, Jane.
A Thousand Acres.

1991
Published

1991
National Book Critics Circle Award for Fiction

1992
Pulitzer Prize for Fiction

1994 WA
Banned at the Lynden High School. The novel was described as having "no literary value in our community right now." School officials note that the protestors have tried to block an anti-drug program, a multicultural program, and a Valentine's Day dance, saying that they did not reflect the values parents want taught.

1996 TX
Retained on the Round Rock Independent High School reading list after a challenge that the book was too violent.

2012 TX
Removed from the Katy Independent School District required reading list following parental complaints about references to sex and violence.
Source: 11, May 1994, p. 88; May 1996, p. 99; Mar. 2013, p. 50.

1613
Smith, Betty.
Joy in the Morning.

1946
Published

1997 WV
Removed from the Jackson County school libraries along with sixteen other titles.
Source: 11, Jan. 1998, p. 13.

1614
Smith, Jeff.
Bone.

2004
Published

2010 MN
Retained in the Rosemount elementary school libraries despite a parent's concern that the series includes smoking, drinking, and gambling in its graphics and storyline. The series is rated suitable for fourth grade and up, has won several awards, and received positive reviews from national publications, including *Time*, which touted the series as the "best all-ages graphic novel ever published."
Source: 11, July 2010, p. 175.

1615

Smith, Lee.
Fair and Tender Ladies.

1988
Published

2007 VA

Challenged in the Washington County schools because of a few "crude" words deemed too graphic for teenage honor students. The author claimed the book provides teens with a safe forum to address issues such as unwanted pregnancy. The novel demonstrates the necessity of a good education and highlights the importance of southwestern Virginia's heritage.
Source: 11, Jan. 2008, pp. 35-36.

1616

Smith, Lillian.
Strange Fruit.

1944
Published

1944 MA
Majority of bookstores in Boston removed the book from sale. The book's distributor was charged in 1945 under the Massachusetts laws governing obscene material, in that he had distributed a publication that was "obscene, indecent, impure, or manifestly tends to corrupt the morals of youth." The court found the bookseller guilty and fined him $200, later reduced to $25. The fact that the novel might promote "lascivious thoughts and...arouse lustful desire" outweighed any artistic merit that the novel might possess.

1944 MI
Majority of bookstores in Detroit removed the book from sale.

1953
Banned in Ireland.
Source: 3, p. 551; 4, pp. 78–79; 15, Vol. IV, p. 698.

1617

Smith, Patrick.
A Land Remembered.

1984
Published

2003 FL
Challenged, but retained, in the Indian River County Schools in Vero Beach despite two parents' complaints about racially offensive language. One of the parents said the book's use of the "N-word" created a hostile learning environment for his children.
Source: 11, Jan. 2004, p. 28.

1618

Smith, Rebecca M.
Family Matters: Concepts in Marriage and Personal Relationships.

1982
Published

1986 NY
Challenged as proposed ninth-grade curriculum textbook in the Buffalo schools because it promotes "secular humanism." In particular, the complainant objected to references to the psychological theories of Erik Erikson, Sigmund Freud, Abraham Maslow, and Jean Piaget.
Source: 11, Mar. 1987, p. 68.

1619

Smith, Robert Kimmell.
Chocolate Fever.

1972
Published

1992 OH
Challenged at the Gahanna-Jefferson Public Schools because it contains the words "damn" and "sucks."
Source: 11, Jan. 1993, p. 12.

1620

Smith, Robert Kimmell.
Jelly Belly.

1981
Published

1992 OH
Challenged at the Gahanna-Jefferson Public Schools because it contains the words "damn" and "sucks."
Source: 11, Jan. 1993, p. 12.

1621

Smith, Robert Kimmell.
Mostly Michael.

1987
Published

1992 OH
Challenged at the Gahanna-Jefferson Public Schools because it contains the words "damn" and "sucks."
Source: 11, Jan. 1993, p. 12.

1622

Smith, Wallace.
Bessie Cotter.

1934
Published

1935
The publisher was charged with selling an "obscene book" and "intent to corrupt" and was ordered to appear before the Bow Street magistrate in London, England. The court fined Heinemann "for publishing an allegedly indecent American book" and ordered the book to be removed from distribution.
Source: 13, pp. 25–26.

1623

Smucker, Barbara Claassen.
Runaway to Freedom: A Story of the Underground Railway.

1978
Published

1991 MD
Challenged, but retained, in the Carroll County schools. Two school board members were offended by its allegedly coarse language.

1993 DE
Challenged at the West Dover Elementary School because it is offensive to African Americans. The objectionable passage reads, "Massa lay on the feather bed and nigger lay on the floor."
Source: 11, Mar. 1992, p. 64; Jan. 1994, p. 15.

1624

Snepp, Frank.
A Decent Interval.

1978
Published

1978
The U.S. Justice Department filed a civil complaint against the author demanding a lifetime ban on his writing or speaking about the CIA.
Source: 4, p. 100; 8, pp. 36–39; 15, Vol. IV, p. 717.

1625
Snow, Edgar.
Red Star Over China.

1938
Published

1985
Banned in South Korea.
Source: 5, Apr. 1986, pp. 30–33.

1626
Snyder, Jane McIntosh.
Sappho.

1995
Published

2000 CA
Removed from the Anaheim school district because school officials said the book is too difficult for middle school students and that it could cause harassment against students seen with it. The American Civil Liberties Union (ACLU) of Southern California filed suit in *Doe v. Anaheim Union High School District* alleging that the removal is "a pretext for viewpoint-based censorship." The ACLU claims no other books have been removed from the junior high library for similar reasons, even though several, such as works by Shakespeare and Dickens, are more difficult reading. The ACLU contends that the school officials engaged in unconstitutional viewpoint discrimination by removing the book because it contains gay and lesbian material. In March 2001, the school board approved a settlement that restored the book to the high school shelves and amended the district's policy to prohibit the removal of books for subject matter involving sexual orientation, but the book will not be returned to the middle school.
Source: 11, Mar. 2001, p. 53; May 2001, p. 95; July 2001, p. 173.

1627
Snyder, Zilpha Keatley.
The Egypt Game.

1967
Published

1968
Newbery Honor Book

1995 TX
Challenged in the Richardson schools because it shows children in dangerous situations, condones trespassing and lying to parents, and teaches children about the occult. The school board declined to ban the award-winning novel but did decide that parents should be notified when it is used in class.

2009 TX
Challenged as part of a reading list in a fourth-grade class at Southern Hills Elementary School in Wichita Falls because the book includes scenes depicting Egyptian worship rituals. The book has been an optional part of the school district's curriculum for years. "I'm not going to stop until it's banned from the school district. I will not quiet down. I will not back down. I don't believe any student should be subjected to anything that has to do with evil gods or black magic," said the student's father.
Source: 11, Mar. 1995, p. 56; Jan. 2010, p. 17.

1628
Snyder, Zilpha Keatley.
The Headless Cupid.

1971
Published

1972
Newbery Honor Book

1989 KS
Challenged at the Hays Public Library because the book "could lead young readers to embrace satanism."

1990 MI
Retained in the Grand Haven school libraries after a parent objected to the book because it "introduces children to the occult and fantasy about immoral acts."

1991 MD
Retained on the approved reading list at Matthew Henson Middle School in Waldorf despite objections to its references to witchcraft.

1992 CA
Challenged in the Escondido school because it contains references to the occult.
Source: 11, July 1989, p. 143; May 1990, p. 106; Sept. 1991, pp. 155–56; Sept. 1992, p. 161.

1629
Snyder, Zilpha Keatley.
The Witches of Worm.

1972
Published

1973
National Book Award for Young People's Literature

1973
Newbery Honor Book

1982 FL
Restricted in Escambia County to sixth graders and above because "it contains 183 pages of rejection, fear, hatred, occult ritual, cruel pranks, lies and even an attempted murder by arson all perpetrated by a twelve-year-old girl."

1988 OR
Challenged at the Kennedy High School in Mt. Angel for its witchcraft theme and scary illustrations.

1990 MI
Retained in the Grand Haven school libraries after a parent objected to the book because it "introduces children to the occult and fantasy about immoral acts."
Source: 11, July 1982, p. 123; Jan. 1989, p. 3; May 1990, p. 106.

1630
Solotareff, Gregoire.
Don't Call Me Little Bunny.

1988
Published

1989 OR
Challenged at the Douglas County Library in Roseburg because the character gets away with bad behavior.

1995 IL
Challenged in the Cook Memorial Library in Libertyville because the actions taken by the bunny character in the book were anti-social and inappropriate for children's reading.
Source: 11, Jan. 1990, pp. 4–5; Jan. 1996, p. 29.

1631
Solzhenitsyn,
Aleksandr Isayevich.
August 1914.

1972
Published

1970
Nobel Prize in Literature

1974
Barred from publication in the USSR; the author was stripped of Soviet citizenship and deported.
Source: 4, p. 91.

1632
Solzhenitsyn, Aleksandr Isayevich.
Cancer Ward.

1966
Published

1974
Barred from publication in the USSR; the author was stripped of Soviet citizenship and deported.
Source: 4, p. 91.

1633
Solzhenitsyn,
Aleksandr Isayevich.
Candle in the Wind.

1973
Published

1974
Barred from publication in the USSR; the author was stripped of Soviet citizenship and deported.
Source: 4, p. 91.

1634
Solzhenitsyn,
Aleksandr Isayevich.
The First Circle.

1964
Published

1974
Barred from publication in the USSR; the author was stripped of Soviet citizenship and deported.
Source: 4, p. 91.

1635
Solzhenitsyn,
Aleksandr Isayevich.
The Gulag Archipelago.

1973
Published

1974
Barred from publication in the USSR; the author was stripped of Soviet citizenship and deported.
Source: 4, p. 91; 8, pp. 76–77.

1636
Solzhenitsyn,
Aleksandr Isayevich.
The Love Girl and the Innocent.

1972
Published

1974
Barred from publication in the USSR; the author was stripped of Soviet citizenship and deported.
Source: 4, p. 91.

1637
Solzhenitsyn,
Aleksandr Isayevich.
One Day in the Life of Ivan Denisovich.

1962
Published

1974
Barred from publication in the USSR; the author was stripped of Soviet citizenship and deported.

1976 NH
Removed from the Milton High School library due to objectionable language.

1976 NJ
Challenged in Mahwah.

1979 WA
Challenged in Omak.

1981 MA
Challenged in the Mohawk Trail Regional High School in Buckland because of profanity in the book.

1995 WY
Removed from the Lincoln Count high school curriculum because of "considerable obscenities."

1999 IA
Retained at the Storm Lake High School despite objections to the novel's profanity.
Source: 4, p. 91; 11, May 1976, p. 61; Jan. 1977, p. 8; July 1979, pp. 10–11; July 1995, p. 100; July 1999, p. 105.

1638
Solzhenitsyn,
Aleksandr Isayevich.
Stories and Prose Poems.

1971
Published

1974
Barred from publication in the USSR; the author was stripped of Soviet citizenship and deported.
Source: 4, p. 91.

1639
Sones, Sonya.
One of Those Hideous Books Where the Mother Dies.

2004
Published

2005
Best Books for Young Adults

2010 WI
Challenged at the Theisen Middle School in Fond du Lac because a parent's belief that the book's "sexual content was too mature for eleven- to fourteen-year-olds." The same parent plans to request removal of six other books from the library, including the *Sisterhood of the Traveling Pants* series, another set of books by Sones, and *Get Well Soon*, by Julie Halpern.
Source: 11, Mar. 2010, p. 54; May 2010, pp. 127-28; July 2010, pp. 156, 176.

1640
Sones, Sonya.
What My Mother Doesn't Know.

2001
Published

2002
Best Books for Young Adults

2003 CA
Removed from the library shelves of the Rosedale Union School District in Bakersfield because of discomfort with Sones's poem, "Ice Capades"—a teenage girl's description of how her breasts react to cold.

2004 TX
Challenged at the Bonnette Junior High School library in Deer Park because the book includes foul language and references to masturbation. The book was selected as a "Young Adults Choice" by the International Reading Association in 2003 and included on the Texas Lone Star State Reading List.

2007 WI
Available only to seventh- and eighth-graders at the Spring Hill School library after a parent wanted the book, which deals with masturbation, groping, and sexual fantasy, among other themes, to be removed from the library and the accelerated reading program.
Source: 11, Nov. 2003, p. 227; Jan. 2005, p. 7; July 2007, pp. 144-45.

1641
Sonnie, Amy, ed.
Revolutionary Voices: A Multicultural Queer Youth Anthology.

2000
Published

2010 NJ
Banned by the Rancocas Valley Board of Education from the Mount Holly High School library shelves after a local conservative group expressed concern that the book was too graphic and obscene. The local group, part of the 9/12 Project, a nationwide government watchdog network launched by the talk-radio and television personality Glenn Beck, called for the banning of three books, all dealing with teenage sexuality and issues of homosexuality. The two other titles challenged, but retained, were: *Love and Sex: Ten Stories of Truth* edited by Michael Cart, and *The Full Spectrum: A New Generation of Writing about Gay, Lesbian, Bisexual, Transgender, Questioning, and Other Identities* edited by David Levithan and Billy Merrell.

2010 NJ
Removed from the Burlington County public library after a member of Glenn Beck's 9/12 Project complained about Sonnie's book. Named as one of the best adult books for high school students by *School Library Journal* in 2001, the book was called "pervasively vulgar, obscene, and inappropriate."
Source: 11, July 2010, pp. 154-56; Sept. 2010, pp. 199-200.

1642
Soyinka, Wole.
The Man Died: Prison Notes of Wole Soyinka.

1971
Published

1986
Nobel Prize in Literature.

1984
Banned in Nigeria. The 1984 Public Officers Decree—Protection Against False Accusation—"made it a criminal offence to publish any article that brought the government or any public official into disrepute." Thus, any published statement, true or false, that could embarrass any government official was forbidden.
Source: 7, p. 321.

1643
Spargo, Edward.
Topics for the Restless.

1974
Published

1986 CO
Challenged at the Jefferson County school libraries in Lakewood. The textbook is a collection of stories and essays designed to promote critical thought among high school students. Parents found "most objectionable" selections from the *Feminine Mystique*, which they said was too favorable to the Equal Rights Amendment; a story on Marilyn Monroe; "Death with Dignity," which addresses what children should be taught about death; and "Hiroshima—Death and Rebirth I and II," stories they claimed "make Americans feel guilty about bombing Hiroshima." The Jefferson County School Board refused to ban the book.
Source: 11, May 1986, p. 82; Sept. 1986, p. 173; Nov. 1986, p. 224.

1644
Sparks, Beatrice.
Jay's Journal.

1978
Published

1998 WA
Challenged for use in the Richland high school English classes along with six other titles because the "books are poor-quality literature and stress suicide, illicit sex, violence, and hopelessness."
Source: 11, Mar. 1999, p. 40.

1645
Speare, Elizabeth George.
The Sign of the Beaver.

1983
Published

1983
Best Books for Young Adults

1984
Newbery Honor Book

2000 FL
Challenged in a Pinellas County elementary school for use of the word "squaw" to refer to Native American women.
Source: 11, May 2000, p. 76.

1646
Speare, Elizabeth George.
Witch of Blackbird Pond.

1958
Published

1959
Newbery Medal

2002 CT
Challenged in the middle school curriculum in Cromwell based on concern that it promotes witchcraft and violence.
Source: 11, Sept. 2002, p. 197; Nov. 2002, pp. 257–58.

1647
Spencer, Scott.
Endless Love.

1979
Published

1991 SC
Banned from the Berkeley County High School media center because of "explicit pornographic passages and adult material for teenage readers."
Source: 11, Mar. 1992, p. 41.

1648

Spiegelman, Art, and
Francoise Mouly.
Raw.

1980
Published

1992 OR
Challenged at the Douglas County
Library in Roseburg because "it's full of
cartoon pornography."
Source: 11, Jan. 1993, p. 9.

1649

Spies, Karen Bornemann.
*Everything You Need to Know
about Incest.*

1992
Published

1996 LA
Pulled from the Ouachita Parish School
library in Monroe because of sexual
content. The Louisiana chapter of the
ACLU filed a lawsuit in the federal courts
on October 3, 1996, claiming that the
principal and the school superintendent
violated First Amendment free speech
rights and also failed to follow established
procedure when they removed the
book. The three-year-old school library
censorship case headed to court after the
Ouachita Parish School Board made no
decision to seek a settlement at a special
meeting on April 12, 1999. On August 17,
1999, the Ouachita Parish School Board
agreed to return the book to the library
and to develop a new book-selection
policy that follows state guidelines for
school media programs.
Source: 11, Sept. 1996, pp. 151–52; Jan. 1997, p. 7;
July 1999, p. 93; Jan. 2000, p. 27.

1650

Spinelli, Jerry.
Jason and Marceline.

1986
Published

1992 NJ
Challenged at the Pitman Middle School
library because the book promotes stealing,
drinking, profanity, and premarital sex.

1993 ND
Challenged, but retained, as part of the
curriculum at Hughes Junior High School
in Bismarck. The controversy centered
around the use of profanity and sexually
explicit language.
Source: 11, July 1992, p. 106; Jan. 1993, p. 27;
Sept. 1993, p. 145; Jan. 1994, p. 38.

1651

Spinelli, Jerry.
Space Station, Seventh Grade.

1982
Published

1988 OR
Challenged at the La Grande Middle
School library because "profanity,
sexual obscenity, immoral values are
throughout the book."
Source: 11, May 1989, p. 93.

1652

Spinoza, Baruch.
Ethics.

1677
Published

1679
His writings were widely banned in
Holland as atheistic and subversive.

1679
The Catholic Church placed all of his
work on the *Index Librorum Prohibitorum*
(Index of Prohibited Books) in Rome, Italy.
His works remained listed until 1966.
Source: 1, pp. 101–3.

1653

Spraggett, Allen.
*Arthur Ford: The Man Who
Talked with the Dead.*

1973
Published

1987 MI
Challenged at the Plymouth-Canton
school system in Canton because the book
deals with witchcraft.
Source: 11, May 1987, p. 110.

1654

St. Stephen's
Community House.
*The Little Black Book for Girlz:
A Book on Healthy Sexuality.*

2006
Published

2013 OR
Challenged at the Taft High library
in Lincoln City because "it is simply
too graphic for a seventh grader."
Each library book is "run by a district
committee made up of district staff and
community members."
Source: 11, July 2013, pp. 141-42.

1655

Stadtmauer, Saul A.
*Visions of the Future:
Magic Boards.*

1977
Published

1984 OR
Removed from the Philomath
Middle School library because it was
"badly written."

1991 OR
Challenged at the Dallas school
library because the book entices
impressionable or emotionally disturbed
children into becoming involved in
witchcraft or the occult.

1992 VA
Pulled, but later placed on reserve to
children with parental permission
at the Forrest Elementary School library
in Hampton.
Source: 11, Sept. 1984, p. 138; Jan. 1992, p. 26;
July 1992, p. 108; Sept. 1992, p. 139.

1656

Stamper, Judith Bauer.
*More Tales for the
Midnight Hour.*

1992
Published

1992 AZ
Challenged at the Neely Elementary
School in Gilbert because the book shows
the dark side of religion through the
occult, the devil, and satanism.
Source: 11, May 1992, p. 78; July 1992, p. 124.

1657

Stanislawski, Michael.
Tsar Nicholas I and the Jews:
The Transformation of Jewish
Society in Russia, 1825-1855.

1983
Published

1983
Banned from the 1983 Moscow
International Book Fair along with more
than fifty other books because it is
"anti-Soviet."
Source: 11, Nov. 1983, p. 201.

1658

Stanley, Lawrence A., ed.
Rap, The Lyrics.

1992
Published

1993 WA
Parent requested that all offensive
materials be labeled at the Sno-Isle
Regional Library in Marysville.
Source: 11, July 1993, p. 103.

1659

Stanway, Andrew.
The Lovers' Guide.

1994
Published

1996 NJ
Removed from the Clifton Public
Library and replaced with a dummy book
made of styrofoam. The library's new
policy restricts to adults any material
containing "patently offensive graphic
illustrations or photographs of sexual or
excretory activities or contact as measured
by contemporary community standards
for minors."
Source: 11, July 1996, pp. 118–19.

1660

Starhawk, and Hilary Valentine.
The Twelve Wild Swans:
A Journey to the Realm of
Magic, Healing, and Action:
Rituals, Exercises and
Magical Training in the
Reclaiming Tradition.

2000
Published

2001 AR
Challenged, but retained, at the
Springdale Public Library despite a
complaint that the book is a "witchcraft
manual" and "turns people away from
God and *Bible* scriptures."
Source: 11, Nov. 2001, p. 277.

1661

Stark, Evan, ed.
Everything You Need to Know
about Sexual Abuse.

1988
Published

1991 WI
Challenged at the Arcadia schools
because the book presents sexual abuse
situations too descriptively.
Source: 11, Sept. 1991, p. 154.

1662

Starkey, Marion Lena.
The Tall Man from Boston.

1975
Published

1985 FL
Challenged at the Sikes Elementary School
media center in Lakeland because the
book "would lead children to believe ideas
contrary to the teachings of the *Bible*."
Source: 11, July 1985, p. 133.

1663

Steel, Danielle.
Changes.

1983
Published

1985 PA
Banned from the Stroudsburg High
School library because it was "blatantly
graphic, pornographic and wholly
unacceptable for a high school library."
Source: 11, May 1985, p. 79.

1664

Steel, Danielle.
Crossings.

1982
Published

1985 PA
Banned from the Stroudsburg High
School library because it was "blatantly
graphic, pornographic and wholly
unacceptable for a high school library."
Source: 11, May 1985, p. 79.

1665

Steel, Danielle.
The Gift.

1994
Published

1996 OH
Challenged at a Coventry school because
"the schools had no business teaching
his children about sex, that it was the job
of the parents."
Source: 11, Jan. 1997, p. 11.

1666

Steer, Dugald.
Wizardology: The Book of
the Secrets of Merlin.

2005
Published

2007 CT
Challenged at the West Haven's Molloy
Elementary School library because the
book exposes children to the occult.
Source: 11, May 2007, p. 91.

1667

Steig, William.
Abel's Island.

1976
Published

1977
Newbery Honor Book

1990 FL
Pulled from the fifth- and sixth-grade
optional reading lists in Clay County
schools because of references to drinking
wine, which administrators determined
violated the district's substance abuse
policy. The objectionable passage reads:
"At home he had to drink some wine to
dispel the chill in his bones. He drank
large draughts of his wine and ran about
everywhere like a wild animal, shouting
and yodeling."
Source: 11, Jan. 1991, p. 16.

1668
Steig, William.
The Amazing Bone.

1976
Published

1977
Caldecott Honor Book

1986 NJ
Challenged at the West Amwell school libraries in Lambertville because a parent objected to "the use of tobacco by the animals."

1993 WA
Challenged at the Discovery Elementary School library in Issaquah because of the graphic and detailed violence.
Source: 11, Mar. 1987, p. 65; Mar. 1994, p. 70.

1669
Steig, William.
Caleb and Kate.

1977
Published

1978
National Book Award for Young People's Literature

1992 PA
Pulled from the Boyertown elementary school library shelves because the book "depicts a dismal outlook on marriage and life." The book was eventually returned.
Source: 11, Mar. 1993, p. 42; May 1993, p. 86.

1670
Steig, William.
Sylvester and the Magic Pebble.

1969
Published

1970
Caldecott Medal

1970
National Book Award for Young People's Literature

1970 CA
In 1970, a nationwide campaign began to remove the book from schools and public libraries across the United States. Challenged in Palo Alto.

1970 IL
Challenged in Wood River.

1970 IL
Removed "for reevaluation" in East Alton.

1970 KS
Challenged in Kansas.

1970 MD
Challenged in Maryland.

1970 MD
The library in Wicomico County answered the challenge by retaining the book.

1970 MD
The library in Prince George County answered the challenge by retaining the book.

1970 NE
Challenged in Lincoln.

1970 NY
Challenged in Queens.

1970 OH
Removed "for reevaluation" in Toledo.

1970 OH
Challenged in Ohio.

1970 PA
Challenged in Pennsylvania.

1970 SC
Challenged in South Carolina.

1970 WY
Challenged in Wyoming.

1971 IL
The Illinois Police Association wrote to librarians asking them to remove the book because its characters, all shown as animals, present police as pigs—although in favorable portrayals. Similar problems reported in eleven other states.
Source: 4, p. 87; 7, pp. 477–80.

1671
Steiger, Brad.
Beyond Belief: True Mysteries of the Unknown.

1991
Published

1995 CA
Challenged at the Hemet Elementary School. The teacher was placed on paid administrative leave after a parent complained that the book deals with the supernatural and the occult.
Source: 11, May 1995, p. 65.

1672
Stein, Sol.
The Magician.

1971
Published

1981 WI
Challenged in Montello.
Source: 11, May 1981, p. 73.

1673
Steinbeck, John.
East of Eden.

1952
Published

1962
Nobel Prize in Literature

1982
Removed from school libraries in Morris, Manitoba, Canada.

1982 AL
Removed from two Anniston high school libraries because it is "ungodly and obscene," but later reinstated on a restrictive basis.

1991 SC
Challenged in the Greenville schools because the book uses the name of God and Jesus in a "vain and profane manner along with inappropriate sexual references."
Source: 11, Mar. 1983, p. 37; July 1991, p. 130.

1674
Steinbeck, John.
Grapes of Wrath.

1939
Published

1940
Pulitzer Prize for Fiction

1939 CA
Banned in Kern County, the scene of Steinbeck's novel.

1939 IL
Burned by the East St. Louis Public Library.

1939 MO
Banned in Kansas City.

1939 NY
Barred from the Buffalo Public Library on the grounds that "vulgar words" were used.

1953
Banned in Ireland.

1973
On February 21, 1973, eleven Turkish book publishers went on trial before an Istanbul martial law tribunal on charges of publishing, possessing, and selling books in violation of an order of the Istanbul martial law command. They faced possible sentences of between one month's and six months' imprisonment "for spreading propaganda unfavorable to the state" and the confiscation of their books. Eight booksellers were also on trial with the publishers on the same charge.

1980 IA
Banned in Kanawha High School classes.

1980 NY
Challenged in Vernon-Verona-Sherill School District.

1981 VT
Challenged as required reading for Richford High School English students due to the book's language and portrayal of a former minister who recounts how he took advantage of a young woman.

1982
Banned in Morris, Manitoba, Canada.

1982 AL
Removed from two Anniston high school libraries, but later reinstated on a restrictive basis.

1986 NC
Challenged at the Moore County school system in Carthage because the book contains the phase "God damn."

1986 NC
Challenged at the Cummings High School in Burlington as an optional reading assignment because the "book is full of filth. My son is being raised in a Christian home and this book takes the Lord's name in vain and has all kinds of profanity in it." Although the parent spoke to the press, a formal complaint with the school demanding the book's removal was not filed.

1991 SC
Challenged in the Greenville schools because the book uses the name of God and Jesus in a "vain and profane manner along with inappropriate sexual references."

1993 TN
Challenged in the Union City High School classes.

Source: 4, p. 82; 5, Summer 1973, p. xii; 8, pp. 61–70; 9, p. 142; 11, May 1980, pp. 52, 62; Jan. 1982, p. 18; Mar. 1983, p. 37; July 1986, p. 120; Nov. 1986, p. 210; Jan. 1987, p. 32; July 1991, p. 130; Mar. 1994, p. 55; 15, Vol. III, pp. 651–52.

1675
Steinbeck, John.
In Dubious Battle.

1936
Published

1953
Banned in Ireland.
Source: 4, p. 83.

1676
Steinbeck, John.
Of Mice and Men.

1937
Published

1953
Banned in Ireland.

1974 IN
Banned in Syracuse.

1977 PA
Banned in Oil City.

1977 SC
Challenged in Greenville by the Fourth Province of the Knights of the Ku Klux Klan.

1979 MI
Challenged, but retained, in the Grand Blanc schools despite the novel being characterized as "vulgar and blasphemous."

1980 NY
Challenged in Vernon-Verona-Sherill School District.

1980 OH
Challenged in Continental.

1981 AZ
Challenged in Saint David.

1982 IN
Challenged in Tell City due to "profanity and using God's name in vain."

1983 AL
Banned from classroom use at the Scottsboro Skyline High School due to "profanity."

1984 TN
The Knoxville School Board chairman vowed to have "filthy books" removed from Knoxville's public schools and picked Steinbeck's novel as the first target due to "its vulgar language."

1987 KY
Reinstated at the Christian County school libraries and English classes after being challenged as vulgar and offensive.

1988 IL
Challenged at the Wheaton-Warrenville Middle School.

1988 MI
Challenged at the Berrien Springs High School because the book contains profanity.

1988 WV
Challenged in the Marion County schools.

1989 AL
Removed from the Northside High School in Tuscaloosa because the book "has profane use of God's name."

1989 AR
Removed from the White Chapel High School in Pine Bluff because of objections to language.

1989 TN
Challenged as a summer youth program reading assignment in Chattanooga because "Steinbeck is known to have had an anti-business attitude." In addition, "he was very questionable as to his patriotism."

1989 TN
Challenged as appropriate for high school reading lists in the Shelby County school system because the novel contained "offensive language."

1990 KS
Challenged, but retained, in a Salina tenth-grade English class despite concerns that it contained "profanity" and "takes the Lord's name in vain."

1990 TX
Challenged in the Riviera schools because it contains profanity.

1991 CA
Challenged by a Fresno parent as a tenth-grade English college preparatory curriculum assignment, citing "profanity" and "racial slurs." The book was retained, and the child of the objecting parent was provided with an alternative reading assignment.

1991 FL
Removed and later returned to the Suwannee High School library because the book is "indecent."

1991 PA
Challenged as curriculum material at the Ringgold High School in Carroll Township because the novel contains terminology offensive to blacks.

1991 TN
Challenged at the Jacksboro High School because the novel contains "blasphemous" language, excessive cursing, and sexual overtones.

1991 VA
Challenged as required reading in the Buckingham County schools because of profanity.

1992 AL
A coalition of community members and clergy in Mobile requested that local school officials form a special textbook screening committee to "weed out objectionable things." Steinbeck's novel was the first target because it contained "profanity" and "morbid and depressing themes."

1992 CA
Challenged at the Modesto High School as recommended reading because of "offensive and racist language." The word "nigger" appears in the book.

1992 FL
Challenged in the Duval County public school libraries because of profanity; lurid passages about sex; and statements defamatory to minorities, God, women, and the disabled.

1992 IA
Challenged in the Waterloo schools.

1992 LA
Challenged at the Oak Hill High School in Alexandria because of profanity.

1992 OH
Temporarily removed from the Hamilton High School reading list after a parent complained about its vulgarity and racial slurs.

1993 AZ
Challenged as an appropriate English curriculum assignment at the Mingus Union High School because of "profane language, moral statement, treatment of the retarded, and the violent ending."

1994 GA
Challenged at the Loganville High School because of its "vulgar language throughout."

1994 TN
Pulled from a classroom by Putnam County school superintendent "due to the language." Later, after discussions with the school district counsel, it was reinstated.

1995 GA
Challenged at the Stephens County High School library in Toccoa Falls because of "curse words." The book was retained.

1995 KS
Challenged in the Galena school library because of the book's language and social implications.

1995 MN
Retained in the Bemidji schools after challenges to the book's "objectionable" language.

1995 VA
Challenged, but retained, in a Warm Springs High School English class.

1997 FL
Removed, restored, restricted, and eventually retained at the Bay County schools in Panama City. A citizen group, the 100 Black United, Inc., requested the novel's removal and "any other inadmissible literary books that have racial slurs in them, such as the using of the word 'nigger.'"

1997 IL
Banned from the Washington Junior High School curriculum in Peru because it was deemed "age inappropriate."

1997 MN
Challenged as a reading list assignment for a ninth-grade literature class, but retained at the Sauk Rapids-Rice High School in St. Cloud. A parent complained that the book's use of racist language led to racist behavior and racial harassment.

1997 OH
Challenged, but retained, in the Louisville high school English classes because of profanity.

1998 AR
Challenged, but retained, in the Bryant school library because of a parent's complaint that the book "takes God's name in vain fifteen times and uses Jesus's name lightly."

1998 CA
Challenged in O'Hara Park Middle School classrooms in Oakley because it contains racial epithets.

1998 WI
Challenged at the Barron School District.

1999 PA
Challenged, but retained, in the sophomore curriculum at West Middlesex High School despite objections to the novel's profanity.

1999 WI
Challenged in the Tomah School District because the novel is violent and contains obscenities.

2002 MI
Challenged as required reading at the high school in Grandville because the book "is full of racism, profanity, and foul language."

2002 MS
Banned from the George County schools because of profanity.

2003 IL
Challenged in the Normal Community High School because the book contains "racial slurs, profanity, violence, and does not represent traditional values." An alternative book, Steinbeck's *The Pearl,* was offered but rejected by the family challenging the novel. The committee then recommended *The House on Mango Street* and *The Way to Rainy Mountain* as alternatives.

2006 PA
Retained in the Greencastle-Antrim tenth-grade English classes. A complaint was filed because of "racial slurs" and profanity used throughout the novel. The book has been used in the high school for more than thirty years, and those who object to its content have the option of reading an alternative reading.

2007 IA
Challenged at the Newton High School because of concerns about profanity and the portrayal of Jesus Christ. Newton High School has required students to read the book since at least the early 1980s. In neighboring Des Moines, it is on the recommended reading list for ninth-grade English; and it is used for some special education students in the eleventh and twelfth grades.

2007 KS

Retained in the Olathe ninth-grade curriculum despite a parent calling the novel a "worthless, profanity-riddled book" that is "derogatory towards African Americans, women, and the developmentally disabled."

2014 MN

Retained in the Brainerd School District curriculum (2014) despite the complaints of two parents who objected to the use of "Jesus Christ" as a curse word, the use of the n-word to describe African Americans, and the term "Japs." They argued this type of language undermines the values of respect they try to instill in their children and the novel should be pulled from the curriculum. Parents and students who object to the language may choose an alternate book by the Nobel Prize-winning author.

Source: 8, pp. 474–76; 9; 11, Mar. 1975, p. 41; Nov. 1977, p. 155; Jan. 1978, p. 7; Mar. 1979, p. 27; May 1980, p. 62; July 1980, p. 77; May 1982, pp. 84–85; July 1983, p. 198; July 1984, p. 104; May 1988, p. 90; July 1988, p. 140; Sept. 1988, pp. 154, 179; Nov. 1988, p. 201; Jan. 1989, p. 28; Nov. 1989, p. 162; Jan. 1990, pp. 10-12; Mar. 1990, p. 45; Mar. 1991, p. 62; July 1991, p. 110; Jan. 1992, p. 25; Mar. 1992, p. 64; July 1992, pp. 111–12, 126; Sept. 1992, pp. 140, 163–64; Jan. 1993, p. 29; Mar. 1994, p. 53; Mar. 1995, pp. 46, 53; May 1995, pp. 84; July 1995, pp. 93, 111–12; Sept. 1995, pp. 157–58; Jan. 1996, p. 29; Mar. 1996, pp. 50, 63; May 1997, pp. 63, 79; Nov. 1997, pp. 167–69; Jan. 1998, pp. 28–29; July 1998, pp. 107, 120; Jan. 1999, p. 9; July 1999, p. 105; Jan. 2000, p. 16; Mar. 2000, p. 52; Nov. 2002, p. 280; Mar. 2003, p. 55; Jan. 2004, p. 11; Sept. 2004, pp. 177-78; Jan. 2007, pp. 29–30; July 2007, pp. 146-47; Jan. 2008, pp. 27-28; May 2014.

1677

Steinbeck, John.
The Red Pony.

1933
Published

1980 NY

Challenged at the Vernon-Verona-Sherill School District as a "filthy, trashy, sex novel."

1994 GA

Challenged in the Oconee County school libraries because a parent complained the book contained profanity. The Oconee School Board voted to evaluate all 40,000 volumes in the system's library and remove any books and teaching materials from the public school that contain "explicit sex and pornography."

1996 NC

Challenged, but retained, on a recommended reading list, at Holmes Middle School in Eden. A parent complained that there were curse words on ten different pages of the book.

1997 AL

Challenged in the Attalla school system because the book contains "profanity and violence."

Source: 11, May 1980, p. 62; Sept. 1994, p. 145; Sept. 1996, p. 170; May 1997, p. 62.

1678

Steinbeck, John.
The Wayward Bus.

1947
Published

1953

Placed on list of books disapproved by the Gathings Committee (a U.S. House of Representatives select committee on indecent literature).

1953
Banned in Ireland.
Source: 4, p. 83.

1679

Stendhal (Marie-Henri Beyle).
The Red and the Black.

1831
Published

1850

Banned in Russia by Czar Nicholas I, whose motto in a campaign to suppress liberal thought was "autocracy, orthodoxy, and nationality."

1864

Placed on the *Index Librorum Prohibitorum* (Index of Prohibited Books) in Rome, Italy, and confirmed by the Index of Pope Leo XIII in 1897. The novel and all of Stendhal's "love stories" remained on the list through the last edition compiled in 1948 and in effect until 1966.

1939

Purged from Spanish libraries by the dictatorship of Francisco Franco.
Source: 8, pp. 284–85.

1680

Stern, Howard.
Miss America.

1995
Published

1996 VA

Challenged at the Prince William County Library. Two newly appointed members of the library board want to limit young people's access to books by removing them from the collection or by creating an "adults-only" section of the library.

1997 CO

Challenged in the Pikes Peak Library District in Colorado Springs because the book is considered "obscene."
Source: 11, Nov. 1996, p. 194; July 1997, p. 93.

1681

Stern, Howard.
Private Parts.

1993
Published

1994 AL

Challenged, but retained, at the Scott Public Library in Alabaster. The Shelby County District Attorney called the book "obscene" and threatened to prosecute the library for circulating it, although no action was taken.

1994 TX

Challenged at the Weslaco Public Library. A petition, with more than 300 signatures, was presented to city officials asking them to more closely monitor books the library purchases. The librarian labeled as "too liberal" subsequently resigned. Former Weslaco librarian filed a federal lawsuit in 1995, charging that she was fired for publicly discussing that city's efforts to ban Stern's work from the library.
Source: 11, Nov. 1994, p. 189; Mar. 1995, p. 53; Sept. 1995, p. 153.

1682

Stewart, Jon, Ben Karlin, and David Javerbaum.
America (The Book): A Citizen's Guide to Democracy Inaction.

2004
Published

2004 MS
Returned to circulation at the Jackson-George Regional Library System in Pascagoula. The library board had banned the best-selling satirical book because the book contained an image of Supreme Court judges' faces superimposed on naked bodies. The book was named a Book of the Year by *Publishers Weekly,* the industry trade magazine.
Source: 11, Mar. 2005, p. 73; 13, pp. 15–17.

1683
Stillman, Peter R.
Introduction to Myth.

1977
Published

1982 WA
Challenged as a text for an elective course for junior and senior high school students in Renton because it was considered anti-Christian by some parents.
Source: 11, Sept. 1982, p. 171.

1684
Stine, R. L.
Beach House.

1992
Published

1996 AR
Challenged at the Pulaski Heights Elementary School library in Little Rock along with similar Stine titles. The book, part of the "Fear Street" series, includes graphic descriptions of boys intimidating and killing girls.
Source: 11, Nov. 1996, p. 211.

1685
Stine, R. L.
Double Date.

2002
Published

2003 GA
Removed from the Crawford County Middle School library because the book deals with complex issues teenagers confront.
Source: 11, Jan. 2004, p. 9.

1686
Stine, R. L.
Ghost Camp.

1996
Published

1997 GA
Challenged, but retained, at the Jackson Elementary School library in Gwinnett County. A concerned parent complained because of graphic content and references to the occult.
Source: 11, Sept. 1997, p. 148.

1687
Stine, R. L.
Goosebumps series.

1996
Published

1996 FL
Challenged at the Bay County elementary schools because of "satanic symbolism, disturbing scenes and dialogue." *The Barking Ghost,* for satanic symbolism and gestures, possession and descriptions of dogs as menacing and attacking; *Night of the Living Dummy II,* for spells or chants, violence and vandalism; *The Haunted Mask,* for graphic description of the ugly mask, demonic possession, violence, disturbing scenes and dialogue; *The Scarecrow Walks at Midnight,* for satanic acts and symbolism, and disturbing scenes; and *Say Cheese and Die!,* for promoting mischief, demonic possession, a reference to Satan and his goals, a disturbing scene describing a death, and a scene that tells of a child disappearing from a birthday party.

1997 MN
Challenged, but retained, in the Anoka-Hennepin school system because "children under the age of twelve may not be able to handle the frightening content of the books."
Source: 11, July 1996, p. 134; Mar. 1997, p. 35; May 1997, p. 77.

1688
Stine, R. L.
The Haunted Mask.

1993
Published

1994 MI
Challenged, but retained, at the Battle Creek Elementary School library despite protests from a parent who said the book is satanic.
Source: 11, Nov. 1994, p. 200.

1689
Stirling, Nora.
You Would If You Loved Me.

1969
Published

1980 UT
Removed from the Utah State Library bookmobile.
Source: 11, Nov. 1980, p. 128.

1690
Stock, Gregory.
The Kid's Book of Questions.

1988
Published

1990 VA
Challenged in the Albemarle County schools in Charlottesville because it is "inappropriate in an academic class." One parent cited a question from the book, which asked whether a child had ever farted and blamed someone else.
Source: 11, Jan. 1991, p. 18.

1691
Stoker, Bram.
Dracula.

1897
Published

1994 TX
Eliminated from required reading lists for juniors and seniors in advanced English classes at the Colony High School in Lewisville because, "the book contains unacceptable descriptions in the introduction, such as 'Dracula is the symptom of a wish, largely sexual, that we wish we did not have.'"
Source: 11, July 1994, p. 116.

1692
Stone, Tanya Lee.
A Bad Boy Can Be Good for a Girl.

2006
Published

2013 NC
Challenged, but retained, at the Currituck High School library. This first novel by Stone, written in a poetry format, follows the story of three girls who fall for the same bad boy intent on seducing every girl in school.
Source: 11, Nov. 2013, p. 243.

1693
Stopes, Marie Carmichael.
Married Love.

1918
Published

1930 PA
Declared "not obscene or immoral" in Philadelphia after two social workers imported copies of the book to use in their work. The case went before Judge Kirkpatrick, U.S. District Judge for the Eastern District of Pennsylvania. Despite the judge's decision, the book was again seized later that year and again went to court, where it was determined was not obscene.

1931
Banned in Ireland by the Irish Censorship Board for its discussion of contraception.
Source: 14, pp. 225–26.

1694
Stoppard, Miriam.
The Magic of Sex.

1992
Published

1996 NJ
Restricted to patrons over eighteen years of age at the Main Memorial Library in Clifton. The book is hidden behind the checkout counter and on the shelves is a dummy book jacket. The book was described as hard-core pornography by the complainant.

1999 CA
Challenged, but retained, at the Auburn-Placer County Library because of sexually explicit material.
Source: 11, Mar. 1996, p. 63; May 1996, p. 83; Nov. 1999, p. 171.

1695
Stoppard, Miriam.
Woman's Body.

1994
Published

1995 GA
Challenged at the Gwinnett-Forsyth Regional Library because it is "too sexually explicit to be on regular library shelves."
Source: 11, Jan. 1996, p. 29.

1696
Storm, Hyemeyohsts.
Seven Arrows.

1972
Published

1985 OR
Challenged at the Creswell High School because the book contains references to masturbation, rape, and incest.
Source: 11, Mar. 1985, p. 45; May 1985, p. 81.

1697
Stowe, Harriet Beecher.
Uncle Tom's Cabin.

1852
Published

1852
Banned in Russia.

1855
Prohibited in Italy and all papal states.

1984 IL
Challenged in the Waukegan School District because the novel contains the word "nigger."
Source: 8, pp. 185-87; 11, July 1984, p. 105.

1698
Strasser, Todd.
Angel Dust Blues.

1979
Published

1983 NY
Challenged as reading material for the Manhasset Public Library's young adult Popsicle series because of "explicit and graphic sex scenes of a most crude and exploitative nature" and "blasphemy."

1987 NC
Challenged at Alexander Central High School and East Junior High School libraries in Taylorsville because of "sexually explicit passages."

1989 OR
Challenged at the Crook County Middle School in Prineville because of explicit language.
Source: 11, Nov. 1983, p. 185; May 1987, p. 87; July 1987, p. 149; Jan. 1990, pp. 4–5.

1699
Strasser, Todd.
Friends Till the End.

1981
Published

1981
Best Books for Young Adults

1985 TX
Challenged at the Arlington junior high school libraries because of "sexually descriptive words."
Source: 11, Mar. 1985, p. 60.

1700
Strasser, Todd.
Give a Boy a Gun.

2000
Published

2007 PA
Retained at the Bangor Area Middle School despite a student's aunt's concerns about the book's depiction of school violence.
Source: 11, Mar. 2008, p. 79.

1701
Stratton-Porter, Jean.
Her Father's Daughter.

1921
Published

1991 OR
Removed from the Clatskanie Library District because of alleged bigotry against the Japanese.
Source: 11, July 1992, p. 103.

1702
Street Law.

1983 MD
Challenged in Linthicum Heights because it is "biased and pressures teenagers to make moral judgments."
Source: 11, Nov. 1983, p. 186; Mar. 1984, p. 53.

1703
Stroud, Jonathan.
The Amulet of Samarkand: Bartimaeus Trilogy, Book One.

2003
Published

2004
Best Books for Young Adults

2008 NY
Restored by the Lackawanna School Board following accusations of censorship by some parents and teachers. The book was pulled from the middle school library recommended list because of concerns that the book deals with the occult.
Source: 11, May 2008, p. 116.

1704
Stroud, Jonathan.
The Golem's Eye.

2004
Published

2005
Best Books for Young Adults

2008 NY
Restored by the Lackawanna School Board along with several other books following accusations of censorship by some parents and teachers. The book was pulled from the middle school library recommended list because of concerns that the book deals with the occult.
Source: 11, May 2008, p. 116.

1705
Stroud, Jonathan.
Ptolemy's Gate.

2007
Published

2008 NY
Restored by the Lackawanna School Board along with several other books following accusations of censorship by some parents and teachers. The book was pulled from the middle school library recommended list because of concerns that the book deals with the occult.
Source: 11, May 2008, p. 116.

1706
Sturges, Jock.
Radiant Identities.

1994
Published

1998 GA
Despite pressure from protestors demanding that Barnes & Noble face child pornography charges, a prosecutor in Cobb County declined to take the nation's largest bookstore chain to court for carrying Sturges's book. Activists from Operation Rescue claimed the book contains children in sexually suggestive positions and should be deemed illegal.

1998 KS
Barnes & Noble officials noted that the decision follows similar rulings by prosecutors in Kansas.

1998 MD
Barnes & Noble officials noted that the decision follows similar rulings by prosecutors in Maryland.

1998 TX
Barnes & Noble officials noted that the decision follows similar rulings by prosecutors in Texas.

1998 WI
Barnes & Noble officials noted that the decision follows similar rulings by prosecutors in Wisconsin.
Source: 11, Jan. 1999, p. 20.

1707
Stwertka, Eve and Albert.
Marijuana.

1979
Published

1997 PA
Challenged at the Stanwood Elementary School in Hempfield because its chapters on purchasing related paraphernalia and marijuana recipes were considered inappropriate.
Source: 11, July 1997, p. 94.

1708
Styron, William.
The Confessions of Nat Turner.

1967
Published

1967
Best Books for Young Adults

1968
Pulitzer Prize for Fiction

1987 IA
Removed from the Thompson High School library in Mason City after a parent objected to some "sexual materials" in the book.
Source: 11, July 1987, p. 126; Sept. 1987, p. 174.

1709
Styron, William.
Sophie's Choice.

1979
Published

1979
National Book Critics Circle Fiction Finalist

1980
National Book Award for Fiction

1979
Banned in South Africa.

2002 CA
Returned to La Mirada High School library after a complaint about its sexual content prompted the school to pull the award-winning novel about a tormented Holocaust survivor.
Source: 5, Apr. 1980, p. 72; 8, pp. 384–85; 11, Mar. 2002, p. 105.

1710
Sullivan, Tim, ed.
Cold Shocks.

1991
Published

1993 NJ
Challenged at the Montclair Public Library because the language in the collection of horror stories "was not conducive to a sixth grader." The complainant demanded that books with possibly offensive contents be labeled with warnings and kept in a limited-access section.
Source: 11, July 1993, p. 100.

1711
Sullivan, Tom, and Derek Gill.
If You Could See What I Hear.

1975
Published

1975
Best Books for Young Adults

1980 UT
Removed from the Utah State
Library bookmobile.
Source: 11, Nov. 1980, p. 128.

1712
Summers, Montague.
The Popular History of Witchcraft.

1937
Published

1986 CA
Challenged by the "God Squad," a group
of three students and their parents, at
the El Camino High School in Oceanside
because the book "glorified the devil
and the occult."
Source: 11, Sept. 1986, p. 151; Nov. 1986, p. 224;
Jan. 1987, p. 9.

1713
Suzuki, Daisetz Teitaro.
Zen Buddhism: Selected Writings.

1983
Published

1987 MI
Challenged at the Plymouth-Canton
school system in Canton because "this
book details the teachings of the religion
of Buddhism in such a way that the reader
could very likely embrace its teachings
and choose this as his religion."
Source: 11, May 1987, p. 109.

1714
Swarthout, Glendon.
Bless the Beasts and the Children.

1970
Published

1970
Best Books for Young Adults

1987 SD
Banned in the Dupree High School English
classes because of what the school board
called "offensive language and vulgarity."
Source: 11, Jan. 1988, p. 12.

1715
Swedenborg, Emanual.
Arcana Coelesta.

1721
Published

1738
His most notable scientific volume,
Principia, which proposed a rational
mathematical explanation of the universe,
was placed on the Catholic Church's
Index Librorum Prohibitorum (Index
of Prohibited Books) in Rome, Italy,
and remained listed for more than
two centuries.

1747
Banned as heretical for contradicting
Lutheran doctrine in Sweden.
Source: 1, pp. 16–18.

1716
Sweedloff, Peter.
Men and Women.

1975
Published

1977 MI
Banned from the Brighton High
School library along with all other sex
education materials.
Source: 11, Sept. 1977, p. 133.

1717
Sweeney, Joyce.
Shadow.

1994
Published

1995
Best Books for Young Adults

1997 KS
Challenged, but retained, on the Anderson
County Junior/Senior High School
library shelves in Garnett. A parent
objected to the book's "graphic language."
Source: 11, July 1997, p. 109.

1718
Swift, Graham.
Waterland.

1983
Published

2012 MI
Challenged as a text in Salem High School
Advanced Placement English courses due to
the book's sexual content. Superintendent
Jeremy Hughes immediately pulled the
book, but later decided to put the book
through the district's review process.
The book was reviewed and retained.
Source: 11, Mar. 2012, pp. 59-60; May 2012, pp. 127-28.

1719
Swift, Jonathan.
Drapier's Letters.

1724
Published

1724
All attempts to prosecute the printer
or to identify the anonymous writer were
frustrated by the aroused Irish nation.
Source: 4, p. 25.

1720
Swift, Jonathan.
Gulliver's Travels.

1726
Published

1726
Denounced as wicked and obscene
in Ireland.
Source: 4, p. 25.

1721
Swift, Jonathan.
Tale of a Tub.

1704
Published

1704
Placed on the *Index Librorum Prohibitorum*
(List of Prohibited Books) in Rome, Italy.
Source: 1, pp. 324–25; 3, p. 259.

1722
Talbert, Marc.
Dead Birds Singing.

1985
Published

1985
Best Books for Young Adults

1993 ND
Challenged, but retained, as part of the
curriculum, at Hughes Junior High School
in Bismarck because it is "offensive."
Source: 11, Sept. 1993, p. 145; Jan. 1994, p. 38.

1723
The Talmud.

200-500 A.D.
Published

600
The history of suppression of the *Talmud*
is many centuries long. Early attempts to

ban it date at least to the seventh and eight centuries.

1144
In Paris, France, the Catholic Church ordered the burning of the *Talmud* on charges of blasphemy and immorality.

1190
With his *Guide for the Perplexed*, Maimonides, the Jewish philosopher, aroused the Christians' resentment, which culminated in the first official burning of Hebrew books by orders of Dominicans, Franciscans, and others in Cairo, Egypt.

1239
Pope Gregory IX ordered the burning of all Jewish books in Rome, Italy.

1244
Pope Innocent IV ordered Louis IX of France to burn all copies in France.

1264
Pope Clement IV appointed a committee of censors in Rome, Italy, to expunge any anti-Christian material. Jews were only allowed to have expurgated copies.

1415
Pope Benedict XII in Rome, Italy, ordered all copies of Talmudic books to be sent to bishops for preservation, but Jews were forbidden to keep copies.

1490
Grand Inquisitor Tomás Torquemada burned thousands of Jewish books by order of Ferdinand and Isabella of Spain.

1492
As Jews were expelled from Spain and Portugal, all Jewish books were confiscated.

1530
At the urging of Martin Luther, German principalities expelled Jews and suppressed their books.

1553
Pope Julius III in Rome, Italy, halted its printing.

1555
Jewish houses were searched throughout Europe. The library of the Hebrew school in Cremona, Italy, was destroyed by the Roman Inquisition and thousands of books were burned.

1555
Pope Pius IV in Rome, Italy, relaxed its prohibition, allowing the distribution of expurgated versions. It was, however,

placed on the newly created *Index Librorum Prohibitorum* (Index of Prohibited Books) the same year.

1592
Pope Clement VIII issued a bull in Rome, Italy, which ordered reinstatement of the ban on its possession by either Jews or Christians.

1926
Along with other religious works, removed from many libraries in the Soviet Union. Printing was also sharply restricted.

1939
Most Jewish schools in Germany were destroyed by the Nazi government, along with Jewish religious texts.

1965
The Second Vatican Council in Rome, Italy, brought about a positive change in attitude, with the Catholic Church formally acknowledging the common foundations of Christianity and Judaism and renouncing anti-Semitism.

Source: 3, p. 110; 4, p. 5; 6, p. 844; 8, pp. 300–303.

1724
Tamar, Erika.
Fair Game.

1993
Published

1994
Best Books for Young Adults

1995 AR
Challenged at the Springdale Public Library because "ethics take a back seat to graphic sexual material. Perhaps there is a less prurient work that explores the issue of rape vs. consensual sex or date rape."

Source: 11, Sept. 1995, p. 157.

1725
Tan, Amy.
The Joy Luck Club.

1989
Published

1989
National Book Critics Circle Fiction Finalist

1990
Best Books for Young Adult

1996 TX
Banned from the Lindale Advanced

Placement English reading list because the book "conflicted with the values of the community."

2004 WI
Challenged at the Arrowhead High School in Waukesha as an elective reading list assignment by a parent because the book contains "sexually explicit and inappropriate material."

Source: 11, Nov. 1996, p. 199; Jan. 2005, p. 11.

1726
Tarbox, Katherine.
A Girl's Life Online.

2004
Published

2008 NY
Challenged in the English 11 Regents class at Baker High School in Baldwinsville because of the book's graphic language. The cautionary tale about Internet safety is one of the five books students could select for the contemporary literature class unit on "teenage struggles."

Source: 11, July 2008, p. 143.

1727
Tateno, Makoto.
Hero-Heel 2.

2008
Published

2012 WA
Challenged at the King County Library System due to yaoi manga's sexually explicit nature.

Source: 11, Jan. 2013, pp. 8-9.

1728
Tax, Meredith.
Families.

1981
Published

1982 WI
Challenged in Mosinee because it teaches family living.

1994 VA
Eliminated from the Fairfax County School's Family Life Education program after "parents complained that it glorifies divorce and shows two women living together."

Source: 9; 11, May 1982, p. 87; May 1994, p. 88; Sept. 1994, p. 153.

1729
Taylor, Mildred D.
The Friendship.

1987
Published

1988
Coretta Scott King Author Award

1997 MD
Challenged, but retained, in the Prince George's County school system after a parent claimed the book has "no redeeming value."
Source: 11, Sept. 1997, p. 149.

1730
Taylor, Mildred D.
The Land.

2001
Published

2002
Best Books for Young Adults

2002
Coretta Scott King Author Award

2002
Scott O'Dell Award for Historical Fiction

2008 FL
Removed from the Turner Elementary School media-center shelves in New Tampa as age inappropriate. A parent challenged the book because the novel contains a racial epithet.
Source: 11, May 2008, p. 96.

1731
Taylor, Mildred D.
Mississippi Bridge.

1990
Published

2001 VA
Challenged, but retained, at the Donahoe Elementary School library in Sandston despite objections of its "negative content and [that] it's riddled with prejudice." The novel by the Newbery Medal-winning author tells the story of a young black man who tries to save white passengers in a bus accident, despite being ordered earlier to give up his seat to "white folks."
Source: 11, May 2001, p. 97; July 2001, p. 174.

1732
Taylor, Mildred D.
Roll of Thunder, Hear My Cry.

1976
Published

1977
Coretta Scott King Author Honor Book

1977
National Book Award for Young People's Literature

1977
Newbery Medal

1993 LA
Removed from the ninth-grade reading list at the Arcadia High School because of racial bias.

1998 CA
Challenged in O'Hara Park Middle School classrooms in Oakley because it contains racial epithets.

2000 AL
Challenged in Chapman Elementary School libraries in Huntsville because it uses racial slurs in dialogue to make points about racism.

2004 FL
Challenged, but retained, as a part of the Seminole County school curriculum despite the concerns of an African-American couple who found the book inappropriate for their thirteen-year-old son. The book depicts the life of an African American family in rural Mississippi in the 1930s and uses the word "nigger."
Source: 11, May 1993, p. 72; July 1998, p. 107; Mar. 2000, p. 47; Mar. 2004, pp. 75–76.

1733
Taylor, Theodore.
The Cay.

1969
Published

1992 CA
Challenged as required reading at the Moorpark schools because it allegedly maligns African Americans.

1995 CA
Removed from the Oak Grove School District's core reading list for seventh-graders in San Jose because of offensive, racist language. Placed on an "extended" list for use in the eighth grade.

1997 MD
Challenged, but retained, at the Prince George's County school system after a parent claimed the book has "no redeeming value."
Source: 11, May 1992, p. 95; July 1995, p. 96; Sept. 1997, p. 149.

1734
Taylor, William.
Agnes the Sheep.

1990
Published

1995 GA
Removed from the Nesbit Elementary School in Gwinnett County because it overused the words "hell, damn, and God." Although other parents wanted the book restored in the elementary school, the County Board of Education refused to reinstate the book.
Source: 11, Jan. 1996, p. 11; Mar. 1996, p. 64.

1735
Tchudi, Stephen.
Probing the Unknown: From Myth to Science.

1990
Published

1995 MI
Challenged in the West Branch-Rose City school district because it discusses occult beliefs.
Source: 11, Jan. 1996, p. 15.

1736
Telander, Rick.
Heaven Is a Playground.

1976
Published

1977
Best Books for Young Adults

1983 WA
Removed from the Evergreen School District of Vancouver along with twenty-nine other titles. The American Civil Liberties Union of Washington filed suit contending that the removals constitute censorship, a violation of plaintiff's rights to free speech and due process, and a violation of the state Open Meetings Act because the removal decisions were made behind closed doors.
Source: 11, Nov. 1983, pp. 185–86.

1737
Teleny: A Novel Attributed to Oscar Wilde.

1893
Published

1984
Seized by the British Customs Office as "indecent and obscene."
Source: 11, Jan. 1985, p. 26.

1738
Terkel, Studs.
Working: People Talk About What They Do All Day and How They Feel About What They Do.

1974
Published

1978 WI
Challenged in Wales due to the book's "obscene language."

1982 PA
Challenged in the senior vocational-technical English class in Girard because some parents and students considered the book obscene.

1983 AZ
Deleted from the seventh- and eighth-grade curriculum in the Washington School District due to "profane language. When we require idealistic and sensitive youth to be burdened with despair, ugliness and hopelessness, we shall be held accountable by the Almighty God."

1983 WA
Removed from an optional reading list at the South Kitsap High School because the chapter "Hooker" demeaned marital status and degraded the sexual act.
Source: 9; 11, July 1978, p. 89; Sept. 1978, p. 123; July 1982, p. 143; Nov. 1983, p. 187; Jan. 1984, pp. 10–11.

1739
Terris, Susan.
Stage Brat.

1980
Published

1990 PA
Removed, but later reinstated, at the Pine Middle School library in Gibsonia because "it talks of adults slithering around in hot tubs, abortions, palm

reading and horoscopes as ways of making life decisions, anti-religious language, and four-letter words."
Source: 11, Nov. 1990, pp. 209–10; Jan. 1991, pp. 28–29.

1740
Terry, Wallace.
Bloods: An Oral History of the Vietnam War by Black Veterans.

1984
Published

1984
Best Books for Young Adults

1987 FL
Banned from the West Hernando Middle School library in Spring Hill because of "harsh language and presents a moral danger to students." The librarian filed a grievance, and the book was returned to the shelves following a ruling by the American Arbitration Association. Forty minutes after the book was returned, the book was removed again, pending a review by an advisory committee.
Source: 7, pp. 60-61; 11, May 1987, p. 85; Sept. 1987, pp. 173-74; Jan. 1988, p. 9.

1741
Thom, James Alexander.
Follow the River.

1981
Published

2002 IN
Removed from the tenth-grade curriculum at the high school in Noblesville after a parent objected to passages about an imagined rape; the book remains in the library collection.
Source: 11, May 2002, p. 117.

1742
Thomas, Piri.
Down These Mean Streets.

1967
Published

1972 NY
Removed from the junior high school library by Community School Board 1250, Queens. Decision upheld by the court's ruling in *President's Council, District 25 v. Community School Board No. 25,* 457 F. 2d 289 (2d Cir. 1972), 409 U.S. 998 (1972).

1976 NY
Removed from the Island Trees Union Free School District High School library along with nine other titles because they were considered "immoral, anti-American, anti-Christian, or just plain filthy." Returned to the library after the U.S. Supreme Court ruling on June 25, 1982, in *Board of Education, Island Trees Union Free School District No. 26 et al. v. Pico et al.,* 457 U.S. 853 (1982).
Source: 11, July 1973, p. 115; Nov. 1982, p. 197; 12, pp. 142–44, 239.

1743
Thompson, Charlotte E.
Single Solutions: An Essential Guide for the Career Woman.

1990
Published

1991 OR
Challenged for technical errors, but retained, at the Multnomah County Library.
Source: 11, Jan. 1992, p. 6.

1744
Thompson, Craig.
Blankets: An Illustrated Novel.

2003
Published

2004
Best Books for Young Adults

2006 MO
Challenged in the Marshall Public Library because some members of the community deemed the book "porno-graphic." The book was moved to the adult book section, from the young-adult area where it had been shelved before.
Source: 11, Nov. 2006, p. 289; Jan. 2007, pp. 9-10; May 2007, p. 115; July 2007, pp. 163-64.

1745
The Three Billy Goats Gruff.

1841-44
Published

1984 OR
Challenged at the Eagle Point Elementary School library because the story was too violent for children.
Source: 11, Sept. 1984, p. 155.

1746

Timberlake, Amy.
The Dirty Cowboy.

2003
Published

2012 PA
Removed from the Annville elementary school library shelves because of its illustrations, involving a cartoon cowboy taking his annual bath. The supposedly true story is of a young cowboy who needs his annual bath and instructs his dog to watch his clothes while he bathes. When the cowboy emerges from his bath in the river, the dog does not recognize his familiar smell and refuses to give back his clothes. In the illustrations, the cowboy's private parts are always covered. The book has received numerous awards, including the International Reading Association award in 2004, the Parents Choice Gold Medal, and the Bulletin Blue Ribbon from *The Bulletin for the Center for Children's Books.*
Source: 11, July 2012, pp. 153-54.

1747

Tindal, Matthew.
Rights of the Christian Church Asserted.

1706
Published

1707
An English grand jury made a presentation against the book, and in 1710, it was proscribed by Parliament and burned.
Source: 1, pp. 287–88.

1748

Toer, Pramoedya Ananta.
The Fugitive.

1950
Published

1950
Banned in Indonesia. The author spent much of his life imprisoned for political reasons and on house arrest for an additional twenty years, from 1979 to 1999. Toer wrote the novel in 1949 while he was imprisoned by the Dutch for his role in Indonesia's anticolonial revolution. With the success of the revolution in 1949, the novel was published in 1950, was acclaimed and then banned because it contained elements of class conflict and was perceived as a potential threat to society. In the following years, his works— thirty novels and books— were burned and banned in Indonesia because they were considered "subversive." Ownership of his books led some to imprisonment and torture. Toer has won many national and international awards for his works.
Source: 8, pp. 55–57.

1749

Toland, John.
Christianity Not Mysterious.

1696
Published

1697
Burned for heresy by the Irish Parliament.

1896
Presented by an English grand jury. Toland escaped arrest by fleeing to Holland.
Source: 1, pp. 39–40.

1750

Tolkien, J. R. R.
[John Ronald Reuel].
Lord of the Rings.

1954
Published

2001 NM
Burned in Alamogordo outside Christ Community Church along with other Tolkien novels as satanic.
Source: 11, Mar. 2002, p. 61.

1751

Tolstoy, Leo.
The Kreutzer Sonata.

1889
Published

1889
Banned from sale in Russia by Czar Nicholas I for "immoral content." Tolstoy's wife appealed personally to the czar, and he relented in 1891 to allow the novel to appear in an expensive-to-produce compendium of the author's works.

1890
Banned by the U.S. Post Office Department.

1890 PA
A Philadelphia vendor was indicted for selling a translation of the novel and taken to court. The court declared the novel to possess "very little dramatic interest or literary merit" and acknowledged as bizarre Tolstoy's recommendation of complete celibacy for all people, married or otherwise, but also stated that "it cannot, on that account, be called an obscene libel."

1926
Banned in Hungary.

1929
Banned in Italy.
Source: 4, p. 49; 10, p. 144; 13, pp. 134–35; 15, Vol. II, pp. 621–22.

1752

Toriyama, Akira.
Dragon Ball: The Monkey King.

2008
Published

2009 MD
Removed from the Wicomico County school media centers because the Japanese graphic novels depict some violence and show nudity.
Source: 11, Jan. 2010, p. 9.

1753

Touchette, Charleen.
It Stops with Me: Memoir of a Canuck Girl.

2004
Published

2005 RI
Removed from the Woonsocket Harris Public Library shelves after the author's father challenged the book. He wrote, "If members of a family wish to harm one another, those actions should be kept private and should not draw in others by involving matters of public policy." The book was later returned to the shelves.
Source: 11, Mar. 2006, p. 91.

1754
The Treasury of American Poetry.

1978
Published

1981 VA
Challenged at the Gretna High School library because it contained eight objectionable words. The review committee recommended to cut out pages or ink over the offending words.
Source: 11, May 1981, p. 66.

1755
Trocchi, Alexander.
Cain's Book.

1960
Published

1964
Police in Sheffield, England, raided a number of bookstores and confiscated the novel. Eventually, the court ruled that the book was obscene. This marked the first time a judgment of obscenity had been made based not on the vulgar language, depiction of sexual activity, or depravity in a work but on the lifestyle it advocated. Lord Chief Justice Parker determined that the narrator's heroin addiction was the reason for censoring the book.
Source: 14, p. 72.

1756
Trotsky, Leon.
Report of the Siberian Delegation.

1903
Published

1903
Banned by the imperial government in 1903 and by the government of the Soviet Union in 1927.

1930 MA
Banned in Boston.

1933
Banned in Germany.

1934
Banned in Italy.
Source: 7, pp. 426–27.

1757
Trueman, Terry.
Stuck in Neutral.

2000
Published

2001
Best Books for Young Adults

2003 WI
Challenged, but retained, on the reading list for eighth graders at the Evansille High School despite concerns about profanity, sexual imagery, and violence.

2012 TX
Challenged at the Creekwood Middle School in Humble because the book was an "inappropriate reading assignment." The fictional book is told in the first person by a teen with cerebral palsy and deals with such subjects as disabilities, quality of life, and euthanasia.
Source: 11, Jan. 2004, p. 13; July 2012, pp. 154-55.

1758
Trumbo, David.
Johnny Got His Gun.

1939
Published

1977 CA
Challenged and/or censored in California for the language and for several passages describing sexual encounters.

1977 CO
Challenged and/or censored in Colorado for the description of the main character after he had been maimed in the war.

1977 MI
Challenged and/or censored in schools in Michigan for too much profanity, too gruesome details of a human being, expressing unpatriotic and anti-American ideas, and sexual passages.

1977 TX
Challenged and/or censored in Texas as unpatriotic and anti-American.

1977 WI
Challenged and/or censored in Wisconsin in 1977 and 1982 for too much profanity and as antiwar.

1982 IL
Challenged and/or censored in Illinois as too violent.

1982 VT
Challenged and/or censored in Vermont.
Source: 8, pp. 107-9.

1759
Tryon, Thomas.
The Other.

1971
Published

1982 NH
Challenged at the Merrimack High School.
Source: 11, Sept. 1982, p. 170.

1760
Tucker, Todd.
Notre Dame vs. the Klan: How the Fighting Irish Defeated the Ku Klux Klan.

2004
Published

2008 IN
Indiana University-Purdue University Indianapolis (IUPUI) administrators have found that a student-employee was guilty of racial harassment merely for reading in a public area a historical account of Notre Dame students' fight with members of the Ku Klux Klan. The student-employee contacted the American Civil Liberties Union of Indiana and six months later received a letter stating that IUPUI "regret[s] this situation took place," is committed to upholding freedom of expression on its campus, and no documents regarding this incident exist in the employee's file.
Source: 11, July 2008, pp. 159-60.

1761
Turkle, Brinton.
Do Not Open.

1981
Published

1990 CA
Challenged at the Jackson Elementary School because of objections to its pictures of supernatural beings.
Source: 11, May 1990, p. 105.

1762

Twain, Mark
[Samuel L. Clemens].
*The Adventures of
Huckleberry Finn.*

1884
Published

1885 MA
Banned in Concord as "trash and
suitable only for the slums."

1905 NY
Excluded from the children's room of the
Brooklyn Public Library on the grounds
that "Huck not only itched but scratched,
and that he said sweat when he should
have said perspiration."

1930
Confiscated at the USSR border.

1957 NY
Dropped from the New York City list of
approved books for senior and junior
high schools, partly because of objections
to frequent use of the term "nigger."

1969 FL
Removed from the Miami-Dade Junior
College required reading list because
the book "creates an emotional block for
black students that inhibits learning."

1976 IL
Challenged as a "racist" novel at the
New Trier High School in Winnetka.

1981 PA
Challenged as a "racist" novel at the
Tamamend Junior High in Warrington.

1982 IA
Challenged as a "racist" novel in
Davenport Public Schools.

1982 TX
Challenged as a "racist" novel at the
Spring Independent School District
in Houston.

1982 VA
Challenged as a "racist" novel at the
Mark Twain Intermediate School in
Fairfax County.

1983 PA
Challenged as a "racist" novel in State
College Area School District.

1984 IL
Challenged as a "racist" novel in
Springfield.

1984 IL
Challenged as a "racist" novel in
Waukegan schools.

1988 IL
Removed from the required reading in
the Rockford public schools because the
book contains the word "nigger."

1988 LA
Removed from a required reading list
and school libraries in Caddo Parish
because of racially offensive passages.

1988 MI
Challenged at the Berrien Springs
High School.

1989 TN
Challenged at the Sevier County High
School in Sevierville because of racial
slurs and dialect.

1990 PA
Challenged on an Erie High School
supplemental English reading list
because of its derogatory references to
African Americans.

1990 TX
Challenged in Plano Independent School
District because the novel is "racist."

1991 AZ
Challenged in the Mesa Unified School
District because the book repeatedly
uses the word "nigger" and damages the
self-esteem of black youth.

1991 LA
Removed from the required reading list
of the Terrebone Parish public schools
in Houma because of the repeated use of
the word "nigger."

1991 MI
Temporarily pulled from the Portage
classrooms after some black parents
complained that their children were
uncomfortable with the book's portrayal
of blacks.

1992 CA
Challenged at the Modesto High School
as a required reading because of "offensive
and racist language." The word "nigger"
appears in the book.

1992 NC
Challenged in the Kinston Middle
School when the superintendent said the
novel could not be assigned because the
students were too young to read the book
because of its use of the word "nigger."

1993 PA
Challenged at the Carlisle area schools
because the book's racial slurs are offensive
to both black and white students.

1994 GA
Challenged in English classes at
Taylor County High School in Butler
because it contains racial slurs and bad
grammar and does not reject slavery.
The book will be taught in the tenth
rather than the ninth grade.

1994 TX
Challenged, but retained, on high
school reading lists, by the Lewisville
school board.

1995 CA
Removed from the required reading lists
in East San Jose high schools in response
to objections raised by African-American
parents. They said the book's use of
racial epithets, including frequent use of
the word "nigger," erodes their children's
self-esteem and affects their performance
in school.

1995 CT
Removed from the eighth-grade curriculum
at a New Haven middle school because
parents complained it undermined the
self-esteem of black youth.

1995 DC
Removed from the curriculum of the
National Cathedral School in Washington,
D.C., because of the novel's content
and language.

1995 WI
Challenged in the Kenosha Unified School
District. The complaint was filed by
the local NAACP, which cited the book as
offensive to African-American students.

1996 AZ
Challenged as required reading in an
honors English class at the McClintock
High School in Tempe by a teacher on
behalf of her daughter and other African-
American students at the school. In May
1996, a class-action lawsuit was filed in
U.S. District Court in Phoenix, alleging
that the district deprived minority students
of educational opportunities by requiring
racially offensive literature as part of class
assignments. In January 1997, a federal
judge dismissed the lawsuit stating he
realized that "language in the novel was
offensive and hurtful to the plaintiff," but
that the suit failed to prove the district

violated students' civil rights or that the works were assigned with discriminatory intent. The U.S. Court of Appeals for the Ninth Circuit in San Francisco ruled that requiring public school students to read literary works that some find racially offensive is not discrimination prohibited by the equal protection clause or Title VI of the 1964 Civil Rights Act. The ruling came in the case *Monteiro v. Tempe Union High School District.*

1996 PA
Dropped from the mandatory required reading list at the Upper Dublin schools because of its allegedly insensitive and offensive language.

1996 TX
Banned from the Lindale Advanced Placement English reading list because the book "conflicted with the values of the community."

1996 WA
Challenged for being on the approved reading list in the Federal Way schools because it "perpetuates hate and racism."

1997 IN
Challenged at the Columbus North High School because the book is "degrading, insensitive, and oppressive."

1997 NJ
Removed from classrooms in the Cherry Hill schools in January 1997 after concerns were raised about its racial epithets and the depiction of its African-American characters. In December 1997, however, the school board approved a new curriculum that places the book in the context of nineteenth-century racial relations and presents the works of African-American writers, including Frederick Douglass, Maya Angelou, and Langston Hughes.

1997 OH
Challenged in the South Euclid-Lyndhurst City Schools because a student complained that some classmates snickered and giggled as the word "nigger" was read aloud by students.

1997 VA
Challenged, but retained, at McLean High School in Fairfax despite a parent's complaint that the book offends African Americans.

1998 GA
Challenged in the Dalton County schools because the book's language is offensive.

1998 GA
Challenged in the Whitfield County schools because the book's language is offensive.

1998 PA
The Pennsylvania NAACP called for the removal of the book from required reading lists in school districts across the state because of its offensive racial language.

1999 AK
Recommended for removal from the Fairbanks North Star Borough School District's required reading lists because of its frequent use of the word "nigger."

2000 OK
Challenged, but retained, in the Enid schools. The novel was previously removed from the curriculum in Enid in 1977 after similar protests. It was returned to the required reading list in 1991.

2001 IL
Challenged in the Kankakee School District because the book uses the word "nigger."

2002 OR
Challenged in the Portland schools by an African-American student who said he was offended by an ethnic slur used in the novel.

2003 IL
Challenged in the Normal Community High School sophomore literature class as being degrading to African Americans. *The Chosen* was offered as an alternative to Twain's novel.

2004 WA
Pulled from the reading lists at the three Renton high schools after an African-American student said the book degraded her and her culture. The novel, which is not required reading in Renton schools but is on a supplemental list of approved books, was eventually retained for classroom usage.

2006 AZ
Challenged as required reading at Cactus High in Peoria. The student and mother have threatened to file a civil-rights complaint because of alleged racial treatment, the segregation of the student, and the use of a racial slur in the classroom.

2006 MI
Pulled from classes in Taylor schools because of complaints about its liberal use of common racial slurs.

2007 MN
Challenged, but retained, in the Lakeville High School as required reading for sophomores. The district will conduct staff training about race issues and revise the way it weighs requests for curriculum changes. The district will also let its staff offer alternative assignments on racially sensitive issues so "students do not feel ostracized because they have opted out of the assignment."

2007 MN
Challenged, but retained, in the St. Louis Park High School in Minneapolis as required reading for sophomores. The district will conduct staff training about race issues and revise the way it weighs requests for curriculum changes. The district will also let its staff offer alternative assignments on racially sensitive issues so "students do not feel ostracized because they have opted out of the assignment."

2007 TX
Challenged at Richland High School in North Richland Hills because of racial epithets.

2008 CT
Retained in the Manchester School District with the requirement that teachers attend seminars on how to deal with issues of race before teaching the book in their classrooms.

Source: 2, pp. 86–87; 4, pp. 49-50; 6, pp. 398-400; 11, May 1969, p. 52; July 1976, p. 87; Sept. 1976, p. 116; Nov. 1981, p. 162; Jan. 1982, pp. 11, 18; May 1982, p. 101; July 1982, p. 126; Sept. 1982, p. 171; Jan. 1984, p. 11; May 1984, p. 72; July 1984, pp. 121–22; Nov. 1984, p. 187; 8, Sept. 1988, pp. 152-53; Nov. 1988, p. 201; Jan. 1989, p. 11; Mar. 1989, p. 43; May 1989, p. 94; Jan. 1991, pp. 17–18; Mar. 1991, pp. 44–45; May 1991, pp. 90-92; Mar. 1992, pp. 43, 64; July 1992, p. 126; Sept. 1992, p. 140; May 1993, p. 73; May 1994, pp. 99–100; Mar. 1995, p. 42; May 1995, pp. 68, 69, 83; July 1995, pp. 96–97; Jan. 1996, p. 13; Mar. 1996, pp. 64–65; May 1996, p. 98; July 1996, p. 120; Sept. 1996, p. 153; Nov. 1996, pp. 198–99; Jan. 1997, p. 12; Mar. 1997, p. 40; May 1997, pp. 65–66, 72; July 1997, pp. 95–96, 97-98; Sept. 1997, p. 149; Nov. 1997, p. 182; Mar. 1998, p. 56; May 1998, pp. 72–73; Nov. 1998, p. 182; Jan. 1999, pp. 13–15; July 1999, pp. 93–94; Mar. 2000, p. 52; July 2000, p. 125; Mar. 2001, p. 57; Jan. 2003, pp. 11–12; Jan. 2004, p. 11; May 2004, p. 91; Jan. 2007, pp. 14-15; Mar. 2007, pp. 50–52; May 2007, p. 99; May 2007, p. 99; July 2007, p. 164; Jan. 2008, pp. 40-41; Mar. 2008, pp. 61-62; Jan. 2009, pp. 22-23; 15, Vol. II, p. 617.

1763
Twain, Mark
[Samuel L. Clemens].
The Adventures of Tom Sawyer.

1876
Published

1876 CO
Excluded from the children's room in the Denver Public Library.

1876 NY
Excluded from the children's room in the Brooklyn Public Library.

1930
Confiscated at the USSR border.

1985
Removed from London, England, school libraries by education officials who found it "racist" and "sexist."

1990 TX
Challenged in the Plano Independent School District because the novel is racist.

1992 IL
Retained in the O'Fallon schools, but parents will be able to request that their children not be required to read the book. A parent had sought the book's removal, charging that its use of the word "nigger" is degrading and offensive to black students.

1997 IN
Challenged in the Columbus schools because the book is "degrading, insensitive, and oppressive." It was suggested that middle school students in the district might use an edited version that deletes controversial language.

Source: 4, pp. 49–50; 11, Sept. 1985, p. 156; Jan. 1991, p. 18; Mar. 1991, pp. 45–46; May 1991, p. 92; May 1992, p. 97; Sept. 1994, p. 152; July 1997, pp. 97–98.

1764
Twain, Mark
[Samuel L. Clemens].
Eve's Diary.

1905
Published

1906 MA
Removed from circulation at the Charlton Library in Worcester because the "Edenic costumes" worn by Eve in the book's fifty illustrations had created an inordinate demand for it among the library's patrons.

Source: 15, Vol. II, p. 626.

1765
Tyndale, William.
The New Testament.

1526
Published

1526
Tyndale's was the first English-language version of the New Testament and the first printed book to be banned in England. Translating the original Greek and Hebrew into the vernacular was illegal in England, so Tyndale attempted to have his translation printed in Cologne in 1525 and eventually published it anonymously in Worms in 1526. Six thousand copies were smuggled into England where they were publicly burned; only one complete copy has survived in the library of the Baptist College at Bristol. Despite the ban, reprints continued to be published.

1534
Church authorities in England opposed Tyndale's translation as undermining their authority and attempted to extradite him from Europe. In 1534 Tyndale published a revision under his own name in Antwerp and continued to live in concealment until his arrest in 1535. Tyndale was imprisoned, strangled at the stake, and burned with copies of his translations of the *Bible* in 1536; at the time of his death, about 50,000 copies in seven editions were in circulation.

1546
The Archbishop of Canterbury issued a new ban, ordering Tyndale's works to be burned specifically for their references to church functionaries as "horse-leeches, maggots, and caterpillars in a kingdom."

1555
Queen Mary again banned his work for containing false doctrines against the Catholic faith.

1939
The Royal Society of Literature reprinted Tyndale's New Testament to celebrate the 400th anniversary of the man who made the first partial English translation.

2000
The first complete reprint issued by the British Library in a pocket-sized edition that mirrors the original.

Source: 1, pp. 213–17; 3, p.319; 4, pp. 12–13; 6, pp. 2,485-86; 8, pp. 208–209, 10.

1766
Ungerer, Tomi.
Beast of Monsieur Racine.

1971
Published

1989 AR
Challenged at the Rogers-Hough Memorial Library because the book is violent.

Source: 11, Sept. 1991, p. 151.

1767
Ungerer, Tomi.
Zeralda's Ogre.

1967
Published

1989 OR
Removed from the Cascades Elementary School in Lebanon because the book had frightening illustrations.

Source: 11, Jan. 1990, pp. 4–5.

1768
Updike, John.
Rabbit Is Rich.

1981
Published

1981
National Book Critics Circle Award for Fiction

1982
National Book Award for Fiction

1982
Pulitzer Prize for Fiction

1996 PA
Removed from the library at Sun Valley High School in Aston because it contains "offensive language and explicit sexual scenes."

Source: 11, May 1996, pp. 83–84.

1769
Updike, John.
Rabbit Run.

1960
Published

1962
Banned in Ireland because the Irish Board of Censors found the work "obscene" and "indecent," objecting particularly to the author's handling of the characters'

sexuality, the "explicit sex acts," and "promiscuity." The work was officially banned from sales in Ireland until the introduction of the revised Censorship Publications Bill in 1967.

1976 ME
Restricted to high school students with parental permission in the six Aroostock County community high school libraries because of passages in the book dealing with sex and an extramarital affair.

1986 WY
Removed from the required reading list for English class at the Medicine Bow Junior High School because of sexual references and profanity in the book.
Source: 8, pp. 376–77; 11, Mar. 1977, p. 36; Mar. 1987, p. 55; 13, pp. 196–97.

1770
Valentine, Johnny.
The Daddy Machine.

1992
Published

1993 MD
Challenged in the Wicomico County Free Library in Salisbury along with three other books on homosexuality intended for juvenile readers.
Source: 11, Jan. 1994, p. 35.

1771
Valentine, Johnny.
The Duke Who Outlawed Jelly Beans.

1991
Published

1993 MD
Challenged in the Wicomico County Free Library in Salisbury along with three other books on homosexuality intended for juvenile readers.

1993 NC
Moved from the children's section to the adult section at the Elizabethtown library.

1993 OH
Retained at the Dayton and Montgomery County Public Library.

1998 FL
Challenged at the Brevard County Library. When the request failed to have the book

banned, the complainant kept the book from other patrons by keeping it checked out for a year.
Source: 11, May 1993, p. 71; July 1993, pp. 100–101; Jan. 1994, p. 35; Mar. 1994, p. 69; July 1998, p. 105.

1772
Van Devanter, Lynda, and Christopher Morgan.
Home Before Morning.

1983
Published

1983
Best Books for Young Adults

1988 MD
Challenged at the Esperanza Middle School library in Lexington because the book's "liberal use of profanity and explicit portrayals of situations."
Source: 11, Nov. 1988, p. 201.

1773
Van Lustbader, Eric.
White Ninja.

1990
Published

1995 VA
Challenged at the Prince William County Library because of passages that describe the vicious rape and flaying of a young woman.
Source: 11, Jan. 1996, p. 12; Nov. 1996, pp. 194, 211; Jan. 1997, p. 26.

1774
Van Slyke, Helen.
Public Smiles, Private Tears.

1982
Published

1989 MI
Challenged at the Public Libraries of Saginaw because the book is "pornographic" with no redeeming value.
Source: 11, May 1989, p. 77.

1775
Van Vooren, Monique.
Night Sanctuary.

1981
Published

1983 AR
Challenged at the White County Library

in Searcy by a local parent, a minister, and a group called the Institute for American Ideals.
Source: 11, Nov. 1983, p. 185; Jan. 1984, p. 25.

1776
Vasilissa the Beautiful: Russian Fairy Tales.

1939
Published

1990 AR
Challenged at the Mena schools because the book contains "violence, voodoo, and cannibalism."
Source: 11, July 1990, p. 147.

1777
Vergil, Polydore.
De Inventoribus Rerum.

1499
Published

1551
Included in a 1551 list of books condemned by the Sorbonne in Paris, France.

1559
Included in the Spanish *Index Librorum Prohibitorum* (Index of Prohibited Books).

1564
Placed on the Roman Catholic Church *Index Librorum Prohibitorum* (Index of Prohibited Books) issued by Pope Paul IV in Rome, Italy.

1569
Included in the Liege Index.
Source: 1, pp. 69–70.

1778
Vidal, Gore.
Live from Golgotha.

1992
Published

1992 TX
Challenged at the Carrollton Public Library because the book is "offensive and pornographic."
Source: 11, Mar. 1993, p. 42.

1779
Vinge, Joan D.
Catspaw.

1988
Published

1995 IA
Restricted to Mediapolis junior high students with parental consent because it was "unredeeming and destructive" as well as "morally decadent."
Source: 11, May 1994, p. 83; July 1995, p. 109.

1780
Voigt, Cynthia.
David and Jonathan.

1992
Published

1998 TX
Placed on the teacher reserve shelf, available for students to check out after they consult with a teacher, at the Colleyville Middle School in Grapevine-Colleyville. The novel, which chronicles the effects of the Holocaust on a group of adolescent boys in the 1950s, was found "to be disturbing and full of sexual references, crude language and adult themes such as suicide, masturbation, and abortion."
Source: 11, May 1998, p. 88; July 1998, p. 106.

1781
Voigt, Cynthia.
Homecoming.

1981
Published

1982
National Book Award for Young People's Literature

1992 VA
Challenged at the Lynchburg middle and high school English classes because it presents readers with negative role models and values.
Source: 11, Sept. 1992, p. 164.

1782
Voigt, Cynthia.
Tell Me If the Lovers Are Losers.

1982
Published

1982
Best Books for Young Adults

1997 WV
Removed from the Jackson County school libraries along with sixteen other titles.
Source: 11, Jan. 1998, p. 13.

1783
Voigt, Cynthia.
When She Hollers.

1994
Published

1995
Best Books for Young Adults

1997 WV
Removed from the Jackson County school libraries along with sixteen other titles.
Source: 11, Jan. 1998, p. 13.

1784
Voltaire, Francois M. [Francois-Marie Arouet].
Candide.

1759
Published

1806
Placed the book on the *Index Librorum Prohibitorum* (List of Prohibited Books) of 1806 by Pope Pius VII in Rome, Italy.

1929 MA
Seized by U.S. Customs in Boston and declared as obscene.

1935
Declared as obscene and suppressed in the USSR.

1944
Voltaire's best-known work remained anathema to American authorities as late as 1944 when Concord Books, issuing a sale catalog that included the book, was informed by the Post Office that such a listing violated U.S. postal regulations on sending obscene matter through the mails.
Source: 2, p. 137; 3, p. 641; 4, p. 27; 8, pp. 323-24; 15, Vol. III, pp. 418–19.

1785
Voltaire, Francois M. [Francois-Marie Arouet].
Letters Concerning the English Nation.

1733
Published

1734
Printed clandestinely, banned by the French Parlement, and burned by the public executioner.

1752
Placed on the Catholic Church's *Index Librorum Prohibitorum* (Index of Prohibited Books) in Rome, Italy, along with thirty-eight other books by Voltaire. The Spanish Index also prohibited all of his writings.
Source: 1, pp. 185–86.

1786
Von Ziegesar, Cecily.
Only in Your Dreams: A Gossip Girl Novel.

2006
Published

2009 FL
Challenged at the Leesburg Public Library because of sexual innuendo, drug references, and other adult topics. Responding to a call by parents, church, and community leaders to remove this novel along with twelve other provocative books available to teens at the Leesburg Public Library, city commissioners voted 4-1 to separate all books based on age groups. High-school books will be placed in a separate area in the library stairwell.

2011 FL
Challenged at the Lake County Public Library by a county commissioner because the book explicitly details the lives and loves of privileged adolescent girls in New York City. The book inspired a popular television series, which premiered in 2007.

2011 MS
Removed from all libraries in the Picayune school district due to the book's explicit language.
Source: 11, July 2009, p. 131; Nov. 2009, p. 201; Nov. 2011, pp. 202-3 .

1787
Vonnegut, Kurt.
Breakfast of Champions.

1973
Published

1995 IL
Challenged in the Monmouth School District Library because it is "pornographic trash."
Source: 11, Mar. 1996, p. 45.

1788
Vonnegut, Kurt.
Cat's Cradle.

1971
Published

1972 OH
The Strongsville School Board voted to withdraw this title from the school library; this action was overturned in 1976 by a U.S. District Court in *Minarcini v. Strongsville City School District*, 541 F. 2d 577 (6th Cir. 1976).

1982 NH
Challenged at the Merrimack High School.
Source: 4, p. 95; 11, Sept. 1982, p. 170; 12, pp. 145–48.

1789
Vonnegut, Kurt.
God Bless You, Mr. Rosewater.

1971
Published

1972 OH
The Strongsville School Board voted to withdraw this title from the school library; this action was overturned in 1976 by a U.S. District Court.
Source: 4, p. 95.

1790
Vonnegut, Kurt.
Slaughterhouse-Five.

1969
Published

1972 MI
Banned in Rochester because the novel "contains and makes references to religious matters" and thus fell within the ban of the establishment clause. An appellate court upheld its usage in the school in *Todd v. Rochester Community Schools*, 41 Mich. App. 320, 200 N. W. 2d 90.

1973 ND
Challenged in many communities, but burned in Drake.

1975 NY
Banned in Levittown.

1979 OH
Banned in North Jackson.

1982 FL
Banned in Lakeland because of the "book's explicit sexual scenes, violence, and obscene language."

1984 WI
Barred from purchase at the Washington Park High School in Racine by the district administrative assistant for instructional services. In 1986, restricted to students who have parental permission at the four Racine Unified District high school libraries because of "language used in the book, depictions of torture, ethnic slurs, and negative portrayals of women."

1985 KY
Challenged at the Owensboro High School library because of "foul language, a section depicting a picture of an act of bestiality, a reference to 'Magic Fingers' attached to the protagonist's bed to help him sleep, and the sentence: 'The gun made a ripping sound like the opening of the fly of God Almighty.'"

1986 WI
Restricted to students who have parental permission at the four Racine Unified District high school libraries because of "language used in the book, depictions of torture, ethnic slurs, and negative portrayals of women."

1987 GA
Banned from the Fitzgerald schools because "it was filled with profanity and full of explicit sexual references."

1987 KY
Challenged at the LaRue County High School library because "the book contains foul language and promotes deviant sexual behavior."

1988 LA
Challenged in the Baton Rouge public high school libraries because the book is "vulgar and offensive."

1989 MI
Challenged in the Monroe public schools as required reading in a modern novel course for high school juniors and senior because of the book's language and the way women are portrayed.

1996 TX
Retained on the Round Rock Independent High School reading list after a challenge that the book was too violent.

1998 VA
Challenged as an eleventh-grade summer reading option in Prince William County because the book "was rife with profanity and explicit sex."

2000 RI
Removed as required reading for sophomores at the Coventry High School after a parent complained that it contained vulgar language, violent imagery, and sexual content.

2006 IL
Retained on the Northwest Suburban High School District 214 reading list in Arlington Heights, along with eight other challenged titles. A board member, elected amid promises to bring her Christian beliefs into all board decision-making, raised the controversy based on excerpts from the books she'd found on the Internet.

2007 MI
Challenged in the Howell High School along with several other books because of strong sexual content. In response to a request from the president of the Livingston Organization for Values in Education, or LOVE, the county's top law enforcement official reviewed the books to see whether laws against distribution of sexually explicit materials to minors had been broken. "After reading the books in question, it is clear that the explicit passages illustrated a larger literary, artistic, or political message and were not included solely to appeal to the prurient interests of minors," the Livingston county prosecutor wrote. "Whether these materials are appropriate for minors is a decision to be made by the school board, but I find that they are not in violation of the criminal laws."

2010 MO
Removed from Republic High School, but later returned and stored in a secure section of the library accessible only to parents. Teachers cannot require the book nor read it aloud in school. A Republic resident filed a complaint about the appropriateness of the book arguing that it teaches principles contrary to the *Bible*.

Source: 8, pp. 165–70; 11, Jan. 1974, p. 4; May 1980, p. 51; Sept. 1982, p. 155; Nov. 1982, p. 197; Sept. 1984, p. 158; Jan. 1986, pp. 9–10; Mar. 1986, p. 57; Mar. 1987, p. 51; July 1987, p. 147; Sept. 1987, pp. 174–75; Nov. 1987, p. 224; May 1988, pp. 86–87; July 1988, pp. 139–40; July 1989, p. 144; May 1996, p. 99; Nov. 1998, p. 183; Jan. 2001, p. 14; July 2006, pp. 210–11; May 2007, pp. 117–18; Nov. 2010, pp. 243-44 ; Sept. 2011, p. 175; Nov. 2011, p. 203; 12, pp. 78–79.

1791
Vonnegut, Kurt.
Welcome to the Monkey House.

1968
Published

1969 AL
A Montgomery teacher was dismissed for assigning this title to her eleventh-grade English class because the book promoted "the killing off of elderly people and free sex." The teacher brought suit and won in *Parducci v. Rutland,* 316 F.Supp. 352, (M. D. Ala 1970).

1977 MN
Pulled from the high school classes in Bloomington.

Source: 11, Jan. 1970, p. 28; July 1977, p. 101; 12, pp. 126–27, 238.

1792
Wagner, Jane.
J. T.

1972
Published

1981 NC
Removed from classroom use in Raleigh due to book's racial stereotyping, but later reinstated by an ad hoc review committee.
Source: 11, Nov. 1981, p. 170.

1793
Walker, Alice.
The Color Purple.

1982
Published

1982
National Book Critics Circle Fiction Finalist

1983
National Book Award for Fiction

1983
Pulitzer Prize for Fiction

1984 CA
Challenged as an appropriate reading for Oakland High School honors class due to the work's "sexual and social explicitness" and its "troubling ideas about race relations, man's relationship to God, African history, and human sexuality." After nine months of haggling and delays, a divided Oakland Board of Education gave formal approval for the book's use.

1985 CA
Rejected for purchase by the Hayward school trustees because of "rough language" and "explicit sex scenes."

1986 VA
Removed from the open shelves of the Newport News school library because of its "profanity and sexual references" and placed in a special section accessible only to students over the age of eighteen or who have written permission from a parent.

1989 MI
Challenged at the public libraries of Saginaw because it was "too sexually graphic for a twelve-year-old."

1989 TN
Challenged as a summer youth program reading assignment in Chattanooga because of its language and "explicitness."

1990 WY
Challenged as an optional reading assignment in the Ten Sleep schools.

1992 NC
Challenged as a reading assignment at the New Bern High School because the main character is raped by her stepfather.

1992 PA
Banned in the Souderton Area School District as appropriate reading for tenth graders because it is "smut."

1995 CT
Challenged on the curricular reading list at Pomperaug High School in Southbury because sexually explicit passages aren't appropriate high school reading.

1995 FL
Challenged at the St. Johns County Schools in St. Augustine.

1995 OR
Retained as an English course reading assignment in the Junction City high school after a challenge to the novel caused months of controversy. Although an alternative assignment was available, the book was challenged due to "inappropriate language, graphic sexual scenes, and book's negative image of black men."

1996 NC
Challenged, but retained, as part of the reading list for Advanced Placement English classes at Northwest High School in High Point. The book was challenged because it is "sexually graphic and violent."

1996 TX
Retained on the Round Rock Independent High School reading list after a challenge that the book was too violent.

1997 WV
Removed from the Jackson County school libraries along with sixteen other titles.

1999 OH
Challenged, but retained, as part of a supplemental reading list at the Shawnee School in Lima. Several parents described its content as vulgar and "X-rated."

1999 VA
Removed from the Ferguson High School library in Newport News. Students may request and borrow the book with parental approval.

2002 VA
Challenged, along with seventeen other titles in the Fairfax County elementary and secondary libraries, by a group called Parents Against Bad Books in Schools. The group contends the books "contain profanity and descriptions of drug abuse, sexually explicit conduct, and torture."

2008 NC
Challenged in Burke County schools in Morgantown by parents concerned about the homosexuality, rape, and incest portrayed in the book.

2013 NC
Challenged, but retained, as a Brunswick County Advanced Placement English eleventh-grade assignment. Language and sexuality or "obscenity" were most often cited as the reason for the majority of the unofficial complaints and criticisms, as was whether or not the book, a Pulitzer Prize-winner that deals with issues of racism, violence against women, and rape, has literary value that was age-appropriate for the students.

Source: 11, July 1984, p. 103; Sept. 1984, p. 156; Mar. 1985, p. 42; May 1985, pp. 75, 91; July 1985, p. 111; Nov. 1986, p. 209; May 1989, p. 77; Sept. 1989, p. 162; May 1990, p. 88; Sept. 1992, p. 142; Mar. 1993, p. 44; May 1993, p. 74; July 1995, p. 98; Sept. 1995, pp. 135, 160-61; Jan. 1996, p. 14; May 1996, p. 99; Mar. 1997, p. 50; May 1997, pp. 78-79; Sept. 1997, p. 149; Jan. 1998, p. 13; Sept. 1999, pp. 131-32; Nov. 1999, p. 163; Jan. 2003, p. 10; Jan. 2009, p. 10; Jan. 2014, p. 12; Mar. 2014, p. 66.

1794
Walker, Alice.
The Temple of My Familiar.

1989
Published

1997 WV
Removed from the Jackson County school libraries along with sixteen other titles.
Source: 11, Jan. 1998, p. 13.

1795
Walker, Alice.
Warrior Marks: Female Genital Mutilation and the Sexual Blinding of Women.

1993
Published

1995 TX
Former Weslaco librarian filed a federal lawsuit charging that she was fired for publicly discussing that city's efforts to ban Walker's work from the library.
Source: 11, Sept. 1995, p. 153.

1796
Walker, Barbara G.
The Woman's Encyclopedia of Myths and Secrets.

1983
Published

1988 OR
Restricted to non-required assignments at the North Bend High School library because the book "is of no benefit to anyone."
Source: 11, Jan. 1990, pp. 4–5.

1797
Walker, Kate.
Peter.

1993
Published

1994
Best Books for Young Adults

1998 WI
Challenged at the Barron School District.

2004 TX
Challenged at the Montgomery County Memorial Library System along with fifteen other young-adult books with gay-positive themes. The objections were posted at the Library Patrons of Texas website. The language describing the books is similar to that posted at the website of the Fairfax County, Virginia-based Parents Against Bad Books in Schools, to which Library Patrons of Texas links.
Source: 11, Jan. 1999, p. 9; Nov. 2004, pp. 231–32.

1798
Walker, Margaret.
Jubilee.

1966
Published

1966
Best Books for Young Adults

1977 SC
Challenged in the Greenville County school libraries by the Titan of the Fourth Province of the Knights of the Ku Klux Klan because the novel produces "racial strife and hatred."

2010 IL
Challenged at the Jacksonville High School by a pastor who said he found the fictionalized story of the author's grandmother, who was born as a slave in Georgia, an "offensive" and "trashy"novel about the way of life in the Old South. "We believe it is to promote superiority for white people and to step on black people and make them feel inferior."
Source: 11, May 1977, p. 73; May 2010, pp. 104-5.

1799
Wallace, Daisy, ed.
Witch Poems.

1976
Published

1993 MT
Challenged at the Bozeman elementary school libraries because it scared a kindergartner.
Source: 11, Sept. 1993, p. 158.

1800
Wallace, Irving.
The Fan Club.

1974
Published

1974 CA
The twenty-six branch librarians of Riverside County were advised that the book was not selected for circulation, and patrons should be told the county selection committee could not in good conscience spend tax money on it; further, that it was not their policy to purchase "formula written commercial fiction."

1982
Malaysian police confiscated the works of Wallace because the books were considered "prejudicial to the public interest."

1988
Destroyed in Beijing, China, and legal authorities threatened to bring criminal charges against the publishers.
Source: 4, p. 91; 5, Jan. 1983, p. 45; 11, Jan. 1989, p. 15.

1801
Walls, Jeannette.
The Glass Castle: A Memoir.

2005
Published

2006
Alex Award

2009 CA
Challenged at the William S. Hart Union High School District in Saugus as required summer reading for the honors English program. The best-selling memoir chronicles the author's harsh childhood and family life and includes profanity, criticisms of Christianity, and accounts of sexual abuse and prostitution. Students have the option of alternative assignments that still meet objectives and teaching goals.

2012 MI
Removed, but later returned as an assigned reading for ninth-grade honors English in the Traverse City West Senior High School.

2012 PA
Challenged, but retained, as part of the tenth-grade English curriculum in the Sade-Central City High School classrooms in Cairnbrook. The best-selling memoir in which Walls describes her hardscrabble upbringing includes sexual assault, casual profanity, drunkenness, seeing the family cat pitched from a moving car, and having to drink ditch water. Even critics of the graphic book praise its theme—overcoming adversity.

2013 KS
Challenged at the McPherson High School pre-AP English freshman class. A school committee unanimously determined the book was appropriately placed in the curriculum noting the district's opt-out policy, which allows all families to opt their children out of any assignment, and ask for an alternate one. The committee made a series of recommendations to the superintendent, who sent a letter to the parents informing them of these recommendations and asking if they desired to appeal the committee's decision. No one appealed the decision.

Source: 11, Jan. 2010, pp. 15-16; May 2012, p. 128; Jan. 2013, pp. 10-11; Mar. 2013, pp. 80-81.

1802
Wambaugh, Joseph.
The Black Marble.

1978
Published

1985 PA
Banned from the Stroudsburg High School library because it was "blatantly graphic, pornographic and wholly unacceptable for a high school library."

Source: 11, May 1985, p. 79.

1803
Wambaugh, Joseph.
The Delta Star.

1983
Published

1985 PA
Banned from the Stroudsburg High School library because it was "blatantly graphic, pornographic and wholly unacceptable for a high school library."

Source: 11, May 1985, p. 79.

1804
Wambaugh, Joseph.
The Glitter Dome.

1981
Published

1985 PA
Banned from the Stroudsburg High School library because it was "blatantly graphic, pornographic and wholly unacceptable for a high school library."

Source: 11, May 1985, 79.

1805
Wambaugh, Joseph.
The New Centurions.

1971
Published

1985 PA
Banned from the Stroudsburg High School library because it was "blatantly graphic, pornographic and wholly unacceptable for a high school library."

Source: 11, May 1985, p. 79.

1806
Warren, Patricia Nell.
The Front Runner.

1974
Published

1982 MI
Challenged at the Three Rivers Public Library because it "promotes homosexuality and perversion."

Source: 11, Mar. 1983, p. 29.

1807
Warren, Robert Penn.
All the King's Men.

1946
Published

1947
Pulitzer Prize for Fiction

1974 TX
Challenged at the Dallas Independent School District high school libraries.

Source: 11, Jan. 1975, pp. 6–7.

1808
Watkins, Yoko Kawashima.
So Far from the Bamboo Grove.

1986
Published

2006 MA
Removed from the sixth-grade English curriculum at Dover-Sherborn Middle School due to scenes hinting at rape, violence against women by Korean men, and a distorted presentation of history. It is part of the state's recommended reading list for the grade level. The book is based on the real-life experiences of Watkins, whose father was a Japanese government official. In a reversal of its decision, the Dover Regional School committee voted unanimously to keep the book as part of a sixth-grade language arts unit on survival. The school is exploring other texts to bring balance to the unit in response to the criticism leveled against the book by some parents and community members.

Source: 11, Jan. 2007, pp. 13-14; Mar. 2007, pp. 73-74.

1809
Watson, Jane Werner, and Sol Chaneles.
The Golden Book of the Mysterious.

1976
Published

1988 MD
Challenged at the Winchester Elementary School because of the book's reference to witchcraft, sorcery, spells, fortune-telling, reincarnation, werewolves, vampires, and ghosts.

Source: 11, July 1988, p. 120; Sept. 1988, p. 178.

1810
Watson, Larry.
Montana 1948: A Novel.

1993
Published

1994
Best Books for Young Adults

2011 WI
Challenged, but eventually retained at the Merrill High School despite some parents complaining that it is "questionable reading material for their tenth-grade students because of language, and sexual and racist themes." School leaders added it to the curriculum twelve years ago, saying it was a less controversial substitute for *Catcher in the Rye*. School leaders also said students have the option of reading a different book if they don't feel comfortable with the one they're assigned.

Source: 11, July 2011, pp. 161-62; Nov. 2011, p. 206; Jan. 2012, p. 35.

1811
Waugh, Evelyn.
Brideshead Revisited.

1945
Published

2005 AL
Alabama Representative Gerald Allen (R-Cottondale) proposed legislation that would prohibit the use of public funds for the "purchase of textbooks or library materials that recognize or promote homosexuality as an acceptable lifestyle." The bill also proposed that novels with gay protagonists and college textbooks that suggest homosexuality is natural would have to be removed from library shelves and destroyed. The bill would impact all Alabama school, public, and university libraries. While it would ban books like *Heather Has Two Mommies*, it could also include classic and popular novels with gay characters such as Evelyn Waugh's *Brideshead Revisited, The Color Purple,* or *The Picture of Dorian Gray.*
Source: 11, Jan. 2005, p. 5.

1812
Waxman, Stephanie.
What Is a Girl? What Is a Boy?

1976
Published

1983 MN
After the Minnesota Civil Liberties Union sued the Elk River School Board, the board reversed its decision to restrict this title to students who have written permission from their parents.

1991 VT
Challenged at the Blue Mountain schools in Wells River.

1994 GA
Placed in a special nonfiction section where an adult must request it for a child at the Lake Lanier Regional Library in Lawrenceville after a group of parents complained that the book is not appropriate for young children.

1994 GA
Moved to the nonfiction section of the Gwinnett-Forsyth Regional Library.
Source: 11, Sept. 1982, pp. 155–56; May 1983, p. 71; Sept. 1983, p. 153; Sept. 1991, p. 178; Nov. 1994, p. 187; Jan. 1995, p. 6.

1813
We the People–History of the U.S.

1981 MS
Removed from the Mississippi state-approved textbook list.
Source: 11, July 1981, p. 93.

1814
Webb, Frances Sienkiewicz Sizer, et al.
Making Life Choices: Health Skills and Concepts.

1994
Published

1997 NC
The Franklin County school board ordered three chapters cut out of the ninth-grade health textbooks. Those chapters dealt with AIDS, HIV, and other sexually transmitted diseases; pairing, marriage, and parenting; and sexual behavior and contraception.
Source: 11, Nov. 1997, p. 169.

1815
Webb, James.
Fields of Fire.

1979
Published

1988 SC
Challenged at the Fort Mill High School because the book contains "offensive language and explicit sex scenes." School officials decided to retain the novel, but to explore the possibility of setting up a "restricted" shelf for "controversial" books.
Source: 11, July 1988, p. 122; Sept. 1988, pp. 178–79.

1816
Wei Hui, Zhou.
Shanghai Baby.

1999
Published

2001
Banned in China because it contains "too much decadence and too much sexual description" and officials believed that it would "give a bad influence to a new generation." Police publicly raided book fairs and confiscated and burned copies of the novel.
Source: 13, p. 217.

1817
Welch, James.
Fools Crow.

1986
Published

1986
American Book Award

1999 MT
Banned from Laurel High School classrooms because the contents are "objectionable, inappropriate, disgusting, and repulsive." Two copies remain in the library.

2000 MT
Challenged, but retained, at the Bozeman High School despite objections to its descriptions of rape, mutilation, sex, and violence.
Source: 11, July 1999, p. 96; Mar. 2000, p. 51; July 2000, p. 125; July 2007, p. 148.

1818
Welch, James.
Winter in the Blood.

1974
Published

1996 TX
Retained on the Round Rock Independent High School reading list after a challenge that the book was too violent.
Source: 11, May 1996, p. 99.

1819
Wells, Rosemary.
Shy Charles.

1988
Published

1991 OR
Challenged because the mother allegedly is portrayed too negatively, but retained, at the Multnomah County Library.
Source: 11, Jan. 1992, p. 6.

1820
Wentworth, Harold, and Stuart B. Flexner.
Dictionary of American Slang.

1967
Published

1979 FL
Returned to the publisher after a parent complained to the Stuart Middle School.

1981 CO
Removed from the Westminster elementary and secondary school libraries.
Source: 11, July 1979, p. 75; Mar. 1982, pp. 42–43.

1821
Wersba, Barbara.
Whistle Me Home.

1997
Published

1998
Best Books for Young Adults

2005 MD
Banned in Carroll County schools. No reason stated.
Source: 11, Mar. 2006, pp. 70–71.

1822
Wertenbaker, Lael Tucker.
The World of Picasso.

1967
Published

1994 AZ
Retained at Maldonado Elementary School in Tucson after being challenged by parents who objected to nudity and "pornographic," "perverted," and "morbid" themes.
Source: 11, July 1994, p. 112.

1823
West, Stanley Gordon.
Finding Laura Buggs.

1999
Published

2007 ND
Challenged in the Fargo School District classrooms because the book includes passages on such topics as sexual bondage, incest, murder, and infanticide. According to district policy, the complainant does not have standing to request either formal or informal reviews because she doesn't have a child in classes using the book. The complainant also contacted the Montana Department of Public Instruction and several state legislators.
Source: 11, July 2007, pp. 148-49.

1824
West, Stanley Gordon.
*Until They Bring
the Streetcars Back.*

1997
Published

2007 ND
Challenged in the Fargo School District classrooms because the book includes passages on such topics as sexual bondage, incest, murder, and infanticide. According to district policy, the complainant does not have standing to request either formal or informal reviews because she doesn't have a child in classes using the book. The complainant also contacted the Montana Department of Public Instruction and several state legislators.
Source: 11, July 2007, pp. 148-49.

1825
Westheimer, David.
Von Ryan's Express.

1964
Published

1977 IL
Challenged at the North Suburban District Library in Loves Park because the novel contains "vulgar sexual expressions, profanity, and a discussion of a scene of gross immorality."
Source: 11, July 1977, p. 99.

1826
Wharton, William.
Birdy.

1979
Published

1979
Best Books for Young Adults

1988 ME
Banned, but later returned to the shelves of the Mary E. Taylor Middle School in Camden. The book was originally removed because it contained ten phrases and sentences that contain sexual material and "offensive" language.
Source: 11, Jan. 1988, pp. 8, 28.

1827
White, Edmund, and
Adam Mars-Jones.
*The Darker Proof: Stories
from a Crisis.*

1988
Published

1993 OR
Challenged at the Deschutes County Library in Bend because it "encourages and condones" homosexuality.
Source: 11, Sept. 1993, pp. 158–59.

1828
White, Edmund, ed.
Faber Book of Gay Short Fiction.

1991
Published

2000 NC
Challenged in the Charlotte Public Library because of its sexual content.
Source: 11, Sept. 2000, p. 143.

1829
White, Ellen Emerson.
Long Live the Queen.

1989
Published

1990
Best Books for Young Adults

1991 WA
Challenged in the Mount Vernon school libraries because it contained a word parents found objectionable.
Source: 11, Mar. 1992, p. 41.

1830
White, Ryan, and
Ann Marie Cunningham.
Ryan White: My Own Story.

1991
Published

1992
Best Books for Young Adults

1996 PA
Removed from the curriculum, but placed on library shelves, with restricted access, at the Stroudsburg middle school because a section "uses a gutter term for sodomy and another approves of teen smoking."
Source: 11, Mar. 1997, p. 37.

1831
Whitlock, Katherine.
*Bridges of Respect: Creating
Support for Lesbian and
Gay Youth.*

1988
Published

1990 IA
Challenged at the Muscatine Public Library because it is "wrong to promote immorality."
Source: 11, Nov. 1990, p. 225.

1832
Whitman, Walt.
Leaves of Grass.

1855
Published

1870 NY
Banned, informally, in New York bookstores. As per their usual practice, the Watch and Ward Society in the New York Society for the Suppression of Vice placed pressure on booksellers to suppress the sale of the book in their shops. Booksellers agreed not to advertise the book nor to suggest its sale to customers.

1870 PA
Banned, informally, in Philadelphia bookstores in the 1870s.

1880 MA
Banned in Boston in the 1880s. As per their usual practice, the Watch and Ward Society in Boston Society for the Suppression of Vice placed pressure on booksellers to suppress the sale of the book in their shops. Booksellers agreed not to advertise the book nor to suggest its sale to customers.
Source: 2, p. 38; 4, p. 45; 8, pp. 465–67; 15, Vol. I, p. 562, II, p. 610.

1833
Wiebe, Rudy Henry, ed.
The Story-Makers: A Selection of Modern Short Stories.

1970
Published

1984
Removed from the Halton County, Ontario, Canada, School District because the short story anthology contains "The Sins of Jesus," by Isaac Babel. According to the complainants, some Christians consider the story "blasphemous because the Lord Jesus appears as a slightly confused comic character who in the end seems to accept that he has made a mistake."
Source: 11, Nov. 1984, p. 188.

1834
Wieler, Diana J.
Bad Boy.

1989
Published

1993
Best Books for Young Adults

1996 PA
Challenged at the State College area middle school libraries. Three parents requested the book's removal, charging that it was full of profanity and portrayed underage drinking and other problems. In addition, the portrayal of the homosexual relationship between two secondary characters "conveys a wrong message."
Source: 11, Nov. 1996, p. 211; Jan. 1997, p. 9.

1835
Wilde, Oscar.
The Happy Prince and Other Stories.

1913
Published

1988 OR
Challenged at the Springfield Public Library because the stories were "distressing and morbid."
Source: 11, Jan. 1989, p. 3.

1836
Wilde, Oscar.
Salome.

1893
Published

1892
Lord Chamberlain withheld the play license in London, England, on the grounds that it introduced biblical characters.

1895 MA
Book banned in Boston.
Source: 4, p. 55.

1837
Wilder, Laura Ingalls.
Little House in the Big Woods.

1932
Published

1996 CA
Removed from the classrooms, but later reinstated, for third-graders at the Lincoln Unified School District in Stockton. Complainants also want the book removed from the library because it "promotes racial epithets and is fueling the fire of racism."
Source: 11, Jan. 1997, p. 9; Mar. 1997, p. 50.

1838
Wilder, Laura Ingalls.
Little House on the Prairie.

1935
Published

1993 LA
Challenged at the Lafourche Parish elementary school libraries in Thibodaux because the book is "offensive to Indians."

1993 SD
Banned in the Sturgis elementary school classrooms due to statements considered derogatory to Native Americans.

1998 MN
Temporarily removed at the Yellow Medicine East Elementary School near Granite Falls due to the book's racist statements against Native Americans.
Source: 11, July 1993, pp. 124–25; Mar. 1994, p. 55; Mar. 1999, p. 36.

1839
Willhoite, Michael.
Daddy's Roommate.

1991
Published

1992 GA
Restricted to adults at the Lake Lanier Regional Library System in Gwinnett County.

1992 NC
Challenged at the Wayne County Public Library in Goldsboro.

1992 NC
Challenged at the Fayetteville Public Library.

1992 NM
Challenged at the Roswell Public Library.

1992 NY
Removed from the Brooklyn School District's curriculum because the school board objected to words that were "age inappropriate."

1992 OR
Challenged at the Tillamook Public Library because it "promotes a dangerous and ungodly lifestyle from which children must be protected."

1992 PA
Challenged at the Dauphin County Library System because the book's intent "is indoctrination into a gay lifestyle."

1992 TX
Challenged at the Grand Prairie Memorial Library.

1992 WA
Challenged at the Timberland Regional Libraries in Olympia because the book promotes homosexuality and is offensive.

1993 AK
Challenged at the Juneau school libraries.

1993 AZ
Challenged at the Mesa Public Library because it "is vile, sick and goes against every law and constitution."

1993 FL
Moved from the children's section to the adult section at the Manatee Public Library.

1993 FL
Challenged at the Alachua County Library in High Springs.

1993 MA
Challenged at the Seekonk library.

1993 MD
Challenged at the Wicomico County Free Library in Salisbury.

1993 MN
Challenged as a reading in the Rosemount-Apple Valley-Eagan Independent School District # 196.

1993 NC
Moved from the children's section to the adult section at the Elizabethtown library.

1993 NC
Challenged at the Cumberland County Public Library.

1993 NJ
Moved from the children's section to the adult section of the Mercer County Library System in Lawrence.

1993 NJ
Challenged at the North Brunswick Public Library.

1993 OH
Retained at the Dayton and Montgomery County Public Library.

1993 TN
Challenged at the Chattanooga-Hamilton County Library Bicentennial Library.

1993 WI
Challenged at the Sussex Public Library.

1994 AZ
Challenged at the Chandler Public Library because the book is a "skillful presentation to the young child about lesbianism/homosexuality."

1994 OR
Removed by Lane County Head Start officials in Cottage Grove from its anti-bias curriculum.

1994 TX
Removed from the children's section of the Fort Worth Public Library because critics say it legitimizes gay relationships.

1998 FL
Challenged at the Brevard County Library. When a request to ban the book failed, the complainant kept the book from other patrons by keeping it checked out for a year.

1998 KS
Challenged, but retained, at the Hays Public Library. A resident objected to "the teaching of the homosexual lifestyle as another way to show love."

1998 TX
Challenged at the Wichita Falls Public Library. When the request to have the book banned failed, the complainant kept the book from other patrons by keeping it checked out for a year. The deacon body of the First Baptist Church requested that any literature that promotes or sanctions a homosexual lifestyle be removed. The Wichita Falls City Council established a policy that allows library card holders who collect three hundred signatures to have children's books moved to an adult portion of the library. U.S. District Court Judge Jerry Buchmeyer struck down the library resolution as unconstitutional and the books were returned.

1999 ID
Challenged, but retained, in the juvenile non-fiction section of the Nampa Public Library.

2000 ID
Challenged, but retained, at the Ada Community Library.

Source: 11, May 1992, pp. 83, 95; Sept. 1992, p. 162; Nov. 1992, pp. 197–99; Jan. 1993, pp. 7, 9, 10, 28; May 1993, pp. 69–71; July 1993, pp. 101, 106-7, 123-26; Sept. 1993, pp. 143–46; Nov. 1993, p. 179; Jan. 1994, pp. 13, 34–36; Mar. 1994, p. 69; July 1994, p. 115; Sept. 1994, pp. 147-48, 166; Nov. 1994, p. 187; Jan. 1995, pp. 4, 6, 8; Sept. 1995, p. 159; May 1998, pp. 69, 88; July 1998, pp. 105–7; Jan. 1999, pp. 8–9; Mar. 1999, p. 36; May 1999, p. 67; Sept. 1999, p. 131; Nov. 1999, p. 172; Mar. 2000, pp. 44, 61; Nov. 2000, pp. 201–202.

1840

Williams-Garcia, Rita.
Like Sisters on the Homefront.

1995
Published

1996
Best Books for Young Adults

1996
Coretta Scott King Author Honor Book

2000 PA
Removed from Central Dauphin school district, Harrisburg elementary and middle school library shelves due to explicit language.

Source: 11, Sept. 2000, p. 144.

1841

Williams, Chancellor.
The Destruction of African Civilization and the Origin of African Civilization.

1971
Published

1993 MD
Challenged at the Prince George's County high school libraries because the two volumes promote "racism against white people." In a complaint filed with the state, the works were called "racist pornography" written "to provoke emotions and actions of racial prejudice, bias, hatred and hostility towards citizens and students in Maryland."

Source: 11, Nov. 1993, p. 177.

1842

Williams, Garth.
The Rabbit's Wedding.

1958
Published

1959 AL
Removed from the "open" shelves to the "reserved" shelves at the Montgomery Public Library because in an illustration, the buck was black while the doe was white. Such miscegenation, stated an editor in Orlando, was "brainwashing.... as soon as you pick up the book and open its pages you realize these rabbits are integrated." *The Home News* of Montgomery, Alabama, added that the book was integrationist propaganda obviously aimed at children in their formative years.
Source: 3, p. 464.

1843
Williams, Jaston; Joe Sears, and Ed Howard.
Greater Tuna.

1983
Published

1991 IL
Challenged at the Grayslake Community High School.
Source: 11, July 1991, pp. 129–30.

1844
Williams, Jay.
The Magic Grandfather.

1979
Published

1989 OR
Challenged at the Little Butte Intermediate School in Eagle Point because the book used swear words and deals with magic and witches.
Source: 11, Jan. 1990, pp. 4–5.

1845
Williams, Roger.
The Bloudy Tenent of Persecution.

1644
Published

1644
Burned publicly by order of the British Parliament.
Source: 8, pp. 215–16.

1846
Willingham, Calder.
End as a Man.

1947
Published

1947 NY
New York Society for Suppression of Vice sought a ban.

1948 PA
Seized in Philadelphia raid.
Source: 4, p. 96; 14, pp. 129–30.

1847
Wilson, August.
Fences.

1986
Published

1987
Drama Desk Award for Outstanding Play

1987
Pulitzer Prize for Drama

1987
Tony Award for Best Play

1993 PA
Challenged in the honors and academic English classes in Carlisle schools because it is "demeaning to women." Teachers must send parents a letter warning about the work's content and explaining that their children may read alternate selections.
Source: 11, July 1993, p. 127.

1848
Wilson, Colin, and Una Woodruff.
Witches.

1981
Published

1986 OR
Challenged at the Albany Library because the book "is satanic in nature, thereby having tremendous drawing power to the curious and unsuspecting."
Source: 11, July 1986, p. 136.

1849
Wilson, Colin.
The Sex Diary of Gerard Orme.

1963
Published

1964 CT
A bookseller in New Britain was arrested for selling this title.
Source: 4, p. 99.

1850
Wilson, Daniel Howard.
Robopocalypse.

2012
Published

2012
Alex Award

2012 TN
Challenged, but retained, as required reading at the Hardin Valley Academy in Knoxville despite objections to "inappropriate language."
Source: 11, Nov. 2012, p. 238; Jan. 2013, pp. 33-34.

1851
Wilson, Edmund.
Memoirs of Hecate County.

1946
Published

1946 CA
Booksellers in San Francisco were arrested for selling the work and taken to trial. A bookseller was charged with selling an "obscene" book, but the first trial was dismissed because it resulted in a hung trial. In the second trial of *People v. Wepplo*, 78 Cal. App. 2D 959, 178 P.2d 853 (1947), the jury acquitted the bookseller.

1946 MA
Shipment ceased because of its censorship laws.

1946 NY
Confiscated by the New York City police from four Doubleday bookshops after the New York Society for Suppression of Vice charged that it was salacious and lascivious. Booksellers in New York City were arrested for selling the work and taken to trial.

1946 PA
Copies of the book were confiscated in Philadelphia and the publisher ceased shipment to Massachusetts because of its censorship laws.

1956
Banned from the U.S. mail.
Source: 4, pp. 76–77; 8, pp. 365-66; 15, Vol. IV, pp. 697–99.

1852

Winship, Elizabeth;
Frank Caparulo,
and Vivian K. Harlin.
Human Sexuality.

1992
Published

1992 GA
Challenged in the Fulton County schools because the "book is a 'how-to' book. It's not only explicit, but it promotes promiscuity in a subtle way that the determined abstainer would have second thoughts about their position." The group alleged that the text "undermines parents' authority, encourages breaking the law, and tears down normal sexual barriers by co-ed, hardcore, adult subject matter covered."

1994 GA
Banned in the Fulton County high schools because the book was too graphic, out-of-date, and did too little to persuade students not to have sex.

1994 MO
Removed from use in health classes by the Belleville School District School Board after parents had complained that the book "didn't stress abstinence from sex by high school students," and because "it didn't say whether sexual relations before marriage, homosexuality, masturbation, or abortion are right or wrong."
Source: 11, May 1992, pp. 82–83; May 1994, p. 87; Sept. 1994, p. 150.

1853

Winship, Elizabeth.
*Perspectives on Health:
Human Sexuality.*

1988
Published

1994 IN
Retained by unanimous school board vote, two mothers nevertheless protested by removing their daughters from classes at an Argos Community School using this textbook because they felt it is "too explicit and sends mixed messages about abstinence." They also objected to treatment of abortion and homosexuality.
Source: 11, May 1994, p. 99.

1854

Winsor, Kathleen.
Forever Amber.

1944
Published

1946
Copies burned at British ports and by the public library in Birmingham, England.

1946 MA
Temporary injunction issued against sale of the book in Springfield. Attorney General George Rowell cited as due cause for banning the book some seventy references to sexual intercourse; thirty-nine illegitimate pregnancies; seven abortions; ten descriptions of women undressing, dressing or bathing in the presence of men; five references to incest; thirteen references ridiculing marriage; and forty-nine "miscellaneous objection-able passages." Rowell lost his case, and Judge Donahue of the Massachusetts Supreme Court defined the book as "a soporific rather an aphrodisiac...while the novel was conducive to sleep, it was not conducive to a desire to sleep with a member of the opposite sex."

1952
Banned in New Zealand after the Minister of Customs, reviewed a copy seized by Customs officers.

1953
Banned in Ireland.
Source: 3, p. 95; 4, p. 93; 8, pp. 336-38; 15, Vol. IV, pp. 696-98.

1855

Winter, Jeanette.
*The Librarian of Basra:
A True Story from Iraq.*

2004
Published

2013 NY
Challenged in Johnson City schools as a suggested reading because of violent illustrations and storyline. The book is about a librarian who sneaks books out of a library during the U.S. bombings in Iraq. The librarian works with members of the community to keep the books safe until the war is over and a new library can be built.
Source: 11, Jan. 2014, pp. 11-12.

1856

Winter, Jeanette.
*Nasreen's Secret School:
A True Story from Afghanistan.*

2009
Published

2013 NY
Challenged in Johnson City schools as a suggested reading because of violent illustrations and storyline. The book is about the Taliban taking control of an Afghan village and preventing girls from going to school. After Nasreen's father is kidnapped and presumed killed, her grandmother smuggles her each day to an underground school where she can learn to read and write.
Source: 11, Jan. 2014, pp. 11-12.

1857

Winthrop, Elizabeth.
The Castle in the Attic.

1985
Published

1995 ME
Challenged at the Medway schools because the book uses swear words and deals with sorcery.
Source: 11, July 1995, p. 97.

1858

Witt, Mary A., et al.
*The Humanities: Cultural
Roots and Continuities.*

1985
Published

1986 FL
Banned from classroom use, but returned to the Columbia High School library in Lake City because of "offensive" language. The school board banned two sections of the text that contained modern adapta-tion of *The Miller's Tale*, by Chaucer and *Lysistrata*, by Aristophanes. In December 1986, four parents filed a lawsuit charging that their children's rights were violated when the textbook was banned from classroom use. On January 30, 1988, the U.S. District Court for the Middle District of Florida ruled that in *Virgil v. School Board of Columbia County* "the school board acted within its broad range of discretion

in determining educational suitability" and thus may constitutionally ban a textbook because of sex and vulgarity. Upholding this ruling, the U.S. Court of Appeals for the Fourth Circuit ruled on January 16, 1989, that the school board did not violate students' constitutional rights when it removed the textbook.

Source: 11, July 1986, p. 119; Nov. 1986, p. 207; Mar. 1987, p. 51; Nov. 1987, p. 223; May 1988, pp. 81, 98; Sept. 1988, p. 150; Mar. 1989, p. 52.

1859
Wittlinger, Ellen.
Sandpiper.

2005
Published

2006
Best Books for Young Adults

2007 AL
Challenged at the Brookwood High School's library due to a complaint that the book has sexual content and language. The grandmother stated that the school should "teach abstinence and no sex before marriage." Wittlinger, the book's author, said in a letter to the school system that she was very surprised to learn that her book was being called "offensive" and "sick" because she said the purpose of the book is not meant to be a how-to guide for oral sex. Instead, it is a cautionary tale to teach kids that oral sex is "real" sex and not just the "cool thing to do." The board decided eventually to retain the book "on the advice of legal counsel."

Source: 11, Nov. 2007, p. 239; Jan. 2008, p. 7; Mar. 2008, p. 77.

1860
Wolf, Eric.
Peasant Wars of the Twentieth Century.

1969
Published

1985
Banned in South Korea.
Source: 5, Apr. 1986, pp. 30–33.

1861
Wolfe, Daniel.
T. E. Lawrence.

1995
Published

2000 CA
Removed from the Anaheim school district because school officials said the book is too difficult for middle school students and that it could cause harassment against students seen with it. The American Civil Liberties Union (ACLU) of Southern California filed suit in *Doe v. Anaheim Union High School District* alleging that the removal is "a pretext for viewpoint-based censorship." The ACLU claims no other books have been removed from the junior high library for similar reasons, even though several, such as works by Shakespeare and Dickens, are more difficult reading. The ACLU contends that the school officials engaged in unconstitutional viewpoint discrimination by removing the book because it contains gay and lesbian material. In March 2001, the school board approved a settlement that restored the book to the high school shelves and amended the district's policy to prohibit the removal of books for subject matter involving sexual orientation, but the book will not be returned to the middle school.

Source: 11, Mar. 2001, p. 53; May 2001, p. 95; July 2001, p. 173.

1862
Wolfe, Thomas.
Of Time and the River.

1935
Published

1983 AL
Four members of the Alabama State Textbook Committee called for the rejection of Wolfe's work for use in Alabama public schools.

Source: 11, Mar. 1983, p. 39; 14, pp. 242–43.

1863
Wolfe, Tom.
The Electric Kool-Aid Acid Test.

1968
Published

2012 PA
Challenged on the Emmaus High School tenth-grade summer reading list because the nonfiction account of the author's drug-induced bus journey across the country has "objectionable sexual content and that there is nothing good about it."

Source: 11, Jan. 2013, p. 12.

1864
Wolff, Tobias.
This Boy's Life: A Memoir.

1989
Published

1990
Best Books for Young Adults

2005 KS
Removed from the Blue Valley School District's high school curriculum in Overland Park. The book was challenged by parents and community members because of "foul language, and references to alcohol and sexual activity."

Source: 11, Nov. 2005, pp. 282–83.

1865
Wolk, Robert L., and Arthur Henley.
The Right to Lie.

1970
Published

1987 MI
Challenged at the Plymouth-Canton school system in Canton because the book is "a psychological guide to everyday deceit."

Source: 11, May 1987, p. 110.

1866
Wood, Audrey.
Elbert's Bad Word.

1988
Published

1992 GA
Challenged in the Columbia County school libraries because Elbert visits a friendly gardener who is a "practicing wizard."

Source: 11, Nov. 1992, p. 197.

1867
Wood, Bari.
Amy Girl.

1987
Published

1988 NJ
Removed from the shelves of the Northern Burlington County Regional

High School library because of its "descriptions of underage drinking and teenage sex."
Source: 11, Mar. 1988, p. 46.

1868
Wood, Maryrose.
Sex Kittens and Horn Dawgs Fall in Love.

2006
Published

2006 FL
Removed along with nine other titles from a library order at the Hernando County schools. Among the other books culled from Nature Coast Technical High School's order were Barbara Kingsolver's first novel, *The Bean Trees; The Clan of the Cave Bear,* by Jean Auel; *Boy's Life,* by Robert McCammon; and the abridged young-adult version of *The Power of One,* by Bryce Courtenay. A board member led the charge against those books, reading profanity-laced passages and castigating the school officials who placed the order. Other books the school system wants to have reviewed are: *Are You in the House Alone?; Rainbow Boys; Rats Saw God;* and *The King Must Die.*
Source: 11, July 2006, p. 182.

1869
Woodroffe, Patrick.
The Second Earth: The Pentateuch Retold.

1988
Published

1992 VA
Removed from the Warrenton Junior High School library because a single parent complained about its "anti-Christian" ideas and its illustrations.
Source: 11, May 1992, pp. 81–82.

1870
Woolley, Persia.
Queen of the Summer Stars.

1990
Published

1991
Best Books for Young Adults

1995 NY
Challenged, but retained, at the Case Junior High School Library in Watertown

because, although the book contains scenes of sex, kidnapping, rape and incest, the themes of love, loyalty, honor and trust are more obvious to the reader.
Source: 11, May 1995, p. 66; July 1995, pp. 109–10.

1871
Wright, Peter.
Spycatcher.

1987
Published

1987
Banned in India.

1987
Banned in England because the author had violated his secrecy oath under the Official Secrets Act. After a two-and-a-half-year battle, the courts determined that three London newspapers could publish excerpts from the former intelligence agent's memoirs.
Source: 8, pp. 173–76; 11, Nov. 1987, p. 229; May 1988, p. 93; Jan. 1989, p. 15.

1872
Wright, Richard.
Black Boy.

1945
Published

1972 MI
Removed from classroom use in Michigan after parents objected to the book's sexual overtones and claimed that it was unsuitable for impressionable sophomores.

1975 LA
Challenged, but retained, in the East Baton Rouge schools despite claims the book contains obscenity, filth, or pornography.

1975 TN
Removed from Tennessee schools for being obscene, instigating hatred between the races, and encouraging immorality.

1976 NY
Restricted to students with parental approval at the Island Trees, N. Y., Union Free School District High School library in 1976; restriction lifted after the U.S. Supreme Court ruling on June 25, 1982, in *Board of Education, Island Trees Union Free School District No. 26 et al. v. Pico et al.,* 457 U.S. 853 (1982).

1987 NE
Challenged in the Lincoln school

libraries because of the novel's "corruptive, obscene nature."

1987 NE
Nebraska Governor Kay Orr's "kitchen cabinet" called for the novel's removal, asserting it had a "corruptive obscene nature" and citing the use of profanity throughout and the incidents of violence. The book was removed from library shelves, then returned after the controversy abated.

1996 TX
Retained on the Round Rock Independent High School reading list after a challenge that the book was too violent.

1997 FL
Challenged in the Jacksonville public schools by a minister who said the book contains "profanity and may spark hard feelings between students of different races."

2007 MI
Challenged in the Howell High School along with several other books because of strong sexual content. In response to a request from the president of the Livingston Organization for Values in Education, or LOVE, the county's top law enforcement official reviewed the books to see whether laws against distribution of sexually explicit materials to minors had been broken. "After reading the books in question, it is clear that the explicit passages illustrated a larger literary, artistic, or political message and were not included solely to appeal to the prurient interests of minors," the Livingston County prosecutor wrote. "Whether these materials are appropriate for minors is a decision to be made by the school board, but I find that they are not in violation of the criminal laws."
Source: 8, pp. 23-28; 11, May 1978, p. 57; Nov. 1982, p. 197; Nov. 1987, p. 225; May 1996, p. 99; Sept. 1997, p. 127; Mar. 2007, pp. 51-52; May 2007, pp. 117-18

1873
Wright, Richard.
Native Son.

1940
Published

1978 NH
Challenged in Goffstown.

1978 NJ
Challenged in Elmwood Park due to "objectionable" language.

1981 MA
Challenged in North Adams due to the book's "violence, sex, and profanity."

1988 MI
Challenged at the Berrien Springs High School in classrooms and libraries because the novel is "vulgar, profane, and sexually explicit."

1994 WA
Retained in the Yakima schools after a five-month dispute over what advanced high school students should read in the classroom. Two parents raised concerns about profanity and images of violence and sexuality in the book and requested that it be removed from the reading list.

1996 NC
Challenged as part of the reading list for Advanced Placement English classes at Northwest High School in High Point. The book was challenged because it is "sexually graphic and violent."

1998 CA
Removed from Irvington High School in Fremont after a few parents complained the book was unnecessarily violent and sexually explicit.

1998 IN
Challenged in the Hamilton High School curriculum in Fort Wayne because of the novel's graphic language and sexual content. Source: 11, May 1978, p. 57; July 1978, p. 98; Sept. 1981, p. 125; Nov. 1981, p. 170; Jan. 1989, p. 28; Nov. 1994, pp. 202–3; Mar. 1997, p. 50; Sept. 1997, p. 149; Sept. 1998, p. 142; Mar. 1999, p. 39.

1874
WritersCorps.
Paint Me Like I Am: Teen Poems.

2003
Published

2009 NJ
The principal at the Landis Intermediate School in Vineyard removed two pages that included the poem "Diary of an Abusive Stepfather" after a thirteen-year-old Landis student's mother questioned its appropriateness. The thirty-one-line poem is peppered with profanity and details a violent relationship between an adult and child. San Francisco-based WritersCorps, an art organization linking writers with teens in urban areas to provide outlets for their experiences, produced the anthology.

2009 WI
Retained in the combined middle and high school library in the North Fond du Lac School District provided it has a label designating it as appropriate for high school students. Younger students could also access the book with prior parental permission. A parent asked the school district to reconsider the book due to mature language. Source: 11, July 2009, pp. 131–32; May 2010, pp. 128-29.

1875
Wycliffe, John.
On Civil Lordship.

1376
Published

1377
Condemned by the Pope in Rome, Italy.

1381
A Council at Oxford, England, prohibited his work as heretical and forbade him from preaching or lecturing.

1415
A church council in Germany ordered his bones exhumed and burned and his ashes thrown into a running stream. Source: 1, pp. 228–29.

1876
Wyden, Peter, and Barbara Wyden.
Growing Up Straight: What Every Thoughtful Parent Should Know About Homosexuality.

1968
Published

1993 OR
Challenged at the Deschutes County Library in Bend because it "encourages and condones" homosexuality. Source: 11, Sept. 1993, pp. 158–59.

1877
Yashima, Taro.
Crow Boy.

1955
Published

1956
Caldecott Honor Book

1994 NY
Challenged by a school board member in the Queens school libraries because it "denigrate[s] white American culture, 'promotes racial separation, and discourages assimilation.'" The rest of the school board voted to retain the book. Source: 11, July 1994, pp. 110–11; Sept. 1994, p. 166.

1878
Yates, Elizabeth.
Amos Fortune, Free Man.

1950
Published

1951
Newbery Medal

1989 MD
Temporarily removed from the classrooms as an optional reading assignment in the Montgomery County schools because the book contained "racist dialogue, fostered stereotypes, and could be degrading to black children who read it." Source: 11, Mar. 1990, p. 62.

1879
Yep, Laurence.
Dragonwings.

1975
Published

1976
Newbery Honor Book

1992 PA
Challenged at the Apollo-Ridge schools in Kittanning because of the frequent use of the word "demon" in the book. The book might encourage children to "commit suicide because they think they can be reincarnated as something or someone else." On September 15, 1992, Judge Joseph Nickleach denied a request seeking to ban the book from the district's curriculum. In his opinion, Nickleach wrote: "The fact that religions and religious concepts are mentioned in school does not automatically constitute a violation of the establishment clause."

1999 IN
Challenged at the Henryville schools because of graphic violence, profanity, references to demons and prostitution,

and alcohol and drug use depicted in a positive light.

Source: 11, Sept. 1992, pp. 142–43; Jan. 1993, p. 18; Nov. 1999, p. 164.

1880
Young, Lawrence A.
Recreational Drugs.

1977
Published

1982 CA
Challenged in the Alameda County Library because it allegedly encourages drug use.

Source: 11, Sept. 1982, p. 169.

1881
Zacks, Richard.
History Laid Bare: Love, Sex, and Perversity from the Ancient Etruscans to Warren G. Harding.

1994
Published

1999 NC
Challenged, but retained, at the Cumberland County Library in Fayetteville despite a complaint that the book deals with sexual history and customs. In addition, the complainant suggested that the library move sexually explicit materials, as well as ones about homosexuality, into an adult section and establish a review committee to screen materials.

Source: 11, July 1999, p. 94; Jan. 2000, pp. 27–28.

1882
Zacks, Richard.
An Underground Education: The Unauthorized and Outrageous Supplement to Everything You Thought You Knew about Art, Sex, Business, Crime, Science, Medicine, and Other Fields of Human Knowledge.

1997
Published

1999 NC
Challenged, but retained, at the Cumberland County Library in Fayetteville despite a

complaint that the book deals with sexual history and customs. In addition, the complainant suggested that the library move sexually explicit materials, as well as ones about homosexuality, into an adult section and establish a review committee to screen materials.

Source: 11, July 1999, p. 94; Jan. 2000, pp. 27–28.

1883
Zemach, Margot.
Jake and Honeybunch Go to Heaven.

1982
Published

1982 CA
The San Francisco Public Library, after surveying librarians employed in their library, refused to acquire the book because it is "racially offensive."
The New York Times stated, "In this case, librarians are deliberately keeping a widely acclaimed book by a major author-artist off their shelves in the name of morality."

1982 IL
The Chicago Public Library, after surveying librarians employed in their library, refused to acquire the book because it is "racially offensive."

1982 WI
The Milwaukee Public Library, after surveying librarians employed in their library, refused to acquire the book because it is "racially offensive."

Source: 14, pp. 189–90.

1884
Zindel, Paul.
Loch.

1994
Published

1997 NV
Challenged due to explicit language, but retained, at the Lander County School District.

Source: 11, Mar. 1998, p. 56.

1885
Zindel, Paul.
My Darling, My Hamburger.

1969
Published

1973 MN
Removed from the Frazee School library.

1976 NY
Removed from the Lyons Elementary School library.

1979 IA
Removed from the Hiawatha Public Library.

1980 IL
Challenged in Champaign.

1982 KY
Challenged in Jefferson County.

1987 SD
Banned in the Dupree High School English classes because of what the school board called "offensive language and vulgarity."

Source: 11, Nov. 1973, p. 135; July 1976, p. 86; Mar. 1979, p. 27; May 1980, p. 61; Mar. 1983, p. 41; Jan. 1988, p. 12.

1886
Zindel, Paul.
Pigman.

1968
Published

1985 MO
Challenged at the Hillsboro School District because the novel features "liars, cheaters and stealers."

1990 CT
Challenged as suitable curriculum material in the Burlington schools because it contains profanity and subject matter that set bad examples and give students negative views of life.

1990 CT
Challenged as suitable curriculum material in the Harwinton schools because it contains profanity and subject matter that set bad examples and give students negative views of life.

1992 VA
Challenged at the Lynchburg middle and high school English classes because the novel contains twenty-nine instances of "destructive, disrespectful, antisocial and illegal behavior… placed in a humorous light, making it seem acceptable."

Source: 11, Mar. 1985, p. 44; Mar. 1991, p. 44; May 1991, p. 90; Sept. 1992, p. 164.

1887
Zinn, Howard.
A People's History of the United States.

1980
Published

2009 VA
Challenged in the North Stafford High School advanced-placement history class, even though it's not the primary textbook because the book is "un-American, leftist propaganda." Students in the advanced placement class also read an article titled, "Howard Zinn's Disappointing History of the United States," which criticizes Zinn's book.
Source: 11, May 2009, pp. 108-9.

1888
Zola, Émile.
J'Accuse.

1898
Published

1894
All Zola's works were placed on the *Index Librorum Prohibitorum* (List of Prohibited Books) in Rome, Italy.

1929
Banned in Yugoslavia.

1953
Banned in Ireland.
Source: 4, pp. 51–52.

1889
Zola, Émile.
Nana.

1880
Published

1888
An English court agreed that all of Zola's works must be withdrawn from circulation, making Zola the only writer to have his works outlawed in England in the nineteenth century. The major complaints centered on the perception that Zola had made a heroine of a prostitute and had discussed "debased man's nature" by uncovering the often sordid sexuality of the period.

1894
Listed on the *Index Librorum Prohibitorum* (List of Prohibited Books) in Rome, Italy.

1929
Banned in Yugoslavia.

1953
Banned in Ireland.
Source: 4, pp. 51–52; 6, pp. 2,718–20; 14, pp. 234–35.

1890
Zwerman, Gilda.
Martina Navratilova.

1995
Published

2000 CA
Removed from the Anaheim school district because school officials said the book is too difficult for middle school students and that it could cause harassment against students seen with it. The American Civil Liberties Union (ACLU) of Southern California filed suit in *Doe v. Anaheim Union High School District* alleging that the removal is "a pretext for viewpoint-based censorship." The ACLU claims no other books have been removed from the junior high library for similar reasons, even though several, such as works by Shakespeare and Dickens, are more difficult reading. The ACLU contends that the school officials engaged in unconstitutional viewpoint discrimination by removing the book because it contains gay and lesbian material. In March 2001, the school board approved a settlement that restored the book to the high school shelves and amended the district's policy to prohibit the removal of books for subject matter involving sexual orientation, but the book will not be returned to the middle school.
Source: 11, Mar. 2001, p. 53; May 2001, p. 95; July 2001, p. 173.

Title Index

Title Index

Geographic Index

Note:
The bibliographic entries are numbered sequentially and the entry number, rather than the page number, is listed below. This index is meant to assist in the development of displays, articles, editorials, and presentations. For example, a display of titles challenged or banned within your state.

Banned Books | Challenging Our Freedom to Read

Irving, 85
Judson, 86
Katy, 1331, 1612
Keller, 1066
LaPorte, 950
Lewisville, 1691, 1762
Lindale, 740, 1024, 1190, 1725, 1762
Lubbock, 1420
Lufkin, 408
Mercedes, 749, 819
Mesquite, 1263, 1463
Montgomery County, 259, 273,
 277, 387, 424, 482, 552, 554, 588, 608,
 609, 660, 729, 738, 912, 1007, 1514, 1797
North Richland Hills, 1762
Olney, 640
Page, 1396
Plano, 1762, 1763
Quitman, 1105
Richardson, 1627
Richmond, 729
Riviera, 1676
Round Rock, 39, 66, 373, 1022, 1221, 1230,
 1252, 1590, 1612, 1790, 1793, 1818, 1872
San Antonio, 282
Santa Fe, 1489, 1490, 1492, 1493
Southlake, 66, 1097, 1159
Stephenville, 268, 1187
Tuscola, 1170
Weslaco, 1364, 1681, 1795
West Brazoria, 1357
Wichita Falls, 8, 306, 1281, 1627, 1839
Wimberley, 66

Utah
172, 264, 887, 1689, 1711
Davis, 800, 1454
Davis County, 287, 444, 1403
Farmington, 612
Magna, 1201
Ogden, 71, 142, 714, 1513
Orem, 231
Payson, 1359
Provo, 729
Salt Lake County, 861

Virginia
Abingdon, 1464, 1483, 1578
Albemarle County, 470, 476
Bedford County, 119, 800
Brentsville, 30, 606, 814
Buckingham County, 1676
Centreville, 451
Charlotte County, 1609
Charlottesville, 765, 1690
Culpeper County, 580
Fairfax, 1762
Fairfax County, 33, 52, 66, 163, 165, 166,
 167, 277, 296, 325, 363, 365, 367, 428,

485, 815, 1063, 1074, 1113, 1230, 1247, 1258,
 1413, 1517, 1728, 1762, 1793
Fauquier, 361
Franklin, 1510
Greene County, 51
Gretna, 1754
Hampton, 326, 1450, 1570, 1655
Harrisonburg, 468
Hillsville, 497
Lake Braddock, 903
Loudoun County, 1454
Lynchburg, 349, 1781, 1886
Newport News, 91, 1793
North Stafford, 1887
Patrick County, 173
Prince William County, 107, 1356, 1680,
 1773, 1790
Richmond, 498
Roanoke, 277
Rockingham County, 1512
Sandston, 1731
South Accomack, 436
Stafford County, 399, 407, 408, 409, 410,
 411, 413
Staunton, 326
Virginia Beach, 1579
Warm Springs, 71, 1676
Warrenton, 1869
Washington County, 1615
Williamsburg, 1191
Wise County, 580
York County, 363
Yorktown, 907

Vermont
480, 1758
Bennington, 227
Chester, 1162
Goochland, 930
Richford, 1674
Shaftsbury, 1365
Townshend, 193
Vergennes, 916, 1129, 1416
Wells River, 1812

Washington
Aberdeen, 904
Arlington, 1165
Bainbridge Island, 434, 1175
Bellevue, 149
Bellingham, 769
Bremerton, 66, 878
Clover Park, 729
Deer Park, 1610
Edmonds, 255
Everett, 627
Evergreen, 659
Federal Way, 1589, 1762
Fort Vancouver, 731

Hockinson, 664, 838
Issaquah, 1509, 1668
Kent, 902, 1270
King County, 1727
Kirkland, 766, 1215, 1411, 1537, 1538, 1539
Kitsap County, 690
Leavenworth, 1261
Longview, 65
Lynden, 1612
Marysville, 192, 1658
Mead, 429, 1337
Mount Vernon, 1829
Mukilteo, 66
North Thurston, 638
Oak Harbor, 188, 221, 1107
Olympia, 1839
Omak, 201, 297, 1637
Othello, 1196
Prosser, 316, 828, 1363
Pullman, 60
Puyallup, 597
Renton, 1683, 1762
Richland, 22, 86, 565, 690, 905, 1297, 1398,
 1400, 1414, 1644
Seattle, 534, 819, 1166, 1196
Sequim, 503
Snohomish, 690
Snoqualmie, 750
South Kitsap, 1738
Spokane, 159, 283, 372, 508, 767, 1041,
 1110, 1196, 1461
Tacoma, 732
Vancouver, 5, 26, 64, 229, 319, 435, 437,
 574, 753, 788, 789, 859, 931, 960, 962,
 994, 1153, 1158, 1180, 1336, 1496, 1537,
 1538, 1539, 1544, 1577, 1582, 1583, 1591, 1736
Washougal, 1028
Yakima, 22, 512, 593, 644, 1873

West Virginia
Boone-Madison, 21
Buckhannon, 71
Chapmanville, 531
Charleston, 780, 782
Eleanor, 779
Jackson County, 291, 334, 394, 485, 529,
 571, 674, 675, 676, 1419, 1581, 1613, 1782,
 1783, 1793, 1794
Jefferson County, 22
Kanawha County, 351, 354, 830
Marion County, 1676
Morgantown, 193
Richwood, 1133

Wisconsin
668, 707, 1321, 1706, 1758
Altoona, 408
Amherst, 21, 193
Antigo, 736, 1504

Topical Index

Banned Books | Challenging Our Freedom to Read

Note:

The bibliographic entries are numbered sequentially and the entry number, rather than the page number, is listed below.

Selected titles in this book have been indexed in the following categories: Art Books, Biographical Works, Black Literature, Children's Literature, Fiction, Folk Tales, Gay and Lesbian Literature, Graphic Novels, Nonfiction, Occult Books, Philosophical Treatises, Plays, Poetry, Political Works, Reference Books, Religious Titles, Sex Education Titles, Short Stories, Textbooks, and Young Adult Literature.

Neither this list nor any of the categories is all-inclusive and comprehensive. Rather, this index is meant to assist in the development of displays, articles, editorials, and presentations.

Children's Literature

About the Author

Robert P. Doyle is the executive director of the Illinois Library Association (ILA). He is a noted authority and frequent speaker on First Amendment rights and the freedom to read. Under his leadership, the association has successfully opposed numerous legislative challenges to intellectual freedom. Prior to joining ILA, Doyle was director of the American Library Association's International Relations Office. Currently, he serves as the vice-president of the Freedom to Read Foundation and is a recipient of their 2009 Roll of Honor Award. He has edited *Banned Books* since 1983. He holds a Bachelor of Arts from the University of Notre Dame, and a Masters in Library Science from the University of Wisconsin-Milwaukee. He was born and raised in Milwaukee, and is a long-time resident of Chicago.

Acknowledgements

Thanks to the American Library Association's Office for Intellectual Freedom—in particular, Barbara Jones, Deborah Caldwell-Stone, and Nanette Perez.

The overall organization of the "incidents" into a searchable database was Mary Kane Trochim's idea. Searching books by title, subject matter, or geographic location became much easier, and the value of this organization in a publication that builds on each year's history has been immeasurable. Gary Sigman constructed and refined the database to accommodate the ever-changing editorial and design needs for the comprehensive list of challenged titles. With his careful guidance, we continue to improve the database's architecture.

Sam Silvio Design provided the thoughtful design for this year's publication. Sam's sophisticated design is clean and elegant. He is a most patient and gentle man.

Catherine Rhodes and Amy Blumstein carefully proofed the designed copy, making sure that no new errors arose in the design phrase.

Chris Watkins is a friend and colleague, and wonderful writer who served as a source of inspiration and a valuable sounding board. As a key strategic thinker, she assisted this publication in every aspect of its development. She certainly saved me from countless embarrassing errors by her fine editing skills.

Judith F. Krug, the first director of the ALA's Office for Intellectual Freedom, empowered me from the inception of Banned Books Week to produce the materials and resources necessary to make the event a reality and a continuing success. Her death was a great loss to the library community and the supporters of the First Amendment. All of us who knew her, worked with her, learned from her and loved her, know how much she would want this work to continue. Her spirit will forever inspire us to be forceful and eloquent in articulating this basic freedom.

The assistance and friendship of those individuals listed above and the friendship of many others unnamed here will be always be remembered and cherished by me.

In Memoriam
Patricia Ann Scarry
1949-2009